SCHOOL OF GOVERNMENT
North Carolina Benchmark...

Final Report on City Services for Fiscal Year 2018–2019

PERFORMANCE AND COST DATA

JUNE 2020

COSPONSORED BY:

THE CITIES OF APEX, ASHEVILLE, CHAPEL HILL, CHARLOTTE, CONCORD, GOLDSBORO, GREENSBORO, GREENVILLE, HICKORY, MOORESVILLE, RALEIGH, WILSON, AND WINSTON-SALEM

SCHOOL OF GOVERNMENT

NORTH CAROLINA LOCAL GOVERNMENT BUDGET ASSOCIATION

The School of Government at the University of North Carolina at Chapel Hill works to improve the lives of North Carolinians by engaging in practical scholarship that helps public officials and citizens understand and improve state and local government. Established in 1931 as the Institute of Government, the School provides educational, advisory, and research services for state and local governments. The School of Government is also home to a nationally ranked Master of Public Administration program, the North Carolina Judicial College, and specialized centers focused on community and economic development, information technology, and environmental finance.

As the largest university-based local government training, advisory, and research organization in the United States, the School of Government offers up to 200 courses, webinars, and specialized conferences for more than 12,000 public officials each year. In addition, faculty members annually publish approximately 50 books, manuals, reports, articles, bulletins, and other print and online content related to state and local government. The School also produces the *Daily Bulletin Online* each day the General Assembly is in session, reporting on activities for members of the legislature and others who need to follow the course of legislation.

Operating support for the School of Government's programs and activities comes from many sources, including state appropriations, local government membership dues, private contributions, publication sales, course fees, and service contracts.

Visit sog.unc.edu or call 919.966.5381 for more information on the School's courses, publications, programs, and services.

Michael R. Smith, DEAN
Aimee N. Wall, SENIOR ASSOCIATE DEAN
Jennifer Willis, ASSOCIATE DEAN FOR DEVELOPMENT
Michael Vollmer, ASSOCIATE DEAN FOR ADMINISTRATION

FACULTY

Whitney Afonso
Trey Allen
Gregory S. Allison
Lydian Altman
David N. Ammons
Maureen Berner
Frayda S. Bluestein
Kirk Boone
Mark F. Botts
Anita R. Brown-Graham
Peg Carlson
Connor Crews
Leisha DeHart-Davis
Shea Riggsbee Denning
Sara DePasquale
Jacquelyn Greene

Margaret F. Henderson
Norma Houston
Cheryl Daniels Howell
Willow S. Jacobson
Robert P. Joyce
Diane M. Juffras
Dona G. Lewandowski
Adam Lovelady
James M. Markham
Christopher B. McLaughlin
Kara A. Millonzi
Jill D. Moore
Jonathan Q. Morgan
Ricardo S. Morse
C. Tyler Mulligan
Kimberly L. Nelson

David W. Owens
Obed Pasha
William C. Rivenbark
Dale J. Roenigk
John Rubin
Jessica Smith
Meredith Smith
Carl W. Stenberg III
John B. Stephens
Charles Szypszak
Thomas H. Thornburg
Shannon H. Tufts
Jeffrey B. Welty (on leave)
Richard B. Whisnant
Brittany L. Williams

© 2020
School of Government
CB# 3330 Knapp Building,
The University of North Carolina at Chapel Hill,
Chapel Hill, NC 27599-3330

Preparation and printing of this report were made possible
by funding from the participating cities.

Printed in the United States of America

24 23 22 21 20   1 2 3 4 5

ISBN 978-1-64238-007-1

CONTENTS

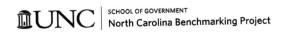

UNC | SCHOOL OF GOVERNMENT
North Carolina Benchmarking Project

PREFACE

North Carolina municipalities are continually looking for ways to improve the efficiency and effectiveness of service delivery. As part of this effort, a group of municipalities joined together with the UNC School of Government and the North Carolina Local Government Budget Association to create an ongoing project to compare performance and cost data for selected governmental services. This joint undertaking is known as the North Carolina Local Government Performance Measurement Project or, more commonly, the North Carolina Benchmarking Project. This report presents performance and cost data for the fiscal year ending June 30, 2019, for the thirteen North Carolina municipalities participating in the benchmarking project: Apex, Asheville, Chapel Hill, Charlotte, Concord, Goldsboro, Greensboro, Greenville, Hickory, Mooresville, Raleigh, Wilson, and Winston-Salem. Twenty-three previous reports regarding municipal services have been published.

The benchmarking project is a collaborative effort. Officials from the participating local governments, including budget and finance staff, program and service staff, and city and town managers, have made vital contributions to the success of the project. Special thanks are owed to the members of the steering committee, who provide the necessary leadership demanded by such a project: Suzanne Parmentier, Accounting and Budget Manager, and Amanda Grogan, Budget and Management Analyst of Apex; Tony McDowell, Budget and Financial Reporting Manager, and Lauren Brune, Budget Analyst of Asheville; David Finley, Budget and Management Analyst of Chapel Hill; Jordan Paschal, Budget Analyst of Charlotte; Lesley Reder, Budget and Performance Manager, Amanda Newton, Management Analyst, and Brandon Edwards, Management Analyst of Concord; Octavius Murphy, Assistant to the Manager of Goldsboro; Tracy Nash, Budget Analyst of Greensboro; Shelley Leach, Financial Analyst of Greenville; Cameron McHargue, Budget Analyst of Hickory; Ryan Rase, Deputy Town Manager of Mooresville; Toy Beeninga, Budget Analyst of Raleigh; Lanette Pridgen, Financial Analyst of Wilson; and Heather Curry, Budget and Evaluation Analyst of Winston-Salem.

The benchmarking project receives contributions from other individuals who strongly support benchmarking and performance measurement. William C. Rivenbark and David N. Ammons, faculty members of the School of Government, serve as project advisors. Special thanks go to Michael R. Smith, dean of the School of Government, and Thomas H. Thornburg, senior associate dean of the School of Government, for their leadership and support of the benchmarking project. The author wishes to acknowledge other School of Government staff who have contributed many hours to the benchmarking project, including Kevin Justice and Melissa Twomey in Strategic Communications.

Dale J. Roenigk
June 2020

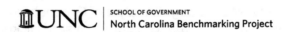

Performance and Cost Data

INTRODUCTION

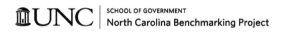

UNC | SCHOOL OF GOVERNMENT
North Carolina Benchmarking Project

INTRODUCTION

Can local governments measure their performance and cost in a meaningful way? Can performance measures in one local government be legitimately compared to the those of another? In the fall of 1995, fourteen large municipalities and counties in North Carolina agreed to participate in a collaborative project to answer these and other questions relating to benchmarking. Seven of the jurisdictions were municipalities, forming Phase I of what is now known as the North Carolina Local Government Performance Measurement Project or, more commonly, the North Carolina Benchmarking Project. The other seven jurisdictions were counties, constituting Phase II of the benchmarking project. A third phase of the benchmarking project began in January 1997, consisting of fourteen municipal and county, small- and medium-sized North Carolina jurisdictions. These phases represented the pilot stage of the benchmarking project.

Since the beginning, the benchmarking project has proceeded with an ongoing agreement to collect, clean, and report comparative performance and cost data from the participating municipalities. Listed below are the thirteen municipalities that are included in this report:

- Apex
- Asheville
- Chapel Hill
- Charlotte
- Concord
- Goldsboro
- Greensboro
- Greenville
- Hickory
- Mooresville
- Raleigh
- Wilson
- Winston-Salem

This project was the result of a joint undertaking of the participating municipalities, the School of Government, and the North Carolina Local Government Budget Association. The North Carolina League of Municipalities and the Local Government Commission also contributed to the development of this project. The goals of the benchmarking project are as follows:

1. To develop/expand the use of performance measurement in local government
2. To produce reliable performance and cost data for comparison
3. To facilitate the use of performance and cost data for service improvement

SERVICES

This report presents performance and cost data and accompanying explanatory information for the following service areas:

- Residential Refuse Collection
- Household Recycling
- Yard Waste/Leaf Collection
- Police Services
- Emergency Communications
- Asphalt Maintenance and Repair
- Fire Services
- Building Inspections
- Fleet Maintenance
- Central Human Resources
- Water Services
- Wastewater Services
- Core Parks and Recreation

The participating units did not agree to continue the benchmarking project to endure the challenges of data collection and "data cleaning" simply to produce a report. They continue with the belief that performance measurement and benchmarking are catalysts to service improvement. No jurisdiction can be the best in every service that it provides, highlighting the notion that even outstanding performers can learn from the practices of others. Performance measurement and benchmarking are about tracking performance and cost data and making changes based on both internal and external comparisons over time.

This report is the twenty-fourth publication representing municipal services. The previous twenty-three reports and their publication dates are listed below:

- *Performance and Cost Data: Phase I City Services* (October 1997)
- *Performance and Cost Data: Phase III City Services* (March 1999)
- *Final Report on City Services for Fiscal Year 1997–98* (March 1999)
- *Final Report on City Services for Fiscal Year 1998–99* (February 2000)
- *Final Report on City Services for Fiscal Year 1999–2000* (February 2001)
- *Final Report on City Services for Fiscal Year 2000–2001* (February 2002)
- *Final Report on City Services for Fiscal Year 2001–2002* (February 2003)
- *Final Report on City Services for Fiscal Year 2002–2003* (February 2004)
- *Final Report on City Services for Fiscal Year 2003–2004* (February 2005)
- *Final Report on City Services for Fiscal Year 2004–2005* (February 2006)
- *Final Report on City Services for Fiscal Year 2005–2006* (February 2007)
- *Final Report on City Services for Fiscal Year 2006–2007* (February 2008)
- *Final Report on City Services for Fiscal Year 2007–2008* (February 2009)
- *Final Report on City Services for Fiscal Year 2008–2009* (February 2010)
- *Final Report on City Services for Fiscal Year 2009–2010* (February 2011)
- *Final Report on City Services for Fiscal Year 2010–2011* (February 2012)
- *Final Report on City Services for Fiscal Year 2011–2012* (February 2013)
- *Final Report on City Services for Fiscal Year 2012–2013* (February 2014)

- *Final Report on City Services for Fiscal Year 2013–2014* (February 2015)
- *Final Report on City Services for Fiscal Year 2014–2015* (February 2016)
- *Final Report on City Services for Fiscal Year 2015–2016* (May 2017)
- *Final Report on City Services for Fiscal Year 2016–2017* (May 2018)
- *Final Report on City Services for Fiscal Year 2017–2018* (April 2019)

REPORTING FORMAT

This is primarily a data report. It incorporates graphs, summary tables, and explanatory information to present the performance and cost results for each service area under study. The results of each service area by municipality are displayed in a standard, two-page format. The following information is contained in this report:

1. **Explanatory Information.** This segment of the report describes how the service is provided and identifies the conditions or dimensions that affect the performance and cost data of service delivery.
2. **Municipal Profile.** This section includes a limited number of characteristics of each municipality, such as population density and median family income, which may affect service performance and cost. Some of the general characteristics, such as population, appear in the municipal profiles for all of the service areas. Others, such as weather and tax base served, appear only in selected profiles.
3. **Service Profile.** This area provides input and output data and identifies important dimensions of service delivery.
4. **Full Cost Profile.** A cost accounting model is used to calculate the full or total cost of providing each service area under study. Although the cost data were collected in detail, using a collection instrument with more than seventy specific line items, the reporting format aggregates the detailed cost data into three general categories for the purpose of presentation: personal services for the direct expenses of salaries, wages, and related fringe benefits; operating costs that include direct operating expenses and indirect cost allocations; and capital costs that represent depreciation of equipment and facilities.
5. **Resource Measures.** These measures gauge the amount of resources or inputs municipalities allocate for the provision of a given service.
6. **Performance Measures.** Three types of performance measures are used and reported: workload, efficiency, and effectiveness. A municipality's performance is compared to the performance average, noting that the average is based on services with numerous variations and should be viewed with caution. The measures used in this report do not assess total service performance. They gauge certain service dimensions and should be approached with an understanding of the service being provided.

SUMMARY OF OVERALL RESULTS

What the project has achieved

1. The project's methodology, consisting of service profiles, performance measures, cost accounting, and an explanation of results, works extremely well for data consistency and comparability. The project's accounting model is especially effective in producing reliable and materially accurate cost data.
2. The performance data have been used in numerous jurisdictions for service improvement, especially in the areas of residential refuse collection, household recycling, police services, and fleet services.
3. The project's success is directly correlates with consensus among numerous local government officials from the participating units regarding service definitions and measurement formulas.

What we have learned

1. Local governments can produce accurate, reliable, and comparable performance and cost data, which can then be used for service improvement.
2. Specific service definitions are vital to performance measurement, including explanatory information.
3. Data availability and quality are very important to performance measurement.
4. Performance measurement and cost accounting are time consuming. However, performance measures provide valuable feedback when the goal is to deliver quality services at a reasonable cost.

READING THE REPORT

This report presents the performance and cost data for the thirteen North Carolina municipalities participating in the benchmarking project for the fiscal year ending June 30, 2019. It also presents multiyear data for participants based on the number of fiscal years each municipality has participated in the benchmarking project. The following table provides the five fiscal years of performance measures contained within the present report and the corresponding municipalities by fiscal year of participation.

Final Report	Jurisdictions
Final Report on City Services for Fiscal Year 2014–2015	Apex, Asheville, Burlington, Cary, Chapel Hill, Concord, Greensboro, Greenville, Hickory, High Point, Salisbury, Wilson, and Winston-Salem
Final Report on City Services for Fiscal Year 2015–2016	Apex, Asheville, Burlington, Cary, Chapel Hill, Charlotte, Concord, Greensboro, Greenville, Hickory, High Point, Raleigh, Salisbury, Wilson, and Winston-Salem
Final Report on City Services for Fiscal Year 2016–2017	Apex, Asheville, Chapel Hill, Charlotte, Concord, Goldsboro, Greensboro, Greenville, Hickory, High Point, Raleigh, Salisbury, Wilson, and Winston-Salem
Final Report on City Services for Fiscal Year 2017–2018	Apex, Asheville, Chapel Hill, Charlotte, Concord, Goldsboro, Greensboro, Greenville, Hickory, High Point, Mooresville, Raleigh, Wilson, and Winston-Salem

Final Report on City Services for Fiscal Year 2018–2019	Apex, Asheville, Chapel Hill, Charlotte, Concord, Goldsboro, Greensboro, Greenville, Hickory, Mooresville, Raleigh, Wilson, and Winston-Salem

The municipal profile, full cost profile, service profile, and explanatory information for each municipality are based solely on performance and cost data for the fiscal year ending June 30, 2019. Readers should be extremely careful when interpreting the performance and cost data of municipalities with multi-year data. Municipal profiles, full cost profiles, service profiles, and explanatory information that support performance measures for the fiscal years ending June 30, 2015, through June 30, 2018, are located in prior year performance and cost data reports and can be obtained from the School of Government.

The benchmarking project considers new service areas and service changes on an annual basis under the guidance of the steering committee. Asphalt Maintenance and Repair represented a new service area for the fiscal year ending June 30, 2000. This service was previously reported as Street Pavement Maintenance. Police Services represented a new service area for the fiscal year ending June 30, 2001. This service was presented as Police Patrol and Police Investigations in prior reports. Fleet Maintenance represented a new service area for the fiscal year ending June 30, 2002. Central Human Resources represented a new service area for the fiscal year ending June 30, 2004. Water Services represented a new service area added in the fiscal year ending June 30, 2007. Wastewater Services was added in the fiscal year ending June 30, 2012. Finally, Core Parks and Recreation was added in the fiscal year ending June 30, 2013.

Municipalities do not participate in every service area for a variety of reasons. Certain ones do not participate in Emergency Communications and Building Inspections because those services are often county functions. In some cases, a municipality may not participate due to organizational structures or other issues. The following table provides the jurisdictions participating in each service area contained in this report.

Service Area	Jurisdictions
Residential Refuse Collection	Apex, Asheville, Chapel Hill, Charlotte, Concord, Goldsboro, Greensboro, Greenville, Hickory, Mooresville, Raleigh, Wilson, and Winston-Salem
Household Recycling	Apex, Asheville, Charlotte, Concord, Goldsboro, Greensboro, Greenville, Hickory, Mooresville, Raleigh, Wilson, and Winston-Salem
Yard Waste/Leaf Collection	Apex, Asheville, Chapel Hill, Charlotte, Concord, Goldsboro, Greensboro, Greenville, Hickory, Mooresville, Raleigh, Wilson, and Winston-Salem
Police Services	Apex, Asheville, Chapel Hill, Concord, Goldsboro, Greensboro, Greenville, Hickory, Mooresville, Raleigh, Wilson, and Winston-Salem
Emergency Communications	Apex, Asheville, Concord, Greensboro, Greenville, Hickory, Raleigh, and Winston-Salem
Asphalt Maintenance and Repair	Apex, Asheville, Chapel Hill, Charlotte, Concord, Goldsboro, Greensboro, Greenville, Hickory, Mooresville, Raleigh, Wilson, and Winston-Salem

Service Area	Jurisdictions
Fire Services	Apex, Asheville, Chapel Hill, Charlotte, Concord, Goldsboro, Greensboro, Greenville, Hickory, Mooresville, Raleigh, Wilson, and Winston-Salem
Building Inspections	Apex, Asheville, Chapel Hill, Goldsboro, Greensboro, Greenville, Raleigh, Wilson, and Winston-Salem
Fleet Maintenance	Apex, Asheville, Chapel Hill, Charlotte, Concord, Goldsboro, Greensboro, Greenville, Hickory, Mooresville, Raleigh, Wilson, and Winston-Salem
Central Human Resources	Apex, Asheville, Chapel Hill, Charlotte, Goldsboro, Greensboro, Greenville, Hickory, Mooresville, Raleigh, Wilson, and Winston-Salem
Water Services	Apex, Asheville, Charlotte, Concord, Goldsboro, Greensboro, Hickory, Mooresville, Raleigh, Wilson, and Winston-Salem
Wastewater Services	Apex, Charlotte, Concord, Goldsboro, Greensboro, Hickory, Mooresville, Raleigh, Wilson, and Winston-Salem
Core Parks and Recreation	Apex, Asheville, Chapel Hill, Concord, Goldsboro, Greensboro, Greenville, Hickory, Mooresville, Raleigh, Wilson, and Winston-Salem

It also should be noted that not all municipalities submit performance and cost data for each performance measure contained within the respective service area. Therefore, data are missing for selected performance measures regardless of service participation.

Performance and Cost Data

RESIDENTIAL REFUSE COLLECTION

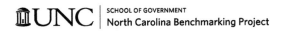

UNC SCHOOL OF GOVERNMENT | North Carolina Benchmarking Project

PERFORMANCE MEASURES FOR RESIDENTIAL REFUSE COLLECTION

SERVICE DEFINITION

This is regularly scheduled collection of household refuse or "garbage" from residential premises and other locations, including small businesses, using containers small enough that residents and/or workers can move or lift them manually. The service excludes collection of waste from dumpsters; regular or special collection of yard waste and leaves; collection of recyclable materials, white goods, or other bulky items; and any special or nonroutine service provided to residences. Transportation of refuse to a landfill or a transfer station is included, but the disposal of refuse and tipping costs is excluded.

NOTES ON PERFORMANCE MEASURES

1. Tons of (Residential) Refuse Collected per 1,000 Population and per 1,000 (Residential) Collection Points

"Tons of refuse collected" is widely used as a measure of workload for this service. A collection point or pickup point is a single locale (active address) from which residential refuse is collected. It can be a single-family residence, a condominium, an apartment, or a small business that uses containers that residents or sanitation workers can move or lift. Pickup points directly generate collection work, so this measure provides a good assessment of workload. "Tons of refuse collected per 1,000 population" and "per 1,000 collection points" also serve as measures of need for this service. Because of citizen expectations and public health requirements, sanitation crews or contractors must pick up all or virtually all household refuse that residents put out for collection.

2. Cost per Ton of Residential Refuse Collected and Cost per Residential Collection Point

These are the project's principal measures of efficiency for this service. Because of differences in the number of people per household and the percentage of the municipal population served by curbside collection, comparisons for these two efficiency measures can vary.

3. Full-Time Equivalent (FTE) Positions

The number of full-time equivalent (FTE) positions for residential refuse collection is the number of employees directly involved in providing the service as approved in the annual operating budget during the fiscal year. This number includes both full-time and part-time workers and both permanent and temporary workers. One FTE equates to 2,080 hours of work per year. Any combination of employees providing 2,080 hours of work annually equals one FTE. Cost data reflect all such workers. The measure "tons collected per collection FTE," however, includes only those workers who actually collect refuse and not supervisory or support personnel.

4. Number of Complaints and Number of Valid Complaints

All of the participating units take calls about residential refuse collection, and nearly all maintain records of one kind or another about such calls. However, the municipalities follow very different procedures in processing and recording these calls and in determining which ones are complaints and which are not. For these reasons, the project is able to present limited comparative data about complaints or valid complaints for residential refuse collection or other solid waste services. Nonetheless, the project recommends that the participating municipalities devise common criteria for identifying complaints and procedures for processing and recording calls.

Residential Refuse Collection

Summary of Key Dimensions of Service

City or Town	Normal Collection Location	Collection Points	Tons Collected	Weekly Routes	Percentage Contracted Service	Crew Size (most commonly used)	City FTE Collection Positions	Main Equipment		Landfill/Transfer	
								Packers	Automated	Trips per Day	Distance
Apex	Curbside	20,963	15,177	5	100%	Contracted	Contracted	Contracted	Contracted	NA	NA
Asheville	Curbside	32,497	22,802	36	0%	1 & 3 person	12	2	7	2	6 miles
Chapel Hill	Curbside	12,195	6,773	28	0%	1 & 3 person	12.71	7	0	1	18 miles
Charlotte	Curbside	220,942	199,400	320	0%	1 & 2 person	79	7	57	1.23	22 miles
Concord	Curbside	33,082	32,948	5	100%	Contracted	Contracted	Contractor - 2	Contractor - 6	1	8 miles
Goldsboro	Curbside	14,372	11,045	16	1%	1 & 3 person	6	1	3	6	11 miles
Greensboro	Curbside	90,625	61,374	68	0%	1 & 2 person	27	5	18	1.8	8 miles
Greenville	Curbside	19,006	27,128	24	0%	1 & 3 person	7	1	5	2	5 miles
Hickory	Curbside	11,940	9,211	15	0%	1 & 2 person	3.75	1	4	2	5 miles
Mooresville	Curbside	14,500	13,121	20	0%	1 & 2 person	11	3	3	2.5	4 miles
Raleigh	Curbside	129,962	92,524	120	0%	1 & 3 person	74	10	22	2	10 miles
Wilson	Curbside	20,900	25,100	24	0%	1 & 3 person	8.5	2	5	1.15	10 miles
Winston-Salem	Curbside	81,589	61,398	96	0%	1 & 3 person	82	8	16	1	10 miles

NOTES

All of the municipalities currently collect residential refuse once per week.
All of the municipalities have special provisions for collecting from the back or side yards of individuals with disabilities or mobility restrictions.

EXPLANATORY FACTORS

These are factors that the project found affected residential refuse collection performance and cost in one or more of the municipalities:

Backyard or curbside collection
Routing
Climate
Topographic conditions
Population density
Size of crews
Type of equipment used (automated)
Privatization
Participation in recycling program
Economies of scale
Distance to landfill/transfer station
Fee policies (volume-based or other)

Fiscal Year 2018–19

Explanatory Information

Service Level and Delivery

Apex contracts with Waste Industries for refuse collection, disposal, and recycling. Only the refuse collection is reflected on this page.

Residents pay $8.30 per month for collection. Refuse is collected once a week at curbside, although backyard collection is provided for disabled customers at no additional charge. Residents receiving service are provided with one ninety-six-gallon container. The service also includes a small number of businesses in the downtown area that use the standard carts but receive service twice a week.

The contractor collects five days a week from different routes. Trash is trucked to the landfill.

The contractor collected 15,177 tons of residential refuse during the fiscal year, at a cost of $73 per ton. The cost per ton does not include the disposal cost at the landfill.

Conditions Affecting Service, Performance, and Costs

Municipal Profile

Population (OSBM 2018)	52,909
Land Area (Square Miles)	21.55
Persons per Square Mile	2,455
Median Household Income	$84,000
U.S. Census 2016	

Service Profile

FTE Positions—Collection	Contractor
FTE Positions—Other	Contractor
Type of Equipment	Contractor
Size of Crews (most commonly used)	Contractor
Weekly Routes	5
Average Distance to Disposal Site	na
Average Daily Trips to Disposal Site	na
Percentage of Service Contracted	100%
Collection Frequency	1 x week
General Collection Location	Curbside
Residential Customers (number represents collection points)	20,963
Tons Collected	15,177
Monthly Service Fee	$8.30

Full Cost Profile

Cost Breakdown by Percentage	
Personal Services	0.0%
Operating Costs	100.0%
Capital Costs	0.0%
TOTAL	100.0%

Cost Breakdown in Dollars	
Personal Services	$0
Operating Costs	$1,104,884
Capital Costs	$0
TOTAL	$1,104,884

Apex

Residential Refuse Collection

Key: Apex ▨   Benchmarking Average —   Fiscal Years 2015 through 2019

Resource Measures

Residential Refuse Collection Costs per Capita

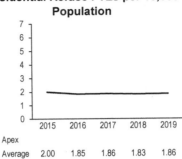

	2015	2016	2017	2018	2019
Apex	$27.10	$29.73	$23.64	$21.00	$20.88
Average	$23.14	$25.44	$23.62	$24.69	$25.82

Residential Refuse FTEs per 10,000 Population

	2015	2016	2017	2018	2019
Apex					
Average	2.00	1.85	1.86	1.83	1.86

Workload Measures

Residential Refuse Tons per 1,000 Population

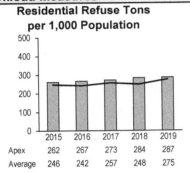

	2015	2016	2017	2018	2019
Apex	262	267	273	284	287
Average	246	242	257	248	275

Residential Refuse Tons per 1,000 Collection Points

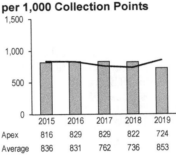

	2015	2016	2017	2018	2019
Apex	816	829	829	822	724
Average	836	831	762	736	853

Efficiency Measures

Residential Refuse Collection Cost per Ton Collected

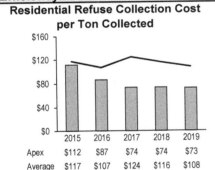

	2015	2016	2017	2018	2019
Apex	$112	$87	$74	$74	$73
Average	$117	$107	$124	$116	$108

Residential Refuse Collection Cost per Collection Point

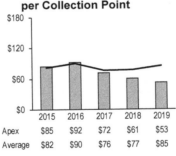

	2015	2016	2017	2018	2019
Apex	$85	$92	$72	$61	$53
Average	$82	$90	$76	$77	$85

Refuse Tons Collected per Municipal Collection FTE

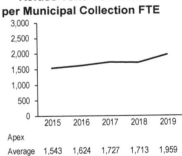

	2015	2016	2017	2018	2019
Apex					
Average	1,543	1,624	1,727	1,713	1,959

Effectiveness Measures

Complaints per 1,000 Collection Points

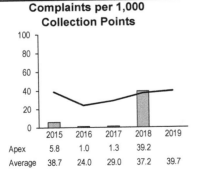

	2015	2016	2017	2018	2019
Apex	5.8	1.0	1.3	39.2	
Average	38.7	24.0	29.0	37.2	39.7

Valid Complaints per 1,000 Collection Points

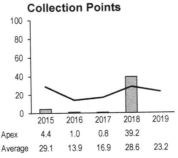

	2015	2016	2017	2018	2019
Apex	4.4	1.0	0.8	39.2	
Average	29.1	13.9	16.9	28.6	23.2

Fiscal Year 2018–19

Explanatory Information

Service Level and Delivery

Asheville collects residential refuse once a week at curbside, although backyard collection is provided for disabled customers at no charge and for other customers for a fee.

The city uses seven automated trucks, each with one driver, from Monday to Thursday working ten-hour days. Two rear packers with two- and three-person crews are used from Monday to Thursday for the collection of bulky items, clean-ups, and streets not accessible by automated trucks.

There are thirty-three main collection routes served by the automated trucks. The average number of trips to the transfer station is two per day per route. Nearly all trash goes to the transfer station before going to the landfill. The average distance to the transfer station is six miles. Two rear packers serve seven collection routes.

The city collected 22,802 tons of residential refuse during the fiscal year, at a cost of $123 per ton. The cost per ton does not include the disposal cost of $43.75 per ton at the transfer station. The transfer station is the primary disposal point for Asheville's trucks.

Residents receiving automated service are provided with one container. The majority of the containers are ninety-five-gallon capacity. Some residents use containers of sixty-five-gallon or thirty-five-gallon capacity. Residents may rent more containers if desired for $14 per month. Residents receiving rear-loading service provide their own containers. They are able to use up to six containers or bags. There is a $14 per month waste fee regardless of container size.

Conditions Affecting Service, Performance, and Costs

Asheville is highly automated in the area of residential refuse collection.

Municipal Profile

Population (OSBM 2018)	93,621
Land Area (Square Miles)	45.53
Persons per Square Mile	2,056
Median Household Income	$40,494
U.S. Census 2016	

Service Profile

FTE Positions—Collection	12.0
FTE Positions—Other	3.4
Type of Equipment	7 automated packers
	2 regular packers
Size of Crews (most commonly used)	1 & 3 person
Weekly Routes	36
Average Distance to Disposal Site	6 miles
Average Daily Trips to Disposal Site	2
Percentage of Service Contracted	0%
Collection Frequency	1 x week
General Collection Location	Curbside
Residential Customers	32,497
(number represents collection points)	
Tons Collected	22,802
Monthly Service Fee	$14.00

Full Cost Profile

Cost Breakdown by Percentage

Personal Services	40.0%
Operating Costs	36.6%
Capital Costs	23.4%
TOTAL	100.0%

Cost Breakdown in Dollars

Personal Services	$1,118,239
Operating Costs	$1,025,356
Capital Costs	$654,249
TOTAL	$2,797,844

Asheville

Residential Refuse Collection

Resource Measures

Residential Refuse Collection Costs per Capita

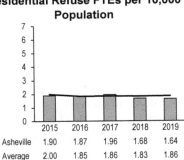

	2015	2016	2017	2018	2019
Asheville	$25.64	$27.57	$16.26	$27.71	$29.88
Average	$23.14	$25.44	$23.62	$24.69	$25.82

Residential Refuse FTEs per 10,000 Population

	2015	2016	2017	2018	2019
Asheville	1.90	1.87	1.96	1.68	1.64
Average	2.00	1.85	1.86	1.83	1.86

Workload Measures

Residential Refuse Tons per 1,000 Population

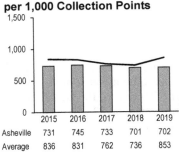

	2015	2016	2017	2018	2019
Asheville	245	247	241	245	244
Average	246	242	257	248	275

Residential Refuse Tons per 1,000 Collection Points

	2015	2016	2017	2018	2019
Asheville	731	745	733	701	702
Average	836	831	762	736	853

Efficiency Measures

Residential Refuse Collection Cost per Ton Collected

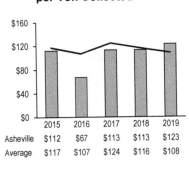

	2015	2016	2017	2018	2019
Asheville	$112	$67	$113	$113	$123
Average	$117	$107	$124	$116	$108

Residential Refuse Collection Cost per Collection Point

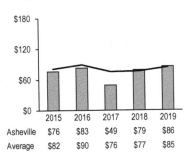

	2015	2016	2017	2018	2019
Asheville	$76	$83	$49	$79	$86
Average	$82	$90	$76	$77	$85

Refuse Tons Collected per Municipal Collection FTE

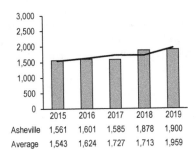

	2015	2016	2017	2018	2019
Asheville	1,561	1,601	1,585	1,878	1,900
Average	1,543	1,624	1,727	1,713	1,959

Effectiveness Measures

Complaints per 1,000 Collection Points

	2015	2016	2017	2018	2019
Asheville	35.3	25.0	31.6	32.4	53.8
Average	38.7	24.0	29.0	37.2	39.7

Valid Complaints per 1,000 Collection Points

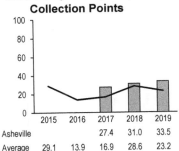

	2015	2016	2017	2018	2019
Asheville			27.4	31.0	33.5
Average	29.1	13.9	16.9	28.6	23.2

Fiscal Year 2018–19

Explanatory Information

Service Level and Delivery

Chapel Hill residential refuse collection is performed by the Solid Waste Services Division under the Public Works Department. The Town provides weekly household waste collection Mondays and Tuesdays with no fees charged.

Residential refuse is collected by seven 3-person crews using rear packers two days per week. The packer crews are staffed with three persons; one driver and two collectors. The trucks average one trip to the transfer station with the distance averaging 18 miles one way. A lift gate truck is also used to collect bulky items and electronics for a fee five days per week. Two pickup trucks are also used to collect medical exemptions, pedestrian trash cans, and streets not accessible to rear packers with one truck running seven days per week and the other running two days per week.

The town collected 6,773 tons of residential refuse during the fiscal year at a cost of $308 per ton or $171 per collection point. The cost does not include the disposal cost of $44.50 per ton at the transfer station for the tipping fee. Residents receive one roll-out cart at no charge but can purchase an additional cart for $60 per cart. Residents can also purchase their own trash cans, but these must be 32 gallons or smaller and weigh less than 60 pounds when full.

Conditions Affecting Service, Performance, and Costs

The Town of Chapel Hill began participation in the benchmarking project in July 2015, with FY 2014–15 being the first reporting year.

The out-of-town transfer station is the primary disposal location for Chapel Hill. Orange County had the highest waste reduction rate (64 percent) in North Carolina in FY 2014–15. The town provides special exemptions for backyard collections for 470 collection points, which represents 3.9 percent of the total collection points.

Municipal Profile

Population (OSBM 2018)	63,178
Land Area (Square Miles)	21.27
Persons per Square Mile	2,971
Median Household Income U.S. Census 2016	$60,802

Service Profile

FTE Positions—Collection	12.7
FTE Positions—Other	1.1
Type of Equipment	7 packers 1 Lift-Gate Truck and 2 Pickups
Size of Crews (most commonly used)	1 & 3 person
Weekly Routes	28
Average Distance to Disposal Site	18 miles
Average Daily Route Trips to Disposal Site	1
Percentage of Service Contracted	0%
Collection Frequency	1 x week
General Collection Location	Curbside
Residential Customers (number represents collection points)	12,195
Tons Collected	6,773
Monthly Service Fee	No

Full Cost Profile

Cost Breakdown by Percentage	
Personal Services	42.2%
Operating Costs	44.9%
Capital Costs	12.9%
TOTAL	100.0%
Cost Breakdown in Dollars	
Personal Services	$880,955
Operating Costs	$936,971
Capital Costs	$270,137
TOTAL	$2,088,063

Chapel Hill

Residential Refuse Collection

Resource Measures

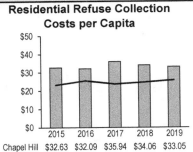

Residential Refuse Collection Costs per Capita

	2015	2016	2017	2018	2019
Chapel Hill	$32.63	$32.09	$35.94	$34.06	$33.05
Average	$23.14	$25.44	$23.62	$24.69	$25.82

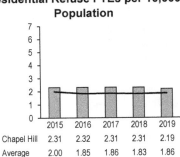

Residential Refuse FTEs per 10,000 Population

	2015	2016	2017	2018	2019
Chapel Hill	2.31	2.32	2.31	2.31	2.19
Average	2.00	1.85	1.86	1.83	1.86

Workload Measures

Residential Refuse Tons per 1,000 Population

	2015	2016	2017	2018	2019
Chapel Hill	111	112	112	112	107
Average	246	242	257	248	275

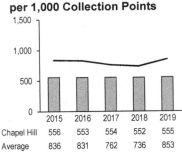

Residential Refuse Tons per 1,000 Collection Points

	2015	2016	2017	2018	2019
Chapel Hill	556	553	554	552	555
Average	836	831	762	736	853

Efficiency Measures

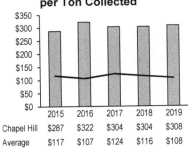

Residential Refuse Collection Cost per Ton Collected

	2015	2016	2017	2018	2019
Chapel Hill	$287	$322	$304	$304	$308
Average	$117	$107	$124	$116	$108

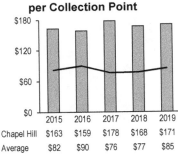

Residential Refuse Collection Cost per Collection Point

	2015	2016	2017	2018	2019
Chapel Hill	$163	$159	$178	$168	$171
Average	$82	$90	$76	$77	$85

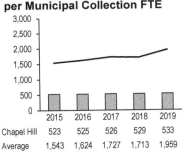

Refuse Tons Collected per Municipal Collection FTE

	2015	2016	2017	2018	2019
Chapel Hill	523	525	526	529	533
Average	1,543	1,624	1,727	1,713	1,959

Effectiveness Measures

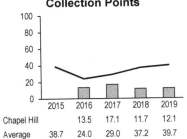

Complaints per 1,000 Collection Points

	2015	2016	2017	2018	2019
Chapel Hill		13.5	17.1	11.7	12.1
Average	38.7	24.0	29.0	37.2	39.7

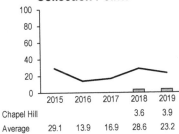

Valid Complaints per 1,000 Collection Points

	2015	2016	2017	2018	2019
Chapel Hill				3.6	3.9
Average	29.1	13.9	16.9	28.6	23.2

Fiscal Year 2018–19

Explanatory Information

Service Level and Delivery

Charlotte collects residential refuse once a week at curbside. Backyard service is available only to those persons with valid medical reasons and physician certification. The city charges an annual fee of $39 for refuse services, which is paid on the property tax bill; the fee applies to both collection and disposal costs and is meant to be just a portion of cost recovery for services.

City crews are composed primarily of one driver, each operating an automated packer. There were fifty-seven of these crews for FY 2018–19. In addition, three crews, each composed of one driver and one laborer, collected refuse using semi-automated packers. These crews are used primarily for backyard service for those citizens with disabilities and some multifamily complexes with less than thirty units. Small business garbage is collected by four crews, each composed of one driver and one laborer, using rear loaders. Costs include reserve crews that were used as needed throughout the year.

The city serviced 320 daily collection routes once each week during the fiscal year, with an average of 1.23 trips to the landfill per day per route at an average one-way distance of twenty-two miles. Each single-family residence is provided one ninety-six-gallon rollout container. An additional receptacle may be purchased for a nominal one-time fee. Charlotte collected 199,400 tons of residential refuse during the fiscal year, at a cost of $92 per ton. The cost per ton does not include the disposal cost of $33, representing the landfill tipping fee.

Conditions Affecting Service, Performance, and Costs

Charlotte did not participate in the Benchmarking Project during FY 2014–15. No data are available for that year.

Charlotte is highly automated in the area of residential refuse collection. It considers all complaints to be valid complaints.

Municipal Profile

Population (OSBM 2018)	852,992
Land Area (Square Miles)	306.31
Persons per Square Mile	2,785
Median Household Income	$46,975
U.S. Census 2016	

Service Profile

FTE Positions—Collection	79.0
FTE Positions—Other	7.0
Type of Equipment	57 automated packers 7 packers
Size of Crews (most commonly used)	1 & 2 person
Weekly Routes	320
Average Distance to Disposal Site	22 miles
Average Daily Trips to Disposal Site	1.23
Percentage of Service Contracted	0%
Collection Frequency	1 x week
General Collection Location	Curbside
Residential Customers (number represents collection points)	220,942
Tons Collected	199,400
Annual Service Fee	46.06

Full Cost Profile

Cost Breakdown by Percentage	
Personal Services	34.6%
Operating Costs	45.0%
Capital Costs	20.4%
TOTAL	100.0%

Cost Breakdown in Dollars	
Personal Services	$6,355,704
Operating Costs	$8,269,521
Capital Costs	$3,742,875
TOTAL	$18,368,100

Charlotte

Residential Refuse Collection

Key: Charlotte ▨   Benchmarking Average —   Fiscal Years 2015 through 2019

Resource Measures

Residential Refuse Collection Costs per Capita

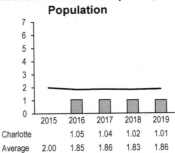

	2015	2016	2017	2018	2019
Charlotte		$20.50	$20.59	$20.64	$21.53
Average	$23.14	$25.44	$23.62	$24.69	$25.82

Residential Refuse FTEs per 10,000 Population

	2015	2016	2017	2018	2019
Charlotte		1.05	1.04	1.02	1.01
Average	2.00	1.85	1.86	1.83	1.86

Workload Measures

Residential Refuse Tons per 1,000 Population

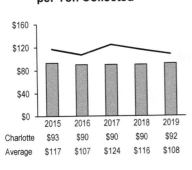

	2015	2016	2017	2018	2019
Charlotte		220	228	229	234
Average	246	242	257	248	275

Residential Refuse Tons per 1,000 Collection Points

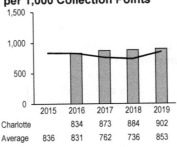

	2015	2016	2017	2018	2019
Charlotte		834	873	884	902
Average	836	831	762	736	853

Efficiency Measures

Residential Refuse Collection Cost per Ton Collected

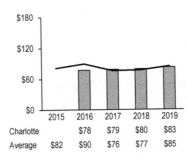

	2015	2016	2017	2018	2019
Charlotte	$93	$90	$90	$90	$92
Average	$117	$107	$124	$116	$108

Residential Refuse Collection Cost per Collection Point

	2015	2016	2017	2018	2019
Charlotte		$78	$79	$80	$83
Average	$82	$90	$76	$77	$85

Refuse Tons Collected per Municipal Collection FTE

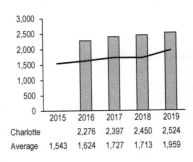

	2015	2016	2017	2018	2019
Charlotte		2,276	2,397	2,450	2,524
Average	1,543	1,624	1,727	1,713	1,959

Effectiveness Measures

Complaints per 1,000 Collection Points

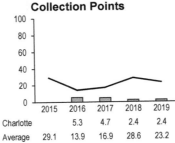

	2015	2016	2017	2018	2019
Charlotte		5.3	4.7	2.4	2.4
Average	38.7	24.0	29.0	37.2	39.7

Valid Complaints per 1,000 Collection Points

	2015	2016	2017	2018	2019
Charlotte		5.3	4.7	2.4	2.4
Average	29.1	13.9	16.9	28.6	23.2

Concord

Fiscal Year 2018–19

Explanatory Information

Service Level and Delivery

Residential refuse collection service is provided once a week at curbside to Concord residents. Backyard service is available for the elderly and disabled. The city has provided residential refuse collection service under contract for many years. The cost of the contract for the year was approximately $1.89 million.

The contractor primarily used five automated packers, each with one person. Residents used one ninety-five-gallon cart, with extra carts available for larger families or unusual circumstances.

The contractor serviced twenty-five collection routes each week, with an average distance per route per day to the landfill of eight miles. The packers made an average of one trip to the landfill per day per route. The contractor collected 32,082 tons of residential refuse during the fiscal year, at a cost of $71 per ton.

Conditions Affecting Service, Performance, and Costs

Concord is one of only two jurisdictions participating in the benchmarking project that contracts 100 percent of its residential refuse collection service. Therefore, "tons collected per collection FTE" is not used for Concord as a performance measure, as this reflects only municipal workers.

Concord's "total tons collected" includes bulk trash, which is collected along with residential refuse and cannot be separated for reporting purposes.

Concord defines valid complaints to mean any missed collection or request for service as determined by the city to result from contractor negligence or omission.

Concord discontinued its old system, which required citizens to schedule the collection of bulky items. Too many collections were not called in, resulting in bulky items being left curbside for days and generating complaints. The drop in complaints in FY 2013–14 was the result of a new system in which the city scouts out items to be picked up and citizens are not required to call in. Pickup is improved and additional costs for the scouting have been offset by savings from avoided costs through improved collection efficiencies.

Municipal Profile

Population (OSBM 2018)	92,568
Land Area (Square Miles)	62.80
Persons per Square Mile	1,474
Median Household Income	$50,863
U.S. Census 2016	

Service Profile

FTE Positions—Collection	1.3 City
FTE Positions—Other	1.64 City
Type of Equipment	6 automated packers 2 packers
Size of Crews (most commonly used)	Contractor
Weekly Routes	25
Average Distance to Disposal Site	8 miles
Average Daily Trips to Disposal Site	1
Percentage of Service Contracted	100%
Collection Frequency	1 x week
General Collection Location	Curbside
Residential Customers (number represents collection points)	33,082
Tons Collected	32,948
Monthly Service Fee	No

Full Cost Profile

Cost Breakdown by Percentage	
Personal Services	6.9%
Operating Costs	92.6%
Capital Costs	0.5%
TOTAL	100.0%

Cost Breakdown in Dollars	
Personal Services	$162,967
Operating Costs	$2,174,471
Capital Costs	$11,386
TOTAL	$2,348,824

Concord

Residential Refuse Collection

Resource Measures

Residential Refuse Collection Costs per Capita

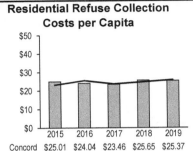

	2015	2016	2017	2018	2019
Concord	$25.01	$24.04	$23.46	$25.65	$25.37
Average	$23.14	$25.44	$23.62	$24.69	$25.82

Residential Refuse FTEs per 10,000 Population

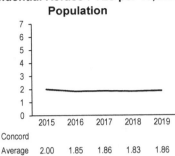

	2015	2016	2017	2018	2019
Concord					
Average	2.00	1.85	1.86	1.83	1.86

Workload Measures

Residential Refuse Tons per 1,000 Population

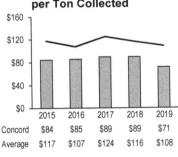

	2015	2016	2017	2018	2019
Concord	285	286	275	287	356
Average	246	242	257	248	275

Residential Refuse Tons per 1,000 Collection Points

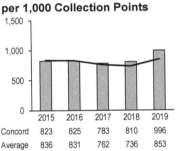

	2015	2016	2017	2018	2019
Concord	823	825	783	810	996
Average	836	831	762	736	853

Efficiency Measures

Residential Refuse Collection Cost per Ton Collected

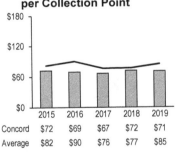

	2015	2016	2017	2018	2019
Concord	$84	$85	$89	$89	$71
Average	$117	$107	$124	$116	$108

Residential Refuse Collection Cost per Collection Point

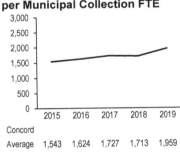

	2015	2016	2017	2018	2019
Concord	$72	$69	$67	$72	$71
Average	$82	$90	$76	$77	$85

Refuse Tons Collected per Municipal Collection FTE

	2015	2016	2017	2018	2019
Concord					
Average	1,543	1,624	1,727	1,713	1,959

Effectiveness Measures

Complaints per 1,000 Collection Points

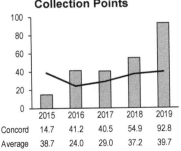

	2015	2016	2017	2018	2019
Concord	14.7	41.2	40.5	54.9	92.8
Average	38.7	24.0	29.0	37.2	39.7

Valid Complaints per 1,000 Collection Points

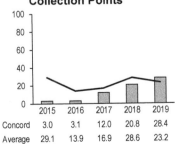

	2015	2016	2017	2018	2019
Concord	3.0	3.1	12.0	20.8	28.4
Average	29.1	13.9	16.9	28.6	23.2

Fiscal Year 2018–19

Explanatory Information

Service Level and Delivery

Goldsboro provides residential refuse collection once a week at curbside for residents. Collection is done by the Solid Waste Division of the Public Works Department. Backyard collection is available for the disabled. Currently the city charges a monthly fee of $22, which includes refuse, recycling, and leaf and limb pickup.

There are three automated trucks with a single driver and one crew with a driver and two collectors using a rear loader. Collection trucks run four days per week. Crews drive eleven miles to a transfer station.

The city collected 11,045 tons of residential refuse during the fiscal year from 14,372 collection points at a cost of $71 per ton. The collection costs do not include a disposal cost at the transfer station of $31.50 per ton.

Conditions Affecting Service, Performance, and Costs

The city of Goldsboro joined the Benchmarking Project in July 2017, with the first year of data showing for FY 2016–17.

Goldsboro contracts refuse collection for one small neighborhood where a hill and tight roads make it infeasible to use city trucks.

Municipal Profile

Population (OSBM 2018)	33,636
Land Area (Square Miles)	29.41
Persons per Square Mile	1,144
Median Household Income U.S. Census 2016	$32,148

Service Profile

FTE Positions—Collection	6.0
FTE Positions—Other	0.8
Type of Equipment	3 automated packers 1 packer
Size of Crews (most commonly used)	1 & 3 person
Weekly Routes	16
Average Distance to Disposal Site	11 miles
Average Daily Trips to Disposal Site	6
Percentage of Service Contracted	0.7%
Collection Frequency	1 x week
General Collection Location	Curbside
Residential Customers (number represents collection points)	14,372
Tons Collected	11,045
Monthly Service Fee	$22

Full Cost Profile

Cost Breakdown by Percentage	
Personal Services	55.9%
Operating Costs	31.9%
Capital Costs	12.2%
TOTAL	100.0%

Cost Breakdown in Dollars	
Personal Services	$439,957
Operating Costs	$251,230
Capital Costs	$95,680
TOTAL	$786,867

Goldsboro

Residential Refuse Collection

Resource Measures

Residential Refuse Collection Costs per Capita

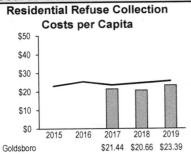

	2015	2016	2017	2018	2019
Goldsboro			$21.44	$20.66	$23.39
Average	$23.14	$25.44	$23.62	$24.69	$25.82

Residential Refuse FTEs per 10,000 Population

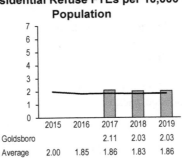

	2015	2016	2017	2018	2019
Goldsboro			2.11	2.03	2.03
Average	2.00	1.85	1.86	1.83	1.86

Workload Measures

Residential Refuse Tons per 1,000 Population

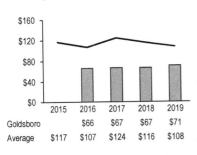

	2015	2016	2017	2018	2019
Goldsboro			323	307	328
Average	246	242	257	248	275

Residential Refuse Tons per 1,000 Collection Points

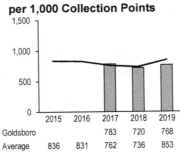

	2015	2016	2017	2018	2019
Goldsboro			783	720	768
Average	836	831	762	736	853

Efficiency Measures

Residential Refuse Collection Cost per Ton Collected

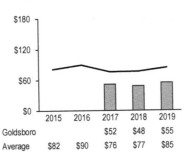

	2015	2016	2017	2018	2019
Goldsboro		$66	$67	$67	$71
Average	$117	$107	$124	$116	$108

Residential Refuse Collection Cost per Collection Point

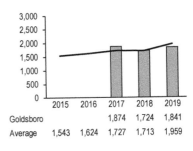

	2015	2016	2017	2018	2019
Goldsboro			$52	$48	$55
Average	$82	$90	$76	$77	$85

Refuse Tons Collected per Municipal Collection FTE

	2015	2016	2017	2018	2019
Goldsboro			1,874	1,724	1,841
Average	1,543	1,624	1,727	1,713	1,959

Effectiveness Measures

Complaints per 1,000 Collection Points

	2015	2016	2017	2018	2019
Goldsboro			81.0		
Average	38.7	24.0	29.0	37.2	39.7

Valid Complaints per 1,000 Collection Points

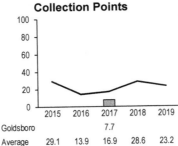

	2015	2016	2017	2018	2019
Goldsboro			7.7		
Average	29.1	13.9	16.9	28.6	23.2

Explanatory Information

Service Level and Delivery

Greensboro provides once-a-week collection of residential refuse at curbside. Each resident is provided up to two ninety-gallon carts. Currently there is no fee for residential collection of refuse.

There were twenty-three city crews for the fiscal year. Eighteen crews each have one driver operating an automated packer. Five crews use rear loaders.

The city used sixty-eight collection routes during the fiscal year, with each packer making an average of 1.8 trips per day to a municipal solid waste transfer station and the travel distance averaging eight miles.

The city collected 61,374 tons of residential refuse during the fiscal year at a cost of $107 per ton.

Greensboro defines automated packers as one-armed automated-loading packers that are operated by one person. Rear loaders are rear-loading packer trucks.

Conditions Affecting Service, Performance, and Costs

Greensboro is highly automated in the area of residential refuse collection.

Municipal Profile

Population (OSBM 2018)	292,306
Land Area (Square Miles)	128.77
Persons per Square Mile	2,270
Median Household Income	$40,760
U.S. Census 2016	

Service Profile

FTE Positions—Collection	27.0
FTE Positions—Other	4.0
Type of Equipment	18 automated packers
	5 packers
Size of Crews (most commonly used)	1 & 2 person
Weekly Routes	68
Average Distance to Disposal Site	8.0
Average Daily Trips to Disposal Site	1.8
Percentage of Service Contracted	0.0%
Collection Frequency	1 x week
General Collection Location	Curbside
Residential Customers	90625
(number represents collection points)	
Tons Collected	61,374
Monthly Service Fee	No

Full Cost Profile

Cost Breakdown by Percentage	
Personal Services	21.5%
Operating Costs	78.5%
Capital Costs	0.0%
TOTAL	100.0%

Cost Breakdown in Dollars	
Personal Services	$1,407,405
Operating Costs	$5,146,965
Capital Costs	$0
TOTAL	$6,554,370

Greensboro

Residential Refuse Collection

Key: Greensboro ▨   Benchmarking Average —   Fiscal Years 2015 through 2019

Resource Measures

Residential Refuse Collection Costs per Capita

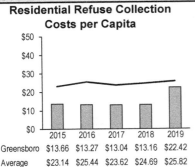

	2015	2016	2017	2018	2019
Greensboro	$13.66	$13.27	$13.04	$13.16	$22.42
Average	$23.14	$25.44	$23.62	$24.69	$25.82

Residential Refuse FTEs per 10,000 Population

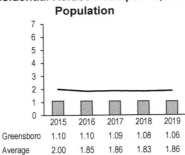

	2015	2016	2017	2018	2019
Greensboro	1.10	1.10	1.09	1.08	1.06
Average	2.00	1.85	1.86	1.83	1.86

Workload Measures

Residential Refuse Tons per 1,000 Population

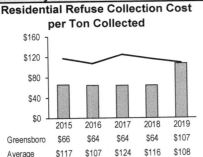

	2015	2016	2017	2018	2019
Greensboro	195	202	203	206	210
Average	246	242	257	248	275

Residential Refuse Tons per 1,000 Collection Points

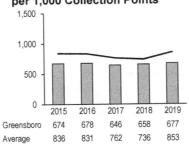

	2015	2016	2017	2018	2019
Greensboro	674	678	646	658	677
Average	836	831	762	736	853

Efficiency Measures

Residential Refuse Collection Cost per Ton Collected

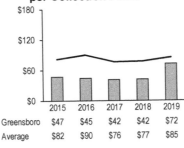

	2015	2016	2017	2018	2019
Greensboro	$66	$64	$64	$64	$107
Average	$117	$107	$124	$116	$108

Residential Refuse Collection Cost per Collection Point

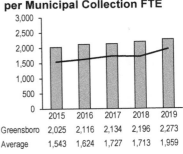

	2015	2016	2017	2018	2019
Greensboro	$47	$45	$42	$42	$72
Average	$82	$90	$76	$77	$85

Refuse Tons Collected per Municipal Collection FTE

	2015	2016	2017	2018	2019
Greensboro	2,025	2,116	2,134	2,196	2,273
Average	1,543	1,624	1,727	1,713	1,959

Effectiveness Measures

Complaints per 1,000 Collection Points

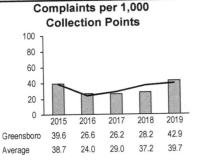

	2015	2016	2017	2018	2019
Greensboro	39.6	26.6	26.2	28.2	42.9
Average	38.7	24.0	29.0	37.2	39.7

Valid Complaints per 1,000 Collection Points

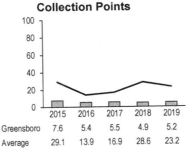

	2015	2016	2017	2018	2019
Greensboro	7.6	5.4	5.5	4.9	5.2
Average	29.1	13.9	16.9	28.6	23.2

Fiscal Year 2018–19

Explanatory Information

Service Level and Delivery

Greenville collects refuse from residential premises once a week at curbside. Curbside collection is priced at $16 per month. Curbside recycling of white goods and electronics is included in the residential refuse fee.

The city uses five one-person crews operating automated trucks and one truck with a crew of three persons using rear-loading vehicles. The crews run collection routes four days a week.

Twenty-four collection routes were used during the fiscal year, with an average of two trips to the transfer station per day per route. The average distance to the transfer station per route was five-and-a-half miles.

Greenville collected 27,128 tons of residential refuse during the fiscal year. The cost per ton does not include the disposal cost of $35.95, representing the tipping fee at the transfer station.

Conditions Affecting Service, Performance, and Costs

The apparent drop in the data in the graphs that look at tons collected is due to reporting improvements. In earlier years, Greenville could not easily separate out refuse collected from multifamily units. Improvements in what the county landfill is able to track and report back to the city mean that the most recent year includes just single-family units. The refuse tonnage, however, for FY 2017–18 was not separated out and represents an estimate.

Municipal Profile

Population (OSBM 2018)	89,790
Land Area (Square Miles)	35.58
Persons per Square Mile	2,523
Median Household Income	$33,339
U.S. Census 2016	

Service Profile

FTE Positions—Collection	7.0
FTE Positions—Other	4.0
Type of Equipment	5 automated packers
	1 packers
Size of Crews (most commonly used)	1 & 3 person
Weekly Routes	24
Average Distance to Disposal Site	5 miles
Average Daily Trips to Disposal Site	2
Percentage of Service Contracted	0%
Collection Frequency	1 x week
General Collection Location	Curbside
Residential Customers	19,006
(number represents collection points)	
Tons Collected	27,128
Monthly Service Fee	$16

Full Cost Profile

Cost Breakdown by Percentage	
Personal Services	36.5%
Operating Costs	44.6%
Capital Costs	18.9%
TOTAL	100.0%

Cost Breakdown in Dollars	
Personal Services	$750,063
Operating Costs	$915,978
Capital Costs	$388,609
TOTAL	$2,054,650

Greenville

Residential Refuse Collection

Key: Greenville ▨   Benchmarking Average —   Fiscal Years 2015 through 2019

Resource Measures

Residential Refuse Collection Costs per Capita

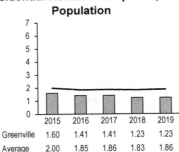

	2015	2016	2017	2018	2019
Greenville	$21.54	$19.73	$23.29	$31.89	$22.88
Average	$23.14	$25.44	$23.62	$24.69	$25.82

Residential Refuse FTEs per 10,000 Population

	2015	2016	2017	2018	2019
Greenville	1.60	1.41	1.41	1.23	1.23
Average	2.00	1.85	1.86	1.83	1.86

Workload Measures

Residential Refuse Tons per 1,000 Population

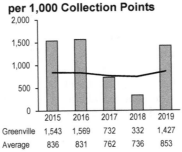

	2015	2016	2017	2018	2019
Greenville	320	325	327	140	302
Average	246	242	257	248	275

Residential Refuse Tons per 1,000 Collection Points

	2015	2016	2017	2018	2019
Greenville	1,543	1,569	732	332	1,427
Average	836	831	762	736	853

Efficiency Measures

Residential Refuse Collection Cost per Ton Collected

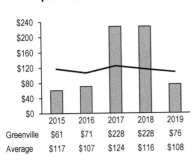

	2015	2016	2017	2018	2019
Greenville	$61	$71	$228	$228	$76
Average	$117	$107	$124	$116	$108

Residential Refuse Collection Cost per Collection Point

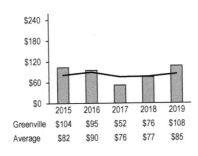

	2015	2016	2017	2018	2019
Greenville	$104	$95	$52	$76	$108
Average	$82	$90	$76	$77	$85

Refuse Tons Collected per Municipal Collection FTE

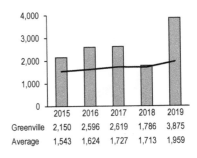

	2015	2016	2017	2018	2019
Greenville	2,150	2,596	2,619	1,786	3,875
Average	1,543	1,624	1,727	1,713	1,959

Effectiveness Measures

Complaints per 1,000 Collection Points

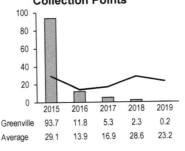

	2015	2016	2017	2018	2019
Greenville	93.7	11.8	5.3	5.6	6.4
Average	38.7	24.0	29.0	37.2	39.7

Valid Complaints per 1,000 Collection Points

	2015	2016	2017	2018	2019
Greenville	93.7	11.8	5.3	2.3	0.2
Average	29.1	13.9	16.9	28.6	23.2

Fiscal Year 2018–19

Explanatory Information

Service Level and Delivery

Hickory collects refuse from residential premises once a week at curbside, although backyard collection is provided for elderly and disabled citizens. A monthly solid waste fee of $19.50 per cart was charged for residential refuse collection service during FY 2016–17. Each residence uses a cart provided by the city for residential refuse collection. Each cart has a capacity of ninety-six gallons and is provided at no charge. Upon request, a second cart is provided to the customer for an additional solid-waste fee.

The city used four one-person crews operating automated packers, with three of these trucks running full-time and one one-fourth of the time. A regular packer truck with one driver and one crew member works about half-time collecting on one-way streets and dead ends.

Fifteen collection routes were used during the fiscal year, with an average of two trips to the transfer station per day per route. The average distance to the transfer station per route was five miles.

Hickory collected 9,211 tons of residential refuse during the fiscal year, at a cost of $39 per ton. The cost per ton does not include the disposal cost of $5.75, representing the tipping fee at the Catawba County landfill.

Hickory defines automated packers as trucks with mechanical arms.

Conditions Affecting Service, Performance, and Costs

Hickory is highly automated in the area of residential refuse collection.

Municipal Profile

Population (OSBM 2018)	40,932
Land Area (Square Miles)	29.92
Persons per Square Mile	1,368
Median Household Income U.S. Census 2016	$35,353

Service Profile

FTE Positions—Collection	3.75
FTE Positions—Other	0.82
Type of Equipment	4 automated packers 1 packer
Size of Crews (most commonly used)	1 & 2 person
Weekly Routes	15
Average Distance to Disposal Site	5 miles
Average Daily Trips to Disposal Site	2
Percentage of Service Contracted	0%
Collection Frequency	1 x week
General Collection Location	Curbside
Residential Customers (number represents collection points)	11,940
Tons Collected	9,211
Monthly Service Fee	22.5

Full Cost Profile

Cost Breakdown by Percentage	
Personal Services	43.9%
Operating Costs	41.8%
Capital Costs	14.3%
TOTAL	100.0%

Cost Breakdown in Dollars	
Personal Services	$158,661
Operating Costs	$151,281
Capital Costs	$51,874
TOTAL	$361,816

Hickory

Residential Refuse Collection

Resource Measures

Residential Refuse Collection Costs per Capita

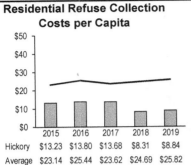

	2015	2016	2017	2018	2019
Hickory	$13.23	$13.80	$13.68	$8.31	$8.84
Average	$23.14	$25.44	$23.62	$24.69	$25.82

Residential Refuse FTEs per 10,000 Population

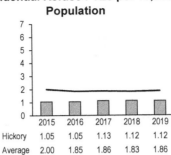

	2015	2016	2017	2018	2019
Hickory	1.05	1.05	1.13	1.12	1.12
Average	2.00	1.85	1.86	1.83	1.86

Workload Measures

Residential Refuse Tons per 1,000 Population

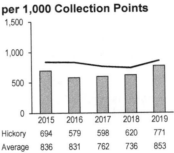

	2015	2016	2017	2018	2019
Hickory	210	175	180	182	225
Average	246	242	257	248	275

Residential Refuse Tons per 1,000 Collection Points

	2015	2016	2017	2018	2019
Hickory	694	579	598	620	771
Average	836	831	762	736	853

Efficiency Measures

Residential Refuse Collection Cost per Ton Collected

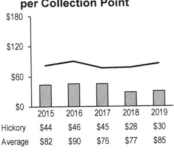

	2015	2016	2017	2018	2019
Hickory	$79	$76	$46	$46	$39
Average	$117	$107	$124	$116	$108

Residential Refuse Collection Cost per Collection Point

	2015	2016	2017	2018	2019
Hickory	$44	$46	$45	$28	$30
Average	$82	$90	$76	$77	$85

Refuse Tons Collected per Municipal Collection FTE

	2015	2016	2017	2018	2019
Hickory	2,259	1,883	1,945	1,973	2,456
Average	1,543	1,624	1,727	1,713	1,959

Effectiveness Measures

Complaints per 1,000 Collection Points

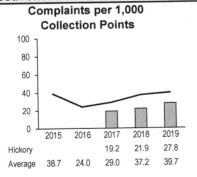

	2015	2016	2017	2018	2019
Hickory			19.2	21.9	27.8
Average	38.7	24.0	29.0	37.2	39.7

Valid Complaints per 1,000 Collection Points

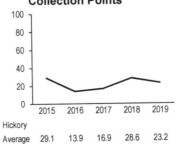

	2015	2016	2017	2018	2019
Hickory					
Average	29.1	13.9	16.9	28.6	23.2

Fiscal Year 2018–19

Explanatory Information

Service Level and Delivery

Mooresville provides residential refuse collection service once per week at curbside. Backyard collection service is provided for disabled customers only. The town charges a monthly fee of $10 for all solid waste collection.

The town used both one-person and two-person crews in six trucks during the fiscal year. Collection routes required an average of 2.5 four-mile trips per route per day to the landfill.

Each resident uses a ninety-five-gallon roll-out cart provided and paid for by the town. There is no limit on the number of carts that can be used. The town collected 13,121 tons of residential refuse during the fiscal year, at a cost per ton of $123.

Conditions Affecting Service, Performance, and Costs

Mooresville joined the Benchmarking project in July 2018, with the first year of data showing for FY2017–18.

The town does not track recycling collection complaints separately. Thus, some of the reported complaints for refuse collection may be about recycling.

Municipal Profile

Population (OSBM 2018)	41,255
Land Area (Square Miles)	22.75
Persons per Square Mile	1,813
Median Household Income	$67,213
U.S. Census 2016	

Service Profile

FTE Positions—Collection	11.0
FTE Positions—Other	2.0
Type of Equipment	3 automated packers
	3 packers
Size of Crews (most commonly used)	1 & 2 person
Weekly Routes	20
Average Distance to Disposal Site	4 miles
Average Daily Trips to Disposal Site	2.5
Percentage of Service Contracted	0%
Collection Frequency	1 x week
General Collection Location	Curbside
Residential Customers	14,500
(number represents collection points)	
Tons Collected	13,121
Monthly Service Fee	$10.00

Full Cost Profile

Cost Breakdown by Percentage

Personal Services	35.4%
Operating Costs	34.9%
Capital Costs	29.7%
TOTAL	100.0%

Cost Breakdown in Dollars

Personal Services	$571,588
Operating Costs	$563,822
Capital Costs	$479,600
TOTAL	$1,615,010

Mooresville

Residential Refuse Collection

Resource Measures

Residential Refuse Collection Costs per Capita

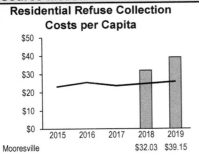

	2015	2016	2017	2018	2019
Mooresville				$32.03	$39.15
Average	$23.14	$25.44	$23.62	$24.69	$25.82

Residential Refuse FTEs per 10,000 Population

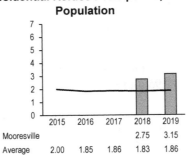

	2015	2016	2017	2018	2019
Mooresville				2.75	3.15
Average	2.00	1.85	1.86	1.83	1.86

Workload Measures

Residential Refuse Tons per 1,000 Population

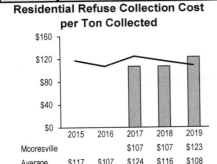

	2015	2016	2017	2018	2019
Mooresville				300	318
Average	246	242	257	248	275

Residential Refuse Tons per 1,000 Collection Points

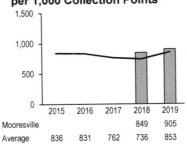

	2015	2016	2017	2018	2019
Mooresville				849	905
Average	836	831	762	736	853

Efficiency Measures

Residential Refuse Collection Cost per Ton Collected

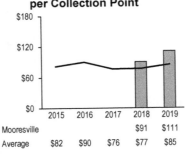

	2015	2016	2017	2018	2019
Mooresville			$107	$107	$123
Average	$117	$107	$124	$116	$108

Residential Refuse Collection Cost per Collection Point

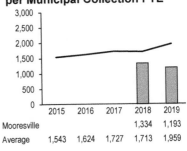

	2015	2016	2017	2018	2019
Mooresville				$91	$111
Average	$82	$90	$76	$77	$85

Refuse Tons Collected per Municipal Collection FTE

	2015	2016	2017	2018	2019
Mooresville				1,334	1,193
Average	1,543	1,624	1,727	1,713	1,959

Effectiveness Measures

Complaints per 1,000 Collection Points

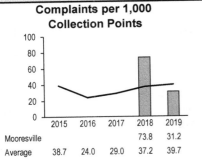

	2015	2016	2017	2018	2019
Mooresville				73.8	31.2
Average	38.7	24.0	29.0	37.2	39.7

Valid Complaints per 1,000 Collection Points

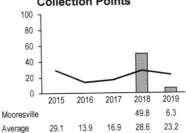

	2015	2016	2017	2018	2019
Mooresville				49.8	6.3
Average	29.1	13.9	16.9	28.6	23.2

Fiscal Year 2018–19

Explanatory Information

Service Level and Delivery

Raleigh provides residential refuse collection service once per week at curbside. Backyard collection service is provided for customers who have been certified by a physician as being unable to move a cart to the curb and who have no able-bodied resident to provide assistance. The city charges a monthly fee of $12.95 for refuse collection.

The city employed twenty-two automated trucks with a single driver and ten crews of three on semi-automated trucks for primary collection. A total of 120 collection routes were used per week with a average truck making two trips per day to the disposal site, covering a distance of ten miles.

Each customer has up to two ninety-five-gallon roll-out carts provided and paid for by the city. The city collected 92,524 tons of residential refuse during the fiscal year, at a cost per ton of $150 or $107 per collection point. Not included in the cost per ton was a $30 landfill tipping fee.

Conditions Affecting Service, Performance, and Costs

Raleigh rejoined the Benchmarking Project in July 2016, with the first year of data showing for FY 2015–16.

Municipal Profile

Population (OSBM 2018)	464,453
Land Area (Square Miles)	145.65
Persons per Square Mile	3,189
Median Household Income	$46,612
U.S. Census 2016	

Service Profile

FTE Positions—Collection	74.0
FTE Positions—Other	4.0
Type of Equipment	22 automated packers
	10 packers
Size of Crews (most commonly used)	1 & 3 person
Weekly Routes	120
Average Distance to Disposal Site	10 miles
Average Daily Trips to Disposal Site	2
Percentage of Service Contracted	0%
Collection Frequency	1 x week
General Collection Location	Curbside
Residential Customers	129,962
(number represents collection points)	
Tons Collected	92,524
Monthly Service Fee	$12.95

Full Cost Profile

Cost Breakdown by Percentage

Personal Services	38.8%
Operating Costs	26.9%
Capital Costs	34.3%
TOTAL	100.0%

Cost Breakdown in Dollars

Personal Services	$5,399,292
Operating Costs	$3,744,361
Capital Costs	$4,775,851
TOTAL	$13,919,504

Raleigh

Residential Refuse Collection

Resource Measures

Residential Refuse Collection Costs per Capita

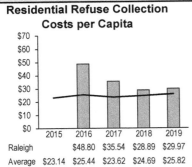

	2015	2016	2017	2018	2019
Raleigh		$48.80	$35.54	$28.89	$29.97
Average	$23.14	$25.44	$23.62	$24.69	$25.82

Residential Refuse FTEs per 10,000 Population

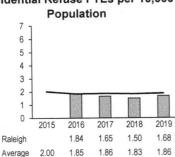

	2015	2016	2017	2018	2019
Raleigh		1.84	1.65	1.50	1.68
Average	2.00	1.85	1.86	1.83	1.86

Workload Measures

Residential Refuse Tons per 1,000 Population

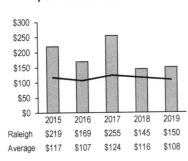

	2015	2016	2017	2018	2019
Raleigh		222	210	200	199
Average	246	242	257	248	275

Residential Refuse Tons per 1,000 Collection Points

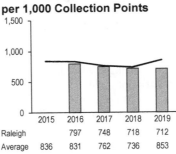

	2015	2016	2017	2018	2019
Raleigh		797	748	718	712
Average	836	831	762	736	853

Efficiency Measures

Residential Refuse Collection Cost per Ton Collected

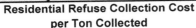

	2015	2016	2017	2018	2019
Raleigh	$219	$169	$255	$145	$150
Average	$117	$107	$124	$116	$108

Residential Refuse Collection Cost per Collection Point

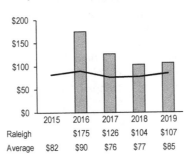

	2015	2016	2017	2018	2019
Raleigh		$175	$126	$104	$107
Average	$82	$90	$76	$77	$85

Refuse Tons Collected per Municipal Collection FTE

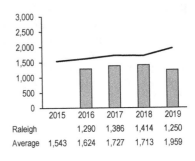

	2015	2016	2017	2018	2019
Raleigh		1,290	1,386	1,414	1,250
Average	1,543	1,624	1,727	1,713	1,959

Effectiveness Measures

Complaints per 1,000 Collection Points

	2015	2016	2017	2018	2019
Raleigh		40.6	46.3	52.5	48.4
Average	38.7	24.0	29.0	37.2	39.7

Valid Complaints per 1,000 Collection Points

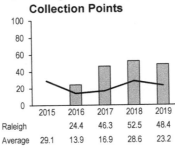

	2015	2016	2017	2018	2019
Raleigh		24.4	46.3	52.5	48.4
Average	29.1	13.9	16.9	28.6	23.2

Fiscal Year 2018–19

Explanatory Information

Service Level and Delivery

Residential refuse collection service is provided once a week at curbside to Wilson residents. Senior citizens and disabled persons may apply for and receive backyard pickup. There is currently a monthly $20.00 fee per household for the residential refuse collection service.

During the fiscal year, the city used five one-person crews working from automated packers. The city also used two three-person crews, each composed of one driver and two collectors working from semi-automated rear loaders. Residents are required to use ninety-six-gallon roll-out containers.

The city serviced twenty-four collection routes each week during the fiscal year. The packers made an average of 1.15 trips to the disposal facility per day per route, with the distance to the transfer station being ten miles.

Wilson collected 25,100 tons of residential refuse during the fiscal year, at a cost of $55 per ton. The cost per ton does not include the disposal cost of $40.87, representing the tipping fee at the transfer station.

Conditions Affecting Service, Performance, and Costs

During FY 2017–18, Wilson made sweeping route changes and added additional entry level positions and two new supervisors.

Wilson began using a new system for tracking all call-ins into "FixIt Wilson" during FY 2017–18. Complaints include missed trash; spilled trash; improper place of container; vehicle or other obstructions blocking pickup; and other issues. Not all of these represent problems with the collection staff. This change in the system increased the reported number of complaints or problems. The city of Wilson considers all complaints to be valid complaints.

Municipal Profile

Population (OSBM 2018)	49,054
Land Area (Square Miles)	30.97
Persons per Square Mile	1,584
Median Household Income	$35,409
U.S. Census 2016	

Service Profile

FTE Positions—Collection	8.5
FTE Positions—Other	0.8
Type of Equipment	5 automated packers
	2 packers
Size of Crews (most commonly used)	1 & 3 person
Weekly Routes	24
Average Distance to Disposal Site	10 miles
Average Daily Trips to Disposal Site	1.15
Percentage of Service Contracted	0%
Collection Frequency	1 x week
General Collection Location	Curbside
Residential Customers (number represents collection points)	20,900
Tons Collected	25,100
Monthly Service Fee	$20.00

Full Cost Profile

Cost Breakdown by Percentage

Personal Services	37.6%
Operating Costs	35.0%
Capital Costs	27.5%
TOTAL	100.0%

Cost Breakdown in Dollars

Personal Services	$522,644
Operating Costs	$486,274
Capital Costs	$382,079
TOTAL	$1,390,997

Wilson

Residential Refuse Collection

Resource Measures

Residential Refuse Collection Costs per Capita

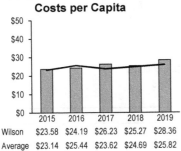

	2015	2016	2017	2018	2019
Wilson	$23.58	$24.19	$26.23	$25.27	$28.36
Average	$23.14	$25.44	$23.62	$24.69	$25.82

Residential Refuse FTEs per 10,000 Population

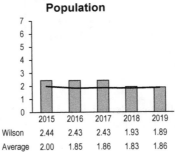

	2015	2016	2017	2018	2019
Wilson	2.44	2.43	2.43	1.93	1.89
Average	2.00	1.85	1.86	1.83	1.86

Workload Measures

Residential Refuse Tons per 1,000 Population

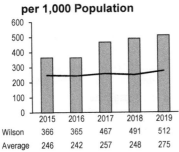

	2015	2016	2017	2018	2019
Wilson	366	365	467	491	512
Average	246	242	257	248	275

Residential Refuse Tons per 1,000 Collection Points

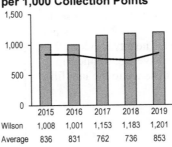

	2015	2016	2017	2018	2019
Wilson	1,008	1,001	1,153	1,183	1,201
Average	836	831	762	736	853

Efficiency Measures

Residential Refuse Collection Cost per Ton Collected

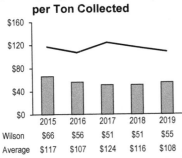

	2015	2016	2017	2018	2019
Wilson	$66	$56	$51	$51	$55
Average	$117	$107	$124	$116	$108

Residential Refuse Collection Cost per Collection Point

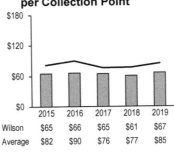

	2015	2016	2017	2018	2019
Wilson	$65	$66	$65	$61	$67
Average	$82	$90	$76	$77	$85

Refuse Tons Collected per Municipal Collection FTE

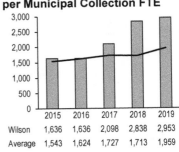

	2015	2016	2017	2018	2019
Wilson	1,636	1,636	2,098	2,838	2,953
Average	1,543	1,624	1,727	1,713	1,959

Effectiveness Measures

Complaints per 1,000 Collection Points

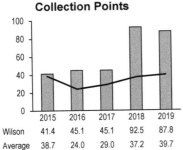

	2015	2016	2017	2018	2019
Wilson	41.4	45.1	45.1	92.5	87.8
Average	38.7	24.0	29.0	37.2	39.7

Valid Complaints per 1,000 Collection Points

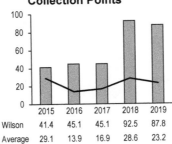

	2015	2016	2017	2018	2019
Wilson	41.4	45.1	45.1	92.5	87.8
Average	29.1	13.9	16.9	28.6	23.2

Fiscal Year 2018–19

Explanatory Information

Service Level and Delivery

Winston-Salem collects residential refuse once from curbside. The city implemented a voluntary curbside collection program in March 2005. In October 2010, the city began the transition to mandatory curbside collection. The transition to a curbside-only collection system was completed during FY 2011–12.

The city uses sixteen one-person crews to collect residential refuse plus eight three-person crews, each composed of a driver and two collectors equipped with rear-loading packers.

Residents may use three thirty-two-gallon containers or one ninety-six-gallon roll-out cart. There was no fee for the residential refuse service during the fiscal year.

The city collected 61,398 tons of residential refuse during the fiscal year from 81,589 collection points. The cost per ton was $119, which does not include the tipping fee of $36 per ton. The city serviced 96 collection routes during the fiscal year, with an average of one trip per route per day to the landfill. The average distance to the landfill was ten miles.

Conditions Affecting Service, Performance, and Costs

Municipal Profile

Population (OSBM 2018)	243,447
Land Area (Square Miles)	132.55
Persons per Square Mile	1,837
Median Household Income U.S. Census 2016	$40,584

Service Profile

FTE Positions—Collection	82.0
FTE Positions—Other	3.0
Type of Equipment	16 automated packers 8 packers
Size of Crews (most commonly used)	1 & 3 person
Weekly Routes	96
Average Distance to Disposal Site	10 miles
Average Daily Trips to Disposal Site	1
Percentage of Service Contracted	0%
Collection Frequency	1 x week
General Collection Location	Curbside
Residential Customers (number represents collection points)	81,589
Tons Collected	61,398
Monthly Service Fee	No

Full Cost Profile

Cost Breakdown by Percentage

Personal Services	45.6%
Operating Costs	35.3%
Capital Costs	19.1%
TOTAL	100.0%

Cost Breakdown in Dollars

Personal Services	$3,317,740
Operating Costs	$2,572,802
Capital Costs	$1,388,026
TOTAL	$7,278,568

Winston-Salem

Residential Refuse Collection

Resource Measures

Residential Refuse Collection Costs per Capita

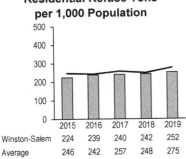

	2015	2016	2017	2018	2019
Winston-Salem	$25.85	$26.13	$30.33	$31.66	$29.90
Average	$23.14	$25.44	$23.62	$24.69	$25.82

Residential Refuse FTEs per 10,000 Population

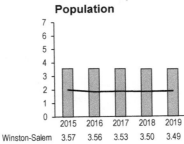

	2015	2016	2017	2018	2019
Winston-Salem	3.57	3.56	3.53	3.50	3.49
Average	2.00	1.85	1.86	1.83	1.86

Workload Measures

Residential Refuse Tons per 1,000 Population

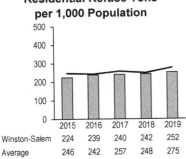

	2015	2016	2017	2018	2019
Winston-Salem	224	239	240	242	252
Average	246	242	257	248	275

Residential Refuse Tons per 1,000 Collection Points

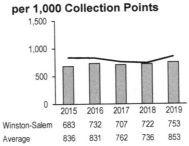

	2015	2016	2017	2018	2019
Winston-Salem	683	732	707	722	753
Average	836	831	762	736	853

Efficiency Measures

Residential Refuse Collection Cost per Ton Collected

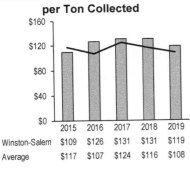

	2015	2016	2017	2018	2019
Winston-Salem	$109	$126	$131	$131	$119
Average	$117	$107	$124	$116	$108

Residential Refuse Collection Cost per Collection Point

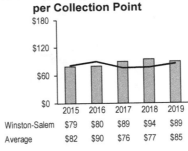

	2015	2016	2017	2018	2019
Winston-Salem	$79	$80	$89	$94	$89
Average	$82	$90	$76	$77	$85

Refuse Tons Collected per Municipal Collection FTE

	2015	2016	2017	2018	2019
Winston-Salem	649	696	704	718	749
Average	1,543	1,624	1,727	1,713	1,959

Effectiveness Measures

Complaints per 1,000 Collection Points

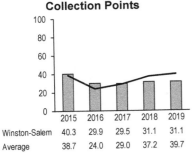

	2015	2016	2017	2018	2019
Winston-Salem	40.3	29.9	29.5	31.1	31.1
Average	38.7	24.0	29.0	37.2	39.7

Valid Complaints per 1,000 Collection Points

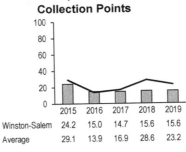

	2015	2016	2017	2018	2019
Winston-Salem	24.2	15.0	14.7	15.6	15.6
Average	29.1	13.9	16.9	28.6	23.2

UNC | SCHOOL OF GOVERNMENT
North Carolina Benchmarking Project

Performance and Cost Data

HOUSEHOLD RECYCLING

PERFORMANCE MEASURES FOR HOUSEHOLD RECYCLING

SERVICE DEFINITION

This includes both curbside collection and processing of household recyclable materials from residences and certain other locations and the drop-off of such materials by citizens at recycling stations or centers. The recyclable materials collected are mainly aluminum and steel cans, plastics, glass bottles, newspapers, magazines, and cardboard. The curbside portion of this service involves regularly scheduled collection that utilizes containers small enough that residents and/or workers can move or lift them. The service definition excludes collection of yard waste, leaves, and commercial recycling.

NOTES ON PERFORMANCE MEASURES

1. Workload and Efficiency Measures

The same sorts of workload and efficiency measures are used for household recycling as for residential refuse collection. The project's workload measures for household recycling are tons of recyclable materials collected per 1,000 population and per 1,000 collection points, and the efficiency measures for this service are cost per ton of recyclable materials collected, cost per collection point, and tons of household recyclable materials collected per full-time equivalent (FTE) position directly involved in household recycling. FTEs for recycling are calculated in the same way as they are for residential refuse collection. Only those FTE positions that actually collect recyclables are used for the measure "tons collected per FTE."

2. Tons of Solid Waste Landfilled per 1,000 Population

"Tons solid waste landfilled per 1,000 population" is used as a workload measure. Although not all residential refuse is recyclable, much more of it is likely to be recycled in the future as recycling technology improves and markets for recyclable materials grow. Thus, tons of solid waste landfilled per 1,000 population serves as a useful indicator of the need for household recycling.

3. Community Set-Out Rate in Household Recycling

The project uses this as a measure the effectiveness of household recycling. Residents in municipalities with curbside recycling choose whether to participate in the program and decide the extent of their participation. As the portion of households participating in household recycling grows, the more effective recycling is likely to be in reducing the volume of residential refuse. This measure combines the set-out rate for those participating and the participation rate to estimate the percentage of potential households that are actually recycling.

4. Tons of Household Recyclable Materials Collected as a Percentage of the Sum of Tons of Residential Refuse Collected Plus Tons of Household Recyclable Materials Collected

This measure assesses the magnitude of household recycling in relation to residential refuse collected for disposal. A household recycling program is effective to the extent it diverts residential refuse from the disposal stream.

Household Recycling

Summary of Key Dimensions of Service

| City or Town | Drop-Off Sites | | Collection Frequency | Collection Points | Community Set-Out Rate | Tons Collected | Percentage of Waste Stream Diverted from Landfill | Percentage Service Contracted | Municipal FTE Collection Positions |
	City Owned	Other							
Apex	0	0	1 x week	15,445	NA	4,241	22%	100%	NA
Asheville	0	1	1 x 2 weeks	29,452	100%	8,525	27%	100%	NA
Charlotte	0	11	1 x 2 weeks	219,839	28%	40,092	17%	100%	NA
Concord	0	1	1 x 2 weeks	33,082	65%	4,348	12%	100%	1.9
Goldsboro	0	0	1 x 2 weeks	14,372	NA	1,020	8%	70%	4.0
Greensboro	20	0	1 x 2 weeks	90,625	45%	16,188	21%	0%	15
Greenville	220	3	1 x week	19,250	65%	3,992	13%	0%	6
Hickory	2	0	1 x 2 weeks	11,940	66%	2,682	23%	92%	0.5
Mooresville	1	1	1 x 2 weeks	11,327	77%	2,591	16%	0%	2
Raleigh	2	1	1 x 2 weeks	189,633	72%	27,966	23%	0%	39
Wilson	0	0	1 x 2 weeks	25,100	65%	1,645	6%	0%	4
Winston-Salem	9	0	1 x 2 weeks	81,589	59%	15,629	20%	100%	NA

NOTES

Community Set-Out Rate is a combination of the participation rate and the participant's set-out rate.

EXPLANATORY FACTORS

These are factors that the project found affected household recycling collection performance and cost in one or more of the municipalities:

Types of items eligible for recycling
Landfill tipping fees for solid waste
Commitment of city officials to recycling
Number of drop-off centers
Community education
Market prices for recyclable materials
Demographic makeup of community

Explanatory Information

Service Level and Delivery

Apex contracts with Waste Industries for refuse collection, disposal, and recycling. Only the recycling collection is reflected on this page. The town offers curbside recycling to all residents. Residents pay a $3.44 fee per container per month. Most residents have a sixty-four-gallon cart though some have eighteen-gallon containers.

The following materials are collected:

- plastics
- paperboard
- chipboard
- paper tubes
- corrugated cardboard
- aluminum
- tin and steel cans
- glass
- newspaper
- magazines and catalogs
- phone books

Residents living within Apex are encouraged to participate in the curbside recycling program. The program serves 15,445 residences.

Conditions Affecting Service, Performance, and Costs

Municipal Profile

Population (OSBM 2018)	52,909
Land Area (Square Miles)	21.55
Persons per Square Mile	2,455
Median Household Income	$84,000
U.S. Census 2016	

Service Profile

FTE Positions—Collection	Contractor
FTE Positions—Other	Contractor
Number of City Drop-Off Centers	0
Other Drop-Off Centers	0
Percentage of Service Contracted	100%
Collection Frequency	1 x week
General Collection Location	Curbside
Recyclables Sorted at Curb	No
Collection Points	15,445
Tons of Recyclables Collected	
Curbside	4,241
City Drop-Off Centers	0
Total Tons Collected	4,241
Monthly Service Fee	$3.44
Revenue from Sale of Recyclables	$0
Sale Revenue as Percentage of Cost	NA

Full Cost Profile

Cost Breakdown by Percentage	
Personal Services	0.0%
Operating Costs	100.0%
Capital Costs	0.0%
TOTAL	100.0%
Cost Breakdown in Dollars	
Personal Services	$0
Operating Costs	$718,596
Capital Costs	$0
TOTAL	$718,596

Apex

Household Recycling

Resource Measures

Recycling Services Cost per Capita

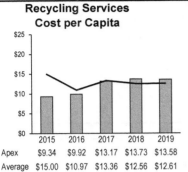

	2015	2016	2017	2018	2019
Apex	$9.34	$9.92	$13.17	$13.73	$13.58
Average	$15.00	$10.97	$13.36	$12.56	$12.61

Recycling Services FTEs per 10,000 Population

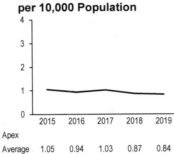

	2015	2016	2017	2018	2019
Apex					
Average	1.05	0.94	1.03	0.87	0.84

Workload Measures

Tons Recyclables Collected per 1,000 Population

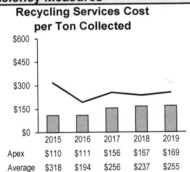

	2015	2016	2017	2018	2019
Apex	84.8	89.7	84.6	82.1	80.1
Average	58.7	63.7	60.8	59.5	56.8

Tons Recyclables Collected per 1,000 Collection Points

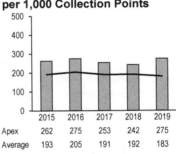

	2015	2016	2017	2018	2019
Apex	262	275	253	242	275
Average	193	205	191	192	183

Tons Solid Waste Landfilled per 1,000 Population

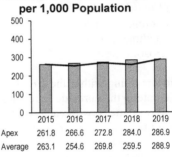

	2015	2016	2017	2018	2019
Apex	261.8	266.6	272.8	284.0	286.9
Average	263.1	254.6	269.8	259.5	288.9

Efficiency Measures

Recycling Services Cost per Ton Collected

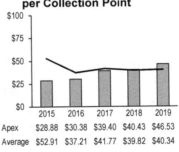

	2015	2016	2017	2018	2019
Apex	$110	$111	$156	$167	$169
Average	$318	$194	$256	$237	$255

Recycling Services Cost per Collection Point

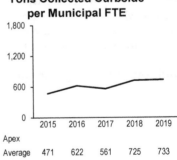

	2015	2016	2017	2018	2019
Apex	$28.88	$30.38	$39.40	$40.43	$46.53
Average	$52.91	$37.21	$41.77	$39.82	$40.34

Tons Collected Curbside per Municipal FTE

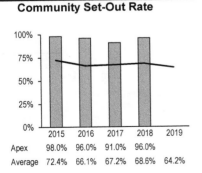

	2015	2016	2017	2018	2019
Apex					
Average	471	622	561	725	733

Effectiveness Measures

Community Set-Out Rate

	2015	2016	2017	2018	2019
Apex	98.0%	96.0%	91.0%	96.0%	
Average	72.4%	66.1%	67.2%	68.6%	64.2%

Tons Recycled as Percentage of Tons Refuse and Recyclables Collected

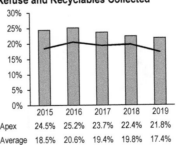

	2015	2016	2017	2018	2019
Apex	24.5%	25.2%	23.7%	22.4%	21.8%
Average	18.5%	20.6%	19.4%	19.8%	17.4%

Fiscal Year 2018–19

Explanatory Information

Service Level and Delivery

The city offers curbside recycling service to all residential customers. The service was provided by contract during the fiscal year by Curbside Management Incorporated. The contracted service also includes daily collection of approximately 276 on-street recycling cans located in the city.

Asheville charged a $14 monthly fee for all solid waste services. The following materials are collected:

- mixed paper
- newspaper
- corrugated cardboard
- clear, green, and brown glass bottles
- all plastic bottles
- aluminum and steel cans
- telephone books (seasonal)
- aerosol cans

Residents living within the city of Asheville are encouraged to participate in the curbside recycling program. The program serves 29,452 residences, with each residence receiving a ninety-five-gallon or in some cases a sixty-five-gallon cart. Recycling is collected every other week on the regular trash day. A curbside recycling truck comes to each neighborhood on a predetermined schedule and separates the recyclables at the curb.

There is one drop-off center within Asheville. This center is set up for people who do not have curbside recycling pickup at their homes or businesses. Anyone can use this center to drop off their recycling during the transfer station's operating times.

Conditions Affecting Service, Performance, and Costs

Municipal Profile

Population (OSBM 2018)	93,621
Land Area (Square Miles)	45.53
Persons per Square Mile	2,056
Median Household Income U.S. Census 2016	$40,494

Service Profile

FTE Positions—Collection	Contractor
FTE Positions—Other	Contractor
Number of City Drop-Off Centers	0
Other Drop-Off Centers	1
Percentage of Service Contracted	100.0%
Collection Frequency	Every 2 weeks
General Collection Location	Curbside
Recyclables Sorted at Curb	No
Collection Points	29,452
Tons of Recyclables Collected	
Curbside	8,525
City Drop-Off Centers	0
Total Tons Collected	8,525
Monthly Service Fee	$0.00
Revenue from Sale of Recyclables	$0
Sale Revenue as Percentage of Cost	NA

Full Cost Profile

Cost Breakdown by Percentage	
Personal Services	0.0%
Operating Costs	100.0%
Capital Costs	0.0%
TOTAL	100.0%
Cost Breakdown in Dollars	
Personal Services	$0
Operating Costs	$1,289,122
Capital Costs	$0
TOTAL	$1,289,122

Asheville

Household Recycling

Resource Measures

Recycling Services Cost per Capita

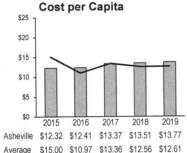

	2015	2016	2017	2018	2019
Asheville	$12.32	$12.41	$13.37	$13.51	$13.77
Average	$15.00	$10.97	$13.36	$12.56	$12.61

Recycling Services FTEs per 10,000 Population

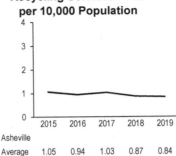

	2015	2016	2017	2018	2019
Asheville					
Average	1.05	0.94	1.03	0.87	0.84

Workload Measures

Tons Recyclables Collected per 1,000 Population

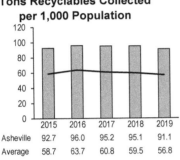

	2015	2016	2017	2018	2019
Asheville	92.7	96.0	95.2	95.1	91.1
Average	58.7	63.7	60.8	59.5	56.8

Tons Recyclables Collected per 1,000 Collection Points

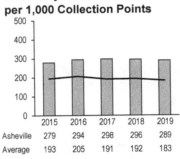

	2015	2016	2017	2018	2019
Asheville	279	294	298	296	289
Average	193	205	191	192	183

Tons Solid Waste Landfilled per 1,000 Population

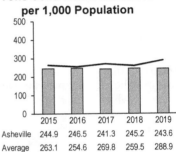

	2015	2016	2017	2018	2019
Asheville	244.9	246.5	241.3	245.2	243.6
Average	263.1	254.6	269.8	259.5	288.9

Efficiency Measures

Recycling Services Cost per Ton Collected

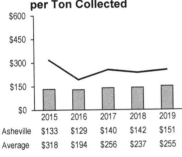

	2015	2016	2017	2018	2019
Asheville	$133	$129	$140	$142	$151
Average	$318	$194	$256	$237	$255

Recycling Services Cost per Collection Point

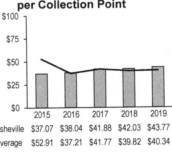

	2015	2016	2017	2018	2019
Asheville	$37.07	$38.04	$41.88	$42.03	$43.77
Average	$52.91	$37.21	$41.77	$39.82	$40.34

Tons Collected Curbside per Municipal FTE

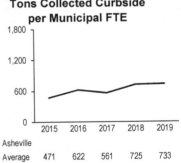

	2015	2016	2017	2018	2019
Asheville					
Average	471	622	561	725	733

Effectiveness Measures

Community Set-Out Rate

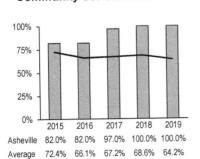

	2015	2016	2017	2018	2019
Asheville	82.0%	82.0%	97.0%	100.0%	100.0%
Average	72.4%	66.1%	67.2%	68.6%	64.2%

Tons Recycled as Percentage of Tons Refuse and Recyclables Collected

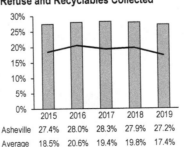

	2015	2016	2017	2018	2019
Asheville	27.4%	28.0%	28.3%	27.9%	27.2%
Average	18.5%	20.6%	19.4%	19.8%	17.4%

Fiscal Year 2018–19

Service Level and Delivery

Charlotte provides curbside recycling collection to single-family residential customers once every two weeks. Recycling collection is entirely provided by a contractor. Materials collected in the recycling program include the following:

- glass
- plastic
- aluminum
- newspaper
- magazines
- catalogs
- phone books
- cardboard
- milk cartons
- aerosol cans
- juice boxes

The majority of users have ninety-five or ninety-six-gallon roll-out containers. The city receives a modest amount from sale of recyclables, which totaled $66,238 for the year.

The county operates several recycling drop-off centers that are available for use by citizens of Charlotte and Mecklenburg County. Tonnage from the drop-off centers is not included in this report.

Conditions Affecting Service, Performance, and Costs

Charlotte did not participate in the Benchmarking Project during FY 2014–15. No data are available for that year.

The set-out rate is calculated daily, as the trucks are outfitted with Radio Frequency Identification (RFID) readers and the recycling carts have RFID chips installed.

Municipal Profile

Population (OSBM 2018)	852,992
Land Area (Square Miles)	306.31
Persons per Square Mile	2,785
Median Household Income	$46,975
U.S. Census 2016	

Service Profile

FTE Positions—Collection	Contractor
FTE Positions—Other	Contractor
Number of City Drop-Off Centers	0
Other Drop-Off Centers	11
Percentage of Service Contracted	100%
Collection Frequency	Every 2 weeks
General Collection Location	Curbside
Recyclables Sorted at Curb	No
Collection Points	219,839
Tons of Recyclables Collected	
Curbside	40,092
City Drop-Off Centers	0
Total Tons Collected	40,092
Monthly Service Fee	0
Revenue from Sale of Recyclables	$66,238
Sale Revenue as Percentage of Cost	0.9%

Full Cost Profile

Cost Breakdown by Percentage	
Personal Services	0.0%
Operating Costs	99.1%
Capital Costs	0.9%
TOTAL	100.0%
Cost Breakdown in Dollars	
Personal Services	$0
Operating Costs	$7,034,262
Capital Costs	$61,649
TOTAL	$7,095,911

Charlotte

Household Recycling

Key: Charlotte ▦   Benchmarking Average —

Fiscal Years 2015 through 2019

Resource Measures

Recycling Services Cost per Capita

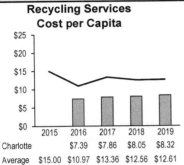

	2015	2016	2017	2018	2019
Charlotte		$7.39	$7.86	$8.05	$8.32
Average	$15.00	$10.97	$13.36	$12.56	$12.61

Recycling Services FTEs per 10,000 Population

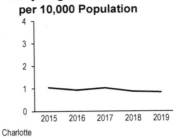

	2015	2016	2017	2018	2019
Charlotte					
Average	1.05	0.94	1.03	0.87	0.84

Workload Measures

Tons Recyclables Collected per 1,000 Population

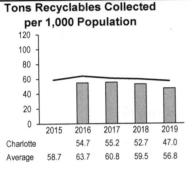

	2015	2016	2017	2018	2019
Charlotte		54.7	55.2	52.7	47.0
Average	58.7	63.7	60.8	59.5	56.8

Tons Recyclables Collected per 1,000 Collection Points

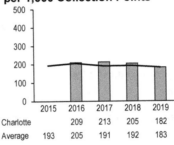

	2015	2016	2017	2018	2019
Charlotte		209	213	205	182
Average	193	205	191	192	183

Tons Solid Waste Landfilled per 1,000 Population

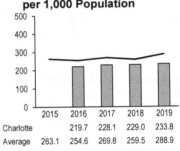

	2015	2016	2017	2018	2019
Charlotte		219.7	228.1	229.0	233.8
Average	263.1	254.6	269.8	259.5	288.9

Efficiency Measures

Recycling Services Cost per Ton Collected

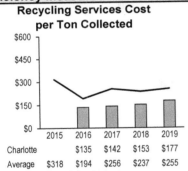

	2015	2016	2017	2018	2019
Charlotte		$135	$142	$153	$177
Average	$318	$194	$256	$237	$255

Recycling Services Cost per Collection Point

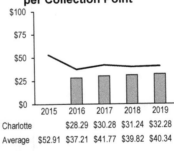

	2015	2016	2017	2018	2019
Charlotte		$28.29	$30.28	$31.24	$32.28
Average	$52.91	$37.21	$41.77	$39.82	$40.34

Tons Collected Curbside per Municipal FTE

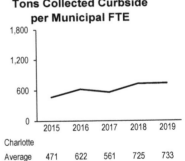

	2015	2016	2017	2018	2019
Charlotte					
Average	471	622	561	725	733

Effectiveness Measures

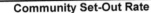

Community Set-Out Rate

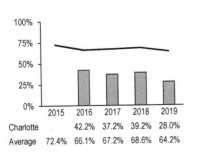

	2015	2016	2017	2018	2019
Charlotte		42.2%	37.2%	39.2%	28.0%
Average	72.4%	66.1%	67.2%	68.6%	64.2%

Tons Recycled as Percentage of Tons Refuse and Recyclables Collected

	2015	2016	2017	2018	2019
Charlotte		19.9%	19.5%	18.7%	16.7%
Average	18.5%	20.6%	19.4%	19.8%	17.4%

Fiscal Year 2018–19

Explanatory Information

Service Level and Delivery

Concord provides biweekly curbside collection of recyclable materials from households. The city uses a contractor to provide recycling collection. Residents place materials into a ninety-five-gallon cart. The recyclable materials collected include:

- glass
- newspaper
- magazines
- mixed paper and mail
- No. 1 and No. 2 plastics
- metal and aluminum food and beverage containers

Concord uses a contract collector for regular residential curbside recycling. The materials are collected on a commingled basis biweekly from each participating resident and delivered to a materials recovery facility (MRF) in Charlotte for separation and marketing.

The city received $64,688 from the sale of recyclables during the year, offsetting some of the costs.

Conditions Affecting Service, Performance, and Costs

Municipal Profile

Population (OSBM 2018)	92,568
Land Area (Square Miles)	62.80
Persons per Square Mile	1,474
Median Household Income U.S. Census 2016	$50,863

Service Profile

FTE Positions—Collection	1.9
FTE Positions—Other	1.44
Number of City Drop-Off Centers	0
Other Drop-Off Centers	1
Percentage of Service Contracted	100%
Collection Frequency	Every 2 weeks
General Collection Location	Curbside
Recyclables Sorted at Curb	No
Collection Points	33,082
Tons of Recyclables Collected	
Curbside	4,348
City Drop-Off Centers	0
Total Tons Collected	4,348
Monthly Service Fee	0
Revenue from Sale of Recyclables	$64,688
Sale Revenue as Percentage of Cost	4.4%

Full Cost Profile

Cost Breakdown by Percentage	
Personal Services	12.7%
Operating Costs	85.6%
Capital Costs	1.8%
TOTAL	100.0%
Cost Breakdown in Dollars	
Personal Services	$185,489
Operating Costs	$1,254,093
Capital Costs	$25,771
TOTAL	$1,465,353

Key: Concord ▨   Benchmarking Average — Fiscal Years 2015 through 2019

Resource Measures

Recycling Services Cost per Capita

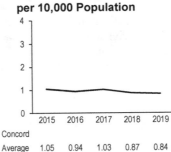

	2015	2016	2017	2018	2019
Concord	$9.91	$9.96	$12.78	$13.62	$15.83
Average	$15.00	$10.97	$13.36	$12.56	$12.61

Recycling Services FTEs per 10,000 Population

	2015	2016	2017	2018	2019
Concord					
Average	1.05	0.94	1.03	0.87	0.84

Workload Measures

Tons Recyclables Collected per 1,000 Population

	2015	2016	2017	2018	2019
Concord	65.0	68.2	67.6	60.2	47.0
Average	58.7	63.7	60.8	59.5	56.8

Tons Recyclables Collected per 1,000 Collection Points

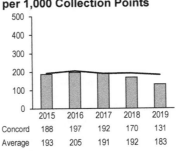

	2015	2016	2017	2018	2019
Concord	188	197	192	170	131
Average	193	205	191	192	183

Tons Solid Waste Landfilled per 1,000 Population

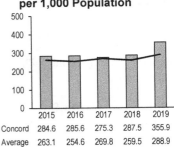

	2015	2016	2017	2018	2019
Concord	284.6	285.6	275.3	287.5	355.9
Average	263.1	254.6	269.8	259.5	288.9

Efficiency Measures

Recycling Services Cost per Ton Collected

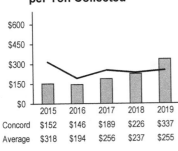

	2015	2016	2017	2018	2019
Concord	$152	$146	$189	$226	$337
Average	$318	$194	$256	$237	$255

Recycling Services Cost per Collection Point

	2015	2016	2017	2018	2019
Concord	$28.65	$28.77	$36.36	$38.36	$44.29
Average	$52.91	$37.21	$41.77	$39.82	$40.34

Tons Collected Curbside per Municipal FTE

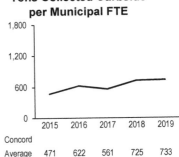

	2015	2016	2017	2018	2019
Concord					
Average	471	622	561	725	733

Effectiveness Measures

Community Set-Out Rate

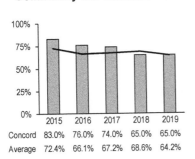

	2015	2016	2017	2018	2019
Concord	83.0%	76.0%	74.0%	65.0%	65.0%
Average	72.4%	66.1%	67.2%	68.6%	64.2%

Tons Recycled as Percentage of Tons Refuse and Recyclables Collected

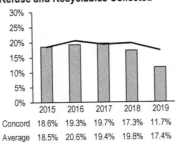

	2015	2016	2017	2018	2019
Concord	18.6%	19.3%	19.7%	17.3%	11.7%
Average	18.5%	20.6%	19.4%	19.8%	17.4%

Explanatory Information

Service Level and Delivery

Goldsboro operates a recycling system with curbside collection for residents. Recycling is picked up by the Solid Waste Division of the Public Works Department. Collection is done every two weeks. Residents pay a fee that covers all solid waste services, including recycling. Residents use a ninety-five-gallon container provided by the city.

Goldsboro's recycling is not sorted curbside. Materials collected by the household recycling program include:

- No. 1 and No. 2 plastics
- newspaper
- magazines
- telephone books
- cardboard
- aluminum and steel cans
- glass jars and bottles
- plastic soda bottles and milk jugs
- office paper

Conditions Affecting Service, Performance, and Costs

The city of Goldsboro joined the Benchmarking Project in July 2017, with the first year of data showing for FY 2016–17.

Goldsboro contracts recycling collection for one small neighborhood where a hill and tight roads make it infeasible to use city trucks.

Municipal Profile

Population (OSBM 2018)	33,636
Land Area (Square Miles)	29.41
Persons per Square Mile	1,144
Median Household Income	$32,148
U.S. Census 2016	

Service Profile

FTE Positions—Collection	4.0
FTE Positions—Other	0.8
Number of City Drop-Off Centers	0
Other Drop-Off Centers	0
Percentage of Service Contracted	0.7%
Collection Frequency	Every 2 weeks
General Collection Location	Curbside
Recyclables Sorted at Curb	No
Collection Points	14,372
Tons of Recyclables Collected	
Curbside	1,020
City Drop-Off Centers	0
Total Tons Collected	1,020
Monthly Service Fee	0
Revenue from Sale of Recyclables	$0
Sale Revenue as Percentage of Cost	NA

Full Cost Profile

Cost Breakdown by Percentage	
Personal Services	55.9%
Operating Costs	31.9%
Capital Costs	12.2%
TOTAL	100.0%
Cost Breakdown in Dollars	
Personal Services	$329,968
Operating Costs	$188,420
Capital Costs	$71,759
TOTAL	$590,147

Goldsboro
Household Recycling

Resource Measures

Recycling Services Cost per Capita

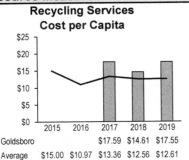

	2015	2016	2017	2018	2019
Goldsboro			$17.59	$14.61	$17.55
Average	$15.00	$10.97	$13.36	$12.56	$12.61

Recycling Services FTEs per 10,000 Population

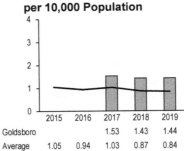

	2015	2016	2017	2018	2019
Goldsboro			1.53	1.43	1.44
Average	1.05	0.94	1.03	0.87	0.84

Workload Measures

Tons Recyclables Collected per 1,000 Population

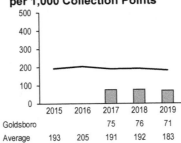

	2015	2016	2017	2018	2019
Goldsboro			31.2	32.6	30.3
Average	58.7	63.7	60.8	59.5	56.8

Tons Recyclables Collected per 1,000 Collection Points

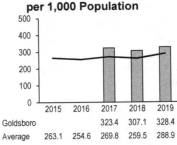

	2015	2016	2017	2018	2019
Goldsboro			75	76	71
Average	193	205	191	192	183

Tons Solid Waste Landfilled per 1,000 Population

	2015	2016	2017	2018	2019
Goldsboro			323.4	307.1	328.4
Average	263.1	254.6	269.8	259.5	288.9

Efficiency Measures

Recycling Services Cost per Ton Collected

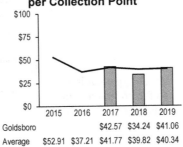

	2015	2016	2017	2018	2019
Goldsboro			$564	$448	$578
Average	$318	$194	$256	$237	$255

Recycling Services Cost per Collection Point

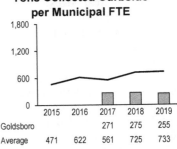

	2015	2016	2017	2018	2019
Goldsboro			$42.57	$34.24	$41.06
Average	$52.91	$37.21	$41.77	$39.82	$40.34

Tons Collected Curbside per Municipal FTE

	2015	2016	2017	2018	2019
Goldsboro			271	275	255
Average	471	622	561	725	733

Effectiveness Measures

Community Set-Out Rate

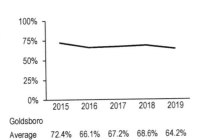

	2015	2016	2017	2018	2019
Goldsboro					
Average	72.4%	66.1%	67.2%	68.6%	64.2%

Tons Recycled as Percentage of Tons Refuse and Recyclables Collected

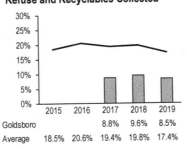

	2015	2016	2017	2018	2019
Goldsboro			8.8%	9.6%	8.5%
Average	18.5%	20.6%	19.4%	19.8%	17.4%

Explanatory Information

Service Level and Delivery

Greensboro operates a voluntary commingled collection process for its recycling customers. Recycling services are provided to the community by means of single ninety-six or sixty-four-gallon automated containers and by green translucent bags. Partnerships also are maintained with fire departments, the county school system, the extension office, and the parks department for providing drop-off sites. There are twenty city-owned drop-off sites, but these collected tons are not reported in Greensboro's data.

Recycling pickup is done every other week. Recycling materials are not sorted curbside. Instead, they are set out in one container, picked up by an automated-collection crew, and taken to an off-site contractor that sorts and recycles the materials. Greensboro provides the collection pickup and delivery to the contractor's location, while the contractor provides for recovery of materials and disposal of the residuals it is unable to recycle.

Materials collected by Greensboro's household recycling program include:

- No. 1 and No. 2 plastics
- newspaper
- magazines
- telephone books
- cardboard
- aluminum and steel cans
- chipboard (cereal boxes)
- glass jars and bottles
- plastic soda bottles and milk jugs
- office paper
- empty aerosol cans

Greensboro contracts with a private firm for separation, packaging, and sale of recyclable materials. City payments to the contractor for the fiscal year are included in total cost. The estimated revenues for sale of recyclables for residential recycling for the fiscal year was $233,318, partially offsetting program costs. Greensboro gets additional revenues from the sale of recyclables from nonresidential sources, but these are not counted here.

Conditions Affecting Service, Performance, and Costs

Greensboro is highly automated in gathering materials from its recycling program.

The set-out rate was based on a manual count done on a biweekly basis.

Municipal Profile

Population (OSBM 2018)	292,306
Land Area (Square Miles)	128.77
Persons per Square Mile	2,270
Median Household Income	$40,760
U.S. Census 2016	

Service Profile

FTE Positions—Collection	15.0
FTE Positions—Other	4.0
Number of City Drop-Off Centers	20
Other Drop-Off Centers	0
Percentage of Service Contracted	0%
Collection Frequency	Every 2 weeks
General Collection Location	Curbside
Recyclables Sorted at Curb	No
Collection Points	90,625
Tons of Recyclables Collected	
Curbside	16,188
City Drop-Off Centers	0
Total Tons Collected	16,188
Monthly Service Fee	0
Revenue from Sale of Recyclables	$233,318
Sale Revenue as Percentage of Cost	9.2%

Full Cost Profile

Cost Breakdown by Percentage	
Personal Services	38.4%
Operating Costs	61.6%
Capital Costs	0.0%
TOTAL	100.0%
Cost Breakdown in Dollars	
Personal Services	$969,728
Operating Costs	$1,553,073
Capital Costs	$0
TOTAL	$2,522,801

Greensboro

Household Recycling

Key: Greensboro ▦   Benchmarking Average —   Fiscal Years 2015 through 2019

Resource Measures

Recycling Services Cost per Capita

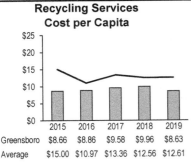

	2015	2016	2017	2018	2019
Greensboro	$8.66	$8.86	$9.58	$9.96	$8.63
Average	$15.00	$10.97	$13.36	$12.56	$12.61

Recycling Services FTEs per 10,000 Population

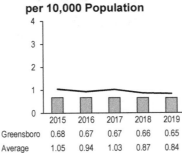

	2015	2016	2017	2018	2019
Greensboro	0.68	0.67	0.67	0.66	0.65
Average	1.05	0.94	1.03	0.87	0.84

Workload Measures

Tons Recyclables Collected per 1,000 Population

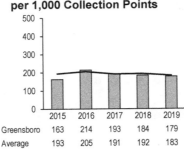

	2015	2016	2017	2018	2019
Greensboro	47.1	63.8	60.5	57.5	55.4
Average	58.7	63.7	60.8	59.5	56.8

Tons Recyclables Collected per 1,000 Collection Points

	2015	2016	2017	2018	2019
Greensboro	163	214	193	184	179
Average	193	205	191	192	183

Tons Solid Waste Landfilled per 1,000 Population

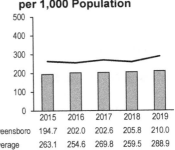

	2015	2016	2017	2018	2019
Greensboro	194.7	202.0	202.6	205.8	210.0
Average	263.1	254.6	269.8	259.5	288.9

Efficiency Measures

Recycling Services Cost per Ton Collected

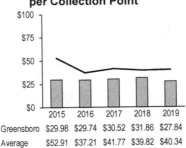

	2015	2016	2017	2018	2019
Greensboro	$184	$139	$158	$173	$156
Average	$318	$194	$256	$237	$255

Recycling Services Cost per Collection Point

	2015	2016	2017	2018	2019
Greensboro	$29.98	$29.74	$30.52	$31.86	$27.84
Average	$52.91	$37.21	$41.77	$39.82	$40.34

Tons Collected Curbside per Municipal FTE

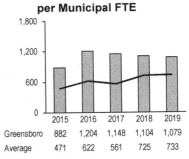

	2015	2016	2017	2018	2019
Greensboro	882	1,204	1,148	1,104	1,079
Average	471	622	561	725	733

Effectiveness Measures

Community Set-Out Rate

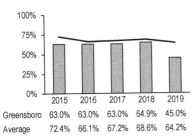

	2015	2016	2017	2018	2019
Greensboro	63.0%	63.0%	63.0%	64.9%	45.0%
Average	72.4%	66.1%	67.2%	68.6%	64.2%

Tons Recycled as Percentage of Tons Refuse and Recyclables Collected

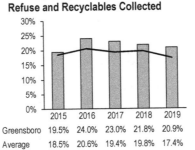

	2015	2016	2017	2018	2019
Greensboro	19.5%	24.0%	23.0%	21.8%	20.9%
Average	18.5%	20.6%	19.4%	19.8%	17.4%

Fiscal Year 2018–19

Explanatory Information

Service Level and Delivery

Greenville offers once-a-week curbside or backyard collection of recyclable materials to its residents through a city-run program. Residents can choose to have backyard collection for a fee. The recycling fee is included in the solid waste fee for residential refuse collection. The recycling materials include:

- newspaper and magazines
- cardboard
- aluminum and steel cans
- No. 1 and No. 2 plastics
- glass of all colors
- white goods

Greenville's household recycling program also uses three city-owned drop-off recycling centers and over 200 other sites connected to multifamily complexes. Tonnage and cost for these other drop-off sites are not included in the performance and cost data.

Conditions Affecting Service, Performance, and Costs

Municipal Profile

Population (OSBM 2018)	89,790
Land Area (Square Miles)	35.58
Persons per Square Mile	2,523
Median Household Income U.S. Census 2016	$33,339

Service Profile

FTE Positions—Collection	6.0
FTE Positions—Other	3.5
Number of City Drop-Off Centers	3
Other Drop-Off Centers	220
Percentage of Service Contracted	0%
Collection Frequency	1 x week
General Collection Location	Curbside
Recyclables Sorted at Curb	No
Collection Points	19,250
Tons of Recyclables Collected	
Curbside	3,992
City Drop-Off Centers	0
Total Tons Collected	3,992
Monthly Service Fee	0
Revenue from Sale of Recyclables	$0
Sale Revenue as Percentage of Cost	NA

Full Cost Profile

Cost Breakdown by Percentage	
Personal Services	34.3%
Operating Costs	45.8%
Capital Costs	19.9%
TOTAL	100.0%
Cost Breakdown in Dollars	
Personal Services	$658,527
Operating Costs	$880,262
Capital Costs	$382,383
TOTAL	$1,921,172

Key: Greenville ▒   Benchmarking Average —   Fiscal Years 2015 through 2019

Resource Measures

Recycling Services Cost per Capita

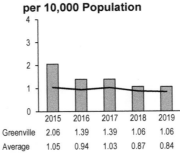

	2015	2016	2017	2018	2019
Greenville	$27.67	$20.49	$22.94	$14.39	$21.40
Average	$15.00	$10.97	$13.36	$12.56	$12.61

Recycling Services FTEs per 10,000 Population

	2015	2016	2017	2018	2019
Greenville	2.06	1.39	1.39	1.06	1.06
Average	1.05	0.94	1.03	0.87	0.84

Workload Measures

Tons Recyclables Collected per 1,000 Population

	2015	2016	2017	2018	2019
Greenville	50.8	44.6	49.9	46.8	44.5
Average	58.7	63.7	60.8	59.5	56.8

Tons Recyclables Collected per 1,000 Collection Points

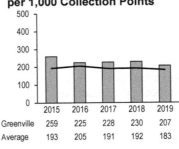

	2015	2016	2017	2018	2019
Greenville	259	225	228	230	207
Average	193	205	191	192	183

Tons Solid Waste Landfilled per 1,000 Population

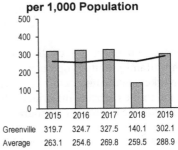

	2015	2016	2017	2018	2019
Greenville	319.7	324.7	327.5	140.1	302.1
Average	263.1	254.6	269.8	259.5	288.9

Efficiency Measures

Recycling Services Cost per Ton Collected

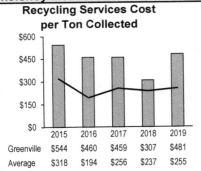

	2015	2016	2017	2018	2019
Greenville	$544	$460	$459	$307	$481
Average	$318	$194	$256	$237	$255

Recycling Services Cost per Collection Point

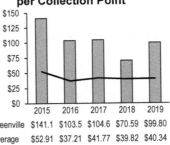

	2015	2016	2017	2018	2019
Greenville	$141.1	$103.5	$104.6	$70.59	$99.80
Average	$52.91	$37.21	$41.77	$39.82	$40.34

Tons Collected Curbside per Municipal FTE

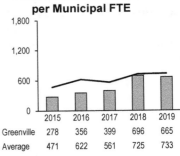

	2015	2016	2017	2018	2019
Greenville	278	356	399	696	665
Average	471	622	561	725	733

Effectiveness Measures

Community Set-Out Rate

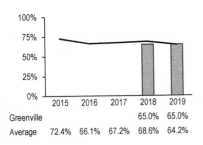

	2015	2016	2017	2018	2019
Greenville				65.0%	65.0%
Average	72.4%	66.1%	67.2%	68.6%	64.2%

Tons Recycled as Percentage of Tons Refuse and Recyclables Collected

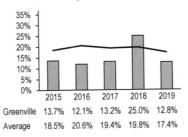

	2015	2016	2017	2018	2019
Greenville	13.7%	12.1%	13.2%	25.0%	12.8%
Average	18.5%	20.6%	19.4%	19.8%	17.4%

Fiscal Year 2018–19

Explanatory Information

Service Level and Delivery

Hickory offers curbside collection of recyclable materials every other week to its residents through a contractual agreement. The recycling materials collected include:

- newspaper and magazines
- aluminum and steel cans
- No. 1 and No. 2 plastics
- glass—all colors
- phone books and junk mail

Hickory's household recycling program also uses two drop-off recycling centers. One is staffed, and the other is not. These centers collect antifreeze and oil in addition to the same household materials that are collected at the curb. Tonnage and costs for this service are included in the performance and cost data.

A separate commercial recycling program that services businesses and multifamily units is operated by the city. The program utilizes city workers and equipment to collect cardboard and paper in addition to the curbside materials. The performance and cost data do not include the commercial program.

The city charges residents a monthly fee for recycling, which is included in the monthly solid waste fee. In the fiscal year, the city collected $23,115 in revenue from the sale of recyclables, partially offsetting program costs.

Conditions Affecting Service, Performance, and Costs

The set-out rate is calculated on a monthly basis by the contractor. While not tracked, missed recycling pickups are minimal and average less than one per month.

Municipal Profile

Population (OSBM 2018)	40,932
Land Area (Square Miles)	29.92
Persons per Square Mile	1,368
Median Household Income U.S. Census 2016	$35,353

Service Profile

FTE Positions—Collection	0.5 City
FTE Positions—Other	0.27 City
Number of City Drop-Off Centers	2
Other Drop-Off Centers	0
Percentage of Service Contracted	92%
Collection Frequency	Every 2 weeks
General Collection Location	Curbside
Recyclables Sorted at Curb	No
Collection Points	11,940
Tons of Recyclables Collected	
Curbside	2,470
City Drop-Off Centers	212
Total Tons Collected	2,682
Monthly Service Fee	0
Revenue from Sale of Recyclables	$23,115
Sale Revenue as Percentage of Cost	5.7%

Full Cost Profile

Cost Breakdown by Percentage	
Personal Services	10.0%
Operating Costs	87.9%
Capital Costs	2.1%
TOTAL	100.0%
Cost Breakdown in Dollars	
Personal Services	$40,845
Operating Costs	$357,594
Capital Costs	$8,382
TOTAL	$406,821

Hickory

Key: Hickory ▨   Benchmarking Average —   Fiscal Years 2015 through 2019

Resource Measures

Recycling Services Cost per Capita

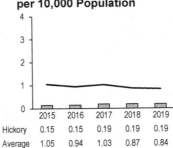

	2015	2016	2017	2018	2019
Hickory	$28.56	$10.68	$8.96	$8.95	$9.94
Average	$15.00	$10.97	$13.36	$12.56	$12.61

Recycling Services FTEs per 10,000 Population

	2015	2016	2017	2018	2019
Hickory	0.15	0.15	0.19	0.19	0.19
Average	1.05	0.94	1.03	0.87	0.84

Workload Measures

Tons Recyclables Collected per 1,000 Population

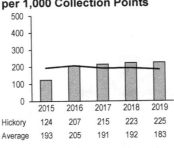

	2015	2016	2017	2018	2019
Hickory	37.4	62.5	64.8	65.6	65.5
Average	58.7	63.7	60.8	59.5	56.8

Tons Recyclables Collected per 1,000 Collection Points

	2015	2016	2017	2018	2019
Hickory	124	207	215	223	225
Average	193	205	191	192	183

Tons Solid Waste Landfilled per 1,000 Population

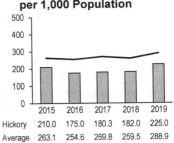

	2015	2016	2017	2018	2019
Hickory	210.0	175.0	180.3	182.0	225.0
Average	263.1	254.6	269.8	259.5	288.9

Efficiency Measures

Recycling Services Cost per Ton Collected

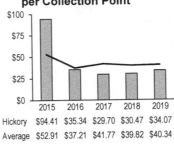

	2015	2016	2017	2018	2019
Hickory	$763	$171	$138	$136	$152
Average	$318	$194	$256	$237	$255

Recycling Services Cost per Collection Point

	2015	2016	2017	2018	2019
Hickory	$94.41	$35.34	$29.70	$30.47	$34.07
Average	$52.91	$37.21	$41.77	$39.82	$40.34

Tons Collected Curbside per Municipal FTE

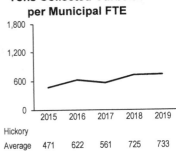

	2015	2016	2017	2018	2019
Hickory					
Average	471	622	561	725	733

Effectiveness Measures

Community Set-Out Rate

	2015	2016	2017	2018	2019
Hickory	84.0%	67.0%	65.0%	63.0%	66.0%
Average	72.4%	66.1%	67.2%	68.6%	64.2%

Tons Recycled as Percentage of Tons Refuse and Recyclables Collected

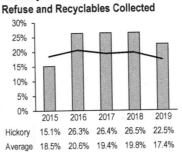

	2015	2016	2017	2018	2019
Hickory	15.1%	26.3%	26.4%	26.5%	22.5%
Average	18.5%	20.6%	19.4%	19.8%	17.4%

Fiscal Year 2018–19

Explanatory Information

Service Level and Delivery

Mooresville provides every other week curbside collection of recyclable materials from households. The town charged a monthly solid waste fee of $10 during the fiscal year, with recycling estimated to be $0.80 of this total.

The town uses staff to provide all collection services. The provides a ninety-five-gallon recycling roll-out container.
The recyclable materials collected include:

- glass (all colors)
- newspaper
- magazines and catalogs
- mixed paper and mail
- telephone books
- cardboard—broken down and cereal boxes
- all plastics
- aluminum cans
- steel cans

Conditions Affecting Service, Performance, and Costs

Mooresville joined the Benchmarking project in July 2018, with the first year of data showing for FY 2017–18.

The set-out rate was reported twice per year. The town does not track recycling complaints separately from residential refuse complaints.

Municipal Profile

Population (OSBM 2018)	41,255
Land Area (Square Miles)	22.75
Persons per Square Mile	1,813
Median Household Income	$67,213
U.S. Census 2016	

Service Profile

FTE Positions—Collection	2.0
FTE Positions—Other	1.0
Number of City Drop-Off Centers	1
Other Drop-Off Centers	1
Percentage of Service Contracted	0%
Collection Frequency	Every 2 weeks
General Collection Location	Curbside
Recyclables Sorted at Curb	No
Collection Points	11,327
Tons of Recyclables Collected	
Curbside	2,587
City Drop-Off Centers	4
Total Tons Collected	2,591
Monthly Service Fee	$10.00
Revenue from Sale of Recyclables	$0
Sale Revenue as Percentage of Cost	NA

Full Cost Profile

Cost Breakdown by Percentage	
Personal Services	19.5%
Operating Costs	58.4%
Capital Costs	22.0%
TOTAL	100.0%
Cost Breakdown in Dollars	
Personal Services	$91,454
Operating Costs	$273,721
Capital Costs	$103,257
TOTAL	$468,432

Mooresville

Household Recycling

Resource Measures

Recycling Services Cost per Capita

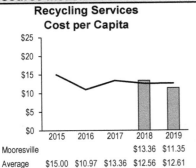

	2015	2016	2017	2018	2019
Mooresville				$13.36	$11.35
Average	$15.00	$10.97	$13.36	$12.56	$12.61

Recycling Services FTEs per 10,000 Population

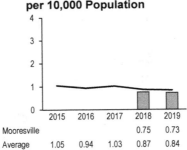

	2015	2016	2017	2018	2019
Mooresville				0.75	0.73
Average	1.05	0.94	1.03	0.87	0.84

Workload Measures

Tons Recyclables Collected per 1,000 Population

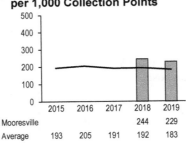

	2015	2016	2017	2018	2019
Mooresville				58.7	62.8
Average	58.7	63.7	60.8	59.5	56.8

Tons Recyclables Collected per 1,000 Collection Points

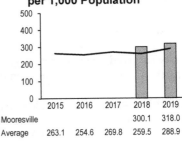

	2015	2016	2017	2018	2019
Mooresville				244	229
Average	193	205	191	192	183

Tons Solid Waste Landfilled per 1,000 Population

	2015	2016	2017	2018	2019
Mooresville				300.1	318.0
Average	263.1	254.6	269.8	259.5	288.9

Efficiency Measures

Recycling Services Cost per Ton Collected

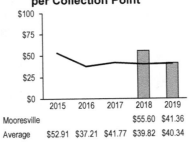

	2015	2016	2017	2018	2019
Mooresville				$228	$181
Average	$318	$194	$256	$237	$255

Recycling Services Cost per Collection Point

	2015	2016	2017	2018	2019
Mooresville				$55.60	$41.36
Average	$52.91	$37.21	$41.77	$39.82	$40.34

Tons Collected Curbside per Municipal FTE

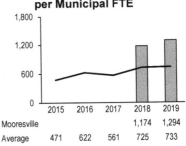

	2015	2016	2017	2018	2019
Mooresville				1,174	1,294
Average	471	622	561	725	733

Effectiveness Measures

Community Set-Out Rate

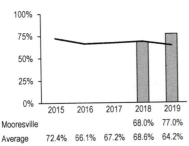

	2015	2016	2017	2018	2019
Mooresville				68.0%	77.0%
Average	72.4%	66.1%	67.2%	68.6%	64.2%

Tons Recycled as Percentage of Tons Refuse and Recyclables Collected

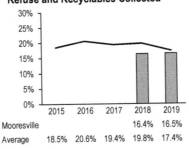

	2015	2016	2017	2018	2019
Mooresville				16.4%	16.5%
Average	18.5%	20.6%	19.4%	19.8%	17.4%

Fiscal Year 2018–19

Explanatory Information

Service Level and Delivery
Raleigh provides curbside collection of recyclables every other week. Three drop-off centers for use by all residents and small businesses are also available. Customers are allowed two ninety-five-gallon carts. A few townhome locations use smaller eighteen-gallon bins due to the difficulty of moving carts to a pickup location.

Recyclables collected include:

- plastic
- glass
- metal and aluminum cans
- magazines
- newspaper
- phone books
- cardboard
- mixed paper

The city received revenue from resale of recyclables of $123,809 during the fiscal year, offsetting some program costs.

Conditions Affecting Service, Performance, and Costs
Raleigh rejoined the Benchmarking Project in July 2016, with the first year of data showing for FY 2015–16.

Municipal Profile

Population (OSBM 2018)	464,453
Land Area (Square Miles)	145.65
Persons per Square Mile	3,189
Median Household Income	$46,612
U.S. Census 2016	

Service Profile

FTE Positions—Collection	39.0
FTE Positions—Other	3.0
Number of City Drop-Off Centers	2
Other Drop-Off Centers	1
Percentage of Service Contracted	0%
Collection Frequency	Every 2 weeks
General Collection Location	Curbside
Recyclables Sorted at Curb	No
Collection Points	189,633
Tons of Recyclables Collected	
Curbside	27,067
City Drop-Off Centers	899
Total Tons Collected	27,966
Monthly Service Fee	$2.60
Revenue from Sale of Recyclables	$0
Sale Revenue as Percentage of Cost	NA

Full Cost Profile

Cost Breakdown by Percentage	
Personal Services	40.3%
Operating Costs	30.6%
Capital Costs	29.1%
TOTAL	100.0%
Cost Breakdown in Dollars	
Personal Services	$2,101,589
Operating Costs	$1,593,728
Capital Costs	$1,516,237
TOTAL	$5,211,554

Raleigh

Household Recycling

Resource Measures

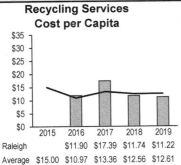

**Recycling Services
Cost per Capita**

	2015	2016	2017	2018	2019
Raleigh		$11.90	$17.39	$11.74	$11.22
Average	$15.00	$10.97	$13.36	$12.56	$12.61

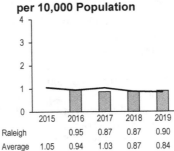

**Recycling Services FTEs
per 10,000 Population**

	2015	2016	2017	2018	2019
Raleigh		0.95	0.87	0.87	0.90
Average	1.05	0.94	1.03	0.87	0.84

Workload Measures

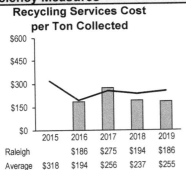

**Tons Recyclables Collected
per 1,000 Population**

	2015	2016	2017	2018	2019
Raleigh		64.1	63.3	60.6	60.2
Average	58.7	63.7	60.8	59.5	56.8

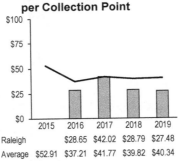

**Tons Recyclables Collected
per 1,000 Collection Points**

	2015	2016	2017	2018	2019
Raleigh		154	153	149	147
Average	193	205	191	192	183

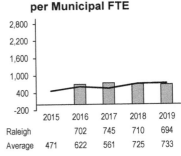

**Tons Solid Waste Landfilled
per 1,000 Population**

	2015	2016	2017	2018	2019
Raleigh		222.4	210.1	199.7	199.2
Average	263.1	254.6	269.8	259.5	288.9

Efficiency Measures

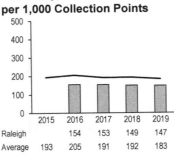

**Recycling Services Cost
per Ton Collected**

	2015	2016	2017	2018	2019
Raleigh		$186	$275	$194	$186
Average	$318	$194	$256	$237	$255

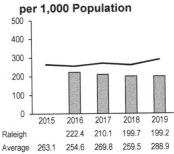

**Recycling Services Cost
per Collection Point**

	2015	2016	2017	2018	2019
Raleigh		$28.65	$42.02	$28.79	$27.48
Average	$52.91	$37.21	$41.77	$39.82	$40.34

**Tons Collected Curbside
per Municipal FTE**

	2015	2016	2017	2018	2019
Raleigh		702	745	710	694
Average	471	622	561	725	733

Effectiveness Measures

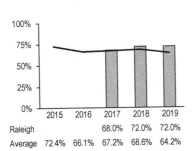

Community Set-Out Rate

	2015	2016	2017	2018	2019
Raleigh			68.0%	72.0%	72.0%
Average	72.4%	66.1%	67.2%	68.6%	64.2%

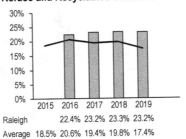

**Tons Recycled as Percentage of Tons
Refuse and Recyclables Collected**

	2015	2016	2017	2018	2019
Raleigh		22.4%	23.2%	23.3%	23.2%
Average	18.5%	20.6%	19.4%	19.8%	17.4%

Explanatory Information

Service Level and Delivery

Wilson's household recycling program provides curbside pickup of materials once each week to residents on the same day as residential refuse collection but by different crews. Wilson began a pilot program in July 2015 that shifted to collection being done once every two weeks. This pilot phase initially covered about 2,800 homes, and each received a ninety-six-gallon roll-out cart. The transition was largely completed in 2018 except for a small number of apartments and town homes that could not be collected with automated trucks but instead required rear loaders. The recycling program is part of the Division of Environmental Services.

The following materials are collected:

- aluminum and steel cans
- No. 1 and No. 2 plastic containers
- newsprint
- clear, green, and brown glass
- waste oil, fluorescent bulbs, electronics, and small appliances, which are collected curbside on a call-in basis

Conditions Affecting Service, Performance, and Costs

The set-out rate was calculated on a monthly basis by drivers on the recycling trucks using counters.

The initial pilot phase for recycling begun in July 2015 helped lower overall costs notably.

Municipal Profile

Population (OSBM 2018)	49,054
Land Area (Square Miles)	30.60
Persons per Square Mile	1,603
Median Household Income	$35,409
U.S. Census 2016	

Service Profile

FTE Positions—Collection	4.0
FTE Positions—Other	0.5
Number of City Drop-Off Centers	0
Other Drop-Off Centers	0
Percentage of Service Contracted	0%
Collection Frequency	
for 96-gallon carts	Every 2 weeks
for 18-gallon cart	Every week
General Collection Location	Curbside
Recyclables Sorted at Curb	No
Collection Points	25,100
Tons of Recyclables Collected	
Curbside	1,645
City Drop-Off Centers	0
Total Tons Collected	1,645
Monthly Service Fee	$20.00
Revenue from Sale of Recyclables	$0

Full Cost Profile

Cost Breakdown by Percentage	
Personal Services	36.8%
Operating Costs	40.8%
Capital Costs	22.3%
TOTAL	100.0%

Cost Breakdown in Dollars	
Personal Services	$234,006
Operating Costs	$259,384
Capital Costs	$141,847
TOTAL	$635,237

Key: Wilson   Benchmarking Average —

Resource Measures

Recycling Services Cost per Capita

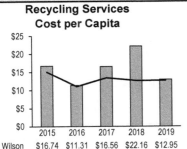

	2015	2016	2017	2018	2019
Wilson	$16.74	$11.31	$16.56	$22.16	$12.95
Average	$15.00	$10.97	$13.36	$12.56	$12.61

Recycling Services FTEs per 10,000 Population

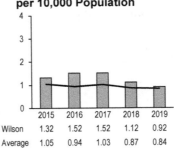

	2015	2016	2017	2018	2019
Wilson	1.32	1.52	1.52	1.12	0.92
Average	1.05	0.94	1.03	0.87	0.84

Workload Measures

Tons Recyclables Collected per 1,000 Population

	2015	2016	2017	2018	2019
Wilson	30.7	32.1	34.5	39.7	33.5
Average	58.7	63.7	60.8	59.5	56.8

Tons Recyclables Collected per 1,000 Collection Points

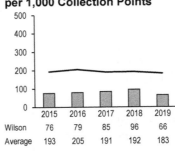

	2015	2016	2017	2018	2019
Wilson	76	79	85	96	66
Average	193	205	191	192	183

Tons Solid Waste Landfilled per 1,000 Population

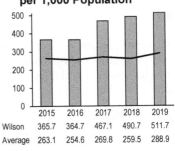

	2015	2016	2017	2018	2019
Wilson	365.7	364.7	467.1	490.7	511.7
Average	263.1	254.6	269.8	259.5	288.9

Efficiency Measures

Recycling Services Cost per Ton Collected

	2015	2016	2017	2018	2019
Wilson	$546	$352	$480	$558	$386
Average	$318	$194	$256	$237	$255

Recycling Services Cost per Collection Point

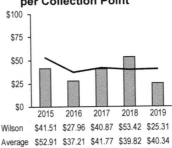

	2015	2016	2017	2018	2019
Wilson	$41.51	$27.96	$40.87	$53.42	$25.31
Average	$52.91	$37.21	$41.77	$39.82	$40.34

Tons Collected Curbside per Municipal FTE

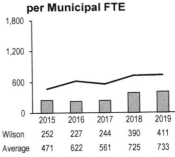

	2015	2016	2017	2018	2019
Wilson	252	227	244	390	411
Average	471	622	561	725	733

Effectiveness Measures

Community Set-Out Rate

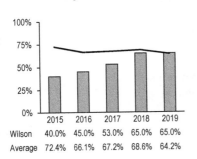

	2015	2016	2017	2018	2019
Wilson	40.0%	45.0%	53.0%	65.0%	65.0%
Average	72.4%	66.1%	67.2%	68.6%	64.2%

Tons Recycled as Percentage of Tons Refuse and Recyclables Collected

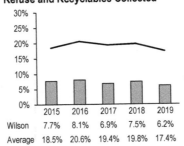

	2015	2016	2017	2018	2019
Wilson	7.7%	8.1%	6.9%	7.5%	6.2%
Average	18.5%	20.6%	19.4%	19.8%	17.4%

Explanatory Information

Service Level and Delivery

Winston-Salem provides biweekly curbside household recycling service to its single-family residences using ninety-six-gallon carts. The city provides nine drop-off sites for cardboard at its fire stations plus two full-service drop-off sites. Items collected in the city's curbside household recycling program include:

- aluminum and steel cans
- all plastic bottles
- green, amber, and clear glass
- newspaper
- magazines, telephone books, and junk mail
- chipboard
- corrugated cardboard (no bundling requirement)
- office paper
- aerosol cans

The city contracts for 100 percent of its curbside household recycling program. The city does not charge a recycling fee. Revenue to the city for the sale of recyclables was $164,241 during the year, partially offsetting program costs.

Conditions Affecting Service, Performance, and Costs

Complaints include calls reported to the city. The contractor has a separate customer service hotline.

Municipal Profile

Population (OSBM 2018)	243,447
Land Area (Square Miles)	132.55
Persons per Square Mile	1,837
Median Household Income U.S. Census 2016	$40,584

Service Profile

FTE Positions—Collection	Contractor
FTE Positions—Other	1.0
Number of City Drop-Off Centers	9
Other Drop-Off Centers	0
Percentage of Service Contracted	100%
Collection Frequency	Every 2 weeks
General Collection Location	Curbside
Recyclables Sorted at Curb	No
Collection Points	81,589
Tons of Recyclables Collected	
Curbside	14,528
City Drop-Off Centers	1,101
Total Tons Collected	15,629
Monthly Service Fee	1.61
Revenue from Sale of Recyclables	$164,241
Sale Revenue as Percentage of Cost	9.9%

Full Cost Profile

Cost Breakdown by Percentage	
Personal Services	5.3%
Operating Costs	94.7%
Capital Costs	0.0%
TOTAL	100.0%

Cost Breakdown in Dollars	
Personal Services	$87,065
Operating Costs	$1,569,793
Capital Costs	$0
TOTAL	$1,656,858

Winston-Salem

Household Recycling

Resource Measures

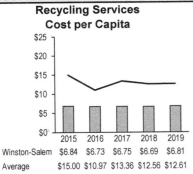

Recycling Services Cost per Capita

	2015	2016	2017	2018	2019
Winston-Salem	$6.84	$6.73	$6.75	$6.69	$6.81
Average	$15.00	$10.97	$13.36	$12.56	$12.61

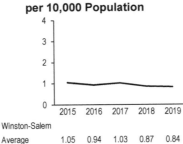

Recycling Services FTEs per 10,000 Population

	2015	2016	2017	2018	2019
Winston-Salem					
Average	1.05	0.94	1.03	0.87	0.84

Workload Measures

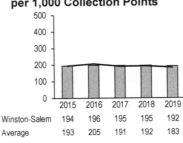

Tons Recyclables Collected per 1,000 Population

	2015	2016	2017	2018	2019
Winston-Salem	61.2	61.7	62.0	62.7	64.2
Average	58.7	63.7	60.8	59.5	56.8

Tons Recyclables Collected per 1,000 Collection Points

	2015	2016	2017	2018	2019
Winston-Salem	194	196	195	195	192
Average	193	205	191	192	183

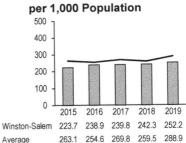

Tons Solid Waste Landfilled per 1,000 Population

	2015	2016	2017	2018	2019
Winston-Salem	223.7	238.9	239.8	242.3	252.2
Average	263.1	254.6	269.8	259.5	288.9

Efficiency Measures

Recycling Services Cost per Ton Collected

	2015	2016	2017	2018	2019
Winston-Salem	$112	$109	$109	$107	$106
Average	$318	$194	$256	$237	$255

Recycling Services Cost per Collection Point

	2015	2016	2017	2018	2019
Winston-Salem	$21.69	$21.44	$21.24	$20.82	$20.31
Average	$52.91	$37.21	$41.77	$39.82	$40.34

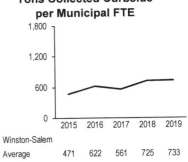

Tons Collected Curbside per Municipal FTE

	2015	2016	2017	2018	2019
Winston-Salem					
Average	471	622	561	725	733

Effectiveness Measures

Community Set-Out Rate

	2015	2016	2017	2018	2019
Winston-Salem	56.8%	57.9%	56.7%	56.0%	59.5%
Average	72.4%	66.1%	67.2%	68.6%	64.2%

Tons Recycled as Percentage of Tons Refuse and Recyclables Collected

	2015	2016	2017	2018	2019
Winston-Salem	21.5%	20.5%	20.5%	20.6%	20.3%
Average	18.5%	20.6%	19.4%	19.8%	17.4%

Performance and Cost Data

YARD WASTE / LEAF COLLECTION

PERFORMANCE MEASURES FOR
YARD WASTE/LEAF COLLECTION

SERVICE DEFINITION

Yard waste and leaf collection includes regularly scheduled or special collection of these items. Such collection may occur from the curb, backyard, or another locale. Yard waste and leaves may be bagged, placed in containers, or loose. The service definition excludes the collection of white goods and other bulky items. Although some municipalities collect yard waste and leaves with household refuse or other trash, they separate the items at some point in the collection process because yard waste and leaves cannot be placed in landfills.

NOTES ON PERFORMANCE MEASURES

1. Tons Collected per 1,000 Population and per 1,000 Collection Points

These are the same performance measures that are used for residential refuse collection, except that tonnage is for yard waste, leaves, and miscellaneous trash rather than residential refuse. "Collection points" refers to the number of residential premises served by regularly scheduled collection of yard waste, leaves, and miscellaneous trash.

2. Cost per Ton Collected

Cost is measured using the project's full cost accounting model, calculating direct, indirect, and capital costs. Tons are as defined above.

3. Tons Collected per Collection FTE

The number of full-time equivalent (FTE) positions refers to the number of employees or laborers who were directly involved in collection of yard waste, leaves, and miscellaneous trash during the fiscal year. This number includes temporary, permanent, full-time, and part-time workers. Such workers can be sanitation, street, or other municipal employees. One FTE equals 2,080 hours of work per year. Any combination of employees providing 2,080 hours of work per year is one FTE.

4. Complaints (and Valid Complaints) per 10,000 Collection Points

Complaints are those tracked by each jurisdiction, using its own criteria and procedures. Collection points are as defined above. The municipalities follow very different procedures in processing and recording these calls and in determining which ones are complaints and which are not. For these reasons, the project is able to present only limited comparative data about complaints or valid complaints. Nonetheless, the project recommends that the participating municipalities devise common criteria for identifying complaints and procedures for processing and recording calls.

Yard Waste/Leaf Collection

Summary of Key Dimensions of Service

City or Town	Yard Waste Collection		Seasonal Loose Leaf Collection	Collection Points	Tons Collected		Collection FTE Positions
	Location	Frequency			Yard Waste	Seasonal Leaves	
Apex	Curbside	1 x week	NA	17,649	7,863	na	15.0
Asheville	Curbside	2 x month	NA	32,497	7,796	na	12.0
Chapel Hill	Curbside	1 x week	2-6 sweeps	12,195	3,313	4,456	14.8
Charlotte	Curbside	1 x week	NA	219,839	61,803	na	71.0
Concord	Curbside	1 x week	3 sweeps	33,082	8,797	2,105	22.4
Goldsboro	Curbside	1 x 2 weeks	1 x 2 weeks	14,372	8,260	3,394	14.0
Greensboro	Curbside	1 x week	2 sweeps	90,625	14,524	13,914	42.2
Greenville	Curbside	1 x week	1 x 2 weeks	20,000	13,500	1,000	20.3
Hickory	Curbside	1 x week	2 sweeps	11,940	5,974	4,240	4.3
Mooresville	Curbside	1 x week	NA	14,500	2,139	3,225	8.0
Raleigh	Curbside	1 x week	2 sweeps	129,962	17,977	14,150	96.0
Wilson	Curbside	1 x week	1 x 3 weeks	25,100	9,022	1,200	11.0
Winston-Salem	Curbside	Yard Waste Cart 1 x week Brush every 10 days	1 x 3 weeks	81,589 for Leaves and brush, 13,828 for Yard Waste	29,010	21,631	70.8

NOTES

Municipalities with no reported seasonal leaf collection collect leaves as part of their yard waste collection programs.

EXPLANATORY FACTORS

These are factors that the project found affected yard waste and leaf collection performance and cost in one or more of the municipalities:

Whether or not a fee is charged for collection
Residential/commercial/industrial nature of the community
Policies regarding sizes and types of items collected
Extent of seasonal leaf collection service
Landfill policies and tipping fees

Fiscal Year 2018–19

Explanatory Information

Service Level and Delivery

The Town of Apex collects yard waste curbside once per week for all city residents. The town collects vegetative matter from residential landscaping. The town does not operate a seasonal leaf collection, but leaves are collected year-round as part of the weekly service. Land clearing debris is not collected. The town charges $7.83 per month for collection of yard waste.

There are three grass/vacuum trucks, two two-person limb-chipping crews, and one grapple-truck operator for larger items. These crews cover the town every week using a five-day-a-week schedule.

Conditions Affecting Service, Performance, and Costs

Municipal Profile

Population (OSBM 2018)	52,909
Land Area (Square Miles)	21.55
Persons per Square Mile	2,455
Median Household Income	$84,000
U.S. Census 2016	

Service Profile

FTE Positions—Collection	16.0
FTE Positions—Other	0.9
Collection Frequency	
Yard Waste	1 x week
Collection Points	17,649
Tons Collected	
Yard Waste	7,863
Seasonal Leaves	with yard waste
Total Tons Collected	7,863
Monthly Service Fee	$7.83

Full Cost Profile

Cost Breakdown by Percentage	
Personal Services	45.0%
Operating Costs	39.3%
Capital Costs	15.7%
TOTAL	100.0%

Cost Breakdown in Dollars	
Personal Services	$937,941
Operating Costs	$818,679
Capital Costs	$328,013
TOTAL	$2,084,633

Apex

Key: Apex ▦   Benchmarking Average —   Fiscal Years 2015 through 2019

Resource Measures

Yard Waste and Leaf Collection Costs per Capita

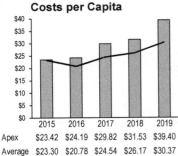

	2015	2016	2017	2018	2019
Apex	$23.42	$24.19	$29.82	$31.53	$39.40
Average	$23.30	$20.78	$24.54	$26.17	$30.37

Yard Waste and Leaf Collection FTEs per 10,000 Population

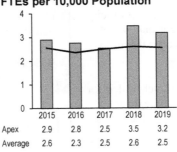

	2015	2016	2017	2018	2019
Apex	2.9	2.8	2.5	3.5	3.2
Average	2.6	2.3	2.5	2.6	2.5

Workload Measures

Yard Waste and Leaf Tons Collected per 1,000 Population

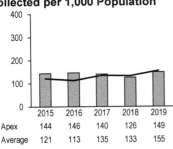

	2015	2016	2017	2018	2019
Apex	144	146	140	126	149
Average	121	113	135	133	155

Yard Waste and Leaf Tons Collected

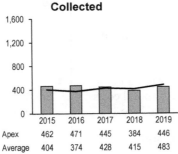

	2015	2016	2017	2018	2019
Apex	462	471	445	384	446
Average	404	374	428	415	483

Efficiency Measures

Yard Waste and Leaf Collection Cost per Collection Point

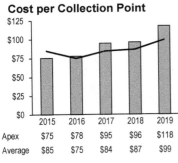

	2015	2016	2017	2018	2019
Apex	$75	$78	$95	$96	$118
Average	$85	$75	$84	$87	$99

Yard Waste and Leaf Collection Cost per Ton Collected

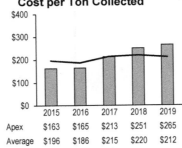

	2015	2016	2017	2018	2019
Apex	$163	$165	$213	$251	$265
Average	$196	$186	$215	$220	$212

Yard Waste and Leaf Tons Collected per Collection FTE

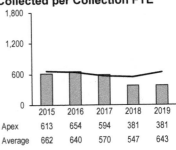

	2015	2016	2017	2018	2019
Apex	613	654	594	381	381
Average	662	640	570	547	643

Effectiveness Measures

Collection Complaints per 10,000 Collection Points

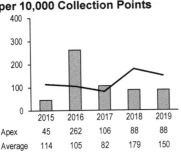

	2015	2016	2017	2018	2019
Apex	45	262	106	88	88
Average	114	105	82	179	150

Valid Complaints per 10,000 Collection Points

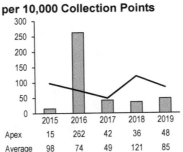

	2015	2016	2017	2018	2019
Apex	15	262	42	36	48
Average	98	74	49	121	85

Asheville

Yard Waste/Leaf Collection

Fiscal Year 2018–19

Explanatory Information

Service Level and Delivery

Asheville collects yard waste curbside twice per month for all city residents. The city collects yard trimmings no longer than 4 feet and no wider than 6 inches. Grass clippings and materials cut by contractors are not collected.

There are three one-person crews on knucklebooms, scheduled for approximately three-and-one-half days per week. Three three-person crews operating rear packers collect yard waste four days per week.

The city does not charge a fee for yard waste collection. A $5 fee is charged for white goods, and a $10 fee is charged for dead animals.

Asheville does not have a separate leaf collection program. Instead, leaves are collected as part of the normal twice-a-month yard waste collection.

The city transfers yard waste to a contractor's site for grinding. The city does not receive any of the grindings. The disposal costs for this are not included in the collection costs reported here.

Conditions Affecting Service, Performance, and Costs

Municipal Profile

Population (OSBM 2018)	93,621
Land Area (Square Miles)	45.53
Persons per Square Mile	2,056
Median Household Income U.S. Census 2016	$40,494

Service Profile

FTE Positions—Collection	13.0
FTE Positions—Other	2.0
Collection Frequency	
Yard Waste	2 x month
Collection Points	32,497
Tons Collected	
Yard Waste	7,796
Seasonal Leaves	with yard waste
Total Tons Collected	7,796
Monthly Service Fee	No

Full Cost Profile

Cost Breakdown by Percentage

Personal Services	43.0%
Operating Costs	40.2%
Capital Costs	16.8%
TOTAL	100.0%

Cost Breakdown in Dollars

Personal Services	$745,494
Operating Costs	$696,618
Capital Costs	$291,539
TOTAL	$1,733,651

Asheville

Yard Waste/Leaf Collection

Key: Asheville ▢   Benchmarking Average —   Fiscal Years 2015 through 2019

Resource Measures

Yard Waste and Leaf Collection Costs per Capita

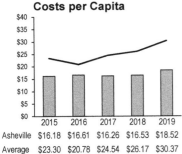

	2015	2016	2017	2018	2019
Asheville	$16.18	$16.61	$16.26	$16.53	$18.52
Average	$23.30	$20.78	$24.54	$26.17	$30.37

Yard Waste and Leaf Collection FTEs per 10,000 Population

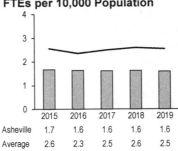

	2015	2016	2017	2018	2019
Asheville	1.7	1.6	1.6	1.6	1.6
Average	2.6	2.3	2.5	2.6	2.5

Workload Measures

Yard Waste and Leaf Tons Collected per 1,000 Population

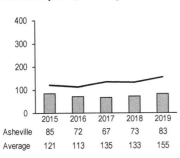

	2015	2016	2017	2018	2019
Asheville	85	72	67	73	83
Average	121	113	135	133	155

Yard Waste and Leaf Tons Collected per 1,000 Collection Points

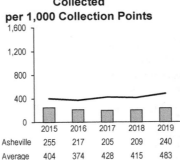

	2015	2016	2017	2018	2019
Asheville	255	217	205	209	240
Average	404	374	428	415	483

Efficiency Measures

Yard Waste and Leaf Collection Cost per Collection Point

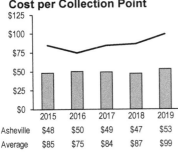

	2015	2016	2017	2018	2019
Asheville	$48	$50	$49	$47	$53
Average	$85	$75	$84	$87	$99

Yard Waste and Leaf Collection Cost per Ton Collected

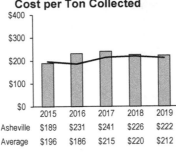

	2015	2016	2017	2018	2019
Asheville	$189	$231	$241	$226	$222
Average	$196	$186	$215	$220	$212

Yard Waste and Leaf Tons Collected per Collection FTE

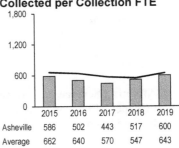

	2015	2016	2017	2018	2019
Asheville	586	502	443	517	600
Average	662	640	570	547	643

Effectiveness Measures

Collection Complaints per 10,000 Collection Points

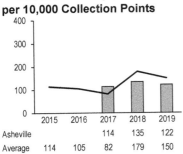

	2015	2016	2017	2018	2019
Asheville			114	135	122
Average	114	105	82	179	150

Valid Complaints per 10,000 Collection Points

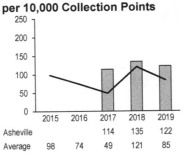

	2015	2016	2017	2018	2019
Asheville			114	135	122
Average	98	74	49	121	85

Explanatory Information

Service Level and Delivery

Yard waste collection is managed by the Solid Waste Services Division of the Public Works Department. Yard waste includes organic materials, such as leaves, stems, grass, limbs, and other residential organic matter. The town does not collect large logs or stumps, or debris from lot clearing.

Yard waste is collected once per week curbside with no monthly fee. Yard waste is collected by seven three-person crews using rear packers two days per week. The Town collects small yard waste materials placed in roll carts, other rigid containers, or paper yard waste bags. The Town collects large yard waste materials in loose piles. Yard waste piles larger than three cubic yards are collected for a fee. The Town does not collect yard waste in plastic bags.

Residents can rent a 10-cubic-yard roll-off container or schedule a paid knuckle boom collection for large projects. These larger loads are collected by a one-person crew using a knuckle boom truck and a hook-lift truck five days per week. Residents pay a fee of $35 per day or $60 per week to rent a roll-off container for collection. The fee for a knuckle boom collection is $125.

Seasonal leaf collection is managed by the Streets and Construction Services Division of the Public Works Department. Seasonal leaf collection is run with five or six cycles in a season from mid-October to early March. Only loose leaves and pine straw free of limbs or other debris are collected curbside. Leaf crews consist of a driver, a raker, and a machine operator. Crews may make use of seasonal labor, and three to six crews are used depending on the volume of leaves at the curb for collection. During peak leaf fall, crews also pull the curb line in conjunction with street sweepers from the Stormwater Program of the Public Works Department.

Conditions Affecting Service, Performance, and Costs

The Town of Chapel Hill began participation in the benchmarking project in July 2015, with FY 2014–15 being the first reporting year.

In FY 2014–15 complaints were not tracked for yard waste.

Municipal Profile

Population (OSBM 2018)	63,178
Land Area (Square Miles)	21.27
Persons per Square Mile	2,971
Median Household Income	$60,802
U.S. Census 2016	

Service Profile

FTE Positions—Collection	15.9
FTE Positions—Other	0.2
Collection Frequency	
Yard Waste	1 x week
Seasonal Leaf Collection	5-6 sweeps
Collection Points	12,195
Tons Collected	
Yard Waste	3,313
Seasonal Leaves	4,456
Total Tons Collected	7,769
Monthly Service Fee	Resdients may purchase cart for $50 but not required

Full Cost Profile

Cost Breakdown by Percentage	
Personal Services	44.0%
Operating Costs	38.1%
Capital Costs	17.9%
TOTAL	100.0%

Cost Breakdown in Dollars	
Personal Services	$1,059,635
Operating Costs	$917,098
Capital Costs	$429,984
TOTAL	$2,406,717

Chapel Hill

Yard Waste/Leaf Collection

Key: Chapel Hill ▨   Benchmarking Average —   Fiscal Years 2015 through 2019

Resource Measures

Yard Waste and Leaf Collection Costs per Capita

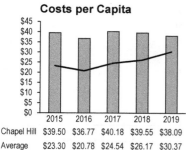

	2015	2016	2017	2018	2019
Chapel Hill	$39.50	$36.77	$40.18	$39.55	$38.09
Average	$23.30	$20.78	$24.54	$26.17	$30.37

Yard Waste and Leaf Collection FTEs per 10,000 Population

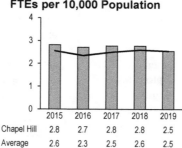

	2015	2016	2017	2018	2019
Chapel Hill	2.8	2.7	2.8	2.8	2.5
Average	2.6	2.3	2.5	2.6	2.5

Workload Measures

Yard Waste and Leaf Tons Collected per 1,000 Population

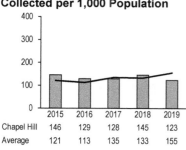

	2015	2016	2017	2018	2019
Chapel Hill	146	129	128	145	123
Average	121	113	135	133	155

Yard Waste and Leaf Tons Collected

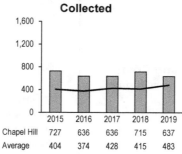

	2015	2016	2017	2018	2019
Chapel Hill	727	636	636	715	637
Average	404	374	428	415	483

Efficiency Measures

Yard Waste and Leaf Collection Cost per Collection Point

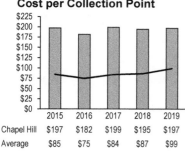

	2015	2016	2017	2018	2019
Chapel Hill	$197	$182	$199	$195	$197
Average	$85	$75	$84	$87	$99

Yard Waste and Leaf Collection Cost per Ton Collected

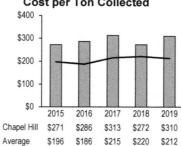

	2015	2016	2017	2018	2019
Chapel Hill	$271	$286	$313	$272	$310
Average	$196	$186	$215	$220	$212

Yard Waste and Leaf Tons Collected per Collection FTE

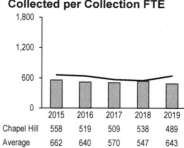

	2015	2016	2017	2018	2019
Chapel Hill	558	519	509	538	489
Average	662	640	570	547	643

Effectiveness Measures

Collection Complaints per 10,000 Collection Points

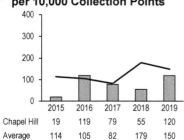

	2015	2016	2017	2018	2019
Chapel Hill	19	119	79	55	120
Average	114	105	82	179	150

Valid Complaints per 10,000 Collection Points

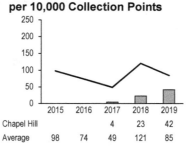

	2015	2016	2017	2018	2019
Chapel Hill			4	23	42
Average	98	74	49	121	85

Fiscal Year 2018–19

Explanatory Information

Service Level and Delivery

Charlotte collects yard waste once per week curbside. The city performs all yard waste collection.

Yard waste includes leaves, stems, grass, limbs, and other residential organic matter. Limbs should be separated into piles small enough for one individual to handle. Leaves and grass clippings must be placed in untied plastic bags or in uncovered trash cans. Yard waste placed at the curb by a commercial landscaping service will not be collected by the city. The city of Charlotte used thirty-four two-person crews working from rear loaders to service the entire city. Additional trucks and staff are allocated as a yard waste reserve.

Leaves are collected in bags and are debagged at the curb as part of the regular yard waste service. A special seasonal leaf collection is not done by the city of Charlotte.

Conditions Affecting Service, Performance, and Costs

Charlotte did not participate in the Benchmarking Project during FY 2014–15. No data are available for that year.

Municipal Profile

Population (OSBM 2018)	852,992
Land Area (Square Miles)	306.31
Persons per Square Mile	2,785
Median Household Income	$46,975
U.S. Census 2016	

Service Profile

FTE Positions—Collection	74.00
FTE Positions—Other	0.00
Collection Frequency	
Yard Waste	1 x week
Collection Points	219,839
Tons Collected	
Yard Waste	61,803
Seasonal Leaves	with yard waste
Total Tons Collected	61,803
Monthly Service Fee	No

Full Cost Profile

Cost Breakdown by Percentage	
Personal Services	40.4%
Operating Costs	44.6%
Capital Costs	15.1%
TOTAL	100.0%

Cost Breakdown in Dollars	
Personal Services	$4,668,897
Operating Costs	$5,155,123
Capital Costs	$1,740,495
TOTAL	$11,564,515

Charlotte

Yard Waste/Leaf Collection

Key: Charlotte ▓   Benchmarking Average —   Fiscal Years 2015 through 2019

Resource Measures

Yard Waste and Leaf Collection Costs per Capita

	2015	2016	2017	2018	2019
Charlotte		$12.25	$12.58	$12.51	$13.56
Average	$23.30	$20.78	$24.54	$26.17	$30.37

Yard Waste and Leaf Collection FTEs per 10,000 Population

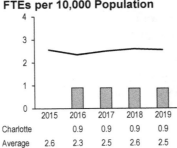

	2015	2016	2017	2018	2019
Charlotte		0.9	0.9	0.9	0.9
Average	2.6	2.3	2.5	2.6	2.5

Workload Measures

Yard Waste and Leaf Tons Collected per 1,000 Population

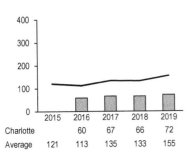

	2015	2016	2017	2018	2019
Charlotte		60	67	66	72
Average	121	113	135	133	155

Yard Waste and Leaf Tons Collected per 1,000 Collection Points

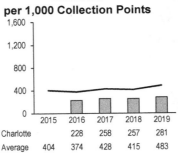

	2015	2016	2017	2018	2019
Charlotte		228	258	257	281
Average	404	374	428	415	483

Efficiency Measures

Yard Waste and Leaf Collection Cost per Collection Point

	2015	2016	2017	2018	2019
Charlotte		$47	$48	$49	$53
Average	$85	$75	$84	$87	$99

Yard Waste and Leaf Collection Cost per Ton Collected

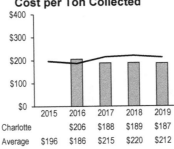

	2015	2016	2017	2018	2019
Charlotte		$206	$188	$189	$187
Average	$196	$186	$215	$220	$212

Yard Waste and Leaf Tons Collected per Collection FTE

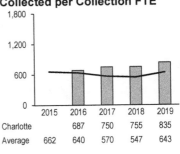

	2015	2016	2017	2018	2019
Charlotte		687	750	755	835
Average	662	640	570	547	643

Effectiveness Measures

Collection Complaints per 10,000 Collection Points

	2015	2016	2017	2018	2019
Charlotte		27	21	6	9
Average	114	105	82	179	150

Valid Complaints per 10,000 Collection Points

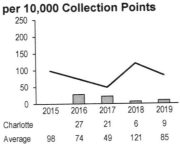

	2015	2016	2017	2018	2019
Charlotte		27	21	6	9
Average	98	74	49	121	85

Concord

Yard Waste/Leaf Collection

Fiscal Year 2018–19

Explanatory Information

Service Level and Delivery

Concord collects all yard waste once per week. Yard waste includes limbs, logs, grass clippings, shrubbery clippings, and leaves.

Concord uses three two-person crews with garbage trucks and a one-person crew with a dump truck to collect yard waste. Four two-person crews also are used to collect limbs and brush with knuckle boom trucks on a weekly basis.

Concord's seasonal loose leaf collection runs from mid-October through mid-February. Each street is serviced following a publicized schedule a minimum of three times for loose leaf collection during this period. Residents who bag their leaves receive weekly collection along with the normal yard waste collection program.

Conditions Affecting Service, Performance, and Costs

Concord provides a high level of service in this area, which make the costs per collection point and per ton appear high.

Municipal Profile

Population (OSBM 2018)	92,568
Land Area (Square Miles)	62.80
Persons per Square Mile	1,474
Median Household Income U.S. Census 2016	$50,863

Service Profile

FTE Positions—Collection	23.70
FTE Positions—Other	2.07
Collection Frequency	
Yard Waste	1 x week
Seasonal Leaf Collection	3 sweeps
Collection Points	33,082
Tons Collected	
Yard Waste	8,797
Seasonal Leaves	2,105
Total Tons Collected	10,902
Monthly Service Fee	No

Full Cost Profile

Cost Breakdown by Percentage	
Personal Services	51.3%
Operating Costs	29.6%
Capital Costs	19.1%
TOTAL	100.0%

Cost Breakdown in Dollars	
Personal Services	$1,387,856
Operating Costs	$799,690
Capital Costs	$516,127
TOTAL	$2,703,673

Concord

Yard Waste/Leaf Collection

Resource Measures

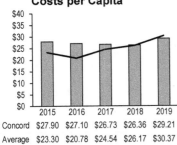

Yard Waste and Leaf Collection Costs per Capita

	2015	2016	2017	2018	2019
Concord	$27.90	$27.10	$26.73	$26.36	$29.21
Average	$23.30	$20.78	$24.54	$26.17	$30.37

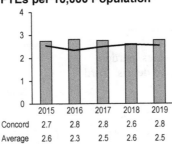

Yard Waste and Leaf Collection FTEs per 10,000 Population

	2015	2016	2017	2018	2019
Concord	2.7	2.8	2.8	2.6	2.8
Average	2.6	2.3	2.5	2.6	2.5

Workload Measures

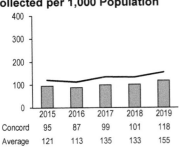

Yard Waste and Leaf Tons Collected per 1,000 Population

	2015	2016	2017	2018	2019
Concord	95	87	99	101	118
Average	121	113	135	133	155

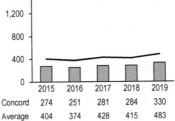

Yard Waste and Leaf Tons Collected

	2015	2016	2017	2018	2019
Concord	274	251	281	284	330
Average	404	374	428	415	483

Efficiency Measures

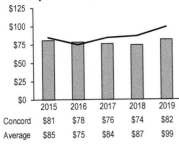

Yard Waste and Leaf Collection Cost per Collection Point

	2015	2016	2017	2018	2019
Concord	$81	$78	$76	$74	$82
Average	$85	$75	$84	$87	$99

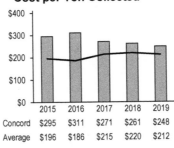

Yard Waste and Leaf Collection Cost per Ton Collected

	2015	2016	2017	2018	2019
Concord	$295	$311	$271	$261	$248
Average	$196	$186	$215	$220	$212

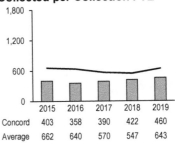

Yard Waste and Leaf Tons Collected per Collection FTE

	2015	2016	2017	2018	2019
Concord	403	358	390	422	460
Average	662	640	570	547	643

Effectiveness Measures

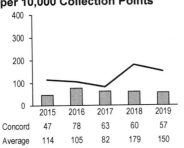

Collection Complaints per 10,000 Collection Points

	2015	2016	2017	2018	2019
Concord	47	78	63	60	57
Average	114	105	82	179	150

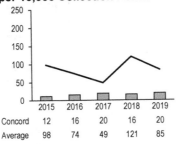

Valid Complaints per 10,000 Collection Points

	2015	2016	2017	2018	2019
Concord	12	16	20	16	20
Average	98	74	49	121	85

Fiscal Year 2018–19

Explanatory Information

Service Level and Delivery

Goldsboro provides yard waste and seasonal leaf collection through the Solid Waste Division of the Public Works Department. Yard waste includes grass clippings, vines, garden and hedge trimmings, shrubbery, and other vegetative debris. Yard waste must be placed at the curbside in loose piles.

Yard waste is collected by four two-person crews consisting of one driver and one collector. Yard waste is collected every two weeks rotating through different sections of the city.

Seasonal leaf collection is done during the months of October through February. Collection is done every two weeks. Five crews are used for seasonal leaf collection consisting of one driver and two collectors per crew. One of the seasonal collectors is a temporary employee, while the driver and the other collector are permanent employees. Leaves must be placed loose or in a leaf cage at the curb.

Conditions Affecting Service, Performance, and Costs

The city of Goldsboro joined the Benchmarking Project in July 2017, with the first year of data showing for FY 2016–17.

Municipal Profile

Population (OSBM 2018)	34,793
Land Area (Square Miles)	29.41
Persons per Square Mile	1,183
Median Household Income	$32,148
U.S. Census 2016	

Service Profile

FTE Positions—Collection	15.00
FTE Positions—Other	1.33
Collection Frequency	
Yard Waste	1 x 2 weeks
Seasonal Leaf Collection	1 x 2 weeks
Collection Points	14,372
Tons Collected	
Yard Waste	8,260
Seasonal Leaves	3,394
Total Tons Collected	11,654
Monthly Service Fee	No

Full Cost Profile

Cost Breakdown by Percentage	
Personal Services	55.9%
Operating Costs	31.9%
Capital Costs	12.2%
TOTAL	100.0%

Cost Breakdown in Dollars	
Personal Services	$1,063,230
Operating Costs	$607,131
Capital Costs	$231,228
TOTAL	$1,901,589

Goldsboro

Yard Waste/Leaf Collection

Resource Measures

Yard Waste and Leaf Collection Costs per Capita

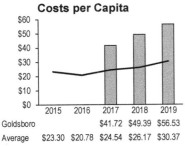

	2015	2016	2017	2018	2019
Goldsboro			$41.72	$49.39	$56.53
Average	$23.30	$20.78	$24.54	$26.17	$30.37

Yard Waste and Leaf Collection FTEs per 10,000 Population

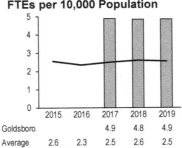

	2015	2016	2017	2018	2019
Goldsboro			4.9	4.8	4.9
Average	2.6	2.3	2.5	2.6	2.5

Workload Measures

Yard Waste and Leaf Tons Collected per 1,000 Population

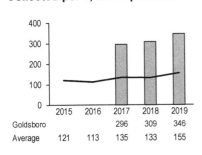

	2015	2016	2017	2018	2019
Goldsboro			296	309	346
Average	121	113	135	133	155

Yard Waste and Leaf Tons Collected per 1,000 Collection Points

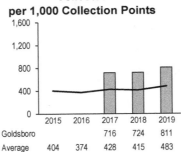

	2015	2016	2017	2018	2019
Goldsboro			716	724	811
Average	404	374	428	415	483

Efficiency Measures

Yard Waste and Leaf Collection Cost per Collection Point

	2015	2016	2017	2018	2019
Goldsboro			$101	$116	$132
Average	$85	$75	$84	$87	$99

Yard Waste and Leaf Collection Cost per Ton Collected

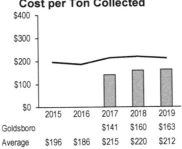

	2015	2016	2017	2018	2019
Goldsboro			$141	$160	$163
Average	$196	$186	$215	$220	$212

Yard Waste and Leaf Tons Collected per Collection FTE

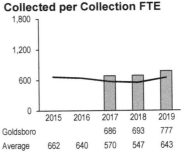

	2015	2016	2017	2018	2019
Goldsboro			686	693	777
Average	662	640	570	547	643

Effectiveness Measures

Collection Complaints per 10,000 Collection Points

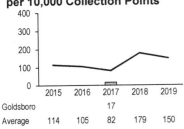

	2015	2016	2017	2018	2019
Goldsboro			17		
Average	114	105	82	179	150

Valid Complaints per 10,000 Collection Points

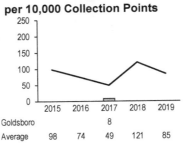

	2015	2016	2017	2018	2019
Goldsboro			8		
Average	98	74	49	121	85

Fiscal Year 2018–19

Explanatory Information

Service Level and Delivery

Greensboro collects yard waste once per week curbside, either in clear plastic bags, thirty-five-gallon containers, or tied in bundles not to exceed 50 pounds or 5 feet in length. Yard waste includes grass, weeds, leaves, tree trimmings, plants, shrubbery trimmings, and other materials generated in yard maintenance. Yard waste does include some bagged leaves during the fall, and this waste is not broken out separately into leaf collection.

The city provides yard waste service to all single-family residences inside the city limits. Yard waste crews include nine two-person crews that rotate between driver and collector. The crews work four days per week, ten hours per day.

Seasonal leaf collection (October through January) is provided by Greensboro's Field Operations Division. Leaves are picked up a minimum of two times from November until mid-January by vacuuming the leaves from the curb.

Conditions Affecting Service, Performance, and Costs

Municipal Profile

Population (OSBM 2018)	292,306
Land Area (Square Miles)	128.77
Persons per Square Mile	2,270
Median Household Income	$40,760
U.S. Census 2016	

Service Profile

FTE Positions—Collection	44.79
FTE Positions—Other	1.15
Collection Frequency	
Yard Waste	1 x week
Seasonal Leaf Collection	2 sweeps
Collection Points	90,625
Tons Collected	
Yard Waste	14,524
Seasonal Leaves	13,914
Total Tons Collected	28,438
Monthly Service Fee	No

Full Cost Profile

Cost Breakdown by Percentage	
Personal Services	37.7%
Operating Costs	62.3%
Capital Costs	0.0%
TOTAL	100.0%

Cost Breakdown in Dollars	
Personal Services	$1,210,312
Operating Costs	$1,999,357
Capital Costs	$0
TOTAL	$3,209,669

Greensboro

Yard Waste/Leaf Collection

Key: Greensboro ▨   Benchmarking Average —   Fiscal Years 2015 through 2019

Resource Measures

Yard Waste and Leaf Collection Costs per Capita

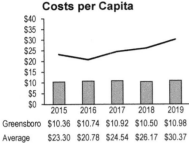

	2015	2016	2017	2018	2019
Greensboro	$10.36	$10.74	$10.92	$10.50	$10.98
Average	$23.30	$20.78	$24.54	$26.17	$30.37

Yard Waste and Leaf Collection FTEs per 10,000 Population

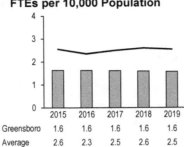

	2015	2016	2017	2018	2019
Greensboro	1.6	1.6	1.6	1.6	1.6
Average	2.6	2.3	2.5	2.6	2.5

Workload Measures

Yard Waste and Leaf Tons Collected per 1,000 Population

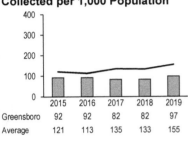

	2015	2016	2017	2018	2019
Greensboro	92	92	82	82	97
Average	121	113	135	133	155

Yard Waste and Leaf Tons Collected

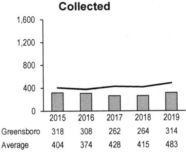

	2015	2016	2017	2018	2019
Greensboro	318	308	262	264	314
Average	404	374	428	415	483

Efficiency Measures

Yard Waste and Leaf Collection Cost per Collection Point

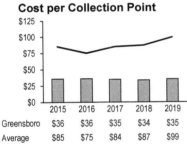

	2015	2016	2017	2018	2019
Greensboro	$36	$36	$35	$34	$35
Average	$85	$75	$84	$87	$99

Yard Waste and Leaf Collection Cost per Ton Collected

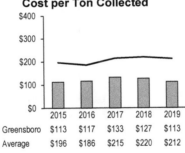

	2015	2016	2017	2018	2019
Greensboro	$113	$117	$133	$127	$113
Average	$196	$186	$215	$220	$212

Yard Waste and Leaf Tons Collected per Collection FTE

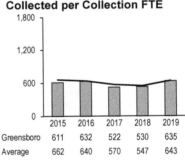

	2015	2016	2017	2018	2019
Greensboro	611	632	522	530	635
Average	662	640	570	547	643

Effectiveness Measures

Collection Complaints per 10,000 Collection Points

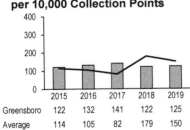

	2015	2016	2017	2018	2019
Greensboro	122	132	141	122	125
Average	114	105	82	179	150

Valid Complaints per 10,000 Collection Points

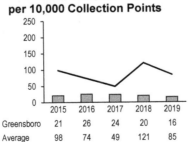

	2015	2016	2017	2018	2019
Greensboro	21	26	24	20	16
Average	98	74	49	121	85

Fiscal Year 2018–19

Explanatory Information

Service Level and Delivery

Greenville collects yard waste once per week curbside. Yard waste includes tree limbs up to 6 feet in length or 4 inches in diameter, bushes, grass clippings, and other vegetative matter. The city does not charge a separate fee for yard waste, leaves, or bulky items. It is part of the solid waste fee.

Greenville uses two-person crews to collect yard waste. Crews are made up of a driver and a collection worker. Each crew has an assigned route for each day.

The city's seasonal leaf collection service runs from November to February. Leaves are collected weekly from the backs of curbs. The city uses five crews, each having a driver and two collection workers. The leaf collection crews are all seasonal employees.

Conditions Affecting Service, Performance, and Costs

Municipal Profile

Population (OSBM 2018)	89,790
Land Area (Square Miles)	35.58
Persons per Square Mile	2,523
Median Household Income	$33,339
U.S. Census 2016	

Service Profile

FTE Positions—Collection	20.3
FTE Positions—Other	6.0
Collection Frequency	
Yard Waste	1 x week
Seasonal Leaf Collection	1 x week
Collection Points	20,000
Tons Collected	
Yard Waste	13,500
Seasonal Leaves	1,000
Total Tons Collected	14,500
Monthly Service Fee	No

Full Cost Profile

Cost Breakdown by Percentage	
Personal Services	41.6%
Operating Costs	42.7%
Capital Costs	15.7%
TOTAL	100.0%

Cost Breakdown in Dollars	
Personal Services	$1,793,332
Operating Costs	$1,837,320
Capital Costs	$676,880
TOTAL	$4,307,532

Greenville
Yard Waste/Leaf Collection

Resource Measures

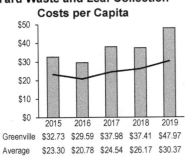

Yard Waste and Leaf Collection Costs per Capita

	2015	2016	2017	2018	2019
Greenville	$32.73	$29.59	$37.98	$37.41	$47.97
Average	$23.30	$20.78	$24.54	$26.17	$30.37

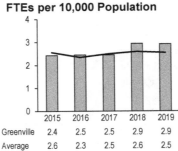

Yard Waste and Leaf Collection FTEs per 10,000 Population

	2015	2016	2017	2018	2019
Greenville	2.4	2.5	2.5	2.9	2.9
Average	2.6	2.3	2.5	2.6	2.5

Workload Measures

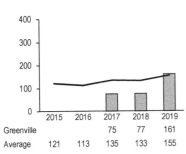

Yard Waste and Leaf Tons Collected per 1,000 Population

	2015	2016	2017	2018	2019
Greenville			75	77	161
Average	121	113	135	133	155

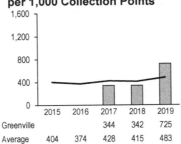

Yard Waste and Leaf Tons Collected per 1,000 Collection Points

	2015	2016	2017	2018	2019
Greenville			344	342	725
Average	404	374	428	415	483

Efficiency Measures

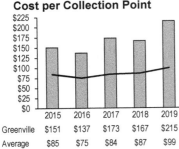

Yard Waste and Leaf Collection Cost per Collection Point

	2015	2016	2017	2018	2019
Greenville	$151	$137	$173	$167	$215
Average	$85	$75	$84	$87	$99

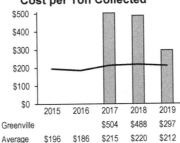

Yard Waste and Leaf Collection Cost per Ton Collected

	2015	2016	2017	2018	2019
Greenville			$504	$488	$297
Average	$196	$186	$215	$220	$212

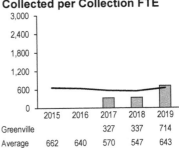

Yard Waste and Leaf Tons Collected per Collection FTE

	2015	2016	2017	2018	2019
Greenville			327	337	714
Average	662	640	570	547	643

Effectiveness Measures

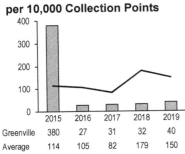

Collection Complaints per 10,000 Collection Points

	2015	2016	2017	2018	2019
Greenville	380	27	31	32	40
Average	114	105	82	179	150

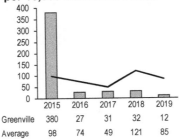

Valid Complaints per 10,000 Collection Points

	2015	2016	2017	2018	2019
Greenville	380	27	31	32	12
Average	98	74	49	121	85

Hickory

Yard Waste/Leaf Collection

Fiscal Year 2018–19

Explanatory Information

Service Level and Delivery

Hickory collects yard waste once per week curbside. Yard waste includes tree limbs less than 6 feet in length and 6 inches in diameter, shrubs, grass clippings, leaves, and other vegetative matter. The city does not charge a separate fee for yard waste, leaves, or bulky items. It is part of the solid waste fee. Residents use either clear plastic bags or open containers.

Hickory is divided into five sections for the yard waste program. Three routes are serviced each day within each section, using three rear loaders with crews comprised of one driver and one laborer each. Large piles are collected with a knuckle boom loader with one driver on a scheduled basis working about half-time.

All yard waste is collected and stockpiled at the city yard waste facility. Debris is ground into mulch or compost and sold back to citizens or used for city projects.

The city's seasonal leaf collection service runs from November to January. There are two sweeps down each city street during this time. City crews use leaf vacuums to collect leaves in box trucks. Hickory uses temporary contract workers to help with leaf collection. These seasonal employees are counted in the total employee count, but only for the one-fourth of the year they work.

Conditions Affecting Service, Performance, and Costs

Hickory's yard waste collection is set up to provide regular service but also takes requests for service when collection is needed. These calls for service cannot be separated out from actual complaints, so complaint data cannot be reported for this service area.

Municipal Profile

Population (OSBM 2018)	40,932
Land Area (Square Miles)	29.92
Persons per Square Mile	1,368
Median Household Income	$35,353
U.S. Census 2016	

Service Profile

FTE Positions—Collection	9.75
FTE Positions—Other	0.7
Collection Frequency	
Yard Waste	1 x week
Seasonal Leaf Collection	2 sweeps
Collection Points	11,940
Tons Collected	
Yard Waste	5,974
Seasonal Leaves	4,240
Total Tons Collected	10,214
Monthly Service Fee	No

Full Cost Profile

Cost Breakdown by Percentage	
Personal Services	39.5%
Operating Costs	47.5%
Capital Costs	12.9%
TOTAL	100.0%

Cost Breakdown in Dollars	
Personal Services	$361,763
Operating Costs	$435,050
Capital Costs	$118,278
TOTAL	$915,091

Hickory

Yard Waste/Leaf Collection

Key: Hickory   Benchmarking Average — Fiscal Years 2015 through 2019

Resource Measures

Yard Waste and Leaf Collection Costs per Capita

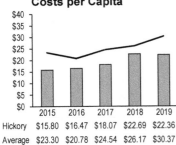

	2015	2016	2017	2018	2019
Hickory	$15.80	$16.47	$18.07	$22.69	$22.36
Average	$23.30	$20.78	$24.54	$26.17	$30.37

Yard Waste and Leaf Collection FTEs per 10,000 Population

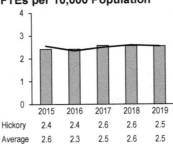

	2015	2016	2017	2018	2019
Hickory	2.4	2.4	2.6	2.6	2.5
Average	2.6	2.3	2.5	2.6	2.5

Workload Measures

Yard Waste and Leaf Tons Collected per 1,000 Population

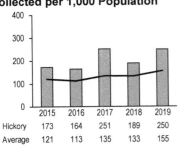

	2015	2016	2017	2018	2019
Hickory	173	164	251	189	250
Average	121	113	135	133	155

Yard Waste and Leaf Tons Collected

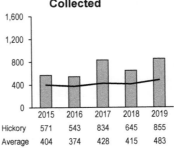

	2015	2016	2017	2018	2019
Hickory	571	543	834	645	855
Average	404	374	428	415	483

Efficiency Measures

Yard Waste and Leaf Collection Cost per Collection Point

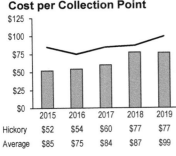

	2015	2016	2017	2018	2019
Hickory	$52	$54	$60	$77	$77
Average	$85	$75	$84	$87	$99

Yard Waste and Leaf Collection Cost per Ton Collected

	2015	2016	2017	2018	2019
Hickory	$92	$100	$72	$120	$90
Average	$196	$186	$215	$220	$212

Yard Waste and Leaf Tons Collected per Collection FTE

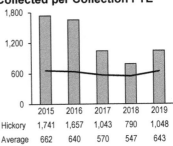

	2015	2016	2017	2018	2019
Hickory	1,741	1,657	1,043	790	1,048
Average	662	640	570	547	643

Effectiveness Measures

Collection Complaints per 10,000 Collection Points

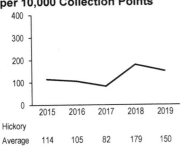

	2015	2016	2017	2018	2019
Hickory					
Average	114	105	82	179	150

Valid Complaints per 10,000 Collection Points

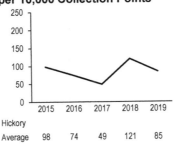

	2015	2016	2017	2018	2019
Hickory					
Average	98	74	49	121	85

Mooresville

Yard Waste/Leaf Collection

Fiscal Year 2018–19

Explanatory Information

Service Level and Delivery

Yard waste is picked up weekly at the curb in Mooresville. Yard waste includes tree and bush trimmings, grass, and leaves. It is collected the day after regularly scheduled garbage pickup.

The town uses two two-person crews, each consisting of a driver and laborer, on packer trucks for yard waste collection. Two additional crews with a single operator in an automated leaf truck collect loose grass and leaves. There is no separate seasonal leaf collection, but during the leaf season, Mooresville runs four automated leaf collection trucks to handle the extra volume.

Conditions Affecting Service, Performance, and Costs

Mooresville joined the Benchmarking project in July 2018, with the first year of data showing for FY 2017–18.

There was a large turnover in staff responsible for yard waste pickup during FY 2017–18. This led to a higher number of complaints due to new staff learning the tasks in the service area.

Municipal Profile

Population (OSBM 2018)	41,255
Land Area (Square Miles)	22.75
Persons per Square Mile	1,813
Median Household Income U.S. Census 2016	$67,213

Service Profile

FTE Positions—Collection	10.0
FTE Positions—Other	0.00
Collection Frequency	
Yard Waste	1 x week
Collection Points	14,500
Tons Collected	
Yard Waste	2,139
Seasonal Leaves	3,225
Total Tons Collected	5,364
Monthly Service Fee	No

Full Cost Profile

Cost Breakdown by Percentage	
Personal Services	24.6%
Operating Costs	28.4%
Capital Costs	47.0%
TOTAL	100.0%

Cost Breakdown in Dollars	
Personal Services	$457,268
Operating Costs	$528,953
Capital Costs	$873,309
TOTAL	$1,859,530

Yard Waste/Leaf Collection

Key: Mooresville ▪   Benchmarking Average —   Fiscal Years 2015 through 2019

Resource Measures

Yard Waste and Leaf Collection Costs per Capita

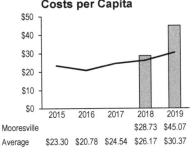

	2015	2016	2017	2018	2019
Mooresville				$28.73	$45.07
Average	$23.30	$20.78	$24.54	$26.17	$30.37

Yard Waste and Leaf Collection FTEs per 10,000 Population

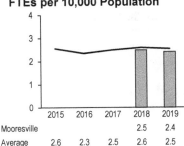

	2015	2016	2017	2018	2019
Mooresville				2.5	2.4
Average	2.6	2.3	2.5	2.6	2.5

Workload Measures

Yard Waste and Leaf Tons Collected per 1,000 Population

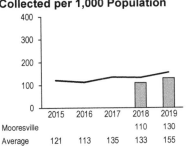

	2015	2016	2017	2018	2019
Mooresville				110	130
Average	121	113	135	133	155

Yard Waste and Leaf Tons Collected

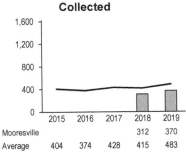

	2015	2016	2017	2018	2019
Mooresville				312	370
Average	404	374	428	415	483

Efficiency Measures

Yard Waste and Leaf Collection Cost per Collection Point

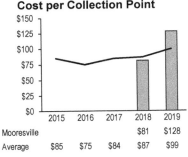

	2015	2016	2017	2018	2019
Mooresville				$81	$128
Average	$85	$75	$84	$87	$99

Yard Waste and Leaf Collection Cost per Ton Collected

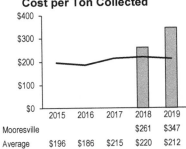

	2015	2016	2017	2018	2019
Mooresville				$261	$347
Average	$196	$186	$215	$220	$212

Yard Waste and Leaf Tons Collected per Collection FTE

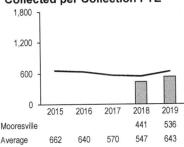

	2015	2016	2017	2018	2019
Mooresville				441	536
Average	662	640	570	547	643

Effectiveness Measures

Collection Complaints per 10,000 Collection Points

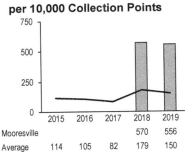

	2015	2016	2017	2018	2019
Mooresville				570	556
Average	114	105	82	179	150

Valid Complaints per 10,000 Collection Points

	2015	2016	2017	2018	2019
Mooresville				208	203
Average	98	74	49	121	85

Raleigh

Yard Waste/Leaf Collection

Fiscal Year 2018–19

Explanatory Information

Service Level and Delivery

Yard waste is picked up weekly at the curb in Raleigh by the Solid Waste Services Department. Yard waste must be bagged or containerized with a limit of fifteen bags. Bags must be clear or biodegradable.

The city uses twelve three-person crews to collect yard waste on the same day as trash collection. Temporary crews are added during leaf season as yard waste volume picks up.

Loose Leaf collection is done by the Transportation Field Services Division. Loose leaves are collected curbside during leaf season, which runs from November to February. Two sweeps of the City are completed during leaf season. The first sweep is usually completed by mid-January, and the second sweep is usually completed by the end of February. Loose leaves must be placed at the street and must be free of debris to be collected.

Conditions Affecting Service, Performance, and Costs

Raleigh rejoined the Benchmarking Project in July 2016, with the first year of data showing for FY 2015–16.

Municipal Profile

Population (OSBM 2018)	464,453
Land Area (Square Miles)	145.65
Persons per Square Mile	3,189
Median Household Income	$46,612
U.S. Census 2016	

Service Profile

FTE Positions—Collection	103.0
FTE Positions—Other	4.5
Collection Frequency	
Yard Waste	1 x week
Seasonal Leaf Collection	2 sweeps
Collection Points	129,962
Tons Collected	
Yard Waste	17,977
Seasonal Leaves	14,150
Total Tons Collected	32,127
Monthly Service Fee	
Yard Waste	Yes
Seasonal Leaf Collection	No

Full Cost Profile

Cost Breakdown by Percentage	
Personal Services	46.2%
Operating Costs	41.5%
Capital Costs	12.3%
TOTAL	100.0%
Cost Breakdown in Dollars	
Personal Services	$3,719,613
Operating Costs	$3,345,776
Capital Costs	$994,050
TOTAL	$8,059,439

Raleigh

Yard Waste/Leaf Collection

Key: Raleigh ▨   Benchmarking Average —   Fiscal Years 2015 through 2019

Resource Measures

Yard Waste and Leaf Collection Costs per Capita

	2015	2016	2017	2018	2019
Raleigh		$10.31	$14.59	$15.66	$17.35
Average	$23.30	$20.78	$24.54	$26.17	$30.37

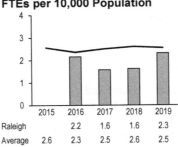

Yard Waste and Leaf Collection FTEs per 10,000 Population

	2015	2016	2017	2018	2019
Raleigh		2.2	1.6	1.6	2.3
Average	2.6	2.3	2.5	2.6	2.5

Workload Measures

Yard Waste and Leaf Tons Collected per 1,000 Population

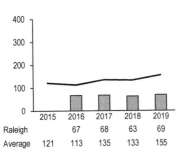

	2015	2016	2017	2018	2019
Raleigh		67	68	63	69
Average	121	113	135	133	155

Yard Waste and Leaf Tons Collected per 1,000 Collection Points

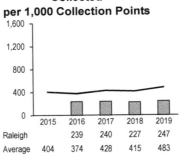

	2015	2016	2017	2018	2019
Raleigh		239	240	227	247
Average	404	374	428	415	483

Efficiency Measures

Yard Waste and Leaf Collection Cost per Collection Point

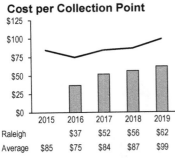

	2015	2016	2017	2018	2019
Raleigh		$37	$52	$56	$62
Average	$85	$75	$84	$87	$99

Yard Waste and Leaf Collection Cost per Ton Collected

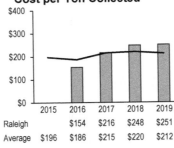

	2015	2016	2017	2018	2019
Raleigh		$154	$216	$248	$251
Average	$196	$186	$215	$220	$212

Yard Waste and Leaf Tons Collected per Collection FTE

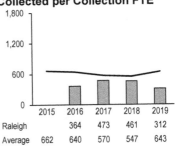

	2015	2016	2017	2018	2019
Raleigh		364	473	461	312
Average	662	640	570	547	643

Effectiveness Measures

Collection Complaints per 10,000 Collection Points

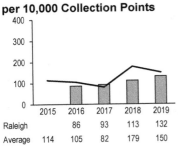

	2015	2016	2017	2018	2019
Raleigh		86	93	113	132
Average	114	105	82	179	150

Valid Complaints per 10,000 Collection Points

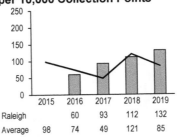

	2015	2016	2017	2018	2019
Raleigh		60	93	112	132
Average	98	74	49	121	85

Wilson

Yard Waste/Leaf Collection

Fiscal Year 2018–19

Explanatory Information

Service Level and Delivery

Yard waste is containerized in bags, sheets, roll-out containers, or other container types for collection by rear-loader packers. Yard waste is collected once per week by compost crews on the same day as residential refuse collection.

The city uses two three-person crews on Tuesdays and Fridays and three or four three-person crews on Mondays and Thursdays to collect yard waste. Each crew is composed of one driver and two workers. These crews rotate collection between residential refuse and yard waste. A one-person crew uses a knuckle boom truck to collect large limbs daily.

The city's leaf season is from mid-October to mid-January. Leaves are collected loose at the curb on a one-to-three-week cycle. The city uses leaf vacuum machines and compacting leaf trucks to collect loose leaves.

Six to eight three-person crews are used to collect loose leaves. The drivers are permanent employees. Collectors are seasonal employees.

Conditions Affecting Service, Performance, and Costs

Wilson began using a new automated system for tracking all call-ins into "Fix-It Wilson" during FY 2017–2018. The contacts for yard waste include all items related to limbs, leaves, and compost. Previously all complaints were received by telephone and documented by hand in a notebook. The jump in complaints is connected to the implementation of this new system rather than changes in service.

Municipal Profile

Population (OSBM 2018)	49,054
Land Area (Square Miles)	30.97
Persons per Square Mile	1,584
Median Household Income	$35,409
U.S. Census 2016	

Service Profile

FTE Positions—Collection	11.5
FTE Positions—Other	0.0
Collection Frequency	
Yard Waste	1 x week
Seasonal Leaf Collection	1 x 3 weeks
Collection Points	25,100
Tons Collected	
Yard Waste	9,022
Seasonal Leaves	1,200
Total Tons Collected	10,222
Monthly Service Fee	Included in solid waste fee

Full Cost Profile

Cost Breakdown by Percentage	
Personal Services	49.5%
Operating Costs	32.5%
Capital Costs	17.9%
TOTAL	100.0%

Cost Breakdown in Dollars	
Personal Services	$679,633
Operating Costs	$446,606
Capital Costs	$246,090
TOTAL	$1,372,329

Wilson

Yard Waste/Leaf Collection

Resource Measures

Yard Waste and Leaf Collection Costs per Capita

	2015	2016	2017	2018	2019
Wilson	$20.76	$21.50	$20.57	$21.28	$27.98
Average	$23.30	$20.78	$24.54	$26.17	$30.37

Yard Waste and Leaf Collection FTEs per 10,000 Population

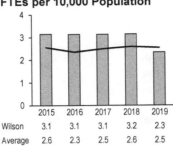

	2015	2016	2017	2018	2019
Wilson	3.1	3.1	3.1	3.2	2.3
Average	2.6	2.3	2.5	2.6	2.5

Workload Measures

Yard Waste and Leaf Tons Collected per 1,000 Population

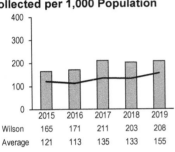

	2015	2016	2017	2018	2019
Wilson	165	171	211	203	208
Average	121	113	135	133	155

Yard Waste and Leaf Tons Collected

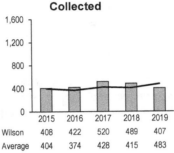

	2015	2016	2017	2018	2019
Wilson	408	422	520	489	407
Average	404	374	428	415	483

Efficiency Measures

Yard Waste and Leaf Collection Cost per Collection Point

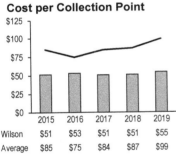

	2015	2016	2017	2018	2019
Wilson	$51	$53	$51	$51	$55
Average	$85	$75	$84	$87	$99

Yard Waste and Leaf Collection Cost per Ton Collected

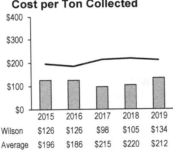

	2015	2016	2017	2018	2019
Wilson	$126	$126	$98	$105	$134
Average	$196	$186	$215	$220	$212

Yard Waste and Leaf Tons Collected per Collection FTE

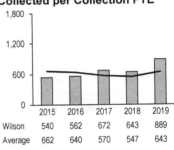

	2015	2016	2017	2018	2019
Wilson	540	562	672	643	889
Average	662	640	570	547	643

Effectiveness Measures

Collection Complaints per 10,000 Collection Points

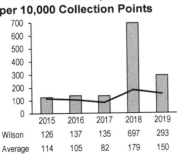

	2015	2016	2017	2018	2019
Wilson	126	137	135	697	293
Average	114	105	82	179	150

Valid Complaints per 10,000 Collection Points

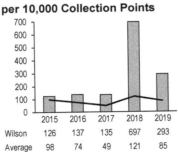

	2015	2016	2017	2018	2019
Wilson	126	137	135	697	293
Average	98	74	49	121	85

Winston-Salem

Yard Waste/Leaf Collection

Fiscal Year 2018–19

Explanatory Information

Service Level and Delivery

The city operates a curbside collection program for brush, leaves, and bulky items. Brush is collected throughout the year, while leaves and bulky items are collected on a seasonal basis. Brush is defined as small tree limbs, branches, and shrubbery clippings. Tree and shrubbery limbs cannot be larger than 6 inches in diameter or 6 feet in length. A city ordinance requires that brush be collected once every ten working days except during leaf season. There are no separate fees for the curbside collection program. The brush collection program gathered 21,963 tons across the city.

The yard waste cart program provides weekly collection of containerized yard waste placed in ninety-six-gallon carts. The city uses six one-person crews using automated packers and one two-person crew using a rear-loading packer to service these carts. Collection is provided Monday through Thursday. Carts are delivered on Friday. Residents who participate in the yard waste cart program pay an annual $60 fee. Residents also pay for the ninety-six-gallon carts at a cost of $60 if the cart is picked up or $65 if the cart is delivered. A household can have up to three carts. The yard cart program serviced 13,828 customers in the fiscal year picking up 7,379 tons.

The city's seasonal leaf collection program picks up leaves that are deposited at the curb between November 1 and January 15. Loose leaves are vacuumed two to three times during this time period. Containerized leaves are collected throughout the year as part of the yard waste program. The city uses thirty-two crews for seasonal leaf collection, with a combination of equipment operators, maintenance workers, and both permanent and seasonal workers.

Conditions Affecting Service, Performance, and Costs

The performance measure "cost per collection point" is based on a total of 81,589 collection points.

Municipal Profile

Population (OSBM 2018)	243,447
Land Area (Square Miles)	132.55
Persons per Square Mile	1,837
Median Household Income	$40,584
U.S. Census 2016	

Service Profile

FTE Positions—Collection	74.5
FTE Positions—Other	1.4
Collection Frequency	
Yard Waste	1 x week
Seasonal Leaf Collection	1 x 3 weeks
Brush	1 x 10 days
Collection Points	81,589
Tons Collected	
Yard Waste	29,010
Seasonal Leaves	21,631
Total Tons Collected	50,641
Monthly Service Fee	$60 per year for cart

Full Cost Profile

Cost Breakdown by Percentage	
Personal Services	50.5%
Operating Costs	29.6%
Capital Costs	19.9%
TOTAL	100.0%

Cost Breakdown in Dollars	
Personal Services	$3,415,231
Operating Costs	$2,000,573
Capital Costs	$1,343,465
TOTAL	$6,759,269

Resource Measures

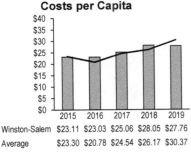

Yard Waste and Leaf Collection Costs per Capita

	2015	2016	2017	2018	2019
Winston-Salem	$23.11	$23.03	$25.06	$28.05	$27.76
Average	$23.30	$20.78	$24.54	$26.17	$30.37

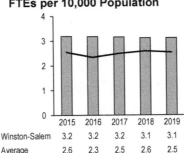

Yard Waste and Leaf Collection FTEs per 10,000 Population

	2015	2016	2017	2018	2019
Winston-Salem	3.2	3.2	3.2	3.1	3.1
Average	2.6	2.3	2.5	2.6	2.5

Workload Measures

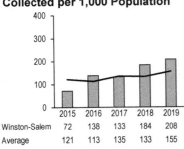

Yard Waste and Leaf Tons Collected per 1,000 Population

	2015	2016	2017	2018	2019
Winston-Salem	72	138	133	184	208
Average	121	113	135	133	155

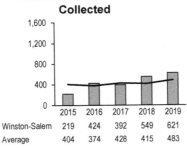

Yard Waste and Leaf Tons Collected

	2015	2016	2017	2018	2019
Winston-Salem	219	424	392	549	621
Average	404	374	428	415	483

Efficiency Measures

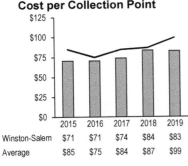

Yard Waste and Leaf Collection Cost per Collection Point

	2015	2016	2017	2018	2019
Winston-Salem	$71	$71	$74	$84	$83
Average	$85	$75	$84	$87	$99

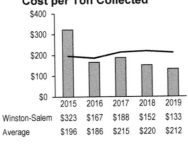

Yard Waste and Leaf Collection Cost per Ton Collected

	2015	2016	2017	2018	2019
Winston-Salem	$323	$167	$188	$152	$133
Average	$196	$186	$215	$220	$212

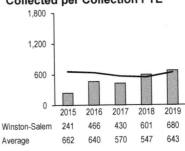

Yard Waste and Leaf Tons Collected per Collection FTE

	2015	2016	2017	2018	2019
Winston-Salem	241	466	430	601	680
Average	662	640	570	547	643

Effectiveness Measures

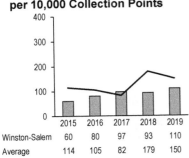

Collection Complaints per 10,000 Collection Points

	2015	2016	2017	2018	2019
Winston-Salem	60	80	97	93	110
Average	114	105	82	179	150

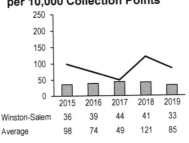

Valid Complaints per 10,000 Collection Points

	2015	2016	2017	2018	2019
Winston-Salem	36	39	44	41	33
Average	98	74	49	121	85

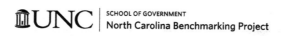

SCHOOL OF GOVERNMENT
North Carolina Benchmarking Project

Performance and Cost Data

POLICE SERVICES

PERFORMANCE MEASURES FOR POLICE SERVICES

SERVICE DEFINITION

Police Services consist of all police activities performed by sworn and non-sworn personnel. This includes, but is not limited to, activities performed by patrol, traffic, investigations, special units, support staff, supervisors, and police administration. This definition captures all functions of the police department except for emergency communications.

NOTES ON PERFORMANCE MEASURES

1. Dispatched Calls

These are calls resulting in the dispatch of an officer. Most dispatches result from calls coming into the emergency communications center or the police department, but some are self-initiated by officers on duty. Multiple calls resulting in the dispatch of several officers are counted as one.

2. Uniform Crime Reporting (UCR) Part I Crimes

Uniform Crime Reporting (UCR) Part I crimes include crimes against persons (criminal homicide, forcible rape, robbery, and aggravated assault) and crimes against property (burglary, larceny, motor vehicle theft, and arson).

3. Incident-Based Reporting (IBR) Part I Crimes

Incident-Based Reporting (IBR) Part I crimes include crimes against persons (criminal homicide, forcible rape, robbery, and aggravated assault) and crimes against property (burglary, larceny, motor vehicle theft, and arson). The difference between the UCR method and the IBR method for reporting crimes is that IBR counts crime and arrest activities at the incident level, as opposed to counting only the most serious crime with multiple offenses.

4. Full-Time Equivalent (FTE) Positions: Sworn Officers

The number of full-time equivalent (FTE) positions is the number of budgeted positions for sworn officers during the fiscal year.

5. Response Time to High Priority Calls

Each police department defines high priority calls somewhat differently. The definitions generally refer to crimes in progress or situations where there are risks of injury or threats to life or property. Response time commences with the dispatch of an officer and ends with the arrival of the officer at the scene of the incident. The officer may be dispatched while on patrol or from the police station.

Police Services

Summary of Key Dimensions of Service

City or Town	Police Department Accredited?	Number of Sworn Officers	Average Length of Service for Sworn Officers (Years)	Number of Patrol Vehicles	Reporting Format	Part I Crimes			Part II Crimes	Dispatched Calls	Number of Traffic Accidents
						Against Persons	Against Property	Total			
Apex	Yes	92.0	13.3	108	IBR	51	640	691	1,721	46,172	1,436
Asheville	Yes	238	7.4	255	IBR	534	5,468	6,002	8,145	136,854	7,174
Chapel Hill	No	118	13.9	77	UCR	85	946	1,031	2,853	31,095	214
Concord	No	185	8.9	217	IBR	81	1,645	1,726	2,100	127,948	3,925
Goldsboro	No	110	9.3	100	UCR	200	1,947	2,147	1,510	52,313	2,242
Greensboro	Yes	675	12.6	242	UCR	1,580	10,639	12,219	14,673	215,008	10,524
Greenville	Yes	205	14.0	238	UCR	445	2,751	3,196	4,788	81,944	4,450
Hickory	No	116	8.7	143	IBR	148	1,751	1,899	4,064	90,024	2,438
Mooresville	Yes	90	8.3	76	NIBRS	71	1,163	1,234	2,448	88,402	2,689
Raleigh	Yes	796	12.5	822	NIBRS	1,755	11,187	12,942	NA	304,972	27,922
Wilson	Yes	125	9.7	128	UCR/INR	209	1,579	1,788	2,538	89,274	2,699
Winston-Salem	Yes	558	12.0	450	NIBRS	2,631	11,658	14,289	35,141	215,260	11,121

EXPLANATORY FACTORS

These are factors that the project found affected police services performance and cost in one or more of the municipalities:

Demographic makeup of the community
Community policing policies
Population density and land area
Downtown area characteristics
Use of incident-based reporting
Presence of unique problems in particular areas, such as drugs or gangs
Emphasis on quick response to all calls
Vehicle take-home policy
Beat structure
Use of special units

Explanatory Information

Service Level and Delivery

The Town of Apex Police Department provides an array of police services, including patrol, investigations, a special response unit, and school resource officers at the high school and middle schools located in the town.

The city had ninety-two sworn officer positions authorized for the year, with an average length of service of over thirteen years. Police services occupies a headquarters located in downtown Apex, newly built in 2010, which houses all divisions in the department. There is also an unmanned substation attached to one of the town fire stations.

Officers in Apex in the patrol division work twelve-hour modified DuPont schedules. Each patrol squad is also assigned a flex officer. The traffic unit works a modified DuPont schedule based on crash statistics. The investigations division works Monday through Friday from 8 a.m. to 5 p.m., with one investigator working from 2 p.m. to 11 p.m. The investigator working the late shift is also the on-call investigator, and this position rotates every week.

Patrol and investigation units are assigned individual vehicles. Command staff also have individually assigned vehicles, which are the only take-home vehicles in the fleet.

The police department was successful in clearing a total of 269 Part I cases during the fiscal year.

The definition of a high-priority call in Apex is any call which the immediate arrival and presence of the police may prevent death or injury or alleviate the threat of death or injury.

Conditions Affecting Service, Performance, and Costs

Municipal Profile

Population (OSBM 2018)	52,909
Land Area (Square Miles)	21.55
Persons per Square Mile	2,455
Median Household Income	$84,000
U.S. Census 2016	

Service Profile

FTE Positions—Sworn	92.0
FTE Positions—Other	7.0
Marked and Unmarked Patrol Vehicles	108
Part I Crimes Reported	
Homicide	0
Rape	8
Robbery	12
Assault	31
Burglary	66
Larceny	559
Auto Theft	14
Arson	1
TOTAL	691
Part II Crimes Reported	1,721
Part I Crimes Cleared	
Persons	42
Property	227
TOTAL	269
Reporting Format	IBR
Number of Calls Dispatched	46,172
Number of Traffic Accidents	1,436
Property Damage for Accidents	$5,407,053

Full Cost Profile

Cost Breakdown by Percentage

Personal Services	61.0%
Operating Costs	25.8%
Capital Costs	13.2%
TOTAL	100.0%

Cost Breakdown in Dollars

Personal Services	$7,616,068
Operating Costs	$3,219,544
Capital Costs	$1,647,905
TOTAL	$12,483,517

Apex

Police Services

Resource Measures

Police Services Costs per Capita

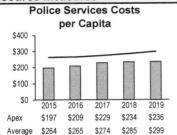

	2015	2016	2017	2018	2019
Apex	$197	$209	$229	$234	$236
Average	$264	$265	$274	$285	$299

Total Police Services Personnel per 10,000 Population

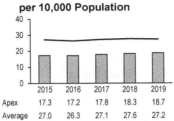

	2015	2016	2017	2018	2019
Apex	17.3	17.2	17.8	18.3	18.7
Average	27.0	26.3	27.1	27.6	27.2

Sworn Police Officers per 10,000 Population

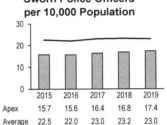

	2015	2016	2017	2018	2019
Apex	15.7	15.6	16.4	16.8	17.4
Average	22.5	22.0	23.0	23.2	23.0

Workload Measures

Calls Dispatched per 1,000 Population

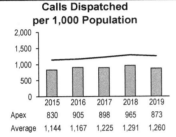

	2015	2016	2017	2018	2019
Apex	830	905	898	965	873
Average	1,144	1,167	1,225	1,291	1,260

Part I Crimes per 1,000 Population

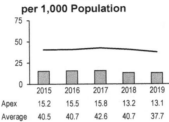

	2015	2016	2017	2018	2019
Apex	15.2	15.5	15.8	13.2	13.1
Average	40.5	40.7	42.6	40.7	37.7

Efficiency Measures

Police Services Cost per Call Dispatched

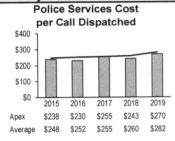

	2015	2016	2017	2018	2019
Apex	$238	$230	$255	$243	$270
Average	$248	$252	$255	$260	$282

Calls Dispatched per Sworn Officer

	2015	2016	2017	2018	2019
Apex	529	578	548	573	502
Average	501	523	524	554	539

Police Services Cost per Part I Case Cleared

	2015	2016	2017	2018	2019
Apex	$34,131	$32,860	$43,413	$58,864	$46,407
Average	$23,091	$19,911	$24,369	$27,864	$30,448

Part I Cases Cleared per Sworn Officer

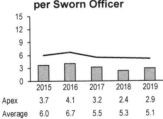

	2015	2016	2017	2018	2019
Apex	3.7	4.1	3.2	2.4	2.9
Average	6.0	6.7	5.5	5.3	5.1

Effectiveness Measures

Percentage of Part I Cases Cleared of Those Reported

	2015	2016	2017	2018	2019
Apex	38.1%	40.9%	33.4%	30.1%	30.1%
Average	33.9%	37.7%	30.5%	31.4%	32.6%

Response Time to High Priority Calls in Minutes

	2015	2016	2017	2018	2019
Apex	4.3	5.4	5.6	3.4	3.4
Average	5.0	5.6	5.5	5.7	5.3

Asheville

Police Services

Fiscal Year 2018–19

Explanatory Information

Service Level and Delivery

The Asheville Police Department provides an array of police services, including patrol, investigations, a telephone response unit, a canine unit, a special response unit, animal control, a drug enforcement unit, a hostage negotiation team, a hazardous device team, and several other special programs.

The city had 238 sworn officer positions authorized for the year, with an average length of service of about 7.41 years. Police services occupies five facilities: the main downtown facility shared by the fire department and four substations.

Officers in Asheville work a varied DuPont schedule based on a fourteen-day period, working six twelve-hour days and one eight-hour day. The schedule requires two or three days on followed by two days off in alternating sequences over the two-week period. A power squad is assigned to work the evening shift during the peak time of calls. Detectives work four ten-hour days, with half the detectives off Mondays and the other half off on Fridays. Detective supervisors work five eight-hour days.

Specialty units such as traffic, SWAT, and detectives have assigned take-home cars. Additionally, sergeants and higher-ranked officers also have assigned vehicles. Patrol cars have multiple users.

The police department was successful in clearing a total of 1,401 Part I cases during the fiscal year. The definition of a high-priority call in Asheville is any call dealing with a crime in progress or a situation where there is immediate danger to a person.

Conditions Affecting Service, Performance, and Costs

The average response time to high priority calls reflects the response time of the first arriving unit. Self-initiated calls are not included in the response time. Due to a better classification of high-priority calls at the Asheville communications unit, police have been able to lower their response time to high-priority calls.

Municipal Profile

Population (OSBM 2018)	93,621
Land Area (Square Miles)	45.53
Persons per Square Mile	2,056
Median Household Income	$40,494
U.S. Census 2016	

Service Profile

FTE Positions—Sworn	238.0
FTE Positions—Other	63.0
Marked and Unmarked Patrol Vehicles	255
Part I Crimes Reported	
Homicide	5
Rape	55
Robbery	146
Assault	328
Burglary	849
Larceny	4,117
Auto Theft	478
Arson	24
TOTAL	6,002
Part II Crimes Reported	8,145
Part I Crimes Cleared	
Persons	247
Property	1,154
TOTAL	1,401
Reporting Format	IBR
Number of Calls Dispatched	136,854
Number of Traffic Accidents	7,174
Property Damage for Accidents	$27,305,711

Full Cost Profile

Cost Breakdown by Percentage

Personal Services	65.6%
Operating Costs	24.8%
Capital Costs	9.6%
TOTAL	100.0%

Cost Breakdown in Dollars

Personal Services	$21,936,668
Operating Costs	$8,280,408
Capital Costs	$3,225,579
TOTAL	$33,442,655

Asheville

Police Services

Resource Measures

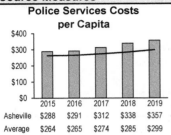

Police Services Costs per Capita

	2015	2016	2017	2018	2019
Asheville	$288	$291	$312	$338	$357
Average	$264	$265	$274	$285	$299

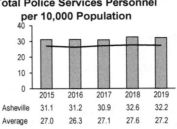

Total Police Services Personnel per 10,000 Population

	2015	2016	2017	2018	2019
Asheville	31.1	31.2	30.9	32.6	32.2
Average	27.0	26.3	27.1	27.6	27.2

Sworn Police Officers per 10,000 Population

	2015	2016	2017	2018	2019
Asheville	25.0	24.4	24.1	25.9	25.4
Average	22.5	22.0	23.0	23.2	23.0

Workload Measures

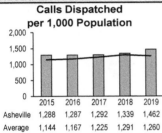

Calls Dispatched per 1,000 Population

	2015	2016	2017	2018	2019
Asheville	1,288	1,287	1,292	1,339	1,462
Average	1,144	1,167	1,225	1,291	1,260

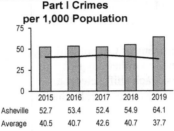

Part I Crimes per 1,000 Population

	2015	2016	2017	2018	2019
Asheville	52.7	53.4	52.4	54.9	64.1
Average	40.5	40.7	42.6	40.7	37.7

Efficiency Measures

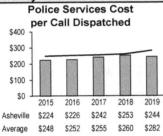

Police Services Cost per Call Dispatched

	2015	2016	2017	2018	2019
Asheville	$224	$226	$242	$253	$244
Average	$248	$252	$255	$260	$282

Calls Dispatched per Sworn Officer

	2015	2016	2017	2018	2019
Asheville	515	527	535	517	575
Average	501	523	524	554	539

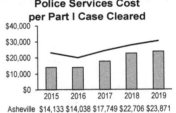

Police Services Cost per Part I Case Cleared

	2015	2016	2017	2018	2019
Asheville	$14,133	$14,038	$17,749	$22,706	$23,871
Average	$23,091	$19,911	$24,369	$27,864	$30,448

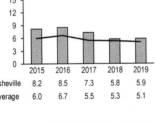

Part I Cases Cleared per Sworn Officer

	2015	2016	2017	2018	2019
Asheville	8.2	8.5	7.3	5.8	5.9
Average	6.0	6.7	5.5	5.3	5.1

Effectiveness Measures

Percentage of Part I Cases Cleared of Those Reported

	2015	2016	2017	2018	2019
Asheville	38.7%	38.8%	33.6%	27.1%	23.3%
Average	33.9%	37.7%	30.5%	31.4%	32.6%

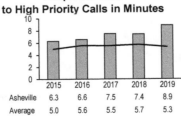

Response Time to High Priority Calls in Minutes

	2015	2016	2017	2018	2019
Asheville	6.3	6.6	7.5	7.4	8.9
Average	5.0	5.6	5.5	5.7	5.3

Fiscal Year 2018–19

Service Level and Delivery

The Town of Chapel Hill Police Department provides an array of police services, including patrol, investigations, a special response unit, bicycle patrol, drug enforcement, limited laboratory work, and a canine unit.

The town had 118 sworn officer positions authorized for the fiscal year, with an average length of service of 13.9 years. Police headquarters is located in a separate building. The department also operates four substations. Three of the substations function as offices for community services, and the fourth is located downtown and functions as a space for report processing but is not regularly staffed.

In order to provide continuous service to the citizens of Chapel Hill, officers work twelve hour shifts and are assigned to either day (6 a.m. to 6 p.m.) or night (6 p.m. to 6 a.m.) shifts. Each shift selects a number of officers to report one to two hours early to cover calls that occur leading up to shift change.

Vehicles are allocated to divisions in the department and are assigned by unit level supervisors. Individual assignments are made for certain positions, but the only officers allowed to take home vehicles are K9 units, administrative officers, and on-call investigators.

The town defines a high-priority call as one that requires immediate police attention to protect persons or render emergency aid.

The police department was successful in clearing a total of 246 Part I cases during the fiscal year.

Conditions Affecting Service, Performance, and Costs

The Town of Chapel Hill began participation in the benchmarking project in July 2015, with FY 2014–15 being the first reporting year.

Reported cases cleared was up in FY 2015–16 by 68 percent for Part I crimes over the prior year. This was due to an improvement in data tracking.

The average response time to high-priority calls reflects the response time of the first arriving unit. Self-initiated calls with a response time of zero are included in the average response time to high-priority calls.

Municipal Profile

Population (OSBM 2018)	63,178
Land Area (Square Miles)	21.27
Persons per Square Mile	2,971
Median Household Income	$60,802
U.S. Census 2016	

Service Profile

FTE Positions—Sworn	118.0
FTE Positions—Other	16.0
Marked and Unmarked Patrol Vehicles	77
Part I Crimes Reported	
Homicide	1
Rape	14
Robbery	22
Assault	48
Burglary	235
Larceny	650
Auto Theft	58
Arson	3
TOTAL	1,031
Part II Crimes Reported	2,853
Part I Crimes Cleared	
Persons	41
Property	205
TOTAL	246
Reporting Format	UCR
Number of Calls Dispatched	31,095
Number of Traffic Accidents	214
Property Damage for Accidents	$5,738,787

Full Cost Profile

Cost Breakdown by Percentage	
Personal Services	63.6%
Operating Costs	29.2%
Capital Costs	7.2%
TOTAL	100.0%

Cost Breakdown in Dollars	
Personal Services	$10,122,661
Operating Costs	$4,651,558
Capital Costs	$1,152,707
TOTAL	$15,926,926

Key: Chapel Hill ▦   Benchmarking Average —   Fiscal Years 2015 through 2019

Resource Measures

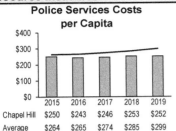

Police Services Costs per Capita

	2015	2016	2017	2018	2019
Chapel Hill	$250	$243	$246	$253	$252
Average	$264	$265	$274	$285	$299

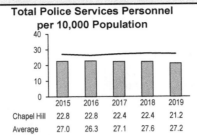

Total Police Services Personnel per 10,000 Population

	2015	2016	2017	2018	2019
Chapel Hill	22.8	22.8	22.4	22.4	21.2
Average	27.0	26.3	27.1	27.6	27.2

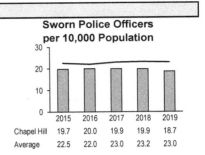

Sworn Police Officers per 10,000 Population

	2015	2016	2017	2018	2019
Chapel Hill	19.7	20.0	19.9	19.9	18.7
Average	22.5	22.0	23.0	23.2	23.0

Workload Measures

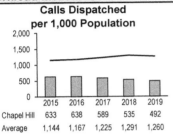

Calls Dispatched per 1,000 Population

	2015	2016	2017	2018	2019
Chapel Hill	633	638	589	535	492
Average	1,144	1,167	1,225	1,291	1,260

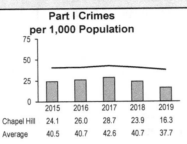

Part I Crimes per 1,000 Population

	2015	2016	2017	2018	2019
Chapel Hill	24.1	26.0	28.7	23.9	16.3
Average	40.5	40.7	42.6	40.7	37.7

Efficiency Measures

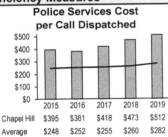

Police Services Cost per Call Dispatched

	2015	2016	2017	2018	2019
Chapel Hill	$395	$381	$418	$473	$512
Average	$248	$252	$255	$260	$282

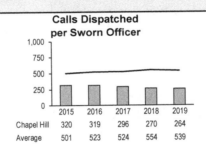

Calls Dispatched per Sworn Officer

	2015	2016	2017	2018	2019
Chapel Hill	320	319	296	270	264
Average	501	523	524	554	539

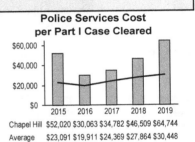

Police Services Cost per Part I Case Cleared

	2015	2016	2017	2018	2019
Chapel Hill	$52,020	$30,063	$34,782	$46,509	$64,744
Average	$23,091	$19,911	$24,369	$27,864	$30,448

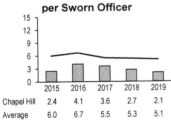

Part I Cases Cleared per Sworn Officer

	2015	2016	2017	2018	2019
Chapel Hill	2.4	4.1	3.6	2.7	2.1
Average	6.0	6.7	5.5	5.3	5.1

Effectiveness Measures

Percentage of Part I Cases Cleared of Those Reported

	2015	2016	2017	2018	2019
Chapel Hill	19.9%	31.1%	24.7%	22.8%	23.9%
Average	33.9%	37.7%	30.5%	31.4%	32.6%

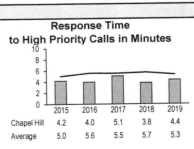

Response Time to High Priority Calls in Minutes

	2015	2016	2017	2018	2019
Chapel Hill	4.2	4.0	5.1	3.8	4.4
Average	5.0	5.6	5.5	5.7	5.3

Concord

Police Services

Fiscal Year 2018–19

Explanatory Information

Service Level and Delivery

Concord's police department provides an array of police services, including patrol, investigations, a traffic unit, a telephone response unit, a canine unit, a special response unit, a bicycle patrol unit, a drug enforcement unit, a limited forensic laboratory, and other programs, such as school resource officers.

The city had 185 sworn officer positions authorized for the fiscal year, with an average length of service of 8.9 years. The police headquarters is in a new separate building located downtown. Four substations are used: two in fire stations and two in shopping malls.

Uniformed patrol officers work twelve-hour rotating shifts. Investigators work five eight-hour days on first and second shifts. District Commanders have the authority to change individual schedules to meet peak demands.

The city defines high-priority emergency calls as those involving an assault in progress, personal injury, breaking and entering, or robbery in progress.

Concord uses a one-on-one car plan. Officers may take their vehicles home if they live in the city or within one mile of the city limits.

The police department was successful in clearing a total of 745 Part I cases during the fiscal year.

Conditions Affecting Service, Performance, and Costs

The average response time to high-priority calls reflects the response time of the first arriving unit. Self-initiated calls are not included.

Concord's high clearance rate has been driven by a focus on clearing larceny cases by arrest or by exhausting leads as quickly as possible. Because larcenies are the largest category of Part I crimes, this effort has substantially improved the overall clearance rate. The lower clearance rates in the last few years is driven mostly by more accurate data reporting rather than a drop in results.

Municipal Profile

Population (OSBM 2018)	92,568
Land Area (Square Miles)	62.80
Persons per Square Mile	1,474
Median Household Income	$50,863
U.S. Census 2016	

Service Profile

FTE Positions—Sworn	185.00
FTE Positions—Other	20.0
Marked and Unmarked Patrol Vehicles	217
Part I Crimes Reported	
Homicide	3
Rape	4
Robbery	33
Assault	41
Burglary	191
Larceny	1,361
Auto Theft	88
Arson	5
TOTAL	1,726
Part II Crimes Reported	2,100
Part I Crimes Cleared	
Persons	61
Property	684
TOTAL	745
Reporting Format	IBR
Number of Calls Dispatched	127,948
Number of Traffic Accidents	3,925
Property Damage for Accidents	$13,494,174

Full Cost Profile

Cost Breakdown by Percentage

Personal Services	65.6%
Operating Costs	25.2%
Capital Costs	9.2%
TOTAL	100.0%

Cost Breakdown in Dollars

Personal Services	$15,952,975
Operating Costs	$6,116,003
Capital Costs	$2,239,226
TOTAL	$24,308,204

Concord

Police Services

Resource Measures

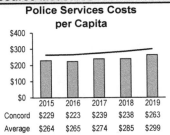

Police Services Costs per Capita

	2015	2016	2017	2018	2019
Concord	$229	$223	$239	$238	$263
Average	$264	$265	$274	$285	$299

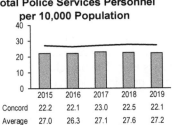

Total Police Services Personnel per 10,000 Population

	2015	2016	2017	2018	2019
Concord	22.2	22.1	23.0	22.5	22.1
Average	27.0	26.3	27.1	27.6	27.2

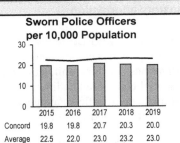

Sworn Police Officers per 10,000 Population

	2015	2016	2017	2018	2019
Concord	19.8	19.8	20.7	20.3	20.0
Average	22.5	22.0	23.0	23.2	23.0

Workload Measures

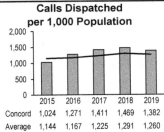

Calls Dispatched per 1,000 Population

	2015	2016	2017	2018	2019
Concord	1,024	1,271	1,411	1,469	1,382
Average	1,144	1,167	1,225	1,291	1,260

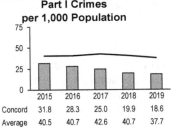

Part I Crimes per 1,000 Population

	2015	2016	2017	2018	2019
Concord	31.8	28.3	25.0	19.9	18.6
Average	40.5	40.7	42.6	40.7	37.7

Efficiency Measures

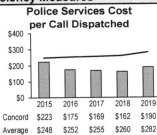

Police Services Cost per Call Dispatched

	2015	2016	2017	2018	2019
Concord	$223	$175	$169	$162	$190
Average	$248	$252	$255	$260	$282

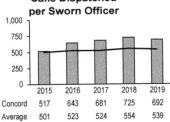

Calls Dispatched per Sworn Officer

	2015	2016	2017	2018	2019
Concord	517	643	681	725	692
Average	501	523	524	554	539

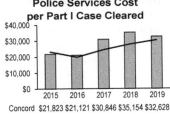

Police Services Cost per Part I Case Cleared

	2015	2016	2017	2018	2019
Concord	$21,823	$21,121	$30,846	$35,154	$32,628
Average	$23,091	$19,911	$24,369	$27,864	$30,448

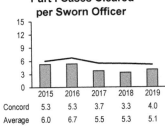

Part I Cases Cleared per Sworn Officer

	2015	2016	2017	2018	2019
Concord	5.3	5.3	3.7	3.3	4.0
Average	6.0	6.7	5.5	5.3	5.1

Effectiveness Measures

Percentage of Part I Cases Cleared of Those Reported

	2015	2016	2017	2018	2019
Concord	33.7%	38.0%	32.0%	34.1%	43.2%
Average	33.9%	37.7%	30.5%	31.4%	32.6%

Response Time to High Priority Calls in Minutes

	2015	2016	2017	2018	2019
Concord	5.1	5.2	5.6	5.6	5.1
Average	5.0	5.6	5.5	5.7	5.3

Explanatory Information

Service Level and Delivery

Goldsboro provides comprehensive police services, including patrol, investigations, a canine unit, a bicycle patrol unit, a drug enforcement unit, animal control, and a limited service forensics unit. The bicycle unit is made up of officers assigned to the housing unit and selective enforcement unit and is not a stand-alone unit.

The city had 110 sworn officers authorized for the fiscal year with an average length of service of 9.3 years. The police department is housed in a complex that is shared with the fire department, with each department having its own entrance but sharing a gym and locker rooms.

Uniformed officers work a total of 2,052 hours per year while investigators work a total of 2,080 hours. Schedules can be adjusted at any time according to call demand, special events, or special incidents. Officers are assigned a vehicle once they are out of field training. They can drive a vehicle home if they live within Wayne County.

Conditions Affecting Service, Performance, and Costs

The city of Goldsboro joined the Benchmarking Project in July 2017, with the first year of data showing for FY 2016–17.

Municipal Profile

Population (OSBM 2018)	33,636
Land Area (Square Miles)	29.41
Persons per Square Mile	1,144
Median Household Income	$32,148
U.S. Census 2016	

Service Profile

FTE Positions—Sworn	110.0
FTE Positions—Other	11.0
Marked and Unmarked Patrol Vehicles	100
Part I Crimes Reported	
Homicide	5
Rape	4
Robbery	49
Assault	142
Burglary	407
Larceny	1,426
Auto Theft	112
Arson	2
TOTAL	2,147
Part II Crimes Reported	1,510
Part I Crimes Cleared	
Persons	59
Property	469
TOTAL	528
Reporting Format	UCR
Number of Calls Dispatched	52,313
Number of Traffic Accidents	2,242
Property Damage for Accidents	NA

Full Cost Profile

Cost Breakdown by Percentage

Personal Services	81.4%
Operating Costs	15.8%
Capital Costs	2.8%
TOTAL	100.0%

Cost Breakdown in Dollars

Personal Services	$7,666,046
Operating Costs	$1,483,407
Capital Costs	$267,241
TOTAL	$9,416,694

Goldsboro

Key: Goldsboro ▨   Benchmarking Average —   Fiscal Years 2015 through 2019

Resource Measures

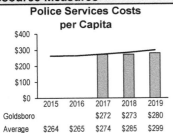

Police Services Costs per Capita

	2015	2016	2017	2018	2019
Goldsboro			$272	$273	$280
Average	$264	$265	$274	$285	$299

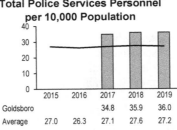

Total Police Services Personnel per 10,000 Population

	2015	2016	2017	2018	2019
Goldsboro			34.8	35.9	36.0
Average	27.0	26.3	27.1	27.6	27.2

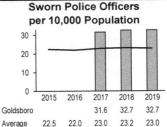

Sworn Police Officers per 10,000 Population

	2015	2016	2017	2018	2019
Goldsboro			31.6	32.7	32.7
Average	22.5	22.0	23.0	23.2	23.0

Workload Measures

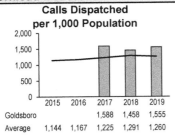

Calls Dispatched per 1,000 Population

	2015	2016	2017	2018	2019
Goldsboro			1,588	1,458	1,555
Average	1,144	1,167	1,225	1,291	1,260

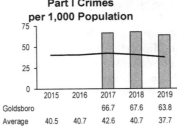

Part I Crimes per 1,000 Population

	2015	2016	2017	2018	2019
Goldsboro			66.7	67.6	63.8
Average	40.5	40.7	42.6	40.7	37.7

Efficiency Measures

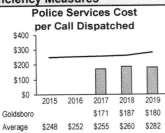

Police Services Cost per Call Dispatched

	2015	2016	2017	2018	2019
Goldsboro			$171	$187	$180
Average	$248	$252	$255	$260	$282

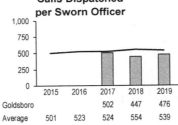

Calls Dispatched per Sworn Officer

	2015	2016	2017	2018	2019
Goldsboro			502	447	476
Average	501	523	524	554	539

Police Services Cost per Part I Case Cleared

	2015	2016	2017	2018	2019
Goldsboro			$15,73	$15,03	$17,83
Average	$23,09	$19,91	$24,36	$27,86	$30,44

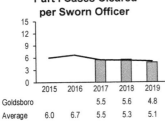

Part I Cases Cleared per Sworn Officer

	2015	2016	2017	2018	2019
Goldsboro			5.5	5.6	4.8
Average	6.0	6.7	5.5	5.3	5.1

Effectiveness Measures

Percentage of Part I Cases Cleared of Those Reported

	2015	2016	2017	2018	2019
Goldsboro			25.9%	26.8%	24.6%
Average	33.9%	37.7%	30.5%	31.4%	32.6%

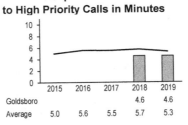

Response Time to High Priority Calls in Minutes

	2015	2016	2017	2018	2019
Goldsboro				4.6	4.6
Average	5.0	5.6	5.5	5.7	5.3

Explanatory Information

Service Level and Delivery

Greensboro provides comprehensive police services, including patrol, investigations, a traffic unit, a telephone response unit, a forensics laboratory, a canine unit, a motorcycle unit, a special response unit, a bicycle patrol unit, a drug enforcement unit, and a student outreach and recruiting program.

The city had 675 sworn officer positions authorized for the fiscal year, with an average length of service of 12.6 years. The police department is housed in a stand-alone headquarters facility. The city also has three substations that serve as remote line-up facilities.

Patrol officers work a four-days-on and four-days-off fixed schedule. There are four shifts each day, with each patrol officer shift lasting eleven hours. Investigators and administrative personnel work Monday through Friday from 8 a.m. to 5 p.m. Schedules can be adjusted at any time according to call demand, special events, or special incidents.

Line patrol officers do take vehicles home during their tour of duty. Patrol supervisors, division commanders, and some investigators take vehicles home, depending on their assignments.

Greensboro defines a high-priority emergency call as one where there is a potential for imminent serious injury or death. The police department was successful in clearing a total of 3,091 Part I cases during the fiscal year.

Conditions Affecting Service, Performance, and Costs

The average response time to high-priority calls reflects the response time of the first arriving unit. Self-initiated calls with a response time of zero are included in the average response time to high-priority calls, with the exception of traffic stops and report-only calls.

Municipal Profile

Population (OSBM 2018)	292,306
Land Area (Square Miles)	128.77
Persons per Square Mile	2,270
Median Household Income	$40,760
U.S. Census 2016	

Service Profile

FTE Positions—Sworn	675.0
FTE Positions—Other	112.0
Marked and Unmarked Patrol Vehicles	242
Part I Crimes Reported	
Homicide	36
Rape	81
Robbery	573
Assault	890
Burglary	2,135
Larceny	7,689
Auto Theft	747
Arson	68
TOTAL	12,219
Part II Crimes Reported	14,673
Part I Crimes Cleared	
Persons	591
Property	2,500
TOTAL	3,091
Reporting Format	UCR
Number of Calls Dispatched	215,008
Number of Traffic Accidents	10,524
Property Damage for Accidents	$43,163,603

Full Cost Profile

Cost Breakdown by Percentage

Personal Services	78.3%
Operating Costs	21.7%
Capital Costs	0.0%
TOTAL	100.0%

Cost Breakdown in Dollars

Personal Services	$67,889,569
Operating Costs	$18,810,616
Capital Costs	$0
TOTAL	$86,700,185

Greensboro

Key: Greensboro ▪   Benchmarking Average —

Resource Measures

Police Services Costs per Capita

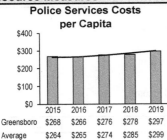

	2015	2016	2017	2018	2019
Greensboro	$268	$266	$276	$278	$297
Average	$264	$265	$274	$285	$299

Total Police Services Personnel per 10,000 Population

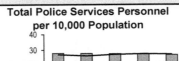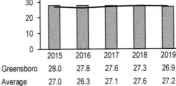

	2015	2016	2017	2018	2019
Greensboro	28.0	27.8	27.6	27.3	26.9
Average	27.0	26.3	27.1	27.6	27.2

Sworn Police Officers per 10,000 Population

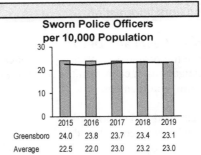

	2015	2016	2017	2018	2019
Greensboro	24.0	23.8	23.7	23.4	23.1
Average	22.5	22.0	23.0	23.2	23.0

Workload Measures

Calls Dispatched per 1,000 Population

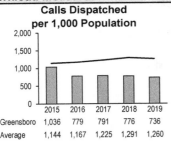

	2015	2016	2017	2018	2019
Greensboro	1,036	779	791	776	736
Average	1,144	1,167	1,225	1,291	1,260

Part I Crimes per 1,000 Population

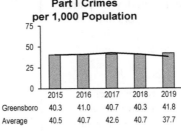

	2015	2016	2017	2018	2019
Greensboro	40.3	41.0	40.7	40.3	41.8
Average	40.5	40.7	42.6	40.7	37.7

Efficiency Measures

Police Services Cost per Call Dispatched

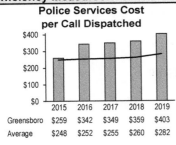

	2015	2016	2017	2018	2019
Greensboro	$259	$342	$349	$359	$403
Average	$248	$252	$255	$260	$282

Calls Dispatched per Sworn Officer

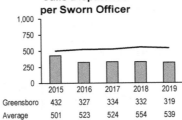

	2015	2016	2017	2018	2019
Greensboro	432	327	334	332	319
Average	501	523	524	554	539

Police Services Cost per Part I Case Cleared

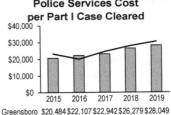

	2015	2016	2017	2018	2019
Greensboro	$20,484	$22,107	$22,942	$26,279	$28,049
Average	$23,091	$19,911	$24,369	$27,864	$30,448

Part I Cases Cleared per Sworn Officer

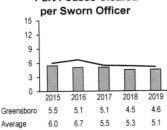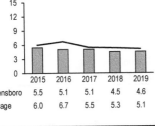

	2015	2016	2017	2018	2019
Greensboro	5.5	5.1	5.1	4.5	4.6
Average	6.0	6.7	5.5	5.3	5.1

Effectiveness Measures

Percentage of Part I Cases Cleared of Those Reported

	2015	2016	2017	2018	2019
Greensboro	32.5%	29.4%	29.6%	26.3%	25.3%
Average	33.9%	37.7%	30.5%	31.4%	32.6%

Response Time to High Priority Calls in Minutes

	2015	2016	2017	2018	2019
Greensboro	6.5	6.9	7.1	7.2	8.4
Average	5.0	5.6	5.5	5.7	5.3

Fiscal Year 2018–19

Explanatory Information

Service Level and Delivery

Greenville provides a full array of police services, including patrol, investigations, a canine unit, a special response unit, bicycle patrol, and drug enforcement.

The city had 205 sworn officer positions authorized for the fiscal year, with an average length of service of fourteen years. The police department occupies space in the city government building.

Patrol officers work a rotating schedule of two on/two off/three on/two off/two on/three off. There are four shifts each day for patrol officers, with the shifts lasting eleven hours. Investigators and administrative personnel work Monday through Friday, with eight-hour shifts. Schedules are subject to change based on call demand, special events, or unusual events.

Some patrol officers have take-home vehicles. There are seven or eight take-home cars per shift. They are assigned by seniority and whether or not the officer lives in the city limits. Officers on a shift who do not have a take-home car are assigned a pool car to drive each day. All investigators and administrative personnel (with one exception) have take-home cars.

Greenville defines high-priority emergency calls as those situations that present a potential for imminent serious injury or death. These calls are dispatched to the first available patrol unit, which may require a citywide dispatch.

The police department was successful in clearing a total of 941 Part I cases during the fiscal year.

Conditions Affecting Service, Performance, and Costs

The average response time to high-priority calls reflects the response time of the first arriving unit. Self-initiated calls are not included in the response times.

Municipal Profile

Population (OSBM 2018)	89,790
Land Area (Square Miles)	35.58
Persons per Square Mile	2,523
Median Household Income	$33,339
U.S. Census 2016	

Service Profile

FTE Positions—Sworn	205.0
FTE Positions—Other	50.0
Marked and Unmarked Patrol Vehicles	238
Part I Crimes Reported	
Homicide	6
Rape	22
Robbery	107
Assault	310
Burglary	451
Larceny	2,198
Auto Theft	94
Arson	8
TOTAL	3,196
Part II Crimes Reported	4,788
Part I Crimes Cleared	
Persons	193
Property	748
TOTAL	941
Reporting Format	UCR
Number of Calls Dispatched	81,944
Number of Traffic Accidents	4,450
Property Damage for Accidents	$14,000,000

Full Cost Profile

Cost Breakdown by Percentage

Personal Services	64.7%
Operating Costs	23.7%
Capital Costs	11.6%
TOTAL	100.0%

Cost Breakdown in Dollars

Personal Services	$17,373,272
Operating Costs	$6,364,213
Capital Costs	$3,125,320
TOTAL	$26,862,805

Greenville

Police Services

Resource Measures

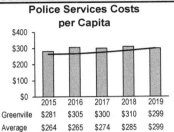

Police Services Costs per Capita

	2015	2016	2017	2018	2019
Greenville	$281	$305	$300	$310	$299
Average	$264	$265	$274	$285	$299

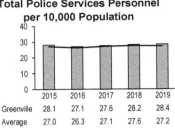

Total Police Services Personnel per 10,000 Population

	2015	2016	2017	2018	2019
Greenville	28.1	27.1	27.6	28.2	28.4
Average	27.0	26.3	27.1	27.6	27.2

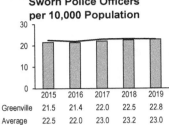

Sworn Police Officers per 10,000 Population

	2015	2016	2017	2018	2019
Greenville	21.5	21.4	22.0	22.5	22.8
Average	22.5	22.0	23.0	23.2	23.0

Workload Measures

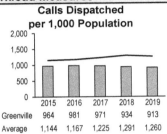

Calls Dispatched per 1,000 Population

	2015	2016	2017	2018	2019
Greenville	964	981	971	934	913
Average	1,144	1,167	1,225	1,291	1,260

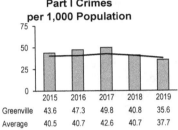

Part I Crimes per 1,000 Population

	2015	2016	2017	2018	2019
Greenville	43.6	47.3	49.8	40.8	35.6
Average	40.5	40.7	42.6	40.7	37.7

Efficiency Measures

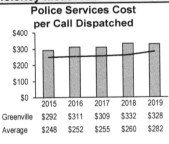

Police Services Cost per Call Dispatched

	2015	2016	2017	2018	2019
Greenville	$292	$311	$309	$332	$328
Average	$248	$252	$255	$260	$282

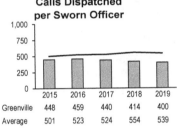

Calls Dispatched per Sworn Officer

	2015	2016	2017	2018	2019
Greenville	448	459	440	414	400
Average	501	523	524	554	539

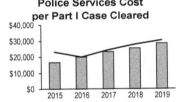

Police Services Cost per Part I Case Cleared

	2015	2016	2017	2018	2019
Greenville	$16,689	$19,992	$23,286	$25,507	$28,547
Average	$23,091	$19,911	$24,369	$27,864	$30,448

Part I Cases Cleared per Sworn Officer

	2015	2016	2017	2018	2019
Greenville	7.8	7.1	5.8	5.4	4.6
Average	6.0	6.7	5.5	5.3	5.1

Effectiveness Measures

Percentage of Part I Cases Cleared of Those Reported

	2015	2016	2017	2018	2019
Greenville	38.7%	32.2%	25.8%	29.8%	29.4%
Average	33.9%	37.7%	30.5%	31.4%	32.6%

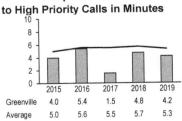

Response Time to High Priority Calls in Minutes

	2015	2016	2017	2018	2019
Greenville	4.0	5.4	1.5	4.8	4.2
Average	5.0	5.6	5.5	5.7	5.3

Fiscal Year 2018–19

Explanatory Information

Service Level and Delivery

Hickory provides a full array of police services, including patrol, investigations, a traffic unit, a small laboratory facility, a canine unit, a special response unit, bicycle patrol, a jail/holding facility, animal control, drug enforcement, and a DARE program.

The city had 116 sworn officer positions authorized for the fiscal year, with an average length of service of 8.7 years. The police department occupies its own three-story facility, completed in January 1996. Each of the five community police areas has an office located in its respective community. These offices are not staffed. They are used for interviews, to obtain information, to store supplies, and to make phone calls.

Patrol officers work a fourteen-day, 80.5-hour cycle. During this period, officers work seven 11.5-hour days. Each of the five districts is commanded by a lieutenant who establishes schedules based on need.

Investigators work Monday through Friday, either from 8:30 a.m. to 5:00 p.m. or 3:30 p.m. to 12:00 a.m. for the second-shift on-call investigators.

Hickory uses the one-officer, one-car plan. Officers take vehicles home if they live in or within one mile of the city. Officers who are members of specialized units needed for emergency response, such as special operations, K-9, or crim020minial investigations, may also take their vehicles home.

Hickory defines high-priority emergency calls as those situations that present an in-progress threat to life or serious property loss. Officers are authorized to utilize blue lights and sirens during responses and may exceed posted speed limits by up to 20 miles per hour.

The police department was successful in clearing a total of 1,162 Part I cases during the fiscal year.

Conditions Affecting Service, Performance, and Costs

The average response time to high-priority calls reflects the response time of the first arriving unit. Self-initiated calls with a response time of zero are included in the average response time to high-priority calls.

Municipal Profile

Population (OSBM 2018)	40,932
Land Area (Square Miles)	29.92
Persons per Square Mile	1,368
Median Household Income	$35,353
U.S. Census 2016	

Service Profile

FTE Positions—Sworn	116.0
FTE Positions—Other	36.0
Marked and Unmarked Patrol Vehicles	143
Part I Crimes Reported	
Homicide	2
Rape	19
Robbery	47
Assault	80
Burglary	249
Larceny	1,323
Auto Theft	175
Arson	4
TOTAL	1,899
Part II Crimes Reported	4,064
Part I Crimes Cleared	
Persons	141
Property	1,021
TOTAL	1,162
Reporting Format	IBR
Number of Calls Dispatched	90,024
Number of Traffic Accidents	2,438
Property Damage for Accidents	$8,718,245

Full Cost Profile

Cost Breakdown by Percentage

Personal Services	67.9%
Operating Costs	23.3%
Capital Costs	8.8%
TOTAL	100.0%

Cost Breakdown in Dollars

Personal Services	$8,611,088
Operating Costs	$2,955,012
Capital Costs	$1,116,728
TOTAL	$12,682,828

Hickory

Police Services

Resource Measures

Police Services Costs per Capita

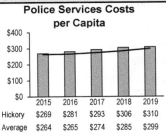

	2015	2016	2017	2018	2019
Hickory	$269	$281	$293	$306	$310
Average	$264	$265	$274	$285	$299

Total Police Services Personnel per 10,000 Population

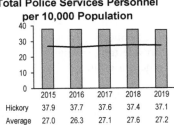

	2015	2016	2017	2018	2019
Hickory	37.9	37.7	37.6	37.4	37.1
Average	27.0	26.3	27.1	27.6	27.2

Sworn Police Officers per 10,000 Population

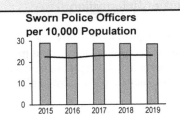

	2015	2016	2017	2018	2019
Hickory	29.0	28.7	28.7	28.5	28.3
Average	22.5	22.0	23.0	23.2	23.0

Workload Measures

Calls Dispatched per 1,000 Population

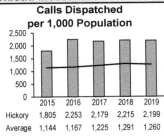

	2015	2016	2017	2018	2019
Hickory	1,805	2,253	2,179	2,215	2,199
Average	1,144	1,167	1,225	1,291	1,260

Part I Crimes per 1,000 Population

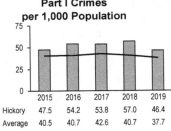

	2015	2016	2017	2018	2019
Hickory	47.5	54.2	53.8	57.0	46.4
Average	40.5	40.7	42.6	40.7	37.7

Efficiency Measures

Police Services Cost per Call Dispatched

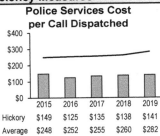

	2015	2016	2017	2018	2019
Hickory	$149	$125	$135	$138	$141
Average	$248	$252	$255	$260	$282

Calls Dispatched per Sworn Officer

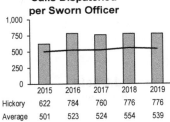

	2015	2016	2017	2018	2019
Hickory	622	784	760	776	776
Average	501	523	524	554	539

Police Services Cost per Part I Case Cleared

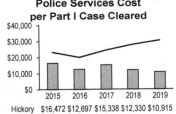

	2015	2016	2017	2018	2019
Hickory	$16,472	$12,697	$15,338	$12,330	$10,915
Average	$23,091	$19,911	$24,369	$27,864	$30,448

Part I Cases Cleared per Sworn Officer

	2015	2016	2017	2018	2019
Hickory	5.6	7.7	6.7	8.7	10.0
Average	6.0	6.7	5.5	5.3	5.1

Effectiveness Measures

Percentage of Part I Cases Cleared of Those Reported

	2015	2016	2017	2018	2019
Hickory	34.4%	40.9%	35.6%	43.5%	61.2%
Average	33.9%	37.7%	30.5%	31.4%	32.6%

Response Time to High Priority Calls in Minutes

	2015	2016	2017	2018	2019
Hickory	6.3	6.3	6.6	7.8	4.4
Average	5.0	5.6	5.5	5.7	5.3

Fiscal Year 2018–19

Explanatory Information

Service Level and Delivery

Mooresville's police department provides an array of police services, including patrol, investigations, canine unit, motorcycle unit, special response, bicycle patrol, drug enforcement, and other programs.

The town had ninety sworn officer positions authorized for the fiscal year, with an average length of service of 8.3 years. The police department is located in a separate facility.

Uniformed officers work a variety of shift schedules. The most common schedule is seven days worked in a fourteen day period that consists of two days on, two days off, three days on, two days off, two days on, and then three days off. The shifts are twelve hours in length with one beginning at 6am and the other at 6pm.

Vehicles are assigned first by type of position and then by availability. Officers are allowed to take vehicles home up to twenty miles from town limits. Certain specialized units are able to take home vehicles with no mileage restrictions.

The police department was successful in clearing a total of 460 Part I cases during the fiscal year.

The town defines high-priority emergency calls as those calls when the immediate presence of police may prevent death or injury or alleviate the threat of death or injury.

Conditions Affecting Service, Performance, and Costs

Mooresville joined the Benchmarking project in July 2018, with the first year of data showing for FY2017–18.

The average response time to high-priority calls reflects the response time of the first arriving unit. Self-initiated calls with a response time of zero are not included in the average response time to high-priority calls.

Municipal Profile

Population (OSBM 2018)	41,255
Land Area (Square Miles)	22.75
Persons per Square Mile	1,813
Median Household Income	$67,213
U.S. Census 2016	

Service Profile

FTE Positions—Sworn	90.0
FTE Positions—Other	24.0
Marked and Unmarked Patrol Vehicles	76
Part I Crimes Reported	
Homicide	1
Rape	16
Robbery	16
Assault	38
Burglary	135
Larceny	968
Auto Theft	53
Arson	7
TOTAL	1,234
Part II Crimes Reported	2,448
Part I Crimes Cleared	
Persons	49
Property	411
TOTAL	460
Reporting Format	NIBRS
Number of Calls Dispatched	88,402
Number of Traffic Accidents	2,689
Property Damage for Accidents	NA

Full Cost Profile

Cost Breakdown by Percentage

Personal Services	59.3%
Operating Costs	27.7%
Capital Costs	13.0%
TOTAL	100.0%

Cost Breakdown in Dollars

Personal Services	$8,650,330
Operating Costs	$4,037,446
Capital Costs	$1,902,027
TOTAL	$14,589,803

Mooresville

Police Services

Resource Measures

Police Services Costs per Capita

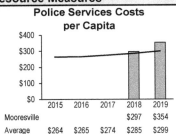

	2015	2016	2017	2018	2019
Mooresville				$297	$354
Average	$264	$265	$274	$285	$299

Total Police Services Personnel per 10,000 Population

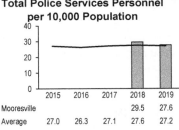

	2015	2016	2017	2018	2019
Mooresville				29.5	27.6
Average	27.0	26.3	27.1	27.6	27.2

Sworn Police Officers per 10,000 Population

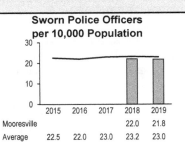

	2015	2016	2017	2018	2019
Mooresville				22.0	21.8
Average	22.5	22.0	23.0	23.2	23.0

Workload Measures

Calls Dispatched per 1,000 Population

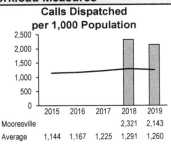

	2015	2016	2017	2018	2019
Mooresville				2,321	2,143
Average	1,144	1,167	1,225	1,291	1,260

Part I Crimes per 1,000 Population

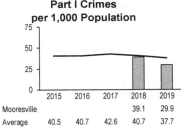

	2015	2016	2017	2018	2019
Mooresville				39.1	29.9
Average	40.5	40.7	42.6	40.7	37.7

Efficiency Measures

Police Services Cost per Call Dispatched

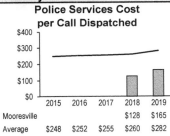

	2015	2016	2017	2018	2019
Mooresville				$128	$165
Average	$248	$252	$255	$260	$282

Calls Dispatched per Sworn Officer

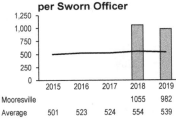

	2015	2016	2017	2018	2019
Mooresville				1055	982
Average	501	523	524	554	539

Police Services Cost per Part I Case Cleared

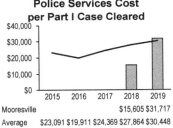

	2015	2016	2017	2018	2019
Mooresville				$15,605	$31,717
Average	$23,091	$19,911	$24,369	$27,864	$30,448

Part I Cases Cleared per Sworn Officer

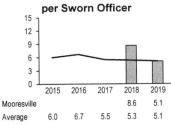

	2015	2016	2017	2018	2019
Mooresville				8.6	5.1
Average	6.0	6.7	5.5	5.3	5.1

Effectiveness Measures

Percentage of Part I Cases Cleared of Those Reported

	2015	2016	2017	2018	2019
Mooresville				48.6%	37.3%
Average	33.9%	37.7%	30.5%	31.4%	32.6%

Response Time to High Priority Calls in Minutes

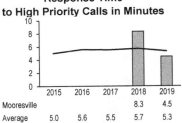

	2015	2016	2017	2018	2019
Mooresville				8.3	4.5
Average	5.0	5.6	5.5	5.7	5.3

Explanatory Information

Service Level and Delivery

Raleigh's police department provides an array of police services, including patrol, investigations, canine unit, special response unit, mounted equine unit, motorcycle unit, drug enforcement units, and other programs.

The city had 796 sworn officer positions authorized for the fiscal year, with an average length of service of 12.52 years. The police department has ten substations around the city.

Patrol officers work a twelve-hour schedule rotating between days and nights every twenty-eight days. Detectives work an 8.4 hour schedule each weekday rotating between a day shift and an evening shift. Most detectives are in a pool that shares responsibilities to cover weekend duty and midnight shifts.

The Field Operations Division has a take-home vehicle program for officers with two years of service and living inside the city limits with a safe driving record. Detectives and Special Operation Divisions have take-home vehicles for units on call or call-back status.

The police department was successful in clearing a total of 3,427 Part I cases during the fiscal year.

The city defines high-priority emergency calls as those involving crimes that are in progress or calls that are life-threatening or potentially life-threatening.

Conditions Affecting Service, Performance, and Costs

Raleigh rejoined the Benchmarking Project in July 2016, with the first year of data showing for FY 2015–16.

The average response time to high-priority calls reflects the response time of each arriving unit. Self-initiated calls are not included in the average response time to high-priority calls.

Municipal Profile

Population (OSBM 2018)	464,453
Land Area (Square Miles)	145.65
Persons per Square Mile	3,189
Median Household Income	$46,612
U.S. Census 2016	

Service Profile

FTE Positions—Sworn	796.0
FTE Positions—Other	105.0
Marked and Unmarked Patrol Vehicles	822
Part I Crimes Reported	
Homicide	21
Rape	171
Robbery	634
Assault	929
Burglary	2,146
Larceny	8,158
Auto Theft	834
Arson	49
TOTAL	12,942
Part II Crimes Reported	NA
Part I Crimes Cleared	
Persons	782
Property	2,645
TOTAL	3,427
Reporting Format	NIBRS
Number of Calls Dispatched	304,972
Number of Traffic Accidents	27,922
Property Damage for Accidents	$3,284,136

Full Cost Profile

Cost Breakdown by Percentage

Personal Services	73.1%
Operating Costs	18.2%
Capital Costs	8.7%
TOTAL	100.0%

Cost Breakdown in Dollars

Personal Services	$88,396,204
Operating Costs	$22,002,286
Capital Costs	$10,531,055
TOTAL	$120,929,545

Key: Raleigh ▨   Benchmarking Average —

Resource Measures

Police Services Costs per Capita

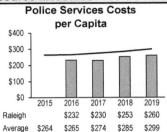

	2015	2016	2017	2018	2019
Raleigh		$232	$230	$253	$260
Average	$264	$265	$274	$285	$299

Total Police Services Personnel per 10,000 Population

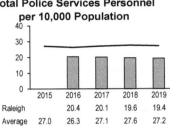

	2015	2016	2017	2018	2019
Raleigh		20.4	20.1	19.6	19.4
Average	27.0	26.3	27.1	27.6	27.2

Sworn Police Officers per 10,000 Population

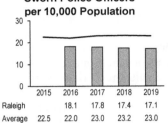

	2015	2016	2017	2018	2019
Raleigh		18.1	17.8	17.4	17.1
Average	22.5	22.0	23.0	23.2	23.0

Workload Measures

Calls Dispatched per 1,000 Population

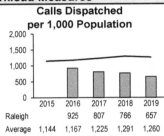

	2015	2016	2017	2018	2019
Raleigh		925	807	766	657
Average	1,144	1,167	1,225	1,291	1,260

Part I Crimes per 1,000 Population

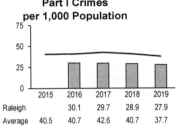

	2015	2016	2017	2018	2019
Raleigh		30.1	29.7	28.9	27.9
Average	40.5	40.7	42.6	40.7	37.7

Efficiency Measures

Police Services Cost per Call Dispatched

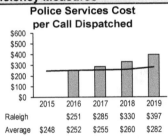

	2015	2016	2017	2018	2019
Raleigh		$251	$285	$330	$397
Average	$248	$252	$255	$260	$282

Calls Dispatched per Sworn Officer

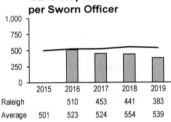

	2015	2016	2017	2018	2019
Raleigh		510	453	441	383
Average	501	523	524	554	539

Police Services Cost per Part I Case Cleared

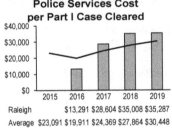

	2015	2016	2017	2018	2019
Raleigh		$13,291	$28,604	$35,008	$35,287
Average	$23,091	$19,911	$24,369	$27,864	$30,448

Part I Cases Cleared per Sworn Officer

	2015	2016	2017	2018	2019
Raleigh		9.6	4.5	4.2	4.3
Average	6.0	6.7	5.5	5.3	5.1

Effectiveness Measures

Percentage of Part I Cases Cleared of Those Reported

	2015	2016	2017	2018	2019
Raleigh		57.9%	27.1%	25.0%	26.5%
Average	33.9%	37.7%	30.5%	31.4%	32.6%

Response Time to High Priority Calls in Minutes

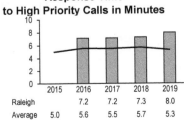

	2015	2016	2017	2018	2019
Raleigh		7.2	7.2	7.3	8.0
Average	5.0	5.6	5.5	5.7	5.3

Fiscal Year 2018–19

Explanatory Information

Service Level and Delivery

Wilson's police department provides an array of police services, including patrol, investigations, a telephone response unit, a forensics laboratory, a canine unit, a part-time mounted equine unit, a special response unit, street crimes, drug enforcement, and other services.

The city had 125 sworn officer positions authorized for the fiscal year, with an average length of service of 9.72 years. The main police department headquarters is located in downtown Wilson, housing administration, records, property, major case investigations, police information services, victim services, evidence, and recruitment and training. There are five substations.

Patrol officers work twelve-hour shifts, working fourteen days of a twenty-eight day cycle (168 hours). Shifts are either 7 a.m. to 7 p.m. or 7 p.m. to 7 a.m. and are rotated every two weeks. Department needs may cause shifts to vary. Investigators generally work eight-hour shifts five days per week. Shifts are 8 a.m. to 5 p.m.

Each patrol officer is assigned a vehicle and may take the vehicle home if he or she resides in the city. Officers living outside the city limits park their vehicles at businesses.

The police department was successful in clearing a total of 623 Part I cases during the fiscal year.

Wilson defines high-priority emergency calls as calls related to crimes in progress that require immediate response: murder, rape, robbery, burglary, arson/fire, and assaults.

Conditions Affecting Service, Performance, and Costs

The average response time to high-priority calls reflects the response time of the first unit to arrive. Self-initiated calls with a response time of zero are not included in the average response time to high-priority calls.

Municipal Profile

Population (OSBM 2018)	49,054
Land Area (Square Miles)	30.97
Persons per Square Mile	1,584
Median Household Income	$35,409
U.S. Census 2016	

Service Profile

FTE Positions—Sworn	125.0
FTE Positions—Other	16.0
Marked and Unmarked Patrol Vehicles	128
Part I Crimes Reported	
Homicide	5
Rape	12
Robbery	60
Assault	132
Burglary	356
Larceny	1,106
Auto Theft	111
Arson	6
TOTAL	1,788
Part II Crimes Reported	2,538
Part I Crimes Cleared	
Persons	125
Property	498
TOTAL	623
Reporting Format	UCR
Number of Calls Dispatched	89,274
Number of Traffic Accidents	2,699
Property Damage for Accidents	NA

Full Cost Profile

Cost Breakdown by Percentage

Personal Services	68.4%
Operating Costs	25.1%
Capital Costs	6.5%
TOTAL	100.0%

Cost Breakdown in Dollars

Personal Services	$12,098,934
Operating Costs	$4,444,553
Capital Costs	$1,150,124
TOTAL	$17,693,611

Wilson

Police Services

Resource Measures

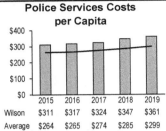

Police Services Costs per Capita

	2015	2016	2017	2018	2019
Wilson	$311	$317	$324	$347	$361
Average	$264	$265	$274	$285	$299

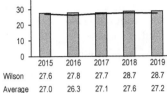

Total Police Services Personnel per 10,000 Population

	2015	2016	2017	2018	2019
Wilson	27.6	27.8	27.7	28.7	28.7
Average	27.0	26.3	27.1	27.6	27.2

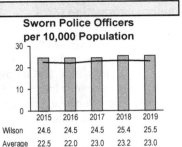

Sworn Police Officers per 10,000 Population

	2015	2016	2017	2018	2019
Wilson	24.6	24.5	24.5	25.4	25.5
Average	22.5	22.0	23.0	23.2	23.0

Workload Measures

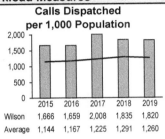

Calls Dispatched per 1,000 Population

	2015	2016	2017	2018	2019
Wilson	1,666	1,659	2,008	1,835	1,820
Average	1,144	1,167	1,225	1,291	1,260

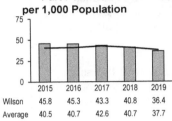

Part I Crimes per 1,000 Population

	2015	2016	2017	2018	2019
Wilson	45.8	45.3	43.3	40.8	36.4
Average	40.5	40.7	42.6	40.7	37.7

Efficiency Measures

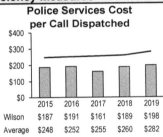

Police Services Cost per Call Dispatched

	2015	2016	2017	2018	2019
Wilson	$187	$191	$161	$189	$198
Average	$248	$252	$255	$260	$282

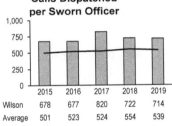

Calls Dispatched per Sworn Officer

	2015	2016	2017	2018	2019
Wilson	678	677	820	722	714
Average	501	523	524	554	539

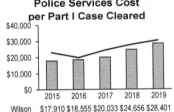

Police Services Cost per Part I Case Cleared

	2015	2016	2017	2018	2019
Wilson	$17,910	$18,555	$20,033	$24,656	$28,401
Average	$23,091	$19,911	$24,369	$27,864	$30,448

Part I Cases Cleared per Sworn Officer

	2015	2016	2017	2018	2019
Wilson	7.1	7.0	6.6	5.5	5.0
Average	6.0	6.7	5.5	5.3	5.1

Effectiveness Measures

Percentage of Part I Cases Cleared of Those Reported

	2015	2016	2017	2018	2019
Wilson	37.9%	37.8%	37.3%	34.5%	34.8%
Average	33.9%	37.7%	30.5%	31.4%	32.6%

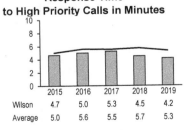

Response Time to High Priority Calls in Minutes

	2015	2016	2017	2018	2019
Wilson	4.7	5.0	5.3	4.5	4.2
Average	5.0	5.6	5.5	5.7	5.3

Winston-Salem

Police Services

Fiscal Year 2018–19

Explanatory Information

Service Level and Delivery

Winston-Salem provides an array of police services to its citizens, including patrol, investigations, a traffic enforcement unit, a DWI Task Force, a telephone response unit, a canine unit, a special response unit, bicycle patrol, drug enforcement, a gang unit, and other crime prevention programs.

The city had 558 sworn officer positions authorized for the fiscal year, with an average length of service of 12.04 years. The police department occupies the public safety center. It houses the police department, emergency communications, and the fire department administration. The special investigations division occupies offices in leased space in another facility. A downtown bike patrol office is maintained in the central downtown area.

The department employs a forward-rotating schedule of five shifts. Officers work five days on and four days off. Shifts are ten hours in length. The majority of investigators work Monday through Friday from 8 a.m. to 5 p.m.

Patrol vehicles are assigned to individual officers. Officers residing within Forsyth County take their vehicles home. If officers reside outside of the county, they park their vehicles in a residential or business area within the city limits.

The police department was successful in clearing a total of 4,546 Part I crimes during the fiscal year.

Winston-Salem defines highest-priority emergency calls as those dealing with a significant threat of imminent injury to persons or with crimes against persons that are in progress or have just occurred and where the suspect is still there.

Conditions Affecting Service, Performance, and Costs

The average response time to high-priority calls reflects the response time of the first arriving unit. Self-initiated calls with a response time of zero are included in the average response time to high-priority calls.

The Winston-Salem Police Department does not investigate arsons, so arsons are not included in the crimes reported here. Arson investigations are handled by the Winston-Salem Fire Department.

Municipal Profile

Population (OSBM 2018)	243,447
Land Area (Square Miles)	132.55
Persons per Square Mile	1,837
Median Household Income	$40,584
U.S. Census 2016	

Service Profile

FTE Positions—Sworn	558.0
FTE Positions—Other	127.0
Marked and Unmarked Patrol Vehicles	450
Part I Crimes Reported	
Homicide	23
Rape	126
Robbery	382
Assault	2,100
Burglary	2,338
Larceny	8,423
Auto Theft	897
Arson	NA
TOTAL	14,289
Part II Crimes Reported	35,141
Part I Crimes Cleared	
Persons	984
Property	3,562
TOTAL	4,546
Reporting Format	NIBRS
Number of Calls Dispatched	215,260
Number of Traffic Accidents	11,121
Property Damage for Accidents	$38,888,571

Full Cost Profile

Cost Breakdown by Percentage

Personal Services	75.6%
Operating Costs	15.2%
Capital Costs	9.3%
TOTAL	100.0%

Cost Breakdown in Dollars

Personal Services	$58,324,103
Operating Costs	$11,695,734
Capital Costs	$7,159,838
TOTAL	$77,179,675

Winston-Salem

Police Services

Resource Measures

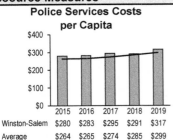

Police Services Costs per Capita

	2015	2016	2017	2018	2019
Winston-Salem	$280	$283	$295	$291	$317
Average	$264	$265	$274	$285	$299

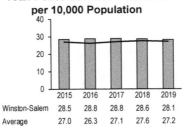

Total Police Services Personnel per 10,000 Population

	2015	2016	2017	2018	2019
Winston-Salem	28.5	28.8	28.8	28.6	28.1
Average	27.0	26.3	27.1	27.6	27.2

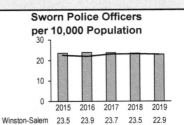

Sworn Police Officers per 10,000 Population

	2015	2016	2017	2018	2019
Winston-Salem	23.5	23.9	23.7	23.5	22.9
Average	22.5	22.0	23.0	23.2	23.0

Workload Measures

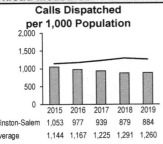

Calls Dispatched per 1,000 Population

	2015	2016	2017	2018	2019
Winston-Salem	1,053	977	939	879	884
Average	1,144	1,167	1,225	1,291	1,260

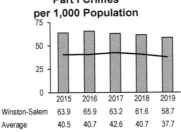

Part I Crimes per 1,000 Population

	2015	2016	2017	2018	2019
Winston-Salem	63.9	65.9	63.2	61.6	58.7
Average	40.5	40.7	42.6	40.7	37.7

Efficiency Measures

Police Services Cost per Call Dispatched

	2015	2016	2017	2018	2019
Winston-Salem	$266	$290	$314	$331	$359
Average	$248	$252	$255	$260	$282

Calls Dispatched per Sworn Officer

	2015	2016	2017	2018	2019
Winston-Salem	447	410	396	375	386
Average	501	523	524	554	539

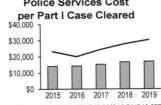

Police Services Cost per Part I Case Cleared

	2015	2016	2017	2018	2019
Winston-Salem	$14,160	$14,381	$15,330	$16,711	$16,977
Average	$23,091	$19,911	$24,369	$27,864	$30,448

Part I Cases Cleared per Sworn Officer

	2015	2016	2017	2018	2019
Winston-Salem	8.4	8.2	8.1	7.4	8.1
Average	6.0	6.7	5.5	5.3	5.1

Effectiveness Measures

Percentage of Part I Cases Cleared of Those Reported

	2015	2016	2017	2018	2019
Winston-Salem	30.9%	29.9%	30.4%	28.3%	31.8%
Average	33.9%	37.7%	30.5%	31.4%	32.6%

Response Time to High Priority Calls in Minutes

	2015	2016	2017	2018	2019
Winston-Salem	3.6	3.9	4.0	3.9	3.9
Average	5.0	5.6	5.5	5.7	5.3

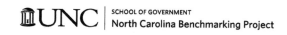

SCHOOL OF GOVERNMENT
North Carolina Benchmarking Project

Performance and Cost Data

EMERGENCY COMMUNICATIONS

SERVICE DEFINITION

This service refers to the receipt and handling of 911 and other calls by an emergency communications center. Such a center must answer all calls, including those that come in over 911 lines and others that come in over regular phone lines. Some calls result in the dispatch of a police or other emergency response unit. Others do not.

NOTES ON PERFORMANCE MEASURES

1. Number of Calls Answered and Number of Calls Dispatched per 1,000 Population

These are used as measures of workload. All calls coming into a police emergency communications center must be answered; therefore, these measures assess service workload. Calls coming into a center also reflect the actual or existing, if not full potential, need for emergency communications services. Many calls coming into a center are dispatched. Others come in over regular telephone lines, and still others may be referred to the center by an external call-taker, such as a county emergency communications center.

2. Telecommunicators

Telecommunicators are the personnel who handle the calls in the communication centers. They may take calls, dispatch calls, or do both. Telecommunicators receive specialized training. They work on a shift schedule that generally allows twenty-four-hour-a-day, seven-day-a-week coverage.

3. Average Number of Seconds from Initial Ring to Answer and Percentage of Calls Answered within Twenty Seconds

These are effectiveness measures that assess how quickly telecommunicators answer calls.

4. Average Processing Time (Seconds)

This is an effectiveness measure representing the average time in seconds between when the telecommunicator answers the telephone and when computer-aided dispatch (CAD) entry begins. This measure is often referred to as "talk time."

5. For Calls Dispatched, Average Number of Seconds from CAD Entry to Dispatch—Highest Priority Calls

Some calls result in the dispatch of a police or other emergency response unit to a life-threatening or other similar emergency situation. Other calls result in a dispatch to a serious—but not emergency—situation. Other calls do not result in a dispatch. This measure assesses dispatch time for high priority, emergency situations.

Emergency Communications

Summary of Key Dimensions of Service

City or Town	Population Served	Number of FTEs	Average Length of Service for Call Takers (in Years)	Total Incoming Calls Handled	Total E-911 Calls Handled	Total Dispatches	Outgoing Calls Other than Dispatches
Apex	52,909	11.3	12.8	41,355	3,834	46,172	8,714
Asheville	93,621	24.0	4.3	171,574	38,441	136,854	32,760
Concord	92,568	25.5	8.9	98,013	29,069	150,809	31,998
Greensboro	533,213	109.0	10.5	589,353	330,522	441,871	152,661
Greenville	89,790	21.0	9.2	96,088	24,682	81,944	3,509
Hickory	40,932	14.0	4.8	119,532	15,861	100,038	26,016
Raleigh	1,073,993	129.0	5.5	835,150	553,997	487,264	288,455
Winston-Salem	243,447	48.0	8.4	469,614	215,222	242,948	63,624

NOTES

The population served by the municipal emergency communications center may go beyond municipal boundaries up to the entire county in cases where the service is a consolidated center.

EXPLANATORY FACTORS

These are factors that the project found affected emergency communication performance and cost in one or more of the municipalities:

Types of emergency response units dispatched, such as police, fire, and EMS
Number and proportion of nonemergency calls received by center
Types of assistance or advice, such as medical, that telecommunicators provide over the phone
Technology available to telecommunication centers
City's definition of what constitutes an "emergency" and "highest priority" call
Service to city only or to city and outlying areas
Training of telecommunicators
Demographic makeup of community
Organizational configuration and staffing for service

Apex

Emergency Communications

Fiscal Year 2018–19

Explanatory Information

Service Level and Delivery

The Apex Emergency Communications Center is a division within the Apex Police Department. This center is a secondary public safety answering point within Wake County, using Raleigh computer-aided dispatch (CAD) as a remote position. The communications center dispatches calls for police, fire, public works, and utilities.

The town owns a 150-foot radio tower that is tied into the Wake County radio system. The system is an 800 MHz system tied into the state VIPER system for radio operations.

Apex's emergency communications center handled a total of 41,355 incoming calls in the fiscal year and dispatched 46,172 calls. The city defines highest-priority emergency calls as those with immediate life or property risk or in-progress calls.

Conditions Affecting Service, Performance, and Costs

CAD entry for Apex does not begin immediately but is activated by operators.

Municipal Profile

Population (OSBM 2018)	52,909
Land Area (Square Miles)	21.55
Persons per Square Mile	2,455
Median Household Income	$84,000
U.S. Census 2016	
County	Wake

Service Profile

Primary or Secondary Answering Point	Secondary
Calls Dispatched	
Police	Yes
Fire	No
Other	Yes
FTE Positions	
Telecommunicators/Call-Takers	9.40
Other	1.93
Total Positions	11.33
Average Length of Service for Call-Takers	12.8 years
Total Incoming Calls	41,355
Total 911 Calls	3,834
Total Calls Dispatched	46,172
Outgoing Calls Other than Dispatch	8,714
Revenue from E-911 Fees	None

Full Cost Profile

Cost Breakdown by Percentage	
Personal Services	72.2%
Operating Costs	22.7%
Capital Costs	5.0%
TOTAL	100.0%
Cost Breakdown in Dollars	
Personal Services	$850,243
Operating Costs	$267,776
Capital Costs	$59,283
TOTAL	$1,177,302

Resource Measures

Emergency Communications Services Costs per Capita

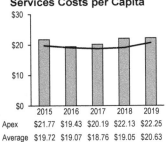

	2015	2016	2017	2018	2019
Apex	$21.77	$19.43	$20.19	$22.13	$22.25
Average	$19.72	$19.07	$18.76	$19.05	$20.63

Emergency Communications FTEs per 10,000 Population

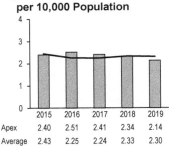

	2015	2016	2017	2018	2019
Apex	2.40	2.51	2.41	2.34	2.14
Average	2.43	2.25	2.24	2.33	2.30

Workload Measures

Total Calls Answered per 1,000 Population

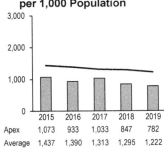

	2015	2016	2017	2018	2019
Apex	1,073	933	1,033	847	782
Average	1,437	1,390	1,313	1,295	1,222

Calls Dispatched per 1,000 Population

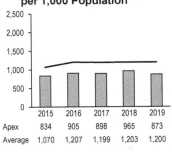

	2015	2016	2017	2018	2019
Apex	834	905	898	965	873
Average	1,070	1,207	1,199	1,203	1,200

E-911 Calls as a Percentage of All Incoming Calls

	2015	2016	2017	2018	2019
Apex	13.0%	8.6%	7.8%	9.1%	9.3%
Average	30.5%	35.9%	36.5%	35.5%	36.5%

Efficiency Measures

Calls Answered per Telecommunicator

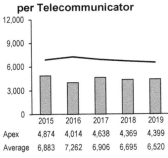

	2015	2016	2017	2018	2019
Apex	4,874	4,014	4,638	4,369	4,399
Average	6,883	7,262	6,906	6,695	6,520

Calls Dispatched per Telecommunicator

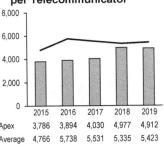

	2015	2016	2017	2018	2019
Apex	3,786	3,894	4,030	4,977	4,912
Average	4,766	5,738	5,531	5,335	5,423

Emergency Communications Cost per Call Dispatched

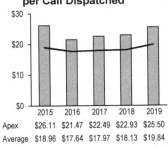

	2015	2016	2017	2018	2019
Apex	$26.11	$21.47	$22.49	$22.93	$25.50
Average	$18.96	$17.64	$17.97	$18.13	$19.84

Effectiveness Measures

Number of Seconds from Initial Ring to Answer

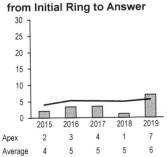

	2015	2016	2017	2018	2019
Apex	2	3	4	1	7
Average	4	5	5	5	6

Percent of E-911 Calls Answered within Twenty Seconds

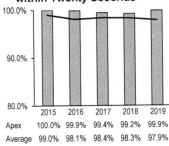

	2015	2016	2017	2018	2019
Apex	100.0%	99.9%	99.4%	99.2%	99.9%
Average	99.0%	98.1%	98.4%	98.3%	97.9%

Average Time in Seconds from CAD Entry to Dispatch for Priority One Calls

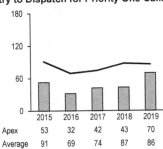

	2015	2016	2017	2018	2019
Apex	53	32	42	43	70
Average	91	69	74	87	86

Asheville

Emergency Communications

Fiscal Year 2018–19

Explanatory Information

Service Level and Delivery

Asheville's Communication Unit handles emergency calls for police and other assistance calls coming into its center from the city. The center is organizationally located in the Support Services Division of the police department. The city handles administrative calls, requests for police response, and E-911 calls. The center is co-located with Buncombe County Emergency Operations Center and Buncombe County Sheriff's Office.

The communications center operates twenty-four hours a day, seven days a week, using four permanent "twelve hour" shifts. A work week consists of three twelve hour shifts and one eight hour shift. The communications center uses a call-taker for its E-911 emergency calls. Buncombe County takes such calls and directs them by computer to the city's communications center. Non-emergency calls, however, come directly into the city's communications center.

The city owns its communications infrastructure, consisting of three towers. One tower is used for repeated radio communications, while the other two towers are stand-alone sites that require officers/telecommunicators to manually switch channels. The city uses the Motorola Simulcast system.

Asheville's emergency communications center handled a total of 171,574 incoming calls in the fiscal year and dispatched 136,854 calls. The city defines highest-priority emergency calls as crimes in progress and situations that are property- or life-threatening.

Conditions Affecting Service, Performance, and Costs

Computer-aided dispatch (CAD) entry is an immediate action beginning when a telecommunicator hits "new call" or "new event."

Asheville's community policing initiative encourages citizens to report criminal activity, and this has generated more calls over time. The wider use of cell phones has also made it easier for citizens to respond immediately, which has probably increased calls as well.

Asheville's Communication Unit has made an effort to better categorize high-priority calls, which has helped reduce the time between the start of CAD entry and dispatch.

Municipal Profile

Population (OSBM 2018)	93,621
Land Area (Square Miles)	45.53
Persons per Square Mile	2,056
Median Household Income	$40,494
U.S. Census 2016	
County	Buncombe

Service Profile

Primary or Secondary Answering Point	Secondary
Calls Dispatched	
Police	Yes
Fire	No
Other	Yes
FTE Positions	
Telecommunicators/Call-Takers	23.0
Other	1.0
Total Positions	24.0
Average Length of Service for Call-Takers	4.3 years
Total Incoming Calls	171,574
Total 911 Calls	38,441
Total Calls Dispatched	136,854
Outgoing Calls Other than Dispatch	32,760
Revenue from E-911 Fees	None

Full Cost Profile

Cost Breakdown by Percentage	
Personal Services	58.2%
Operating Costs	40.8%
Capital Costs	1.1%
TOTAL	100.0%

Cost Breakdown in Dollars	
Personal Services	$1,216,772
Operating Costs	$852,985
Capital Costs	$22,502
TOTAL	$2,092,259

Resource Measures

Emergency Communications Services Costs per Capita

	2015	2016	2017	2018	2019
Asheville	$21.68	$21.78	$22.79	$21.73	$22.35
Average	$19.72	$19.07	$18.76	$19.05	$20.63

Emergency Communications FTEs per 10,000 Population

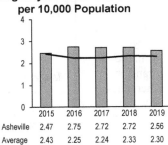

	2015	2016	2017	2018	2019
Asheville	2.47	2.75	2.72	2.72	2.56
Average	2.43	2.25	2.24	2.33	2.30

Workload Measures

Total Calls Answered per 1,000 Population

	2015	2016	2017	2018	2019
Asheville	1,945	1,991	1,657	1,837	1,833
Average	1,437	1,390	1,313	1,295	1,222

Calls Dispatched per 1,000 Population

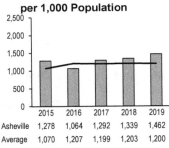

	2015	2016	2017	2018	2019
Asheville	1,278	1,064	1,292	1,339	1,462
Average	1,070	1,207	1,199	1,203	1,200

E-911 Calls as a Percentage of All Incoming Calls

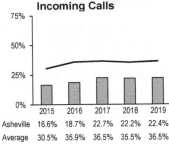

	2015	2016	2017	2018	2019
Asheville	16.6%	18.7%	22.7%	22.2%	22.4%
Average	30.5%	35.9%	36.5%	35.5%	36.5%

Efficiency Measures

Calls Answered per Telecommunicator

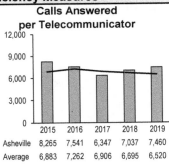

	2015	2016	2017	2018	2019
Asheville	8,265	7,541	6,347	7,037	7,460
Average	6,883	7,262	6,906	6,695	6,520

Calls Dispatched per Telecommunicator

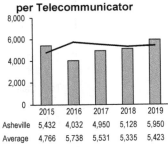

	2015	2016	2017	2018	2019
Asheville	5,432	4,032	4,950	5,128	5,950
Average	4,766	5,738	5,531	5,335	5,423

Emergency Communications Cost per Call Dispatched

	2015	2016	2017	2018	2019
Asheville	$16.96	$20.46	$17.64	$16.23	$15.29
Average	$18.96	$17.64	$17.97	$18.13	$19.84

Effectiveness Measures

Number of Seconds from Initial Ring to Answer

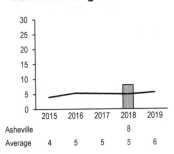

	2015	2016	2017	2018	2019
Asheville				8	
Average	4	5	5	5	6

Percent of E-911 Calls Answered within Twenty Seconds

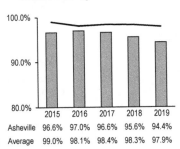

	2015	2016	2017	2018	2019
Asheville	96.6%	97.0%	96.6%	95.6%	94.4%
Average	99.0%	98.1%	98.4%	98.3%	97.9%

Average Time in Seconds from CAD Entry to Dispatch for Priority One Calls

	2015	2016	2017	2018	2019
Asheville	115	94	94	94	96
Average	91	69	74	87	86

Explanatory Information

Service Level and Delivery

Concord's emergency communications center handles E-911 and non-emergency calls for the city. The emergency communications function of the city is separate from the police and fire functions and does not answer or transfer administrative calls for those departments. The emergency communications center does answer calls for utility and other city departments after hours, which is reflected in the number of incoming calls.

The city uses an 800 MHz system, which is a twelve-channel, five-site system shared with Cabarrus County and the City of Kannapolis.

Concord's center handled a total of 98,013 calls in the fiscal year, dispatching 150,809 calls.

Conditions Affecting Service, Performance, and Costs

Municipal Profile

Population (OSBM 2018)	92,568
Land Area (Square Miles)	62.80
Persons per Square Mile	1,474
Median Household Income	$50,863
U.S. Census 2016	
County	Cabarrus

Service Profile

Primary or Secondary Answering Point	Primary
Calls Dispatched	
Police	Yes
Fire	Yes
Other	Yes
FTE Positions	
Telecommunicators/Call-Takers	23.5
Other	2.0
Total Positions	25.5
Average Length of Service for Call-Takers	8.9 years
Total Incoming Calls	98,013
Total 911 Calls	29,069
Total Calls Dispatched	150,809
Outgoing Calls Other than Dispatch	31,998
Revenue from E-911 Fees	None

Full Cost Profile

Cost Breakdown by Percentage	
Personal Services	82.5%
Operating Costs	15.9%
Capital Costs	1.7%
TOTAL	100.0%
Cost Breakdown in Dollars	
Personal Services	$1,456,503
Operating Costs	$280,060
Capital Costs	$29,876
TOTAL	$1,766,439

Concord

Emergency Communications

Resource Measures

Emergency Communications Services Costs per Capita

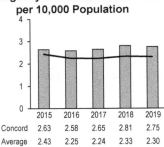

	2015	2016	2017	2018	2019
Concord	$16.62	$15.91	$17.16	$17.91	$19.08
Average	$19.72	$19.07	$18.76	$19.05	$20.63

Emergency Communications FTEs per 10,000 Population

	2015	2016	2017	2018	2019
Concord	2.63	2.58	2.65	2.81	2.75
Average	2.43	2.25	2.24	2.33	2.30

Workload Measures

Total Calls Answered per 1,000 Population

	2015	2016	2017	2018	2019
Concord	1,181	1,177	1,204	1,104	1,059
Average	1,437	1,390	1,313	1,295	1,222

Calls Dispatched per 1,000 Population

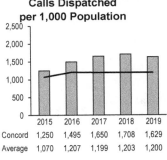

	2015	2016	2017	2018	2019
Concord	1,250	1,495	1,650	1,708	1,629
Average	1,070	1,207	1,199	1,203	1,200

E-911 Calls as a Percentage of All Incoming Calls

	2015	2016	2017	2018	2019
Concord	26.2%	27.0%	27.1%	28.3%	29.7%
Average	30.5%	35.9%	36.5%	35.5%	36.5%

Efficiency Measures

Calls Answered per Telecommunicator

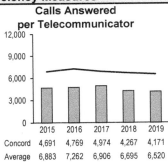

	2015	2016	2017	2018	2019
Concord	4,691	4,769	4,974	4,267	4,171
Average	6,883	7,262	6,906	6,695	6,520

Calls Dispatched per Telecommunicator

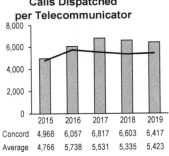

	2015	2016	2017	2018	2019
Concord	4,968	6,057	6,817	6,603	6,417
Average	4,766	5,738	5,531	5,335	5,423

Emergency Communications Cost per Call Dispatched

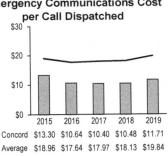

	2015	2016	2017	2018	2019
Concord	$13.30	$10.64	$10.40	$10.48	$11.71
Average	$18.96	$17.64	$17.97	$18.13	$19.84

Effectiveness Measures

Number of Seconds from Initial Ring to Answer

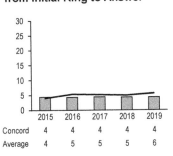

	2015	2016	2017	2018	2019
Concord	4	4	4	4	4
Average	4	5	5	5	6

Percent of E-911 Calls Answered within Twenty Seconds

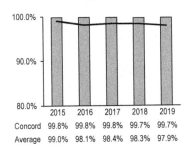

	2015	2016	2017	2018	2019
Concord	99.8%	99.8%	99.8%	99.7%	99.7%
Average	99.0%	98.1%	98.4%	98.3%	97.9%

Average Time in Seconds from CAD Entry to Dispatch for Priority One Calls

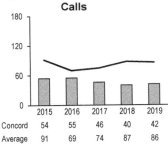

	2015	2016	2017	2018	2019
Concord	54	55	46	40	42
Average	91	69	74	87	86

Greensboro   # Emergency Communications

Fiscal Year 2018–19

Explanatory Information

Service Level and Delivery

Guilford Metro 911 operates under an interlocal agreement between the City of Greensboro and Guilford County. The public safety answering point serves as a separate department providing emergency communications for the City of Greensboro, Guilford County, and Gibsonville (except for the City of High Point Police and Fire departments). The services include dispatch and call intake for all law agencies, fire agencies, and EMS. The consolidation process enabled the first update of all 911 equipment in ten years and the creation of a back-up E-911 center to improve disaster preparedness. These changes contributed to slightly higher operational costs.

Guilford Metro 911 uses Motorola Trunked P25 Regional radio system. The system has nine tower sites and is jointly owned with Guilford County.

Greensboro's communications center handled a total of 589,353 incoming calls in the fiscal year, dispatching 441,871 calls. The city defines highest-priority emergency calls as call types that require the fastest response, such as shootings, robberies, and domestic violence.

Greensboro received $2,518,081 in E-911 revenues to support system operations.

Conditions Affecting Service, Performance, and Costs

Municipal Profile

Population (OSBM 2018)–Guilford County	533,213
Land Area (Square Miles)	649.42
Persons per Square Mile	821
Median Household Income	$40,760
U.S. Census 2016	
County	Guilford

Service Profile

Primary or Secondary Answering Point	Primary
Calls Dispatched	
Police	Yes
Fire	Yes
Other	Yes
FTE Positions	
Telecommunicators/Call-Takers	92.0
Other	17.0
Total Positions	109.0
Average Length of Service for Call-Takers	10.5 years
Total Incoming Calls	589,353
Total 911 Calls	330,522
Total Calls Dispatched	441,871
Outgoing Calls Other than Dispatch	152,661
Revenue from E-911 Fees	$2,518,081

Full Cost Profile

Cost Breakdown by Percentage	
Personal Services	80.6%
Operating Costs	19.4%
Capital Costs	0.0%
TOTAL	100.0%

Cost Breakdown in Dollars	
Personal Services	$6,649,375
Operating Costs	$1,597,535
Capital Costs	$0
TOTAL	$8,246,910

Resource Measures

Emergency Communications Services Costs per Capita

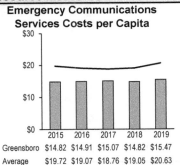

	2015	2016	2017	2018	2019
Greensboro	$14.82	$14.91	$15.07	$14.82	$15.47
Average	$19.72	$19.07	$18.76	$19.05	$20.63

Emergency Communications FTEs per 10,000 Population

	2015	2016	2017	2018	2019
Greensboro	2.03	2.01	1.98	1.95	2.04
Average	2.43	2.25	2.24	2.33	2.30

Workload Measures

Total Calls Answered per 1,000 Population

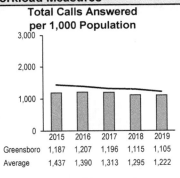

	2015	2016	2017	2018	2019
Greensboro	1,187	1,207	1,196	1,115	1,105
Average	1,437	1,390	1,313	1,295	1,222

Calls Dispatched per 1,000 Population

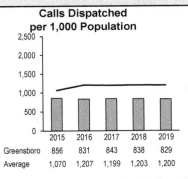

	2015	2016	2017	2018	2019
Greensboro	856	831	843	838	829
Average	1,070	1,207	1,199	1,203	1,200

E-911 Calls as a Percentage of All Incoming Calls

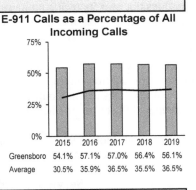

	2015	2016	2017	2018	2019
Greensboro	54.1%	57.1%	57.0%	56.4%	56.1%
Average	30.5%	35.9%	36.5%	35.5%	36.5%

Efficiency Measures

Calls Answered per Telecommunicator

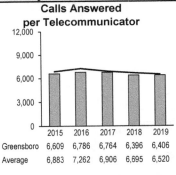

	2015	2016	2017	2018	2019
Greensboro	6,609	6,786	6,764	6,396	6,406
Average	6,883	7,262	6,906	6,695	6,520

Calls Dispatched per Telecommunicator

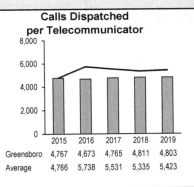

	2015	2016	2017	2018	2019
Greensboro	4,767	4,673	4,765	4,811	4,803
Average	4,766	5,738	5,531	5,335	5,423

Emergency Communications Cost per Call Dispatched

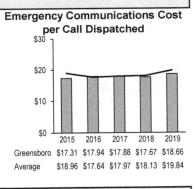

	2015	2016	2017	2018	2019
Greensboro	$17.31	$17.94	$17.88	$17.67	$18.66
Average	$18.96	$17.64	$17.97	$18.13	$19.84

Effectiveness Measures

Number of Seconds from Initial Ring to Answer

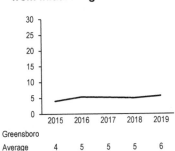

	2015	2016	2017	2018	2019
Greensboro					
Average	4	5	5	5	6

Percent of E-911 Calls Answered within Twenty Seconds

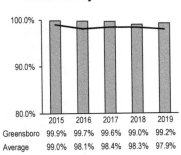

	2015	2016	2017	2018	2019
Greensboro	99.9%	99.7%	99.6%	99.0%	99.2%
Average	99.0%	98.1%	98.4%	98.3%	97.9%

Average Time in Seconds from CAD Entry to Dispatch for Priority One Calls

	2015	2016	2017	2018	2019
Greensboro	56	56	58	58	97
Average	91	69	74	87	86

Greenville
Emergency Communications

Fiscal Year 2018–19

Explanatory Information

Service Level and Delivery
Greenville's emergency communications center is a secondary public safety answering point, with Pitt County being the primary answering point. Pitt County initially receives all 911 calls and dispatches fire and EMS calls inside the city limits. All 911 calls for police services are transferred to the Greenville Police Department emergency communications center for dispatch. Calls can also be made directly to the police department over a dedicated emergency line.

The city does not own its own communications system and infrastructure. Greenville operates on the VIPER system maintained by the North Carolina State Highway Patrol. This system is fully maintained and operated by the state. The system has one tower located within the city limits and fully supports communication interoperability among all law enforcement agencies in Pitt County and with Greenville Fire/Rescue and East Care medical transport.

Greenville's center took in 96,088 incoming calls in the fiscal year and dispatched 81,944 calls.

Conditions Affecting Service, Performance, and Costs
Telecommunicators in Greenville are also tasked with overseeing public safety cameras through several large monitors. When needed, they are instructed to log events requiring a response as service calls. This video monitoring results in higher staffing needs in the emergency communications center.

Municipal Profile

Population (OSBM 2018)	89,790
Land Area (Square Miles)	35.58
Persons per Square Mile	2,523
Median Household Income U.S. Census 2016	$33,339
County	Pitt

Service Profile

Primary or Secondary Answering Point	Secondary
Calls Dispatched	
Police	Yes
Fire	No
Other	Yes
FTE Positions	
Telecommunicators/Call-Takers	20.0
Other	1.0
Total Positions	21.0
Average Length of Service for Call-Takers	9.2 years
Total Incoming Calls	96,088
Total 911 Calls	24,682
Total Calls Dispatched	81,944
Outgoing Calls Other than Dispatch	3,509
Revenue from E-911 Fees	None

Full Cost Profile

Cost Breakdown by Percentage	
Personal Services	70.5%
Operating Costs	29.5%
Capital Costs	0.0%
TOTAL	100.0%

Cost Breakdown in Dollars	
Personal Services	$1,581,016
Operating Costs	$662,563
Capital Costs	$0
TOTAL	$2,243,579

Greenville

Emergency Communications

Resource Measures

Emergency Communications Services Costs per Capita

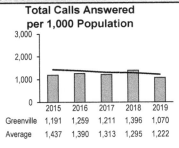

	2015	2016	2017	2018	2019
Greenville	$25.30	$27.81	$21.79	$21.40	$24.99
Average	$19.72	$19.07	$18.76	$19.05	$20.63

Emergency Communications FTEs per 10,000 Population

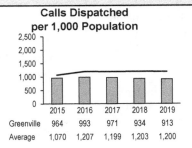

	2015	2016	2017	2018	2019
Greenville	1.94	1.93	1.93	2.13	2.34
Average	2.43	2.25	2.24	2.33	2.30

Workload Measures

Total Calls Answered per 1,000 Population

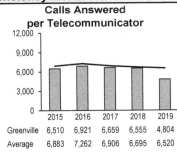

	2015	2016	2017	2018	2019
Greenville	1,191	1,259	1,211	1,396	1,070
Average	1,437	1,390	1,313	1,295	1,222

Calls Dispatched per 1,000 Population

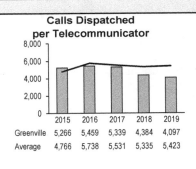

	2015	2016	2017	2018	2019
Greenville	964	993	971	934	913
Average	1,070	1,207	1,199	1,203	1,200

E-911 Calls as a Percentage of All Incoming Calls

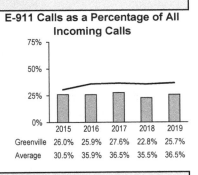

	2015	2016	2017	2018	2019
Greenville	26.0%	25.9%	27.6%	22.8%	25.7%
Average	30.5%	35.9%	36.5%	35.5%	36.5%

Efficiency Measures

Calls Answered per Telecommunicator

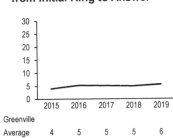

	2015	2016	2017	2018	2019
Greenville	6,510	6,921	6,659	6,555	4,804
Average	6,883	7,262	6,906	6,695	6,520

Calls Dispatched per Telecommunicator

	2015	2016	2017	2018	2019
Greenville	5,266	5,459	5,339	4,384	4,097
Average	4,766	5,738	5,531	5,335	5,423

Emergency Communications Cost per Call Dispatched

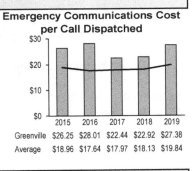

	2015	2016	2017	2018	2019
Greenville	$26.25	$28.01	$22.44	$22.92	$27.38
Average	$18.96	$17.64	$17.97	$18.13	$19.84

Effectiveness Measures

Number of Seconds from Initial Ring to Answer

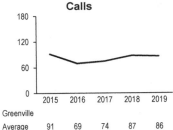

	2015	2016	2017	2018	2019
Greenville					
Average	4	5	5	5	6

Percent of E-911 Calls Answered within Twenty Seconds

	2015	2016	2017	2018	2019
Greenville					
Average	99.0%	98.1%	98.4%	98.3%	97.9%

Average Time in Seconds from CAD Entry to Dispatch for Priority One Calls

	2015	2016	2017	2018	2019
Greenville					
Average	91	69	74	87	86

Fiscal Year 2018–19

Explanatory Information

Service Level and Delivery

Hickory's emergency communications center is a secondary public safety answering point, with Catawba County being the primary answering point. Catawaba County initially receives all 911 calls and dispatches fire and EMS calls inside the city limits. All 911 calls for police services are transferred to the emergency communications center for dispatch. Any emergency calls for other city services are transferred to the emergency communications center between 3:30 p.m. and 7:00 a.m.

The city owns its communications system and infrastructure. It uses an Ericsson 800 MHz radio system. There is one 1,350-foot tower and antennas at two other sites. The system serves approximately 200 users in five city departments.

Hickory's communications center took in 119,532 incoming calls during the year. The center dispatched 100,038 calls during the year.

Hickory received $198,926 in E-911 revenues to support system operations.

Conditions Affecting Service, Performance, and Costs

Incoming calls in Hickory are down over time because of changes in how calls are routed. Several special units now have their own administrative phones, so calls no longer come through the emergency communications center. Additionally, the animal control unit's operations were moved out of the police department, so their calls are now being fed through code enforcement.

Municipal Profile

Population (OSBM 2018)	40,932
Land Area (Square Miles)	29.92
Persons per Square Mile	1,368
Median Household Income	$35,353
U.S. Census 2016	
County	Catawba

Service Profile

Primary or Secondary Answering Point	Secondary
Calls Dispatched	
Police	Yes
Fire	No
Other	No
FTE Positions	
Telecommunicators/Call-Takers	14.0
Other	0.0
Total Positions	14.0
Average Length of Service for Call-Takers	4.8 years
Total Incoming Calls	119,532
Total 911 Calls	15,861
Total Calls Dispatched	100,038
Outgoing Calls Other than Dispatch	26,016
Revenue from E-911 Fees	$198,926

Full Cost Profile

Cost Breakdown by Percentage	
Personal Services	63.2%
Operating Costs	35.4%
Capital Costs	1.3%
TOTAL	100.0%
Cost Breakdown in Dollars	
Personal Services	$703,296
Operating Costs	$394,236
Capital Costs	$14,948
TOTAL	$1,112,480

Hickory
Emergency Communications

Resource Measures

Emergency Communications Services Costs per Capita

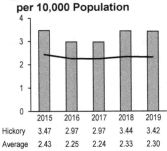

	2015	2016	2017	2018	2019
Hickory	$18.77	$20.62	$20.12	$23.68	$27.18
Average	$19.72	$19.07	$18.76	$19.05	$20.63

Emergency Communications FTEs per 10,000 Population

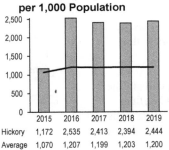

	2015	2016	2017	2018	2019
Hickory	3.47	2.97	2.97	3.44	3.42
Average	2.43	2.25	2.24	2.33	2.30

Workload Measures

Total Calls Answered per 1,000 Population

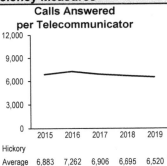

	2015	2016	2017	2018	2019
Hickory					
Average	1,437	1,390	1,313	1,295	1,222

Calls Dispatched per 1,000 Population

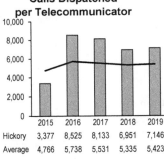

	2015	2016	2017	2018	2019
Hickory	1,172	2,535	2,413	2,394	2,444
Average	1,070	1,207	1,199	1,203	1,200

E-911 Calls as a Percentage of All Incoming Calls

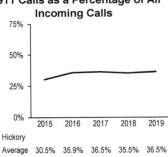

	2015	2016	2017	2018	2019
Hickory					
Average	30.5%	35.9%	36.5%	35.5%	36.5%

Efficiency Measures

Calls Answered per Telecommunicator

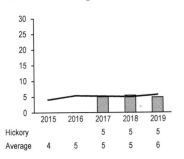

	2015	2016	2017	2018	2019
Hickory					
Average	6,883	7,262	6,906	6,695	6,520

Calls Dispatched per Telecommunicator

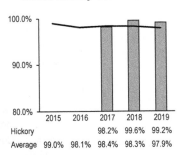

	2015	2016	2017	2018	2019
Hickory	3,377	8,525	8,133	6,951	7,146
Average	4,766	5,738	5,531	5,335	5,423

Emergency Communications Cost per Call Dispatched

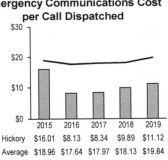

	2015	2016	2017	2018	2019
Hickory	$16.01	$8.13	$8.34	$9.89	$11.12
Average	$18.96	$17.64	$17.97	$18.13	$19.84

Effectiveness Measures

Number of Seconds from Initial Ring to Answer

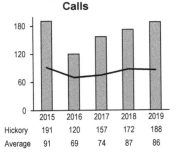

	2015	2016	2017	2018	2019
Hickory			5	5	5
Average	4	5	5	5	6

Percent of E-911 Calls Answered within Twenty Seconds

	2015	2016	2017	2018	2019
Hickory			98.2%	99.6%	99.2%
Average	99.0%	98.1%	98.4%	98.3%	97.9%

Average Time in Seconds from CAD Entry to Dispatch for Priority One Calls

	2015	2016	2017	2018	2019
Hickory	191	120	157	172	188
Average	91	69	74	87	86

Fiscal Year 2018–19

Explanatory Information

Service Level and Delivery

The Emergency Communications Center (ECC) is the answering and dispatch agency for all of Wake County. It provides dispatch services for forty-four law enforcement, fire, EMS, rescue, and public service agencies. The ECC takes 911 calls for the Wake County Sheriff's Department, but these calls are transferred to the sheriff's telecommunicators.

The Town of Cary provides its own services for fire and police, but the ECC provides EMS call service for Cary.

The ECC uses a combination of city-owned and leased tower and transmitter sites. The system uses an 800 MHz system. Over 7,000 mobile and portable radios have been issued to public safety and non-public safety users within Wake County for use of the system.

The ECC handled a total of 835,150 incoming calls in the fiscal year, dispatching 487,264 calls. The ECC defines highest-priority emergency calls as all fire and EMS calls and also police calls with a priority of "0" or "1" as defined by the police agency being dispatched.

Raleigh received $2,780,251 in E-911 revenues to support system operations.

Conditions Affecting Service, Performance, and Costs

Raleigh rejoined the Benchmarking Project in July 2016, with the first year of data showing for FY 2015–16.

At the start of FY 2015–16, the ECC switched from all positions being on automatic call distribution to specific positions utilizing the automatic system. This decreased answering efficiency, but it helped increase responder safety issues that were identified when all positions used the automatic system. Additionally during this year, the ECC had a one-fourth attrition rate, which impacted answering efficiencies as well.

Municipal Profile

Population (OSBM 2017)-Wake County	1,073,993
Land Area (Square Miles)	831.92
Persons per Square Mile	1,291
Median Household Income	$46,612
U.S. Census 2016	
County	Wake

Service Profile

Primary or Secondary Answering Point	Primary
Calls Dispatched	
Police	Yes
Fire	Yes
Other	Yes
FTE Positions	
Telecommunicators/Call-Takers	102.0
Other	27.0
Total Positions	129.0
Average Length of Service for Call-Takers	5.5 years
Total Incoming Calls	835,150
Total 911 Calls	553,997
Total Calls Dispatched	487,264
Outgoing Calls Other than Dispatch	288,455
Revenue from E-911 Fees	$2,780,251

Full Cost Profile

Cost Breakdown by Percentage	
Personal Services	59.9%
Operating Costs	38.5%
Capital Costs	1.6%
TOTAL	100.0%
Cost Breakdown in Dollars	
Personal Services	$8,131,318
Operating Costs	$5,233,006
Capital Costs	$214,942
TOTAL	$13,579,266

Raleigh

Emergency Communications

Resource Measures

Emergency Communications Services Costs per Capita

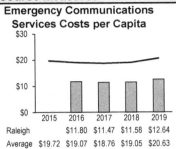

	2015	2016	2017	2018	2019
Raleigh		$11.80	$11.47	$11.58	$12.64
Average	$19.72	$19.07	$18.76	$19.05	$20.63

Emergency Communications FTEs per 10,000 Population

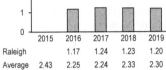

	2015	2016	2017	2018	2019
Raleigh		1.17	1.24	1.23	1.20
Average	2.43	2.25	2.24	2.33	2.30

Workload Measures

Total Calls Answered per 1,000 Population

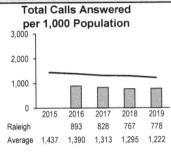

	2015	2016	2017	2018	2019
Raleigh		893	828	767	778
Average	1,437	1,390	1,313	1,295	1,222

Calls Dispatched per 1,000 Population

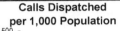
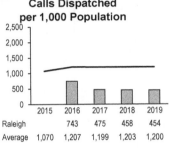

	2015	2016	2017	2018	2019
Raleigh		743	475	458	454
Average	1,070	1,207	1,199	1,203	1,200

E-911 Calls as a Percentage of All Incoming Calls

	2015	2016	2017	2018	2019
Raleigh		67.9%	68.0%	65.7%	66.3%
Average	30.5%	35.9%	36.5%	35.5%	36.5%

Efficiency Measures

Calls Answered per Telecommunicator

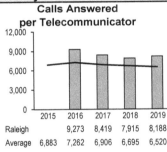

	2015	2016	2017	2018	2019
Raleigh		9,273	8,419	7,915	8,188
Average	6,883	7,262	6,906	6,695	6,520

Calls Dispatched per Telecommunicator

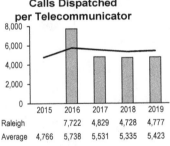

	2015	2016	2017	2018	2019
Raleigh		7,722	4,829	4,728	4,777
Average	4,766	5,738	5,531	5,335	5,423

Emergency Communications Cost per Call Dispatched

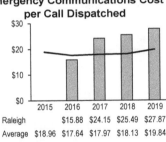

	2015	2016	2017	2018	2019
Raleigh		$15.88	$24.15	$25.49	$27.87
Average	$18.96	$17.64	$17.97	$18.13	$19.84

Effectiveness Measures

Number of Seconds from Initial Ring to Answer

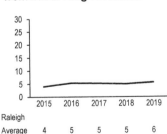

	2015	2016	2017	2018	2019
Raleigh					
Average	4	5	5	5	6

Percent of E-911 Calls Answered within Twenty Seconds

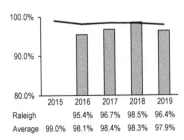

	2015	2016	2017	2018	2019
Raleigh		95.4%	96.7%	98.5%	96.4%
Average	99.0%	98.1%	98.4%	98.3%	97.9%

Average Time in Seconds from CAD Entry to Dispatch for Priority One Calls

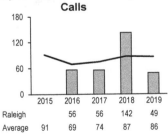

	2015	2016	2017	2018	2019
Raleigh		56	56	142	49
Average	91	69	74	87	86

Winston-Salem   # Emergency Communications

Fiscal Year 2018–19

Explanatory Information

Service Level and Delivery

Winston-Salem's Emergency Communications Division is part of the police department and handles 911 and non-emergency calls for police and fire. Calls received for EMS, the sheriff's office, county fire, and the highway patrol are transferred to the appropriate agency. All telecommunicators are hired and trained as call-takers and dispatchers.

The city owns the infrastructure but contracts with local vendors to provide telecommunications services. The City of Winston-Salem and Forsyth County implemented a voice radio system in October 2004. The Motorola ASTRO 800 MHz Trunked Simulcast system is made up of eight tower sites utilizing fifteen channels. The Winston-Salem Police Department uses a non-trunked 800 MHz system for the mobile data system, with one transmitter site using three channels.

Winston-Salem's center handled a total of 469,614 calls in the fiscal year, dispatching 242,948 calls. The city defines highest-priority emergency calls as calls with a significant threat of imminent injury to persons or calls for crimes against persons that are in progress or have just occurred and the suspect is still there.

Winston-Salem received $521,156 in E-911 revenues to support system operations.

Conditions Affecting Service, Performance, and Costs

The Emergency Communications Division has been short operators from its authorized total during some of the years.

The system has not been able to provide data on calls answered in the 20-second interval in the past, but improvements now show this data.

Municipal Profile

Population (OSBM 2018)	243,447
Land Area (Square Miles)	132.55
Persons per Square Mile	1,837
Median Household Income	$40,584
U.S. Census 2016	
County	Forsyth

Service Profile

Primary or Secondary Answering Point	Primary
Calls Dispatched	
Police	Yes
Fire	Yes
Other	No
FTE Positions	
Telecommunicators/Call-Takers	46.0
Other	2.0
Total Positions	48.0
Average Length of Service for Call-Takers	8.4 years
Total Incoming Calls	469,614
Total 911 Calls	215,222
Total Calls Dispatched	242,948
Outgoing Calls Other than Dispatch	63,624
Revenue from E-911 Fees	$521,156

Full Cost Profile

Cost Breakdown by Percentage	
Personal Services	69.9%
Operating Costs	25.8%
Capital Costs	4.3%
TOTAL	100.0%
Cost Breakdown in Dollars	
Personal Services	$3,592,865
Operating Costs	$1,324,523
Capital Costs	$221,174
TOTAL	$5,138,562

Winston-Salem

Emergency Communications

Resource Measures

Emergency Communications Services Costs per Capita

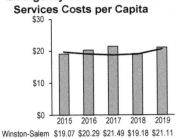

	2015	2016	2017	2018	2019
Winston-Salem	$19.07	$20.29	$21.49	$19.18	$21.11
Average	$19.72	$19.07	$18.76	$19.05	$20.63

Emergency Communications FTEs per 10,000 Population

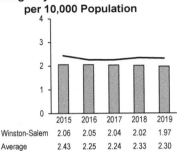

	2015	2016	2017	2018	2019
Winston-Salem	2.06	2.05	2.04	2.02	1.97
Average	2.43	2.25	2.24	2.33	2.30

Workload Measures

Total Calls Answered per 1,000 Population

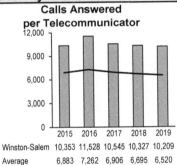

	2015	2016	2017	2018	2019
Winston-Salem	2,045	2,268	2,060	1,997	1,929
Average	1,437	1,390	1,313	1,295	1,222

Calls Dispatched per 1,000 Population

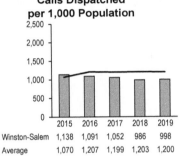

	2015	2016	2017	2018	2019
Winston-Salem	1,138	1,091	1,052	986	998
Average	1,070	1,207	1,199	1,203	1,200

E-911 Calls as a Percentage of All Incoming Calls

	2015	2016	2017	2018	2019
Winston-Salem	46.9%	45.8%	45.2%	44.2%	45.8%
Average	30.5%	35.9%	36.5%	35.5%	36.5%

Efficiency Measures

Calls Answered per Telecommunicator

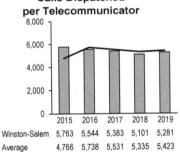

	2015	2016	2017	2018	2019
Winston-Salem	10,353	11,528	10,545	10,327	10,209
Average	6,883	7,262	6,906	6,695	6,520

Calls Dispatched per Telecommunicator

	2015	2016	2017	2018	2019
Winston-Salem	5,763	5,544	5,383	5,101	5,281
Average	4,766	5,738	5,531	5,335	5,423

Emergency Communications Cost per Call Dispatched

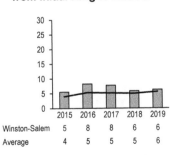

	2015	2016	2017	2018	2019
Winston-Salem	$16.75	$18.60	$20.43	$19.44	$21.15
Average	$18.96	$17.64	$17.97	$18.13	$19.84

Effectiveness Measures

Number of Seconds from Initial Ring to Answer

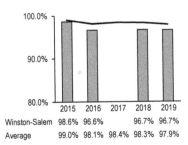

	2015	2016	2017	2018	2019
Winston-Salem	5	8	8	6	6
Average	4	5	5	5	6

Percent of E-911 Calls Answered within Twenty Seconds

	2015	2016	2017	2018	2019
Winston-Salem	98.6%	96.6%		96.7%	96.7%
Average	99.0%	98.1%	98.4%	98.3%	97.9%

Average Time in Seconds from CAD Entry to Dispatch for Priority One Calls

	2015	2016	2017	2018	2019
Winston-Salem	77	72	69	63	58
Average	91	69	74	87	86

Performance and Cost Data

ASPHALT MAINTENANCE AND REPAIR

PERFORMANCE MEASURES FOR ASPHALT MAINTENANCE AND REPAIR

SERVICE DEFINITION

Asphalt Maintenance and Repair includes the activities of pothole repair, repaving, surface treatment, structure adjustments, milling, and utility cuts. It does not include work on reconstruction, handicap ramps, storm drainage, sidewalks, curb and gutter, right-of-way maintenance, street cleaning and sweeping, pavement marking, lane widening, unpaved street maintenance, or snow and ice removal.

NOTES ON PERFORMANCE MEASURES

1. Lane Miles Maintained

This measure refers to total lane miles that a municipality maintains, including state streets and municipal streets. The standard lane mile is 12 feet in width and 5,280 feet in length. Some jurisdictions do not track lane miles. Therefore, a methodology must be employed to calculate lane miles for participation.

2. Potholes and Utility Cuts per Lane Mile

Breaks in pavement due to potholes or to intentional utility cuts affect asphalt maintenance workload in the short term and long term because of breaks in the pavement integrity.

3. Cost of Road Treatment per Lane Mile

This is the cost of different types of asphalt treatment that a municipality may use to maintain or repair roads. Treatments include preservation work, such as crack or slurry sealing; resurfacing, which is typically one to two inches of new asphalt; and rehabilitation, which combines resurfacing with milling work to repair more damaged roads.

4. Cost of Asphalt Maintenance and Repair

Total cost of asphalt maintenance and repair represents the total direct, indirect, and capital costs taken from the accounting form. "Cost of maintenance" represents total cost from the accounting form minus cost of any treatment efforts by contract and municipal crews.

5. Percentage of Street Segments Rated 85 or Better and Below 45

Many municipalities use standard rating systems for assessing street pavement condition. These systems apply professionally determined criteria and embody scales that provide relatively objective ratings. These measures indicate the proportion of street segments that are rated 85 or better, which is good condition, and those rated below 45, which is poor condition, on the most recent street pavement assessment.

6. Percentage of Potholes Repaired within Twenty-Four Hours

Repair of potholes in a timely manner is important for maintaining pavement integrity and minimizing further damage to the street and vehicle traffic.

Asphalt Maintenance and Repair

Summary of Key Dimensions of Service

City or Town	Lane Miles Maintained	Total Lane Miles Treated by Type			Percent Treated			FTE Positions for City Staff
		Preservation	Resurfacing	Rehabilitation	Preservation	Resurfacing	Rehabilitation	
Apex	414.78	43.2	0.0	2.6	10.4%	0.0%	0.6%	8.3
Asheville	805.00	0.0	3.3	2.5	0.0%	0.4%	0.3%	17.1
Chapel Hill	333.40	0.0	0.0	10.4	0.0%	0.0%	3.1%	6.7
Charlotte	5,414.58	0.6	0.5	158.3	0.0%	0.0%	2.9%	122.0
Concord	711.55	0.0	24.9	0.0	0.0%	3.5%	0.0%	12.3
Goldsboro	324.68	0.0	0.0	21.4	0.0%	0.0%	6.6%	6.0
Greensboro	2,431.00	27.5	67.0	0.0	1.1%	2.8%	0.0%	51.0
Greenville	682.68	0.0	0.0	31.3	0.0%	0.0%	4.6%	8.5
Hickory	721.30	0.0	9.0	0.0	0.0%	1.2%	0.0%	7.0
Mooresville	304.00	0.0	0.0	11.8	0.0%	0.0%	3.9%	21.0
Raleigh	2,317.00	0.0	32.0	0.0	0.0%	1.4%	0.0%	41.0
Wilson	695.37	8.6	0.0	0.3	1.2%	0.0%	0.0%	5.5
Winston-Salem	2,805.50	14.0	209.0	0.0	0.5%	7.5%	0.0%	43.4

EXPLANATORY FACTORS

These are factors that the project found affected asphalt maintenance and repair performance and cost in one or more of the municipalities:

Costs of materials in different cities
Weather conditions and terrain
Vehicle burden placed on streets
Age of street infrastructure
Depth of materials applied in repaving
Extent of contracting

Fiscal Year 2018–19

Explanatory Information

Service Level and Delivery
The Town of Apex's Streets Department was responsible for maintaining approximately 414.8 lane miles during the fiscal year. The Streets Department is part of the Public Works and Utilities Division for the town.

The town rehabilitated 2.6 lane miles during the year, which involves milling and resurfacing. The Town also did preservation work on 43.2 lane miles. This represented treatment of about 11.1 percent of total lane miles maintained.

The city reported that 25 percent of its lane miles were rated 85 or better on the pavement condition rating. The rating was performed by US Infrastructure of Carolina, Inc. using surveying in 2017.

The number of potholes reported for the fiscal year was eighty-one. The town only repairs within one day those potholes that are considered large and dangerous. Smaller potholes are repaired when the streets crews can get to them.

The Streets Department also repaired thirty-two utility cuts and eighty-three maintenance patches.

Conditions Affecting Service, Performance, and Costs
Hurricane Matthew in September 2016 had impacts on Apex, which raised the event to a Federal Emergency Management Agency (FEMA) event and response.

Municipal Profile

Population (OSBM 2018)	52,909
Land Area (Square Miles)	21.55
Persons per Square Mile	2,455
Topography	Flat; gently rolling
Climate	Temperate; little ice and snow

Service Profile

FTE Positions—Crews	7.00
FTE Positions—Other	1.25
Lane Miles Maintained	414.8
Lane Miles Treated	
Preservation	43.2
Resurfacing	0.0
Rehabilitation	2.6
TOTAL	45.8
Total Costs for All Treatment Types	$696,311
Potholes Repaired	81
Number of Utility Cuts	45
Number of Maintenance Patches (exclusive of potholes and utility cuts)	81
Average Cost per Ton of Hot Asphalt during Year	$106.27

Full Cost Profile

Cost Breakdown by Percentage	
Personal Services	17.5%
Operating Costs	77.1%
Capital Costs	5.4%
TOTAL	100.0%
Cost Breakdown in Dollars	
Personal Services	$256,886
Operating Costs	$1,128,533
Capital Costs	$78,890
TOTAL	$1,464,309

Apex

Asphalt Maintenance and Repair

Key: Apex ▨　　Benchmarking Average —　　Fiscal Years 2015 through 2019

Resource Measures

Asphalt Maintenance and Repair Services Costs per Capita

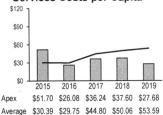

	2015	2016	2017	2018	2019
Apex	$51.70	$26.08	$36.24	$37.60	$27.68
Average	$30.39	$29.75	$44.80	$50.06	$53.59

Asphalt Maintenance and Repair FTEs per 10,000 Population

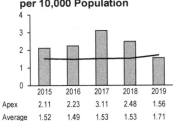

	2015	2016	2017	2018	2019
Apex	2.11	2.23	3.11	2.48	1.56
Average	1.52	1.49	1.53	1.53	1.71

Service Costs per Lane Mile of Road Maintained

	2015	2016	2017	2018	2019
Apex	$7,868	$3,863	$4,949	$4,714	$3,530
Average	$3,593	$3,700	$5,949	$6,793	$6,500

Workload Measures

Number of Lane Miles Maintained per 1,000 Population

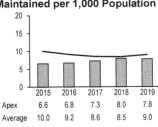

	2015	2016	2017	2018	2019
Apex	6.6	6.8	7.3	8.0	7.8
Average	10.0	9.2	8.6	8.5	9.0

Reported Potholes per Lane Mile Maintained

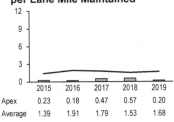

	2015	2016	2017	2018	2019
Apex	0.23	0.18	0.47	0.57	0.20
Average	1.39	1.91	1.79	1.53	1.68

Repaired Utility Cuts per Lane Mile Maintained

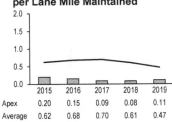

	2015	2016	2017	2018	2019
Apex	0.20	0.15	0.09	0.08	0.11
Average	0.62	0.68	0.70	0.61	0.47

Efficiency Measures

Cost of Maintenance per Lane Mile Maintained

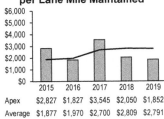

	2015	2016	2017	2018	2019
Apex	$2,827	$1,827	$3,545	$2,050	$1,852
Average	$1,877	$1,970	$2,700	$2,809	$2,791

Cost per Lane Mile for Preservation Treatment

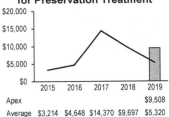

	2015	2016	2017	2018	2019
Apex					$9,508
Average	$3,214	$4,648	$14,370	$9,697	$5,320

Cost per Lane Mile for Resurfacing Treatment

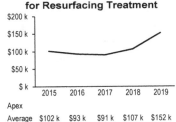

	2015	2016	2017	2018	2019
Apex					
Average	$102 k	$93 k	$91 k	$107 k	$152 k

Cost per Lane Mile for Rehabilitation Treatment

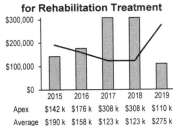

	2015	2016	2017	2018	2019
Apex	$142 k	$176 k	$308 k	$308 k	$110 k
Average	$190 k	$158 k	$123 k	$123 k	$275 k

Cost per Ton for Contract Resurfacing

	2015	2016	2017	2018	2019
Apex		$89	$192	$231	$136
Average	$86	$132	$129	$152	$192

Effectiveness Measures

Percent of Lane Miles Rated 85 or Better

	2015	2016	2017	2018	2019
Apex	57%	57%	56%	25%	25%
Average	43%	48%	46%	40%	40%

Percent of Lane Miles Rated Below 45

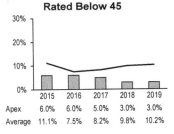

	2015	2016	2017	2018	2019
Apex	6.0%	6.0%	5.0%	3.0%	3.0%
Average	11.1%	7.5%	8.2%	9.8%	10.2%

Percentage of Potholes Repaired within 24 hours

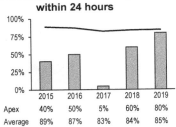

	2015	2016	2017	2018	2019
Apex	40%	50%	5%	60%	80%
Average	89%	87%	83%	84%	85%

Asheville

Asphalt Maintenance

Fiscal Year 2018–19

Explanatory Information

Service Level and Delivery

The City of Asheville was responsible for maintaining approximately 805 lane miles during the fiscal year. The city treated 5.8 lane miles during the year, equating to approximately 0.7 percent of total lane miles.

The city used contractors to do rehabilitation work on 1.04 lane miles, which includes milling and resurfacing. City crews also completed 1.44 lane miles of rehabilitation work. Contractors did resurfacing work on an additional 3.3 lane miles.

The city reported that eight percent of its lane miles were rated 85 or above on its most recent street pavement condition rating. This rating was done by in-house staff using the Institute for Transportation Research and Education (ITRE) system.

The number of potholes reported for the year was 4,974. The percentage of potholes repaired within twenty-four hours was approximately 95 percent.

The city has a permitting system for any utility cuts that must be made either by city or contractor crews. A total of 1,443 utility cuts were repaired during the year.

Conditions Affecting Service, Performance, and Costs

Due to the somewhat harsher mountain weather in Asheville compared to the other benchmarking partners, problems with pavement, such as potholes, tend to be more common.

Municipal Profile

Population (OSBM 2018)	93,621
Land Area (Square Miles)	45.53
Persons per Square Mile	2,056
Topography	Hill, mountains
Climate	Moderate; ice and snow

Service Profile

FTE Positions—Crews	15.00
FTE Positions—Other	2.09
Lane Miles Maintained	805.0
Lane Miles Treated	
Preservation	0.0
Resurfacing	3.3
Rehabilitation	2.5
TOTAL	5.8
Total Costs for All Treatment Types	$2,542,552
Potholes Repaired	4,974
Number of Utility Cuts	1,443
Number of Maintenance Patches (exclusive of potholes and utility cuts)	18
Average Cost per Ton of Hot Asphalt during Year	$85.59

Full Cost Profile

Cost Breakdown by Percentage	
Personal Services	24.4%
Operating Costs	64.1%
Capital Costs	11.5%
TOTAL	100.0%
Cost Breakdown in Dollars	
Personal Services	$1,475,514
Operating Costs	$3,876,865
Capital Costs	$697,479
TOTAL	$6,049,858

Asheville

Asphalt Maintenance and Repair

Key: Asheville   Benchmarking Average —   Fiscal Years 2015 through 2019

Resource Measures

Asphalt Maintenance and Repair Services Costs per Capita

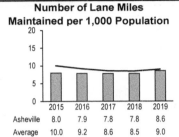

	2015	2016	2017	2018	2019
Asheville	$52.27	$58.07	$58.17	$94.25	$64.62
Average	$30.39	$29.75	$44.80	$50.06	$53.59

Asphalt Maintenance and Repair FTEs per 10,000 Population

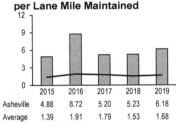

	2015	2016	2017	2018	2019
Asheville	1.91	1.88	1.86	1.86	1.82
Average	1.52	1.49	1.53	1.53	1.71

Service Costs per Lane Mile of Road Maintained

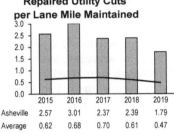

	2015	2016	2017	2018	2019
Asheville	$6,540	$7,390	$7,477	$12,098	$7,515
Average	$3,593	$3,700	$5,949	$6,793	$6,500

Workload Measures

Number of Lane Miles Maintained per 1,000 Population

	2015	2016	2017	2018	2019
Asheville	8.0	7.9	7.8	7.8	8.6
Average	10.0	9.2	8.6	8.5	9.0

Reported Potholes per Lane Mile Maintained

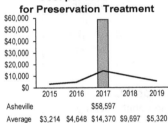

	2015	2016	2017	2018	2019
Asheville	4.88	8.72	5.20	5.23	6.18
Average	1.39	1.91	1.79	1.53	1.68

Repaired Utility Cuts per Lane Mile Maintained

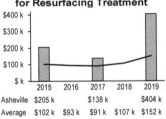

	2015	2016	2017	2018	2019
Asheville	2.57	3.01	2.37	2.39	1.79
Average	0.62	0.68	0.70	0.61	0.47

Efficiency Measures

Cost of Maintenance per Lane Mile Maintained

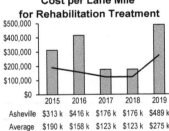

	2015	2016	2017	2018	2019
Asheville	$4,635	$4,664	$4,082	$3,828	$4,357
Average	$1,877	$1,970	$2,700	$2,809	$2,791

Cost per Lane Mile for Preservation Treatment

	2015	2016	2017	2018	2019
Asheville			$58,597		
Average	$3,214	$4,648	$14,370	$9,697	$5,320

Cost per Lane Mile for Resurfacing Treatment

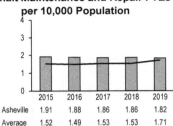

	2015	2016	2017	2018	2019
Asheville	$205 k		$138 k		$404 k
Average	$102 k	$93 k	$91 k	$107 k	$152 k

Cost per Lane Mile for Rehabilitation Treatment

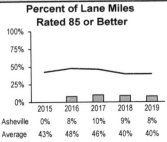

	2015	2016	2017	2018	2019
Asheville	$313 k	$416 k	$176 k	$176 k	$489 k
Average	$190 k	$158 k	$123 k	$123 k	$275 k

Cost per Ton for Contract Resurfacing

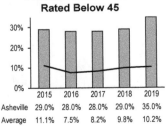

	2015	2016	2017	2018	2019
Asheville	$48	$206	$197	$227	$429
Average	$86	$132	$129	$152	$192

Effectiveness Measures

Percent of Lane Miles Rated 85 or Better

	2015	2016	2017	2018	2019
Asheville	0%	8%	10%	9%	8%
Average	43%	48%	46%	40%	40%

Percent of Lane Miles Rated Below 45

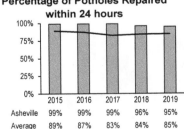

	2015	2016	2017	2018	2019
Asheville	29.0%	28.0%	28.0%	29.0%	35.0%
Average	11.1%	7.5%	8.2%	9.8%	10.2%

Percentage of Potholes Repaired within 24 hours

	2015	2016	2017	2018	2019
Asheville	99%	99%	99%	96%	95%
Average	89%	87%	83%	84%	85%

Chapel Hill

Asphalt Maintenance

Fiscal Year 2018–19

Explanatory Information

Service Level and Delivery

Asphalt maintenance is performed by the Town of Chapel Hill Streets and Construction Services Division of the Public Works Department. The Town provides services in asphalt maintenance, sidewalk maintenance, storm debris cleanup, gravel road maintenance, snow and ice removal, and cleanup following special events. During the fiscal year the town was responsible for maintaining approximately 333 lane miles. During the year 10.4 lane miles were treated or about 3.1 percent of total lane miles.

Contract crews did rehabilitation work on 10.4 lane miles during the year.

The town reported that 43.6 percent of its lane miles rated 85 or above on its most recent pavement condition rating conducted in 2018. The roads were rated by US Infrastructure of Carolina using the system relying on the Institute for Transportation Research and Education (ITRE) degradation curves.

The number of potholes reported for the year was ninety-six. Permit holders repaired thirty-four utility cuts during the year. A permit is required for any non-town entity cutting inside the right-of-way. The permit holder is responsible for all repairs. Because one permit can involve multiple cuts, the actual number of cuts is higher than the number listed. The streets inspector monitors the work and bills the responsible party. The Public Works Engineering Division inspects larger projects involving a water or sewer line replacement.

Conditions Affecting Service, Performance, and Costs

The Town of Chapel Hill began participation in the benchmarking project in July 2015, with FY 2014–15 being the first reporting year.

Though the FY 2015–16 Chapel Hill budget included $585,222 for annual resurfacing work, this funding was encumbered and carried forward into FY 2016–17 and was not reflected in the costs for this service area for that report year. A total of 5.5 lane miles were resurfaced using FY 2015–16 funds but at the beginning of FY 2016–17. These costs were reported in that year.

The town experienced two significant snow storms in the FY 2017–18 fiscal year which impacted operations and funding.

Municipal Profile

Population (OSBM 2018)	63,178
Land Area (Square Miles)	21.27
Persons per Square Mile	2,971
Topography	Flat; gently rolling
Climate	Temperate; little ice and snow

Service Profile

FTE Positions—Crews	5.20
FTE Positions—Other	1.50
Lane Miles Maintained	333.4
Lane Miles Treated	
Preservation	0.0
Resurfacing	0.0
Rehabilitation	10.4
TOTAL	10.4
Total Costs for All Treatment Types	$1,479,595
Potholes Repaired	96
Number of Utility Cuts	34
Number of Maintenance Patches (exclusive of potholes and utility cuts)	NA
Average Cost per Ton of Hot Asphalt during Year	$59.00

Full Cost Profile

Cost Breakdown by Percentage	
Personal Services	16.3%
Operating Costs	74.6%
Capital Costs	9.1%
TOTAL	100.0%

Cost Breakdown in Dollars	
Personal Services	$483,131
Operating Costs	$2,209,806
Capital Costs	$270,934
TOTAL	$2,963,871

Asphalt Maintenance and Repair

Resource Measures

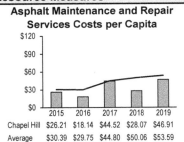

Asphalt Maintenance and Repair Services Costs per Capita

	2015	2016	2017	2018	2019
Chapel Hill	$26.21	$18.14	$44.52	$28.07	$46.91
Average	$30.39	$29.75	$44.80	$50.06	$53.59

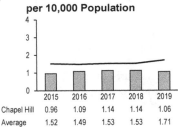

Asphalt Maintenance and Repair FTEs per 10,000 Population

	2015	2016	2017	2018	2019
Chapel Hill	0.96	1.09	1.14	1.14	1.06
Average	1.52	1.49	1.53	1.53	1.71

Service Costs per Lane Mile of Road Maintained

	2015	2016	2017	2018	2019
Chapel Hill	$4,615	$3,242	$7,992	$5,044	$8,890
Average	$3,593	$3,700	$5,949	$6,793	$6,500

Workload Measures

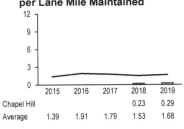

Number of Lane Miles Maintained per 1,000 Population

	2015	2016	2017	2018	2019
Chapel Hill	5.7	5.6	5.6	5.6	5.3
Average	10.0	9.2	8.6	8.5	9.0

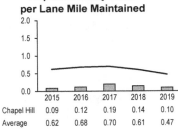

Reported Potholes per Lane Mile Maintained

	2015	2016	2017	2018	2019
Chapel Hill				0.23	0.29
Average	1.39	1.91	1.79	1.53	1.68

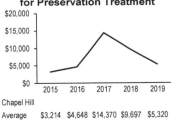

Repaired Utility Cuts per Lane Mile Maintained

	2015	2016	2017	2018	2019
Chapel Hill	0.09	0.12	0.19	0.14	0.10
Average	0.62	0.68	0.70	0.61	0.47

Efficiency Measures

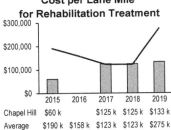

Cost of Maintenance per Lane Mile Maintained

	2015	2016	2017	2018	2019
Chapel Hill	$2,886	$3,242	$3,479	$3,282	$4,452
Average	$1,877	$1,970	$2,700	$2,809	$2,791

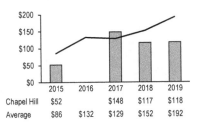

Cost per Lane Mile for Preservation Treatment

	2015	2016	2017	2018	2019
Chapel Hill					
Average	$3,214	$4,648	$14,370	$9,697	$5,320

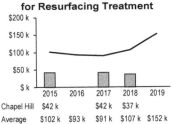

Cost per Lane Mile for Resurfacing Treatment

	2015	2016	2017	2018	2019
Chapel Hill	$42 k		$42 k	$37 k	
Average	$102 k	$93 k	$91 k	$107 k	$152 k

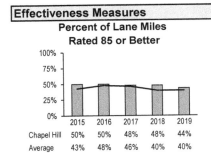

Cost per Lane Mile for Rehabilitation Treatment

	2015	2016	2017	2018	2019
Chapel Hill	$60 k		$125 k	$125 k	$133 k
Average	$190 k	$158 k	$123 k	$123 k	$275 k

Cost per Ton for Contract Resurfacing

	2015	2016	2017	2018	2019
Chapel Hill	$52		$148	$117	$118
Average	$86	$132	$129	$152	$192

Effectiveness Measures

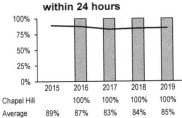

Percent of Lane Miles Rated 85 or Better

	2015	2016	2017	2018	2019
Chapel Hill	50%	50%	48%	48%	44%
Average	43%	48%	46%	40%	40%

Percent of Lane Miles Rated Below 45

	2015	2016	2017	2018	2019
Chapel Hill	6.0%	6.0%	11.0%	11.0%	13.9%
Average	11.1%	7.5%	8.2%	9.8%	10.2%

Percentage of Potholes Repaired within 24 hours

	2015	2016	2017	2018	2019
Chapel Hill		100%	100%	100%	100%
Average	89%	87%	83%	84%	85%

Charlotte

Asphalt Maintenance

Fiscal Year 2018–19

Explanatory Information

Service Level and Delivery

The City of Charlotte Street Maintenance Division provides service in the areas of maintenance and repair of street drainage structures; sidewalks; storm debris cleanup; and specialty repair items, such as brick walls, decorative pavers, fences, and guardrails. During the fiscal year, the city was responsible for maintaining approximately 5,415 lane miles and treated 159.4 lane miles, equating to approximately 2.9 percent of total lane miles.

Of the treatment work done during the year, 0.63 lane miles received preservation work, completed by city crews, such as crack sealing or thin overlays. Resurfacing work covered 0.52 lane miles and was done by contractors. Additionally, 146.37 lane miles were rehabilitated by contractors with milling followed by resurfacing. City crews completed a further 11.9 lane miles of rehabilitation work as well.

The city reported that 40.81 percent of its lane miles rated 85 or above on its most recent pavement condition rating conducted in 2019.

The number of potholes reported for the fiscal year was 2,889. The percentage of potholes repaired within twenty-four hours was 45 percent. A total of 1,351 utility cuts was also repaired during the year by contractors and the Street Maintenance Division.

Conditions Affecting Service, Performance, and Costs

Charlotte did not participate in the Benchmarking Project during FY 2014–15. No data are available for that year.

Municipal Profile

Population (OSBM 2018)	852,992
Land Area (Square Miles)	306.31
Persons per Square Mile	2,785
Topography	Flat; gently rolling
Climate	Temperate; little ice and snow

Service Profile

FTE Positions—Crews	104.00
FTE Positions—Other	18.00
Lane Miles Maintained	5,414.6
Lane Miles Treated	
Preservation	0.6
Resurfacing	0.5
Rehabilitation	158.3
TOTAL	159.4
Total Costs for All Treatment Types	$12,531,773
Potholes Repaired	2,889
Number of Utility Cuts	1,351
Number of Maintenance Patches (exclusive of potholes and utility cuts)	NA
	50
Average Cost per Ton of Hot Asphalt during Year	$45.05

Full Cost Profile

Cost Breakdown by Percentage	
Personal Services	25.2%
Operating Costs	62.7%
Capital Costs	12.1%
TOTAL	100.0%
Cost Breakdown in Dollars	
Personal Services	$7,540,835
Operating Costs	$18,738,364
Capital Costs	$3,620,378
TOTAL	$29,899,577

Asphalt Maintenance and Repair

Key: Charlotte ▨   Benchmarking Average —   Fiscal Years 2015 through 2019

Resource Measures

Asphalt Maintenance and Repair Services Costs per Capita

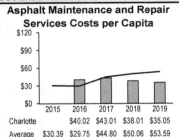

	2015	2016	2017	2018	2019
Charlotte		$40.02	$43.01	$38.01	$35.05
Average	$30.39	$29.75	$44.80	$50.06	$53.59

Asphalt Maintenance and Repair FTEs per 10,000 Population

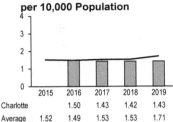

	2015	2016	2017	2018	2019
Charlotte		1.50	1.43	1.42	1.43
Average	1.52	1.49	1.53	1.53	1.71

Service Costs per Lane Mile of Road Maintained

	2015	2016	2017	2018	2019
Charlotte		$6,199	$6,709	$5,982	$5,522
Average	$3,593	$3,700	$5,949	$6,793	$6,500

Workload Measures

Number of Lane Miles Maintained per 1,000 Population

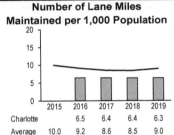

	2015	2016	2017	2018	2019
Charlotte		6.5	6.4	6.4	6.3
Average	10.0	9.2	8.6	8.5	9.0

Reported Potholes per Lane Mile Maintained

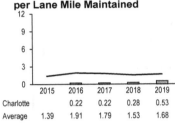

	2015	2016	2017	2018	2019
Charlotte		0.22	0.22	0.28	0.53
Average	1.39	1.91	1.79	1.53	1.68

Repaired Utility Cuts per Lane Mile Maintained

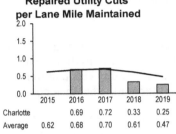

	2015	2016	2017	2018	2019
Charlotte		0.69	0.72	0.33	0.25
Average	0.62	0.68	0.70	0.61	0.47

Efficiency Measures

Cost of Maintenance per Lane Mile Maintained

	2015	2016	2017	2018	2019
Charlotte		$3,237	$3,273	$3,317	$3,208
Average	$1,877	$1,970	$2,700	$2,809	$2,791

Cost per Lane Mile for Preservation Treatment

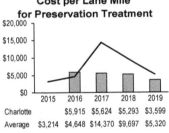

	2015	2016	2017	2018	2019
Charlotte		$5,915	$5,624	$5,293	$3,599
Average	$3,214	$4,648	$14,370	$9,697	$5,320

Cost per Lane Mile for Resurfacing Treatment

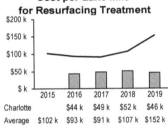

	2015	2016	2017	2018	2019
Charlotte		$44 k	$49 k	$52 k	$46 k
Average	$102 k	$93 k	$91 k	$107 k	$152 k

Cost per Lane Mile for Rehabilitation Treatment

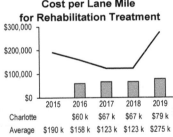

	2015	2016	2017	2018	2019
Charlotte		$60 k	$67 k	$67 k	$79 k
Average	$190 k	$158 k	$123 k	$123 k	$275 k

Cost per Ton for Contract Resurfacing

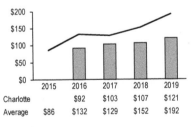

	2015	2016	2017	2018	2019
Charlotte		$92	$103	$107	$121
Average	$86	$132	$129	$152	$192

Effectiveness Measures

Percent of Lane Miles Rated 85 or Better

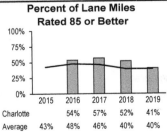

	2015	2016	2017	2018	2019
Charlotte		54%	57%	52%	41%
Average	43%	48%	46%	40%	40%

Percent of Lane Miles Rated Below 45

	2015	2016	2017	2018	2019
Charlotte		0.9%	0.5%	0.8%	0.2%
Average	11.1%	7.5%	8.2%	9.8%	10.2%

Percentage of Potholes Repaired within 24 hours

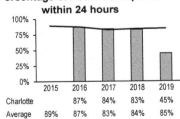

	2015	2016	2017	2018	2019
Charlotte		87%	84%	83%	45%
Average	89%	87%	83%	84%	85%

Service Level and Delivery
The City of Concord was responsible for maintaining approximately 712 lane miles during the fiscal year. A total of 24.9 lane miles was treated during the year or about 3.5 percent of the total.

Contractors resurfaced 24.92 lane miles.

The city reported that 46.6 percent of its lane miles rated 85 or above on its most recent pavement condition rating, conducted in 2017 using a city system based on North Carolina Department of Transportation ratings.

The number of potholes reported for the year was 162, including those reported by citizens and the city. The percentage of potholes repaired within twenty-four hours was 100 percent. Concord also reported 291 utility cuts that were repaired and 135 maintenance patches for work other than potholes or utility cuts.

Conditions Affecting Service, Performance, and Costs
The costs associated with asphalt maintenance and resurfacing are influenced by competition among providers due to the location of three asphalt plants within the city limits.

Municipal Profile

Population (OSBM 2018)	92,568
Land Area (Square Miles)	62.80
Persons per Square Mile	1,474
Topography	Flat; gently rolling
Climate	Temperate; little ice and snow

Service Profile

FTE Positions—Crews	10.75
FTE Positions—Other	1.55
Lane Miles Maintained	711.6
Lane Miles Treated	
Preservation	0.0
Resurfacing	24.9
Rehabilitation	0.0
TOTAL	24.9
Total Costs for All Treatment Types	$2,375,024
Potholes Repaired	162
Number of Utility Cuts	291
Number of Maintenance Patches (exclusive of potholes and utility cuts)	135
Average Cost per Ton of Hot Asphalt during Year	$67.00

Full Cost Profile

Cost Breakdown by Percentage	
Personal Services	20.2%
Operating Costs	74.6%
Capital Costs	5.2%
TOTAL	100.0%
Cost Breakdown in Dollars	
Personal Services	$760,331
Operating Costs	$2,812,995
Capital Costs	$197,386
TOTAL	$3,770,712

Resource Measures

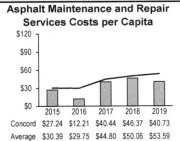

Asphalt Maintenance and Repair Services Costs per Capita

	2015	2016	2017	2018	2019
Concord	$27.24	$12.21	$40.44	$46.37	$40.73
Average	$30.39	$29.75	$44.80	$50.06	$53.59

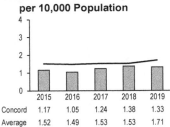

Asphalt Maintenance and Repair FTEs per 10,000 Population

	2015	2016	2017	2018	2019
Concord	1.17	1.05	1.24	1.38	1.33
Average	1.52	1.49	1.53	1.53	1.71

Service Costs per Lane Mile of Road Maintained

	2015	2016	2017	2018	2019
Concord	$3,331	$1,515	$5,046	$5,973	$5,299
Average	$3,593	$3,700	$5,949	$6,793	$6,500

Workload Measures

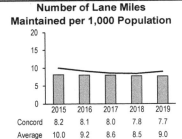

Number of Lane Miles Maintained per 1,000 Population

	2015	2016	2017	2018	2019
Concord	8.2	8.1	8.0	7.8	7.7
Average	10.0	9.2	8.6	8.5	9.0

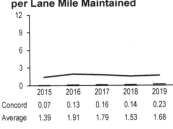

Reported Potholes per Lane Mile Maintained

	2015	2016	2017	2018	2019
Concord	0.07	0.13	0.16	0.14	0.23
Average	1.39	1.91	1.79	1.53	1.68

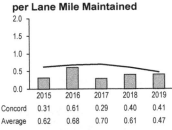

Repaired Utility Cuts per Lane Mile Maintained

	2015	2016	2017	2018	2019
Concord	0.31	0.61	0.29	0.40	0.41
Average	0.62	0.68	0.70	0.61	0.47

Efficiency Measures

Cost of Maintenance per Lane Mile Maintained

	2015	2016	2017	2018	2019
Concord	$1,620	$1,515	$1,740	$1,949	$1,961
Average	$1,877	$1,970	$2,700	$2,809	$2,791

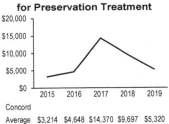

Cost per Lane Mile for Preservation Treatment

	2015	2016	2017	2018	2019
Concord					
Average	$3,214	$4,648	$14,370	$9,697	$5,320

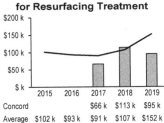

Cost per Lane Mile for Resurfacing Treatment

	2015	2016	2017	2018	2019
Concord			$66 k	$113 k	$95 k
Average	$102 k	$93 k	$91 k	$107 k	$152 k

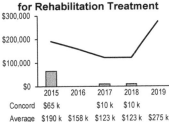

Cost per Lane Mile for Rehabilitation Treatment

	2015	2016	2017	2018	2019
Concord	$65 k		$10 k	$10 k	
Average	$190 k	$158 k	$123 k	$123 k	$275 k

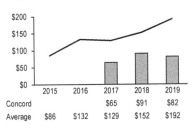

Cost per Ton for Contract Resurfacing

	2015	2016	2017	2018	2019
Concord			$65	$91	$82
Average	$86	$132	$129	$152	$192

Effectiveness Measures

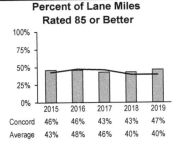

Percent of Lane Miles Rated 85 or Better

	2015	2016	2017	2018	2019
Concord	46%	46%	43%	43%	47%
Average	43%	48%	46%	40%	40%

Percent of Lane Miles Rated Below 45

	2015	2016	2017	2018	2019
Concord	9.0%	9.0%	5.0%	5.8%	7.0%
Average	11.1%	7.5%	8.2%	9.8%	10.2%

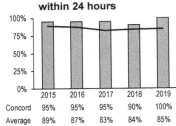

Percentage of Potholes Repaired within 24 hours

	2015	2016	2017	2018	2019
Concord	95%	95%	95%	90%	100%
Average	89%	87%	83%	84%	85%

Fiscal Year 2018–19

Explanatory Information

Service Level and Delivery

The City of Goldsboro was responsible for maintaining 325 lane miles during the fiscal year. Goldsboro treated a total of 21.4 lane miles during the year, equating to about 15.5 percent of total lane miles.

Of the treatment work done on Goldsboro's streets, all 21.36 lane miles received rehabilitation work done by contractors. Rehabiltation work requires milling work and is then followed by resurfacing.

The number of potholes reported for the year was 315. The percentage of potholes repaired within twenty-four hours was estimated at 98 percent. The city has one person driving around the city every day looking for potholes that need to be repaired and fixing them on the spot. A total of 135 utility cuts were also repaired, with city crews repairing water and sewer cuts reported by the city's Distribution and Collections Division.

Conditions Affecting Service, Performance, and Costs

The city of Goldsboro joined the Benchmarking Project in July 2017, with the first year of data showing for FY 2016–17.

Hurricane Matthew in October 2016 impacted asphalt work significantly. Crews were diverted to recovery efforts such as tree removal. Additionally, fifty-one sink holes developed over the year in roads due to storm water infrastructure failures under the asphalt surfaces.

The amount of street work done in FY 2017–18 was up significantly due the use of street bonds to fund the work.

Municipal Profile

Population (OSBM 2018)	33,636
Land Area (Square Miles)	29.41
Persons per Square Mile	1,144
Topography	Flat
Climate	Temperate; little ice and snow

Service Profile

FTE Positions—Crews	4.00
FTE Positions—Other	2.00
Lane Miles Maintained	324.7
Lane Miles Treated	
Preservation	0.0
Resurfacing	0.0
Rehabilitation	21.4
TOTAL	21.4
Total Costs for All Treatment Types	$2,627,358
Potholes Repaired	315
Number of Utility Cuts	135
Number of Maintenance Patches (exclusive of potholes and utility cuts)	NA
Average Cost per Ton of Hot Asphalt during Year	$72.50

Full Cost Profile

Cost Breakdown by Percentage	
Personal Services	8.3%
Operating Costs	91.7%
Capital Costs	0.0%
TOTAL	100.0%

Cost Breakdown in Dollars	
Personal Services	$257,222
Operating Costs	$2,851,845
Capital Costs	$0
TOTAL	$3,109,067

Key: Goldsboro ▪ Benchmarking Average — Fiscal Years 2015 through 2019

Resource Measures

Asphalt Maintenance and Repair Services Costs per Capita

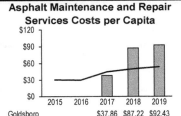

	2015	2016	2017	2018	2019
Goldsboro			$37.86	$87.22	$92.43
Average	$30.39	$29.75	$44.80	$50.06	$53.59

Asphalt Maintenance and Repair FTEs per 10,000 Population

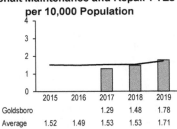

	2015	2016	2017	2018	2019
Goldsboro			1.29	1.48	1.78
Average	1.52	1.49	1.53	1.53	1.71

Service Costs per Lane Mile of Road Maintained

	2015	2016	2017	2018	2019
Goldsboro			$8,094	$18,072	$9,576
Average	$3,593	$3,700	$5,949	$6,793	$6,500

Workload Measures

Number of Lane Miles Maintained per 1,000 Population

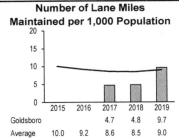

	2015	2016	2017	2018	2019
Goldsboro			4.7	4.8	9.7
Average	10.0	9.2	8.6	8.5	9.0

Reported Potholes per Lane Mile Maintained

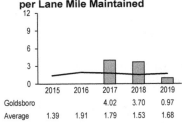

	2015	2016	2017	2018	2019
Goldsboro			4.02	3.70	0.97
Average	1.39	1.91	1.79	1.53	1.68

Repaired Utility Cuts per Lane Mile Maintained

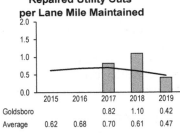

	2015	2016	2017	2018	2019
Goldsboro			0.82	1.10	0.42
Average	0.62	0.68	0.70	0.61	0.47

Efficiency Measures

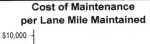

Cost of Maintenance per Lane Mile Maintained

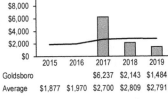

	2015	2016	2017	2018	2019
Goldsboro			$6,237	$2,143	$1,484
Average	$1,877	$1,970	$2,700	$2,809	$2,791

Cost per Lane Mile for Preservation Treatment

	2015	2016	2017	2018	2019
Goldsboro					
Average	$3,214	$4,648	$14,370	$9,697	$5,320

Cost per Lane Mile for Resurfacing Treatment

	2015	2016	2017	2018	2019
Goldsboro			$39 k	$103 k	
Average	$102 k	$93 k	$91 k	$107 k	$152 k

Cost per Lane Mile for Rehabilitation Treatment

	2015	2016	2017	2018	2019
Goldsboro			$47 k	$47 k	$123 k
Average	$190 k	$158 k	$123 k	$123 k	$275 k

Cost per Ton for Contract Resurfacing

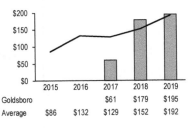

	2015	2016	2017	2018	2019
Goldsboro			$61	$179	$195
Average	$86	$132	$129	$152	$192

Effectiveness Measures

Percent of Lane Miles Rated 85 or Better

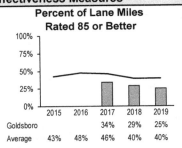

	2015	2016	2017	2018	2019
Goldsboro			34%	29%	25%
Average	43%	48%	46%	40%	40%

Percent of Lane Miles Rated Below 45

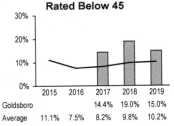

	2015	2016	2017	2018	2019
Goldsboro			14.4%	19.0%	15.0%
Average	11.1%	7.5%	8.2%	9.8%	10.2%

Percentage of Potholes Repaired within 24 hours

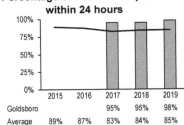

	2015	2016	2017	2018	2019
Goldsboro			95%	95%	98%
Average	89%	87%	83%	84%	85%

Greensboro

Asphalt Maintenance

Fiscal Year 2018–19

Explanatory Information

Service Level and Delivery

The City of Greensboro was responsible for maintaining 2,431 lane miles during the fiscal year. Greensboro treated a total of 94.5 lane miles during the year, equating to about 3.9 percent of total lane miles.

Of the treatment work done on Greensboro's streets, 27.5 of the lane miles had preservation work performed, such as crack sealing or thin overlays. All of this preservation work was done by city crews. Resurfacing work was done on 67.0 lane miles by contract crews.

The number of potholes reported for the year was 7,801. The percentage of potholes repaired within twenty-four hours was 63 percent. A total of 400 utility cuts were also repaired, with city crews repairing water and sewer cuts but private contractors repairing others after getting permits from the city. A further 103 maintenance patches were completed beyond potholes and utility cuts.

Conditions Affecting Service, Performance, and Costs

Changes in tracking software have improved the accuracy of potholes reported and asphalt used over time.

Municipal Profile

Population (OSBM 2018)	292,306
Land Area (Square Miles)	128.77
Persons per Square Mile	2,270
Topography	Flat; gently rolling
Climate	Temperate; little ice and snow

Service Profile

FTE Positions—Crews	45.00
FTE Positions—Other	6.00
Lane Miles Maintained	2,431.0
Lane Miles Treated	
Preservation	27.5
Resurfacing	67.0
Rehabilitation	0.0
TOTAL	94.5
Total Costs for All Treatment Types	$7,611,200
Potholes Repaired	7,801
Number of Utility Cuts	400
Number of Maintenance Patches (exclusive of potholes and utility cuts)	103
Average Cost per Ton of Hot Asphalt during Year	$68.29

Full Cost Profile

Cost Breakdown by Percentage	
Personal Services	19.9%
Operating Costs	80.1%
Capital Costs	0.0%
TOTAL	100.0%
Cost Breakdown in Dollars	
Personal Services	$2,622,463
Operating Costs	$10,582,063
Capital Costs	$0
TOTAL	$13,204,526

Greensboro

Key: Greensboro ▨   Benchmarking Average —   Fiscal Years 2015 through 2019

Resource Measures

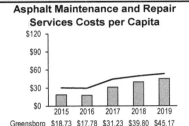

Asphalt Maintenance and Repair Services Costs per Capita

	2015	2016	2017	2018	2019
Greensboro	$18.73	$17.78	$31.23	$39.80	$45.17
Average	$30.39	$29.75	$44.80	$50.06	$53.59

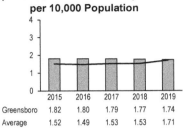

Asphalt Maintenance and Repair FTEs per 10,000 Population

	2015	2016	2017	2018	2019
Greensboro	1.82	1.80	1.79	1.77	1.74
Average	1.52	1.49	1.53	1.53	1.71

Service Costs per Lane Mile of Road Maintained

	2015	2016	2017	2018	2019
Greensboro	$1,447	$1,498	$3,652	$4,716	$5,432
Average	$3,593	$3,700	$5,949	$6,793	$6,500

Workload Measures

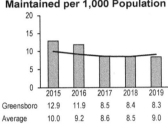

Number of Lane Miles Maintained per 1,000 Population

	2015	2016	2017	2018	2019
Greensboro	12.9	11.9	8.5	8.4	8.3
Average	10.0	9.2	8.6	8.5	9.0

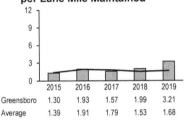

Reported Potholes per Lane Mile Maintained

	2015	2016	2017	2018	2019
Greensboro	1.30	1.93	1.57	1.99	3.21
Average	1.39	1.91	1.79	1.53	1.68

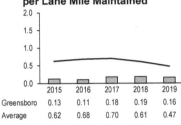

Repaired Utility Cuts per Lane Mile Maintained

	2015	2016	2017	2018	2019
Greensboro	0.13	0.11	0.18	0.19	0.16
Average	0.62	0.68	0.70	0.61	0.47

Efficiency Measures

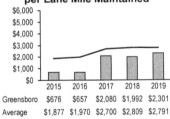

Cost of Maintenance per Lane Mile Maintained

	2015	2016	2017	2018	2019
Greensboro	$676	$657	$2,080	$1,992	$2,301
Average	$1,877	$1,970	$2,700	$2,809	$2,791

Cost per Lane Mile for Preservation Treatment

	2015	2016	2017	2018	2019
Greensboro	$2,560	$3,282	$2,148	$3,128	$4,044
Average	$3,214	$4,648	$14,370	$9,697	$5,320

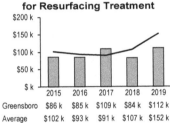

Cost per Lane Mile for Resurfacing Treatment

	2015	2016	2017	2018	2019
Greensboro	$86 k	$85 k	$109 k	$84 k	$112 k
Average	$102 k	$93 k	$91 k	$107 k	$152 k

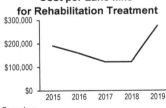

Cost per Lane Mile for Rehabilitation Treatment

	2015	2016	2017	2018	2019
Greensboro					
Average	$190 k	$158 k	$123 k	$123 k	$275 k

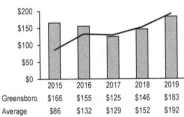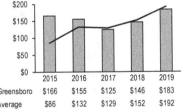

Cost per Ton for Contract Resurfacing

	2015	2016	2017	2018	2019
Greensboro	$166	$155	$125	$146	$183
Average	$86	$132	$129	$152	$192

Effectiveness Measures

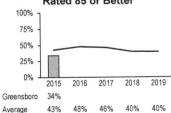

Percent of Lane Miles Rated 85 or Better

	2015	2016	2017	2018	2019
Greensboro	34%				
Average	43%	48%	46%	40%	40%

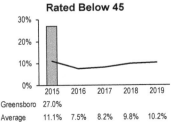

Percent of Lane Miles Rated Below 45

	2015	2016	2017	2018	2019
Greensboro	27.0%				
Average	11.1%	7.5%	8.2%	9.8%	10.2%

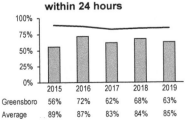

Percentage of Potholes Repaired within 24 hours

	2015	2016	2017	2018	2019
Greensboro	56%	72%	62%	68%	63%
Average	89%	87%	83%	84%	85%

Fiscal Year 2018–19

Explanatory Information

Service Level and Delivery
The City of Greenville was responsible for maintaining approximately 683 lane miles during the fiscal year. During the year, Greenville reported that 31.3 lane miles were given rehabilitation treatment, which involves milling and resurfacing, equating to 4.6 percent of total lane miles.

Greenville reported that 63.1 percent of lane miles were rated 85 or better on its most recent pavement condition rating, conducted in 2014 by a consultant.

Conditions Affecting Service, Performance, and Costs
Above average rainfall and extreme temperatures during the winter months has resulted in higher than normal numbers of pothole repairs and pavement failures.

Municipal Profile

Population (OSBM 2018)	89,790
Land Area (Square Miles)	35.58
Persons per Square Mile	2,523
Topography	Flat
Climate	Temperate; little ice and snow

Service Profile

FTE Positions—Crews	7.00
FTE Positions—Other	1.50
Lane Miles Maintained	682.7
Lane Miles Treated	
Preservation	0.0
Resurfacing	0.0
Rehabilitation	31.3
TOTAL	31.3
Total Costs for All Treatment Types	$4,315,854
Potholes Repaired	1,027
Number of Utility Cuts	333
	$105
Number of Maintenance Patches (exclusive of potholes and utility cuts)	136
Average Cost per Ton of Hot Asphalt during Year	$89.00

Full Cost Profile

Cost Breakdown by Percentage	
Personal Services	9.6%
Operating Costs	79.7%
Capital Costs	10.6%
TOTAL	100.0%
Cost Breakdown in Dollars	
Personal Services	$617,341
Operating Costs	$5,114,599
Capital Costs	$681,545
TOTAL	$6,413,485

Key: Greenville ▪   Benchmarking Average —   Fiscal Years 2015 through 2019

Resource Measures

Asphalt Maintenance and Repair Services Costs per Capita

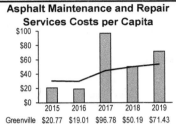

	2015	2016	2017	2018	2019
Greenville	$20.77	$19.01	$96.78	$50.19	$71.43
Average	$30.39	$29.75	$44.80	$50.06	$53.59

Asphalt Maintenance and Repair FTEs per 10,000 Population

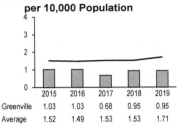

	2015	2016	2017	2018	2019
Greenville	1.03	1.03	0.68	0.95	0.95
Average	1.52	1.49	1.53	1.53	1.71

Service Costs per Lane Mile of Road Maintained

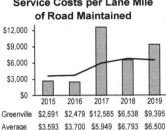

	2015	2016	2017	2018	2019
Greenville	$2,691	$2,479	$12,585	$6,538	$9,395
Average	$3,593	$3,700	$5,949	$6,793	$6,500

Workload Measures

Number of Lane Miles Maintained per 1,000 Population

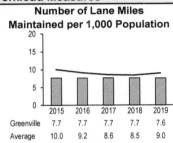

	2015	2016	2017	2018	2019
Greenville	7.7	7.7	7.7	7.7	7.6
Average	10.0	9.2	8.6	8.5	9.0

Reported Potholes per Lane Mile Maintained

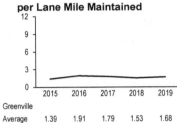

	2015	2016	2017	2018	2019
Greenville					
Average	1.39	1.91	1.79	1.53	1.68

Repaired Utility Cuts per Lane Mile Maintained

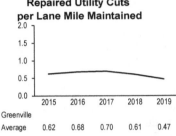

	2015	2016	2017	2018	2019
Greenville					
Average	0.62	0.68	0.70	0.61	0.47

Efficiency Measures

Cost of Maintenance per Lane Mile Maintained

	2015	2016	2017	2018	2019
Greenville	$960	$748	$1,353	$2,275	$3,073
Average	$1,877	$1,970	$2,700	$2,809	$2,791

Cost per Lane Mile for Preservation Treatment

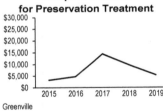

	2015	2016	2017	2018	2019
Greenville					
Average	$3,214	$4,648	$14,370	$9,697	$5,320

Cost per Lane Mile for Resurfacing Treatment

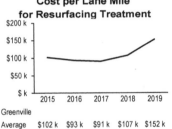

	2015	2016	2017	2018	2019
Greenville					
Average	$102 k	$93 k	$91 k	$107 k	$152 k

Cost per Lane Mile for Rehabilitation Treatment

	2015	2016	2017	2018	2019
Greenville	$68 k	$68 k	$177 k	$177 k	$138 k
Average	$190 k	$158 k	$123 k	$123 k	$275 k

Cost per Ton for Contract Resurfacing

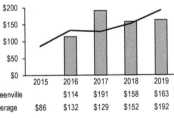
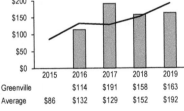

	2015	2016	2017	2018	2019
Greenville		$114	$191	$158	$163
Average	$86	$132	$129	$152	$192

Effectiveness Measures

Percent of Lane Miles Rated 85 or Better

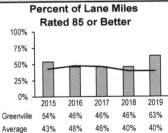

	2015	2016	2017	2018	2019
Greenville	54%	46%	46%	46%	63%
Average	43%	48%	46%	40%	40%

Percent of Lane Miles Rated Below 45

	2015	2016	2017	2018	2019
Greenville	1.1%	1.0%	1.0%	1.0%	0.6%
Average	11.1%	7.5%	8.2%	9.8%	10.2%

Percentage of Potholes Repaired within 24 hours

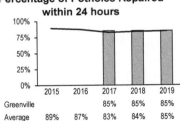

	2015	2016	2017	2018	2019
Greenville			85%	85%	85%
Average	89%	87%	83%	84%	85%

Fiscal Year 2018–19

Explanatory Information

Service Level and Delivery

The City of Hickory was responsible for maintaining approximately 721 lane miles during the fiscal year, including 238.8 lane miles of state roads. The city treated a total of nine lane miles with resurfacing, equating to 1.2 percent of total lane miles.

The city resurfaced nine lane miles using contractors.
The city reported that 29 percent of its lane miles rated 85 or above on its most recent pavement condition rating, conducted in 2017. The city used the Institute for Transportation Research and Education (ITRE) to conduct its rating system.

The number of potholes reported for the year was 339, including self-reported and citizen-reported potholes. The percentage of potholes repaired within twenty-four hours was 96 percent.

Conditions Affecting Service, Performance, and Costs

Wet winter weather during the fiscal year led to more potholes. A tornado during the prior year also affected service levels for three months during the cleanup phase after the storm.

Municipal Profile

Population (OSBM 2018)	40,932
Land Area (Square Miles)	29.92
Persons per Square Mile	1,368
Topography	Gently rolling
Climate	Temperate; some ice and snow

Service Profile

FTE Positions—Crews	6.00
FTE Positions—Other	1.00
Lane Miles Maintained	721.3
Lane Miles Treated	
Preservation	0.0
Resurfacing	9.0
Rehabilitation	0.0
TOTAL	9.0
Total Costs for All Treatment Types	$949,000
Potholes Repaired	339
Number of Utility Cuts	NA
Number of Maintenance Patches (exclusive of potholes and utility cuts)	NA
Average Cost per Ton of Hot Asphalt during Year	NA

Full Cost Profile

Cost Breakdown by Percentage	
Personal Services	15.2%
Operating Costs	82.9%
Capital Costs	1.9%
TOTAL	100.0%

Cost Breakdown in Dollars	
Personal Services	$270,894
Operating Costs	$1,480,492
Capital Costs	$34,356
TOTAL	$1,785,742

Hickory

Key: Hickory ▪   Benchmarking Average —   Fiscal Years 2015 through 2019

Resource Measures

Asphalt Maintenance and Repair Services Costs per Capita

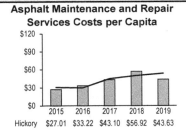

	2015	2016	2017	2018	2019
Hickory	$27.01	$33.22	$43.10	$56.92	$43.63
Average	$30.39	$29.75	$44.80	$50.06	$53.59

Asphalt Maintenance and Repair FTEs per 10,000 Population

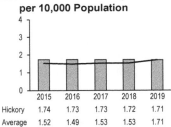

	2015	2016	2017	2018	2019
Hickory	1.74	1.73	1.73	1.72	1.71
Average	1.52	1.49	1.53	1.53	1.71

Service Costs per Lane Mile of Road Maintained

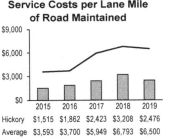

	2015	2016	2017	2018	2019
Hickory	$1,515	$1,862	$2,423	$3,208	$2,476
Average	$3,593	$3,700	$5,949	$6,793	$6,500

Workload Measures

Number of Lane Miles Maintained per 1,000 Population

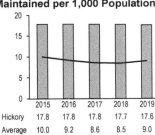

	2015	2016	2017	2018	2019
Hickory	17.8	17.8	17.8	17.7	17.6
Average	10.0	9.2	8.6	8.5	9.0

Reported Potholes per Lane Mile Maintained

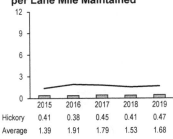

	2015	2016	2017	2018	2019
Hickory	0.41	0.38	0.45	0.41	0.47
Average	1.39	1.91	1.79	1.53	1.68

Repaired Utility Cuts per Lane Mile Maintained

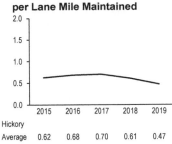

	2015	2016	2017	2018	2019
Hickory					
Average	0.62	0.68	0.70	0.61	0.47

Efficiency Measures

Cost of Maintenance per Lane Mile Maintained

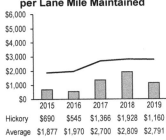

	2015	2016	2017	2018	2019
Hickory	$690	$545	$1,366	$1,928	$1,160
Average	$1,877	$1,970	$2,700	$2,809	$2,791

Cost per Lane Mile for Preservation Treatment

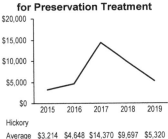

	2015	2016	2017	2018	2019
Hickory					
Average	$3,214	$4,648	$14,370	$9,697	$5,320

Cost per Lane Mile for Resurfacing Treatment

	2015	2016	2017	2018	2019
Hickory	$44 k	$53 k	$44 k	$52 k	$105 k
Average	$102 k	$93 k	$91 k	$107 k	$152 k

Cost per Lane Mile for Rehabilitation Treatment

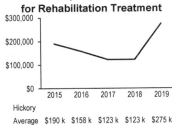

	2015	2016	2017	2018	2019
Hickory					
Average	$190 k	$158 k	$123 k	$123 k	$275 k

Cost per Ton for Contract Resurfacing

	2015	2016	2017	2018	2019
Hickory	$77	$92	$77	$90	$182
Average	$86	$132	$129	$152	$192

Effectiveness Measures

Percent of Lane Miles Rated 85 or Better

	2015	2016	2017	2018	2019
Hickory	38%	39%	37%	27%	29%
Average	43%	48%	46%	40%	40%

Percent of Lane Miles Rated Below 45

	2015	2016	2017	2018	2019
Hickory	7.0%	7.0%	12.0%	14.0%	13.0%
Average	11.1%	7.5%	8.2%	9.8%	10.2%

Percentage of Potholes Repaired within 24 hours

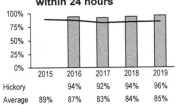

	2015	2016	2017	2018	2019
Hickory		94%	92%	94%	96%
Average	89%	87%	83%	84%	85%

Mooresville

Asphalt Maintenance

Fiscal Year 2018–19

Explanatory Information

Service Level and Delivery

Road work is done by the Streets Division of the Public Works Department in Mooresville. The town was responsible for 304 lane miles. During the year, contract crews rehabilitated 11.8 lane miles, which is about 3.9 percent of total lane miles maintained. Rehabilitation involves milling before resurfacing.

The town reported that 35 percent of its lane miles rated 85 or above on its most recent pavement condition rating, conducted in 2016. The town used a consultant for the rating.

The number of potholes reported for the year was 168. The percentage of potholes repaired within twenty-four hours was not available. A total of ninety cuts were also made, with the city repairing all of these. Additionally, eighty maintenance patches were done, which are not included in the pothole or utility cut numbers.

Conditions Affecting Service, Performance, and Costs

Mooresville joined the Benchmarking project in July 2018, with the first year of data showing for FY2017–18.

Municipal Profile

Population (OSBM 2018)	41,255
Land Area (Square Miles)	22.75
Persons per Square Mile	1,813
Topography	Flat; gently rolling
Climate	Temperate; little ice and snow

Service Profile

FTE Positions—Crews	19.00
FTE Positions—Other	2.00
Lane Miles Maintained	304.0
Lane Miles Treated	
Preservation	0.0
Resurfacing	0.0
Rehabilitation	11.8
TOTAL	11.8
Total Costs for All Treatment Types	$1,257,602
Potholes Repaired	168
Number of Utility Cuts	90
Number of Maintenance Patches (exclusive of potholes and utility cuts)	80
Average Cost per Ton of Hot Asphalt during Year	$95.00

Full Cost Profile

Cost Breakdown by Percentage	
Personal Services	16.3%
Operating Costs	76.0%
Capital Costs	7.8%
TOTAL	100.0%
Cost Breakdown in Dollars	
Personal Services	$454,525
Operating Costs	$2,124,255
Capital Costs	$217,537
TOTAL	$2,796,317

Key: Mooresville   Benchmarking Average —   Fiscal Years 2015 through 2019

Resource Measures

Asphalt Maintenance and Repair Services Costs per Capita

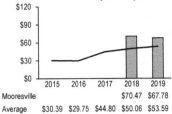

	2015	2016	2017	2018	2019
Mooresville				$70.47	$67.78
Average	$30.39	$29.75	$44.80	$50.06	$53.59

Asphalt Maintenance and Repair FTEs per 10,000 Population

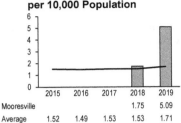

	2015	2016	2017	2018	2019
Mooresville				1.75	5.09
Average	1.52	1.49	1.53	1.53	1.71

Service Costs per Lane Mile of Road Maintained

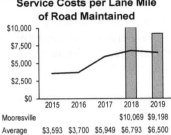

	2015	2016	2017	2018	2019
Mooresville				$10,069	$9,198
Average	$3,593	$3,700	$5,949	$6,793	$6,500

Workload Measures

Number of Lane Miles Maintained per 1,000 Population

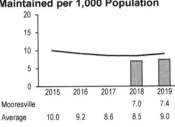

	2015	2016	2017	2018	2019
Mooresville				7.0	7.4
Average	10.0	9.2	8.6	8.5	9.0

Reported Potholes per Lane Mile Maintained

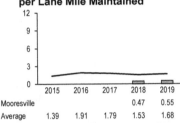

	2015	2016	2017	2018	2019
Mooresville				0.47	0.55
Average	1.39	1.91	1.79	1.53	1.68

Repaired Utility Cuts per Lane Mile Maintained

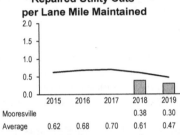

	2015	2016	2017	2018	2019
Mooresville				0.38	0.30
Average	0.62	0.68	0.70	0.61	0.47

Efficiency Measures

Cost of Maintenance per Lane Mile Maintained

	2015	2016	2017	2018	2019
Mooresville				$6,380	$5,062
Average	$1,877	$1,970	$2,700	$2,809	$2,791

Cost per Lane Mile for Preservation Treatment

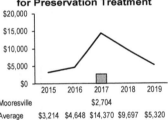

	2015	2016	2017	2018	2019
Mooresville			$2,704		
Average	$3,214	$4,648	$14,370	$9,697	$5,320

Cost per Lane Mile for Resurfacing Treatment

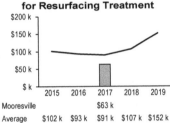

	2015	2016	2017	2018	2019
Mooresville			$63 k		
Average	$102 k	$93 k	$91 k	$107 k	$152 k

Cost per Lane Mile for Rehabilitation Treatment

	2015	2016	2017	2018	2019
Mooresville					$107 k
Average	$190 k	$158 k	$123 k	$123 k	$275 k

Cost per Ton for Contract Resurfacing

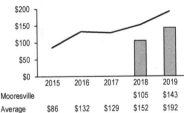
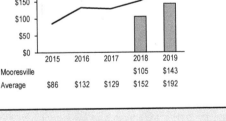

	2015	2016	2017	2018	2019
Mooresville				$105	$143
Average	$86	$132	$129	$152	$192

Effectiveness Measures

Percent of Lane Miles Rated 85 or Better

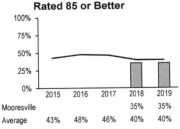

	2015	2016	2017	2018	2019
Mooresville				35%	35%
Average	43%	48%	46%	40%	40%

Percent of Lane Miles Rated Below 45

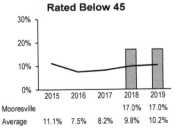

	2015	2016	2017	2018	2019
Mooresville				17.0%	17.0%
Average	11.1%	7.5%	8.2%	9.8%	10.2%

Percentage of Potholes Repaired within 24 hours

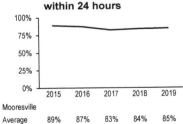

	2015	2016	2017	2018	2019
Mooresville					
Average	89%	87%	83%	84%	85%

Raleigh
Asphalt Maintenance

Fiscal Year 2018–19

Explanatory Information

Service Level and Delivery

The City of Raleigh's Department of Transportation is responsible for for street maintenance. During the year the city was responsible for maintaining approximately 2,317 lane miles.

The city used contractors to resurface 32.0 lane miles (1.4 percent of total lane miles).

The city reported that 64 percent of its lane miles rated 85 or above on its most recent pavement condition rating, conducted in 2018. The city used city staff conducting a windshield survey following the Institute for Transportation Research and Education (ITRE) rating system.

The number of potholes reported for the year was 5,157. A total of 1,278 utility cuts were also made, with the city repairing all of these. Additionally, 343 maintenance patches were completed, which are exclusive of potholes and utility cut repairs.

Conditions Affecting Service, Performance, and Costs

Raleigh rejoined the Benchmarking Project in July 2016, with the first year of data showing for FY 2015–16.

Municipal Profile

Population (OSBM 2018)	464,453
Land Area (Square Miles)	145.65
Persons per Square Mile	3,189
Topography	Flat; gently rolling
Climate	Temperate; little ice and snow

Service Profile

FTE Positions—Crews	33.00
FTE Positions—Other	8.00
Lane Miles Maintained	2,317.0
Lane Miles Treated	
Preservation	0.0
Resurfacing	32.0
Rehabilitation	0.0
TOTAL	32.0
Total Costs for All Treatment Types	$6,768,651
Potholes Repaired	5,157
Number of Utility Cuts	1,278
Number of Maintenance Patches (exclusive of potholes and utility cuts)	343
Average Cost per Ton of Hot Asphalt during Year	$56.00

Full Cost Profile

Cost Breakdown by Percentage	
Personal Services	18.8%
Operating Costs	68.1%
Capital Costs	13.1%
TOTAL	100.0%
Cost Breakdown in Dollars	
Personal Services	$3,239,730
Operating Costs	$11,733,722
Capital Costs	$2,247,505
TOTAL	$17,220,957

Raleigh

Asphalt Maintenance and Repair

Key: Raleigh ▨   Benchmarking Average —   Fiscal Years 2015 through 2019

Resource Measures

Asphalt Maintenance and Repair Services Costs per Capita

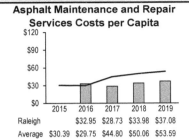

	2015	2016	2017	2018	2019
Raleigh		$32.95	$28.73	$33.98	$37.08
Average	$30.39	$29.75	$44.80	$50.06	$53.59

Asphalt Maintenance and Repair FTEs per 10,000 Population

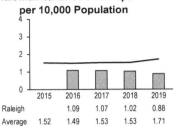

	2015	2016	2017	2018	2019
Raleigh		1.09	1.07	1.02	0.88
Average	1.52	1.49	1.53	1.53	1.71

Service Costs per Lane Mile of Road Maintained

	2015	2016	2017	2018	2019
Raleigh		$6,180	$5,621	$6,656	$7,432
Average	$3,593	$3,700	$5,949	$6,793	$6,500

Workload Measures

Number of Lane Miles Maintained per 1,000 Population

	2015	2016	2017	2018	2019
Raleigh		5.3	5.1	5.1	5.0
Average	10.0	9.2	8.6	8.5	9.0

Reported Potholes per Lane Mile Maintained

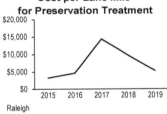

	2015	2016	2017	2018	2019
Raleigh		2.91	2.40	1.37	2.23
Average	1.39	1.91	1.79	1.53	1.68

Repaired Utility Cuts per Lane Mile Maintained

	2015	2016	2017	2018	2019
Raleigh		0.32	0.45	0.49	0.55
Average	0.62	0.68	0.70	0.61	0.47

Efficiency Measures

Cost of Maintenance per Lane Mile Maintained

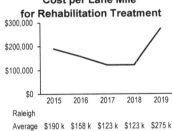

	2015	2016	2017	2018	2019
Raleigh		$3,030	$2,662	$3,603	$4,511
Average	$1,877	$1,970	$2,700	$2,809	$2,791

Cost per Lane Mile for Preservation Treatment

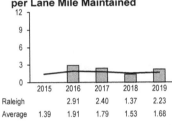

	2015	2016	2017	2018	2019
Raleigh					
Average	$3,214	$4,648	$14,370	$9,697	$5,320

Cost per Lane Mile for Resurfacing Treatment

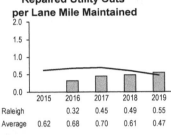

	2015	2016	2017	2018	2019
Raleigh		$206 k	$261 k	$295 k	$212 k
Average	$102 k	$93 k	$91 k	$107 k	$152 k

Cost per Lane Mile for Rehabilitation Treatment

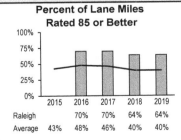

	2015	2016	2017	2018	2019
Raleigh					
Average	$190 k	$158 k	$123 k	$123 k	$275 k

Cost per Ton for Contract Resurfacing

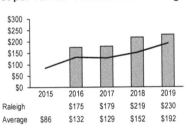

	2015	2016	2017	2018	2019
Raleigh		$175	$179	$219	$230
Average	$86	$132	$129	$152	$192

Effectiveness Measures

Percent of Lane Miles Rated 85 or Better

	2015	2016	2017	2018	2019
Raleigh		70%	70%	64%	64%
Average	43%	48%	46%	40%	40%

Percent of Lane Miles Rated Below 45

	2015	2016	2017	2018	2019
Raleigh		2.0%	2.0%	1.3%	1.3%
Average	11.1%	7.5%	8.2%	9.8%	10.2%

Percentage of Potholes Repaired within 24 hours

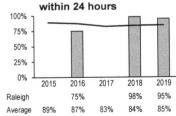

	2015	2016	2017	2018	2019
Raleigh		75%		98%	95%
Average	89%	87%	83%	84%	85%

Wilson

Asphalt Maintenance

Fiscal Year 2018–19

Explanatory Information

Service Level and Delivery
The City of Wilson was responsible for maintaining approximately 695 lane miles of city streets during the year. The city treated a total of 8.9 lane miles during the year, or 1.3 percent of the total lane miles maintained.

Contract crews treated 0.3 lane miles with rehabilitation. This project was a complete rebuild with extensive work needed. The road had no stone base requiring a cut of 6 inches of soil, replaced with aggregate and paved with 3 inches of asphalt. City crews performed preservation work on 8.6 lane miles. Preservation techniques include methods such as crack sealing or thin overlays.

The city reported that 47 percent of its lane miles rated 85 or above on its most recent pavement condition rating, conducted in 2018. The city relied on a consultant for the rating, who used a customized rating based on the Institute for Transportation Research and Education (ITRE) system.

The number of potholes reported for the year was 2,774. The percentage of potholes repaired within twenty-four hours was 90 percent. Repairs to 691 utility cuts were also made during the year.

Conditions Affecting Service, Performance, and Costs
The cost of asphalt and maintenance materials is directly related to fluctuations in the price of petroleum.

Municipal Profile

Population (OSBM 2018)	49,054
Land Area (Square Miles)	30.97
Persons per Square Mile	1,584
Topography	Flat
Climate	Temperate; little ice and snow

Service Profile

FTE Positions—Crews	5.00
FTE Positions—Other	0.50
Lane Miles Maintained	695.4
Lane Miles Treated	
Preservation	8.6
Resurfacing	0.0
Rehabilitation	0.3
TOTAL	8.9
Total Costs for All Treatment Types	$337,767
Potholes Repaired	2,774
Number of Utility Cuts	691
Number of Maintenance Patches (exclusive of potholes and utility cuts)	311
Average Cost per Ton of Hot Asphalt during Year	$79.24

Full Cost Profile

Cost Breakdown by Percentage	
Personal Services	25.7%
Operating Costs	67.5%
Capital Costs	6.7%
TOTAL	100.0%

Cost Breakdown in Dollars	
Personal Services	$419,949
Operating Costs	$1,102,651
Capital Costs	$109,750
TOTAL	$1,632,350

Asphalt Maintenance and Repair

Key: Wilson ▥   Benchmarking Average —   Fiscal Years 2015 through 2019

Resource Measures

Asphalt Maintenance and Repair Services Costs per Capita

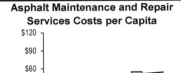

	2015	2016	2017	2018	2019
Wilson	$27.48	$28.44	$36.32	$54.57	$33.28
Average	$30.39	$29.75	$44.80	$50.06	$53.59

Asphalt Maintenance and Repair FTEs per 10,000 Population

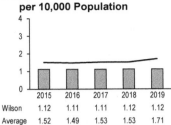

	2015	2016	2017	2018	2019
Wilson	1.12	1.11	1.11	1.12	1.12
Average	1.52	1.49	1.53	1.53	1.71

Service Costs per Lane Mile of Road Maintained

	2015	2016	2017	2018	2019
Wilson	$1,945	$2,019	$2,580	$3,859	$2,347
Average	$3,593	$3,700	$5,949	$6,793	$6,500

Workload Measures

Number of Lane Miles Maintained per 1,000 Population

	2015	2016	2017	2018	2019
Wilson	14.1	14.1	14.1	14.1	14.2
Average	10.0	9.2	8.6	8.5	9.0

Reported Potholes per Lane Mile Maintained

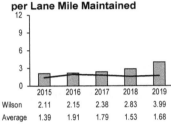

	2015	2016	2017	2018	2019
Wilson	2.11	2.15	2.38	2.83	3.99
Average	1.39	1.91	1.79	1.53	1.68

Repaired Utility Cuts per Lane Mile Maintained

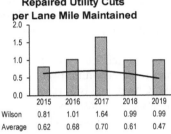

	2015	2016	2017	2018	2019
Wilson	0.81	1.01	1.64	0.99	0.99
Average	0.62	0.68	0.70	0.61	0.47

Efficiency Measures

Cost of Maintenance per Lane Mile Maintained

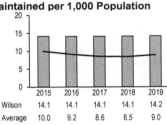

	2015	2016	2017	2018	2019
Wilson	$1,418	$1,548	$1,626	$2,404	$1,862
Average	$1,877	$1,970	$2,700	$2,809	$2,791

Cost per Lane Mile for Preservation Treatment

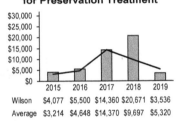

	2015	2016	2017	2018	2019
Wilson	$4,077	$5,500	$14,360	$20,671	$3,536
Average	$3,214	$4,648	$14,370	$9,697	$5,320

Cost per Lane Mile for Resurfacing Treatment

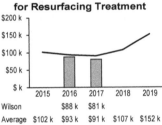

	2015	2016	2017	2018	2019
Wilson		$88 k	$81 k		
Average	$102 k	$93 k	$91 k	$107 k	$152 k

Cost per Lane Mile for Rehabilitation Treatment

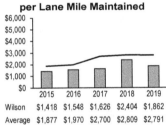

	2015	2016	2017	2018	2019
Wilson	$590 k				$1024 k
Average	$190 k	$158 k	$123 k	$123 k	$275 k

Cost per Ton for Contract Resurfacing

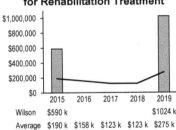

	2015	2016	2017	2018	2019
Wilson		$118	$113	$154	$272
Average	$86	$132	$129	$152	$192

Effectiveness Measures

Percent of Lane Miles Rated 85 or Better

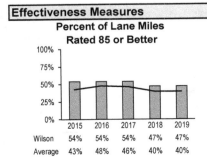

	2015	2016	2017	2018	2019
Wilson	54%	54%	54%	47%	47%
Average	43%	48%	46%	40%	40%

Percent of Lane Miles Rated Below 45

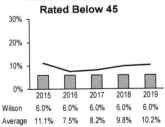

	2015	2016	2017	2018	2019
Wilson	6.0%	6.0%	6.0%	6.0%	6.0%
Average	11.1%	7.5%	8.2%	9.8%	10.2%

Percentage of Potholes Repaired within 24 hours

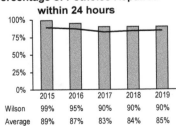

	2015	2016	2017	2018	2019
Wilson	99%	95%	90%	90%	90%
Average	89%	87%	83%	84%	85%

Winston-Salem

Asphalt Maintenance

Fiscal Year 2018–19

Explanatory Information

Service Level and Delivery

The City of Winston-Salem was responsible for maintaining approximately 2,805.5 lane miles of city streets during the fiscal year. The city treated 223 lane miles or approximately 7.9% of total lane miles for the city.

Contractors did 14 lane miles of preservation work and 208.91 lane miles of resurfacing, City crews did an additional 0.11 lane miles of resurfacing work as well.

The city reported that 48 percent of its lane miles rated 85 or above on its most recent pavement condition rating, conducted in 2018. The city used the Pavement Tracking System (PTS).

The city reported 3,696 potholes for the year. The percentage of potholes repaired within twenty-four hours was estimated at 67 percent. City policy is to repair potholes within twenty-four hours, but the lower response level is a result of calls on weekends and sick or vacation time of repair crews.

Conditions Affecting Service, Performance, and Costs

Winston-Salem's Department of Transportation had three major snow storm events and higher than normal rainfall for the fiscal year, which lowered road repair work and maintenance activities and expenses.

Municipal Profile

Population (OSBM 2018)	243,447
Land Area (Square Miles)	132.55
Persons per Square Mile	1,837
Topography	Gently rolling
Climate	Temperate; some ice and snow

Service Profile

FTE Positions—Crews	40.00
FTE Positions—Other	3.40
Lane Miles Maintained	2,805.5
Lane Miles Treated	
Preservation	14.0
Resurfacing	209.0
Rehabilitation	0.0
TOTAL	223.0
Total Costs for All Treatment Types	$19,296,242
Potholes Repaired	3,696
Number of Utility Cuts	262
Number of Maintenance Patches (exclusive of potholes and utility cuts)	8
Average Cost per Ton of Hot Asphalt during Year	$57.93

Full Cost Profile

Cost Breakdown by Percentage	
Personal Services	5.8%
Operating Costs	92.4%
Capital Costs	1.8%
TOTAL	100.0%
Cost Breakdown in Dollars	
Personal Services	$1,279,129
Operating Costs	$20,440,638
Capital Costs	$393,565
TOTAL	$22,113,332

Resource Measures

Asphalt Maintenance and Repair Services Costs per Capita

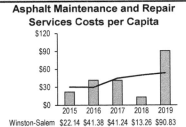

	2015	2016	2017	2018	2019
Winston-Salem	$22.14	$41.38	$41.24	$13.26	$90.83
Average	$30.39	$29.75	$44.80	$50.06	$53.59

Asphalt Maintenance and Repair FTEs per 10,000 Population

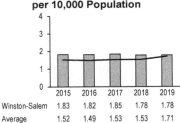

	2015	2016	2017	2018	2019
Winston-Salem	1.83	1.82	1.85	1.78	1.78
Average	1.52	1.49	1.53	1.53	1.71

Service Costs per Lane Mile of Road Maintained

	2015	2016	2017	2018	2019
Winston-Salem	$2,385	$4,455	$4,259	$1,382	$7,882
Average	$3,593	$3,700	$5,949	$6,793	$6,500

Workload Measures

Number of Lane Miles Maintained per 1,000 Population

	2015	2016	2017	2018	2019
Winston-Salem	9.3	9.3	9.7	9.6	11.5
Average	10.0	9.2	8.6	8.5	9.0

Reported Potholes per Lane Mile Maintained

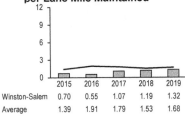

	2015	2016	2017	2018	2019
Winston-Salem	0.70	0.55	1.07	1.19	1.32
Average	1.39	1.91	1.79	1.53	1.68

Repaired Utility Cuts per Lane Mile Maintained

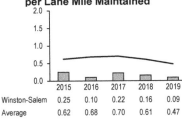

	2015	2016	2017	2018	2019
Winston-Salem	0.25	0.10	0.22	0.16	0.09
Average	0.62	0.68	0.70	0.61	0.47

Efficiency Measures

Cost of Maintenance per Lane Mile Maintained

	2015	2016	2017	2018	2019
Winston-Salem	$1,179	$652	$955	$1,363	$1,004
Average	$1,877	$1,970	$2,700	$2,809	$2,791

Cost per Lane Mile for Preservation Treatment

	2015	2016	2017	2018	2019
Winston-Salem	$3,004	$3,895	$2,791		$5,914
Average	$3,214	$4,648	$14,370	$9,697	$5,320

Cost per Lane Mile for Resurfacing Treatment

	2015	2016	2017	2018	2019
Winston-Salem	$131 k	$85 k	$105 k	$123 k	$92 k
Average	$102 k	$93 k	$91 k	$107 k	$152 k

Cost per Lane Mile for Rehabilitation Treatment

	2015	2016	2017	2018	2019
Winston-Salem	$95 k	$73 k	$71 k	$71 k	
Average	$190 k	$158 k	$123 k	$123 k	$275 k

Cost per Ton for Contract Resurfacing

	2015	2016	2017	2018	2019
Winston-Salem		$148	$92		$240
Average	$86	$132	$129	$152	$192

Effectiveness Measures

Percent of Lane Miles Rated 85 or Better

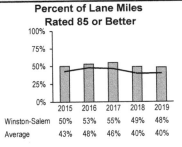

	2015	2016	2017	2018	2019
Winston-Salem	50%	53%	55%	49%	48%
Average	43%	48%	46%	40%	40%

Percent of Lane Miles Rated Below 45

	2015	2016	2017	2018	2019
Winston-Salem	9.0%	9.0%	5.0%	10.0%	11.0%
Average	11.1%	7.5%	8.2%	9.8%	10.2%

Percentage of Potholes Repaired within 24 hours

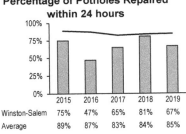

	2015	2016	2017	2018	2019
Winston-Salem	75%	47%	65%	81%	67%
Average	89%	87%	83%	84%	85%

Performance and Cost Data

FIRE SERVICES

PERFORMANCE MEASURES FOR FIRE SERVICES

SERVICE DEFINITION

Fire Services refers to activities and programs relating to the prevention and suppression of fires, responses to calls for service, rescue service (if provided), fire inspections (if provided), responses to hazardous materials calls (if provided), and fire education services. The services provided by fire departments vary from city to city, but the common goal remains the same: to protect the lives and property of the community served.

NOTES ON PERFORMANCE MEASURES

1. Number of Actual Fires per 1,000 Population

The total number of actual fires includes all types of fires, including structural fires.

2. Fire Inspections Completed per 1,000 Population

Fire inspections include Level I, II, and III inspections.

3. Number of Fire Department Responses per 1,000 Population

Responses include those to fires, medical emergencies, false alarms, and other types of situations that result in mobilization of fire equipment and personnel.

4. Cost per Fire Department Response

The cost represents the total cost of fire services and is calculated using a full cost accounting model that captures direct, indirect, and capital costs. Response is as defined above.

5. Number of Inspections Completed per Fire Inspector FTE

One full-time equivalent (FTE) position equals 2,080 hours of work per year. Any combination of employees providing 2,080 hours of work per year is counted as one FTE.

6. Average Turnout and Travel Time for First Unit Dispatched under "Priority One" Situations

Fast response is a critical determinant in how successful fire responders will be. Response time is calculated by adding both the turnout time (the time the dispatch is received until the first unit is out the door) and the travel time (the time the first unit is out the door until the unit arrives on the scene).

7. Percentage of Full Responses within Eight Minutes

The speed of fire department responses can be judged both by the time for the first unit arriving and also by how long it takes a full complement of trucks and personnel to respond to an emergency. The percentage within eight minutes takes into account travel time.

8. Percentage of Fires Confined to Object or Room of Origin

Containment of fires to as small an area as possible limits total damages. The degree of containment depends on how quickly the fire department is called and is also an effectiveness measure that is reported to the state.

9. Percentage of Fires for Which Cause Is Determined

Investigation of the causes of fires can be an important part of prevention and suppression efforts. While the cause of all fires cannot always be determined, being able to identify causes is important if lessons are to be learned from the investigations.

10. Percentage of Fire Code Violations "Cleared" by Correction or Imposition of Penalty within Ninety Days

Fire code violations are violations of state and local laws and regulations as found through fire inspections. The violators are given time to correct the violation before a penalty is imposed. This is an effectiveness measure that provides an indication of timeliness of follow-up.

11. Percentage of Cases with Lost Pulse Where Pulse Is Recovered at Time of Transfer for Transport

Fire departments frequently are the first responders to medical calls, including cases where an individual has no pulse either at the time of arrival or during the response. This effectiveness measure reports the percentage of these cases in which the patient has recovered a pulse by the time responsibility for care has been transferred to emergency responders who will transport the patient to a hospital. Many patients cannot be saved, and recovery of pulse does not guarantee survival at the hospital.

Fire Services

Summary of Key Dimensions of Service

City or Town	Population Served	Land Area Served (in Square Miles)	Value of Property in Service Area (in Billions)	Total Number of Fire Department Responses	Fire Code Violations Found	Number of Community Fire Stations	Number of Fire Services FTEs	ISO* Rating
Apex	59,095	67.8	$7.9	3,238	1,287	5	82	3—town 6—outlying
Asheville	93,621	45.5	$15.1	20,427	6,533	12	271	2
Chapel Hill	63,761	22.9	$8.3	4,896	na	5	98	2
Charlotte	881,480	320.8	$101.9	130,128	46,518	41 + 1 airport	1,172	1
Concord	96,270	69.7	$11.8	12,313	6,829	10 + 1 airport	213	1
Goldsboro	33,636	29.4	$2.4	2,623	412	5	83	3
Greensboro	301,437	140.2	$28.8	42,277	9,250	26	584	1
Greenville	90,201	37.2	$6.6	18,598	4,147	6	164	3
Hickory	46,051	42.9	$5.4	6,740	3,407	6 + 1 airport	137	3
Mooresville	41,255	23.1	$6.5	7,497	22,380	5	95	1
Raleigh	464,453	146.1	$60.3	43,047	24,695	28	622	1
Wilson	49,054	31.0	$4.1	4,433	4,540	5	100	1
Winston-Salem	243,447	132.5	$22.4	27,303	5,775	19	368	2

NOTES
*ISO—Insurance Service Office

EXPLANATORY FACTORS
These are factors that the project found affected fire services performance and cost in one or more of the municipalities:

Population and area served
Value of property area protected in service area
Number of engine companies
Number of fire department responses
Fire code violations
ISO rating
Age of housing stock

Apex

Fiscal Year 2018–19

Explanatory Information

Service Level and Delivery

The mission of the Apex Fire Department is to protect life, property, and the environment from fire, medical emergencies, natural disasters, and other emergencies for those who live, work, and travel in and through the town and surrounding area. In addition to the town, the fire department serves an additional forty-nine square miles in surrounding fire districts.

The fire department uses a shift schedule with one twenty-four-hour shift on schedule and one off every three days, followed by a four-day break. On average, shift personnel work ten to eleven days per twenty-eight-day cycle.

The area within the Town of Apex has an ISO rating of 3, while the surrounding fire districts served have an ISO rating of 6. The rating was done during 2013 and was an upgrade from the prior rating for both areas.

The Apex Fire Department conducted 983 fire maintenance, construction, and reinspections during the fiscal year. The fire department handles all inspections within town limits and coordinates with the Wake County Fire Marshal for joint inspections in the extra-territorial jurisdiction for new construction, fire alarms, and sprinkler reviews and inspections. Apex has a fire marshal and one inspector.

All fire investigations in Apex are handled by the Wake County Fire Marshal. Apex assists in investigations but does not provide the investigative reports.

Conditions Affecting Service, Performance, and Costs

Municipal Profile

Service Population	59,095
Land Area (Square Miles)	67.76
Persons per Square Mile	872
Median Household Income	$84,000
U.S. Census 2016	

Service Profile

FTE Positions—Firefighters	72.0
FTE Positions—Other	10.0
Fire Stations	5
First-Line Fire Apparatus	
Pumpers	4
Aerial Trucks	1
Quints	1
Squads	0
Rescue	1
Other	6
Fire Department Responses	3,238
Responses for Fires	89
Structural Fires Reported	33
Inspections Completed for Maintenance, Construction, and Reinspections	983
Fire Code Violations Reported	1,287
Estimated Fire Loss (millions)	$1.39
Amount of Property Protected in Service Area (millions)	$7,942
Number of Fire Education Programs or Events	58

Full Cost Profile

Cost Breakdown by Percentage	
Personal Services	65.6%
Operating Costs	20.8%
Capital Costs	13.6%
TOTAL	100.0%
Cost Breakdown in Dollars	
Personal Services	$6,918,989
Operating Costs	$2,193,155
Capital Costs	$1,433,301
TOTAL	$10,545,445

Resource Measures

Fire Services Costs per Capita

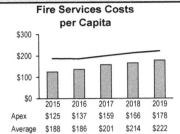

	2015	2016	2017	2018	2019
Apex	$125	$137	$159	$166	$178
Average	$188	$186	$201	$214	$222

Fire Services Total FTEs per 10,000 Population

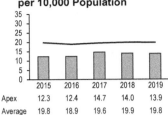

	2015	2016	2017	2018	2019
Apex	12.3	12.4	14.7	14.0	13.9
Average	19.8	18.9	19.6	19.9	19.8

Fire Services Cost per Thousand Dollars of Property Protected

	2015	2016	2017	2018	2019
Apex	$1.16	$1.16	$1.35	$1.24	$1.33
Average	$1.90	$1.83	$2.05	$1.97	$2.01

Workload Measures

Actual Fires per 1,000 Population

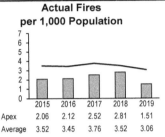

	2015	2016	2017	2018	2019
Apex	2.06	2.12	2.52	2.81	1.51
Average	3.52	3.45	3.76	3.52	3.06

Fire Department Responses per 1,000 Population

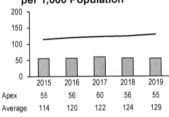

	2015	2016	2017	2018	2019
Apex	55	56	60	56	55
Average	114	120	122	124	129

Fire Inspections Completed per 1,000 Population

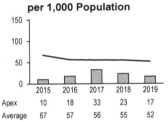

	2015	2016	2017	2018	2019
Apex	10	18	33	23	17
Average	67	57	56	55	52

Efficiency Measures

Fire Services Cost per Fire Department Response

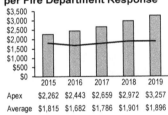

	2015	2016	2017	2018	2019
Apex	$2,262	$2,443	$2,659	$2,972	$3,257
Average	$1,815	$1,682	$1,786	$1,901	$1,896

Inspections Completed per Inspector FTE

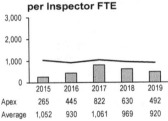

	2015	2016	2017	2018	2019
Apex	265	445	822	630	492
Average	1,052	930	1,061	969	920

Effectiveness Measures

Average Response Time to Priority One Calls in Minutes

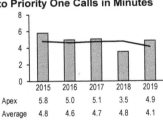

	2015	2016	2017	2018	2019
Apex	5.8	5.0	5.1	3.5	4.9
Average	4.8	4.6	4.7	4.8	4.1

Percentage of Fire Code Violations Cleared within 90 Days

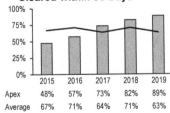

	2015	2016	2017	2018	2019
Apex	48%	57%	73%	82%	89%
Average	67%	71%	64%	71%	63%

Percentage of Fires Confined to Rooms or Objects Involved on Arrival

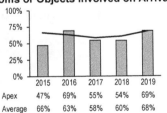

	2015	2016	2017	2018	2019
Apex	47%	69%	55%	54%	69%
Average	66%	63%	58%	60%	68%

Percentage of Fires for Which Cause Was Determined

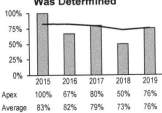

	2015	2016	2017	2018	2019
Apex	100%	67%	80%	50%	76%
Average	83%	82%	79%	73%	76%

Percentage of Full Response within 8 Minutes Travel Time

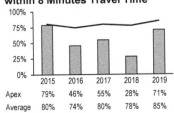

	2015	2016	2017	2018	2019
Apex	79%	46%	55%	28%	71%
Average	80%	74%	80%	78%	85%

Percentage of Lost Pulse Cases Recovered Pulse at Transfer of Care

	2015	2016	2017	2018	2019
Apex		44.4%	42.9%	33.3%	35.0%
Average	42.0%	37.0%	36.6%	37.1%	46.0%

Explanatory Information

Service Level and Delivery

The mission of the Asheville Fire Department is to protect the lives, property, and environment of all people within Asheville by preventing the occurrence and minimizing the adverse effects of fires, accidents, and all other emergencies.

The fire department contains the following divisions: emergency response, technical services, and fire marshal.

The fire department uses a modified shift schedule that includes twenty-four hours on duty and twenty-four hours off duty, averaging fifty-six hours per week. The work schedule is as follows: twenty-four hours on, twenty-four hours off; twenty-four hours on, forty-eight hours off; twenty-four hours on, twenty-four hours off; twenty-four hours on, ninety-six hours off. This works out to an average work week of fifty-six hours.

The city has an ISO rating of 2, as rated in 2018. The Asheville Fire Department has been accredited since 2005.

The fire and rescue department conducted 7,877 fire maintenance, construction, and reinspections during the fiscal year. The fire marshal's office is comprised of two sections. One section is responsible for existing construction and another for new construction. Deputy fire marshals (DFMs) are responsible for conducting periodic fire prevention inspections inside the corporate limits of the City of Asheville, as required by the N.C. Office of the State Fire Marshal. The Asheville City Council adopted a fee schedule for periodic fire inspections. These fees are based on cost recovery. Each DFM conducts fire inspections of every commercial premise located within Asheville. Most personnel work a day shift, while several work a twenty-four-hour shift. These DFMs are liaisons to the other divisions on matters regarding code enforcement, fire investigations, and pre-incident planning.

Conditions Affecting Service, Performance, and Costs

Municipal Profile

Service Population	93,621
Land Area (Square Miles)	45.53
Persons per Square Mile	2,056
Median Household Income	$40,494
U.S. Census 2016	

Service Profile

FTE Positions—Firefighters	238.0
FTE Positions—Other	32.8
Fire Stations	12
First-Line Fire Apparatus	
Pumpers	9
Aerial Trucks	3
Quints	2
Squads	1
Rescue	1
Other	1
Fire Department Responses	20,427
Responses for Fires	422
Structural Fires Reported	58
Inspections Completed for Maintenance, Construction, and Reinspections	7,877
Fire Code Violations Reported	6,533
Estimated Fire Loss (millions)	$2.15
Amount of Property Protected in Service Area (millions)	$15,081
Number of Fire Education Programs or Events	334

Full Cost Profile

Cost Breakdown by Percentage

Personal Services	69.5%
Operating Costs	20.4%
Capital Costs	10.1%
TOTAL	100.0%

Cost Breakdown in Dollars

Personal Services	$22,835,493
Operating Costs	$6,696,771
Capital Costs	$3,310,663
TOTAL	$32,842,927

Asheville   # Fire Services

Resource Measures

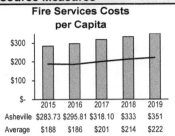

Fire Services Costs per Capita

	2015	2016	2017	2018	2019
Asheville	$283.73	$295.81	$318.10	$333	$351
Average	$188	$186	$201	$214	$222

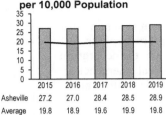

Fire Services Total FTEs per 10,000 Population

	2015	2016	2017	2018	2019
Asheville	27.2	27.0	28.4	28.5	28.9
Average	19.8	18.9	19.6	19.9	19.8

Fire Services Cost per Thousand Dollars of Property Protected

	2015	2016	2017	2018	2019
Asheville	$2.28	$2.37	$2.57	$2.10	$2.18
Average	$1.90	$1.83	$2.05	$1.97	$2.01

Workload Measures

Actual Fires per 1,000 Population

	2015	2016	2017	2018	2019
Asheville	4.37	4.79	4.91	4.33	4.51
Average	3.52	3.45	3.76	3.52	3.06

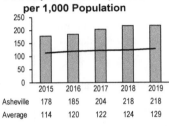

Fire Department Responses per 1,000 Population

	2015	2016	2017	2018	2019
Asheville	178	185	204	218	218
Average	114	120	122	124	129

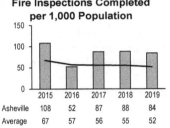

Fire Inspections Completed per 1,000 Population

	2015	2016	2017	2018	2019
Asheville	108	52	87	88	84
Average	67	57	56	55	52

Efficiency Measures

Fire Services Cost per Fire Department Response

	2015	2016	2017	2018	2019
Asheville	$1,591	$1,597	$1,556	$1,530	$1,608
Average	$1,815	$1,682	$1,786	$1,901	$1,896

Inspections Completed per Inspector FTE

	2015	2016	2017	2018	2019
Asheville	787	624	1,003	1,012	788
Average	1,052	930	1,061	969	920

Effectiveness Measures

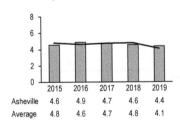

Average Response Time to Priority One Calls in Minutes

	2015	2016	2017	2018	2019
Asheville	4.6	4.9	4.7	4.6	4.4
Average	4.8	4.6	4.7	4.8	4.1

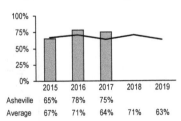

Percentage of Fire Code Violations Cleared within 90 Days

	2015	2016	2017	2018	2019
Asheville	65%	78%	75%		
Average	67%	71%	64%	71%	63%

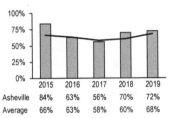

Percentage of Fires Confined to Rooms or Objects Involved on Arrival

	2015	2016	2017	2018	2019
Asheville	84%	63%	56%	70%	72%
Average	66%	63%	58%	60%	68%

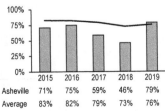

Percentage of Fires for Which Cause Was Determined

	2015	2016	2017	2018	2019
Asheville	71%	75%	59%	46%	79%
Average	83%	82%	79%	73%	76%

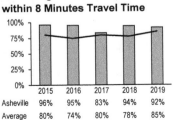

Percentage of Full Response within 8 Minutes Travel Time

	2015	2016	2017	2018	2019
Asheville	96%	95%	83%	94%	92%
Average	80%	74%	80%	78%	85%

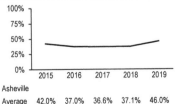

Percentage of Lost Pulse Cases Recovered Pulse at Transfer of Care

	2015	2016	2017	2018	2019
Asheville					
Average	42.0%	37.0%	36.6%	37.1%	46.0%

Fiscal Year 2018–19

Explanatory Information

Service Level and Delivery

The Town of Chapel Hill's Fire Department mission is to minimize the risk of fire and other hazards to the life and property of the citizens of Chapel Hill. To accomplish this mission, the department provides response to and mitigation of fires, medical emergencies, hazardous materials incidents, and other emergencies as they arise.

The fire department is organized into three divisions: operations, administration, and life safety. Operations and life safety are administered by a deputy chief with support staff. Administration consists of the fire chief and support staff.

The fire department works a 3/4 system, where personnel are on duty for 24 hours starting at 7 a.m. The town has five community stations with six primary vehicles for response.

The town has an ISO rating of 2 received in 2016, which was an upgrade from the year before.

Fire inspections are performed by fire inspectors and are designed to be completed in accordance with the State of North Carolina's inspection schedule. Initial inspections may generate findings for reinspection. The department counts malls as one inspection per occupancy and one per building structure. High rises have one inspection per building plus one per commercial occupancy. Multi-structure apartment complexes have just one inspection per complex.

Conditions Affecting Service, Performance, and Costs

The Town of Chapel Hill began participation in the benchmarking project in July 2015, with FY 2014–15 being the first reporting year.

Complete data on fire code violations and fire safety complaints was not available for the last few years.

Municipal Profile

Service Population	63,761
Land Area (Square Miles)	22.91
Persons per Square Mile	2,784
Median Household Income	$60,802
U.S. Census 2016	

Service Profile

FTE Positions—Firefighters	79.0
FTE Positions—Other	19.0
Fire Stations	5
First-Line Fire Apparatus	
Pumpers	5
Aerial Trucks	1
Quints	1
Squads	0
Rescue	1
Other	0
Fire Department Responses	4,896
Responses for Fires	112
Structural Fires Reported	37
Inspections Completed for Maintenance, Construction, and Reinspections	3,307
Fire Code Violations Reported	NA
Estimated Fire Loss (millions)	$0.33
Amount of Property Protected in Service Area (millions)	$8,315
Number of Fire Education Programs or Events	NA

Full Cost Profile

Cost Breakdown by Percentage

Personal Services	62.5%
Operating Costs	28.3%
Capital Costs	9.2%
TOTAL	100.0%

Cost Breakdown in Dollars

Personal Services	$7,807,570
Operating Costs	$3,539,292
Capital Costs	$1,152,707
TOTAL	$12,499,569

Chapel Hill

Fire Services

Resource Measures

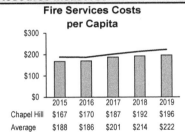

Fire Services Costs per Capita

	2015	2016	2017	2018	2019
Chapel Hill	$167	$170	$187	$192	$196
Average	$188	$186	$201	$214	$222

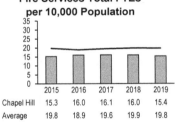

Fire Services Total FTEs per 10,000 Population

	2015	2016	2017	2018	2019
Chapel Hill	15.3	16.0	16.1	16.0	15.4
Average	19.8	18.9	19.6	19.9	19.8

Fire Services Cost per Thousand Dollars of Property Protected

	2015	2016	2017	2018	2019
Chapel Hill	$1.35	$1.35	$1.49	$1.44	$1.50
Average	$1.90	$1.83	$2.05	$1.97	$2.01

Workload Measures

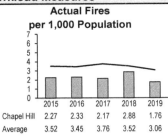

Actual Fires per 1,000 Population

	2015	2016	2017	2018	2019
Chapel Hill	2.27	2.33	2.17	2.88	1.76
Average	3.52	3.45	3.76	3.52	3.06

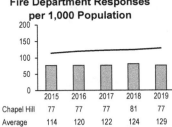

Fire Department Responses per 1,000 Population

	2015	2016	2017	2018	2019
Chapel Hill	77	77	77	81	77
Average	114	120	122	124	129

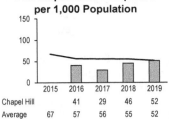

Fire Inspections Completed per 1,000 Population

	2015	2016	2017	2018	2019
Chapel Hill		41	29	46	52
Average	67	57	56	55	52

Efficiency Measures

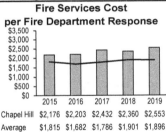

Fire Services Cost per Fire Department Response

	2015	2016	2017	2018	2019
Chapel Hill	$2,176	$2,203	$2,432	$2,360	$2,553
Average	$1,815	$1,682	$1,786	$1,901	$1,896

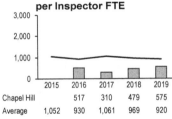

Inspections Completed per Inspector FTE

	2015	2016	2017	2018	2019
Chapel Hill		517	310	479	575
Average	1,052	930	1,061	969	920

Effectiveness Measures

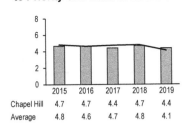

Average Response Time to Priority One Calls in Minutes

	2015	2016	2017	2018	2019
Chapel Hill	4.7	4.7	4.4	4.7	4.4
Average	4.8	4.6	4.7	4.8	4.1

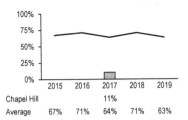

Percentage of Fire Code Violations Cleared within 90 Days

	2015	2016	2017	2018	2019
Chapel Hill			11%		
Average	67%	71%	64%	71%	63%

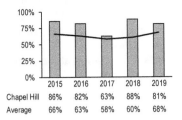

Percentage of Fires Confined to Rooms or Objects Involved on Arrival

	2015	2016	2017	2018	2019
Chapel Hill	86%	82%	63%	88%	81%
Average	66%	63%	58%	60%	68%

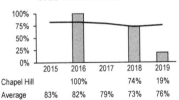

Percentage of Fires for Which Cause Was Determined

	2015	2016	2017	2018	2019
Chapel Hill		100%		74%	19%
Average	83%	82%	79%	73%	76%

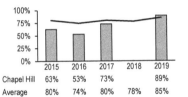

Percentage of Full Response within 8 Minutes Travel Time

	2015	2016	2017	2018	2019
Chapel Hill	63%	53%	73%		89%
Average	80%	74%	80%	78%	85%

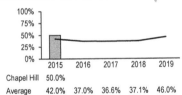

Percentage of Lost Pulse Cases Recovered Pulse at Transfer of Care

	2015	2016	2017	2018	2019
Chapel Hill	50.0%				
Average	42.0%	37.0%	36.6%	37.1%	46.0%

Fiscal Year 2018–19

Explanatory Information

Service Level and Delivery

The mission of the Charlotte Fire Department is to minimize the risk of fire and other hazards to the life and property of the citizens of Charlotte. To accomplish this mission, the department provides response to and mitigation of fires, medical emergencies, hazardous materials incidents, aircraft emergencies, technical rescues, and other emergencies as they arise. These services are provided immediately to any person who has a need anywhere within the corporate limits of Charlotte.

The divisions of the Charlotte Fire Department are operations (A, B, C), training, administration, communications, logistics, fire prevention, and fire investigation.

The city uses a modified twenty-four-hour/forty-eight-hour shift schedule, using four twenty-four-hour shifts in a twelve-day cycle. The cycle is on one day, off one day, on one day, off two days, on one day, off one day, on one day, off four days. In addition, firefighters receive a Kelley day (ten hours) off and a Kelley night (fourteen hours) off every seven weeks to maintain the number of hours worked per week at fifty-two.

The city has an ISO rating of 1, which is the highest level possible. The Charlotte Fire Department has been accredited since 2000.

The fire department conducted 47,899 fire maintenance, construction, and reinspections during the fiscal year. All inspections are performed by certified fire inspectors who are employees of the Fire Prevention Bureau. The inspectors handle certificate of occupancy inspections, permit inspections and issuances, regular code enforcement inspections, and reinspections. The Bureau currently uses separate inspections on each building of an apartment complex.

Conditions Affecting Service, Performance, and Costs

Charlotte did not participate in the Benchmarking Project during FY 2014–15. No data are available for that year.

Charlotte staffs a fire station at the airport in addition to forty-one community fire stations.

Municipal Profile	
Service Population	881,480
Land Area (Square Miles)	320.82
Persons per Square Mile	2,748
Median Household Income	$46,975
U.S. Census 2016	

Service Profile	
FTE Positions—Firefighters	1,036.0
FTE Positions—Other	136.0
Fire Stations	42
First-Line Fire Apparatus	
Pumpers	42
Aerial Trucks	0
Quints	16
Squads	0
Rescue	2
Other	36
Fire Department Responses	130,128
Responses for Fires	2,059
Structural Fires Reported	427
Inspections Completed for Maintenance, Construction, and Reinspections	47,899
Fire Code Violations Reported	46,518
Estimated Fire Loss (millions)	$16.20
Amount of Property Protected in Service Area (millions)	$101,862
Number of Fire Education Programs or Events	1,500

Full Cost Profile	
Cost Breakdown by Percentage	
Personal Services	66.5%
Operating Costs	21.7%
Capital Costs	11.8%
TOTAL	100.0%
Cost Breakdown in Dollars	
Personal Services	$114,520,844
Operating Costs	$22,057,035
Capital Costs	$11,884,789
TOTAL	$148,462,668

Charlotte

Fire Services

Resource Measures

Fire Services Costs per Capita

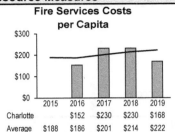

	2015	2016	2017	2018	2019
Charlotte		$152	$230	$230	$168
Average	$188	$186	$201	$214	$222

Fire Services Total FTEs per 10,000 Population

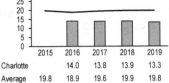

	2015	2016	2017	2018	2019
Charlotte		14.0	13.8	13.9	13.3
Average	19.8	18.9	19.6	19.9	19.8

Fire Services Cost per Thousand Dollars of Property Protected

	2015	2016	2017	2018	2019
Charlotte		$1.36	$2.09	$2.03	$1.46
Average	$1.90	$1.83	$2.05	$1.97	$2.01

Workload Measures

Actual Fires per 1,000 Population

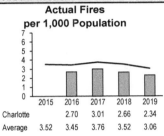

	2015	2016	2017	2018	2019
Charlotte		2.70	3.01	2.66	2.34
Average	3.52	3.45	3.76	3.52	3.06

Fire Department Responses per 1,000 Population

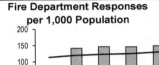
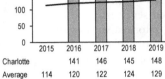

	2015	2016	2017	2018	2019
Charlotte		141	146	145	148
Average	114	120	122	124	129

Fire Inspections Completed per 1,000 Population

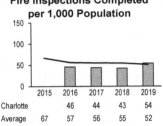

	2015	2016	2017	2018	2019
Charlotte		46	44	43	54
Average	67	57	56	55	52

Efficiency Measures

Fire Services Cost per Fire Department Response

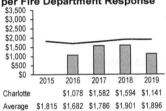

	2015	2016	2017	2018	2019
Charlotte		$1,078	$1,582	$1,594	$1,141
Average	$1,815	$1,682	$1,786	$1,901	$1,896

Inspections Completed per Inspector FTE

	2015	2016	2017	2018	2019
Charlotte		1,421	1,387	1,184	1,409
Average	1,052	930	1,061	969	920

Effectiveness Measures

Average Response Time to Priority One Calls in Minutes

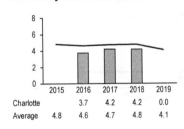

	2015	2016	2017	2018	2019
Charlotte		3.7	4.2	4.2	0.0
Average	4.8	4.6	4.7	4.8	4.1

Percentage of Fire Code Violations Cleared within 90 Days

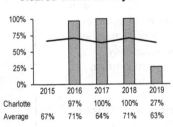

	2015	2016	2017	2018	2019
Charlotte		97%	100%	100%	27%
Average	67%	71%	64%	71%	63%

Percentage of Fires Confined to Rooms or Objects Involved on Arrival

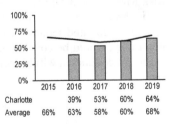

	2015	2016	2017	2018	2019
Charlotte		39%	53%	60%	64%
Average	66%	63%	58%	60%	68%

Percentage of Fires for Which Cause Was Determined

	2015	2016	2017	2018	2019
Charlotte		89%	91%	92%	95%
Average	83%	82%	79%	73%	76%

Percentage of Full Response within 8 Minutes Travel Time

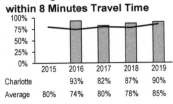

	2015	2016	2017	2018	2019
Charlotte		93%	82%	87%	90%
Average	80%	74%	80%	78%	85%

Percentage of Lost Pulse Cases Recovered Pulse at Transfer of Care

	2015	2016	2017	2018	2019
Charlotte		41.7%	44.7%	43.4%	63.7%
Average	42.0%	37.0%	36.6%	37.1%	46.0%

Concord

Fire Services

Fiscal Year 2018–19

Explanatory Information

Service Level and Delivery
The City of Concord Fire Department is committed to providing a positive work environment to enable the department and its personnel to strive for and achieve excellence in fire protection services.

The department is committed to the following: providing leadership through a management/employee team organizational concept that is dedicated to modern-day management principles and practices; providing the citizens with the best possible modern-day fire protection and life safety services in a courteous, professional, and cost-effective manner; providing equal opportunity for all employees to excel in their job performance and career development; striving to continually increase the public's awareness through fire prevention activities, public education, and community-based services; maintaining and striving to improve on an open, informative flow of correct information so that all employees and employee teams reach their goals and objectives; subscribing to departmental values of honesty, professionalism, teamwork, loyalty, dedication, and commitment to serving the public; and planning for change to develop and prepare the department to always strive for excellence.

The fire department in Concord contains the following divisions: administration, suppression, operations, training and career development, fire-risk management, and emergency management.

The fire department utilizes a shift schedule that includes twenty-four hours on and forty-eight hours off.

The city has an ISO rating of 1, as rated in 2018. This is the highest level rating possible and was an upgrade from the last rating.

The fire department conducted 6,829 fire maintenance, construction, and reinspections during the fiscal year. Inspections are conducted by the Fire-Risk Management Division. Each inspector has an assigned area of the city and a specific number of inspections to complete. Each occupancy is counted separately in the inspections number. An apartment complex would be considered as one occupancy. Reinspections are conducted within forty-five days to confirm corrections.

Conditions Affecting Service, Performance, and Costs
Concord staffs a fire station at the airport in addition to ten community fire stations.

Municipal Profile

Service Population	96,270
Land Area (Square Miles)	69.74
Persons per Square Mile	1,381
Median Household Income	$50,863
U.S. Census 2016	

Service Profile

FTE Positions—Firefighters	195.0
FTE Positions—Other	18.0
Fire Stations	11
First-Line Fire Apparatus	
Pumpers	9
Aerial Trucks	3
Quints	0
Squads	0
Rescue	1
Other	12
Fire Department Responses	12,313
Responses for Fires	261
Structural Fires Reported	64
Inspections Completed for Maintenance, Construction, and Reinspections	8,117
Fire Code Violations Reported	6,829
Estimated Fire Loss (millions)	$3.12
Amount of Property Protected in Service Area (millions)	$11,750
Number of Fire Education Programs or Events	194

Full Cost Profile

Cost Breakdown by Percentage

Personal Services	66.9%
Operating Costs	20.8%
Capital Costs	12.3%
TOTAL	100.0%

Cost Breakdown in Dollars

Personal Services	$15,787,771
Operating Costs	$4,910,866
Capital Costs	$2,893,569
TOTAL	$23,592,206

Concord

Fire Services

Resource Measures

Fire Services Costs per Capita

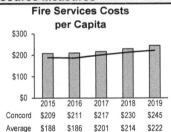

	2015	2016	2017	2018	2019
Concord	$209	$211	$217	$230	$245
Average	$188	$186	$201	$214	$222

Fire Services Total FTEs per 10,000 Population

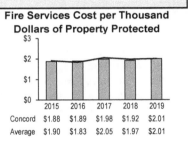

	2015	2016	2017	2018	2019
Concord	21.6	22.1	22.4	21.9	22.1
Average	19.8	18.9	19.6	19.9	19.8

Fire Services Cost per Thousand Dollars of Property Protected

	2015	2016	2017	2018	2019
Concord	$1.88	$1.89	$1.98	$1.92	$2.01
Average	$1.90	$1.83	$2.05	$1.97	$2.01

Workload Measures

Actual Fires per 1,000 Population

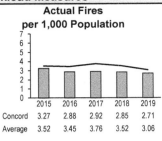

	2015	2016	2017	2018	2019
Concord	3.27	2.88	2.92	2.85	2.71
Average	3.52	3.45	3.76	3.52	3.06

Fire Department Responses per 1,000 Population

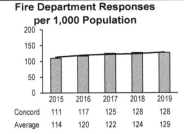

	2015	2016	2017	2018	2019
Concord	111	117	125	128	128
Average	114	120	122	124	129

Fire Inspections Completed per 1,000 Population

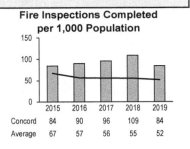

	2015	2016	2017	2018	2019
Concord	84	90	96	109	84
Average	67	57	56	55	52

Efficiency Measures

Fire Services Cost per Fire Department Response

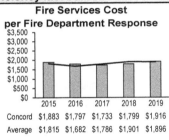

	2015	2016	2017	2018	2019
Concord	$1,883	$1,797	$1,733	$1,799	$1,916
Average	$1,815	$1,682	$1,786	$1,901	$1,896

Inspections Completed per Inspector FTE

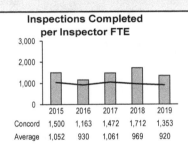

	2015	2016	2017	2018	2019
Concord	1,500	1,163	1,472	1,712	1,353
Average	1,052	930	1,061	969	920

Effectiveness Measures

Average Response Time to Priority One Calls in Minutes

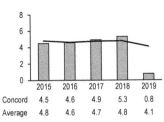

	2015	2016	2017	2018	2019
Concord	4.5	4.6	4.9	5.3	0.8
Average	4.8	4.6	4.7	4.8	4.1

Percentage of Fire Code Violations Cleared within 90 Days

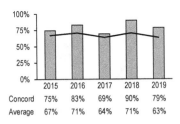

	2015	2016	2017	2018	2019
Concord	75%	83%	69%	90%	79%
Average	67%	71%	64%	71%	63%

Percentage of Fires Confined to Rooms or Objects Involved on Arrival

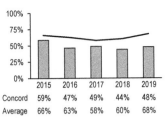

	2015	2016	2017	2018	2019
Concord	59%	47%	49%	44%	48%
Average	66%	63%	58%	60%	68%

Percentage of Fires for Which Cause Was Determined

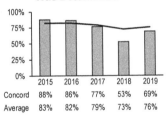

	2015	2016	2017	2018	2019
Concord	88%	86%	77%	53%	69%
Average	83%	82%	79%	73%	76%

Percentage of Full Response within 8 Minutes Travel Time

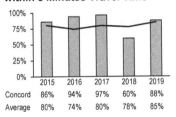

	2015	2016	2017	2018	2019
Concord	86%	94%	97%	60%	88%
Average	80%	74%	80%	78%	85%

Percentage of Lost Pulse Cases Recovered Pulse at Transfer of Care

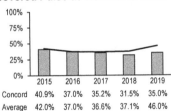

	2015	2016	2017	2018	2019
Concord	40.9%	37.0%	35.2%	31.5%	35.0%
Average	42.0%	37.0%	36.6%	37.1%	46.0%

Explanatory Information

Service Level and Delivery

The mission of the Goldsboro Fire Department is to protect lives, the environment, and property by providing prompt, skillful, and cost-effective fire protection, EMS, and life safety service. The Department maintains a receptive and ethical work environment that is conducive to the development of innovative and creative solutions by employees to meet the ever-changing needs of the community.

The fire department utilizes a shift schedule that includes alternates twenty-four hours on and twenty-four hours off for five days followed by four days off. This works out to fifty-six hour work weeks with shifts starting and ending at 8 a.m.

The city has an ISO rating of 3 as rated in 2010.

The fire department in Goldsboro conducted 1,449 fire maintenance, construction, and reinspections during the fiscal year. General inspections are performed according to the mandated inspection schedule, which is based on occupancy type established in the International Fire Code. Maintenance fire inspections are assigned by the fire marshal to the fire inspectors, fire company inspectors, and the fire marshal's office as well. The fire inspector or fire marshal perform all site plan reviews, fumigation, tent inspections, and construction inspections for fire suppression and sprinklers, tanks, and fire alarm systems.

Conditions Affecting Service, Performance, and Costs

The city of Goldsboro joined the Benchmarking Project in July 2017, with the first year of data showing for FY 2016–17.

Municipal Profile

Service Population	34,793
Land Area (Square Miles)	29.35
Persons per Square Mile	1,186
Median Household Income	$32,148
U.S. Census 2016	

Service Profile

FTE Positions—Firefighters	74.0
FTE Positions—Other	9.0
Fire Stations	5
First-Line Fire Apparatus	
Pumpers	4
Aerial Trucks	1
Quints	1
Squads	0
Rescue	0
Other	1
Fire Department Responses	2,623
Responses for Fires	157
Structural Fires Reported	35
Inspections Completed for Maintenance, Construction, and Reinspections	1,449
Fire Code Violations Reported	412
Estimated Fire Loss (millions)	$0.78
Amount of Property Protected in Service Area (millions)	$2,418
Number of Fire Education Programs or Events	148

Full Cost Profile

Cost Breakdown by Percentage

Personal Services	88.7%
Operating Costs	8.8%
Capital Costs	2.5%
TOTAL	100.0%

Cost Breakdown in Dollars

Personal Services	$5,579,337
Operating Costs	$552,034
Capital Costs	$155,968
TOTAL	$6,287,339

Goldsboro

Fire Services

Resource Measures

Fire Services Costs per Capita

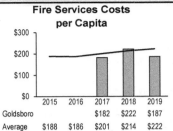

	2015	2016	2017	2018	2019
Goldsboro			$182	$222	$187
Average	$188	$186	$201	$214	$222

Fire Services Total FTEs per 10,000 Population

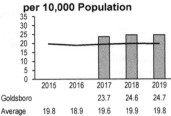

	2015	2016	2017	2018	2019
Goldsboro			23.7	24.6	24.7
Average	19.8	18.9	19.6	19.9	19.8

Fire Services Cost per Thousand Dollars of Property Protected

	2015	2016	2017	2018	2019
Goldsboro			$2.65	$3.11	$2.60
Average	$1.90	$1.83	$2.05	$1.97	$2.01

Workload Measures

Actual Fires per 1,000 Population

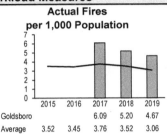

	2015	2016	2017	2018	2019
Goldsboro			6.09	5.20	4.67
Average	3.52	3.45	3.76	3.52	3.06

Fire Department Responses per 1,000 Population

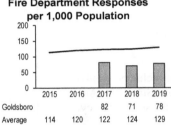

	2015	2016	2017	2018	2019
Goldsboro			82	71	78
Average	114	120	122	124	129

Fire Inspections Completed per 1,000 Population

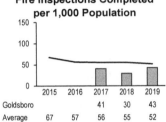

	2015	2016	2017	2018	2019
Goldsboro			41	30	43
Average	67	57	56	55	52

Efficiency Measures

Fire Services Cost per Fire Department Response

	2015	2016	2017	2018	2019
Goldsboro			$2,236	$3,125	$2,397
Average	$1,815	$1,682	$1,786	$1,901	$1,896

Inspections Completed per Inspector FTE

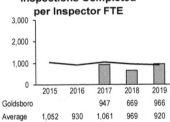

	2015	2016	2017	2018	2019
Goldsboro			947	669	966
Average	1,052	930	1,061	969	920

Effectiveness Measures

Average Response Time to Priority One Calls in Minutes

	2015	2016	2017	2018	2019
Goldsboro			5.7	5.0	5.8
Average	4.8	4.6	4.7	4.8	4.1

Percentage of Fire Code Violations Cleared within 90 Days

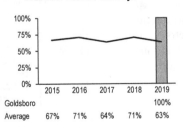

	2015	2016	2017	2018	2019
Goldsboro					100%
Average	67%	71%	64%	71%	63%

Percentage of Fires Confined to Rooms or Objects Involved on Arrival

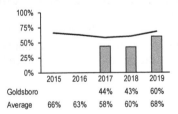

	2015	2016	2017	2018	2019
Goldsboro			44%	43%	60%
Average	66%	63%	58%	60%	68%

Percentage of Fires for Which Cause Was Determined

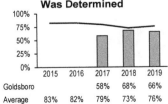

	2015	2016	2017	2018	2019
Goldsboro			58%	68%	66%
Average	83%	82%	79%	73%	76%

Percentage of Full Response within 8 Minutes Travel Time

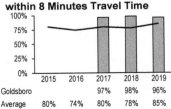

	2015	2016	2017	2018	2019
Goldsboro			97%	98%	96%
Average	80%	74%	80%	78%	85%

Percentage of Lost Pulse Cases Recovered Pulse at Transfer of Care

	2015	2016	2017	2018	2019
Goldsboro					
Average	42.0%	37.0%	36.6%	37.1%	46.0%

Greensboro

Fire Services

Fiscal Year 2018–19

Explanatory Information

Service Level and Delivery

The mission of the Greensboro Fire Department is to provide the public the best possible service in a courteous, professional, and cost-effective manner; to provide leadership through a well-defined management team committed to the departmental management philosophy; to provide equal opportunity for all employees in job performance and career development; to enhance public awareness through education, activities, and services; to maintain an open, informative flow of information so that all municipal departments may reach their goals and objectives; and to subscribe to honesty, integrity, and fairness.

The fire department contains two branches: emergency services and support services.

The fire department utilizes a shift schedule that includes twenty-four hours on and forty-eight hours off. For Fair Labor Standards Act (FLSA) purposes, the department utilizes a twenty-seven-day cycle.

The city has an ISO rating of 1, the highest rating possible, as rated in 2019. The Greensboro Fire Department has been accredited since 1997.

The fire department in Greensboro conducted 11,215 fire maintenance, construction, and reinspections during the fiscal year. General inspections are performed according to the mandated inspection schedule, which is based on occupancy type established in the International Fire Code. Complaints are addressed within twenty-four hours and are handled twenty-four hours a day as shift personnel are available. Inspectors generally work in districts and work in specialized areas, including educational, institutional, high rise, privilege licenses, and certificates of compliance. Apartment complexes are assigned one file number for the entire complex.

Conditions Affecting Service, Performance, and Costs

For clearance of fire code violations, Greensboro requires the violation to be cleared by witness of an inspector in person. With a backlog of inspections, this has meant some violations have not been cleared per the definition but may have been addressed.

Municipal Profile

Service Population	301,437
Land Area (Square Miles)	140.19
Persons per Square Mile	2,150
Median Household Income	$40,760
U.S. Census 2016	

Service Profile

FTE Positions—Firefighters	527.0
FTE Positions—Other	57.0
Fire Stations	26
First-Line Fire Apparatus	
Pumpers	24
Aerial Trucks	0
Quints	11
Squads	0
Rescue	1
Other	0
Fire Department Responses	42,277
Responses for Fires	956
Structural Fires Reported	212
Inspections Completed for Maintenance, Construction, and Reinspections	11,215
Fire Code Violations Reported	9,250
Estimated Fire Loss (millions)	$5.82
Amount of Property Protected in Service Area (millions)	$28,820
Number of Fire Education Programs or Events	1,633

Full Cost Profile

Cost Breakdown by Percentage

Personal Services	80.5%
Operating Costs	19.5%
Capital Costs	0.0%
TOTAL	100.0%

Cost Breakdown in Dollars

Personal Services	$46,793,179
Operating Costs	$11,319,149
Capital Costs	$0
TOTAL	$58,112,328

Key: Greensboro ▦   Benchmarking Average —   Fiscal Years 2015 through 2019

Resource Measures

Fire Services Costs per Capita

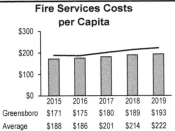

	2015	2016	2017	2018	2019
Greensboro	$171	$175	$180	$189	$193
Average	$188	$186	$201	$214	$222

Fire Services Total FTEs per 10,000 Population

	2015	2016	2017	2018	2019
Greensboro	19.8	20.2	19.9	19.6	19.4
Average	19.8	18.9	19.6	19.9	19.8

Fire Services Cost per Thousand Dollars of Property Protected

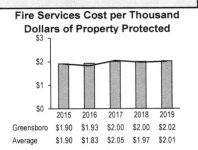

	2015	2016	2017	2018	2019
Greensboro	$1.90	$1.93	$2.00	$2.00	$2.02
Average	$1.90	$1.83	$2.05	$1.97	$2.01

Workload Measures

Actual Fires per 1,000 Population

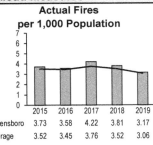

	2015	2016	2017	2018	2019
Greensboro	3.73	3.58	4.22	3.81	3.17
Average	3.52	3.45	3.76	3.52	3.06

Fire Department Responses per 1,000 Population

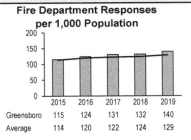

	2015	2016	2017	2018	2019
Greensboro	115	124	131	132	140
Average	114	120	122	124	129

Fire Inspections Completed per 1,000 Population

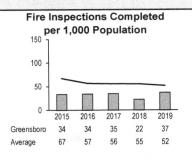

	2015	2016	2017	2018	2019
Greensboro	34	34	35	22	37
Average	67	57	56	55	52

Efficiency Measures

Fire Services Cost per Fire Department Response

	2015	2016	2017	2018	2019
Greensboro	$1,482	$1,406	$1,376	$1,438	$1,375
Average	$1,815	$1,682	$1,786	$1,901	$1,896

Inspections Completed per Inspector FTE

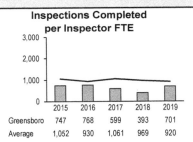

	2015	2016	2017	2018	2019
Greensboro	747	768	599	393	701
Average	1,052	930	1,061	969	920

Effectiveness Measures

Average Response Time to Priority One Calls in Minutes

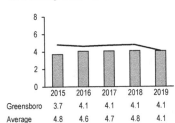

	2015	2016	2017	2018	2019
Greensboro	3.7	4.1	4.1	4.1	4.1
Average	4.8	4.6	4.7	4.8	4.1

Percentage of Fire Code Violations Cleared within 90 Days

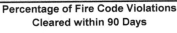
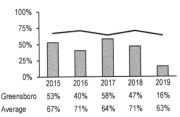

	2015	2016	2017	2018	2019
Greensboro	53%	40%	58%	47%	16%
Average	67%	71%	64%	71%	63%

Percentage of Fires Confined to Rooms or Objects Involved on Arrival

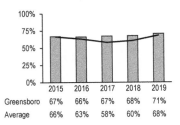

	2015	2016	2017	2018	2019
Greensboro	67%	66%	67%	68%	71%
Average	66%	63%	58%	60%	68%

Percentage of Fires for Which Cause Was Determined

	2015	2016	2017	2018	2019
Greensboro	63%	61%	71%	82%	86%
Average	83%	82%	79%	73%	76%

Percentage of Full Response within 8 Minutes Travel Time

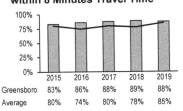

	2015	2016	2017	2018	2019
Greensboro	83%	86%	88%	89%	88%
Average	80%	74%	80%	78%	85%

Percentage of Lost Pulse Cases Recovered Pulse at Transfer of Care

	2015	2016	2017	2018	2019
Greensboro	24.0%	34.5%	34.8%	30.4%	
Average	42.0%	37.0%	36.6%	37.1%	46.0%

Greenville

Fire Services

Fiscal Year 2018–19

Explanatory Information

Service Level and Delivery
The primary goals of the Greenville Fire and Rescue Department are to prevent fires and save lives and property by providing emergency response services for fires or medical emergencies. The city provides fire services in areas beyond the city boundaries covering thirty-two square miles.

Emergency personnel work a 24.25-hour shift followed by 47.75 hours off.

The city has an ISO rating of 3, as rated in 2015. Greenville became an accredited department in 2019.

The fire department in Greenville conducted 2,944 fire maintenance, construction, and reinspections during the fiscal year. The Life Safety Services Division handles all inspection-related matters following the International Fire Code.

Conditions Affecting Service, Performance, and Costs
Greenville is the only city in the benchmarking project that has emergency medical services transports (EMS) provided through the city fire department. In the other jurisdictions, EMS transports are provided by county departments.

Complications with data tracking prevented Greenville from being able to submit numbers on fire incidents and several other measures for previous fiscal years.

Municipal Profile

Service Population	90,201
Land Area (Square Miles)	37.16
Persons per Square Mile	2,427
Median Household Income	$33,339
U.S. Census 2016	

Service Profile

FTE Positions—Firefighters	144.0
FTE Positions—Other	20.0
Fire Stations	6
First-Line Fire Apparatus	
Pumpers	1
Aerial Trucks	1
Quints	4
Squads	0
Rescue	1
Other	2
Fire Department Responses	18,598
Responses for Fires	327
Structural Fires Reported	72
Inspections Completed for Maintenance, Construction, and Reinspections	3,287
Fire Code Violations Reported	4,147
Estimated Fire Loss (millions)	$1.77
Amount of Property Protected in Service Area (millions)	$6,572
Number of Fire Education Programs or Events	254

Full Cost Profile

Cost Breakdown by Percentage

Personal Services	66.1%
Operating Costs	22.7%
Capital Costs	11.3%
TOTAL	100.0%

Cost Breakdown in Dollars

Personal Services	$12,255,765
Operating Costs	$4,203,291
Capital Costs	$2,089,226
TOTAL	$18,548,282

Resource Measures

Fire Services Costs per Capita

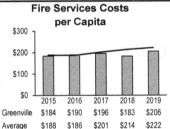

	2015	2016	2017	2018	2019
Greenville	$184	$190	$196	$183	$206
Average	$188	$186	$201	$214	$222

Fire Services Total FTEs per 10,000 Population

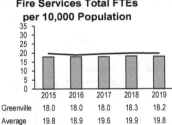

	2015	2016	2017	2018	2019
Greenville	18.0	18.0	18.0	18.3	18.2
Average	19.8	18.9	19.6	19.9	19.8

Fire Services Cost per Thousand Dollars of Property Protected

	2015	2016	2017	2018	2019
Greenville	$2.73	$2.77	$2.86	$2.46	$2.82
Average	$1.90	$1.83	$2.05	$1.97	$2.01

Workload Measures

Actual Fires per 1,000 Population

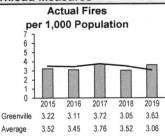

	2015	2016	2017	2018	2019
Greenville	3.22	3.11	3.72	3.05	3.63
Average	3.52	3.45	3.76	3.52	3.06

Fire Department Responses per 1,000 Population

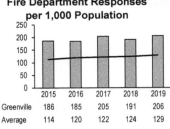

	2015	2016	2017	2018	2019
Greenville	186	185	205	191	206
Average	114	120	122	124	129

Fire Inspections Completed per 1,000 Population

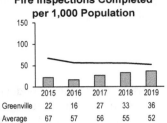

	2015	2016	2017	2018	2019
Greenville	22	16	27	33	36
Average	67	57	56	55	52

Efficiency Measures

Fire Services Cost per Fire Department Response

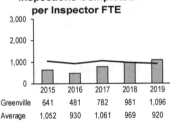

	2015	2016	2017	2018	2019
Greenville	$986	$1,027	$956	$954	$997
Average	$1,815	$1,682	$1,786	$1,901	$1,896

Inspections Completed per Inspector FTE

	2015	2016	2017	2018	2019
Greenville	641	481	782	981	1,096
Average	1,052	930	1,061	969	920

Effectiveness Measures

Average Response Time to Priority One Calls in Minutes

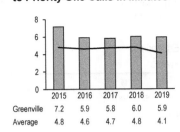

	2015	2016	2017	2018	2019
Greenville	7.2	5.9	5.8	6.0	5.9
Average	4.8	4.6	4.7	4.8	4.1

Percentage of Fire Code Violations Cleared within 90 Days

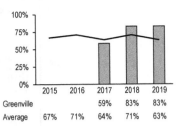

	2015	2016	2017	2018	2019
Greenville			59%	83%	83%
Average	67%	71%	64%	71%	63%

Percentage of Fires Confined to Rooms or Objects Involved on Arrival

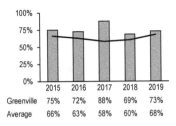

	2015	2016	2017	2018	2019
Greenville	75%	72%	88%	69%	73%
Average	66%	63%	58%	60%	68%

Percentage of Fires for Which Cause Was Determined

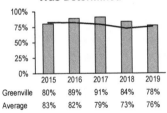

	2015	2016	2017	2018	2019
Greenville	80%	89%	91%	84%	78%
Average	83%	82%	79%	73%	76%

Percentage of Full Response within 8 Minutes Travel Time

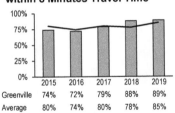

	2015	2016	2017	2018	2019
Greenville	74%	72%	79%	88%	89%
Average	80%	74%	80%	78%	85%

Percentage of Lost Pulse Cases Recovered Pulse at Transfer of Care

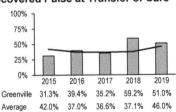

	2015	2016	2017	2018	2019
Greenville	31.3%	39.4%	35.2%	59.2%	51.0%
Average	42.0%	37.0%	36.6%	37.1%	46.0%

Fiscal Year 2018–19

Explanatory Information

Service Level and Delivery

The goal of the Hickory Fire Department is to provide high quality emergency services, education, and prevention that protect the community through professional coworkers focused on customer service, compassion, commitment, and innovation. The city provides fire coverage for an area of 13 square miles beyond city boundaries.

The fire department contains the following divisions: administration, fire and life safety, training, maintenance, and fire suppression.

Fire suppression personnel work a twenty-four-hour shift with forty-eight hours off between shifts. The twenty-four-hour shift begins at 8 a.m.

The city has an ISO rating of 3, as rated in 2005.

The fire department in Hickory conducted 6,740 fire maintenance, construction, and reinspections during the fiscal year. Fire prevention inspectors are assigned Level I, Level II, and Level III inspections. They also review construction and fire protection plans and inspect the installation of fire protection systems. The inspectors also accompany building inspectors during certificate of occupancy inspections and are responsible for conducting fire investigations, fire hydrant flow tests, occupancy and site visits, and other activities as assigned.

Conditions Affecting Service, Performance, and Costs

Hickory has a fire station staffed at the regional airport in addition to the six community fire stations.

Municipal Profile

Service Population	46,051
Land Area (Square Miles)	42.86
Persons per Square Mile	1,075
Median Household Income	$35,353
U.S. Census 2016	

Service Profile

FTE Positions—Firefighters	117.0
FTE Positions—Other	20.0
Fire Stations	7
First-Line Fire Apparatus	
Pumpers	6
Aerial Trucks	2
Quints	0
Squads	0
Rescue	1
Other	3
Fire Department Responses	6,740
Responses for Fires	182
Structural Fires Reported	34
Inspections Completed for Maintenance, Construction, and Reinspections	4,887
Fire Code Violations Reported	3,407
Estimated Fire Loss (millions)	$1.49
Amount of Property Protected in Service Area (millions)	$5,386
Number of Fire Education Programs or Events	463

Full Cost Profile

Cost Breakdown by Percentage	
Personal Services	67.6%
Operating Costs	27.7%
Capital Costs	4.7%
TOTAL	100.0%

Cost Breakdown in Dollars	
Personal Services	$9,101,941
Operating Costs	$3,725,174
Capital Costs	$638,096
TOTAL	$13,465,211

Hickory

Fire Services

Resource Measures

Fire Services Costs per Capita

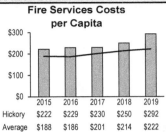

	2015	2016	2017	2018	2019
Hickory	$222	$229	$230	$250	$292
Average	$188	$186	$201	$214	$222

Fire Services Total FTEs per 10,000 Population

	2015	2016	2017	2018	2019
Hickory	30.0	30.0	29.4	29.3	29.7
Average	19.8	18.9	19.6	19.9	19.8

Fire Services Cost per Thousand Dollars of Property Protected

	2015	2016	2017	2018	2019
Hickory	$1.92	$2.08	$2.09	$2.22	$2.50
Average	$1.90	$1.83	$2.05	$1.97	$2.01

Workload Measures

Actual Fires per 1,000 Population

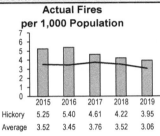

	2015	2016	2017	2018	2019
Hickory	5.25	5.40	4.61	4.22	3.95
Average	3.52	3.45	3.76	3.52	3.06

Fire Department Responses per 1,000 Population

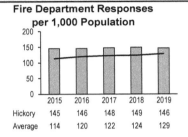

	2015	2016	2017	2018	2019
Hickory	145	146	148	149	146
Average	114	120	122	124	129

Fire Inspections Completed per 1,000 Population

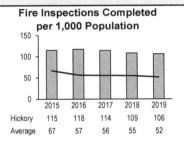

	2015	2016	2017	2018	2019
Hickory	115	118	114	109	106
Average	67	57	56	55	52

Efficiency Measures

Fire Services Cost per Fire Department Response

	2015	2016	2017	2018	2019
Hickory	$1,524	$1,575	$1,555	$1,680	$1,998
Average	$1,815	$1,682	$1,786	$1,901	$1,896

Inspections Completed per Inspector FTE

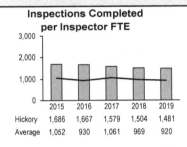

	2015	2016	2017	2018	2019
Hickory	1,686	1,667	1,579	1,504	1,481
Average	1,052	930	1,061	969	920

Effectiveness Measures

Average Response Time to Priority One Calls in Minutes

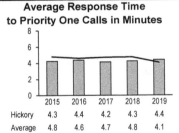

	2015	2016	2017	2018	2019
Hickory	4.3	4.4	4.2	4.3	4.4
Average	4.8	4.6	4.7	4.8	4.1

Percentage of Fire Code Violations Cleared within 90 Days

	2015	2016	2017	2018	2019
Hickory		100%	100%	100%	100%
Average	67%	71%	64%	71%	63%

Percentage of Fires Confined to Rooms or Objects Involved on Arrival

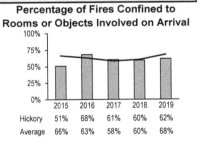

	2015	2016	2017	2018	2019
Hickory	51%	68%	61%	60%	62%
Average	66%	63%	58%	60%	68%

Percentage of Fires for Which Cause Was Determined

	2015	2016	2017	2018	2019
Hickory	93%	93%	92%	85%	95%
Average	83%	82%	79%	73%	76%

Percentage of Full Response within 8 Minutes Travel Time

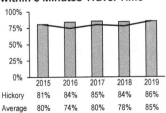

	2015	2016	2017	2018	2019
Hickory	81%	84%	85%	84%	86%
Average	80%	74%	80%	78%	85%

Percentage of Lost Pulse Cases Recovered Pulse at Transfer of Care

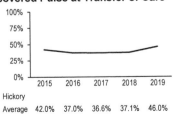

	2015	2016	2017	2018	2019
Hickory					
Average	42.0%	37.0%	36.6%	37.1%	46.0%

Explanatory Information

Service Level and Delivery

The purpose of the Mooresville Fire Department is to provide capable, well-trained personnel and necessary equipment to suppress fires; to provide rescue services as needed; and to work toward a more fire-safe community through loss-prevention activities, including inspections, code enforcement, and public education programs.

The fire department contains the following three divisions: administration, operations, and prevention/inspection.

The shift schedule for the fire department is twenty-four hours on and forty-eight hours off with three shifts. Administrative, fire marshal office and squads work a regular five-day work week from 8am to 5pm.

The town has an ISO rating of 1, as rated in 2017. This is the highest rating possible.

The fire department in Mooresville conducted 937 fire maintenance, construction, and reinspections during the fiscal year. All inspections are conducted by the fire marshal's office.

Conditions Affecting Service, Performance, and Costs

Mooresville joined the Benchmarking project in July 2018, with the first year of data showing for FY 2017–18.

Municipal Profile	
Service Population	41,255
Land Area (Square Miles)	23.06
Persons per Square Mile	1,789
Median Household Income	$67,213
U.S. Census 2016	

Service Profile	
FTE Positions—Firefighters	84.0
FTE Positions—Other	11.0
Fire Stations	5
First-Line Fire Apparatus	
Pumpers	5
Aerial Trucks	1
Quints	0
Squads	1
Rescue	0
Other	0
Fire Department Responses	7,497
Responses for Fires	125
Structural Fires Reported	11
Inspections Completed for Maintenance, Construction, and Reinspections	937
Fire Code Violations Reported	22,380
Estimated Fire Loss (millions)	$0.71
Amount of Property Protected in Service Area (millions)	$6,492
Number of Fire Education Programs or Events	199

Full Cost Profile	
Cost Breakdown by Percentage	
Personal Services	55.1%
Operating Costs	27.3%
Capital Costs	17.6%
TOTAL	100.0%
Cost Breakdown in Dollars	
Personal Services	$7,567,895
Operating Costs	$3,758,193
Capital Costs	$2,416,332
TOTAL	$13,742,420

Mooresville

Fire Services

Resource Measures

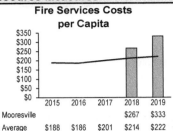

Fire Services Costs per Capita

	2015	2016	2017	2018	2019
Mooresville				$267	$333
Average	$188	$186	$201	$214	$222

Fire Services Total FTEs per 10,000 Population

	2015	2016	2017	2018	2019
Mooresville				23.5	23.0
Average	19.8	18.9	19.6	19.9	19.8

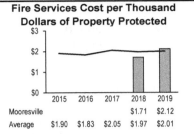

Fire Services Cost per Thousand Dollars of Property Protected

	2015	2016	2017	2018	2019
Mooresville				$1.71	$2.12
Average	$1.90	$1.83	$2.05	$1.97	$2.01

Workload Measures

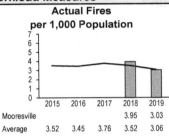

Actual Fires per 1,000 Population

	2015	2016	2017	2018	2019
Mooresville				3.95	3.03
Average	3.52	3.45	3.76	3.52	3.06

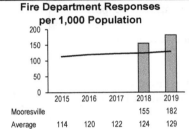

Fire Department Responses per 1,000 Population

	2015	2016	2017	2018	2019
Mooresville				155	182
Average	114	120	122	124	129

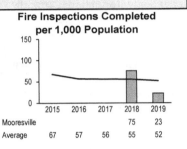

Fire Inspections Completed per 1,000 Population

	2015	2016	2017	2018	2019
Mooresville				75	23
Average	67	57	56	55	52

Efficiency Measures

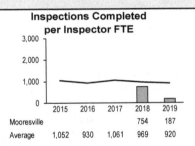

Fire Services Cost per Fire Department Response

	2015	2016	2017	2018	2019
Mooresville				$1,721	$1,833
Average	$1,815	$1,682	$1,786	$1,901	$1,896

Inspections Completed per Inspector FTE

	2015	2016	2017	2018	2019
Mooresville				754	187
Average	1,052	930	1,061	969	920

Effectiveness Measures

Average Response Time to Priority One Calls in Minutes

	2015	2016	2017	2018	2019
Mooresville				6.4	4.8
Average	4.8	4.6	4.7	4.8	4.1

Percentage of Fire Code Violations Cleared within 90 Days

	2015	2016	2017	2018	2019
Mooresville				4%	
Average	67%	71%	64%	71%	63%

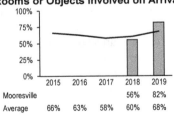

Percentage of Fires Confined to Rooms or Objects Involved on Arrival

	2015	2016	2017	2018	2019
Mooresville				56%	82%
Average	66%	63%	58%	60%	68%

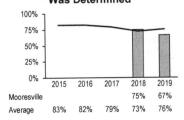

Percentage of Fires for Which Cause Was Determined

	2015	2016	2017	2018	2019
Mooresville				75%	67%
Average	83%	82%	79%	73%	76%

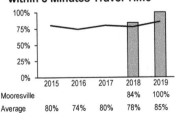

Percentage of Full Response within 8 Minutes Travel Time

	2015	2016	2017	2018	2019
Mooresville				84%	100%
Average	80%	74%	80%	78%	85%

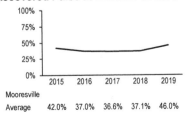

Percentage of Lost Pulse Cases Recovered Pulse at Transfer of Care

	2015	2016	2017	2018	2019
Mooresville					
Average	42.0%	37.0%	36.6%	37.1%	46.0%

Fiscal Year 2018–19

Explanatory Information

Service Level and Delivery

The Raleigh Fire Department provides the following services in carrying out its mission: fire protection, emergency medical first response, extrication, confined space and high-angle rescue, hazardous materials response, fire inspections, and fire education.

The fire department is broken into five primary function areas. The Office of the Fire Chief provides administrative services and oversight; the Office of the Fire Marshal is the enforcement, educational, and informational arm; the Operations Division responds to and manages incidents and special events; the Support Services Division supplies and maintains infrastructure, equipment, clothing, and apparatus; and the Training Division recruits, hires, trains, and manages career development.

The shift schedule for the fire department is a nine-day cycle as follows: five twenty-four-hour days alternating on and off followed by four days off.

The city received an ISO rating of 1 in 2016. This is the highest rating possible.

The fire department in Raleigh conducted 21,783 fire maintenance, construction, and reinspections during the fiscal year. Fire inspections are scheduled by the Office of the Fire Marshal through an automated process based on a priority basis and consistent with section 106 of the NC State Fire Code. Other inspections are scheduled as requested for special events, operational permits, and special requests. Apartment complexes are counted as one inspection per building, and high rises are considered as one inspection with one file.

Conditions Affecting Service, Performance, and Costs

Raleigh rejoined the Benchmarking Project in July 2016, with the first year of data showing for FY 2015–16.

Raleigh currently marks some violations as repaired but not yet completely resolved. This creates more open violations in the system while decisions are made about referrals or penalties before the violation can be cleared.

Municipal Profile

Service Population	464,453
Land Area (Square Miles)	146.07
Persons per Square Mile	3,180
Median Household Income	$46,612
U.S. Census 2016	

Service Profile

FTE Positions—Firefighters	552.0
FTE Positions—Other	70.0
Fire Stations	28
First-Line Fire Apparatus	
Pumpers	27
Aerial Trucks	9
Quints	0
Squads	2
Rescue	1
Other	12
Fire Department Responses	43,047
Responses for Fires	896
Structural Fires Reported	255
Inspections Completed for Maintenance, Construction, and Reinspections	21,783
Fire Code Violations Reported	24,695
Estimated Fire Loss (millions)	$14.50
Amount of Property Protected in Service Area (millions)	$60,313
Number of Fire Education Programs or Events	337

Full Cost Profile

Cost Breakdown by Percentage	
Personal Services	74.4%
Operating Costs	16.6%
Capital Costs	9.0%
TOTAL	100.0%

Cost Breakdown in Dollars	
Personal Services	$54,830,482
Operating Costs	$12,190,009
Capital Costs	$6,631,835
TOTAL	$73,652,326

Raleigh

Fire Services

Resource Measures

Fire Services Costs per Capita

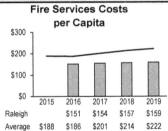

	2015	2016	2017	2018	2019
Raleigh		$151	$154	$157	$159
Average	$188	$186	$201	$214	$222

Fire Services Total FTEs per 10,000 Population

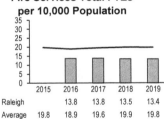

	2015	2016	2017	2018	2019
Raleigh		13.8	13.8	13.5	13.4
Average	19.8	18.9	19.6	19.9	19.8

Fire Services Cost per Thousand Dollars of Property Protected

	2015	2016	2017	2018	2019
Raleigh		$1.24	$1.29	$1.22	$1.22
Average	$1.90	$1.83	$2.05	$1.97	$2.01

Workload Measures

Actual Fires per 1,000 Population

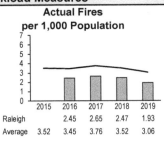

	2015	2016	2017	2018	2019
Raleigh		2.45	2.65	2.47	1.93
Average	3.52	3.45	3.76	3.52	3.06

Fire Department Responses per 1,000 Population

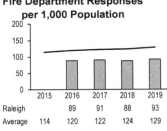

	2015	2016	2017	2018	2019
Raleigh		89	91	88	93
Average	114	120	122	124	129

Fire Inspections Completed per 1,000 Population

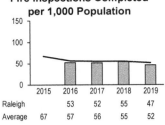

	2015	2016	2017	2018	2019
Raleigh		53	52	55	47
Average	67	57	56	55	52

Efficiency Measures

Fire Services Cost per Fire Department Response

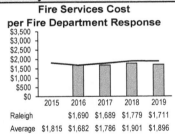

	2015	2016	2017	2018	2019
Raleigh		$1,690	$1,689	$1,779	$1,711
Average	$1,815	$1,682	$1,786	$1,901	$1,896

Inspections Completed per Inspector FTE

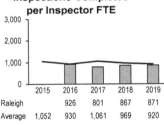

	2015	2016	2017	2018	2019
Raleigh		926	801	867	871
Average	1,052	930	1,061	969	920

Effectiveness Measures

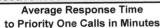

Average Response Time to Priority One Calls in Minutes

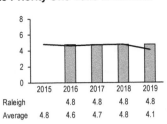

	2015	2016	2017	2018	2019
Raleigh		4.8	4.8	4.8	4.8
Average	4.8	4.6	4.7	4.8	4.1

Percentage of Fire Code Violations Cleared within 90 Days

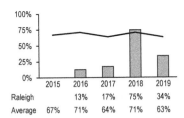

	2015	2016	2017	2018	2019
Raleigh		13%	17%	75%	34%
Average	67%	71%	64%	71%	63%

Percentage of Fires Confined to Rooms or Objects Involved on Arrival

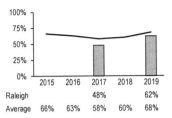

	2015	2016	2017	2018	2019
Raleigh			48%		62%
Average	66%	63%	58%	60%	68%

Percentage of Fires for Which Cause Was Determined

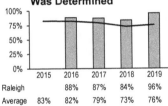

	2015	2016	2017	2018	2019
Raleigh		88%	87%	84%	96%
Average	83%	82%	79%	73%	76%

Percentage of Full Response within 8 Minutes Travel Time

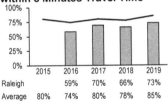

	2015	2016	2017	2018	2019
Raleigh		59%	70%	66%	73%
Average	80%	74%	80%	78%	85%

Percentage of Lost Pulse Cases Recovered Pulse at Transfer of Care

	2015	2016	2017	2018	2019
Raleigh					54.8%
Average	42.0%	37.0%	36.6%	37.1%	46.0%

Fiscal Year 2018–19

Explanatory Information

Service Level and Delivery

Wilson Fire/Rescue Services is a public safety organization whose mission is to assist the public in the protection of life and property by minimizing the impact of fire, medical emergencies, and potential disasters or events that affect the community and the environment.

Wilson Fire/Rescue Services has two major divisions. Operations handles emergency responses and equipment maintenance. Support Services handles fire prevention and education, facility maintenance, IM/GIS, and budget.

Firefighters work twenty-four hours on and twenty-four hours off. Each work cycle consists of three twenty-four-hour shifts with a day off between shifts. A four-day break is then provided before the cycle repeats itself.

The city has an ISO rating of 1, as rated in 2018. This is the highest rating that can be achieved. The Wilson Fire Department has been accredited since 2002.

The fire department in Wilson conducted 3,350 fire maintenance, construction, and reinspections during the fiscal year. Fire inspections are conducted by the Fire Prevention Bureau on a daily basis. Each inspector is assigned a district in which he or she handles all inspections. A charge is made on the third reinspection.

Conditions Affecting Service, Performance, and Costs

Municipal Profile

Service Population	49,054
Land Area (Square Miles)	31.01
Persons per Square Mile	1,582
Median Household Income	$35,409
U.S. Census 2016	

Service Profile

FTE Positions—Firefighters	85.0
FTE Positions—Other	15.0
Fire Stations	5
First-Line Fire Apparatus	
Pumpers	4
Aerial Trucks	1
Quints	1
Squads	0
Rescue	0
Other	1
Fire Department Responses	4,433
Responses for Fires	188
Structural Fires Reported	42
Inspections Completed for Maintenance, Construction, and Reinspections	3,350
Fire Code Violations Reported	4,540
Estimated Fire Loss (millions)	$0.70
Amount of Property Protected in Service Area (millions)	$4,127
Number of Fire Education Programs or Events	70

Full Cost Profile

Cost Breakdown by Percentage	
Personal Services	72.5%
Operating Costs	18.3%
Capital Costs	9.2%
TOTAL	100.0%
Cost Breakdown in Dollars	
Personal Services	$8,065,367
Operating Costs	$2,037,500
Capital Costs	$1,026,494
TOTAL	$11,129,361

Wilson

Fire Services

Resource Measures

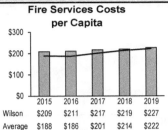

Fire Services Costs per Capita

	2015	2016	2017	2018	2019
Wilson	$209	$211	$217	$219	$227
Average	$188	$186	$201	$214	$222

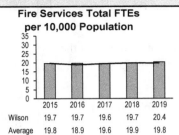

Fire Services Total FTEs per 10,000 Population

	2015	2016	2017	2018	2019
Wilson	19.7	19.7	19.6	19.7	20.4
Average	19.8	18.9	19.6	19.9	19.8

Fire Services Cost per Thousand Dollars of Property Protected

	2015	2016	2017	2018	2019
Wilson	$2.45	$2.44	$2.51	$2.66	$2.70
Average	$1.90	$1.83	$2.05	$1.97	$2.01

Workload Measures

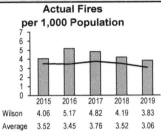

Actual Fires per 1,000 Population

	2015	2016	2017	2018	2019
Wilson	4.06	5.17	4.82	4.19	3.83
Average	3.52	3.45	3.76	3.52	3.06

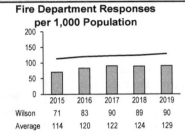

Fire Department Responses per 1,000 Population

	2015	2016	2017	2018	2019
Wilson	71	83	90	89	90
Average	114	120	122	124	129

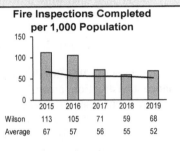

Fire Inspections Completed per 1,000 Population

	2015	2016	2017	2018	2019
Wilson	113	105	71	59	68
Average	67	57	56	55	52

Efficiency Measures

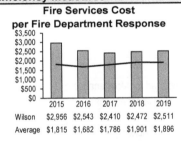

Fire Services Cost per Fire Department Response

	2015	2016	2017	2018	2019
Wilson	$2,956	$2,543	$2,410	$2,472	$2,511
Average	$1,815	$1,682	$1,786	$1,901	$1,896

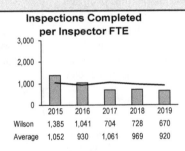

Inspections Completed per Inspector FTE

	2015	2016	2017	2018	2019
Wilson	1,385	1,041	704	728	670
Average	1,052	930	1,061	969	920

Effectiveness Measures

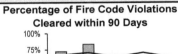

Average Response Time to Priority One Calls in Minutes

	2015	2016	2017	2018	2019
Wilson	4.2	4.2	4.4	4.5	4.1
Average	4.8	4.6	4.7	4.8	4.1

Percentage of Fire Code Violations Cleared within 90 Days

	2015	2016	2017	2018	2019
Wilson	73%	83%	56%	36%	24%
Average	67%	71%	64%	71%	63%

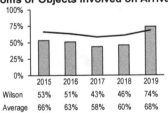

Percentage of Fires Confined to Rooms or Objects Involved on Arrival

	2015	2016	2017	2018	2019
Wilson	53%	51%	43%	46%	74%
Average	66%	63%	58%	60%	68%

Percentage of Fires for Which Cause Was Determined

	2015	2016	2017	2018	2019
Wilson	74%	68%	84%	76%	82%
Average	83%	82%	79%	73%	76%

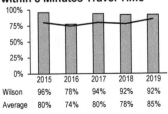

Percentage of Full Response within 8 Minutes Travel Time

	2015	2016	2017	2018	2019
Wilson	96%	78%	94%	92%	92%
Average	80%	74%	80%	78%	85%

Percentage of Lost Pulse Cases Recovered Pulse at Transfer of Care

	2015	2016	2017	2018	2019
Wilson	34.0%	33.3%	25.8%	34.7%	17.1%
Average	42.0%	37.0%	36.6%	37.1%	46.0%

Winston-Salem

Fire Services

Fiscal Year 2018–19

Explanatory Information

Service Level and Delivery

The mission of the Winston-Salem Fire Department is to protect the lives and property of all people within Winston-Salem by reducing the occurrence and minimizing the effects of fires.

The Winston-Salem Fire Department contains the following six divisions: fire suppression, vehicle maintenance, planning, community education, fire prevention, and administration.

Fire suppression personnel work a twenty-one-day cycle with an average of fifty-six hours per week.

The city has an ISO rating of 2, as rated in 2015.

The fire department in Winston-Salem conducted 5,480 fire maintenance, construction, and reinspections during the fiscal year. The fire department inspection program includes inspections that (1) ensure reasonable life safety conditions within a structure; (2) identify fire hazards; and (3) determine the proper installation, operation, and maintenance of fire protection features, systems, and appliances within buildings. The fire department inspection program involves both the Fire Prevention Bureau and the fire engine companies. Similar to the Fire Prevention Bureau, all fire stations have inspection responsibilities and conduct building inspections within their assigned territories. Each business within the city limits is inspected annually and receives as many return visits as necessary for fire code compliance.

Conditions Affecting Service, Performance, and Costs

Winston-Salem has a high number of inspections per inspector full-time equivalent (FTE) when compared to the other jurisdictions due to the fact that many inspections are performed by fire company personnel. The city defines an inspection as a site interior and/or exterior survey of a building, operation, event, condition, and/or activity for the purpose of verifying fire and building code compliance.

Municipal Profile

Service Population	243,447
Land Area (Square Miles)	132.55
Persons per Square Mile	1,837
Median Household Income	$40,584
U.S. Census 2016	

Service Profile

FTE Positions—Firefighters	339.0
FTE Positions—Other	29.0
Fire Stations	19
First-Line Fire Apparatus	
Pumpers	18
Aerial Trucks	5
Quints	0
Squads	0
Rescue	2
Other	13
Fire Department Responses	27,303
Responses for Fires	681
Structural Fires Reported	220
Inspections Completed for Maintenance, Construction, and Reinspections	5,480
Fire Code Violations Reported	5,775
Estimated Fire Loss (millions)	$4.33
Amount of Property Protected in Service Area (millions)	$22,384
Number of Fire Education Programs or Events	223

Full Cost Profile

Cost Breakdown by Percentage

Personal Services	78.9%
Operating Costs	13.9%
Capital Costs	7.3%
TOTAL	100.0%

Cost Breakdown in Dollars

Personal Services	$29,109,421
Operating Costs	$5,114,457
Capital Costs	$2,684,659
TOTAL	$36,908,537

Winston-Salem

Fire Services

Key: Winston-Salem ▨   Benchmarking Average —   Fiscal Years 2015 through 2019

Resource Measures

Fire Services Costs per Capita

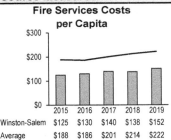

	2015	2016	2017	2018	2019
Winston-Salem	$125	$130	$140	$138	$152
Average	$188	$186	$201	$214	$222

Fire Services Total FTEs per 10,000 Population

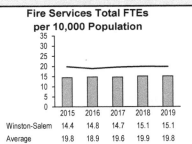

	2015	2016	2017	2018	2019
Winston-Salem	14.4	14.8	14.7	15.1	15.1
Average	19.8	18.9	19.6	19.9	19.8

Fire Services Cost per Thousand Dollars of Property Protected

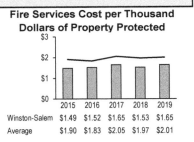

	2015	2016	2017	2018	2019
Winston-Salem	$1.49	$1.52	$1.65	$1.53	$1.65
Average	$1.90	$1.83	$2.05	$1.97	$2.01

Workload Measures

Actual Fires per 1,000 Population

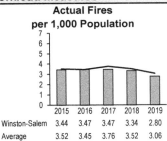

	2015	2016	2017	2018	2019
Winston-Salem	3.44	3.47	3.47	3.34	2.80
Average	3.52	3.45	3.76	3.52	3.06

Fire Department Responses per 1,000 Population

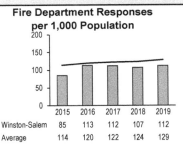

	2015	2016	2017	2018	2019
Winston-Salem	85	113	112	107	112
Average	114	120	122	124	129

Fire Inspections Completed per 1,000 Population

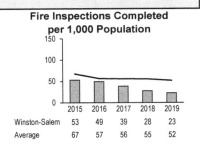

	2015	2016	2017	2018	2019
Winston-Salem	53	49	39	28	23
Average	67	57	56	55	52

Efficiency Measures

Fire Services Cost per Fire Department Response

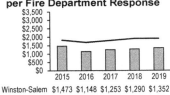

	2015	2016	2017	2018	2019
Winston-Salem	$1,473	$1,148	$1,253	$1,290	$1,352
Average	$1,815	$1,682	$1,786	$1,901	$1,896

Inspections Completed per Inspector FTE

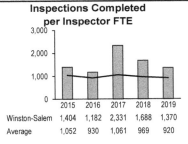

	2015	2016	2017	2018	2019
Winston-Salem	1,404	1,182	2,331	1,688	1,370
Average	1,052	930	1,061	969	920

Effectiveness Measures

Average Response Time to Priority One Calls in Minutes

	2015	2016	2017	2018	2019
Winston-Salem	4.5	4.7	4.7	4.8	4.9
Average	4.8	4.6	4.7	4.8	4.1

Percentage of Fire Code Violations Cleared within 90 Days

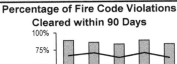

	2015	2016	2017	2018	2019
Winston-Salem	89%	86%	83%	89%	83%
Average	67%	71%	64%	71%	63%

Percentage of Fires Confined to Rooms or Objects Involved on Arrival

	2015	2016	2017	2018	2019
Winston-Salem	76%	73%	72%	69%	70%
Average	66%	63%	58%	60%	68%

Percentage of Fires for Which Cause Was Determined

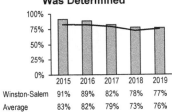

	2015	2016	2017	2018	2019
Winston-Salem	91%	89%	82%	78%	77%
Average	83%	82%	79%	73%	76%

Percentage of Full Response within 8 Minutes Travel Time

	2015	2016	2017	2018	2019
Winston-Salem	65%	60%	57%	62%	56%
Average	80%	74%	80%	78%	85%

Percentage of Lost Pulse Cases Recovered Pulse at Transfer of Care

	2015	2016	2017	2018	2019
Winston-Salem	72.2%	28.6%	37.7%	27.5%	65.1%
Average	42.0%	37.0%	36.6%	37.1%	46.0%

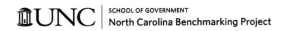

SCHOOL OF GOVERNMENT
North Carolina Benchmarking Project

Performance and Cost Data

BUILDING INSPECTIONS

PERFORMANCE MEASURES FOR BUILDING INSPECTIONS

SERVICE DEFINITION

Building Inspection Services refers to permit issuance and inspections for building, electrical, mechanical (including heating and cooling), and plumbing work on new residential and commercial construction or additions and alterations to enforce the North Carolina State Building Code and related local building regulations. The inspection process includes the receipt of permit applications, review of plans and specifications, issuance of permits, and follow-up field inspections to ensure compliance. Excluded are the enforcement of zoning and subdivision regulations, fire codes, minimum housing codes, erosion and sedimentation control regulations, watershed regulations, historic preservation ordinances, and other development regulations or plans.

NOTES ON PERFORMANCE MEASURES

1. Building Inspections per 1,000 Population

Building inspections are those required by the North Carolina State Building Code for general building, electrical, mechanical (including heating and cooling), and plumbing work associated with construction projects. Inspections include re-inspections. They do not include non–building code inspections or consultation visits.

2. Value of Total Building Permits as Percentage of Tax Base of Area Served

When a building permit is issued, the dollar amount of the work specified in the contract(s) authorizing the work is recorded as the value of the building permit. Tax base refers to the taxable valuation used for levying the fiscal year property tax for the area served.

3. Value of Commercial Permits as Percentage of Tax Base of Area Served

Commercial building permits are issued for construction of business, manufacturing, institutional, and other nonresidential buildings or improvements. Tax base is defined above.

4. Cost per Building Inspection and Inspections per Day per Inspector

Building inspections are defined above. Cost is determined using the project's full cost accounting model, including direct, indirect, and capital costs. An inspector full-time equivalent (FTE) is calculated using a work year of 235 days. Inspector FTEs include permanent, temporary, part-time, and full-time inspectors.

5. Value of Building Permits per FTE

Value of building permits is defined above. Inspectors must be certified by the state to enforce the state building code and be able to review plans and conduct inspections to enforce that code. Inspector FTEs exclude supervisors, who may be certified but who spend less than 50 percent of their time performing inspections. Inspector FTEs also exclude support personnel who are not certified.

6. Number of Plan Reviews per Reviewer FTE

The state building code requires that plans and specifications for most commercial and residential construction be reviewed before permits are issued for such construction. Reviewer FTEs are calculated using a 2,080-hour work year, the actual number of plan reviews conducted during the fiscal year, and the number of plan reviewers.

7. Percentage of Inspection Responses within One Working Day of Request

A request for inspection may be made by phone, in person, or in writing. A response refers to at least beginning an inspection, regardless of whether approval of the work occurs. The majority of inspections are completed the same day as initiated. A response to a request within one working day means that the inspection is initiated before the end of the workday following the day on which the request is made.

8. Percentage of Inspections That Are Re-inspections

A re-inspection occurs when a building inspector must inspect work that has previously been inspected. A re-inspection can occur due to problems found in the original inspection or for other reasons.

Building Inspections

Summary of Key Dimensions of Service

City or Town	Area Served (in Square Miles)	Population Growth from 2010 to 2017	Building Inspections by Trade					Number of Plan Reviewers	Building Inspector FTEs	Total Staff FTEs
			Building	Electrical	Mechanical	Plumbing	Total			
Apex	37.2	29.3%	25,489	12,855	10,041	14,254	62,639	3.0	11.0	20.0
Asheville	45.8	10.2%	14,326	10,734	8,575	6,571	40,206	5.0	15.0	25.0
Chapel Hill	27.5	4.7%	2,881	2,588	2,620	1,800	9,889	2.0	6.0	14.0
Goldsboro	57.6	-7.6%	1,520	2,184	1,692	855	6,251	1.0	4.0	8.0
Greensboro	134.6	6.9%	18,126	19,134	15,766	10,767	63,793	4.5	16.0	30.0
Greenville	61.8	5.5%	4,037	3,590	3,129	2,715	13,471	1.0	7.0	12.0
Raleigh	147.0	14.0%	28,945	39,634	31,403	19,167	119,149	18.0	42.0	80.0
Wilson	58.5	0.0%	2,981	2,347	2,219	1,346	8,893	1.0	4.0	7.0
Winston-Salem	396.0	5.8%	17,675	22,335	17,629	12,938	70,577	3.0	18.0	38.4

* Total Inspections for Chapel Hill includes 347 that did not fit into the four major categories.

EXPLANATORY FACTORS

These are factors that the project found affected building inspection performance and cost in one or more of the municipalities:

Rate of growth and development in city
Size and complexity of construction projects
Geographic area served by county building inspections
Inspectors' enforcement of local development regulations
Emphasis given to plan review in each jurisdiction
Inspector specialization
Organization of the building inspection function

Explanatory Information

Service Level and Delivery

The Town of Apex provides building inspection services though the Building Inspections and Permits Department. The department is organized into two major divisions: building inspections and engineering. The department provides inspections for all of Apex and just over twenty-one square miles of area in its extraterritorial jurisdiction (ETJ).

All building inspectors in Apex serve each of the major trades. The department enforces the North Carolina State Building Code.

The department has a goal of having all inspectors fully qualified for the technical, administrative, and customer service aspects of their job. Training is accomplished primarily by off-site seminars and conferences offered by state-approved sponsors.

Apex has a standard that all inspection requests recorded by a permit technician or the permit office voicemail by 3 a.m. are to be performed on the next business day. Due to high workload during the latter part of the fiscal year, the city was not able to always meet this standard of service.

Total revenue received from inspection fees amounted to $3,912,682 for the fiscal year.

Conditions Affecting Service, Performance, and Costs

The population served is calculated by adding the population of Apex with the population of the ETJ. The tax base served is calculated by adding the tax base of Apex with the tax base of the ETJ. The population and the tax base of the ETJ are calculated by taking the population and tax base per square mile of Wake County and multiplying them by the square miles of the ETJ.

Apex does not track multifamily as a category of reporting for inspections or plan reviews. Instead, townhomes are included with residential, and condos and apartments are included with commercial.

While Apex has the goal of providing next-day service for building inspections, the large volume of work in the strong growth community has made this goal difficult to achieve at all times.

Municipal Profile

Population Served	70,417
Land Area Inspected (Square Miles)	37.21
Persons per Square Mile	1,892
Estimated Tax Base in Service Area (billions)	$8.69
Median Household Income	$84,000
U.S. Census 2016	

Service Profile

FTE Inspectors	
Building	0.0
Electrical	0.0
Mechanical	0.0
Plumbing	0.0
All Trades	11.0
Total Inspectors	11.0
FTE Plan Reviewers	3.0
Other FTE Positions	6.0
Total of All Positions	20.0
Number of Inspections by Type	
Building	25,489
Electrical	12,855
Mechanical	10,041
Plumbing	14,254
TOTAL	62,639
Building Permit Values	
Residential	$365,424,000
Multifamily	with other categories
Commercial	$62,553,964
TOTAL	$427,977,964
Inspection Fee Revenue	$3,912,682

Full Cost Profile

Cost Breakdown by Percentage	
Personal Services	70.1%
Operating Costs	22.9%
Capital Costs	6.9%
TOTAL	100.0%
Cost Breakdown in Dollars	
Personal Services	$1,919,885
Operating Costs	$627,744
Capital Costs	$189,262
TOTAL	$2,736,891

Apex

Building Inspections

Resource Measures

Building Inspections Services Costs per Capita

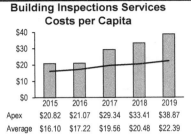

	2015	2016	2017	2018	2019
Apex	$20.82	$21.07	$29.34	$33.41	$38.87
Average	$16.10	$17.22	$19.56	$20.48	$22.39

Building Inspections Services FTEs per 10,000 Population

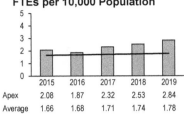

	2015	2016	2017	2018	2019
Apex	2.08	1.87	2.32	2.53	2.84
Average	1.66	1.68	1.71	1.74	1.78

Building Inspections Services Cost per Million Dollars of Tax Base

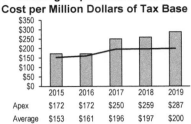

	2015	2016	2017	2018	2019
Apex	$172	$172	$250	$259	$287
Average	$153	$161	$196	$197	$200

Workload Measures

Inspections per 1,000 Population in Service Area

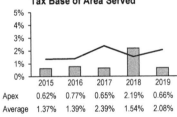

	2015	2016	2017	2018	2019
Apex	461	450	739	1016	890
Average	243	257	276	300	307

Inspections per Square Mile in Service Area

	2015	2016	2017	2018	2019
Apex	817	828	1,323	1,814	1,683
Average	417	504	504	544	554

Value of Building Permits as Percentage of Tax Base of Area Served

	2015	2016	2017	2018	2019
Apex	2.45%	2.39%	3.73%	5.94%	4.49%
Average	2.24%	2.37%	3.69%	3.09%	3.12%

Value of Commercial Permits as Percentage of Tax Base of Area Served

	2015	2016	2017	2018	2019
Apex	0.62%	0.77%	0.65%	2.19%	0.66%
Average	1.37%	1.39%	2.39%	1.54%	2.08%

Value of Building Permits per Inspector FTE in Millions of Dollars

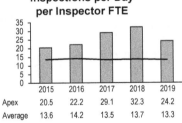

	2015	2016	2017	2018	2019
Apex	$30.9	$34.1	$40.6	$57.4	$38.9
Average	$29.4	$32.4	$41.6	$36.2	$36.4

Efficiency Measures

Building Services Cost per Inspection—All Types

	2015	2016	2017	2018	2019
Apex	$45.13	$46.84	$39.71	$32.89	$43.69
Average	$69.09	$69.47	$81.73	$86.79	$90.08

Inspections per Day per Inspector FTE

	2015	2016	2017	2018	2019
Apex	20.5	22.2	29.1	32.3	24.2
Average	13.6	14.2	13.5	13.7	13.3

Plan Reviews per Year per Reviewer FTE

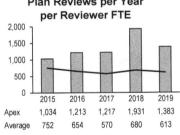

	2015	2016	2017	2018	2019
Apex	1,034	1,213	1,217	1,931	1,383
Average	752	654	570	680	613

Effectiveness Measures

Percentage of Inspection Responses within One Working Day of Request

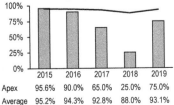

	2015	2016	2017	2018	2019
Apex	95.6%	90.0%	65.0%	25.0%	75.0%
Average	95.2%	94.3%	92.8%	88.0%	93.1%

Percentage of Inspections That Are Reinspections

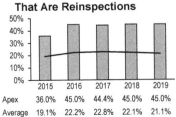

	2015	2016	2017	2018	2019
Apex	36.0%	45.0%	44.4%	45.0%	45.0%
Average	19.1%	22.2%	22.8%	22.1%	21.1%

Fiscal Year 2018–19

Explanatory Information

Service Level and Delivery

The City of Asheville Building Safety Division provides building inspection and permitting services to all areas within the Asheville city limits.

Inspectors include those who function in all trades and those who are certified in one of the following four trades: building, electrical, plumbing, or mechanical. The Building Safety Division enforces the North Carolina State Building Code and the Asheville Minimum Housing Code. The costs and the positions associated with enforcing the housing code are excluded from the project's performance and cost data.

The division has a goal of twelve training days per inspector per year. Inspectors are required to obtain certification in their primary trade plus two others. A career ladder encourages inspectors to work toward obtaining Level III certification in their primary trade and Level II certification in two other trades. Training is a high priority for the department, with an emphasis on code consistency. Training for contractors and designers also is a high priority for the department.

Asheville's policy is that all inspection requests received by phone before 4:30 p.m. and online by 6:00 p.m. will be performed the following business day.

Total revenue received from inspection fees amounted to $3.1 million for the fiscal year. The fee schedule separates fees for each type of permit, with specific fees depending on type of work, cost, square footage, and other factors. One free reinspection is granted per trade per project. Additional inspections are provided for a fee of $75 that must be paid prior to the inspection.

Conditions Affecting Service, Performance, and Costs

The city has many old and historic buildings that are difficult to renovate and bring into compliance with the state code. The city also has days during which snow and ice impact service delivery for this city function.

Municipal Profile

Population Served	93,621
Land Area Inspected (Square Miles)	45.79
Persons per Square Mile	2,045
Estimated Tax Base in Service Area (billions)	$14.60
Median Household Income	$40,494
U.S. Census 2016	

Service Profile

FTE Inspectors	
Building	0.0
Electrical	0.0
Mechanical	0.0
Plumbing	0.0
All Trades	15.0
Total Inspectors	15.0
FTE Plan Reviewers	5.0
Other FTE Positions	5.0
Total of All Positions	25.0
Number of Inspections by Type	
Building	14,326
Electrical	10,734
Mechanical	8,575
Plumbing	6,571
TOTAL	40,206
Building Permit Values	
Residential	$113,539,274
Multifamily	$58,276,332
Commercial	$194,676,164
TOTAL	$366,491,770
Inspection Fee Revenue	$3,121,828

Full Cost Profile

Cost Breakdown by Percentage	
Personal Services	71.8%
Operating Costs	23.8%
Capital Costs	4.4%
TOTAL	100.0%
Cost Breakdown in Dollars	
Personal Services	$2,516,673
Operating Costs	$834,469
Capital Costs	$155,924
TOTAL	$3,507,066

Resource Measures

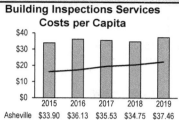

Building Inspections Services Costs per Capita

	2015	2016	2017	2018	2019
Asheville	$33.90	$36.13	$35.53	$34.75	$37.46
Average	$16.10	$17.22	$19.56	$20.48	$22.39

Building Inspections Services FTEs per 10,000 Population

	2015	2016	2017	2018	2019
Asheville	3.59	3.52	2.72	2.72	2.67
Average	1.66	1.68	1.71	1.74	1.78

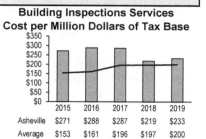

Building Inspections Services Cost per Million Dollars of Tax Base

	2015	2016	2017	2018	2019
Asheville	$271	$288	$287	$219	$233
Average	$153	$161	$196	$197	$200

Workload Measures

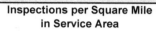

Inspections per 1,000 Population in Service Area

	2015	2016	2017	2018	2019
Asheville	388	400	392	358	429
Average	243	257	276	300	307

Inspections per Square Mile in Service Area

	2015	2016	2017	2018	2019
Asheville	755	800	788	719	878
Average	417	504	504	544	554

Value of Building Permits as Percentage of Tax Base of Area Served

	2015	2016	2017	2018	2019
Asheville	4.19%	3.68%	5.77%	1.90%	2.43%
Average	2.24%	2.37%	3.69%	3.09%	3.12%

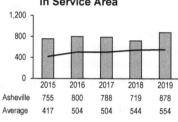

Value of Commercial Permits as Percentage of Tax Base of Area Served

	2015	2016	2017	2018	2019
Asheville	2.67%	2.59%	4.29%	1.04%	1.29%
Average	1.37%	1.39%	2.39%	1.54%	2.08%

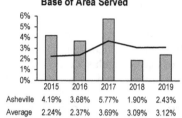

Value of Building Permits per Inspector FTE in Millions of Dollars

	2015	2016	2017	2018	2019
Asheville	$33.4	$26.2	$43.8	$18.5	$24.4
Average	$29.4	$32.4	$41.6	$36.2	$36.4

Efficiency Measures

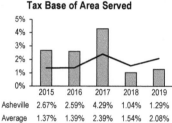

Building Services Cost per Inspection—All Types

	2015	2016	2017	2018	2019
Asheville	$87.47	$90.26	$90.56	$96.97	$87.23
Average	$69.09	$69.47	$81.73	$86.79	$90.08

Inspections per Day per Inspector FTE

	2015	2016	2017	2018	2019
Asheville	10.5	9.7	10.2	9.3	11.4
Average	13.6	14.2	13.5	13.7	13.3

Plan Reviews per Year per Reviewer FTE

	2015	2016	2017	2018	2019
Asheville	585	630	669	569	549
Average	752	654	570	680	613

Effectiveness Measures

Percentage of Inspection Responses within One Working Day of Request

	2015	2016	2017	2018	2019
Asheville	99.0%	99.0%	99.0%	99.0%	99.0%
Average	95.2%	94.3%	92.8%	88.0%	93.1%

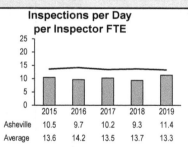

Percentage of Inspections That Are Reinspections

	2015	2016	2017	2018	2019
Asheville	16.8%	17.2%	15.3%	14.2%	11.2%
Average	19.1%	22.2%	22.8%	22.1%	21.1%

Explanatory Information

Service Level and Delivery

The Town of Chapel Hill provides building inspection services within its corporate limits and extra-territorial jurisdiction (ETJ) through its Permits and Inspections Division within the Office of Community Safety. The division is a full-service entity, meeting all requirements mandated by the N.C. General Statutes.

Inspectors have a main discipline in one of the building trades and usually perform Level 3 inspections, plus they perform inspections in other disciplines when needed. On occasion retired part-time inspectors are brought in to help with overloads and the need for plan review in field inspections.

Total revenue received from inspection fees amounted to $2.16 million for the fiscal year. The fee schedule separates fees for each type of permit, with specific fees depending on a minimum amount, square footage, and other factors. There is a fee for reinspections.

Conditions Affecting Service, Performance, and Costs

The Town of Chapel Hill began participation in the benchmarking project in July 2015, with FY 2014–15 being the first reporting year.

Although data for the earlier years are not shown here, Chapel Hill has noted an uptick in permits and construction over prior years. There has particularly been an increase in larger and more complex projects requiring staff attention.

The population served is calculated by adding the population of Chapel Hill with the population of the ETJ. The tax base served is calculated by adding the tax base of Chapel Hill with the tax base of the ETJ. The population and the tax base of the ETJ are calculated by taking the population and tax base per square mile of Orange County and multiplying them by the square miles of the ETJ.

Municipal Profile

Population Served	65,435
Land Area Inspected (Square Miles)	27.50
Persons per Square Mile	2,379
Estimated Tax Base in Service Area (billions)	$8.29
Median Household Income	$60,802
U.S. Census 2016	

Service Profile

FTE Inspectors	
Building	0.0
Electrical	0.0
Mechanical	0.0
Plumbing	0.0
All Trades	6.0
Total Inspectors	6.0
FTE Plan Reviewers	2.0
Other FTE Positions	6.0
Total of All Positions	14.0
Number of Inspections by Type	
Building	2,881
Electrical	2,588
Mechanical	2,620
Plumbing	1,800
TOTAL	10,260
Building Permit Values	
Residential	$61,739
Multifamily	included with commercial
Commercial	$235,996,718
TOTAL	$236,058,457
Inspection Fee Revenue	$2,159,773

Full Cost Profile

Cost Breakdown by Percentage	
Personal Services	55.2%
Operating Costs	21.9%
Capital Costs	23.0%
TOTAL	100.0%
Cost Breakdown in Dollars	
Personal Services	$1,443,421
Operating Costs	$572,699
Capital Costs	$601,086
TOTAL	$2,617,206

Chapel Hill

Building Inspections

Resource Measures

Building Inspections Services Costs per Capita

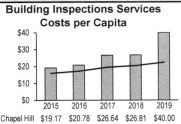

	2015	2016	2017	2018	2019
Chapel Hill	$19.17	$20.78	$26.64	$26.81	$40.00
Average	$16.10	$17.22	$19.56	$20.48	$22.39

Building Inspections Services FTEs per 10,000 Population

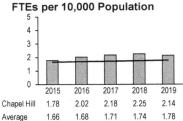

	2015	2016	2017	2018	2019
Chapel Hill	1.78	2.02	2.18	2.25	2.14
Average	1.66	1.68	1.71	1.74	1.78

Building Inspections Services Cost per Million Dollars of Tax Base

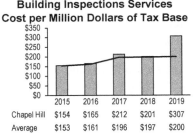

	2015	2016	2017	2018	2019
Chapel Hill	$154	$165	$212	$201	$307
Average	$153	$161	$196	$197	$200

Workload Measures

Inspections per 1,000 Population in Service Area

	2015	2016	2017	2018	2019
Chapel Hill	184	270	178	169	157
Average	243	257	276	300	307

Inspections per Square Mile in Service Area

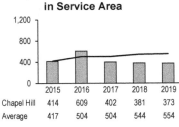

	2015	2016	2017	2018	2019
Chapel Hill	414	609	402	381	373
Average	417	504	504	544	554

Value of Building Permits as Percentage of Tax Base of Area Served

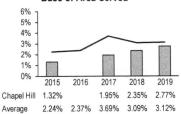

	2015	2016	2017	2018	2019
Chapel Hill	1.32%		1.95%	2.35%	2.77%
Average	2.24%	2.37%	3.69%	3.09%	3.12%

Value of Commercial Permits as Percentage of Tax Base of Area Served

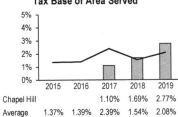

	2015	2016	2017	2018	2019
Chapel Hill			1.10%	1.69%	2.77%
Average	1.37%	1.39%	2.39%	1.54%	2.08%

Value of Building Permits per Inspector FTE in Millions of Dollars

	2015	2016	2017	2018	2019
Chapel Hill	$16.9		$21.6	$32.5	$39.3
Average	$29.4	$32.4	$41.6	$36.2	$36.4

Efficiency Measures

Building Services Cost per Inspection—All Types

	2015	2016	2017	2018	2019
Chapel Hill	$104.21	$76.95	$149.46	$158.76	$255.09
Average	$69.09	$69.47	$81.73	$86.79	$90.08

Inspections per Day per Inspector FTE

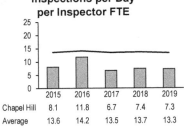

	2015	2016	2017	2018	2019
Chapel Hill	8.1	11.8	6.7	7.4	7.3
Average	13.6	14.2	13.5	13.7	13.3

Plan Reviews per Year per Reviewer FTE

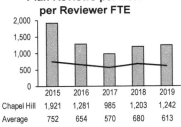

	2015	2016	2017	2018	2019
Chapel Hill	1,921	1,281	985	1,203	1,242
Average	752	654	570	680	613

Effectiveness Measures

Percentage of Inspection Responses within One Working Day of Request

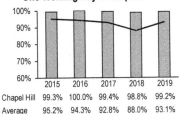

	2015	2016	2017	2018	2019
Chapel Hill	99.3%	100.0%	99.4%	98.8%	99.2%
Average	95.2%	94.3%	92.8%	88.0%	93.1%

Percentage of Inspections That Are Reinspections

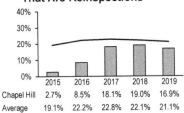

	2015	2016	2017	2018	2019
Chapel Hill	2.7%	8.5%	18.1%	19.0%	16.9%
Average	19.1%	22.2%	22.8%	22.1%	21.1%

Fiscal Year 2018–19

Service Level and Delivery

Goldsboro Inspections is a separate department that operates independently of the Wayne County inspections function. Goldsboro performs all residential and commercial inspections within the city limits and the extraterritorial jurisdiction areas. The Department performs single-phase inspections for commercial and residential properties.

Inspectors for the city are trade-specific. Inspectors are required to take at least six hours of trade specific training each year in addition to thirty hours of state mandated training.

All requests for inspections have a goal of a response within twenty-four hours. Re-inspections are charged $75 for the first time and $125 for each subsequent time.

Conditions Affecting Service, Performance, and Costs

The city of Goldsboro joined the Benchmarking Project in July 2017, with the first year of data showing for FY 2016–17.

Goldsboro combines residential and multifamily when reporting the dollar value of permits.

The city of Goldsboro had a noticeably higher level of residential and building permits for FY 2016–17 due to recovery work following Hurricane Matthew in October 2016.

Municipal Profile

Population Served	40,154
Land Area Inspected (Square Miles)	57.55
Persons per Square Mile	698
Estimated Tax Base in Service Area (billions)	$2.71
Median Household Income	$32,148
U.S. Census 2016	

Service Profile

FTE Inspectors	
Building	1.0
Electrical	1.0
Mechanical	1.0
Plumbing	1.0
All Trades	0.0
Total Inspectors	4.0
FTE Plan Reviewers	1.0
Other FTE Positions	3.0
Total of All Positions	8.0
Number of Inspections by Type	
Building	1,520
Electrical	2,184
Mechanical	1,692
Plumbing	855
TOTAL	12,502
Building Permit Values	
Residential	$12,000,000
Multifamily	included with residential
Commercial	$57,000,000
TOTAL	$69,000,000
Inspection Fee Revenue	$494,057

Full Cost Profile

Cost Breakdown by Percentage	
Personal Services	90.5%
Operating Costs	9.5%
Capital Costs	0.0%
TOTAL	100.0%
Cost Breakdown in Dollars	
Personal Services	$576,288
Operating Costs	$60,252
Capital Costs	$0
TOTAL	$636,540

Resource Measures

Building Inspections Services Costs per Capita

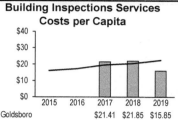

	2015	2016	2017	2018	2019
Goldsboro			$21.41	$21.85	$15.85
Average	$16.10	$17.22	$19.56	$20.48	$22.39

Building Inspections Services FTEs per 10,000 Population

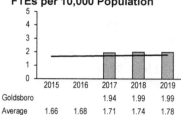

	2015	2016	2017	2018	2019
Goldsboro			1.94	1.99	1.99
Average	1.66	1.68	1.71	1.74	1.78

Building Inspections Services Cost per Million Dollars of Tax Base

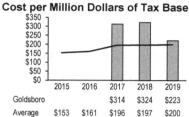

	2015	2016	2017	2018	2019
Goldsboro			$314	$324	$223
Average	$153	$161	$196	$197	$200

Workload Measures

Inspections per 1,000 Population in Service Area

	2015	2016	2017	2018	2019
Goldsboro			182	152	311
Average	243	257	276	300	307

Inspections per Square Mile in Service Area

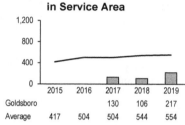

	2015	2016	2017	2018	2019
Goldsboro			130	106	217
Average	417	504	504	544	554

Value of Building Permits as Percentage of Tax Base of Area Served

	2015	2016	2017	2018	2019
Goldsboro			3.94%	2.84%	2.42%
Average	2.24%	2.37%	3.69%	3.09%	3.12%

Value of Commercial Permits as Percentage of Tax Base of Area Served

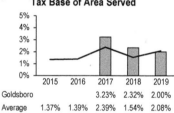

	2015	2016	2017	2018	2019
Goldsboro			3.23%	2.32%	2.00%
Average	1.37%	1.39%	2.39%	1.54%	2.08%

Value of Building Permits per Inspector FTE in Millions of Dollars

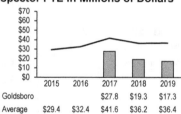

	2015	2016	2017	2018	2019
Goldsboro			$27.8	$19.3	$17.3
Average	$29.4	$32.4	$41.6	$36.2	$36.4

Efficiency Measures

Building Services Cost per Inspection—All Types

	2015	2016	2017	2018	2019
Goldsboro			$117.66	$144.20	$50.92
Average	$69.09	$69.47	$81.73	$86.79	$90.08

Inspections per Day per Inspector FTE

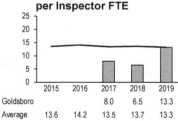

	2015	2016	2017	2018	2019
Goldsboro			8.0	6.5	13.3
Average	13.6	14.2	13.5	13.7	13.3

Plan Reviews per Year per Reviewer FTE

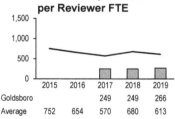

	2015	2016	2017	2018	2019
Goldsboro			249	249	266
Average	752	654	570	680	613

Effectiveness Measures

Percentage of Inspection Responses within One Working Day of Request

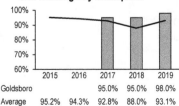

	2015	2016	2017	2018	2019
Goldsboro			95.0%	95.0%	98.0%
Average	95.2%	94.3%	92.8%	88.0%	93.1%

Percentage of Inspections That Are Reinspections

	2015	2016	2017	2018	2019
Goldsboro			19.9%	23.2%	12.0%
Average	19.1%	22.2%	22.8%	22.1%	21.1%

Explanatory Information

Service Level and Delivery
Inspections is a division of the Engineering and Inspections Department of the City of Greensboro. The inspections division consists of plans review, building inspections, plumbing inspections, mechanical inspections, electrical inspections, and local code enforcement. The city services the incorporated portion of the city but not the extraterritorial jurisdiction areas.

Trade inspectors are required to attain a Level III certification of their primary building trade within two years. Mechanical and plumbing inspectors are required to attain a secondary certification. Local ordinance inspectors are required to attain a Level I certification. All certified inspectors are required to take and pass a law and administrative course.

All requests for inspections are responded to within forty-eight hours or less. Nearly all requests are called into the city's automated system or entered via its website.

Total revenue received from inspection fees amounted to $2.5 million for the fiscal year. If a request for inspection is made and the job is not ready or corrections have not been made, a $45 fee for each reinspection is assessed.

Conditions Affecting Service, Performance, and Costs
The broad downturn in the economy reduced building activity and the number of requests for inspections in the earlier years.

Municipal Profile

Population Served	292,306
Land Area Inspected (Square Miles)	134.62
Persons per Square Mile	2,171
Estimated Tax Base in Service Area (billions)	$27.51
Median Household Income	$40,760

U.S. Census 2016

Service Profile

FTE Inspectors	
Building	5.0
Electrical	5.0
Mechanical	3.0
Plumbing	3.0
All Trades	0.0
Total Inspectors	16.0
FTE Plan Reviewers	4.5
Other FTE Positions	9.5
Total of All Positions	30.0
Number of Inspections by Type	
Building	18,126
Electrical	19,134
Mechanical	15,766
Plumbing	10,767
TOTAL	63,793
Building Permit Values	
Residential	$136,971,102
Multifamily	$84,484,849
Commercial	$30,773,821
TOTAL	$252,229,772
Inspection Fee Revenue	$2,465,641

Full Cost Profile

Cost Breakdown by Percentage	
Personal Services	81.9%
Operating Costs	18.1%
Capital Costs	0.0%
TOTAL	100.0%
Cost Breakdown in Dollars	
Personal Services	$2,562,387
Operating Costs	$565,859
Capital Costs	$0
TOTAL	$3,128,246

Greensboro

Building Inspections

Resource Measures

Building Inspections Services Costs per Capita

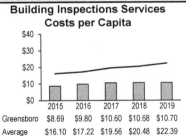

	2015	2016	2017	2018	2019
Greensboro	$8.69	$9.80	$10.60	$10.68	$10.70
Average	$16.10	$17.22	$19.56	$20.48	$22.39

Building Inspections Services FTEs per 10,000 Population

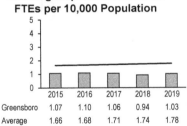

	2015	2016	2017	2018	2019
Greensboro	1.07	1.10	1.06	0.94	1.03
Average	1.66	1.68	1.71	1.74	1.78

Building Inspections Services Cost per Million Dollars of Tax Base

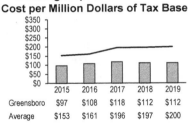

	2015	2016	2017	2018	2019
Greensboro	$97	$108	$118	$112	$112
Average	$153	$161	$196	$197	$200

Workload Measures

Inspections per 1,000 Population in Service Area

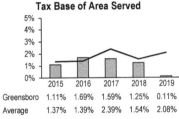

	2015	2016	2017	2018	2019
Greensboro	220	234	249	233	218
Average	243	257	276	300	307

Inspections per Square Mile in Service Area

	2015	2016	2017	2018	2019
Greensboro	464	516	529	501	474
Average	417	504	504	544	554

Value of Building Permits as Percentage of Tax Base of Area Served

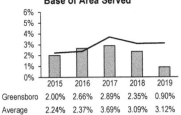

	2015	2016	2017	2018	2019
Greensboro	2.00%	2.66%	2.89%	2.35%	0.90%
Average	2.24%	2.37%	3.69%	3.09%	3.12%

Value of Commercial Permits as Percentage of Tax Base of Area Served

	2015	2016	2017	2018	2019
Greensboro	1.11%	1.69%	1.59%	1.25%	0.11%
Average	1.37%	1.39%	2.39%	1.54%	2.08%

Value of Building Permits per Inspector FTE in Millions of Dollars

	2015	2016	2017	2018	2019
Greensboro	$33.6	$45.4	$46.3	$40.5	$15.8
Average	$29.4	$32.4	$41.6	$36.2	$36.4

Efficiency Measures

Building Services Cost per Inspection—All Types

	2015	2016	2017	2018	2019
Greensboro	$39.52	$41.90	$42.56	$45.90	$49.04
Average	$69.09	$69.47	$81.73	$86.79	$90.08

Inspections per Day per Inspector FTE

	2015	2016	2017	2018	2019
Greensboro	17.5	18.8	18.8	17.8	17.0
Average	13.6	14.2	13.5	13.7	13.3

Plan Reviews per Year per Reviewer FTE

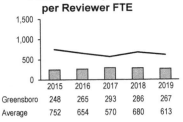

	2015	2016	2017	2018	2019
Greensboro	248	265	293	286	267
Average	752	654	570	680	613

Effectiveness Measures

Percentage of Inspection Responses within One Working Day of Request

	2015	2016	2017	2018	2019
Greensboro	87.0%	89.0%	95.0%	95.0%	89.0%
Average	95.2%	94.3%	92.8%	88.0%	93.1%

Percentage of Inspections That Are Reinspections

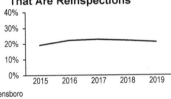

	2015	2016	2017	2018	2019
Greensboro					
Average	19.1%	22.2%	22.8%	22.1%	21.1%

Explanatory Information

Service Level and Delivery

The City of Greenville provides detailed inspections services within city limits and its extraterritorial jurisdiction (ETJ). The city provides building, plumbing, electrical, and mechanical code enforcement services.

Total revenue received from inspection fees amounted to $1.1 million for the fiscal year. Inspection and permit fees depend on the type of construction or work, value of construction, and other factors.

Conditions Affecting Service, Performance, and Costs

The population served is calculated by adding the population of Greenville with the population of the ETJ. The tax base served is calculated by adding the tax base of Greenville with the tax base of the ETJ. The population and the tax base of the ETJ are calculated by taking the population and tax base per square mile of Pitt County and multiplying them by the square miles of the ETJ.

The earlier broad downturn in the economy reduced building activity and the number of requests for inspections.

Municipal Profile

Population Served	96,709
Land Area Inspected (Square Miles)	61.82
Persons per Square Mile	1,564
Estimated Tax Base in Service Area (billions)	$7.11
Median Household Income	$33,339
U.S. Census 2016	

Service Profile

FTE Inspectors	
Building	0.0
Electrical	0.0
Mechanical	0.0
Plumbing	0.0
All Trades	7.0
Total Inspectors	6.0
FTE Plan Reviewers	1.0
Other FTE Positions	4.0
Total of All Positions	12.0
Number of Inspections by Type	
Building	4,037
Electrical	3,590
Mechanical	3,129
Plumbing	2,715
TOTAL	13,471
Building Permit Values	
Residential	$72,569,729
Multifamily	$22,888,918
Commercial	$79,170,316
TOTAL	$174,628,963
Inspection Fee Revenue	$1,096,988

Full Cost Profile

Cost Breakdown by Percentage	
Personal Services	73.7%
Operating Costs	21.5%
Capital Costs	4.8%
TOTAL	100.0%

Cost Breakdown in Dollars	
Personal Services	$963,829
Operating Costs	$281,440
Capital Costs	$63,364
TOTAL	$1,308,633

Greenville

Key: Greenville ▨   Benchmarking Average —   Fiscal Years 2015 through 2019

Resource Measures

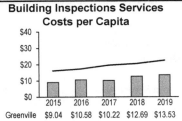

Building Inspections Services Costs per Capita

	2015	2016	2017	2018	2019
Greenville	$9.04	$10.58	$10.22	$12.69	$13.53
Average	$16.10	$17.22	$19.56	$20.48	$22.39

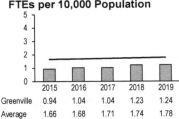

Building Inspections Services FTEs per 10,000 Population

	2015	2016	2017	2018	2019
Greenville	0.94	1.04	1.04	1.23	1.24
Average	1.66	1.68	1.71	1.74	1.78

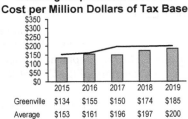

Building Inspections Services Cost per Million Dollars of Tax Base

	2015	2016	2017	2018	2019
Greenville	$134	$155	$150	$174	$185
Average	$153	$161	$196	$197	$200

Workload Measures

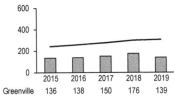

Inspections per 1,000 Population in Service Area

	2015	2016	2017	2018	2019
Greenville	136	138	150	176	139
Average	243	257	276	300	307

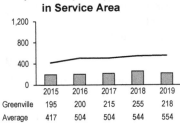

Inspections per Square Mile in Service Area

	2015	2016	2017	2018	2019
Greenville	195	200	215	255	218
Average	417	504	504	544	554

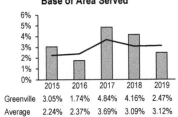

Value of Building Permits as Percentage of Tax Base of Area Served

	2015	2016	2017	2018	2019
Greenville	3.05%	1.74%	4.84%	4.16%	2.47%
Average	2.24%	2.37%	3.69%	3.09%	3.12%

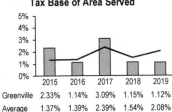

Value of Commercial Permits as Percentage of Tax Base of Area Served

	2015	2016	2017	2018	2019
Greenville	2.33%	1.14%	3.09%	1.15%	1.12%
Average	1.37%	1.39%	2.39%	1.54%	2.08%

Value of Building Permits per Inspector FTE in Millions of Dollars

	2015	2016	2017	2018	2019
Greenville	$43.8	$23.0	$63.8	$49.3	$24.9
Average	$29.4	$32.4	$41.6	$36.2	$36.4

Efficiency Measures

Building Services Cost per Inspection—All Types

	2015	2016	2017	2018	2019
Greenville	$66.57	$76.87	$67.94	$72.21	$97.14
Average	$69.09	$69.47	$81.73	$86.79	$90.08

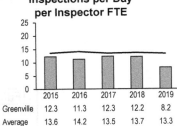

Inspections per Day per Inspector FTE

	2015	2016	2017	2018	2019
Greenville	12.3	11.3	12.3	12.2	8.2
Average	13.6	14.2	13.5	13.7	13.3

Plan Reviews per Year per Reviewer FTE

	2015	2016	2017	2018	2019
Greenville	957	879	593	721	709
Average	752	654	570	680	613

Effectiveness Measures

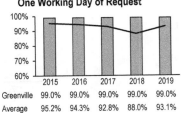

Percentage of Inspection Responses within One Working Day of Request

	2015	2016	2017	2018	2019
Greenville	99.0%	99.0%	99.0%	99.0%	99.0%
Average	95.2%	94.3%	92.8%	88.0%	93.1%

Percentage of Inspections That Are Reinspections

	2015	2016	2017	2018	2019
Greenville	19.4%	26.6%	26.5%	22.1%	
Average	19.1%	22.2%	22.8%	22.1%	21.1%

Explanatory Information

Service Level and Delivery

The City of Raleigh conducts building inspections through its Building and Safety Division of the Development Services Department. The Development Services Department serves the entire jurisdictional territory of the City of Raleigh.

Inspection services are currently provided by inspectors specializing in each of the major service trades as well as inspectors who cover all trades. A staff of plan reviewers and support specialists further the work in the division.

It is the policy of the inspection work team to respond to an inspection request within twenty-four hours for each type of construction. Most inspections are completed within one day of a request.

Total revenue received from inspection fees was $10.8 million for the fiscal year. Inspection and permit fees depend on the type of construction or work, the value of construction, and other factors. Reinspections are not charged for the first time. Reinspections of the same inspection item that has failed for a second time are subject to a reinspection fee.

Conditions Affecting Service, Performance, and Costs

Raleigh rejoined the Benchmarking Project in July 2016, with the first year of data showing for FY 2015–16.

The permit value of multifamily building projects is included in the totals for commercial projects.

Municipal Profile

Population Served	464,453
Land Area Inspected (Square Miles)	147.00
Persons per Square Mile	3,160
Estimated Tax Base in Service Area (billions)	$59.20
Median Household Income	$46,612
U.S. Census 2016	

Service Profile

FTE Inspectors	
Building	7.0
Electrical	10.0
Mechanical	7.0
Plumbing	5.0
All Trades	13.0
Total Inspectors	42.0
FTE Plan Reviewers	18.0
Other FTE Positions	20.0
Total of All Positions	80.0
Number of Inspections by Type	
Building	28,945
Electrical	39,634
Mechanical	31,403
Plumbing	19,167
TOTAL	119,149
Building Permit Values	
Residential	$458,143,683
Multifamily	with commercial
Commercial	$1,338,800,520
TOTAL	$1,796,944,203
Inspection Fee Revenue	$10,830,063

Full Cost Profile

Cost Breakdown by Percentage	
Personal Services	66.7%
Operating Costs	25.5%
Capital Costs	7.7%
TOTAL	100.0%
Cost Breakdown in Dollars	
Personal Services	$4,896,076
Operating Costs	$1,875,165
Capital Costs	$568,197
TOTAL	$7,339,438

Key: Raleigh ▓   Benchmarking Average —   Fiscal Years 2015 through 2019

Resource Measures

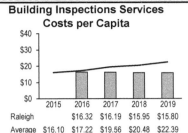

Building Inspections Services Costs per Capita

	2015	2016	2017	2018	2019
Raleigh		$16.32	$16.19	$15.95	$15.80
Average	$16.10	$17.22	$19.56	$20.48	$22.39

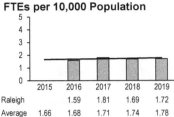

Building Inspections Services FTEs per 10,000 Population

	2015	2016	2017	2018	2019
Raleigh		1.59	1.81	1.69	1.72
Average	1.66	1.68	1.71	1.74	1.78

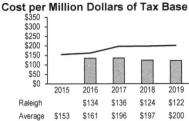

Building Inspections Services Cost per Million Dollars of Tax Base

	2015	2016	2017	2018	2019
Raleigh		$134	$136	$124	$122
Average	$153	$161	$196	$197	$200

Workload Measures

Inspections per 1,000 Population in Service Area

	2015	2016	2017	2018	2019
Raleigh		266	274	257	257
Average	243	257	276	300	307

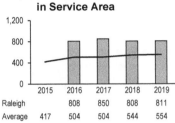

Inspections per Square Mile in Service Area

	2015	2016	2017	2018	2019
Raleigh		808	850	808	811
Average	417	504	504	544	554

Value of Building Permits as Percentage of Tax Base of Area Served

	2015	2016	2017	2018	2019
Raleigh		3.18%	5.29%	2.46%	2.98%
Average	2.24%	2.37%	3.69%	3.09%	3.12%

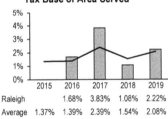

Value of Commercial Permits as Percentage of Tax Base of Area Served

	2015	2016	2017	2018	2019
Raleigh		1.68%	3.83%	1.08%	2.22%
Average	1.37%	1.39%	2.39%	1.54%	2.08%

Value of Building Permits per Inspector FTE in Millions of Dollars

	2015	2016	2017	2018	2019
Raleigh		$46.0	$61.6	$35.5	$42.8
Average	$29.4	$32.4	$41.6	$36.2	$36.4

Efficiency Measures

Building Services Cost per Inspection—All Types

	2015	2016	2017	2018	2019
Raleigh		$61.30	$58.98	$62.01	$61.60
Average	$69.09	$69.47	$81.73	$86.79	$90.08

Inspections per Day per Inspector FTE

	2015	2016	2017	2018	2019
Raleigh		13.5	11.4	12.3	12.1
Average	13.6	14.2	13.5	13.7	13.3

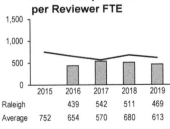

Plan Reviews per Year per Reviewer FTE

	2015	2016	2017	2018	2019
Raleigh		439	542	511	469
Average	752	654	570	680	613

Effectiveness Measures

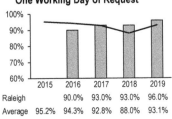

Percentage of Inspection Responses within One Working Day of Request

	2015	2016	2017	2018	2019
Raleigh		90.0%	93.0%	93.0%	96.0%
Average	95.2%	94.3%	92.8%	88.0%	93.1%

Percentage of Inspections That Are Reinspections

	2015	2016	2017	2018	2019
Raleigh		10.7%	11.8%	10.3%	15.6%
Average	19.1%	22.2%	22.8%	22.1%	21.1%

Fiscal Year 2018–19

Explanatory Information

Service Level and Delivery

The City of Wilson's inspection team serves the area within the city's corporate limits and the extraterritorial zoning jurisdiction (ETJ) that is approximately one mile beyond city limits.

Inspection services are currently provided by three inspectors, one field supervisor, and the inspections divisions manager. Two permit technicians provide support to this function. For commercial jobs, each inspector is assigned a primary inspection field. For residential jobs, inspectors hold certificates in all trade areas. Fire inspections are typically handled by certified inspectors in the fire department but are occasionally conducted by building inspectors who have fire inspection certification.

It is the policy of the inspection work team to respond to an inspection request on the same working day if the request is made prior to 8:30 a.m. and to respond to an inspection request by the following working day if the request is made after 8:30 a.m. Most inspections are completed on the same day the request is made.

Total revenue received from inspection fees was $347,018 for the fiscal year. Inspection and permit fees depend on the type of construction or work, the value of construction, and other factors. A reinspection fee is assessed when making an inspection for the same trade that had been previously rejected.

Conditions Affecting Service, Performance, and Costs

The population served is calculated by adding the population of Wilson with the population of the ETJ. The tax base served is calculated by adding the tax base of Wilson with the tax base of the ETJ. The population and the tax base of the ETJ are calculated by taking the population and tax base per square mile of Wilson County and multiplying them by the square miles of the ETJ.

The broad downturn in the economy reduced building activity and the number of requests for inspections in the earlier years, but in FY 2018–19 activity in commercial buildings has picked up.

Municipal Profile

Population Served	54,933
Land Area Inspected (Square Miles)	58.54
Persons per Square Mile	938
Estimated Tax Base in Service Area (billions)	$4.62
Median Household Income	$35,409
U.S. Census 2016	

Service Profile

FTE Inspectors	
Building	0.0
Electrical	0.0
Mechanical	0.0
Plumbing	0.0
All Trades	4.0
Total Inspectors	4.0
FTE Plan Reviewers	1.0
Other FTE Positions	2.0
Total of All Positions	7.0
Number of Inspections by Type	
Building	2,981
Electrical	2,347
Mechanical	2,219
Plumbing	1,346
TOTAL	8,893
Building Permit Values	
Residential	$15,450,047
Multifamily	$0
Commercial	$349,519,461
TOTAL	$364,969,508
Inspection Fee Revenue	$347,018

Full Cost Profile

Cost Breakdown by Percentage	
Personal Services	75.0%
Operating Costs	18.4%
Capital Costs	6.6%
TOTAL	100.0%
Cost Breakdown in Dollars	
Personal Services	$693,099
Operating Costs	$169,993
Capital Costs	$61,043
TOTAL	$924,135

Resource Measures

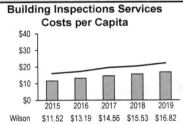

Building Inspections Services Costs per Capita

	2015	2016	2017	2018	2019
Wilson	$11.52	$13.19	$14.56	$15.53	$16.82
Average	$16.10	$17.22	$19.56	$20.48	$22.39

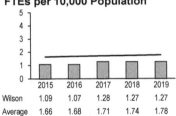

Building Inspections Services FTEs per 10,000 Population

	2015	2016	2017	2018	2019
Wilson	1.09	1.07	1.28	1.27	1.27
Average	1.66	1.68	1.71	1.74	1.78

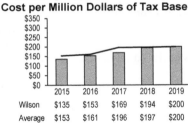

Building Inspections Services Cost per Million Dollars of Tax Base

	2015	2016	2017	2018	2019
Wilson	$135	$153	$169	$194	$200
Average	$153	$161	$196	$197	$200

Workload Measures

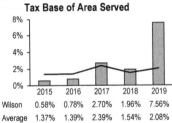

Inspections per 1,000 Population in Service Area

	2015	2016	2017	2018	2019
Wilson	133	126	139	157	162
Average	243	257	276	300	307

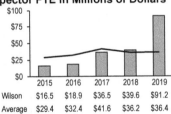

Inspections per Square Mile in Service Area

	2015	2016	2017	2018	2019
Wilson	125	114	138	148	152
Average	417	504	504	544	554

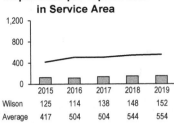

Value of Building Permits as Percentage of Tax Base of Area Served

	2015	2016	2017	2018	2019
Wilson	1.05%	1.17%	3.10%	3.60%	7.89%
Average	2.24%	2.37%	3.69%	3.09%	3.12%

Value of Commercial Permits as Percentage of Tax Base of Area Served

	2015	2016	2017	2018	2019
Wilson	0.58%	0.78%	2.70%	1.96%	7.56%
Average	1.37%	1.39%	2.39%	1.54%	2.08%

Value of Building Permits per Inspector FTE in Millions of Dollars

	2015	2016	2017	2018	2019
Wilson	$16.5	$18.9	$36.5	$39.6	$91.2
Average	$29.4	$32.4	$41.6	$36.2	$36.4

Efficiency Measures

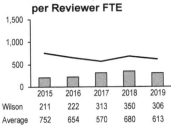

Building Services Cost per Inspection—All Types

	2015	2016	2017	2018	2019
Wilson	$86.64	$104.80	$104.40	$98.95	$103.92
Average	$69.09	$69.47	$81.73	$86.79	$90.08

Inspections per Day per Inspector FTE

	2015	2016	2017	2018	2019
Wilson	10.4	10.0	8.1	9.2	9.5
Average	13.6	14.2	13.5	13.7	13.3

Plan Reviews per Year per Reviewer FTE

	2015	2016	2017	2018	2019
Wilson	211	222	313	350	306
Average	752	654	570	680	613

Effectiveness Measures

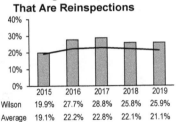

Percentage of Inspection Responses within One Working Day of Request

	2015	2016	2017	2018	2019
Wilson	100.0%	100.0%	100.0%	99.0%	99.0%
Average	95.2%	94.3%	92.8%	88.0%	93.1%

Percentage of Inspections That Are Reinspections

	2015	2016	2017	2018	2019
Wilson	19.9%	27.7%	28.8%	25.8%	25.9%
Average	19.1%	22.2%	22.8%	22.1%	21.1%

Fiscal Year 2018–19

Explanatory Information

Service Level and Delivery

The Inspections Division is a combined program for Winston-Salem and Forsyth County, providing building inspections services for all areas of the county, with the exception of the Town of Kernersville.

Inspectors are certified in one of the following four trades: building, electrical, mechanical, or plumbing. Inspectors drive to and from inspection sites in city-owned vehicles. Besides the North Carolina State Building Code, the Inspections Division enforces zoning codes and soil and sedimentation control regulations. Full-time equivalent positions and costs for these responsibilities are excluded from the project's figures for building inspections.

It is the policy of the Inspections Division to respond to inspection requests within one working day; 90 percent of the time it achieves this goal.

Total revenue received from inspection fees amounted to $4.2 million for the fiscal year. Inspection and permit fees depend on the type of construction or work, value of the construction, and other factors. An extra trip charge of $40 is assessed for each reinspection due to a second and subsequent failed inspection on each permit.

Conditions Affecting Service, Performance, and Costs

Municipal Profile

Population Served	350,216
Land Area Inspected (Square Miles)	396.00
Persons per Square Mile	884
Estimated Tax Base in Service Area (billions)	$26.08
Median Household Income	$40,584
U.S. Census 2016	

Service Profile

FTE Inspectors	
Building	4.0
Electrical	5.0
Mechanical	6.0
Plumbing	3.0
All Trades	0.0
Total Inspectors	18.0
FTE Plan Reviewers	3.0
Other FTE Positions	17.4
Total of All Positions	38.4
Number of Inspections by Type	
Building	17,675
Electrical	22,335
Mechanical	17,629
Plumbing	12,938
TOTAL	70,577
Building Permit Values	
Residential	$259,703,967
Multifamily	with residential
Commercial	$337,291,592
TOTAL	$596,995,559
Inspection Fee Revenue	$4,208,720

Full Cost Profile

Cost Breakdown by Percentage	
Personal Services	61.0%
Operating Costs	33.2%
Capital Costs	5.8%
TOTAL	100.0%
Cost Breakdown in Dollars	
Personal Services	$2,670,273
Operating Costs	$1,456,434
Capital Costs	$254,036
TOTAL	$4,380,743

Resource Measures

Building Inspections Services Costs per Capita

	2015	2016	2017	2018	2019
Winston-Salem	$9.52	$9.93	$11.53	$12.62	$12.51
Average	$16.10	$17.22	$19.56	$20.48	$22.39

Building Inspections Services FTEs per 10,000 Population

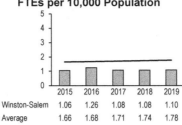

	2015	2016	2017	2018	2019
Winston-Salem	1.06	1.26	1.08	1.08	1.10
Average	1.66	1.68	1.71	1.74	1.78

Building Inspections Services Cost per Million Dollars of Tax Base

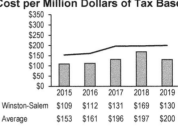

	2015	2016	2017	2018	2019
Winston-Salem	$109	$112	$131	$169	$130
Average	$153	$161	$196	$197	$200

Workload Measures

Inspections per 1,000 Population in Service Area

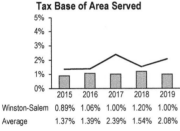

	2015	2016	2017	2018	2019
Winston-Salem	176	175	179	182	202
Average	243	257	276	300	307

Inspections per Square Mile in Service Area

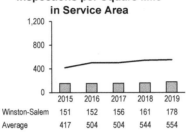

	2015	2016	2017	2018	2019
Winston-Salem	151	152	156	161	178
Average	417	504	504	544	554

Value of Building Permits as Percentage of Tax Base of Area Served

	2015	2016	2017	2018	2019
Winston-Salem	1.64%	1.77%	1.73%	2.18%	1.77%
Average	2.24%	2.37%	3.69%	3.09%	3.12%

Value of Commercial Permits as Percentage of Tax Base of Area Served

	2015	2016	2017	2018	2019
Winston-Salem	0.89%	1.06%	1.00%	1.20%	1.00%
Average	1.37%	1.39%	2.39%	1.54%	2.08%

Value of Building Permits per Inspector FTE in Millions of Dollars

	2015	2016	2017	2018	2019
Winston-Salem	$30.5	$33.4	$32.7	$33.4	$33.2
Average	$29.4	$32.4	$41.6	$36.2	$36.4

Efficiency Measures

Building Services Cost per Inspection—All Types

	2015	2016	2017	2018	2019
Winston-Salem	$54.09	$56.83	$64.31	$69.18	$62.07
Average	$69.09	$69.47	$81.73	$86.79	$90.08

Inspections per Day per Inspector FTE

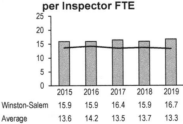

	2015	2016	2017	2018	2019
Winston-Salem	15.9	15.9	16.4	15.9	16.7
Average	13.6	14.2	13.5	13.7	13.3

Plan Reviews per Year per Reviewer FTE

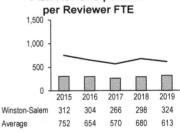

	2015	2016	2017	2018	2019
Winston-Salem	312	304	266	298	324
Average	752	654	570	680	613

Effectiveness Measures

Percentage of Inspection Responses within One Working Day of Request

	2015	2016	2017	2018	2019
Winston-Salem	86.2%	87.4%	90.1%	87.9%	83.3%
Average	95.2%	94.3%	92.8%	88.0%	93.1%

Percentage of Inspections That Are Reinspections

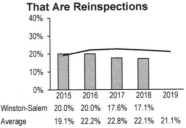

	2015	2016	2017	2018	2019
Winston-Salem	20.0%	20.0%	17.6%	17.1%	
Average	19.1%	22.2%	22.8%	22.1%	21.1%

UNC SCHOOL OF GOVERNMENT
North Carolina Benchmarking Project

Performance and Cost Data

FLEET MAINTENANCE

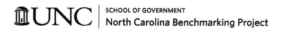

PERFORMANCE MEASURES FOR FLEET MAINTENANCE

SERVICE DEFINITION

Fleet Maintenance represents the scheduled and unscheduled maintenance of rolling stock performed by the central garage and contractual work assigned by the central garage. This includes preventive, predictive, corrective, and breakdown maintenance. Excluded from this definition are rolling stock not maintained by the central garage and the broader activities of fleet services, such as rolling stock replacement and disposal, fuel station operation, and pool vehicle management.

NOTES ON PERFORMANCE MEASURES

1. Number of Vehicle Equivalent Units (VEUs) per Technician FTE

Vehicle Equivalent Units (VEUs) are a weighted measure of the maintenance effort associated with different classes of vehicles. A normal-use car is considered equal to one VEU. Vehicles such as fire trucks or police cars have higher VEUs, reflecting greater expected levels of maintenance effort. The number of VEUs in a municipality is determined by taking the number of rolling stock units in different classes of vehicles and multiplying them by a class weight for that category of vehicle. Vehicle categories include cars; light, medium, and heavy vehicles; trailed equipment; off-road/construction/tractor units; and buses. The number of full-time equivalent (FTE) positions for technicians is the number of employees directly involved in providing the maintenance services for the municipality's rolling stock as approved in the annual operating budget for the fiscal year.

2. Number of Preventive Maintenances Completed In-House per Technician FTE

The number of preventive maintenance jobs (PMs) completed in-house is the total number completed for the fiscal year ending June 30 that are done by the municipality's staff. The number of FTE positions for technicians is the same as defined above.

3. Cost per Work Order

This measure represents the total cost of fleet maintenance and is calculated using the full cost accounting model that captures direct, indirect, and capital costs. Work orders include the total number of work orders produced, including those related to contractual work, for the fiscal year ending June 30.

4. Cost per Vehicle Equivalent Unit (VEU)

This measure represents the total cost of fleet maintenance and is calculated using the full cost accounting model that captures direct, indirect, and capital costs. VEUs are calculated as defined above for the fiscal year ending June 30.

5. Hours Billed as a Percentage of Total Hours

The total number of billable hours includes all hours for technicians available for work during the fiscal year. Billable hours are calculated by multiplying 2,080 (hours in a normal working year) by the number of FTE positions for technicians as defined above. However, this number of FTEs is adjusted for vacancies. Hours billed represents actual hours billed during the fiscal year by the central garage to departments, divisions, and programs.

5. Preventive Maintenances (PMs) as a Percentage of All Work Orders

This measure is based on the total number of PMs (done in-house or by outside contractors) completed during the fiscal year divided by the total number of work orders (including contractual work) completed during the fiscal year for that jurisdiction.

7. Percentage of PMs Completed on Schedule

Based on the total number of PMs as defined above, this measure represents the percentage of PMs completed as scheduled as defined by the respective jurisdiction's standards.

8. Percentage of Work Orders Completed within Twenty-Four Hours

Based on the total number of work orders as defined above, this measure represents the percentage of work orders completed during the fiscal year within twenty-four hours of being received.

9. Percentage of Rolling Stock Available per Day

Based on the total number of rolling stock units as defined above, this measure represents the average percentage of rolling stock available for use per working day of the jurisdiction.

10. Percentage of Work Orders Requiring Repeat Repair within Thirty Days

Based on the total number of work orders as defined above, this measure represents the percentage of work orders (completed work on a unit of rolling stock) requiring repeat repair for the same problem within thirty days.

Fleet Maintenance

Summary of Key Dimensions of Service

City or Town	Number of Rolling Stock Maintained	Average Age of Rolling Stock (in Years)	Number of Work Orders	Number of Preventive Maintenances	Number of Work Bays	Authorized Technician FTEs	Labor Rate (per Hour)	Fund Type
Apex	479	8.0	2,118	1,935	6	4.0	NA	General Fund
Asheville	898	NA	6,764	1,590	16	9.0	Light-$50, Heavy $60	General Fund
Chapel Hill	425	7.7	1,759	774	10	5.5	$100.00	Internal Service
Charlotte	4,191	6.6	39,787	14,427	90	78.0	$80.75	General Fund
Concord	978	7.6	3,958	1,784	8	8.0	$60.00	General Fund
Goldsboro	520	10.8	3,800	911	11	6.0	$13.50	General Fund
Greensboro	1,696	9.2	12,211	5,301	34	31.0	$52.00	Internal Service
Greenville	707	7.1	5,797	2,394	12	13.0	$60.00	Internal Service
Hickory	465	12.5	5,452	1,287	14	7.0	$60.00	Internal Service
Mooresville	471	8.1	4,968	1,872	9	6.5	$59.00	General Fund
Raleigh	2,798	6.2	22,906	7,793	51	47.0	Heavy&Lead Mech - $65, Motor Mech - $55, Welder - $40, Auto Specialist - $40, Auto Tire-$40, PM Tech - $27	Internal Service
Wilson	882	11.0	6,955	1,570	15	11.0	$44.00	General Fund
Winston-Salem	1,931	8.9	10,697	2,237	31	19.0	$50.00	Internal Service

EXPLANATORY FACTORS

These are factors that the project found affected fleet maintenance performance and cost in one or more of the municipalities:

Number of vehicles maintained
Types of vehicles maintained
Fleet replacement plan
Average age of vehicles by type
Average miles driven for each type of vehicle
Preventive maintenance classification system
Preventive maintenance schedule

Fiscal Year 2018–19

Explanatory Information

Service Level and Delivery

Fleet Services is a division of the Facility and Fleet Services Department in the Town of Apex. The activities for this operation are accounted for in the general fund.

The town does not charge departments for labor but does track time technicians spend on work orders. There is no charge to departments for parts or sublet work. Parts inventory turned over approximately nine times during the fiscal year.

The following services were contracted out:

- transmission repairs
- extended repair order work
- major engine repairs
- body work
- EMS ambulance body service work
- electric line truck repairs
- major hydraulic cylinder repairs
- fire truck pump repairs

Conditions Affecting Service, Performance, and Costs

Vehicle Equivalent Units (VEUs) are a weighted measure of the maintenance effort associated with different classes of vehicles. A normal-use car is considered equal to one VEU. Vehicles such as fire trucks or police cars have higher VEUs, reflecting greater expected levels of maintenance.

The measure "hours billed as a percentage of total hours" is based on a work year of 2,080 hours and only counts those positions that were filled. It should be noted that technicians have responsibilities that do not result in billable hours, and they take normal vacation and sick leave. Therefore, this percentage should not be expected to be near 100 percent.

In Apex the preventive maintenance (PM) completion standard for "percentage of PMs completed as scheduled" is within thirty days of the scheduled date or within mileage parameters.

In addition to rolling stock, Apex's fleet services has maintenance responsibilities for other pieces of equipment, including asphalt rollers, whacker and roller tamps, portable generators, ballfield conditioners, various types of ATVs, weedeaters, lawnmowers, chainsaws, sump pumps, water pumps, snow plows, flail mowers, boat motors, light towers, and stump grinders.

The Apex Fleet Services supervisor provides technician support on an as needed basis.

Municipal Profile

Population (OSBM 2018)	52,909
Land Area (Square Miles)	21.55
Persons per Square Mile	2,455

Service Profile

FTE Positions—Technician	5.0
FTE Positions—Other	1.5
Work Bays	6

Rolling Stock Maintained	No.	Average Age
Cars—Normal Usage	9	5.5 Years
Cars—Severe Usage	111	5.0 Years
Motorcycles	3	3.0 Years
Light Utility Vehicles	12	10.0 Years
Light Vehicles	132	7.0 Years
Medium Vehicles	33	10.0 Years
Heavy—Sanitation	2	NA
Heavy—Sewer	3	5.5 Years
Heavy—Fire Apparatus	12	10.0 Years
Heavy—Other	26	7.5 Years
Trailed Equipment	81	12.5 Years
Off-Road/Construction/Tractors	55	9.0 Years
Buses	0	NA
TOTAL	479	

Vehicle Equivalent Units (VEUs)	1,388
Average Rolling Stock Units Available per Day	467
Hours Billed	6,962
Work Orders	2,118
Repeat Repairs within 30 Days	5
Work Orders Completed within 24 hours	1,589
Preventive Maintenance Jobs (PMs)	1,935
PMs Completed as Scheduled	1,896

Full Cost Profile

Cost Breakdown by Percentage

Personal Services	35.8%
Operating Costs	58.5%
Capital Costs	5.7%
TOTAL	100.0%

Cost Breakdown in Dollars

Personal Services	$412,098
Operating Costs	$674,018
Capital Costs	$65,851
TOTAL	$1,151,967

Resource Measures

Fleet Maintenance Services Cost per Capita

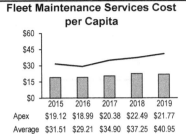

	2015	2016	2017	2018	2019
Apex	$19.12	$18.99	$20.38	$22.49	$21.77
Average	$31.51	$29.21	$34.90	$37.25	$40.95

Fleet Maintenance FTEs per 10,000 Population

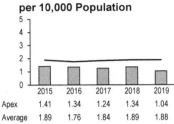

	2015	2016	2017	2018	2019
Apex	1.41	1.34	1.24	1.34	1.04
Average	1.89	1.76	1.84	1.89	1.88

Fleet Maintenance FTEs per 100 Municipal Employees

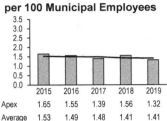

	2015	2016	2017	2018	2019
Apex	1.65	1.55	1.39	1.56	1.32
Average	1.53	1.49	1.48	1.41	1.41

Workload Measures

Number of Vehicle Equivalent Units (VEUs) per Technician FTE

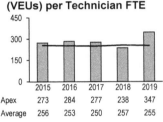

	2015	2016	2017	2018	2019
Apex	273	284	277	238	347
Average	256	253	250	257	255

Preventive Maintenances (PMs) Completed In-House per Tech FTE

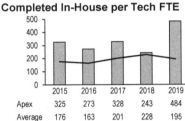

	2015	2016	2017	2018	2019
Apex	325	273	328	243	484
Average	176	163	201	228	195

Efficiency Measures

Fleet Maintenance Cost per Work Order

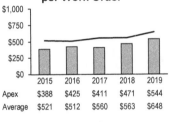

	2015	2016	2017	2018	2019
Apex	$388	$425	$411	$471	$544
Average	$521	$512	$560	$563	$648

Fleet Maintenance Cost per Vehicle Equivalent Unit (VEU)

	2015	2016	2017	2018	2019
Apex	$747	$749	$800	$917	$830
Average	$974	$1,039	$1,207	$1,249	$1,416

Hours Billed as a Percentage of Total Hours

	2015	2016	2017	2018	2019
Apex	86%	74%	86%	74%	84%
Average	76%	74%	71%	67%	67%

Effectiveness Measures

Preventive Maintenances (PMs) as a Percentage of All Work Orders

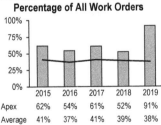

	2015	2016	2017	2018	2019
Apex	62%	54%	61%	52%	91%
Average	41%	37%	41%	39%	38%

Percentage of Preventive Maintenances (PMs) Completed as Scheduled

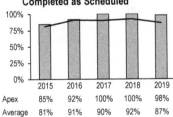

	2015	2016	2017	2018	2019
Apex	85%	92%	100%	100%	98%
Average	81%	91%	90%	92%	87%

Percentage of Work Orders Completed within 24 Hours

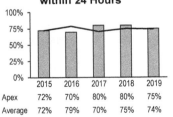

	2015	2016	2017	2018	2019
Apex	72%	70%	80%	80%	75%
Average	72%	79%	70%	75%	74%

Percentage of Rolling Stock Available per Day

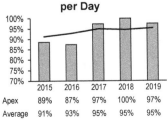

	2015	2016	2017	2018	2019
Apex	89%	87%	97%	100%	97%
Average	91%	93%	95%	95%	95%

Percentage of Work Orders Requiring Repeat Repair within 30 Days

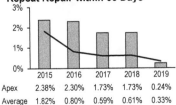

	2015	2016	2017	2018	2019
Apex	2.38%	2.30%	1.73%	1.73%	0.24%
Average	1.82%	0.80%	0.59%	0.61%	0.33%

Fiscal Year 2018–19

Explanatory Information

Service Level and Delivery

Fleet Management is a division of the Asheville Public Works Department, consisting of the fleet maintenance garage and a fueling station. The activities for this operation are accounted for in the general fund.

Charges for maintenance services are charged at a $60-an-hour labor rate for heavy vehicles and $50-an-hour rate for light vehicles. There is a 30 percent markup on parts stocked, a 5 percent markup on parts immediately installed, and a 5 percent markup on sublet work.

The following services were contracted out:

- major automatic and manual transmission repairs
- front-end alignments
- major emergency generator repairs
- aerial inspections
- paint and body repairs
- tire repairs on trucks over one ton
- major hydraulic cylinder repairs

Conditions Affecting Service, Performance, and Costs

Vehicle Equivalent Units (VEUs) are a weighted measure of the maintenance effort associated with different classes of vehicles. A normal-use car is considered equal to one VEU. Vehicles such as fire trucks or police cars have higher VEUs, reflecting greater expected levels of maintenance.

The measure "hours billed as a percentage of total hours" is based on a work year of 2,080 hours and only counts those positions that were filled. It should be noted that technicians have responsibilities that do not result in billable hours, and they take normal vacation, sick leave, and time for training. Therefore, this percentage should not be expected to be near 100 percent.

In addition to rolling stock, Asheville's fleet services has maintenance responsibilities for other pieces of equipment, including snow plows, sand spreaders, a curb builder, and other city equipment.

Municipal Profile

Population (OSBM 2018)	93,621
Land Area (Square Miles)	45.53
Persons per Square Mile	2,056

Service Profile

FTE Positions—Technician	9.0
FTE Positions—Other	7.0
Work Bays	16

Rolling Stock Maintained	No.	Average Age
Cars—Normal Usage	26	NA
Cars—Severe Usage	271	NA
Motorcycles	4	1.5 Years
Light Utility Vehicles	15	NA
Light Vehicles	259	NA
Medium Vehicles	33	NA
Heavy—Sanitation	25	4.3 Years
Heavy—Sewer	5	NA
Heavy—Fire Apparatus	28	NA
Heavy—Other	4	NA
Trailed Equipment	96	NA
Off-Road/Construction/Tractors	110	NA
Buses	22	NA
TOTAL	898	

Vehicle Equivalent Units (VEUs)	2,948
Average Rolling Stock Units Available per Day	NA
Hours Billed	7,270
Work Orders	6,764
Repeat Repairs within 30 Days	48
Work Orders Completed within 24 hours	NA
Preventive Maintenance Jobs (PMs)	1,590
PMs Completed as Scheduled	1,577

Full Cost Profile

Cost Breakdown by Percentage

Personal Services	22.8%
Operating Costs	73.2%
Capital Costs	4.1%
TOTAL	100.0%

Cost Breakdown in Dollars

Personal Services	$1,015,735
Operating Costs	$3,266,964
Capital Costs	$180,884
TOTAL	$4,463,583

Asheville

Fleet Maintenance

Resource Measures

Fleet Maintenance Services Cost per Capita

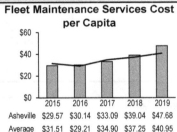

	2015	2016	2017	2018	2019
Asheville	$29.57	$30.14	$33.09	$39.04	$47.68
Average	$31.51	$29.21	$34.90	$37.25	$40.95

Fleet Maintenance FTEs per 10,000 Population

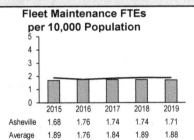

	2015	2016	2017	2018	2019
Asheville	1.68	1.76	1.74	1.74	1.71
Average	1.89	1.76	1.84	1.89	1.88

Fleet Maintenance FTEs per 100 Municipal Employees

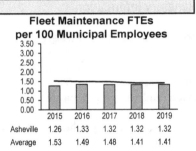

	2015	2016	2017	2018	2019
Asheville	1.26	1.33	1.32	1.32	1.32
Average	1.53	1.49	1.48	1.41	1.41

Workload Measures

Number of Vehicle Equivalent Units (VEUs) per Technician FTE

	2015	2016	2017	2018	2019
Asheville	287	290	330	320	328
Average	256	253	250	257	255

Preventive Maintenances (PMs) Completed In-House per Tech FTE

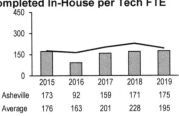

	2015	2016	2017	2018	2019
Asheville	173	92	159	171	175
Average	176	163	201	228	195

Efficiency Measures

Fleet Maintenance Cost per Work Order

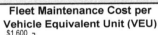

	2015	2016	2017	2018	2019
Asheville	$560	$555	$579	$478	$660
Average	$521	$512	$560	$563	$648

Fleet Maintenance Cost per Vehicle Equivalent Unit (VEU)

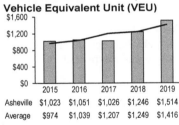

	2015	2016	2017	2018	2019
Asheville	$1,023	$1,051	$1,026	$1,246	$1,514
Average	$974	$1,039	$1,207	$1,249	$1,416

Hours Billed as a Percentage of Total Hours

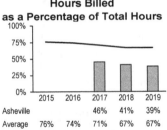

	2015	2016	2017	2018	2019
Asheville			46%	41%	39%
Average	76%	74%	71%	67%	67%

Effectiveness Measures

Preventive Maintenances (PMs) as a Percentage of All Work Orders

	2015	2016	2017	2018	2019
Asheville	33%	17%	27%	21%	24%
Average	41%	37%	41%	39%	38%

Percentage of Preventive Maintenances (PMs) Completed as Scheduled

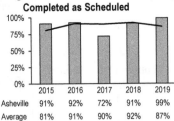

	2015	2016	2017	2018	2019
Asheville	91%	92%	72%	91%	99%
Average	81%	91%	90%	92%	87%

Percentage of Work Orders Completed within 24 Hours

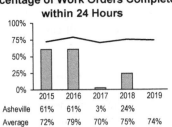

	2015	2016	2017	2018	2019
Asheville	61%	61%	3%	24%	
Average	72%	79%	70%	75%	74%

Percentage of Rolling Stock Available per Day

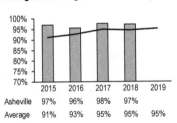

	2015	2016	2017	2018	2019
Asheville	97%	96%	98%	97%	
Average	91%	93%	95%	95%	95%

Percentage of Work Orders Requiring Repeat Repair within 30 Days

	2015	2016	2017	2018	2019
Asheville		1.22%	1.39%	1.32%	0.71%
Average	1.82%	0.80%	0.59%	0.61%	0.33%

Explanatory Information

Service Level and Delivery

The Town of Chapel Hill provides fleet maintenance through the Fleet Management Program in the Public Works Department Administration Division. The program is operated as an internal service fund charging departments for services.

A labor rate of $100 per hour is charged for maintenance work. Additionally, a parts markup of 15 percent is applied to the cost of parts, and a 10 percent markup is charged for overseeing sublet work.

The town contracted out some maintenance services during the fiscal year, including towing, body work, lift truck inspections, and parts inventory. The overall turnover in parts was estimated at three times per year.

Conditions Affecting Service, Performance, and Costs

The Town of Chapel Hill began participation in the benchmarking project in July 2015, with FY 2014–15 being the first reporting year.

Chapel Hill improved its tracking of repeat repairs to more closely follow the benchmarking directions of repairs to the same component, as opposed to repairs to address the same complaint.

Vehicle Equivalent Units (VEUs) are a weighted measure of the maintenance effort associated with different classes of vehicles. A normal-use car is considered equal to one VEU. Vehicles such as fire trucks or police cars have higher VEUs, reflecting greater expected levels of maintenance.

The measure "hours billed as a percentage of total hours" is based on a work year of 2,080 hours and only counts those positions that were filled. It should be noted that technicians have responsibilities that do not result in billable hours, and they take normal vacation and sick leave. Therefore, this percentage should not be expected to be near 100 percent. There was a large degree of turnover in the shop during the prior year, with a full complement only reached at the start of FY 2015–16.

In Chapel Hill the preventive maintenance (PM) completion standard for "percentage of PMs completed as scheduled" includes varying standards depending on the work but must occur within thirty days of the scheduled date, within the scheduled month, or within mileage parameters.

In addition to rolling stock, Chapel Hill's fleet services has maintenance responsibilities for generators, light towers, mowers, weed wackers, leaf blowers, leaf vacuum machines, and sign towers.

Municipal Profile

Population (OSBM 2018)	63,178
Land Area (Square Miles)	21.27
Persons per Square Mile	2,971

Service Profile

FTE Positions—Technician	5.50
FTE Positions—Other	2.25
Work Bays	10

Rolling Stock Maintained	No.	Average Age
Cars—Normal Usage	123	7.8 Years
Cars—Severe Usage	66	6.8 Years
Motorcycles	0	NA
Light Utility Vehicles	33	8.5 Years
Light Vehicles	84	6.4 Years
Medium Vehicles	18	8.8 Years
Heavy—Sanitation	15	9.8 Years
Heavy—Sewer	1	12.8 Years
Heavy—Fire Apparatus	11	13.5 Years
Heavy—Other	15	8.6 Years
Trailed Equipment	36	8.0 Years
Off-Road/Construction/Tractors	23	7.3 Years
Buses	0	NA
TOTAL	425	

Vehicle Equivalent Units (VEUs)	1,188
Average Rolling Stock Units Available per Day	NA
Hours Billed	7,684
Work Orders	1,759
Repeat Repairs within 30 Days	2
Work Orders Completed within 24 hours	911
Preventive Maintenance Jobs (PMs)	774
PMs Completed as Scheduled	695

Full Cost Profile

Cost Breakdown by Percentage

Personal Services	26.0%
Operating Costs	43.0%
Capital Costs	31.0%
TOTAL	100.0%

Cost Breakdown in Dollars

Personal Services	$620,301
Operating Costs	$1,025,036
Capital Costs	$739,345
TOTAL	$2,384,682

Chapel Hill

Fleet Maintenance

Resource Measures

Fleet Maintenance Services Cost per Capita

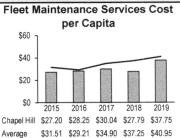

	2015	2016	2017	2018	2019
Chapel Hill	$27.20	$28.25	$30.04	$27.79	$37.75
Average	$31.51	$29.21	$34.90	$37.25	$40.95

Fleet Maintenance FTEs per 10,000 Population

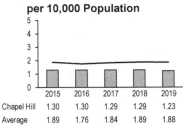

	2015	2016	2017	2018	2019
Chapel Hill	1.30	1.30	1.29	1.29	1.23
Average	1.89	1.76	1.84	1.89	1.88

Fleet Maintenance FTEs per 100 Municipal Employees

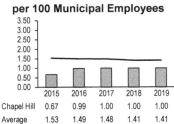

	2015	2016	2017	2018	2019
Chapel Hill	0.67	0.99	1.00	1.00	1.00
Average	1.53	1.49	1.48	1.41	1.41

Workload Measures

Number of Vehicle Equivalent Units (VEUs) per Technician FTE

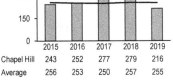

	2015	2016	2017	2018	2019
Chapel Hill	243	252	277	279	216
Average	256	253	250	257	255

Preventive Maintenances (PMs) Completed In-House per Tech FTE

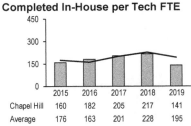

	2015	2016	2017	2018	2019
Chapel Hill	160	182	205	217	141
Average	176	163	201	228	195

Efficiency Measures

Fleet Maintenance Cost per Work Order

	2015	2016	2017	2018	2019
Chapel Hill	$911	$824	$822	$732	$1,356
Average	$521	$512	$560	$563	$648

Fleet Maintenance Cost per Vehicle Equivalent Unit (VEU)

	2015	2016	2017	2018	2019
Chapel Hill	$1,113	$1,114	$1,179	$1,083	$2,008
Average	$974	$1,039	$1,207	$1,249	$1,416

Hours Billed as a Percentage of Total Hours

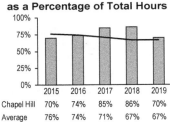

	2015	2016	2017	2018	2019
Chapel Hill	70%	74%	85%	86%	70%
Average	76%	74%	71%	67%	67%

Effectiveness Measures

Preventive Maintenances (PMs) as a Percentage of All Work Orders

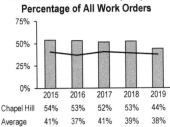

	2015	2016	2017	2018	2019
Chapel Hill	54%	53%	52%	53%	44%
Average	41%	37%	41%	39%	38%

Percentage of Preventive Maintenances (PMs) Completed as Scheduled

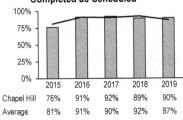

	2015	2016	2017	2018	2019
Chapel Hill	76%	91%	92%	89%	90%
Average	81%	91%	90%	92%	87%

Percentage of Work Orders Completed within 24 Hours

	2015	2016	2017	2018	2019
Chapel Hill	86%	92%	87%	85%	52%
Average	72%	79%	70%	75%	74%

Percentage of Rolling Stock Available per Day

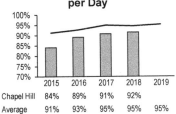

	2015	2016	2017	2018	2019
Chapel Hill	84%	89%	91%	92%	
Average	91%	93%	95%	95%	95%

Percentage of Work Orders Requiring Repeat Repair within 30 Days

	2015	2016	2017	2018	2019
Chapel Hill	2.75%	1.08%	0.78%	0.53%	0.11%
Average	1.82%	0.80%	0.59%	0.61%	0.33%

Fiscal Year 2018–19

Explanatory Information

Service Level and Delivery

The City of Charlotte and the County of Mecklenburg merged fleet maintenance services under a city-operated program beginning July 1, 2009. The data reported here are inclusive of both fleets. The services are provided by Charlotte's Fleet Management Division, which is part of the Engineering and Property Management Department. All activities for this operation are accounted for in the general fund. The Fleet Management Division currently charges an administrative fee per unit to compensate for the overhead of administrative staff, including tags and title work, specification writing, and fleet analysis.

Charges for maintenance services included a $80.75-per-hour labor rate, a 13.4 percent markup charge on parts sold, and a 20.8 percent markup charge on sublet work. Part caps are negotiated individually, based on very special and specific needs. All sublet transactions are subject to a $500 cap.

The following services were contracted out during the year: accident repair, body work, spring repairs, front-end alignment, glass replacement, fuel system repair, engine overhauls, transmission overhauls, towing, some tire service, police car preparation, heavy tire replacement and repair, some light-vehicle preventive maintenance, painting/graphic installation, and radio/computer installation or removal.

Conditions Affecting Service, Performance, and Costs

Charlotte did not participate in the Benchmarking Project during FY 2014–15. No data are available for that year.

Vehicle Equivalent Units (VEUs) are a weighted measure of the maintenance effort associated with different classes of vehicles. A normal-use car is considered equal to one VEU.

The measure "hours billed as a percentage of total hours" is based on a work year of 2,080 hours and only counts those positions that were filled. Technicians have responsibilities that do not result in billable hours, and they take normal vacation and sick leave. Therefore, this percentage should not be expected to be near 100 percent.

In Charlotte the preventive maintenance (PM) completion standard for "percentage of PMs completed as scheduled" is within thirty days of the scheduled date and mileage parameters.

The city provides motorpool services. These include reservations, tracking, cleaning, parking, and check-in. In addition to rolling stock, Charlotte's fleet services had maintenance responsibilities for generators, mowers, weed whackers, compressors, saws, blowers, fans, asphalt-tar/kettles, edgers, snow plows, spreaders, tamps, mixers, chippers, posthole diggers, grinders, pressure washers, and other city equipment.

Municipal Profile

Population (OSBM 2018)	852,992
Land Area (Square Miles)	306.31
Persons per Square Mile	2,785

Service Profile

FTE Positions—Technician	78.00
FTE Positions—Other	46.0
Work Bays	90

Rolling Stock Maintained	No.	Average Age
Cars—Normal Usage	336	6.4 Years
Cars—Severe Usage	839	3.3 Years
Motorcycles	84	4.9 Years
Light Utility Vehicles	87	5.5 Years
Light Vehicles	1,541	5.4 Years
Medium Vehicles	136	10.2 Years
Heavy—Sanitation	174	5.8 Years
Heavy—Sewer	33	7.0 Years
Heavy—Fire Apparatus	109	8.3 Years
Heavy—Other	146	7.4 Years
Trailed Equipment	353	11.8 Years
Off-Road/Construction/Tractors	351	11.9 Years
Buses	2	10.4 Years
TOTAL	4,191	

Vehicle Equivalent Units (VEUs)	13,513
Average Rolling Stock Units Available per Day	3,451
Hours Billed	NA
Work Orders	39,787
Repeat Repairs within 30 Days	0
Work Orders Completed within 24 hours	9,940
Preventive Maintenance Jobs (PMs)	14,427
PMs Completed as Scheduled	NA

Full Cost Profile

Cost Breakdown by Percentage

Personal Services	40.6%
Operating Costs	58.9%
Capital Costs	0.5%
TOTAL	100.0%

Cost Breakdown in Dollars

Personal Services	$9,686,879
Operating Costs	$14,071,025
Capital Costs	$123,117
TOTAL	$23,881,021

Charlotte

Fleet Maintenance

Resource Measures

Fleet Maintenance Services Cost per Capita

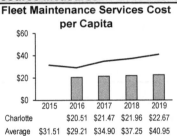

	2015	2016	2017	2018	2019
Charlotte		$20.51	$21.47	$21.96	$22.67
Average	$31.51	$29.21	$34.90	$37.25	$40.95

Fleet Maintenance FTEs per 10,000 Population

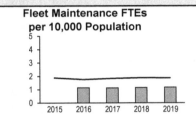

	2015	2016	2017	2018	2019
Charlotte		1.14	1.13	1.15	1.18
Average	1.89	1.76	1.84	1.89	1.88

Fleet Maintenance FTEs per 100 Municipal Employees

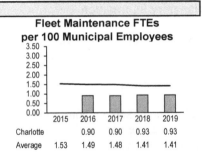

	2015	2016	2017	2018	2019
Charlotte		0.90	0.90	0.93	0.93
Average	1.53	1.49	1.48	1.41	1.41

Charlotte includes county employees too.

Workload Measures

Number of Vehicle Equivalent Units (VEUs) per Technician FTE

	2015	2016	2017	2018	2019
Charlotte		206	176	166	173
Average	256	253	250	257	255

Preventive Maintenances (PMs) Completed In-House per Tech FTE

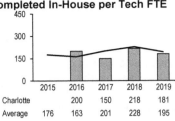

	2015	2016	2017	2018	2019
Charlotte		200	150	218	181
Average	176	163	201	228	195

Efficiency Measures

Fleet Maintenance Cost per Work Order

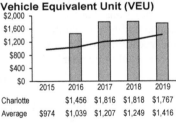

	2015	2016	2017	2018	2019
Charlotte		$601	$692	$582	$600
Average	$521	$512	$560	$563	$648

Fleet Maintenance Cost per Vehicle Equivalent Unit (VEU)

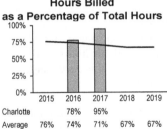

	2015	2016	2017	2018	2019
Charlotte		$1,456	$1,816	$1,818	$1,767
Average	$974	$1,039	$1,207	$1,249	$1,416

Hours Billed as a Percentage of Total Hours

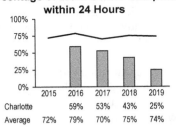

	2015	2016	2017	2018	2019
Charlotte		78%	95%		
Average	76%	74%	71%	67%	67%

Effectiveness Measures

Preventive Maintenances (PMs) as a Percentage of All Work Orders

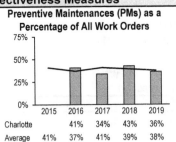

	2015	2016	2017	2018	2019
Charlotte		41%	34%	43%	36%
Average	41%	37%	41%	39%	38%

Percentage of Preventive Maintenances (PMs) Completed as Scheduled

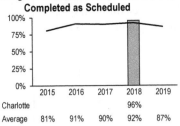

	2015	2016	2017	2018	2019
Charlotte				96%	
Average	81%	91%	90%	92%	87%

Percentage of Work Orders Completed within 24 Hours

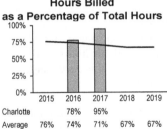

	2015	2016	2017	2018	2019
Charlotte		59%	53%	43%	25%
Average	72%	79%	70%	75%	74%

Percentage of Rolling Stock Available per Day

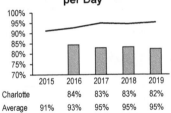

	2015	2016	2017	2018	2019
Charlotte		84%	83%	83%	82%
Average	91%	93%	95%	95%	95%

Percentage of Work Orders Requiring Repeat Repair within 30 Days

	2015	2016	2017	2018	2019
Charlotte		0.02%	0.02%	0.00%	0.00%
Average	1.82%	0.80%	0.59%	0.61%	0.33%

Fiscal Year 2018–19

Explanatory Information

Service Level and Delivery

Concord's Fleet Department operates as a separate city department through an internal service fund, charging other departments for services rendered.

A labor rate of $60 per hour is charged for all maintenance services. There is a 25 percent markup charge for parts and a 10 percent markup on sublet work.

The following services were contracted out:

- body repairs
- aerial device repairs
- front-end alignments

Conditions Affecting Service, Performance, and Costs

Vehicle Equivalent Units (VEUs) are a weighted measure of the maintenance effort associated with different classes of vehicles. A normal-use car is considered equal to one VEU. Vehicles such as fire trucks or police cars have higher VEUs, reflecting greater expected levels of maintenance.

The measure "hours billed as a percentage of total hours" is based on a work year of 2,080 hours and only counts those positions that were filled. It should be noted that technicians have responsibilities that do not result in billable hours, and they take normal vacation and sick leave. Therefore, this percentage should not be expected to be near 100 percent.

In Concord, the preventive maintenance (PM) completion standard for "percentage of PMs completed as scheduled" is within thirty days of the scheduled date.

In addition to rolling stock, Concord's fleet services has maintenance responsibilities for generators, mowers, weedeaters, chainsaws, chop saws, leaf blowers, tamps, pumps, power washers, and other city equipment.

A drop in repeat repairs was driven by an analysis that showed that a large portion of comebacks were due to A/C and charging system issues. Better equipment was purchased for these repairs, and a master mechanic was hired to do most of the A/C repair work, leading to lower repeat repairs.

Municipal Profile

Population (OSBM 2018)	92,568
Land Area (Square Miles)	62.80
Persons per Square Mile	1,474

Service Profile

FTE Positions—Technician	8.00
FTE Positions—Other	6.0
Work Bays	8

Rolling Stock Maintained	No.	Average Age
Cars—Normal Usage	5	6.0 Years
Cars—Severe Usage	188	4.8 Years
Motorcycles	5	1.8 Years
Light Utility Vehicles	61	8.5 Years
Light Vehicles	251	6.4 Years
Medium Vehicles	56	6.3 Years
Heavy—Sanitation	14	5.1 Years
Heavy—Sewer	3	3.2 Years
Heavy—Fire Apparatus	24	11.2 Years
Heavy—Other	66	8.3 Years
Trailed Equipment	182	11.8 Years
Off-Road/Construction/Tractors	112	8.3 Years
Buses	11	5.3 Years
TOTAL	978	

Vehicle Equivalent Units (VEUs)	2,974
Average Rolling Stock Units Available per Day	966
Hours Billed	9,743
Work Orders	3,958
Repeat Repairs within 30 Days	14
Work Orders Completed within 24 hours	3,910
Preventive Maintenance Jobs (PMs)	1,784
PMs Completed as Scheduled	1,748

Full Cost Profile

Cost Breakdown by Percentage

Personal Services	45.4%
Operating Costs	49.1%
Capital Costs	5.5%
TOTAL	100.0%

Cost Breakdown in Dollars

Personal Services	$1,009,201
Operating Costs	$1,091,095
Capital Costs	$122,319
TOTAL	$2,222,615

Concord

Key: Concord ▨   Benchmarking Average —   Fiscal Years 2015 through 2019

Resource Measures

Fleet Maintenance Services Cost per Capita

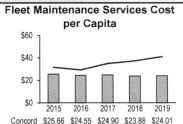

	2015	2016	2017	2018	2019
Concord	$25.66	$24.55	$24.90	$23.88	$24.01
Average	$31.51	$29.21	$34.90	$37.25	$40.95

Fleet Maintenance FTEs per 10,000 Population

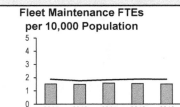

	2015	2016	2017	2018	2019
Concord	1.52	1.49	1.58	1.54	1.51
Average	1.89	1.76	1.84	1.89	1.88

Fleet Maintenance FTEs per 100 Municipal Employees

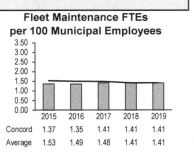

	2015	2016	2017	2018	2019
Concord	1.37	1.35	1.41	1.41	1.41
Average	1.53	1.49	1.48	1.41	1.41

Workload Measures

Number of Vehicle Equivalent Units (VEUs) per Technician FTE

	2015	2016	2017	2018	2019
Concord	348	354	348	360	372
Average	256	253	250	257	255

Preventive Maintenances (PMs) Completed In-House per Tech FTE

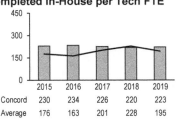

	2015	2016	2017	2018	2019
Concord	230	234	226	220	223
Average	176	163	201	228	195

Efficiency Measures

Fleet Maintenance Cost per Work Order

	2015	2016	2017	2018	2019
Concord	$573	$552	$561	$537	$562
Average	$521	$512	$560	$563	$648

Fleet Maintenance Cost per Vehicle Equivalent Unit (VEU)

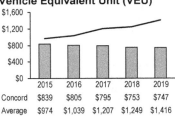

	2015	2016	2017	2018	2019
Concord	$839	$805	$795	$753	$747
Average	$974	$1,039	$1,207	$1,249	$1,416

Hours Billed as a Percentage of Total Hours

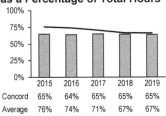

	2015	2016	2017	2018	2019
Concord	65%	64%	65%	65%	65%
Average	76%	74%	71%	67%	67%

Effectiveness Measures

Preventive Maintenances (PMs) as a Percentage of All Work Orders

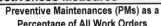
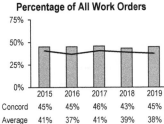

	2015	2016	2017	2018	2019
Concord	45%	45%	46%	43%	45%
Average	41%	37%	41%	39%	38%

Percentage of Preventive Maintenances (PMs) Completed as Scheduled

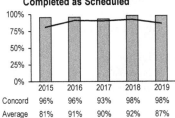

	2015	2016	2017	2018	2019
Concord	96%	96%	93%	98%	98%
Average	81%	91%	90%	92%	87%

Percentage of Work Orders Completed within 24 Hours

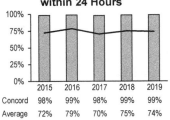

	2015	2016	2017	2018	2019
Concord	98%	99%	98%	99%	99%
Average	72%	79%	70%	75%	74%

Percentage of Rolling Stock Available per Day

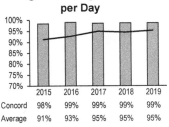

	2015	2016	2017	2018	2019
Concord	98%	99%	99%	99%	99%
Average	91%	93%	95%	95%	95%

Percentage of Work Orders Requiring Repeat Repair within 30 Days

	2015	2016	2017	2018	2019
Concord	0.44%	0.36%	0.43%	0.35%	0.35%
Average	1.82%	0.80%	0.59%	0.61%	0.33%

Goldsboro

Fleet Maintenance

Fiscal Year 2018–19

Explanatory Information

Service Level and Delivery

Goldsboro's fleet maintenance operation is housed within the Garage Division of the Public Works Department. The division is funded out of the city's General Fund.

The labor rate for the fiscal year was $13.50 an hour. No markup charges are placed on parts or sublet work performed by the Garage Division.

The following services were contracted out:

- body work
- engine repairs requiring specialized tools
- engine diagnostics
- wheel alignments
- hydraulics

Conditions Affecting Service, Performance, and Costs

The city of Goldsboro joined the Benchmarking Project in July 2017, with the first year of data showing for FY 2016–17.

Vehicle Equivalent Units (VEUs) are a weighted measure of the maintenance effort associated with different classes of vehicles. A normal-use car is considered equal to one VEU. Vehicles such as fire trucks or police cars have higher VEUs, reflecting greater expected levels of maintenance.

The measure "hours billed as a percentage of total hours" is based on a work year of 2,080 hours and only counts those positions that were filled. It should be noted that technicians have responsibilities that do not result in billable hours, and they take normal vacation and sick leave. Therefore, this percentage should not be expected to be near 100 percent.

In Goldsboro, the preventive maintenance (PM) completion standard for "percentage of PMs completed as scheduled" uses scheduled dates within the calendar month or within thirty days of schedule.

In addition to rolling stock, Goldsboro's Garage Division has maintenance responsibilities for portable generators, mowers, blowers, weed wackers, pressure washers, and other equipment.

Municipal Profile

Population (OSBM 2018)	33,636
Land Area (Square Miles)	29.41
Persons per Square Mile	1,144

Service Profile

FTE Positions—Technician	6.0
FTE Positions—Other	4.0
Work Bays	11

Rolling Stock Maintained	No.	Average Age
Cars—Normal Usage	10	13.0 Years
Cars—Severe Usage	111	6.0 Years
Motorcycles	0	NA
Light Utility Vehicles	132	13.0 Years
Light Vehicles	85	8.0 Years
Medium Vehicles	4	11.0 Years
Heavy—Sanitation	40	13.0 Years
Heavy—Sewer	3	5.0 Years
Heavy—Fire Apparatus	12	24.0 Years
Heavy—Other	20	11.0 Years
Trailed Equipment	64	14.0 Years
Off-Road/Construction/Tractors	37	12.0 Years
Buses	2	2.0 Years
TOTAL	520	

Vehicle Equivalent Units (VEUs)	1,771
Average Rolling Stock Units Available per Day	516
Hours Billed	4,297
Work Orders	3,800
Repeat Repairs within 30 Days	0
Work Orders Completed within 24 hours	NA
Preventive Maintenance Jobs (PMs)	911
PMs Completed as Scheduled	911

Full Cost Profile

Cost Breakdown by Percentage

Personal Services	41.9%
Operating Costs	58.1%
Capital Costs	0.0%
TOTAL	100.0%

Cost Breakdown in Dollars

Personal Services	$630,798
Operating Costs	$875,170
Capital Costs	$0
TOTAL	$1,505,968

Resource Measures

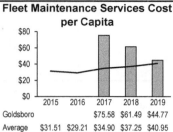

Fleet Maintenance Services Cost per Capita

	2015	2016	2017	2018	2019
Goldsboro			$75.58	$61.49	$44.77
Average	$31.51	$29.21	$34.90	$37.25	$40.95

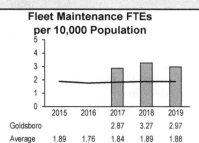

Fleet Maintenance FTEs per 10,000 Population

	2015	2016	2017	2018	2019
Goldsboro			2.87	3.27	2.97
Average	1.89	1.76	1.84	1.89	1.88

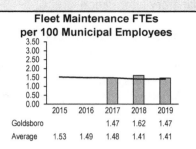

Fleet Maintenance FTEs per 100 Municipal Employees

	2015	2016	2017	2018	2019
Goldsboro			1.47	1.62	1.47
Average	1.53	1.49	1.48	1.41	1.41

Workload Measures

Number of Vehicle Equivalent Units (VEUs) per Technician FTE

	2015	2016	2017	2018	2019
Goldsboro			170	227	295
Average	256	253	250	257	255

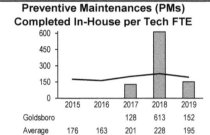

Preventive Maintenances (PMs) Completed In-House per Tech FTE

	2015	2016	2017	2018	2019
Goldsboro			128	613	152
Average	176	163	201	228	195

Efficiency Measures

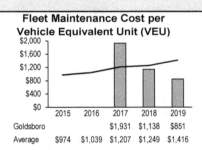

Fleet Maintenance Cost per Work Order

	2015	2016	2017	2018	2019
Goldsboro			$689	$526	$396
Average	$521	$512	$560	$563	$648

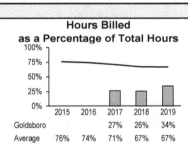

Fleet Maintenance Cost per Vehicle Equivalent Unit (VEU)

	2015	2016	2017	2018	2019
Goldsboro			$1,931	$1,138	$851
Average	$974	$1,039	$1,207	$1,249	$1,416

Hours Billed as a Percentage of Total Hours

	2015	2016	2017	2018	2019
Goldsboro			27%	26%	34%
Average	76%	74%	71%	67%	67%

Effectiveness Measures

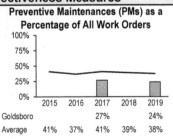

Preventive Maintenances (PMs) as a Percentage of All Work Orders

	2015	2016	2017	2018	2019
Goldsboro			27%		24%
Average	41%	37%	41%	39%	38%

Percentage of Preventive Maintenances (PMs) Completed as Scheduled

	2015	2016	2017	2018	2019
Goldsboro			100%	100%	100%
Average	81%	91%	90%	92%	87%

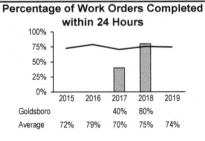

Percentage of Work Orders Completed within 24 Hours

	2015	2016	2017	2018	2019
Goldsboro			40%	80%	
Average	72%	79%	70%	75%	74%

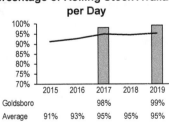

Percentage of Rolling Stock Available per Day

	2015	2016	2017	2018	2019
Goldsboro			98%		99%
Average	91%	93%	95%	95%	95%

Percentage of Work Orders Requiring Repeat Repair within 30 Days

	2015	2016	2017	2018	2019
Goldsboro			0.03%	0.23%	0.00%
Average	1.82%	0.80%	0.59%	0.61%	0.33%

Greensboro

Fleet Maintenance

Fiscal Year 2018–19

Explanatory Information

Service Level and Delivery

Greensboro's fleet maintenance operation is housed within the Equipment Services Division of the Finance Department. The division consists of four sections: administration, services, parts, and tires. All activities for this operation are accounted for in an internal service fund, with other departments and programs charged for its maintenance services on a cost recovery basis.

The labor rate for the fiscal year was $52 an hour. Charges included a 25 percent markup for parts sold and a 5 percent markup for sublet work.

The following services were contracted out:

- body work
- glass repair
- upholstery repair
- most automotive and light-duty oil changes
- other repairs when workload exceeded in-house capacity

Conditions Affecting Service, Performance, and Costs

Vehicle Equivalent Units (VEUs) are a weighted measure of the maintenance effort associated with different classes of vehicles. A normal-use car is considered equal to one VEU. Vehicles such as fire trucks or police cars have higher VEUs, reflecting greater expected levels of maintenance.

The measure "hours billed as a percentage of total hours" is based on a work year of 2,080 hours and only counts those positions that were filled. It should be noted that technicians have responsibilities that do not result in billable hours, and they take normal vacation and sick leave. Therefore, this percentage should not be expected to be near 100 percent.

In Greensboro, the preventive maintenance (PM) completion standard for "percentage of PMs completed as scheduled" uses mileage parameters and scheduled dates within the calendar month or within thirty days of schedule.

In addition to rolling stock, Greensboro's fleet services has maintenance responsibilities for generators, saws, blowers, various police equipment, asphalt pavers, sprayers, hydraulic hammers, a motor mixer, pumps, snow plows, spreaders, and other equipment.

In Greensboro, maintenance on fire vehicles is performed by mechanics in the fire department. The work performed is not counted here.

Municipal Profile

Population (OSBM 2018)	292,306
Land Area (Square Miles)	128.77
Persons per Square Mile	2,270

Service Profile

FTE Positions—Technician	31.0
FTE Positions—Other	17.0
Work Bays	34

Rolling Stock Maintained	No.	Average Age
Cars—Normal Usage	239	12.0 Years
Cars—Severe Usage	352	7.0 Years
Motorcycles	7	1.4 Years
Light Utility Vehicles	33	15.0 Years
Light Vehicles	397	10.0 Years
Medium Vehicles	61	9.0 Years
Heavy—Sanitation	101	6.0 Years
Heavy—Sewer	8	11.0 Years
Heavy—Fire Apparatus	0	NA
Heavy—Other	157	8.0 Years
Trailed Equipment	224	11.0 Years
Off-Road/Construction/Tractors	114	7.0 Years
Buses	3	3.0 Years
TOTAL	1,696	

Vehicle Equivalent Units (VEUs)	5,484
Average Rolling Stock Units Available per Day	1,574
Hours Billed	43,370
Work Orders	12,211
Repeat Repairs within 30 Days	40
Work Orders Completed within 24 hours	11,331
Preventive Maintenance Jobs (PMs)	5,301
PMs Completed as Scheduled	5,301

Full Cost Profile

Cost Breakdown by Percentage

Personal Services	30.7%
Operating Costs	69.3%
Capital Costs	0.0%
TOTAL	100.0%

Cost Breakdown in Dollars

Personal Services	$3,576,627
Operating Costs	$8,079,573
Capital Costs	$0
TOTAL	$11,656,200

Key: Greensboro ▪ Benchmarking Average — Fiscal Years 2015 through 2019

Resource Measures

Fleet Maintenance Services Cost per Capita

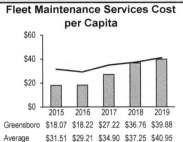

	2015	2016	2017	2018	2019
Greensboro	$18.07	$18.22	$27.22	$36.76	$39.88
Average	$31.51	$29.21	$34.90	$37.25	$40.95

Fleet Maintenance FTEs per 10,000 Population

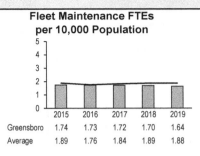

	2015	2016	2017	2018	2019
Greensboro	1.74	1.73	1.72	1.70	1.64
Average	1.89	1.76	1.84	1.89	1.88

Fleet Maintenance FTEs per 100 Municipal Employees

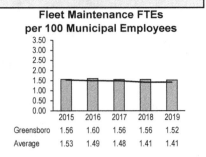

	2015	2016	2017	2018	2019
Greensboro	1.56	1.60	1.56	1.56	1.52
Average	1.53	1.49	1.48	1.41	1.41

Workload Measures

Number of Vehicle Equivalent Units (VEUs) per Technician FTE

	2015	2016	2017	2018	2019
Greensboro	170	165	175	168	177
Average	256	253	250	257	255

Preventive Maintenances (PMs) Completed In-House per Tech FTE

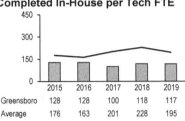

	2015	2016	2017	2018	2019
Greensboro	128	128	100	118	117
Average	176	163	201	228	195

Efficiency Measures

Fleet Maintenance Cost per Work Order

	2015	2016	2017	2018	2019
Greensboro	$420	$422	$648	$832	$955
Average	$521	$512	$560	$563	$648

Fleet Maintenance Cost per Vehicle Equivalent Unit (VEU)

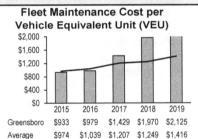

	2015	2016	2017	2018	2019
Greensboro	$933	$979	$1,429	$1,970	$2,125
Average	$974	$1,039	$1,207	$1,249	$1,416

Hours Billed as a Percentage of Total Hours

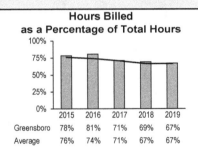

	2015	2016	2017	2018	2019
Greensboro	78%	81%	71%	69%	67%
Average	76%	74%	71%	67%	67%

Effectiveness Measures

Preventive Maintenances (PMs) as a Percentage of All Work Orders

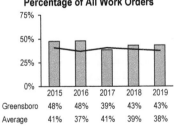

	2015	2016	2017	2018	2019
Greensboro	48%	48%	39%	43%	43%
Average	41%	37%	41%	39%	38%

Percentage of Preventive Maintenances (PMs) Completed as Scheduled

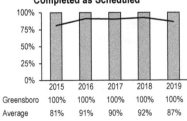

	2015	2016	2017	2018	2019
Greensboro	100%	100%	100%	100%	100%
Average	81%	91%	90%	92%	87%

Percentage of Work Orders Completed within 24 Hours

	2015	2016	2017	2018	2019
Greensboro	92%	93%	93%	92%	93%
Average	72%	79%	70%	75%	74%

Percentage of Rolling Stock Available per Day

	2015	2016	2017	2018	2019
Greensboro	92%	93%	93%	92%	93%
Average	91%	93%	95%	95%	95%

Percentage of Work Orders Requiring Repeat Repair within 30 Days

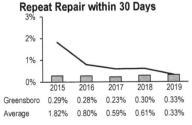

	2015	2016	2017	2018	2019
Greensboro	0.29%	0.28%	0.23%	0.30%	0.33%
Average	1.82%	0.80%	0.59%	0.61%	0.33%

Greenville

Fleet Maintenance

Fiscal Year 2018–19

Explanatory Information

Service Level and Delivery

The Fleet Division is a part of Greenville's Public Works Department. All activities for this operation are accounted for as part of an internal service fund.

The division charges the Transit and Sanitation departments a $60-per-hour labor rate for maintenance services and has a 15 percent markup on parts and a 15 percent markup on sublet work.

The following services were contracted out:

- alignments
- major body and paint repair
- two-way radio installs
- emergency light installs
- exhaust repair
- glass repair or replacement
- transmission overhaul
- major engine repair
- warranty repairs
- towing

Conditions Affecting Service, Performance, and Costs

Vehicle Equivalent Units (VEUs) are a weighted measure of the maintenance effort associated with different classes of vehicles. A normal-use car is considered equal to one VEU. Vehicles such as fire trucks or police cars have higher VEUs, reflecting greater expected levels of maintenance.

In Greenville, the preventive maintenance (PM) completion standard for "percentage of PMs completed as scheduled" is within thirty days of the scheduled date or mileage parameters.

In addition to rolling stock, Greenville's fleet division has maintenance responsibilities for generators, lawnmowers, blowers, weedeaters, light towers, tampers, chainsaws, golf carts, utility carts, bush hogs, sprayers, fog machines, tractors, salt spreaders, leaf vacuums, concrete saws, an asphalt melter, rollers, a stump grinder, trail mowers, and other equipment.

Municipal Profile

Population (OSBM 2018)	89,790
Land Area (Square Miles)	35.58
Persons per Square Mile	2,523

Service Profile

FTE Positions—Technician	13.0
FTE Positions—Other	5.0
Work Bays	12

Rolling Stock Maintained	No.	Average Age
Cars—Normal Usage	25	8.0 Years
Cars—Severe Usage	191	4.0 Years
Motorcycles	6	6.0 Years
Light Utility Vehicles	42	10.0 Years
Light Vehicles	174	6.0 Years
Medium Vehicles	33	5.0 Years
Heavy—Sanitation	48	5.0 Years
Heavy—Sewer	1	4.0 Years
Heavy—Fire Apparatus	16	10.0 Years
Heavy—Other	26	8.0 Years
Trailed Equipment	77	12.0 Years
Off-Road/Construction/Tractors	51	14.0 Years
Buses	17	8.0 Years
TOTAL	707	

Vehicle Equivalent Units (VEUs)	2,604
Average Rolling Stock Units Available per Day	672
Hours Billed	22,118
Work Orders	5,797
Repeat Repairs within 30 Days	NA
Work Orders Completed within 24 hours	NA
Preventive Maintenance Jobs (PMs)	2,394
PMs Completed as Scheduled	NA

Full Cost Profile

Cost Breakdown by Percentage

Personal Services	30.0%
Operating Costs	68.2%
Capital Costs	1.8%
TOTAL	100.0%

Cost Breakdown in Dollars

Personal Services	$1,654,885
Operating Costs	$3,761,410
Capital Costs	$99,977
TOTAL	$5,516,272

Greenville

Key: Greenville ▨   Benchmarking Average —   Fiscal Years 2015 through 2019

Resource Measures

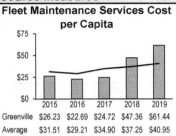

Fleet Maintenance Services Cost per Capita

	2015	2016	2017	2018	2019
Greenville	$26.23	$22.69	$24.72	$47.36	$61.44
Average	$31.51	$29.21	$34.90	$37.25	$40.95

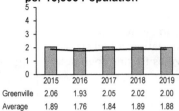

Fleet Maintenance FTEs per 10,000 Population

	2015	2016	2017	2018	2019
Greenville	2.06	1.93	2.05	2.02	2.00
Average	1.89	1.76	1.84	1.89	1.88

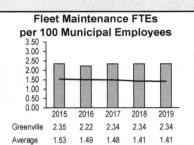

Fleet Maintenance FTEs per 100 Municipal Employees

	2015	2016	2017	2018	2019
Greenville	2.35	2.22	2.34	2.34	2.34
Average	1.53	1.49	1.48	1.41	1.41

Workload Measures

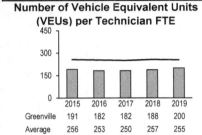

Number of Vehicle Equivalent Units (VEUs) per Technician FTE

	2015	2016	2017	2018	2019
Greenville	191	182	182	188	200
Average	256	253	250	257	255

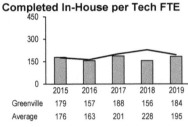

Preventive Maintenances (PMs) Completed In-House per Tech FTE

	2015	2016	2017	2018	2019
Greenville	179	157	188	156	184
Average	176	163	201	228	195

Efficiency Measures

Fleet Maintenance Cost per Work Order

	2015	2016	2017	2018	2019
Greenville	$439	$402	$364	$735	$952
Average	$521	$512	$560	$563	$648

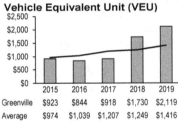

Fleet Maintenance Cost per Vehicle Equivalent Unit (VEU)

	2015	2016	2017	2018	2019
Greenville	$923	$844	$918	$1,730	$2,119
Average	$974	$1,039	$1,207	$1,249	$1,416

Hours Billed as a Percentage of Total Hours

	2015	2016	2017	2018	2019
Greenville	81%	72%	88%	92%	83%
Average	76%	74%	71%	67%	67%

Effectiveness Measures

Preventive Maintenances (PMs) as a Percentage of All Work Orders

	2015	2016	2017	2018	2019
Greenville	45%	41%	41%	35%	41%
Average	41%	37%	41%	39%	38%

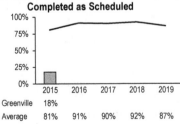

Percentage of Preventive Maintenances (PMs) Completed as Scheduled

	2015	2016	2017	2018	2019
Greenville	18%				
Average	81%	91%	90%	92%	87%

Percentage of Work Orders Completed within 24 Hours

	2015	2016	2017	2018	2019
Greenville	17%				
Average	72%	79%	70%	75%	74%

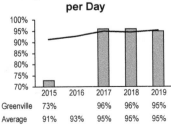

Percentage of Rolling Stock Available per Day

	2015	2016	2017	2018	2019
Greenville	73%		96%	96%	95%
Average	91%	93%	95%	95%	95%

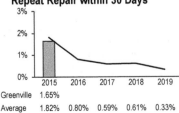

Percentage of Work Orders Requiring Repeat Repair within 30 Days

	2015	2016	2017	2018	2019
Greenville	1.65%				
Average	1.82%	0.80%	0.59%	0.61%	0.33%

Fiscal Year 2018–19

Explanatory Information

Service Level and Delivery

Fleet Maintenance is a division of Hickory's Public Services Department and consists of a garage office, a parts warehouse, a welding shop, a maintenance shop, a fleet wash station, a fuel station, and a compressed natural gas station. All activities for this operation are accounted for in an internal service fund.

The division charges a $60-per-hour labor rate for maintenance services and a 25 percent markup charge on parts sold. There is no markup charge for sublet work.

The following services were contracted out:

- alignments
- body work
- large wrecker service
- special machine work
- starter/alternator repair
- glass repair or replacement
- transmission repairs

Conditions Affecting Service, Performance, and Costs

Vehicle Equivalent Units (VEUs) are a weighted measure of the maintenance effort associated with different classes of vehicles. A normal-use car is considered equal to one VEU. Vehicles such as fire trucks or police cars have higher VEUs, reflecting greater expected levels of maintenance.

The measure "hours billed as a percentage of total hours" is based on a work year of 2,080 hours and only counts those positions that were filled. It should be noted that technicians have responsibilities that do not result in billable hours, and they take normal vacation and sick leave. Therefore, this percentage should not be expected to be near 100 percent.

In Hickory, the preventive maintenance (PM) completion standard for "percentage of PMs completed as scheduled" is within thirty days of the scheduled date.

In addition to rolling stock, Hickory's fleet services has maintenance responsibilities for electronic signs, saws, weedeaters, sewer machines, hole piercing tools, boring machines, pumps, mowers, edgers, a sand blaster, pressure washers, blowers, mules, spreaders, generators, tamps, vacuums, airport equipment, grinders, a fleet wash station, a compressed natural gas fuel station, a gasoline and diesel fuel station, and other equipment.

In Hickory, maintenance on fire vehicles is performed by mechanics in the fire department. The work performed is not counted here.

Municipal Profile

Population (OSBM 2018)	40,932
Land Area (Square Miles)	29.92
Persons per Square Mile	1,368

Service Profile

FTE Positions—Technician	7.0
FTE Positions—Other	4.0
Work Bays	14

Rolling Stock Maintained	No.	Average Age
Cars—Normal Usage	17	13.4 Years
Cars—Severe Usage	115	8.3 Years
Motorcycles	0	NA
Light Utility Vehicles	11	9.0 Years
Light Vehicles	73	10.8 Years
Medium Vehicles	29	15.8 Years
Heavy—Sanitation	28	11.8 Years
Heavy—Sewer	5	9.4 Years
Heavy—Fire Apparatus	0	NA
Heavy—Other	18	19.3 Years
Trailed Equipment	48	10.0 Years
Off-Road/Construction/Tractors	121	17.0 Years
Buses	0	NA
TOTAL	465	

Vehicle Equivalent Units (VEUs)	1,668
Average Rolling Stock Units Available per Day	445
Hours Billed	10,486
Work Orders	5,452
Repeat Repairs within 30 Days	6
Work Orders Completed within 24 hours	5,400
Preventive Maintenance Jobs (PMs)	1,287
PMs Completed as Scheduled	883

Full Cost Profile

Cost Breakdown by Percentage	
Personal Services	29.4%
Operating Costs	69.6%
Capital Costs	1.0%
TOTAL	100.0%

Cost Breakdown in Dollars	
Personal Services	$594,039
Operating Costs	$1,405,003
Capital Costs	$20,400
TOTAL	$2,019,442

Hickory

Fleet Maintenance

Resource Measures

Fleet Maintenance Services Cost per Capita

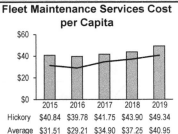

	2015	2016	2017	2018	2019
Hickory	$40.84	$39.78	$41.75	$43.90	$49.34
Average	$31.51	$29.21	$34.90	$37.25	$40.95

Fleet Maintenance FTEs per 10,000 Population

	2015	2016	2017	2018	2019
Hickory	2.73	2.48	2.22	2.46	2.69
Average	1.89	1.76	1.84	1.89	1.88

Fleet Maintenance FTEs per 100 Municipal Employees

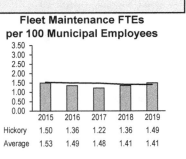

	2015	2016	2017	2018	2019
Hickory	1.50	1.36	1.22	1.36	1.49
Average	1.53	1.49	1.48	1.41	1.41

Workload Measures

Number of Vehicle Equivalent Units (VEUs) per Technician FTE

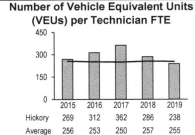

	2015	2016	2017	2018	2019
Hickory	269	312	362	286	238
Average	256	253	250	257	255

Preventive Maintenances (PMs) Completed In-House per Tech FTE

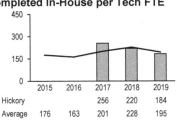

	2015	2016	2017	2018	2019
Hickory			256	220	184
Average	176	163	201	228	195

Efficiency Measures

Fleet Maintenance Cost per Work Order

	2015	2016	2017	2018	2019
Hickory	$301	$322	$336	$364	$370
Average	$521	$512	$560	$563	$648

Fleet Maintenance Cost per Vehicle Equivalent Unit (VEU)

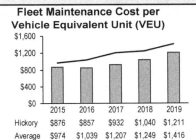

	2015	2016	2017	2018	2019
Hickory	$876	$857	$932	$1,040	$1,211
Average	$974	$1,039	$1,207	$1,249	$1,416

Hours Billed as a Percentage of Total Hours

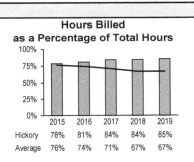

	2015	2016	2017	2018	2019
Hickory	78%	81%	84%	84%	85%
Average	76%	74%	71%	67%	67%

Effectiveness Measures

Preventive Maintenances (PMs) as a Percentage of All Work Orders

	2015	2016	2017	2018	2019
Hickory			25%	27%	24%
Average	41%	37%	41%	39%	38%

Percentage of Preventive Maintenances (PMs) Completed as Scheduled

	2015	2016	2017	2018	2019
Hickory				66%	69%
Average	81%	91%	90%	92%	87%

Percentage of Work Orders Completed within 24 Hours

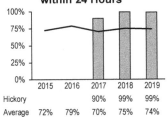

	2015	2016	2017	2018	2019
Hickory			90%	99%	99%
Average	72%	79%	70%	75%	74%

Percentage of Rolling Stock Available per Day

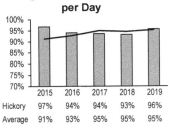

	2015	2016	2017	2018	2019
Hickory	97%	94%	94%	93%	96%
Average	91%	93%	95%	95%	95%

Percentage of Work Orders Requiring Repeat Repair within 30 Days

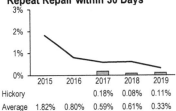

	2015	2016	2017	2018	2019
Hickory			0.18%	0.08%	0.11%
Average	1.82%	0.80%	0.59%	0.61%	0.33%

Explanatory Information

Service Level and Delivery

Fleet Services is part of the Public Works Division under the Public Services Department. Fleet Services maintains the town's vehicles and equipment. All activities in this operation are accounted for in Mooresville's general fund.

Labor is billed at $59 per hour. There is no markup on any parts sold or sublet work performed on town vehicles.

The following services were contracted out:

- body work
- exhaust system repairs
- towing

Conditions Affecting Service, Performance, and Costs

Mooresville joined the Benchmarking project in July 2018, with the first year of data showing for FY2017–18.

Vehicle Equivalent Units (VEUs) are a weighted measure of the maintenance effort associated with different classes of vehicles. A normal-use car is considered equal to one VEU. Vehicles such as fire trucks or police cars have higher VEUs, reflecting greater expected levels of maintenance.

In Mooresville, the preventive maintenance (PM) completion standard for "percentage of PMs completed as scheduled" is within thirty days of scheduled maintenance or within defined mileage parameters.

In addition to maintenance responsibilities for the town's rolling stock, Fleet Services is also responsible for equipment, including rollers, generators, pumps, tack machines, pavers, air compressors, weed wackers, mowers, snow equipment, saws, and other town-owned equipment.

Municipal Profile

Population (OSBM 2018)	41,255
Land Area (Square Miles)	22.75
Persons per Square Mile	1,813

Service Profile

FTE Positions—Technician	6.5
FTE Positions—Other	2.5
Work Bays	9

Rolling Stock Maintained	No.	Average Age
Cars—Normal Usage	22	7.1 Years
Cars—Severe Usage	128	5.7 Years
Motorcycles	2	8.0 Years
Light Utility Vehicles	31	6.7 Years
Light Vehicles	120	8.1 Years
Medium Vehicles	31	8.3 Years
Heavy—Sanitation	10	5.2 Years
Heavy—Sewer	4	7.2 Years
Heavy—Fire Apparatus	12	10.4 Years
Heavy—Other	9	7.5 Years
Trailed Equipment	64	12.8 Years
Off-Road/Construction/Tractors	38	10.7 Years
Buses	0	NA
TOTAL	471	

Vehicle Equivalent Units (VEUs)	1,376
Average Rolling Stock Units Available per Day	456
Hours Billed	7,977
Work Orders	4,968
Repeat Repairs within 30 Days	20
Work Orders Completed within 24 hours	NA
Preventive Maintenance Jobs (PMs)	1,872
PMs Completed as Scheduled	1,872

Full Cost Profile

Cost Breakdown by Percentage

Personal Services	31.8%
Operating Costs	64.3%
Capital Costs	3.9%
TOTAL	100.0%

Cost Breakdown in Dollars

Personal Services	$627,638
Operating Costs	$1,268,143
Capital Costs	$77,035
TOTAL	$1,972,816

Mooresville

Fleet Maintenance

Resource Measures

Fleet Maintenance Services Cost per Capita

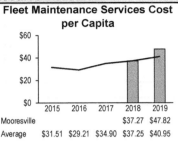

	2015	2016	2017	2018	2019
Mooresville				$37.27	$47.82
Average	$31.51	$29.21	$34.90	$37.25	$40.95

Fleet Maintenance FTEs per 10,000 Population

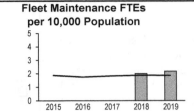

	2015	2016	2017	2018	2019
Mooresville				2.00	2.18
Average	1.89	1.76	1.84	1.89	1.88

Fleet Maintenance FTEs per 100 Municipal Employees

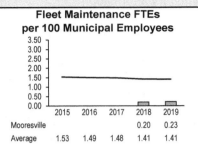

	2015	2016	2017	2018	2019
Mooresville				0.20	0.23
Average	1.53	1.49	1.48	1.41	1.41

Workload Measures

Number of Vehicle Equivalent Units (VEUs) per Technician FTE

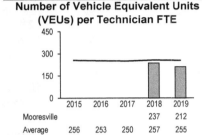

	2015	2016	2017	2018	2019
Mooresville				237	212
Average	256	253	250	257	255

Preventive Maintenances (PMs) Completed In-House per Tech FTE

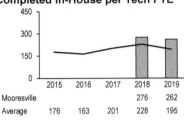

	2015	2016	2017	2018	2019
Mooresville				276	262
Average	176	163	201	228	195

Efficiency Measures

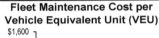

Fleet Maintenance Cost per Work Order

	2015	2016	2017	2018	2019
Mooresville				$467	$397
Average	$521	$512	$560	$563	$648

Fleet Maintenance Cost per Vehicle Equivalent Unit (VEU)

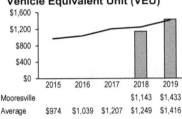

	2015	2016	2017	2018	2019
Mooresville				$1,143	$1,433
Average	$974	$1,039	$1,207	$1,249	$1,416

Hours Billed as a Percentage of Total Hours

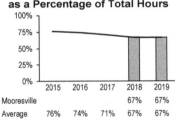

	2015	2016	2017	2018	2019
Mooresville				67%	67%
Average	76%	74%	71%	67%	67%

Effectiveness Measures

Preventive Maintenances (PMs) as a Percentage of All Work Orders

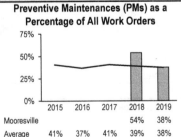

	2015	2016	2017	2018	2019
Mooresville				54%	38%
Average	41%	37%	41%	39%	38%

Percentage of Preventive Maintenances (PMs) Completed as Scheduled

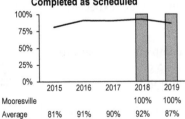

	2015	2016	2017	2018	2019
Mooresville				100%	100%
Average	81%	91%	90%	92%	87%

Percentage of Work Orders Completed within 24 Hours

	2015	2016	2017	2018	2019
Mooresville					
Average	72%	79%	70%	75%	74%

Percentage of Rolling Stock Available per Day

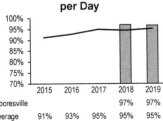

	2015	2016	2017	2018	2019
Mooresville				97%	97%
Average	91%	93%	95%	95%	95%

Percentage of Work Orders Requiring Repeat Repair within 30 Days

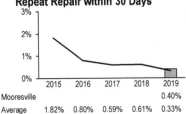

	2015	2016	2017	2018	2019
Mooresville					0.40%
Average	1.82%	0.80%	0.59%	0.61%	0.33%

Explanatory Information

Service Level and Delivery

The Vehicle Fleet Service Division is under the Engineering Services Department for the City of Raleigh. The division provides maintenance and repair services for all city vehicles and motorized equipment except for Fire Department vehicles and city buses, which are handled by their own department. The city operates three separate locations to service vehicles. The division also handles replacement of new vehicles and equipment, managing fuel operations, and the city motor pool. The division is run as an internal service fund for the city.

Varying labor rates are used for different types of workers ranging from $27 per hour for preventative maintenance technicians up to $65 for heavy equipment mechanics. A markup of 25 percent is added for parts, and a 15 percent markup is added for sublet work.

The following services were contracted out:

- body work
- painting of new vehicles
- transmission work and overhauls
- some engine replacements
- spring work
- natural gas tank inspections
- onsite lubrication services for refuse vehicles
- towing

Conditions Affecting Service, Performance, and Costs

Raleigh rejoined the Benchmarking Project in July 2016, with the first year of data showing for FY 2015–16.

Vehicle Equivalent Units (VEUs) are a weighted measure of the maintenance effort associated with different classes of vehicles. A normal-use car is considered equal to one VEU. Vehicles such as fire trucks or police cars have higher VEUs, reflecting greater expected levels of maintenance.

In Raleigh, the preventive maintenance (PM) completion standard for "percentage of PMs completed as scheduled" is 45 days and a 30 percent variance for meters, which could be miles or hours.

In addition to maintenance responsibilities for the city's rolling stock, the division also has responsibility for equipment, including pumps, weed eaters, concrete saws, mowers, blowers, compressors, light towers, scissor lifts, vacuums, pipe saws, flashing light arrows, chippers, spray washes, line markers, leaf vacuums, outboard motors, spreaders, generators, paint sprayers, grass trimmers, yard waste handlers, power rodders, golf carts, forklifts, and other city equipment.

Municipal Profile

Population (OSBM 2018)	464,453
Land Area (Square Miles)	145.65
Persons per Square Mile	3,189

Service Profile

FTE Positions—Technician	47.0
FTE Positions—Other	30.0

Work Bays

Rolling Stock Maintained	No.	Average Age
Cars—Normal Usage	242	5.2 Years
Cars—Severe Usage	478	3.9 Years
Motorcycles	8	2.3 Years
Light Utility Vehicles	87	6.4 Years
Light Vehicles	900	5.6 Years
Medium Vehicles	153	6.3 Years
Heavy—Sanitation	108	4.3 Years
Heavy—Sewer	24	5.5 Years
Heavy—Fire Apparatus	0	NA
Heavy—Other	149	6.5 Years
Trailed Equipment	417	9.8 Years
Off-Road/Construction/Tractors	211	8.6 Years
Buses	21	10.4 Years
TOTAL	2,798	

Vehicle Equivalent Units (VEUs)	8,098
Average Rolling Stock Units Available per Day	2,658
Hours Billed	55,420
Work Orders	22,906
Repeat Repairs within 30 Days	194
Work Orders Completed within 24 hours	16,935
Preventive Maintenance Jobs (PMs)	7,793
PMs Completed as Scheduled	6,242

Full Cost Profile

Cost Breakdown by Percentage

Personal Services	47.8%
Operating Costs	46.1%
Capital Costs	6.0%
TOTAL	100.0%

Cost Breakdown in Dollars

Personal Services	$5,273,980
Operating Costs	$5,086,965
Capital Costs	$666,423
TOTAL	$11,027,368

Resource Measures

Fleet Maintenance Services Cost per Capita

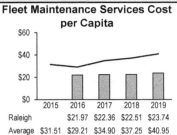

	2015	2016	2017	2018	2019
Raleigh		$21.97	$22.36	$22.51	$23.74
Average	$31.51	$29.21	$34.90	$37.25	$40.95

Fleet Maintenance FTEs per 10,000 Population

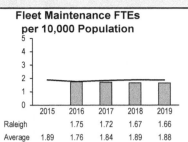

	2015	2016	2017	2018	2019
Raleigh		1.75	1.72	1.67	1.66
Average	1.89	1.76	1.84	1.89	1.88

Fleet Maintenance FTEs per 100 Municipal Employees

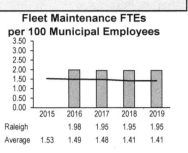

	2015	2016	2017	2018	2019
Raleigh		1.98	1.95	1.95	1.95
Average	1.53	1.49	1.48	1.41	1.41

Workload Measures

Number of Vehicle Equivalent Units (VEUs) per Technician FTE

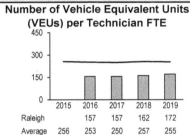

	2015	2016	2017	2018	2019
Raleigh		157	157	162	172
Average	256	253	250	257	255

Preventive Maintenances (PMs) Completed In-House per Tech FTE

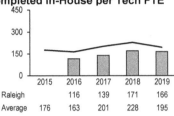

	2015	2016	2017	2018	2019
Raleigh		116	139	171	166
Average	176	163	201	228	195

Efficiency Measures

Fleet Maintenance Cost per Work Order

	2015	2016	2017	2018	2019
Raleigh		$416	$459	$522	$481
Average	$521	$512	$560	$563	$648

Fleet Maintenance Cost per Vehicle Equivalent Unit (VEU)

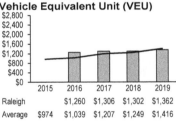

	2015	2016	2017	2018	2019
Raleigh		$1,260	$1,306	$1,302	$1,362
Average	$974	$1,039	$1,207	$1,249	$1,416

Hours Billed as a Percentage of Total Hours

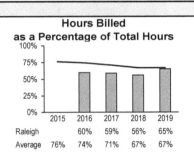

	2015	2016	2017	2018	2019
Raleigh		60%	59%	56%	65%
Average	76%	74%	71%	67%	67%

Effectiveness Measures

Preventive Maintenances (PMs) as a Percentage of All Work Orders

	2015	2016	2017	2018	2019
Raleigh		24%	31%	42%	34%
Average	41%	37%	41%	39%	38%

Percentage of Preventive Maintenances (PMs) Completed as Scheduled

	2015	2016	2017	2018	2019
Raleigh		76%	76%	78%	80%
Average	81%	91%	90%	92%	87%

Percentage of Work Orders Completed within 24 Hours

	2015	2016	2017	2018	2019
Raleigh		80%	79%	72%	74%
Average	72%	79%	70%	75%	74%

Percentage of Rolling Stock Available per Day

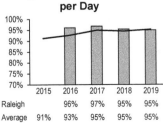

	2015	2016	2017	2018	2019
Raleigh		96%	97%	95%	95%
Average	91%	93%	95%	95%	95%

Percentage of Work Orders Requiring Repeat Repair within 30 Days

	2015	2016	2017	2018	2019
Raleigh		0.62%	0.61%	1.06%	0.85%
Average	1.82%	0.80%	0.59%	0.61%	0.33%

Wilson

Fleet Maintenance

Fiscal Year 2018–19

<table>
<tr><td colspan="2">

Explanatory Information

</td></tr>
</table>

Service Level and Delivery

Wilson's Fleet Maintenance Division is housed within the Department of Public Services. All activities in this operation are accounted for in the general fund.

Charges for maintenance services included a $44-per-hour labor rate, a 25 percent markup charge on parts sold, and a 5 percent markup charge on sublet work.

The following services were contracted out:

- body repairs
- paint work
- wrecker service
- radiator repairs
- alignment
- muffler repairs

Conditions Affecting Service, Performance, and Costs

Vehicle Equivalent Units (VEUs) are a weighted measure of the maintenance effort associated with different classes of vehicles. A normal-use car is considered equal to one VEU. Vehicles such as fire trucks or police cars have higher VEUs, reflecting greater expected levels of maintenance.

The measure "hours billed as a percentage of total hours" is based on a work year of 2,080 hours and only counts those positions that were filled. It should be noted that technicians have responsibilities that do not result in billable hours, and they take normal vacation and sick leave. Therefore, this percentage should not be expected to be near 100 percent.

In Wilson, the preventive maintenance (PM) completion standard for "percentage of PMs completed as scheduled" varies, including both calendar and mileage standards.

In addition to rolling stock, Wilson's fleet services has maintenance responsibilities for generators, mowers, tamps, leaf machines, water pumps, and other city equipment.

Municipal Profile

Population (OSBM 2018)	49,054
Land Area (Square Miles)	30.97
Persons per Square Mile	1,584

Service Profile

FTE Positions—Technician	11.0
FTE Positions—Other	5.0
Work Bays	15

Rolling Stock Maintained	No.	Average Age
Cars—Normal Usage	32	8.7 Years
Cars—Severe Usage	120	7.0 Years
Motorcycles	3	3.0 Years
Light Utility Vehicles	12	8.0 Years
Light Vehicles	202	9.0 Years
Medium Vehicles	59	13.0 Years
Heavy—Sanitation	33	8.5 Years
Heavy—Sewer	5	10.2 Years
Heavy—Fire Apparatus	10	12.6 Years
Heavy—Other	65	9.6 Years
Trailed Equipment	165	14.0 Years
Off-Road/Construction/Tractors	172	14.0 Years
Buses	4	14.0 Years
TOTAL	882	

Vehicle Equivalent Units (VEUs)	2,929
Average Rolling Stock Units Available per Day	847
Hours Billed	16,703
Work Orders	6,955
Repeat Repairs within 30 Days	34
Work Orders Completed within 24 hours	5,911
Preventive Maintenance Jobs (PMs)	1,570
PMs Completed as Scheduled	1,413

Full Cost Profile

Cost Breakdown by Percentage

Personal Services	30.3%
Operating Costs	65.3%
Capital Costs	4.4%
TOTAL	100.0%

Cost Breakdown in Dollars

Personal Services	$1,308,397
Operating Costs	$2,820,671
Capital Costs	$188,849
TOTAL	$4,317,917

Wilson

Fleet Maintenance

Resource Measures

Fleet Maintenance Services Cost per Capita

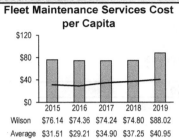

	2015	2016	2017	2018	2019
Wilson	$76.14	$74.36	$74.24	$74.80	$88.02
Average	$31.51	$29.21	$34.90	$37.25	$40.95

Fleet Maintenance FTEs per 10,000 Population

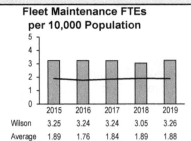

	2015	2016	2017	2018	2019
Wilson	3.25	3.24	3.24	3.05	3.26
Average	1.89	1.76	1.84	1.89	1.88

Fleet Maintenance FTEs per 100 Municipal Employees

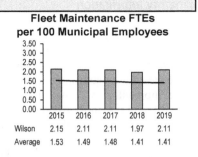

	2015	2016	2017	2018	2019
Wilson	2.15	2.11	2.11	1.97	2.11
Average	1.53	1.49	1.48	1.41	1.41

Workload Measures

Number of Vehicle Equivalent Units (VEUs) per Technician FTE

	2015	2016	2017	2018	2019
Wilson	248	257	250	281	266
Average	256	253	250	257	255

Preventive Maintenances (PMs) Completed In-House per Tech FTE

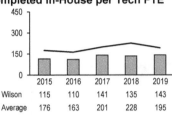

	2015	2016	2017	2018	2019
Wilson	115	110	141	135	143
Average	176	163	201	228	195

Efficiency Measures

Fleet Maintenance Cost per Work Order

	2015	2016	2017	2018	2019
Wilson	$536	$475	$495	$505	$621
Average	$521	$512	$560	$563	$648

Fleet Maintenance Cost per Vehicle Equivalent Unit (VEU)

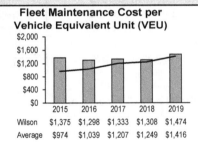

	2015	2016	2017	2018	2019
Wilson	$1,375	$1,298	$1,333	$1,308	$1,474
Average	$974	$1,039	$1,207	$1,249	$1,416

Hours Billed as a Percentage of Total Hours

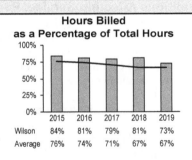

	2015	2016	2017	2018	2019
Wilson	84%	81%	79%	81%	73%
Average	76%	74%	71%	67%	67%

Effectiveness Measures

Preventive Maintenances (PMs) as a Percentage of All Work Orders

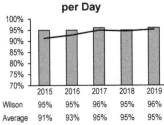

	2015	2016	2017	2018	2019
Wilson	18%	16%	21%	19%	23%
Average	41%	37%	41%	39%	38%

Percentage of Preventive Maintenances (PMs) Completed as Scheduled

	2015	2016	2017	2018	2019
Wilson	90%	90%	90%	90%	90%
Average	81%	91%	90%	92%	87%

Percentage of Work Orders Completed within 24 Hours

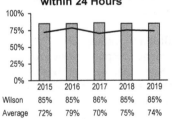

	2015	2016	2017	2018	2019
Wilson	85%	85%	86%	85%	85%
Average	72%	79%	70%	75%	74%

Percentage of Rolling Stock Available per Day

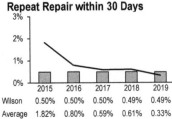

	2015	2016	2017	2018	2019
Wilson	95%	95%	96%	95%	96%
Average	91%	93%	95%	95%	95%

Percentage of Work Orders Requiring Repeat Repair within 30 Days

	2015	2016	2017	2018	2019
Wilson	0.50%	0.50%	0.50%	0.49%	0.49%
Average	1.82%	0.80%	0.59%	0.61%	0.33%

Winston-Salem   # Fleet Maintenance

Fiscal Year 2018–19

Explanatory Information

Service Level and Delivery

Fleet Services is a division of the Property and Facilities Management Department, consisting of eight units: vehicle maintenance administration, contract monitoring administration, heavy equipment, service station, vehicle leasing, parts, light equipment, and tire shop. All activities in this operation are accounted for in an internal service fund.

Charges for maintenance services included a $50-per-hour labor rate, a 26 percent markup charge for parts sold, and a 13 percent markup charge for sublet work.

The following services were contracted out:

- body work
- welding
- hydraulic cylinder and pump repair
- glass repair
- towing
- transmission repair

Conditions Affecting Service, Performance, and Costs

Vehicle Equivalent Units (VEUs) are a weighted measure of the maintenance effort associated with different classes of vehicles. A normal-use car is considered equal to one VEU. Vehicles such as fire trucks or police cars have higher VEUs, reflecting greater expected levels of maintenance.

The measure "hours billed as a percentage of total hours" is based on a work year of 2,080 hours and only counts those positions that were filled. It should be noted that technicians have responsibilities that do not result in billable hours, and they take normal vacation and sick leave. Therefore, this percentage should not be expected to be near 100 percent. Winston-Salem indicated that seventeen technician FTEs were actually working during the fiscal year for this calculation.

In addition to rolling stock, Winston-Salem's Fleet Services has maintenance responsibilities for mowers, weedeaters, water pumps, chain saws, whacker tamps, pavement stripers, tractor implements, leaf blowers, power trimmers, salt spreaders, snow plows, and other city equipment.

In Winston-Salem, maintenance on fire vehicles is performed by mechanics in the fire department. Those mechanics and that work performed are not counted here.

Municipal Profile

Population (OSBM 2018)	243,447
Land Area (Square Miles)	132.55
Persons per Square Mile	1,837

Service Profile

FTE Positions—Technician	19.0
FTE Positions—Other	14.0
Work Bays	31

Rolling Stock Maintained	No.	Average Age
Cars—Normal Usage	276	7.9 Years
Cars—Severe Usage	481	7.8 Years
Motorcycles	13	4.1 Years
Light Utility Vehicles	10	8.2 Years
Light Vehicles	432	7.3 Years
Medium Vehicles	147	12.5 Years
Heavy—Sanitation	57	5.5 Years
Heavy—Sewer	11	2.8 Years
Heavy—Fire Apparatus	30	NA
Heavy—Other	65	5.2 Years
Trailed Equipment	160	14.3 Years
Off-Road/Construction/Tractors	249	12.8 Years
Buses	0	NA
TOTAL	1,931	

Vehicle Equivalent Units (VEUs)	5,929
Average Rolling Stock Units Available per Day	1,917
Hours Billed	26,840
Work Orders	10,697
Repeat Repairs within 30 Days	NA
Work Orders Completed within 24 hours	7,106
Preventive Maintenance Jobs (PMs)	2,237
PMs Completed as Scheduled	628

Full Cost Profile

Cost Breakdown by Percentage	
Personal Services	29.5%
Operating Costs	69.0%
Capital Costs	1.5%
TOTAL	100.0%

Cost Breakdown in Dollars	
Personal Services	$1,687,589
Operating Costs	$3,952,854
Capital Costs	$87,345
TOTAL	$5,727,788

Winston-Salem

Fleet Maintenance

Key: Winston-Salem ▫   Benchmarking Average —   Fiscal Years 2015 through 2019

Resource Measures

Fleet Maintenance Services Cost per Capita

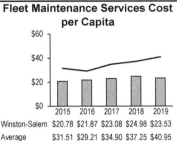

	2015	2016	2017	2018	2019
Winston-Salem	$20.78	$21.87	$23.08	$24.98	$23.53
Average	$31.51	$29.21	$34.90	$37.25	$40.95

Fleet Maintenance FTEs per 10,000 Population

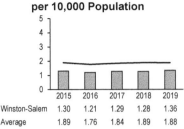

	2015	2016	2017	2018	2019
Winston-Salem	1.30	1.21	1.29	1.28	1.36
Average	1.89	1.76	1.84	1.89	1.88

Fleet Maintenance FTEs per 100 Municipal Employees

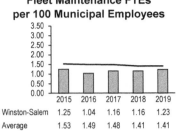

	2015	2016	2017	2018	2019
Winston-Salem	1.25	1.04	1.16	1.16	1.23
Average	1.53	1.49	1.48	1.41	1.41

Workload Measures

Number of Vehicle Equivalent Units (VEUs) per Technician FTE

	2015	2016	2017	2018	2019
Winston-Salem	278	320	302	425	312
Average	256	253	250	257	255

Preventive Maintenances (PMs) Completed In-House per Tech FTE

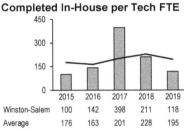

	2015	2016	2017	2018	2019
Winston-Salem	100	142	398	211	118
Average	176	163	201	228	195

Efficiency Measures

Fleet Maintenance Cost per Work Order

	2015	2016	2017	2018	2019
Winston-Salem	$563	$642	$661	$572	$535
Average	$521	$512	$560	$563	$648

Fleet Maintenance Cost per Vehicle Equivalent Unit (VEU)

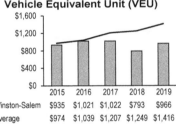

	2015	2016	2017	2018	2019
Winston-Salem	$935	$1,021	$1,022	$793	$966
Average	$974	$1,039	$1,207	$1,249	$1,416

Hours Billed as a Percentage of Total Hours

	2015	2016	2017	2018	2019
Winston-Salem	64%	77%	65%	58%	68%
Average	76%	74%	71%	67%	67%

Effectiveness Measures

Preventive Maintenances (PMs) as a Percentage of All Work Orders

	2015	2016	2017	2018	2019
Winston-Salem	22%	28%	85%	36%	21%
Average	41%	37%	41%	39%	38%

Percentage of Preventive Maintenances (PMs) Completed as Scheduled

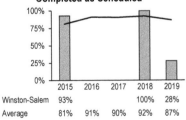

	2015	2016	2017	2018	2019
Winston-Salem	93%			100%	28%
Average	81%	91%	90%	92%	87%

Percentage of Work Orders Completed within 24 Hours

	2015	2016	2017	2018	2019
Winston-Salem	67%	70%	67%	68%	66%
Average	72%	79%	70%	75%	74%

Percentage of Rolling Stock Available per Day

	2015	2016	2017	2018	2019
Winston-Salem	97%	94%	99%	95%	99%
Average	91%	93%	95%	95%	95%

Percentage of Work Orders Requiring Repeat Repair within 30 Days

	2015	2016	2017	2018	2019
Winston-Salem	4.71%			0.57%	
Average	1.82%	0.80%	0.59%	0.61%	0.33%

Performance and Cost Data

CENTRAL HUMAN RESOURCES

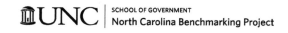

PERFORMANCE MEASURES FOR CENTRAL HUMAN RESOURCES

SERVICE DEFINITION

Central Human Resources represents an internal support service. It is characterized by various functions related to the daily management of human capital or personnel, including compensation analysis; position classification; benefits administration; management of employee training and development; employee relations; position control; employee performance evaluations; recruitment and selection; occupational health, wellness, and safety programs; administration of the Human Resources Information System (HRIS); and general administration of the central human resources office. Excluded from the counts here are staff who may be assisting with certain human resource functions but who are not in the central human resources department, such as employees who might be assigned to individual departments. Also excluded from this service area is risk financing, including general liability insurance and workers' compensation.

NOTES ON PERFORMANCE MEASURES

1. Total Workforce FTEs per 10,000 Population

The number of full-time equivalent (FTE) positions includes all permanent full-time and permanent part-time employees budgeted for the municipality. One FTE equates to 2,080 hours of work per year. Any combination of employees providing 2,080 hours of annual work equals one FTE.

2. Number of Applications Received per 100 Employees

Human resources is responsible for the recruitment and selection of applicants to fill new or vacant positions.

3. Number of Position Requisitions per 100 Employees

Position requisitions are submitted to the human resources office by departments seeking to fill vacant positions.

4. Cost per Employee

This measure represents the total cost of human resources for the fiscal year ending June 30 and is calculated using the project's full cost accounting model, which captures direct, indirect, and capital costs. Cost per employee is the primary measure of cost efficiency for this service area.

5. Ratio of Human Resources Staff to Total Workforce

This is a calculation of human resource FTEs divided by the total number of employees in the permanent municipal workforce, including full- and part-time staff.

6. Probationary Period Completion Rate (New Hires)

Most organizations require that new employees complete a probationary employment period, typically lasting three to eighteen months from the hire date, depending on the job classification. This effectiveness measure is calculated by dividing the total number of employees that completed the probationary period by the number of employees eligible to complete the probationary period during the fiscal year.

7. Employee Total Turnover Rate

The employee turnover rate is calculated by dividing the total number of separated staff during the fiscal year by the total number of authorized positions.

8. Employee Voluntary Turnover Rate

The employee voluntary turnover rate is calculated by dividing the number of voluntarily separated staff during the fiscal year by the total number of authorized positions. Voluntary separations include retirements and resignations.

9. Percentage of Grievances Resolved at Department Level

Most jurisdictions have a process in place for handling formal grievances filed by employees. This effectiveness measure is calculated by dividing the number of formal grievances that were resolved within the respective department (prior to going to a higher level or third party for resolution) by the total number of grievances filed during the fiscal year.

10. Average Number of Days from Position Post Date to Hire Date

This includes the number of working days from the date a job is posted to the hire date (first day of employment). It includes only recruitments for permanent full-time and part-time positions that were completed during the fiscal year. This measure excludes recruitment of temporary workers.

Central Human Resources

Summary of Key Dimensions of Service

City or Town	Total Number of Authorized Municipal Positions	Average Length of Service (in Years)	Number of Position Requisitions	Number of Employment Applications Processed	Number of Retirees Serviced	Probationary Period	Turnover Rate	Number of HR FTEs
Apex	466	7.4	79	5,820	51	6 & 12 months	11.8%	4.0
Asheville	1,281	8.5	408	8,707	234	6 months	13.8%	21.6
Chapel Hill	703	9.7	270	7,523	50	6 & 12 months	12.8%	8.0
Charlotte	7,510	10.0	678	76,791	na	6 & 12 months	9.0%	46.0
Goldsboro	617	8.6	225	3,781	5	6 & 12 months	8.1%	5.0
Greensboro	3,167	10.5	473	33,059	500	6 & 12 months	8.6%	44.0
Greenville	767	10.1	190	9,757	300	6 & 12 months	11.9%	11.0
Hickory	737	9.7	70	3,566	95	12 months	12.9%	8.0
Mooresville	471	9.2	68	2,612	70	6 months	8.3%	5.0
Raleigh	4,284	10.0	876	53,836	157	6 & 12 months	9.5%	32.0
Wilson	779	9.5	95	5,600	95	12 months	10.7%	6.0
Winston-Salem	2,834	10.5	582	23,460	1,119	6 & 12 months	11.3%	15.0

NOTES
For municipalities with varying probationary periods, typically fire and/or police personnel have longer probationary periods.

EXPLANATORY FACTORS
These are factors that the project found affected human resources performance and cost in one or more of the municipalities:

Decentralization of HR functions
Personnel policies
External economic climate
Unemployment rate
Extent of contracting out for services
Departmental discretion regarding vacancies
Hiring freezes
State and/or federal mandates

Apex

Central Human Resources

Fiscal Year 2018–19

Explanatory Information

Service Level and Delivery

The Human Resources Department for Apex provides a comprehensive assortment of services, including occupational health and wellness, benefits, recruitment and selection, compensation, employee relations, and training and development programs.

Two employee compensation studies were completed during the fiscal year covering thirty positions. The Town of Apex tries to study one-third of the job classifications every three years and uses a consultant to assist in this process.

The town's probationary period for new employees is six months for general employees and twelve months for sworn police, fire, and EMS personnel.

Conditions Affecting Service, Performance, and Costs

Municipal Profile

Population (OSBM 2018)	52,909
Land Area (Square Miles)	21.55
Persons per Square Mile	2,455
Median Household Income	$84,000
U.S. Census 2016	
County Unemployment Rate (2018)	3.3%
U.S. Bureau of Labor Statistics	

Service Profile

Central HR FTE Positions	
Administration	1.0
Generalist/Specialist	2.0
Staff Support/Clerical	1.00
Total Authorized Workforce	466.0
Authorized FTEs	464.9
Average Length of Service (Months)	89
Number of Position Requisitions	79
Employment Applications Processed	5,820
Length of Probationary Employment Period	6 & 12 months
Compensation Studies Completed	2
Positions Studied	30
Employee Turnover	
Voluntary Separations	50
Involuntary Separations	5
TOTAL SEPARATIONS	55
Formal Grievances Filed by Employees	1
Equal Employment Opportunity Commission (EEOC) Complaints Filed	1

Full Cost Profile

Cost Breakdown by Percentage	
Personal Services	59.6%
Operating Costs	39.0%
Capital Costs	1.5%
TOTAL	100.0%
Cost Breakdown in Dollars	
Personal Services	$391,715
Operating Costs	$256,157
Capital Costs	$9,620
TOTAL	$657,492

Key: Apex □   Benchmarking Average —   Fiscal Years 2015 through 2019

Resource Measures

Human Resources Services Cost per Capita

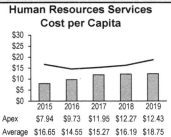

	2015	2016	2017	2018	2019
Apex	$7.94	$9.73	$11.95	$12.27	$12.43
Average	$16.65	$14.55	$15.27	$16.19	$18.75

Human Resources FTEs per 10,000 Population

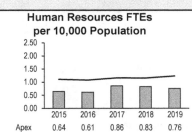

	2015	2016	2017	2018	2019
Apex	0.64	0.61	0.86	0.83	0.76
Average	1.10	1.08	1.16	1.15	1.23

Workload Measures

Total Municipal FTEs per 10,000 Population

	2015	2016	2017	2018	2019
Apex	85	86	89	92	88
Average	118	114	121	122	117

Applications Processed per 100 Municipal Employees

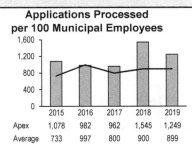

	2015	2016	2017	2018	2019
Apex	1,078	982	962	1,545	1,249
Average	733	997	800	900	899

Position Requisitions per 100 Municipal Employees

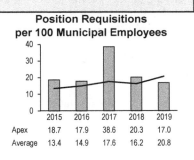

	2015	2016	2017	2018	2019
Apex	18.7	17.9	38.6	20.3	17.0
Average	13.4	14.9	17.6	16.2	20.8

Efficiency Measures

Human Resources Cost per Municipal Employee

	2015	2016	2017	2018	2019
Apex	$932	$1,128	$1,338	$1,324	$1,411
Average	$1,341	$1,261	$1,272	$1,325	$1,601

Ratio of Human Resources Staff to 100 Municipal Employees

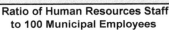
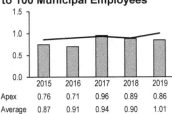

	2015	2016	2017	2018	2019
Apex	0.76	0.71	0.96	0.89	0.86
Average	0.87	0.91	0.94	0.90	1.01

Effectiveness Measures

Probationary Period Completion Rate (New Hires)

	2015	2016	2017	2018	2019
Apex	86%	86%	89%	97%	92%
Average	90%	85%	87%	85%	84%

Employee Turnover Rate (All Separations)

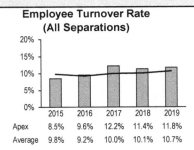

	2015	2016	2017	2018	2019
Apex	8.5%	9.6%	12.2%	11.4%	11.8%
Average	9.8%	9.2%	10.0%	10.1%	10.7%

Employee Turnover Rate (Voluntary Separations)

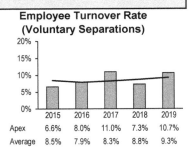

	2015	2016	2017	2018	2019
Apex	6.6%	8.0%	11.0%	7.3%	10.7%
Average	8.5%	7.9%	8.3%	8.8%	9.3%

Percentage of Grievances Resolved at Department Level

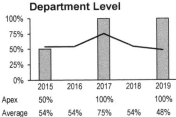

	2015	2016	2017	2018	2019
Apex	50%		100%		100%
Average	54%	54%	75%	54%	48%

Average Days from Post Date to Hire Date (First Day of Employment)

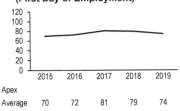

	2015	2016	2017	2018	2019
Apex					
Average	70	72	81	79	74

Explanatory Information

Service Level and Delivery

The Human Resources Department provides a comprehensive assortment of services, including occupational health and wellness, benefits, recruitment and selection, compensation, and employee relations.

The city's probationary period for new employees is six months.

Conditions Affecting Service, Performance, and Costs

The city's data include the following positions (and related costs) as part of the city's Human Resources Department: health services supervisor, registered nurse, and administrative staff.

Employee relations issues are resolved through the city's administration.

All advertising costs for vacant positions are now paid for out of the Human Resources budget, with the exception of industry-specific websites or publications specifically requested by the individual departments.

Asheville did not conduct a broad compensation study in the city but did evaluate seventy-six individual positions.

Municipal Profile

Population (OSBM 2018)	93,621
Land Area (Square Miles)	45.53
Persons per Square Mile	2,056
Median Household Income	$40,494
U.S. Census 2016	
County Unemployment Rate (2018)	3.0%
U.S. Bureau of Labor Statistics	

Service Profile

Central HR FTE Positions	
Administration	5.00
Generalist/Specialist	14.00
Staff Support/Clerical	2.60
Total Authorized Workforce	1,281.0
Authorized FTEs	1,275.0
Average Length of Service (Months)	101.4
Number of Position Requisitions	408
Employment Applications Processed	8,707
Length of Probationary Employment Period	6 months
Compensation Studies Completed	0
Positions Studied	76
Employee Turnover	
Voluntary Separations	160
Involuntary Separations	17
TOTAL SEPARATIONS	177
Formal Grievances Filed by Employees	9
Equal Employment Opportunity Commission (EEOC) Complaints Filed	1

Full Cost Profile

Cost Breakdown by Percentage	
Personal Services	64.7%
Operating Costs	31.9%
Capital Costs	3.4%
TOTAL	100.0%

Cost Breakdown in Dollars	
Personal Services	$1,817,588
Operating Costs	$897,460
Capital Costs	$95,664
TOTAL	$2,810,712

Asheville

Central Human Resources

Resource Measures

Human Resources Services Cost per Capita

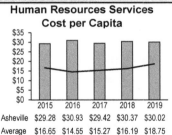

	2015	2016	2017	2018	2019
Asheville	$29.28	$30.93	$29.42	$30.37	$30.02
Average	$16.65	$14.55	$15.27	$16.19	$18.75

Human Resources FTEs per 10,000 Population

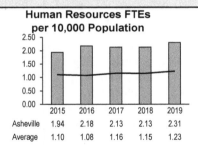

	2015	2016	2017	2018	2019
Asheville	1.94	2.18	2.13	2.13	2.31
Average	1.10	1.08	1.16	1.15	1.23

Workload Measures

Total Municipal FTEs per 10,000 Population

	2015	2016	2017	2018	2019
Asheville	121	131	131	138	136
Average	118	114	121	122	117

Applications Processed per 100 Municipal Employees

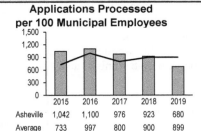

	2015	2016	2017	2018	2019
Asheville	1,042	1,100	976	923	680
Average	733	997	800	900	899

Position Requisitions per 100 Municipal Employees

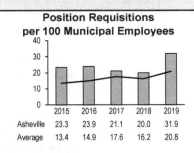

	2015	2016	2017	2018	2019
Asheville	23.3	23.9	21.1	20.0	31.9
Average	13.4	14.9	17.6	16.2	20.8

Efficiency Measures

Human Resources Cost per Municipal Employee

	2015	2016	2017	2018	2019
Asheville	$2,198	$2,345	$2,230	$2,176	$2,194
Average	$1,341	$1,261	$1,272	$1,325	$1,601

Ratio of Human Resources Staff to 100 Municipal Employees

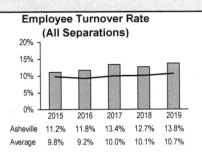

	2015	2016	2017	2018	2019
Asheville	1.46	1.65	1.62	1.53	1.69
Average	0.87	0.91	0.94	0.90	1.01

Effectiveness Measures

Probationary Period Completion Rate (New Hires)

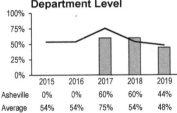

	2015	2016	2017	2018	2019
Asheville	88%	88%	91%	91%	84%
Average	90%	85%	87%	85%	84%

Employee Turnover Rate (All Separations)

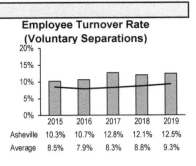

	2015	2016	2017	2018	2019
Asheville	11.2%	11.8%	13.4%	12.7%	13.8%
Average	9.8%	9.2%	10.0%	10.1%	10.7%

Employee Turnover Rate (Voluntary Separations)

	2015	2016	2017	2018	2019
Asheville	10.3%	10.7%	12.8%	12.1%	12.5%
Average	8.5%	7.9%	8.3%	8.8%	9.3%

Percentage of Grievances Resolved at Department Level

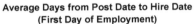

	2015	2016	2017	2018	2019
Asheville	0%	0%	60%	60%	44%
Average	54%	54%	75%	54%	48%

Average Days from Post Date to Hire Date (First Day of Employment)

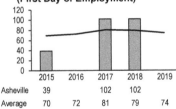

	2015	2016	2017	2018	2019
Asheville	39		102	102	
Average	70	72	81	79	74

Chapel Hill

Central Human Resources

Fiscal Year 2018–19

Explanatory Information

Service Level and Delivery

The Town of Chapel Hill's Human Resource Development Department is organized into one centralized HR department using a specialist structure with several departmental HR liasons who facilitate communication of the town'sprocesses and procedures, benefits paperwork, and predisciplinary conferences. The department ensures standard operating procedures are followed and coordinates departmental interviews for job openings.

The town provides an employee assistance program at no cost to town staff. Chapel Hill also provides some life insurance coverage and short and long-term disability at no cost to employees. The town has an on-site wellness clinic staffed with a nurse practitioner and registered nurse. The town also offers a variety of other wellness programs at reduced cost such, as gym membership, nutritionists, and Weight Watchers.

There were 7,523 applications processed for open positions.

The town's probationary period for most new employees is six months. Department heads and police personnel serve a twelve-month period.

Conditions Affecting Service, Performance, and Costs

The Town of Chapel Hill began participation in the benchmarking project in July 2015, with FY 2014–15 being the first reporting year.

Municipal Profile

Population (OSBM 2018)	63,178
Land Area (Square Miles)	21.27
Persons per Square Mile	2,971
Median Household Income	$60,802
U.S. Census 2016	
County Unemployment Rate (2018)	3.3%
U.S. Bureau of Labor Statistics	

Service Profile

Central HR FTE Positions	
Administration	3.0
Generalist/Specialist	4.0
Staff Support/Clerical	1.0
Total Authorized Workforce	703.0
Authorized FTEs	698.00
Average Length of Service (Months)	116.76
Number of Position Requisitions	270
Employment Applications Processed	7,523
Length of Probationary Employment Period	6 & 12 months
Compensation Studies Completed	0
Positions Studied	0
Employee Turnover	
Voluntary Separations	86
Involuntary Separations	4
TOTAL SEPARATIONS	90
Formal Grievances Filed by Employees	3
Equal Employment Opportunity Commission (EEOC) Complaints Filed	2

Full Cost Profile

Cost Breakdown by Percentage	
Personal Services	25.4%
Operating Costs	55.7%
Capital Costs	18.9%
TOTAL	100.0%
Cost Breakdown in Dollars	
Personal Services	$746,657
Operating Costs	$1,636,981
Capital Costs	$557,080
TOTAL	$2,940,718

Key: Chapel Hill ▨   Benchmarking Average —   Fiscal Years 2015 through 2019

Resource Measures

Human Resources Services Cost per Capita

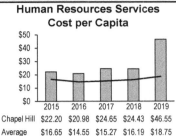

	2015	2016	2017	2018	2019
Chapel Hill	$22.20	$20.98	$24.65	$24.43	$46.55
Average	$16.65	$14.55	$15.27	$16.19	$18.75

Human Resources FTEs per 10,000 Population

	2015	2016	2017	2018	2019
Chapel Hill	1.34	1.34	1.17	1.34	1.27
Average	1.10	1.08	1.16	1.15	1.23

Workload Measures

Total Municipal FTEs per 10,000 Population

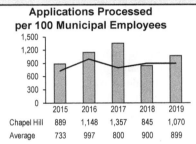

	2015	2016	2017	2018	2019
Chapel Hill	121	128	128	128	110
Average	118	114	121	122	117

Applications Processed per 100 Municipal Employees

	2015	2016	2017	2018	2019
Chapel Hill	889	1,148	1,357	845	1,070
Average	733	997	800	900	899

Position Requisitions per 100 Municipal Employees

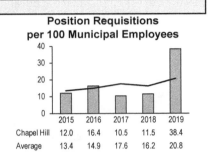

	2015	2016	2017	2018	2019
Chapel Hill	12.0	16.4	10.5	11.5	38.4
Average	13.4	14.9	17.6	16.2	20.8

Efficiency Measures

Human Resources Cost per Municipal Employee

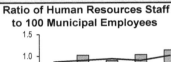
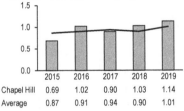

	2015	2016	2017	2018	2019
Chapel Hill	$1,149	$1,599	$1,904	$1,894	$4,183
Average	$1,341	$1,261	$1,272	$1,325	$1,601

Ratio of Human Resources Staff to 100 Municipal Employees

	2015	2016	2017	2018	2019
Chapel Hill	0.69	1.02	0.90	1.03	1.14
Average	0.87	0.91	0.94	0.90	1.01

Effectiveness Measures

Probationary Period Completion Rate (New Hires)

	2015	2016	2017	2018	2019
Chapel Hill	98%	69%	90%	88%	39%
Average	90%	85%	87%	85%	84%

Employee Turnover Rate (All Separations)

	2015	2016	2017	2018	2019
Chapel Hill	6.3%	9.1%	10.6%	11.0%	12.8%
Average	9.8%	9.2%	10.0%	10.1%	10.7%

Employee Turnover Rate (Voluntary Separations)

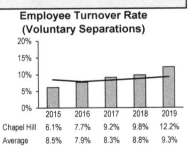

	2015	2016	2017	2018	2019
Chapel Hill	6.1%	7.7%	9.2%	9.8%	12.2%
Average	8.5%	7.9%	8.3%	8.8%	9.3%

Percentage of Grievances Resolved at Department Level

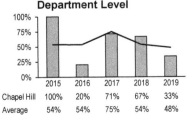

	2015	2016	2017	2018	2019
Chapel Hill	100%	20%	71%	67%	33%
Average	54%	54%	75%	54%	48%

Average Days from Post Date to Hire Date (First Day of Employment)

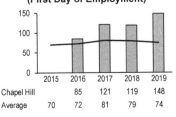

	2015	2016	2017	2018	2019
Chapel Hill		85	121	119	148
Average	70	72	81	79	74

Explanatory Information

Service Level and Delivery

Charlotte's Human Resources Department is organized into six core services: benefits, organization development and learning, human resources management systems and payroll, employee relations and compliance, talent acquisition, and compensation planning. These functional areas perform a variety of strategic, tactical, and transactional services. Some of the transactional services are outsourced.

There were 76,791 employment applications processed for open positions. All applicants must use the PeopleSoft online job application software for each position for which they wish to apply.

The city is self-insured for medical, prescription drug, and dental insurance, and third-party administrators are retained to administer the plans. The wellness program, Wellness Works, includes a wide variety of programs, such as tobacco cessation, annual flu shots, blood pressure screenings, on-site fitness education programs, and weight loss programs. The city partners with OurHealth for health clinic operations for employees, retirees, and dependents, which in addition to health coaching and health risk assessments, provides many health care services. In 2011, the city began offering a premium differential to employees who take a health screening.

Conditions Affecting Service, Performance, and Costs

Charlotte did not participate in the Benchmarking Project during FY 2014–15. No data are available for that year.

Charlotte has a very robust wellness program, including a health clinic. Many resources are devoted to the success of this program. There are wellness ambassadors in every department in the city.

The payroll function in many cities is located in finance; it resides in Human Resources in Charlotte.

Municipal Profile

Population (OSBM 2018)	852,992
Land Area (Square Miles)	306.31
Persons per Square Mile	2,785
Median Household Income	$46,975
U.S. Census 2016	
County Unemployment Rate (2018)	3.7%
U.S. Bureau of Labor Statistics	

Service Profile

Central HR FTE Positions	
Administration	2.0
Generalist/Specialist	42.0
Staff Support/Clerical	2.0
Total Authorized Workforce	7,510.0
Authorized FTEs	7,498.0
Average Length of Service (Months)	120.26
Number of Position Requisitions	678
Employment Applications Processed	76,791
Length of Probationary Employment Period	6 & 12 months
Compensation Studies Completed	11
Positions Studied	220
Employee Turnover	
Voluntary Separations	589
Involuntary Separations	87
TOTAL SEPARATIONS	676
Formal Grievances Filed by Employees	31
Equal Employment Opportunity Commission (EEOC) Complaints Filed	15

Full Cost Profile

Cost Breakdown by Percentage	
Personal Services	70.4%
Operating Costs	27.6%
Capital Costs	2.0%
TOTAL	100.0%
Cost Breakdown in Dollars	
Personal Services	$5,414,460
Operating Costs	$2,124,341
Capital Costs	$152,164
TOTAL	$7,690,965

Charlotte

Central Human Resources

Key: Charlotte ▦ Benchmarking Average — Fiscal Years 2015 through 2019

Resource Measures

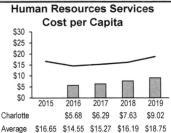

Human Resources Services Cost per Capita

	2015	2016	2017	2018	2019
Charlotte		$5.68	$6.29	$7.63	$9.02
Average	$16.65	$14.55	$15.27	$16.19	$18.75

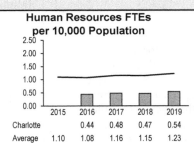

Human Resources FTEs per 10,000 Population

	2015	2016	2017	2018	2019
Charlotte		0.44	0.48	0.47	0.54
Average	1.10	1.08	1.16	1.15	1.23

Workload Measures

Total Municipal FTEs per 10,000 Population

	2015	2016	2017	2018	2019
Charlotte		88	91	87	88
Average	118	114	121	122	117

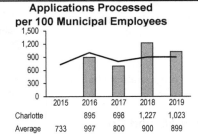

Applications Processed per 100 Municipal Employees

	2015	2016	2017	2018	2019
Charlotte		895	698	1,227	1,023
Average	733	997	800	900	899

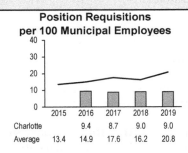

Position Requisitions per 100 Municipal Employees

	2015	2016	2017	2018	2019
Charlotte		9.4	8.7	9.0	9.0
Average	13.4	14.9	17.6	16.2	20.8

Efficiency Measures

Human Resources Cost per Municipal Employee

	2015	2016	2017	2018	2019
Charlotte		$643	$688	$880	$1,024
Average	$1,341	$1,261	$1,272	$1,325	$1,601

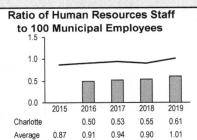

Ratio of Human Resources Staff to 100 Municipal Employees

	2015	2016	2017	2018	2019
Charlotte		0.50	0.53	0.55	0.61
Average	0.87	0.91	0.94	0.90	1.01

Effectiveness Measures

Probationary Period Completion Rate (New Hires)

	2015	2016	2017	2018	2019
Charlotte		82%	89%	82%	83%
Average	90%	85%	87%	85%	84%

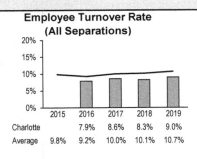

Employee Turnover Rate (All Separations)

	2015	2016	2017	2018	2019
Charlotte		7.9%	8.6%	8.3%	9.0%
Average	9.8%	9.2%	10.0%	10.1%	10.7%

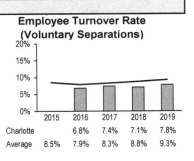

Employee Turnover Rate (Voluntary Separations)

	2015	2016	2017	2018	2019
Charlotte		6.8%	7.4%	7.1%	7.8%
Average	8.5%	7.9%	8.3%	8.8%	9.3%

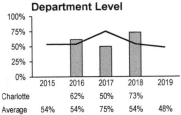

Percentage of Grievances Resolved at Department Level

	2015	2016	2017	2018	2019
Charlotte		62%	50%	73%	
Average	54%	54%	75%	54%	48%

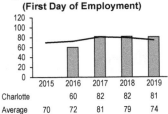

Average Days from Post Date to Hire Date (First Day of Employment)

	2015	2016	2017	2018	2019
Charlotte		60	82	82	81
Average	70	72	81	79	74

Explanatory Information

Service Level and Delivery

The mission of the Human Resources Department for the City of Goldsboro is to provide services that promote a work environment that is characterized by fair treatment of staff, open communications, personal accountability, trust, and mutual respect. The department provides a comprehensive array of services that includes employee selection and recruitment, salary and compensation, benefits, professional development, employee relations, employee health/wellness, and compliance with federal and state safety regulations.

The city's probationary period for new employees is six months for non-public safety employees and twelve months for public safety employees.

During the fiscal year, the city conducted five compensation studies covering twenty-one positions.

Conditions Affecting Service, Performance, and Costs

The city of Goldsboro joined the Benchmarking Project in July 2017, with the first year of data showing for FY 2016–17.

The city provides a $20,000 life insurance policy for all active full-time employees.

Municipal Profile

Population (OSBM 2018)	33,636
Land Area (Square Miles)	29.41
Persons per Square Mile	1,144
Median Household Income	$32,148
U.S. Census 2016	
County Unemployment Rate (2018)	4.4%
U.S. Bureau of Labor Statistics	

Service Profile

Central HR FTE Positions	
Administration	1.0
Generalist/Specialist	3.0
Staff Support/Clerical	1.0
Total Authorized Workforce	617.0
Authorized FTEs	501.5
Average Length of Service (Months)	102.83
Number of Position Requisitions	225
Employment Applications Processed	3,781
Length of Probationary Employment Period	6 & 12 months
Compensation Studies Completed	5
Positions Studied	21
Employee Turnover	
Voluntary Separations	44
Involuntary Separations	6
TOTAL SEPARATIONS	50
Formal Grievances Filed by Employees	3
Equal Employment Opportunity Commission (EEOC) Complaints Filed	0

Full Cost Profile

Cost Breakdown by Percentage	
Personal Services	67.5%
Operating Costs	32.5%
Capital Costs	0.0%
TOTAL	100.0%
Cost Breakdown in Dollars	
Personal Services	$427,097
Operating Costs	$205,280
Capital Costs	$0
TOTAL	$632,377

Goldsboro

Central Human Resources

Resource Measures

Human Resources Services Cost per Capita

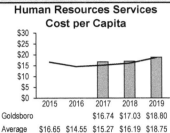

	2015	2016	2017	2018	2019
Goldsboro			$16.74	$17.03	$18.80
Average	$16.65	$14.55	$15.27	$16.19	$18.75

Human Resources FTEs per 10,000 Population

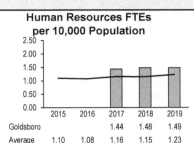

	2015	2016	2017	2018	2019
Goldsboro			1.44	1.48	1.49
Average	1.10	1.08	1.16	1.15	1.23

Workload Measures

Total Municipal FTEs per 10,000 Population

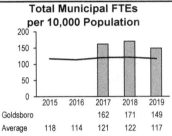

	2015	2016	2017	2018	2019
Goldsboro			162	171	149
Average	118	114	121	122	117

Applications Processed per 100 Municipal Employees

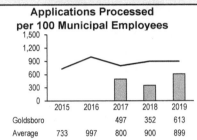

	2015	2016	2017	2018	2019
Goldsboro			497	352	613
Average	733	997	800	900	899

Position Requisitions per 100 Municipal Employees

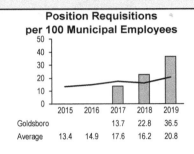

	2015	2016	2017	2018	2019
Goldsboro			13.7	22.8	36.5
Average	13.4	14.9	17.6	16.2	20.8

Efficiency Measures

Human Resources Cost per Municipal Employee

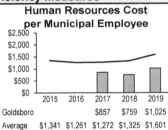

	2015	2016	2017	2018	2019
Goldsboro			$857	$759	$1,025
Average	$1,341	$1,261	$1,272	$1,325	$1,601

Ratio of Human Resources Staff to 100 Municipal Employees

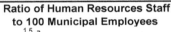
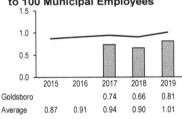

	2015	2016	2017	2018	2019
Goldsboro			0.74	0.66	0.81
Average	0.87	0.91	0.94	0.90	1.01

Effectiveness Measures

Probationary Period Completion Rate (New Hires)

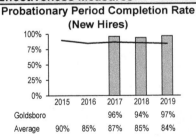

	2015	2016	2017	2018	2019
Goldsboro			96%	94%	97%
Average	90%	85%	87%	85%	84%

Employee Turnover Rate (All Separations)

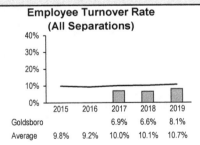

	2015	2016	2017	2018	2019
Goldsboro			6.9%	6.6%	8.1%
Average	9.8%	9.2%	10.0%	10.1%	10.7%

Employee Turnover Rate (Voluntary Separations)

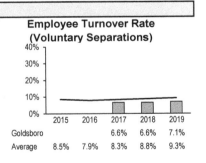

	2015	2016	2017	2018	2019
Goldsboro			6.6%	6.6%	7.1%
Average	8.5%	7.9%	8.3%	8.8%	9.3%

Percentage of Grievances Resolved at Department Level

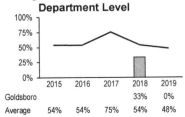

	2015	2016	2017	2018	2019
Goldsboro				33%	0%
Average	54%	54%	75%	54%	48%

Average Days from Post Date to Hire Date (First Day of Employment)

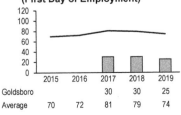

	2015	2016	2017	2018	2019
Goldsboro			30	30	25
Average	70	72	81	79	74

Greensboro

Explanatory Information

Service Level and Delivery

The Human Resources Department for the City of Greensboro provides comprehensive personnel services, including recruitment and selection, compensation, benefits, employee relations, safety, and occupational health and wellness. The total number of full-time equivalent (FTE) positions includes staff from the Training Division, which is housed in a separate department from Human Resources. The HR department has a staff attorney who is able to provide legal consultation on a variety of issues confronting the HR department.

The city conducted one compensation study for the year covering 125 positions.

The city's probationary period for new employees is six months for non-public safety employees and twelve months for public safety employees.

Conditions Affecting Service, Performance, and Costs

Municipal Profile

Population (OSBM 2018)	292,306
Land Area (Square Miles)	128.77
Persons per Square Mile	2,270
Median Household Income	$40,760
U.S. Census 2016	
County Unemployment Rate (2018)	4.1%
U.S. Bureau of Labor Statistics	

Service Profile

Central HR FTE Positions	
Administration	3.0
Generalist/Specialist	39.0
Staff Support/Clerical	2.0
Total Authorized Workforce	3,167.0
Authorized FTEs	3,154.0
Average Length of Service (Months)	126.12
Number of Position Requisitions	473
Employment Applications Processed	33,059
Length of Probationary Employment Period	6 & 12 months
Compensation Studies Completed	1
Positions Studied	125
Employee Turnover	
Voluntary Separations	220
Involuntary Separations	52
TOTAL SEPARATIONS	272
Formal Grievances Filed by Employees	29
Equal Employment Opportunity Commission (EEOC) Complaints Filed	4

Full Cost Profile

Cost Breakdown by Percentage	
Personal Services	74.3%
Operating Costs	25.7%
Capital Costs	0.0%
TOTAL	100.0%
Cost Breakdown in Dollars	
Personal Services	$2,534,794
Operating Costs	$878,981
Capital Costs	$0
TOTAL	$3,413,775

Greensboro

Central Human Resources

Key: Greensboro ▨   Benchmarking Average —   Fiscal Years 2015 through 2019

Resource Measures

Human Resources Services Cost per Capita

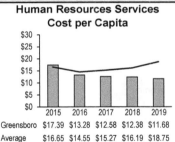

	2015	2016	2017	2018	2019
Greensboro	$17.39	$13.28	$12.58	$12.38	$11.68
Average	$16.65	$14.55	$15.27	$16.19	$18.75

Human Resources FTEs per 10,000 Population

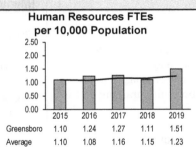

	2015	2016	2017	2018	2019
Greensboro	1.10	1.24	1.27	1.11	1.51
Average	1.10	1.08	1.16	1.15	1.23

Workload Measures

Total Municipal FTEs per 10,000 Population

	2015	2016	2017	2018	2019
Greensboro	108	108	110	104	108
Average	118	114	121	122	117

Applications Processed per 100 Municipal Employees

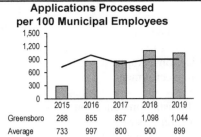

	2015	2016	2017	2018	2019
Greensboro	288	855	857	1,098	1,044
Average	733	997	800	900	899

Position Requisitions per 100 Municipal Employees

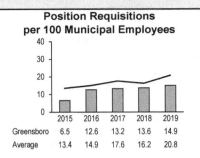

	2015	2016	2017	2018	2019
Greensboro	6.5	12.6	13.2	13.6	14.9
Average	13.4	14.9	17.6	16.2	20.8

Efficiency Measures

Human Resources Cost per Municipal Employee

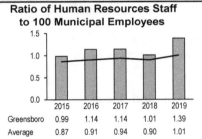

	2015	2016	2017	2018	2019
Greensboro	$1,555	$1,226	$1,137	$1,126	$1,078
Average	$1,341	$1,261	$1,272	$1,325	$1,601

Ratio of Human Resources Staff to 100 Municipal Employees

	2015	2016	2017	2018	2019
Greensboro	0.99	1.14	1.14	1.01	1.39
Average	0.87	0.91	0.94	0.90	1.01

Effectiveness Measures

Probationary Period Completion Rate (New Hires)

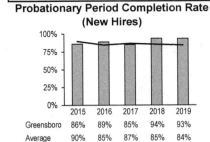

	2015	2016	2017	2018	2019
Greensboro	86%	89%	85%	94%	93%
Average	90%	85%	87%	85%	84%

Employee Turnover Rate (All Separations)

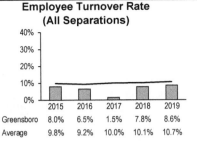

	2015	2016	2017	2018	2019
Greensboro	8.0%	6.5%	1.5%	7.8%	8.6%
Average	9.8%	9.2%	10.0%	10.1%	10.7%

Employee Turnover Rate (Voluntary Separations)

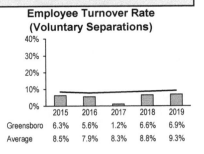

	2015	2016	2017	2018	2019
Greensboro	6.3%	5.6%	1.2%	6.6%	6.9%
Average	8.5%	7.9%	8.3%	8.8%	9.3%

Percentage of Grievances Resolved at Department Level

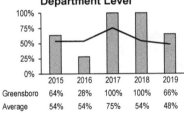

	2015	2016	2017	2018	2019
Greensboro	64%	28%	100%	100%	66%
Average	54%	54%	75%	54%	48%

Average Days from Post Date to Hire Date (First Day of Employment)

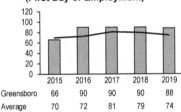

	2015	2016	2017	2018	2019
Greensboro	66	90	90	90	88
Average	70	72	81	79	74

Explanatory Information

Service Level and Delivery

The Human Resources Department for the City of Greenville is responsible for recruitment and selection, salary and benefits administration, position classification, employee relations, affirmative action and equal employment opportunity, training and development, risk administration, and safety.

The city's probationary period is twelve months for all law enforcement personnel and employees in a trainee status, such as fire/rescue trainees. All other employees serve a six-month probationary period.

Nearly all employment applications are processed online. The Human Resources Department screens applications to ensure that applicants meet the position minimum qualifications. Applications are only accepted for positions that are open for recruitment.

Greenville has a voluntary wellness program focusing on education, fitness, mental health, nutrition, weight management, personal health, and personal safety. A safety specialist provides technical safety and occupational illness and injury prevention training.

A formal grievance by an employee in Greenville requires a written notice appealing a disciplinary action given to a supervisor. The grievance process is an internal one, moving up the chain of command with specific timeframes for responses and appeals to the next level.

Conditions Affecting Service, Performance, and Costs

Municipal Profile

Population (OSBM 2018)	89,790
Land Area (Square Miles)	35.58
Persons per Square Mile	2,523
Median Household Income	$33,339
U.S. Census 2016	
County Unemployment Rate (2018)	4.3%
U.S. Bureau of Labor Statistics	

Service Profile

Central HR FTE Positions	
Administration	3.0
Generalist/Specialist	6.0
Staff Support/Clerical	2.0
Total Authorized Workforce	766.8
Authorized FTEs	766.75
Average Length of Service (Months)	121
Number of Position Requisitions	190
Employment Applications Processed	9,757
Length of Probationary Employment Period	6 & 12 months
Compensation Studies Completed	0
Positions Studied	0
Employee Turnover	
Voluntary Separations	80
Involuntary Separations	11
TOTAL SEPARATIONS	91
Formal Grievances Filed by Employees	6
Equal Employment Opportunity Commission (EEOC) Complaints Filed	2

Full Cost Profile

Cost Breakdown by Percentage	
Personal Services	67.1%
Operating Costs	32.4%
Capital Costs	0.5%
TOTAL	100.0%
Cost Breakdown in Dollars	
Personal Services	$902,072
Operating Costs	$435,296
Capital Costs	$7,050
TOTAL	$1,344,418

Key: Greenville ▨ Benchmarking Average — Fiscal Years 2015 through 2019

Resource Measures

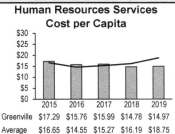

Human Resources Services Cost per Capita

	2015	2016	2017	2018	2019
Greenville	$17.29	$15.76	$15.99	$14.78	$14.97
Average	$16.65	$14.55	$15.27	$16.19	$18.75

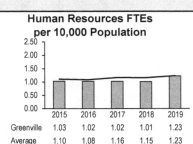

Human Resources FTEs per 10,000 Population

	2015	2016	2017	2018	2019
Greenville	1.03	1.02	1.02	1.01	1.23
Average	1.10	1.08	1.16	1.15	1.23

Workload Measures

Total Municipal FTEs per 10,000 Population

	2015	2016	2017	2018	2019
Greenville	87	86	87	86	85
Average	118	114	121	122	117

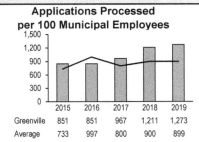

Applications Processed per 100 Municipal Employees

	2015	2016	2017	2018	2019
Greenville	851	851	967	1,211	1,273
Average	733	997	800	900	899

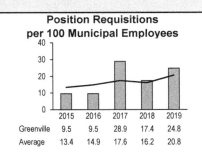

Position Requisitions per 100 Municipal Employees

	2015	2016	2017	2018	2019
Greenville	9.5	9.5	28.9	17.4	24.8
Average	13.4	14.9	17.6	16.2	20.8

Efficiency Measures

Human Resources Cost per Municipal Employee

	2015	2016	2017	2018	2019
Greenville	$1,976	$1,812	$1,830	$1,712	$1,753
Average	$1,341	$1,261	$1,272	$1,325	$1,601

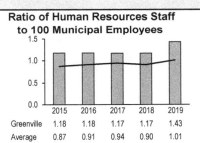

Ratio of Human Resources Staff to 100 Municipal Employees

	2015	2016	2017	2018	2019
Greenville	1.18	1.18	1.17	1.17	1.43
Average	0.87	0.91	0.94	0.90	1.01

Effectiveness Measures

Probationary Period Completion Rate (New Hires)

	2015	2016	2017	2018	2019
Greenville	95%	95%	97%	93%	91%
Average	90%	85%	87%	85%	84%

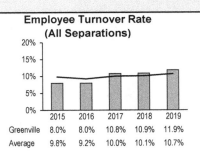

Employee Turnover Rate (All Separations)

	2015	2016	2017	2018	2019
Greenville	8.0%	8.0%	10.8%	10.9%	11.9%
Average	9.8%	9.2%	10.0%	10.1%	10.7%

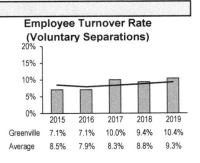

Employee Turnover Rate (Voluntary Separations)

	2015	2016	2017	2018	2019
Greenville	7.1%	7.1%	10.0%	9.4%	10.4%
Average	8.5%	7.9%	8.3%	8.8%	9.3%

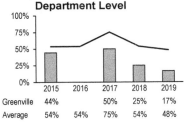

Percentage of Grievances Resolved at Department Level

	2015	2016	2017	2018	2019
Greenville	44%		50%	25%	17%
Average	54%	54%	75%	54%	48%

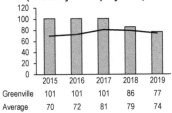

Average Days from Post Date to Hire Date (First Day of Employment)

	2015	2016	2017	2018	2019
Greenville	101	101	101	86	77
Average	70	72	81	79	74

Fiscal Year 2018–19

Explanatory Information

Service Level and Delivery

The human resources function for the City of Hickory contains a director, an organizational development coordinator, a city nurse, two human resources analysts (one oversees benefits administration and the other oversees general employment), and one clerical position. Risk management is a division of the human resources function, which includes a risk manager and a clerical support position.

The city's probationary period is twelve months for all new city employees. The city conducted six compensation studies during the fiscal year for 300 positions.

Conditions Affecting Service, Performance, and Costs

Municipal Profile

Population (OSBM 2018)	40,932
Land Area (Square Miles)	29.92
Persons per Square Mile	1,368
Median Household Income	$35,353
U.S. Census 2016	
County Unemployment Rate (2018)	3.5%
U.S. Bureau of Labor Statistics	

Service Profile

Central HR FTE Positions	
Administration	1.00
Generalist/Specialist	5.0
Staff Support/Clerical	2.00
Total Authorized Workforce	737.0
Authorized FTEs	697.5
Average Length of Service (Months)	116.4
Number of Position Requisitions	70
Employment Applications Processed	3,566
Length of Probationary	12 months
Employment Period	
Compensation Studies Completed	6
Positions Studied	300
Employee Turnover	
Voluntary Separations	86
Involuntary Separations	9
TOTAL SEPARATIONS	95
Formal Grievances Filed by Employees	2
Equal Employment Opportunity	0
Commission (EEOC) Complaints Filed	

Full Cost Profile

Cost Breakdown by Percentage	
Personal Services	76.0%
Operating Costs	22.8%
Capital Costs	1.2%
TOTAL	100.0%
Cost Breakdown in Dollars	
Personal Services	$437,856
Operating Costs	$131,384
Capital Costs	$7,180
TOTAL	$576,420

Hickory

Central Human Resources

Resource Measures

Human Resources Services Cost per Capita

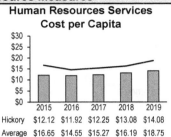

	2015	2016	2017	2018	2019
Hickory	$12.12	$11.92	$12.25	$13.08	$14.08
Average	$16.65	$14.55	$15.27	$16.19	$18.75

Human Resources FTEs per 10,000 Population

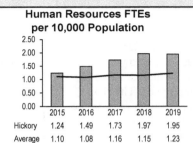

	2015	2016	2017	2018	2019
Hickory	1.24	1.49	1.73	1.97	1.95
Average	1.10	1.08	1.16	1.15	1.23

Workload Measures

Total Municipal FTEs per 10,000 Population

	2015	2016	2017	2018	2019
Hickory	172	172	182	181	170
Average	118	114	121	122	117

Applications Processed per 100 Municipal Employees

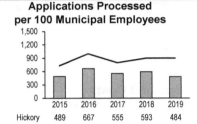

	2015	2016	2017	2018	2019
Hickory	489	667	555	593	484
Average	733	997	800	900	899

Position Requisitions per 100 Municipal Employees

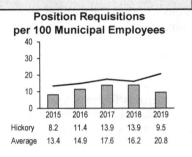

	2015	2016	2017	2018	2019
Hickory	8.2	11.4	13.9	13.9	9.5
Average	13.4	14.9	17.6	16.2	20.8

Efficiency Measures

Human Resources Cost per Municipal Employee

	2015	2016	2017	2018	2019
Hickory	$667	$654	$673	$723	$782
Average	$1,341	$1,261	$1,272	$1,325	$1,601

Ratio of Human Resources Staff to 100 Municipal Employees

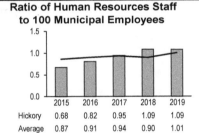

	2015	2016	2017	2018	2019
Hickory	0.68	0.82	0.95	1.09	1.09
Average	0.87	0.91	0.94	0.90	1.01

Effectiveness Measures

Probationary Period Completion Rate (New Hires)

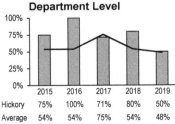

	2015	2016	2017	2018	2019
Hickory	93%	72%	80%	69%	74%
Average	90%	85%	87%	85%	84%

Employee Turnover Rate (All Separations)

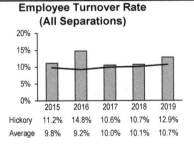

	2015	2016	2017	2018	2019
Hickory	11.2%	14.8%	10.6%	10.7%	12.9%
Average	9.8%	9.2%	10.0%	10.1%	10.7%

Employee Turnover Rate (Voluntary Separations)

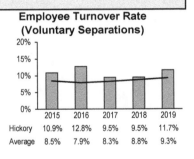

	2015	2016	2017	2018	2019
Hickory	10.9%	12.8%	9.5%	9.5%	11.7%
Average	8.5%	7.9%	8.3%	8.8%	9.3%

Percentage of Grievances Resolved at Department Level

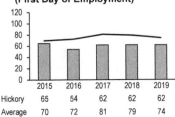

	2015	2016	2017	2018	2019
Hickory	75%	100%	71%	80%	50%
Average	54%	54%	75%	54%	48%

Average Days from Post Date to Hire Date (First Day of Employment)

	2015	2016	2017	2018	2019
Hickory	65	54	62	62	62
Average	70	72	81	79	74

Mooresville

Central Human Resources

Fiscal Year 2018–19

Explanatory Information

Service Level and Delivery

The Town of Mooresville's Human Resources Department oversees and coordinates several programs and services for the town's employees. The HR Department organizationally includes five HR employees but also three risk management employees. The risk management employees are not included here, as this is outside the benchmarking service definition. The Town also provides HR support for the jurisdiction's cable company, but their data is not included in this report.

The city's probationary period for new general employees is six months.

One compensation study covering 103 positions was conducted during the fiscal year.

Conditions Affecting Service, Performance, and Costs

Mooresville joined the Benchmarking project in July 2018, with the first year of data showing for FY2017–18.

Employment applications are screened on a daily basis so that departments are only one working day away from receiving applications from candidates.

Mooresville has centralized costs associated with tuition assistance and professional development within the Human Resources Department.

Municipal Profile	
Population (OSBM 2018)	41,255
Land Area (Square Miles)	22.75
Persons per Square Mile	1,813
Median Household Income	$67,213
U.S. Census 2016	
County Unemployment Rate (2018)	3.5%
U.S. Bureau of Labor Statistics	

Service Profile	
Central HR FTE Positions	
Administration	2.0
Generalist/Specialist	2.0
Staff Support/Clerical	1.0
Total Authorized Workforce	471.0
Authorized FTEs	470.8
Average Length of Service (Months)	110.28
Number of Position Requisitions	68
Employment Applications Processed	2,612
Length of Probationary Employment Period	6 months
Compensation Studies Completed	1
Positions Studied	103
Employee Turnover	
Voluntary Separations	32
Involuntary Separations	7
TOTAL SEPARATIONS	39
Formal Grievances Filed by Employees	8
Equal Employment Opportunity Commission (EEOC) Complaints Filed	5

Full Cost Profile	
Cost Breakdown by Percentage	
Personal Services	43.6%
Operating Costs	55.2%
Capital Costs	1.2%
TOTAL	100.0%
Cost Breakdown in Dollars	
Personal Services	$483,757
Operating Costs	$612,046
Capital Costs	$13,631
TOTAL	$1,109,434

Key: Mooresville   Benchmarking Average —   Fiscal Years 2015 through 2019

Resource Measures

Human Resources Services Cost per Capita

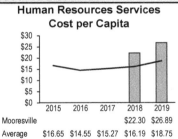

	2015	2016	2017	2018	2019
Mooresville				$22.30	$26.89
Average	$16.65	$14.55	$15.27	$16.19	$18.75

Human Resources FTEs per 10,000 Population

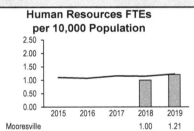

	2015	2016	2017	2018	2019
Mooresville				1.00	1.21
Average	1.10	1.08	1.16	1.15	1.23

Workload Measures

Total Municipal FTEs per 10,000 Population

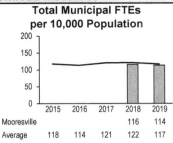

	2015	2016	2017	2018	2019
Mooresville				116	114
Average	118	114	121	122	117

Applications Processed per 100 Municipal Employees

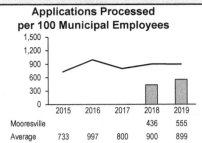

	2015	2016	2017	2018	2019
Mooresville				436	555
Average	733	997	800	900	899

Position Requisitions per 100 Municipal Employees

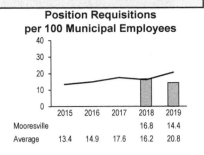

	2015	2016	2017	2018	2019
Mooresville				16.8	14.4
Average	13.4	14.9	17.6	16.2	20.8

Efficiency Measures

Human Resources Cost per Municipal Employee

	2015	2016	2017	2018	2019
Mooresville				$1,919	$2,355
Average	$1,341	$1,261	$1,272	$1,325	$1,601

Ratio of Human Resources Staff to 100 Municipal Employees

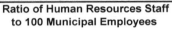
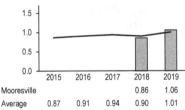

	2015	2016	2017	2018	2019
Mooresville				0.86	1.06
Average	0.87	0.91	0.94	0.90	1.01

Effectiveness Measures

Probationary Period Completion Rate (New Hires)

	2015	2016	2017	2018	2019
Mooresville				83%	90%
Average	90%	85%	87%	85%	84%

Employee Turnover Rate (All Separations)

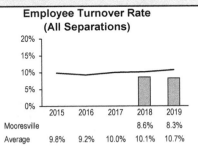

	2015	2016	2017	2018	2019
Mooresville				8.6%	8.3%
Average	9.8%	9.2%	10.0%	10.1%	10.7%

Employee Turnover Rate (Voluntary Separations)

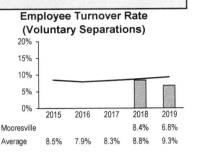

	2015	2016	2017	2018	2019
Mooresville				8.4%	6.8%
Average	8.5%	7.9%	8.3%	8.8%	9.3%

Percentage of Grievances Resolved at Department Level

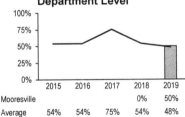

	2015	2016	2017	2018	2019
Mooresville				0%	50%
Average	54%	54%	75%	54%	48%

Average Days from Post Date to Hire Date (First Day of Employment)

	2015	2016	2017	2018	2019
Mooresville				46	69
Average	70	72	81	79	74

Raleigh

Central Human Resources

Fiscal Year 2018–19

Explanatory Information

Service Level and Delivery

The City of Raleigh's Human Resource Department is organized around work units covering benefits and wellness, employee training and organizational development, talent acquisition, classification and compensation, HRIS administration, and health, safety, and worker's compensation. In addition, the department has three business partners who align with the city's assistant city managers and their respective departments.

The city's probationary period for law enforcement officers is twelve months from the date of employment or successful completion of field training. For firefighters, the probationary period is from the date of employment to six months after graduation from the academy. For all other employees, the probation period lasts six months from the date of employment.

One compensation study covering 2,413 positions was conducted during the fiscal year. A market review of benchmark jobs was conducted for comparison.

All applications for employment must be completed electronically. HR conducts an initial scan based on minimum qualifications and secondarily by screening questions developed by the hiring manager.

Conditions Affecting Service, Performance, and Costs

Raleigh rejoined the Benchmarking Project in July 2016, with the first year of data showing for FY 2015–16.

Municipal Profile

Population (OSBM 2018)	464,453
Land Area (Square Miles)	145.65
Persons per Square Mile	3,189
Median Household Income	$46,612
U.S. Census 2016	
County Unemployment Rate (2018)	3.3%
U.S. Bureau of Labor Statistics	

Service Profile

Central HR FTE Positions	
Administration	7.0
Generalist/Specialist	21.0
Staff Support/Clerical	4.0
Total Authorized Workforce	4,284.0
Authorized FTEs	4,284.0
Average Length of Service (Months)	120
Number of Position Requisitions	876
Employment Applications Processed	53,836
Length of Probationary Employment Period	6 & 12 months
Compensation Studies Completed	1
Positions Studied	2,413
Employee Turnover	
Voluntary Separations	333
Involuntary Separations	72
TOTAL SEPARATIONS	405
Formal Grievances Filed by Employees	16
Equal Employment Opportunity Commission (EEOC) Complaints Filed	2

Full Cost Profile

Cost Breakdown by Percentage	
Personal Services	63.0%
Operating Costs	36.3%
Capital Costs	0.7%
TOTAL	100.0%

Cost Breakdown in Dollars	
Personal Services	$2,794,018
Operating Costs	$1,609,411
Capital Costs	$30,398
TOTAL	$4,433,827

Raleigh

Central Human Resources

Key: Raleigh ▪   Benchmarking Average —   Fiscal Years 2015 through 2019

Resource Measures

Human Resources Services Cost per Capita

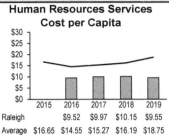

	2015	2016	2017	2018	2019
Raleigh		$9.52	$9.97	$10.15	$9.55
Average	$16.65	$14.55	$15.27	$16.19	$18.75

Human Resources FTEs per 10,000 Population

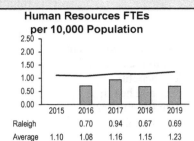

	2015	2016	2017	2018	2019
Raleigh		0.70	0.94	0.67	0.69
Average	1.10	1.08	1.16	1.15	1.23

Workload Measures

Total Municipal FTEs per 10,000 Population

	2015	2016	2017	2018	2019
Raleigh		88	88	92	92
Average	118	114	121	122	117

Applications Processed per 100 Municipal Employees

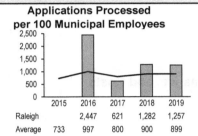

	2015	2016	2017	2018	2019
Raleigh		2,447	621	1,282	1,257
Average	733	997	800	900	899

Position Requisitions per 100 Municipal Employees

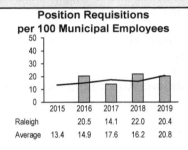

	2015	2016	2017	2018	2019
Raleigh		20.5	14.1	22.0	20.4
Average	13.4	14.9	17.6	16.2	20.8

Efficiency Measures

Human Resources Cost per Municipal Employee

	2015	2016	2017	2018	2019
Raleigh		$1,080	$1,133	$1,108	$1,035
Average	$1,341	$1,261	$1,272	$1,325	$1,601

Ratio of Human Resources Staff to 100 Municipal Employees

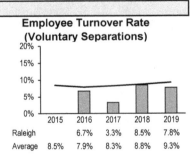

	2015	2016	2017	2018	2019
Raleigh		0.80	1.06	0.73	0.75
Average	0.87	0.91	0.94	0.90	1.01

Effectiveness Measures

Probationary Period Completion Rate (New Hires)

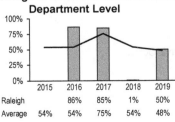

	2015	2016	2017	2018	2019
Raleigh		83%	72%	87%	92%
Average	90%	85%	87%	85%	84%

Employee Turnover Rate (All Separations)

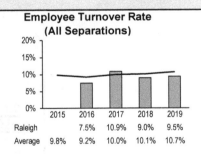

	2015	2016	2017	2018	2019
Raleigh		7.5%	10.9%	9.0%	9.5%
Average	9.8%	9.2%	10.0%	10.1%	10.7%

Employee Turnover Rate (Voluntary Separations)

	2015	2016	2017	2018	2019
Raleigh		6.7%	3.3%	8.5%	7.8%
Average	8.5%	7.9%	8.3%	8.8%	9.3%

Percentage of Grievances Resolved at Department Level

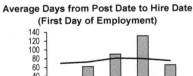

	2015	2016	2017	2018	2019
Raleigh		86%	85%	1%	50%
Average	54%	54%	75%	54%	48%

Average Days from Post Date to Hire Date (First Day of Employment)

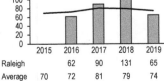

	2015	2016	2017	2018	2019
Raleigh		62	90	131	65
Average	70	72	81	79	74

Wilson

Central Human Resources

Fiscal Year 2018–19

Explanatory Information

Service Level and Delivery

The City of Wilson has a centralized Human Resources Department that includes policy development and implementation, classification and pay administration, recruitment and selection, benefits administration, and employee relations. The safety and health program is a function of the Risk Management Division under another department. Occupational health needs are met through a contract with the Wilson Medical Center.

The city conducted one compensation study during the fiscal year, covering 249 positions.

The city's probationary period is twelve months for new city employees.

Conditions Affecting Service, Performance, and Costs

Municipal Profile

Population (OSBM 2018)	49,054
Land Area (Square Miles)	30.97
Persons per Square Mile	1,584
Median Household Income	$35,409
U.S. Census 2016	
County Unemployment Rate (2018)	6.2%
U.S. Bureau of Labor Statistics	

Service Profile

Central HR FTE Positions	
Administration	1.0
Generalist/Specialist	3.0
Staff Support/Clerical	2.0
Total Authorized Workforce	779.0
Authorized FTEs	771.0
Average Length of Service (Months)	114
Number of Position Requisitions	95
Employment Applications Processed	5,600
Length of Probationary Employment Period	12 months
Compensation Studies Completed	1
Positions Studied	249
Employee Turnover	
Voluntary Separations	64
Involuntary Separations	19
TOTAL SEPARATIONS	83
Formal Grievances Filed by Employees	3
Equal Employment Opportunity Commission (EEOC) Complaints Filed	1

Full Cost Profile

Cost Breakdown by Percentage	
Personal Services	76.0%
Operating Costs	21.6%
Capital Costs	2.4%
TOTAL	100.0%
Cost Breakdown in Dollars	
Personal Services	$487,135
Operating Costs	$138,413
Capital Costs	$15,437
TOTAL	$640,985

Wilson

Central Human Resources

Resource Measures

Human Resources Services Cost per Capita

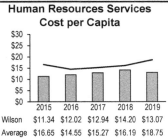

	2015	2016	2017	2018	2019
Wilson	$11.34	$12.02	$12.94	$14.20	$13.07
Average	$16.65	$14.55	$15.27	$16.19	$18.75

Human Resources FTEs per 10,000 Population

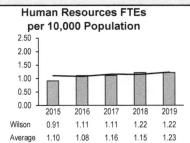

	2015	2016	2017	2018	2019
Wilson	0.91	1.11	1.11	1.22	1.22
Average	1.10	1.08	1.16	1.15	1.23

Workload Measures

Total Municipal FTEs per 10,000 Population

	2015	2016	2017	2018	2019
Wilson	145	147	152	155	157
Average	118	114	121	122	117

Applications Processed per 100 Municipal Employees

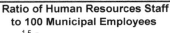
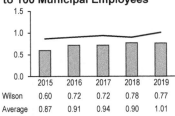

	2015	2016	2017	2018	2019
Wilson	236	315	251	343	719
Average	733	997	800	900	899

Position Requisitions per 100 Municipal Employees

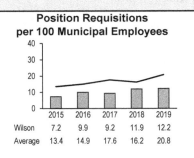

	2015	2016	2017	2018	2019
Wilson	7.2	9.9	9.2	11.9	12.2
Average	13.4	14.9	17.6	16.2	20.8

Efficiency Measures

Human Resources Cost per Municipal Employee

	2015	2016	2017	2018	2019
Wilson	$750	$781	$841	$907	$823
Average	$1,341	$1,261	$1,272	$1,325	$1,601

Ratio of Human Resources Staff to 100 Municipal Employees

	2015	2016	2017	2018	2019
Wilson	0.60	0.72	0.72	0.78	0.77
Average	0.87	0.91	0.94	0.90	1.01

Effectiveness Measures

Probationary Period Completion Rate (New Hires)

	2015	2016	2017	2018	2019
Wilson	82%	94%	71%	66%	91%
Average	90%	85%	87%	85%	84%

Employee Turnover Rate (All Separations)

	2015	2016	2017	2018	2019
Wilson	15.2%	7.8%	10.1%	10.8%	10.7%
Average	9.8%	9.2%	10.0%	10.1%	10.7%

Employee Turnover Rate (Voluntary Separations)

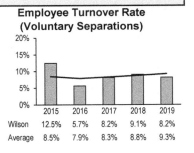

	2015	2016	2017	2018	2019
Wilson	12.5%	5.7%	8.2%	9.1%	8.2%
Average	8.5%	7.9%	8.3%	8.8%	9.3%

Percentage of Grievances Resolved at Department Level

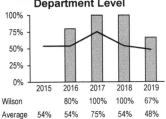

	2015	2016	2017	2018	2019
Wilson		80%	100%	100%	67%
Average	54%	54%	75%	54%	48%

Average Days from Post Date to Hire Date (First Day of Employment)

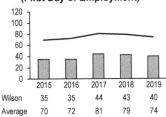

	2015	2016	2017	2018	2019
Wilson	35	35	44	43	40
Average	70	72	81	79	74

Winston-Salem

Central Human Resources

Fiscal Year 2018–19

Explanatory Information

Service Level and Delivery

The human resources function is housed under two separate departments: Human Resources (HR) and Finance. The finance department is responsible for benefits administration and employee safety. The human resources department has three separate sections: general human resources management, employee health, and employee training.

The city conducted one compensation study during the fiscal year, covering 293 positions.

Winston-Salem began having employees go through a probationary period in FY 2015–16 for the first time. The city's probationary period for new general employees is six months and twelve months for police and fire personnel. No data are available for the measure "probationary period completion rate (new hires)" before FY 2015–16.

Conditions Affecting Service, Performance, and Costs

Winston-Salem now requires all job applications to be submitted online. This process has made it substantially easier to apply for jobs, pushing up the number of applications.

The city has two health insurance plans: a basic plan and the Basic Plus Plan, which has richer benefits and more expensive premiums for employees. The city offers a dental reimbursement plan instead of a dental insurance plan.

The City Attorney's Office handles all Equal Employment Opportunity Commission (EEOC) charges.

Winston-Salem's HR department manually calculates the time from post date to hire by subtracting the "approved for posting date" from the actual hire date as noted in the department's system. Certain current policies can effectively stretch this time period, which accounts for the long time reported in the length of time to hire new employees. For example, graduates from the fire academy may sometimes require five months before all evaluations are completed.

Municipal Profile	
Population (OSBM 2018)	243,447
Land Area (Square Miles)	132.55
Persons per Square Mile	1,837
Median Household Income	$40,584
U.S. Census 2016	
County Unemployment Rate (2018)	3.8%
U.S. Bureau of Labor Statistics	

Service Profile	
Central HR FTE Positions	
Administration	3.0
Generalist/Specialist	10.0
Staff Support/Clerical	2.0
Total Authorized Workforce	2,834.0
Authorized FTEs	2,643.0
Average Length of Service (Months)	126
Number of Position Requisitions	582
Employment Applications Processed	23,460
Length of Probationary Employment Period	6 & 12 months
Compensation Studies Completed	1
Positions Studied	293
Employee Turnover	
Voluntary Separations	257
Involuntary Separations	64
TOTAL SEPARATIONS	321
Formal Grievances Filed by Employees	84
Equal Employment Opportunity Commission (EEOC) Complaints Filed	3

Full Cost Profile	
Cost Breakdown by Percentage	
Personal Services	37.6%
Operating Costs	59.5%
Capital Costs	2.8%
TOTAL	100.0%
Cost Breakdown in Dollars	
Personal Services	$1,646,474
Operating Costs	$2,603,329
Capital Costs	$123,532
TOTAL	$4,373,335

Winston-Salem

Central Human Resources

Key: Winston-Salem ▧   Benchmarking Average —   Fiscal Years 2015 through 2019

Resource Measures

Human Resources Services Cost per Capita

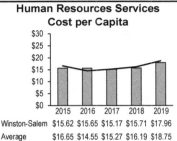

	2015	2016	2017	2018	2019
Winston-Salem	$15.62	$15.65	$15.17	$15.71	$17.96
Average	$16.65	$14.55	$15.27	$16.19	$18.75

Human Resources FTEs per 10,000 Population

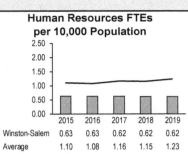

	2015	2016	2017	2018	2019
Winston-Salem	0.63	0.63	0.62	0.62	0.62
Average	1.10	1.08	1.16	1.15	1.23

Workload Measures

Total Municipal FTEs per 10,000 Population

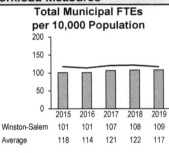

	2015	2016	2017	2018	2019
Winston-Salem	101	101	107	108	109
Average	118	114	121	122	117

Applications Processed per 100 Municipal Employees

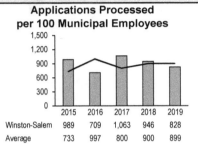

	2015	2016	2017	2018	2019
Winston-Salem	989	709	1,063	946	828
Average	733	997	800	900	899

Position Requisitions per 100 Municipal Employees

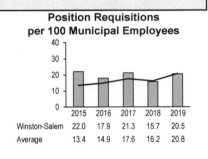

	2015	2016	2017	2018	2019
Winston-Salem	22.0	17.9	21.3	15.7	20.5
Average	13.4	14.9	17.6	16.2	20.8

Efficiency Measures

Human Resources Cost per Municipal Employee

	2015	2016	2017	2018	2019
Winston-Salem	$1,502	$1,338	$1,364	$1,373	$1,543
Average	$1,341	$1,261	$1,272	$1,325	$1,601

Ratio of Human Resources Staff to 100 Municipal Employees

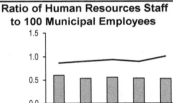

	2015	2016	2017	2018	2019
Winston-Salem	0.61	0.54	0.56	0.54	0.53
Average	0.87	0.91	0.94	0.90	1.01

Effectiveness Measures

Probationary Period Completion Rate (New Hires)

	2015	2016	2017	2018	2019
Winston-Salem		86%	91%	82%	86%
Average	90%	85%	87%	85%	84%

Employee Turnover Rate (All Separations)

	2015	2016	2017	2018	2019
Winston-Salem	10.4%	9.6%	14.3%	13.6%	11.3%
Average	9.8%	9.2%	10.0%	10.1%	10.7%

Employee Turnover Rate (Voluntary Separations)

	2015	2016	2017	2018	2019
Winston-Salem	8.1%	8.1%	12.1%	10.9%	9.1%
Average	8.5%	7.9%	8.3%	8.8%	9.3%

Percentage of Grievances Resolved at Department Level

	2015	2016	2017	2018	2019
Winston-Salem	43%		67%	53%	52%
Average	54%	54%	75%	54%	48%

Average Days from Post Date to Hire Date (First Day of Employment)

	2015	2016	2017	2018	2019
Winston-Salem	112	90	86	82	89
Average	70	72	81	79	74

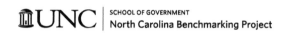

Performance and Cost Data

WATER SERVICES

PERFORMANCE MEASURES FOR WATER SERVICES

SERVICE DEFINITION
This service area includes the collection, treatment, distribution, and billing related to drinking water services. It includes reservoirs where appropriate, pumping stations, pipes to and from treatment plants, storage tanks, and treatment plants. Activities and costs include the operation, maintenance, and installation of infrastructure. Also included are costs and activities associated with the installation, upkeep, and reading of meters; billing and collection costs for drinking water services; and administrative activities, such as planning, engineering, and testing. Excluded are reclaimed water, sewer collection, and wastewater treatment services.

NOTES ON PERFORMANCE MEASURES

1. Thousands of Gallons Billed Water per Meter
This workload measure captures the amount of water provided per meter in the system. Water that does not make it to customer taps is not included.

2. Miles of Main Line Pipe per Square Mile of Service Area
The amount of pipe per square mile shows the density of the pipe infrastructure to be maintained relative to the geographic size of the area served.

3. Total Cost per Thousand Gallons of Billed Water
This efficiency measure shows the total system costs per 1,000 gallons of water that is actually billed to customers.

4. Million Gallons of Billed Water per All Staff FTEs
Large numbers of staff including treatment staff, line maintenance staff, meter readers, billing staff, and others are required to bring drinking water to customer taps. Based on all staff who help support the delivery of drinking water to customers, this efficiency measure shows how much billable water is produced per full-time equivalent (FTE) staff member.

5. Billed Water as a Percentage of Finished Water
Not all water produced at treatment plants makes it to customer meters. Some water is lost through leaks or breaks in the system. Other water is unbilled but authorized for uses such as fighting fires or flushing lines. This efficiency measure shows the percentage of water produced that makes it to customer taps.

6. Percentage of Existing Pipeline Renewed
Replacement or rehabilitation of existing pipeline is needed to ensure that the distribution infrastructure can continue to function. This effectiveness measure shows the percentage of existing water lines that are renewed each year.

7. Percentage of Bills Not Collected

Collection of water bills sent to customers is necessary to ensure revenues for system operation. Adjustments to bills reflecting water loss adjustments are not included in the amount of billings.

8. Peak Daily Demand as a Percentage of Treatment Capacity

A water system needs sufficient capacity to meet not only average demands, but also peak demands. This measure looks at peak historical demand relative to the water system treatment capacity in a day.

9. Breaks and Leaks per Mile of Main Line Pipe

Breaks or leaks in water distribution lines mean the loss of treated water.

10. Customer Complaints about Water Quality per Thousand Meters

Concerns for the adequacy of water are matched with the quality of the water delivered to customers. This effectiveness measure assesses customers' perceptions about their water quality.

Water Services

Summary of Key Dimensions of Service

City or Town	Estimated Residential Population in Service Area	Service Area (in Square Miles)	Average Daily Demand for Water (in MGD)	Operating Treatment Plants	Total Treatment Capacity for Finished Water (in MGD)	Miles of Water Main Lines	Number of Water Meters	Water System FTE Positions
Apex	58,726	24.0	3.8	Shared with Cary	Shared with Cary	310.5	21,663	28.0
Asheville	124,300	183.0	20.3	3	43.5	203.4	63,980	155.0
Charlotte	1,093,901	546.0	108.0	3	252.0	4,393.0	300,418	442.0
Concord	92,567	142.8	12.8	2	24.0	743.1	41,156	63.0
Goldsboro	34,234	25.0	6.5	1	12.0	270.0	14,438	26.0
Greensboro	294,722	148.0	32.0	2	54.0	1,511.2	106,478	162.0
Hickory	99,530	326.0	11.4	1	32.0	947.7	30,133	55.0
Mooresville	41,000	36.0	6.7	2	18.0	313.0	16,357	31.8
Raleigh	582,098	299.0	49.3	2	100.0	2,324.0	202,039	297.0
Wilson	54,500	40.0	9.1	2	22.0	428.0	22,659	47.0
Winston-Salem	348,596	280.0	36.2	3	91.0	2,359.0	131,218	170.2

NOTES
MGD stands for millions of gallons per day.

EXPLANATORY FACTORS
These are factors that the project found affected water services performance and cost in one or more of the municipalities:

Topography
Water quality of source water
Size of service area
Population density
Age of infrastructure
Growth of population and businesses

Explanatory Information

Service Level and Delivery
The Town of Apex Water Distribution Division is housed within the Department of Public Works. It consists of repairs, preventive maintenance, meter installation and replacement, and testing. The town is co-owner of the Cary/Apex water treatment facility, which draws raw water from Jordan Lake. The Town of Cary provides the operational staff for the treatment plant, but Apex shares in the costs of operation and capital.

Apex bases replacement of water lines on customer complaints, frequency of repairs, street rehabilitation needs, age and material of pipes, and flow concerns.

Currently, most water meters are read by automatic means. Replacement of meters is based on a combination of factors, as is water line replacement.

Conditions Affecting Service, Performance, and Costs
The costs of water services as captured here do not include debt service but do capture depreciation.

Municipal Profile

Estimated Service Population	58,726
Service Land Area (Square Miles)	24.0
Persons per Square Mile	2,447
Topography	Flat; gently rolling
Climate	Temperate; little ice and snow
Median Household Income	$84,000
U.S. Census 2016	

Service Profile

FTE Staff Positions	
Treatment Plant	0.0
Line Crews	17.0
Meter Readers	5.0
Billing/Collection	4.0
Other	2.0
Total	28.0
Number of Treatment Plants	NA
Total Treatment Capacity	NA
Average Daily Demand	3.8 MGD
Miles of Main Line Pipe	311
Average Age of Main Line Pipe	16 years
Number of Breaks/Leaks	61
Number of Water Meters	21,663
Percent of Meters Read Automatically	93.9%
Total Revenues Collected	$12,510,314

Full Cost Profile

Cost Breakdown by Percentage	
Personal Services	20.7%
Operating Costs	47.3%
Capital Costs	32.1%
TOTAL	100.0%
Cost Breakdown in Dollars	
Personal Services	$1,612,061
Operating Costs	$3,690,302
Capital Costs	$2,503,095
TOTAL	$7,805,458

Key: Apex ▪   Benchmarking Average —   Fiscal Years 2015 through 2019

Resource Measures

Water Services Cost per Capita

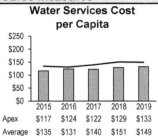

	2015	2016	2017	2018	2019
Apex	$117	$124	$122	$129	$133
Average	$135	$131	$140	$151	$149

Water Services FTEs per 10,000 Population

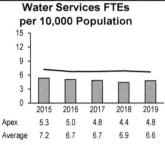

	2015	2016	2017	2018	2019
Apex	5.3	5.0	4.8	4.4	4.8
Average	7.2	6.7	6.7	6.9	6.6

Water Services Cost per Meter

	2015	2016	2017	2018	2019
Apex	$336	$387	$380	$387	$360
Average	$343	$353	$368	$389	$381

Workload Measures

Thousands of Gallons of Billed Water per Meter

	2015	2016	2017	2018	2019
Apex	67.0	70.8	70.0	65.8	52.4
Average	92.9	95.6	95.0	95.2	93.9

Miles of Main Line Pipe per Square Mile of Service Area

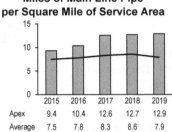

	2015	2016	2017	2018	2019
Apex	9.4	10.4	12.6	12.7	12.9
Average	7.5	7.8	8.3	8.6	7.9

Efficiency Measures

Total Cost per Thousand Gallons of Billed Water

	2015	2016	2017	2018	2019
Apex	$5.01	$5.47	$5.43	$5.88	$6.87
Average	$3.88	$3.87	$4.04	$4.26	$4.25

Million Gallons of Billed Water per Water Services FTEs

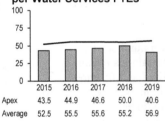

	2015	2016	2017	2018	2019
Apex	43.5	44.9	46.6	50.0	40.6
Average	52.5	55.5	55.6	55.2	56.9

Billed Water as a Percentage of Finished Water

	2015	2016	2017	2018	2019
Apex	89%	88%	85%	87%	83%
Average	86%	87%	82%	84%	83%

Effectiveness Measures

Percentage of Existing Pipeline Replaced or Rehabbed

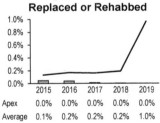

	2015	2016	2017	2018	2019
Apex	0.0%	0.0%	0.0%	0.0%	0.0%
Average	0.1%	0.2%	0.2%	0.2%	1.0%

Percentage of Water Bills Not Collected

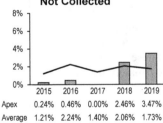

	2015	2016	2017	2018	2019
Apex	0.24%	0.46%	0.00%	2.46%	3.47%
Average	1.21%	2.24%	1.40%	2.06%	1.73%

Peak Daily Demand as a Percentage of Treatment Capacity

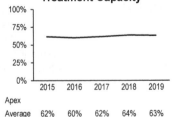

	2015	2016	2017	2018	2019
Apex					
Average	62%	60%	62%	64%	63%

Breaks and Leaks per Mile of Main Line Pipe

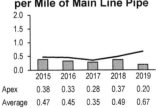

	2015	2016	2017	2018	2019
Apex	0.38	0.33	0.28	0.37	0.20
Average	0.47	0.45	0.35	0.49	0.67

Customer Complaints about Water Quality per 1,000 Meters

	2015	2016	2017	2018	2019
Apex	5.00	4.73	1.69	1.54	1.06
Average	7.41	6.26	5.72	6.88	5.82

Fiscal Year 2018–19

Explanatory Information

Service Level and Delivery

The City of Asheville Water Resources Department is a publicly owned water utility that produces and supplies water for residential, business, industrial, and wholesale bulk customers. The utility serves the city of Asheville, approximately 27 percent of Buncombe County, and approximately 2 percent of Henderson County. Approximately 124,000 people are served over a 183-square-mile area.

Asheville has three water treatment plants drawing from a city reservoir, the Mills River, and may also take water from the French Broad River as needed. The estimated safe yield for water is 35 million gallons per day.

Asheville has an asset management program in place to assist with identifying replacement and refurbishment needs. The goal is for water main lines to be replaced every eighty years.

Currently nearly all water meters are read by various automatic systems, including radio-read and touch-read meters. The goal is to replace all meters in the next few years with radio-read meters.

Conditions Affecting Service, Performance, and Costs

The costs of water services as captured here do not include debt service but do capture depreciation.

The topography and climate in Asheville create a number of problems for water systems operation. The mountainous terrain makes it difficult to install water lines. The utility has fifty-three pressure zones, ranging from 20 to 643 psi, with an average from 180 to 200 psi. Colder temperatures can also make maintenance harder to complete and lead to breaks due to freezing. Due to the Sullivan Acts, Asheville is not allowed to refuse water line installation in any areas of Buncombe County or to charge differential rates.

The number of breaks and leaks in the system has been declining. The Water Resources Department has worked actively to better identify situations with repeated leaks in time and, when identified, to replace pipe for a more permanent solution. These efforts with the help of an engineering firm have led to an approximately ten percent reduction in water losses.

Municipal Profile	
Estimated Service Population	124,300
Service Land Area (Square Miles)	183.0
Persons per Square Mile	679
Topography	Hilly, mountains
Climate	Moderate; ice and snow
Median Household Income	$40,494
U.S. Census 2016	

Service Profile	
FTE Staff Positions	
Treatment Plant	43.0
Line Crews	44.0
Meter Readers	2.0
Billing/Collection	24.0
Other	42.0
Total	155.0
Number of Treatment Plants	3
Total Treatment Capacity	43.5 MGD
Average Daily Demand	20.3 MGD
Miles of Main Line Pipe	203
Average Age of Main Line Pipe	55 years
Number of Breaks/Leaks	746
Number of Water Meters	63,980
Percent of Meters Read Automatically	99.9%
Total Revenues Collected	$40,246,882

Full Cost Profile	
Cost Breakdown by Percentage	
Personal Services	33.9%
Operating Costs	37.8%
Capital Costs	28.3%
TOTAL	100.0%
Cost Breakdown in Dollars	
Personal Services	$9,922,821
Operating Costs	$11,062,091
Capital Costs	$8,292,778
TOTAL	$29,277,690

Asheville

Water Services

Resource Measures

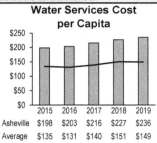

Water Services Cost per Capita

	2015	2016	2017	2018	2019
Asheville	$198	$203	$216	$227	$236
Average	$135	$131	$140	$151	$149

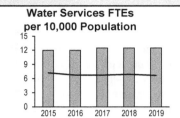

Water Services FTEs per 10,000 Population

	2015	2016	2017	2018	2019
Asheville	12.0	12.0	12.5	12.5	12.5
Average	7.2	6.7	6.7	6.9	6.6

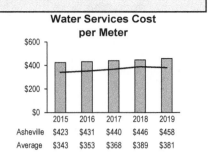

Water Services Cost per Meter

	2015	2016	2017	2018	2019
Asheville	$423	$431	$440	$446	$458
Average	$343	$353	$368	$389	$381

Workload Measures

Thousands of Gallons of Billed Water per Meter

	2015	2016	2017	2018	2019
Asheville	85.6	89.2	90.6	85.5	83.3
Average	92.9	95.6	95.0	95.2	93.9

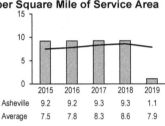

Miles of Main Line Pipe per Square Mile of Service Area

	2015	2016	2017	2018	2019
Asheville	9.2	9.2	9.3	9.3	1.1
Average	7.5	7.8	8.3	8.6	7.9

Efficiency Measures

Total Cost per Thousand Gallons of Billed Water

	2015	2016	2017	2018	2019
Asheville	$4.95	$4.83	$4.86	$5.21	$5.49
Average	$3.88	$3.87	$4.04	$4.26	$4.25

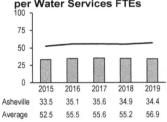

Million Gallons of Billed Water per Water Services FTEs

	2015	2016	2017	2018	2019
Asheville	33.5	35.1	35.6	34.9	34.4
Average	52.5	55.5	55.6	55.2	56.9

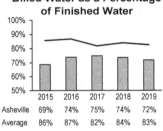

Billed Water as a Percentage of Finished Water

	2015	2016	2017	2018	2019
Asheville	69%	74%	75%	74%	72%
Average	86%	87%	82%	84%	83%

Effectiveness Measures

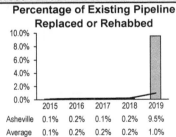

Percentage of Existing Pipeline Replaced or Rehabbed

	2015	2016	2017	2018	2019
Asheville	0.1%	0.2%	0.1%	0.2%	9.5%
Average	0.1%	0.2%	0.2%	0.2%	1.0%

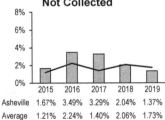

Percentage of Water Bills Not Collected

	2015	2016	2017	2018	2019
Asheville	1.67%	3.49%	3.29%	2.04%	1.37%
Average	1.21%	2.24%	1.40%	2.06%	1.73%

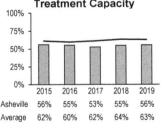

Peak Daily Demand as a Percentage of Treatment Capacity

	2015	2016	2017	2018	2019
Asheville	56%	55%	53%	55%	56%
Average	62%	60%	62%	64%	63%

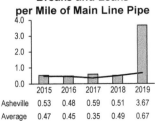

Breaks and Leaks per Mile of Main Line Pipe

	2015	2016	2017	2018	2019
Asheville	0.53	0.48	0.59	0.51	3.67
Average	0.47	0.45	0.35	0.49	0.67

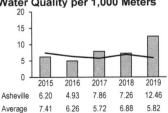

Customer Complaints about Water Quality per 1,000 Meters

	2015	2016	2017	2018	2019
Asheville	6.20	4.93	7.86	7.26	12.46
Average	7.41	6.26	5.72	6.88	5.82

Fiscal Year 2018–19

Explanatory Information

Service Level and Delivery

Charlotte Water (CLTWater) is a combined water and sewer utility for Mecklenburg County and the City of Charlotte. The department is run as an official City of Charlotte department. The area served is generally considered to be Mecklenburg County but also includes a small number of metered drinking water interconnections with the City of Concord and the counties of Union in North Carolina and Lancaster and York in South Carolina. The service area covers approximately 546 square miles and serves over one million people.

Source water for the system is drawn from two impounded lakes on the Catawba River, Lake Norman and Mountain Island Lake, which are operated by Duke Energy. The combined estimated safe yield is between 376 and 503 million gallons per day. The system operates three treatment plants with a combined treatment capacity of 242 million gallons per day. The treatment plants are conventional facilities using rapid mix, flocculation, settling, filtration, and chemical application.

The estimated average age of main line pipes in the system is twenty-nine years. CMU's replacement policy for pipe is based on flow and quality standards.

All meters are now read automatically. CMU uses a system that allows vans traveling the city to read meters as they drive by. The replacement standard is every fifteen years for water meters.

Conditions Affecting Service, Performance, and Costs

Charlotte did not participate in the Benchmarking Project during FY 2014–15. No data are available for that year.

The costs of water services as captured here do not include debt service but do capture depreciation.

The reduction in reported leaks and breaks over time is in large part due to improvements in tracking and data reporting. CMU staff worked on improving how the work order system is used to determine the number of leaks or breaks in the water system.

Municipal Profile

Estimated Service Population	1,093,901
Service Land Area (Square Miles)	546.0
Persons per Square Mile	2,003
Topography	Flat; gently rolling
Climate	Temperate; little ice and snow
Median Household Income U.S. Census 2016	$46,975

Service Profile

FTE Staff Positions	
Treatment Plant	67.0
Line Crews	179.0
Meter Readers	4.0
Billing/Collection	12.0
Other	180.0
Total	442.0
Number of Treatment Plants	3
Total Treatment Capacity	242.0 MGD
Average Daily Demand	108.0 MGD
Miles of Main Line Pipe	4,393
Average Age of Main Line Pipe	32 years
Number of Breaks/Leaks	3,805
Number of Water Meters	300,418
Percent of Meters Read Automatically	100.0%
Total Revenues Collected	$188,207,631

Full Cost Profile

Cost Breakdown by Percentage	
Personal Services	28.9%
Operating Costs	31.7%
Capital Costs	39.4%
TOTAL	100.0%
Cost Breakdown in Dollars	
Personal Services	$28,256,068
Operating Costs	$31,002,607
Capital Costs	$38,559,560
TOTAL	$97,818,235

Charlotte

Water Services

Key: Charlotte ▪ Benchmarking Average — Fiscal Years 2015 through 2019

Resource Measures

Water Services Cost per Capita

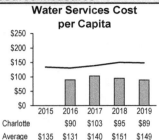

	2015	2016	2017	2018	2019
Charlotte		$90	$103	$95	$89
Average	$135	$131	$140	$151	$149

Water Services FTEs per 10,000 Population

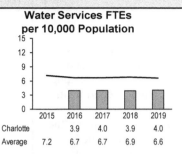

	2015	2016	2017	2018	2019
Charlotte		3.9	4.0	3.9	4.0
Average	7.2	6.7	6.7	6.9	6.6

Water Services Cost per Meter

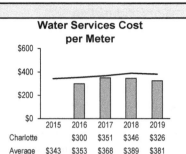

	2015	2016	2017	2018	2019
Charlotte		$300	$351	$346	$326
Average	$343	$353	$368	$389	$381

Workload Measures

Thousands of Gallons of Billed Water per Meter

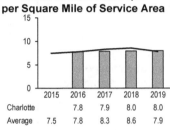

	2015	2016	2017	2018	2019
Charlotte		112.3	113.7	107.6	107.3
Average	92.9	95.6	95.0	95.2	93.9

Miles of Main Line Pipe per Square Mile of Service Area

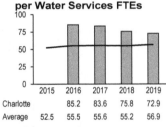

	2015	2016	2017	2018	2019
Charlotte		7.8	7.9	8.0	8.0
Average	7.5	7.8	8.3	8.6	7.9

Efficiency Measures

Total Cost per Thousand Gallons of Billed Water

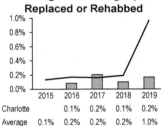

	2015	2016	2017	2018	2019
Charlotte		$2.67	$3.09	$3.22	$3.03
Average	$3.88	$3.87	$4.04	$4.26	$4.25

Million Gallons of Billed Water per Water Services FTEs

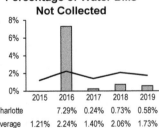

	2015	2016	2017	2018	2019
Charlotte		85.2	83.6	75.8	72.9
Average	52.5	55.5	55.6	55.2	56.9

Billed Water as a Percentage of Finished Water

	2015	2016	2017	2018	2019
Charlotte		82%	85%	82%	82%
Average	86%	87%	82%	84%	83%

Effectiveness Measures

Percentage of Existing Pipeline Replaced or Rehabbed

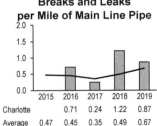

	2015	2016	2017	2018	2019
Charlotte		0.1%	0.2%	0.1%	0.2%
Average	0.1%	0.2%	0.2%	0.2%	1.0%

Percentage of Water Bills Not Collected

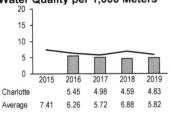

	2015	2016	2017	2018	2019
Charlotte		7.29%	0.24%	0.73%	0.58%
Average	1.21%	2.24%	1.40%	2.06%	1.73%

Peak Daily Demand as a Percentage of Treatment Capacity

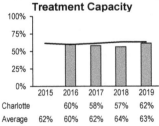

	2015	2016	2017	2018	2019
Charlotte		60%	58%	57%	62%
Average	62%	60%	62%	64%	63%

Breaks and Leaks per Mile of Main Line Pipe

	2015	2016	2017	2018	2019
Charlotte		0.71	0.24	1.22	0.87
Average	0.47	0.45	0.35	0.49	0.67

Customer Complaints about Water Quality per 1,000 Meters

	2015	2016	2017	2018	2019
Charlotte		5.45	4.98	4.59	4.83
Average	7.41	6.26	5.72	6.88	5.82

Concord

Water Services

Explanatory Information

Service Level and Delivery

The City of Concord Water Resources Department is a water-only utility. The department has three divisions: one for operations and maintenance and one for each of two treatment plants. Meter reading, billing, and collections are handled by the city Finance Department.

Concord's system serves approximately 93,000 people and covers the City of Concord, the Town of Midland, and approximately one-fourth of Cabarrus County. Water sources for the system are Lake Fisher, owned by the city, and Lakes Howell and Concord, reservoirs owned by the Water and Sewer Authority of Cabarrus County. The combined estimated safe yield is 24 million gallons per day.

The city operates two treatment plants with a combined treatment capacity of 24 million gallons per day. Concord has emergency connections with the City of Charlotte and the City of Kannapolis and sells small amounts of water to the Town of Harrisburg and the Town of Midland.

The estimated average age of main line pipes in the system is thirty-five years. Water meters are read monthly, with all being read using automatic means. The replacement standard for water meters is fifteen years.

Conditions Affecting Service, Performance, and Costs

The costs of water services as captured here do not include debt service but do capture depreciation.

Municipal Profile

Estimated Service Population	92,567
Service Land Area (Square Miles)	142.8
Persons per Square Mile	648
Topography	Flat; gently rolling
Climate	Temperate; little ice and snow
Median Household Income U.S. Census 2016	$50,863

Service Profile

FTE Staff Positions	
Treatment Plant	26.0
Line Crews	25.0
Meter Readers	0.0
Billing/Collection	0.0
Other	12.0
Total	63.0
Number of Treatment Plants	2
Total Treatment Capacity	24.0 MGD
Average Daily Demand	12.8 MGD
Miles of Main Line Pipe	743
Average Age of Main Line Pipe	35 years
Number of Breaks/Leaks	49
Number of Water Meters	41,156
Percent of Meters Read Automatically	100.0%
Total Revenues Collected	$25,835,009

Full Cost Profile

Cost Breakdown by Percentage	
Personal Services	28.7%
Operating Costs	49.4%
Capital Costs	21.9%
TOTAL	100.0%
Cost Breakdown in Dollars	
Personal Services	$5,191,178
Operating Costs	$8,941,232
Capital Costs	$3,966,683
TOTAL	$18,099,093

Resource Measures

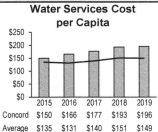

Water Services Cost per Capita

	2015	2016	2017	2018	2019
Concord	$150	$166	$177	$193	$196
Average	$135	$131	$140	$151	$149

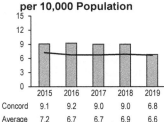

Water Services FTEs per 10,000 Population

	2015	2016	2017	2018	2019
Concord	9.1	9.2	9.0	9.0	6.8
Average	7.2	6.7	6.7	6.9	6.6

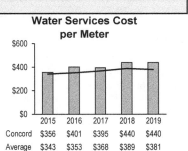

Water Services Cost per Meter

	2015	2016	2017	2018	2019
Concord	$356	$401	$395	$440	$440
Average	$343	$353	$368	$389	$381

Workload Measures

Thousands of Gallons of Billed Water per Meter

	2015	2016	2017	2018	2019
Concord	93.2	97.4	94.0	95.6	96.5
Average	92.9	95.6	95.0	95.2	93.9

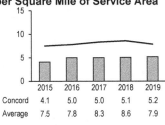

Miles of Main Line Pipe per Square Mile of Service Area

	2015	2016	2017	2018	2019
Concord	4.1	5.0	5.0	5.1	5.2
Average	7.5	7.8	8.3	8.6	7.9

Efficiency Measures

Total Cost per Thousand Gallons of Billed Water

	2015	2016	2017	2018	2019
Concord	$3.82	$4.12	$4.21	$4.60	$4.56
Average	$3.88	$3.87	$4.04	$4.26	$4.25

Million Gallons of Billed Water per Water Services FTEs

	2015	2016	2017	2018	2019
Concord	43.4	43.6	46.8	46.5	63.1
Average	52.5	55.5	55.6	55.2	56.9

Billed Water as a Percentage of Finished Water

	2015	2016	2017	2018	2019
Concord	95%	100%	100%	86%	85%
Average	86%	87%	82%	84%	83%

Effectiveness Measures

Percentage of Existing Pipeline Replaced or Rehabbed

	2015	2016	2017	2018	2019
Concord	0.0%	0.0%	0.0%	0.0%	0.0%
Average	0.1%	0.2%	0.2%	0.2%	1.0%

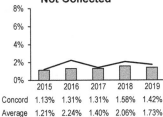

Percentage of Water Bills Not Collected

	2015	2016	2017	2018	2019
Concord	1.13%	1.31%	1.31%	1.58%	1.42%
Average	1.21%	2.24%	1.40%	2.06%	1.73%

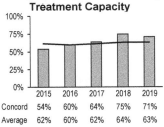

Peak Daily Demand as a Percentage of Treatment Capacity

	2015	2016	2017	2018	2019
Concord	54%	60%	64%	75%	71%
Average	62%	60%	62%	64%	63%

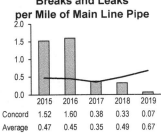

Breaks and Leaks per Mile of Main Line Pipe

	2015	2016	2017	2018	2019
Concord	1.52	1.60	0.38	0.33	0.07
Average	0.47	0.45	0.35	0.49	0.67

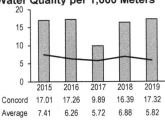

Customer Complaints about Water Quality per 1,000 Meters

	2015	2016	2017	2018	2019
Concord	17.01	17.26	9.89	16.39	17.32
Average	7.41	6.26	5.72	6.88	5.82

Goldsboro

Water Services

Fiscal Year 2018–19

Explanatory Information

Service Level and Delivery

Goldsboro's drinking water services are a joint responsibility between the Public Works and Public Utilities Departments. Both departments are overseen by the Public Works Director. Public Works is responsible for the collection and distribution system lines. Public Utilities is responsible for the operations of the water treatment plant, the water reclamation facility, and pump stations.

The Goldsboro system serves approximately 34,000 people in an area covering twenty-five square miles. Water is collected from the Neuse River. The system also has an emergency option to collect from the Littler River, but this option has not been needed for several years. The estimated safe yield of the system is 6 million gallons per day based on an analysis performed by consultants. The system has emergency connections with Eastern Wayne, Belfast-Patetown, Fork Town, and Southern Wayne Sanitary districts.

The city runs one treatment plant with a capacity of 12 million gallons per day. The plant uses traditional surface water treatment consisting of coagulation, flocculation, sedimentation, filtration, and disinfection.

Goldsboro handles pipe placement by focusing on breaks in the system.

Conditions Affecting Service, Performance, and Costs

The city of Goldsboro joined the Benchmarking Project in July 2017, with the first year of data showing for FY 2016–17.

The costs of water services as captured here do not include debt service but do capture depreciation.

Hurricane Matthew in October 2016 put stress on the water system due to the extensive flooding.

Municipal Profile

Estimated Service Population	34,234
Service Land Area (Square Miles)	25.0
Persons per Square Mile	1,369
Topography	Flat
Climate	Temperate; little ice and snow
Median Household Income U.S. Census 2016	$32,148

Service Profile

FTE Staff Positions	
Treatment Plant	9.0
Line Crews	5.0
Meter Readers	4.0
Billing/Collection	6.0
Other	2.0
Total	26.0
Number of Treatment Plants	1
Total Treatment Capacity	12.0 MGD
Average Daily Demand	6.5 MGD
Miles of Main Line Pipe	270
Average Age of Main Line Pipe	NA
Number of Breaks/Leaks	359
Number of Water Meters	14,438
Percent of Meters Read Automatically	100.0%
Total Revenues Collected	$6,277,394

Full Cost Profile

Cost Breakdown by Percentage	
Personal Services	13.6%
Operating Costs	84.4%
Capital Costs	2.0%
TOTAL	100.0%
Cost Breakdown in Dollars	
Personal Services	$668,096
Operating Costs	$4,139,612
Capital Costs	$98,206
TOTAL	$4,905,914

Goldsboro

Water Services

Resource Measures

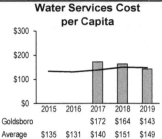

Water Services Cost per Capita

	2015	2016	2017	2018	2019
Goldsboro			$172	$164	$143
Average	$135	$131	$140	$151	$149

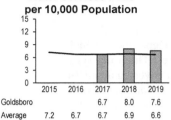

Water Services FTEs per 10,000 Population

	2015	2016	2017	2018	2019
Goldsboro			6.7	8.0	7.6
Average	7.2	6.7	6.7	6.9	6.6

Water Services Cost per Meter

	2015	2016	2017	2018	2019
Goldsboro			$457	$346	$340
Average	$343	$353	$368	$389	$381

Workload Measures

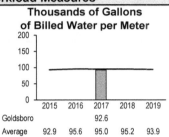

Thousands of Gallons of Billed Water per Meter

	2015	2016	2017	2018	2019
Goldsboro			92.6		
Average	92.9	95.6	95.0	95.2	93.9

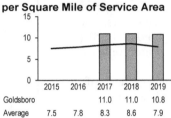

Miles of Main Line Pipe per Square Mile of Service Area

	2015	2016	2017	2018	2019
Goldsboro			11.0	11.0	10.8
Average	7.5	7.8	8.3	8.6	7.9

Efficiency Measures

Total Cost per Thousand Gallons of Billed Water

	2015	2016	2017	2018	2019
Goldsboro			$4.93		$3.38
Average	$3.88	$3.87	$4.04	$4.26	$4.25

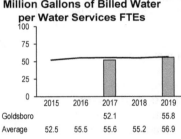

Million Gallons of Billed Water per Water Services FTEs

	2015	2016	2017	2018	2019
Goldsboro			52.1		55.8
Average	52.5	55.5	55.6	55.2	56.9

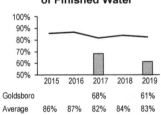

Billed Water as a Percentage of Finished Water

	2015	2016	2017	2018	2019
Goldsboro			68%		61%
Average	86%	87%	82%	84%	83%

Effectiveness Measures

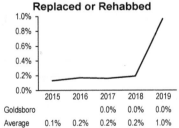

Percentage of Existing Pipeline Replaced or Rehabbed

	2015	2016	2017	2018	2019
Goldsboro			0.0%	0.0%	0.0%
Average	0.1%	0.2%	0.2%	0.2%	1.0%

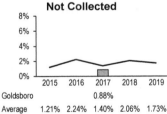

Percentage of Water Bills Not Collected

	2015	2016	2017	2018	2019
Goldsboro			0.88%		
Average	1.21%	2.24%	1.40%	2.06%	1.73%

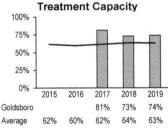

Peak Daily Demand as a Percentage of Treatment Capacity

	2015	2016	2017	2018	2019
Goldsboro			81%	73%	74%
Average	62%	60%	62%	64%	63%

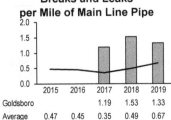

Breaks and Leaks per Mile of Main Line Pipe

	2015	2016	2017	2018	2019
Goldsboro			1.19	1.53	1.33
Average	0.47	0.45	0.35	0.49	0.67

Customer Complaints about Water Quality per 1,000 Meters

	2015	2016	2017	2018	2019
Goldsboro			2.45	0.56	1.94
Average	7.41	6.26	5.72	6.88	5.82

Greensboro   # Water Services

Fiscal Year 2018–19

Explanatory Information

Service Level and Delivery

Greensboro's drinking water is provided by the Water Supply Division, which is part of the Water Resources Department, which also includes wastewater and stormwater services. The water system serves approximately 295,000 people in an area covering about 148 square miles. In addition to City of Greensboro residents, the system serves many addresses in Guilford County in areas adjacent to the city limits.

Water sources for the system are three city-owned reservoirs in the Haw River basin, which is part of the Upper Cape Fear River basin. The estimated safe yield of the system is 36.7 million gallons per day, based on a fifty-year estimate as certified by engineers. The system has emergency interconnections with High Point, Burlington, Reidsville, Winston-Salem, and Piedmont Triad Water Authority.

The city runs two treatment plants with a combined capacity of 54 million gallons. Both plants use conventional surface water treatment.

The estimated average age of main line pipes in the system is forty years. Greensboro has begun a spending program on water line rehabilitation and plans to increase funding for this activity for the next several years.

Water meters are read and billed monthly. All meters are read automatically using a radio system.

Conditions Affecting Service, Performance, and Costs

Greensboro has a very high collection rate for water bills. The city has a lien law, so only a small portion of billed amounts goes unpaid. The lien law was changed during FY 2010–11 so that it now only includes owners and not tenants.

Greensboro has a large public education program to encourage water conservation.

The costs of water services as captured here do not include debt service but do capture depreciation.

Municipal Profile

Estimated Service Population	294,722
Service Land Area (Square Miles)	148.0
Persons per Square Mile	1,991
Topography	Flat; gently rolling
Climate	Temperate; little ice and snow
Median Household Income	$40,760
U.S. Census 2016	

Service Profile

FTE Staff Positions	
Treatment Plant	52.0
Line Crews	68.0
Meter Readers	16.0
Billing/Collection	7.5
Other	18.5
Total	162.0
Number of Treatment Plants	2
Total Treatment Capacity	54.0 MGD
Average Daily Demand	32.0 MGD
Miles of Main Line Pipe	1,511
Average Age of Main Line Pipe	40 years
Number of Breaks/Leaks	319
Number of Water Meters	106,478
Percent of Meters Read Automatically	100.0%
Total Revenues Collected	$58,124,053

Full Cost Profile

Cost Breakdown by Percentage	
Personal Services	17.1%
Operating Costs	66.0%
Capital Costs	16.9%
TOTAL	100.0%
Cost Breakdown in Dollars	
Personal Services	$6,930,554
Operating Costs	$26,737,876
Capital Costs	$6,867,123
TOTAL	$40,535,553

Key: Greensboro ▨   Benchmarking Average —   Fiscal Years 2015 through 2019

Resource Measures

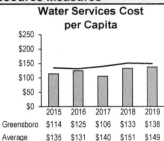

Water Services Cost per Capita

	2015	2016	2017	2018	2019
Greensboro	$114	$125	$106	$133	$138
Average	$135	$131	$140	$151	$149

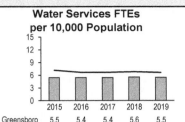

Water Services FTEs per 10,000 Population

	2015	2016	2017	2018	2019
Greensboro	5.5	5.4	5.4	5.6	5.5
Average	7.2	6.7	6.7	6.9	6.6

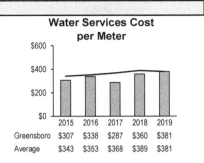

Water Services Cost per Meter

	2015	2016	2017	2018	2019
Greensboro	$307	$338	$287	$360	$381
Average	$343	$353	$368	$389	$381

Workload Measures

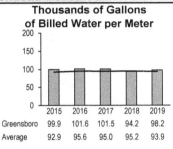

Thousands of Gallons of Billed Water per Meter

	2015	2016	2017	2018	2019
Greensboro	99.9	101.6	101.5	94.2	98.2
Average	92.9	95.6	95.0	95.2	93.9

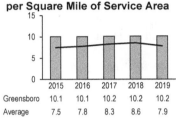
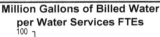

Miles of Main Line Pipe per Square Mile of Service Area

	2015	2016	2017	2018	2019
Greensboro	10.1	10.1	10.2	10.2	10.2
Average	7.5	7.8	8.3	8.6	7.9

Efficiency Measures

Total Cost per Thousand Gallons of Billed Water

	2015	2016	2017	2018	2019
Greensboro	$3.08	$3.33	$2.83	$3.82	$3.88
Average	$3.88	$3.87	$4.04	$4.26	$4.25

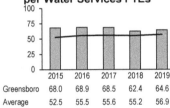

Million Gallons of Billed Water per Water Services FTEs

	2015	2016	2017	2018	2019
Greensboro	68.0	68.9	68.5	62.4	64.6
Average	52.5	55.5	55.6	55.2	56.9

Billed Water as a Percentage of Finished Water

	2015	2016	2017	2018	2019
Greensboro	86%	89%	85%	84%	90%
Average	86%	87%	82%	84%	83%

Effectiveness Measures

Percentage of Existing Pipeline Replaced or Rehabbed

	2015	2016	2017	2018	2019
Greensboro	0.5%	0.4%	0.5%	0.3%	0.3%
Average	0.1%	0.2%	0.2%	0.2%	1.0%

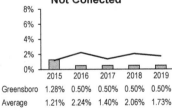

Percentage of Water Bills Not Collected

	2015	2016	2017	2018	2019
Greensboro	1.28%	0.50%	0.50%	0.50%	0.50%
Average	1.21%	2.24%	1.40%	2.06%	1.73%

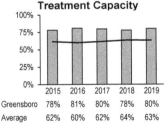

Peak Daily Demand as a Percentage of Treatment Capacity

	2015	2016	2017	2018	2019
Greensboro	78%	81%	80%	78%	80%
Average	62%	60%	62%	64%	63%

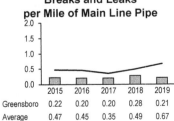

Breaks and Leaks per Mile of Main Line Pipe

	2015	2016	2017	2018	2019
Greensboro	0.22	0.20	0.20	0.28	0.21
Average	0.47	0.45	0.35	0.49	0.67

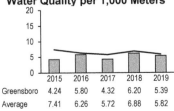

Customer Complaints about Water Quality per 1,000 Meters

	2015	2016	2017	2018	2019
Greensboro	4.24	5.80	4.32	6.20	5.39
Average	7.41	6.26	5.72	6.88	5.82

Hickory   # Water Services

Fiscal Year 2018–19

Explanatory Information

Service Level and Delivery

Water services in Hickory are provided by a combined water distribution division under the Public Services Department. The water system services an area covering roughly 326 square miles and approximately 100,000 people. Water is provided for the city of Hickory and also for the towns of Hildenbran, Brookford, and Catawba; the Sherrill's Ford, Mountain View, and Cooksville communities of Catawba County; and the Bethlehem, Sugarloaf, and Highway 16 communities of Alexander County.

Source water is from the Catawba River basin, with an estimated safe yield of 54 million gallons per day. Hickory sells water to the systems in Conover, Claremont, and Icard Township. The system has one treatment plant with a capacity of 32 million gallons per day.

Water meters are read monthly. Hickory's replacement standard for water meters is twenty years. About 17.1 percent of water meters in the system are read by automatic means.

Conditions Affecting Service, Performance, and Costs

The costs of water services as captured here do not include debt service but do capture depreciation.

Municipal Profile

Estimated Service Population	99,530
Service Land Area (Square Miles)	326.0
Persons per Square Mile	305
Topography	Flat; gently rolling
Climate	Temperate; some ice and snow
Median Household Income	$35,353
U.S. Census 2016	

Service Profile

FTE Staff Positions	
Treatment Plant	13.0
Line Crews	25.0
Meter Readers	6.0
Billing/Collection	5.0
Other	6.0
Total	55.0
Number of Treatment Plants	1
Total Treatment Capacity	32.0 MGD
Average Daily Demand	11.4 MGD
Miles of Main Line Pipe	948
Average Age of Main Line Pipe	40 years
Number of Breaks/Leaks	285
Number of Water Meters	30,133
Percent of Meters Read Automatically	17.1%
Total Revenues Collected	$16,230,771

Full Cost Profile

Cost Breakdown by Percentage	
Personal Services	28.4%
Operating Costs	46.4%
Capital Costs	25.2%
TOTAL	100.0%
Cost Breakdown in Dollars	
Personal Services	$2,745,644
Operating Costs	$4,478,057
Capital Costs	$2,428,298
TOTAL	$9,651,999

Hickory

Water Services

Resource Measures

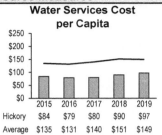

Water Services Cost per Capita

	2015	2016	2017	2018	2019
Hickory	$84	$79	$80	$90	$97
Average	$135	$131	$140	$151	$149

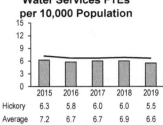

Water Services FTEs per 10,000 Population

	2015	2016	2017	2018	2019
Hickory	6.3	5.8	6.0	6.0	5.5
Average	7.2	6.7	6.7	6.9	6.6

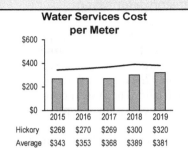

Water Services Cost per Meter

	2015	2016	2017	2018	2019
Hickory	$268	$270	$269	$300	$320
Average	$343	$353	$368	$389	$381

Workload Measures

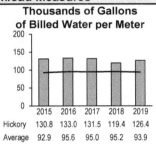

Thousands of Gallons of Billed Water per Meter

	2015	2016	2017	2018	2019
Hickory	130.8	133.0	131.5	119.4	126.4
Average	92.9	95.6	95.0	95.2	93.9

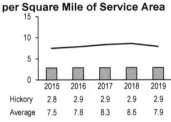

Miles of Main Line Pipe per Square Mile of Service Area

	2015	2016	2017	2018	2019
Hickory	2.8	2.9	2.9	2.9	2.9
Average	7.5	7.8	8.3	8.6	7.9

Efficiency Measures

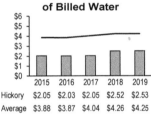

Total Cost per Thousand Gallons of Billed Water

	2015	2016	2017	2018	2019
Hickory	$2.05	$2.03	$2.05	$2.52	$2.53
Average	$3.88	$3.87	$4.04	$4.26	$4.25

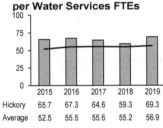

Million Gallons of Billed Water per Water Services FTEs

	2015	2016	2017	2018	2019
Hickory	65.7	67.3	64.6	59.3	69.3
Average	52.5	55.5	55.6	55.2	56.9

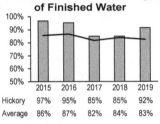

Billed Water as a Percentage of Finished Water

	2015	2016	2017	2018	2019
Hickory	97%	95%	85%	85%	92%
Average	86%	87%	82%	84%	83%

Effectiveness Measures

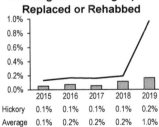

Percentage of Existing Pipeline Replaced or Rehabbed

	2015	2016	2017	2018	2019
Hickory	0.1%	0.1%	0.1%	0.1%	0.2%
Average	0.1%	0.2%	0.2%	0.2%	1.0%

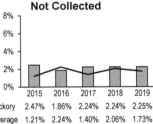

Percentage of Water Bills Not Collected

	2015	2016	2017	2018	2019
Hickory	2.47%	1.86%	2.24%	2.24%	2.25%
Average	1.21%	2.24%	1.40%	2.06%	1.73%

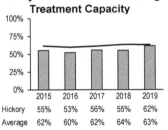

Peak Daily Demand as a Percentage of Treatment Capacity

	2015	2016	2017	2018	2019
Hickory	55%	53%	56%	55%	62%
Average	62%	60%	62%	64%	63%

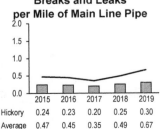

Breaks and Leaks per Mile of Main Line Pipe

	2015	2016	2017	2018	2019
Hickory	0.24	0.23	0.20	0.25	0.30
Average	0.47	0.45	0.35	0.49	0.67

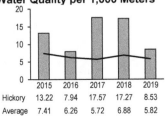

Customer Complaints about Water Quality per 1,000 Meters

	2015	2016	2017	2018	2019
Hickory	13.22	7.94	17.57	17.27	8.53
Average	7.41	6.26	5.72	6.88	5.82

Fiscal Year 2018–19

Service Level and Delivery

The Town of Mooresville provides water service and wastewater services through the Public Services Department as an enterprise fund. Only the data for the water services portion of the system are reported here. The system covers 36 square miles and serves approximately 41,000 people.

The water source for the system is Lake Norman. The estimated safe yield for the system is 188 million gallons per day. The system has two treatment plants with a capacity of 18 million gallons per day. The plants use conventional surface water treatment. Disinfection is provided through on-site generation of sodium hypochlorite.

Water meters are read once per month. Currently, nearly all meters are read by automatic means. The standard for meter replacement is twenty years.

Conditions Affecting Service, Performance, and Costs

Mooresville joined the Benchmarking project in July 2018, with the first year of data showing for FY 2017–18.

Mooresville has two industries that are very large users of water, a water bottler and a company producing energy drinks. These two users significantly push up water use per meter for the overall town numbers.

The costs of water services as captured here do not include debt service but do capture depreciation.

Mooresville's system includes two pressure zones. The higher pressure zone primarily serves the town's industrial parks. Studies are underway to increase the high-pressure zones based on future needs.

Municipal Profile

Estimated Service Population	41,000
Service Land Area (Square Miles)	36.0
Persons per Square Mile	1,139
Topography	Flat; gently rolling
Climate	Temperate; little ice and snow
Median Household Income	$67,213
U.S. Census 2016	

Service Profile

FTE Staff Positions	
Treatment Plant	13.3
Line Crews	12.0
Meter Readers	4.0
Billing/Collection	2.5
Other	0.0
Total	31.8
Number of Treatment Plants	2
Total Treatment Capacity	18.0 MGD
Average Daily Demand	6.7 MGD
Miles of Main Line Pipe	313
Average Age of Main Line Pipe	22 years
Number of Breaks/Leaks	64
Number of Water Meters	16,357
Percent of Meters Read Automatically	98.0%
Total Revenues Collected	$13,983,988

Full Cost Profile

Cost Breakdown by Percentage	
Personal Services	28.2%
Operating Costs	48.8%
Capital Costs	22.9%
TOTAL	100.0%
Cost Breakdown in Dollars	
Personal Services	$2,059,748
Operating Costs	$3,561,362
Capital Costs	$1,671,068
TOTAL	$7,292,178

Mooresville

Water Services

Resource Measures

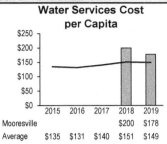

Water Services Cost per Capita

	2015	2016	2017	2018	2019
Mooresville				$200	$178
Average	$135	$131	$140	$151	$149

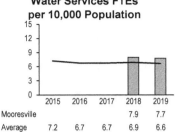

Water Services FTEs per 10,000 Population

	2015	2016	2017	2018	2019
Mooresville				7.9	7.7
Average	7.2	6.7	6.7	6.9	6.6

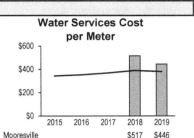

Water Services Cost per Meter

	2015	2016	2017	2018	2019
Mooresville				$517	$446
Average	$343	$353	$368	$389	$381

Workload Measures

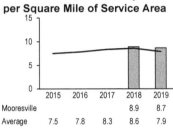

Thousands of Gallons of Billed Water per Meter

	2015	2016	2017	2018	2019
Mooresville				124.3	122.8
Average	92.9	95.6	95.0	95.2	93.9

Miles of Main Line Pipe per Square Mile of Service Area

	2015	2016	2017	2018	2019
Mooresville				8.9	8.7
Average	7.5	7.8	8.3	8.6	7.9

Efficiency Measures

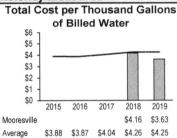

Total Cost per Thousand Gallons of Billed Water

	2015	2016	2017	2018	2019
Mooresville				$4.16	$3.63
Average	$3.88	$3.87	$4.04	$4.26	$4.25

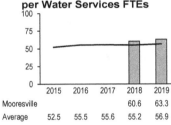

Million Gallons of Billed Water per Water Services FTEs

	2015	2016	2017	2018	2019
Mooresville				60.6	63.3
Average	52.5	55.5	55.6	55.2	56.9

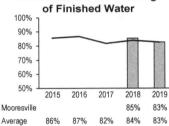

Billed Water as a Percentage of Finished Water

	2015	2016	2017	2018	2019
Mooresville				85%	83%
Average	86%	87%	82%	84%	83%

Effectiveness Measures

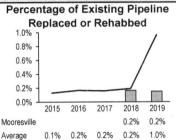

Percentage of Existing Pipeline Replaced or Rehabbed

	2015	2016	2017	2018	2019
Mooresville				0.2%	0.2%
Average	0.1%	0.2%	0.2%	0.2%	1.0%

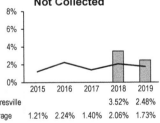

Percentage of Water Bills Not Collected

	2015	2016	2017	2018	2019
Mooresville				3.52%	2.48%
Average	1.21%	2.24%	1.40%	2.06%	1.73%

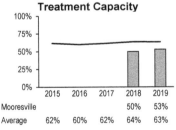

Peak Daily Demand as a Percentage of Treatment Capacity

	2015	2016	2017	2018	2019
Mooresville				50%	53%
Average	62%	60%	62%	64%	63%

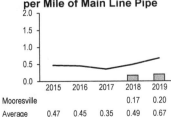

Breaks and Leaks per Mile of Main Line Pipe

	2015	2016	2017	2018	2019
Mooresville				0.17	0.20
Average	0.47	0.45	0.35	0.49	0.67

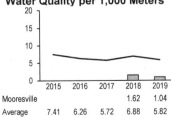

Customer Complaints about Water Quality per 1,000 Meters

	2015	2016	2017	2018	2019
Mooresville				1.62	1.04
Average	7.41	6.26	5.72	6.88	5.82

Explanatory Information

Service Level and Delivery

Public Utilities is a department within the City of Raleigh. It is a combined enterprise system which provides drinking water and sewage treatment services to the City of Raleigh and six merger towns: Garner, Rolesville, Knightdale, Wake Forest, Wendell, and Zebulon. As of FY 2019, approximately 580,000 people live in the contractual service area of 299 square miles. Source water supply is from Falls Lake located in the Neuse River watershed and from Lake Wheeler and Lake Benson, which are in the Swift Creek watershed. During FY 2019, the Utility received a reallocation of its water supply that increased the system's 50-year reliable yield to 98 million gallons per day.

The Utility operates two surface water treatment plants with a total permitted treatment capacity of 106 million gallons per day. The E.M. Johnson plant provides 86 percent of the potable water using an enhanced coagulation treatment process with the addition of settled water ozone. The Dempsey E. Benton plant also utilizes an enhanced coagulation treatment process using raw water ozone, solids contact sedimentation, a two-stage filter process, and ultraviolet disinfection prior to clearwell storage.

Water meters are read once per month. Currently, nearly all meters are read by automatic means. The standard for meter replacement is fifteen years.

Conditions Affecting Service, Performance, and Costs

Raleigh rejoined the Benchmarking Project in July 2016, with the first year of data showing for FY 2015–16.

The approved reallocation of supply water resources in FY 2019 comes with increased costs to maintain and finance the improvement. Due to source water organics both treatment plants utilize enhanced coagulation with ferric sulfate and chloramine disinfection to control disinfection byproducts. These processes have higher chemical and operating costs than traditional treatment processes. Additionally, Raleigh has a specialized program to manage water age and disinfection byproducts in the distribution system.

The costs of water services as captured here do not include debt service but do capture depreciation.

Municipal Profile

Estimated Service Population	582,098
Service Land Area (Square Miles)	299.0
Persons per Square Mile	1,947
Topography	Flat; gently rolling
Climate	Temperate; little ice and snow
Median Household Income U.S. Census 2016	$46,612

Service Profile

FTE Staff Positions	
Treatment Plant	61.0
Line Crews	82.0
Meter Readers	2.0
Billing/Collection	27.0
Other	125.0
Total	297.0
Number of Treatment Plants	2
Total Treatment Capacity	106.0 MGD
Average Daily Demand	49.3 MGD
Miles of Main Line Pipe	2,324
Average Age of Main Line Pipe	30 years
Number of Breaks/Leaks	408
Number of Water Meters	202,039
Percent of Meters Read Automatically	94.4%
Total Revenues Collected	$115,410,048

Full Cost Profile

Cost Breakdown by Percentage	
Personal Services	35.3%
Operating Costs	45.1%
Capital Costs	19.6%
TOTAL	100.0%
Cost Breakdown in Dollars	
Personal Services	$23,573,101
Operating Costs	$30,166,265
Capital Costs	$13,121,252
TOTAL	$66,860,618

Raleigh

Water Services

Resource Measures

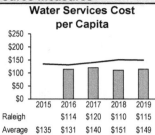

Water Services Cost per Capita

	2015	2016	2017	2018	2019
Raleigh		$114	$120	$110	$115
Average	$135	$131	$140	$151	$149

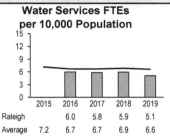

Water Services FTEs per 10,000 Population

	2015	2016	2017	2018	2019
Raleigh		6.0	5.8	5.9	5.1
Average	7.2	6.7	6.7	6.9	6.6

Water Services Cost per Meter

	2015	2016	2017	2018	2019
Raleigh		$337	$356	$336	$331
Average	$343	$353	$368	$389	$381

Workload Measures

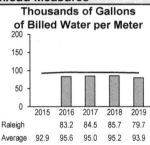

Thousands of Gallons of Billed Water per Meter

	2015	2016	2017	2018	2019
Raleigh		83.2	84.5	85.7	79.7
Average	92.9	95.6	95.0	95.2	93.9

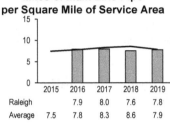

Miles of Main Line Pipe per Square Mile of Service Area

	2015	2016	2017	2018	2019
Raleigh		7.9	8.0	7.6	7.8
Average	7.5	7.8	8.3	8.6	7.9

Efficiency Measures

Total Cost per Thousand Gallons of Billed Water

	2015	2016	2017	2018	2019
Raleigh		$4.06	$4.21	$3.92	$4.15
Average	$3.88	$3.87	$4.04	$4.26	$4.25

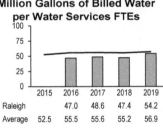

Million Gallons of Billed Water per Water Services FTEs

	2015	2016	2017	2018	2019
Raleigh		47.0	48.6	47.4	54.2
Average	52.5	55.5	55.6	55.2	56.9

Billed Water as a Percentage of Finished Water

	2015	2016	2017	2018	2019
Raleigh		87%	89%	90%	90%
Average	86%	87%	82%	84%	83%

Effectiveness Measures

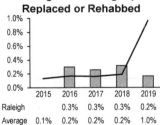

Percentage of Existing Pipeline Replaced or Rehabbed

	2015	2016	2017	2018	2019
Raleigh		0.3%	0.3%	0.3%	0.2%
Average	0.1%	0.2%	0.2%	0.2%	1.0%

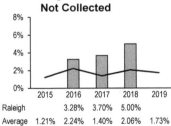

Percentage of Water Bills Not Collected

	2015	2016	2017	2018	2019
Raleigh		3.28%	3.70%	5.00%	
Average	1.21%	2.24%	1.40%	2.06%	1.73%

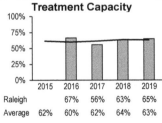

Peak Daily Demand as a Percentage of Treatment Capacity

	2015	2016	2017	2018	2019
Raleigh		67%	56%	63%	65%
Average	62%	60%	62%	64%	63%

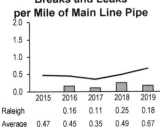

Breaks and Leaks per Mile of Main Line Pipe

	2015	2016	2017	2018	2019
Raleigh		0.16	0.11	0.25	0.18
Average	0.47	0.45	0.35	0.49	0.67

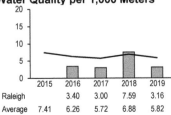

Customer Complaints about Water Quality per 1,000 Meters

	2015	2016	2017	2018	2019
Raleigh		3.40	3.00	7.59	3.16
Average	7.41	6.26	5.72	6.88	5.82

Wilson

Water Services

Fiscal Year 2018–19

Explanatory Information

Service Level and Delivery

Water services in Wilson are handled by a combined water/sewer division under the Department of Public Works. Billing services are handled by the Wilson Finance Department. The water system serves approximately 54,500 people over forty square miles.

Source water for the system comes from four city-owned reservoirs. Water is also pumped from two different reservoirs in the Neuse River basin. The estimated safe yield for the system is 29 million gallons per day.

The system has two treatment plants with a combined treatment capacity of 22 million gallons per day. The plants use conventional surface water treatment with flocculation, sedimentation, and filtration.

Water meters are read once per month in Wilson. Approximately half of the water meters in the system are read by automatic remote means using a radio system by Itron.

Conditions Affecting Service, Performance, and Costs

The costs of water services as captured here do not include debt service but do capture depreciation. Large capital improvements are being made to the Buckhorn Lake Dam and Wastewater Projects, which have been required to meet advanced nutrient removal.

Municipal Profile

Estimated Service Population	54,500
Service Land Area (Square Miles)	40.0
Persons per Square Mile	1,363
Topography	Flat; gently rolling
Climate	Temperate; little ice and snow
Median Household Income	$35,409
U.S. Census 2016	

Service Profile

FTE Staff Positions	
Treatment Plant	18.0
Line Crews	20.0
Meter Readers	3.0
Billing/Collection	3.0
Other	3.0
Total	47.0
Number of Treatment Plants	2
Total Treatment Capacity	22.0 MGD
Average Daily Demand	9.1 MGD
Miles of Main Line Pipe	428
Average Age of Main Line Pipe	44 years
Number of Breaks/Leaks	55
Number of Water Meters	22,659
Percent of Meters Read Automatically	44.1%
Total Revenues Collected	$12,721,000

Full Cost Profile

Cost Breakdown by Percentage	
Personal Services	25.4%
Operating Costs	46.8%
Capital Costs	27.8%
TOTAL	100.0%
Cost Breakdown in Dollars	
Personal Services	$3,050,944
Operating Costs	$5,615,548
Capital Costs	$3,339,108
TOTAL	$12,005,600

Resource Measures

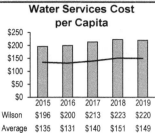

Water Services Cost per Capita

	2015	2016	2017	2018	2019
Wilson	$196	$200	$213	$223	$220
Average	$135	$131	$140	$151	$149

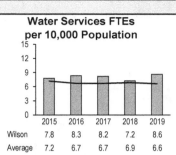

Water Services FTEs per 10,000 Population

	2015	2016	2017	2018	2019
Wilson	7.8	8.3	8.2	7.2	8.6
Average	7.2	6.7	6.7	6.9	6.6

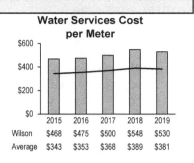

Water Services Cost per Meter

	2015	2016	2017	2018	2019
Wilson	$468	$475	$500	$548	$530
Average	$343	$353	$368	$389	$381

Workload Measures

Thousands of Gallons of Billed Water per Meter

	2015	2016	2017	2018	2019
Wilson	84.2	84.1	82.2	87.1	85.6
Average	92.9	95.6	95.0	95.2	93.9

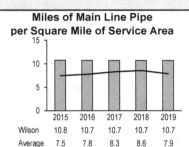

Miles of Main Line Pipe per Square Mile of Service Area

	2015	2016	2017	2018	2019
Wilson	10.8	10.7	10.7	10.7	10.7
Average	7.5	7.8	8.3	8.6	7.9

Efficiency Measures

Total Cost per Thousand Gallons of Billed Water

	2015	2016	2017	2018	2019
Wilson	$5.56	$5.65	$6.08	$6.30	$6.19
Average	$3.88	$3.87	$4.04	$4.26	$4.25

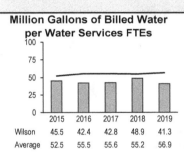

Million Gallons of Billed Water per Water Services FTEs

	2015	2016	2017	2018	2019
Wilson	45.5	42.4	42.8	48.9	41.3
Average	52.5	55.5	55.6	55.2	56.9

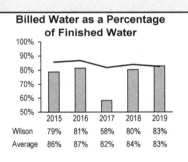

Billed Water as a Percentage of Finished Water

	2015	2016	2017	2018	2019
Wilson	79%	81%	58%	80%	83%
Average	86%	87%	82%	84%	83%

Effectiveness Measures

Percentage of Existing Pipeline Replaced or Rehabbed

	2015	2016	2017	2018	2019
Wilson	0.2%	0.1%	0.1%	0.2%	0.1%
Average	0.1%	0.2%	0.2%	0.2%	1.0%

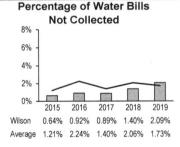

Percentage of Water Bills Not Collected

	2015	2016	2017	2018	2019
Wilson	0.64%	0.92%	0.89%	1.40%	2.09%
Average	1.21%	2.24%	1.40%	2.06%	1.73%

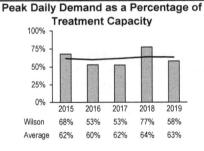

Peak Daily Demand as a Percentage of Treatment Capacity

	2015	2016	2017	2018	2019
Wilson	68%	53%	53%	77%	58%
Average	62%	60%	62%	64%	63%

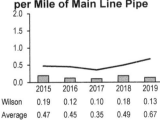

Breaks and Leaks per Mile of Main Line Pipe

	2015	2016	2017	2018	2019
Wilson	0.19	0.12	0.10	0.18	0.13
Average	0.47	0.45	0.35	0.49	0.67

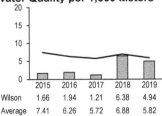

Customer Complaints about Water Quality per 1,000 Meters

	2015	2016	2017	2018	2019
Wilson	1.66	1.94	1.21	6.38	4.94
Average	7.41	6.26	5.72	6.88	5.82

Winston-Salem

Water Services

Fiscal Year 2018–19

Explanatory Information

Service Level and Delivery

The Winston-Salem and Forsyth County Utilities Division operates a combined water and sewer system that covers the city and most of the remaining population of Forsyth County. Approximately 349,000 people are served in an area covering roughly 280 square miles.

The system has an eleven-member utility commission that was created by an interlocal agreement between the City of Winston-Salem and Forsyth County. The commission sets policy for publicly owned water, wastewater, and solid waste disposal facilities. The commission is also charged with the responsibility for long-range planning, authorizing funding for projects, operation and maintenance of facilities, and setting policies and rate structures. The commission is not authorized to issue bonds to finance capital improvements.

Water sources for the system are drawn from two separate points on the Yadkin River. The city also uses Salem Lake as a water source. The estimated safe yield for the system is 100 million gallons per day.

The city uses three treatment plants with a daily treatment capacity of 91 million gallons. The plants all use conventional treatment, employing coagulation, flocculation, and sedimentation followed by rapid sand filtration and then chlorine treatment for disinfection.

The system has 2,359 miles of pipeline. The replacement goal for pipes is seventy-five years.

Water meters are read both monthly and bi-monthly depending on the account type. Currently the system has a small number of meters read by automatic means, totaling approximately 13 percent. The replacement standard for water meters is approximately every ten years. The goal is to have completely switched to automatically read meters within ten years.

Conditions Affecting Service, Performance, and Costs

The costs of water services as captured here do not include debt service but do capture depreciation.

Winston-Salem made improvements in their calculation of population served and area covered to improve the accuracy of their data. This had the effect of decreasing the reported population and size of area served from earlier years. The changes seen in FY 2017–18 are due to this improved estimation and not a change in services.

Municipal Profile

Estimated Service Population	348,596
Service Land Area (Square Miles)	280.0
Persons per Square Mile	1,245
Topography	Gently rolling
Climate	Temperate; some ice and snow
Median Household Income	$40,584
U.S. Census 2016	

Service Profile

FTE Staff Positions	
Treatment Plant	53.0
Line Crews	74.0
Meter Readers	15.0
Billing/Collection	8.2
Other	20.0
Total	170.2
Number of Treatment Plants	3
Total Treatment Capacity	91.0 MGD
Average Daily Demand	36.2 MGD
Miles of Main Line Pipe	2,359
Average Age of Main Line Pipe	75 years
Number of Breaks/Leaks	425
Number of Water Meters	128,931
Percent of Meters Read Automatically	13.3%
Total Revenues Collected	$62,831,795

Full Cost Profile

Cost Breakdown by Percentage	
Personal Services	26.9%
Operating Costs	38.1%
Capital Costs	35.0%
TOTAL	100.0%
Cost Breakdown in Dollars	
Personal Services	$9,218,344
Operating Costs	$13,061,263
Capital Costs	$12,013,787
TOTAL	$34,293,394

Winston-Salem

Water Services

Resource Measures

Water Services Cost per Capita

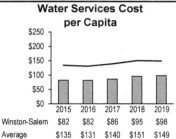

	2015	2016	2017	2018	2019
Winston-Salem	$82	$82	$86	$95	$98
Average	$135	$131	$140	$151	$149

Water Services FTEs per 10,000 Population

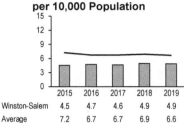

	2015	2016	2017	2018	2019
Winston-Salem	4.5	4.7	4.6	4.9	4.9
Average	7.2	6.7	6.7	6.9	6.6

Water Services Cost per Meter

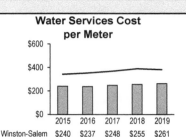

	2015	2016	2017	2018	2019
Winston-Salem	$240	$237	$248	$255	$261
Average	$343	$353	$368	$389	$381

Workload Measures

Thousands of Gallons of Billed Water per Meter

	2015	2016	2017	2018	2019
Winston-Salem	89.6	88.9	89.7	87.2	86.5
Average	92.9	95.6	95.0	95.2	93.9

Miles of Main Line Pipe per Square Mile of Service Area

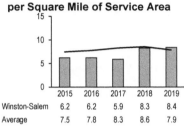

	2015	2016	2017	2018	2019
Winston-Salem	6.2	6.2	5.9	8.3	8.4
Average	7.5	7.8	8.3	8.6	7.9

Efficiency Measures

Total Cost per Thousand Gallons of Billed Water

	2015	2016	2017	2018	2019
Winston-Salem	$2.68	$2.66	$2.76	$2.92	$3.02
Average	$3.88	$3.87	$4.04	$4.26	$4.25

Million Gallons of Billed Water per Water Services FTEs

	2015	2016	2017	2018	2019
Winston-Salem	67.8	65.1	67.1	66.1	66.7
Average	52.5	55.5	55.6	55.2	56.9

Billed Water as a Percentage of Finished Water

	2015	2016	2017	2018	2019
Winston-Salem	85%	84%	87%	86%	86%
Average	86%	87%	82%	84%	83%

Effectiveness Measures

Percentage of Existing Pipeline Replaced or Rehabbed

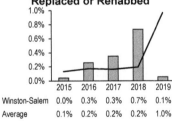

	2015	2016	2017	2018	2019
Winston-Salem	0.0%	0.3%	0.3%	0.7%	0.1%
Average	0.1%	0.2%	0.2%	0.2%	1.0%

Percentage of Water Bills Not Collected

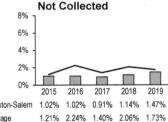

	2015	2016	2017	2018	2019
Winston-Salem	1.02%	1.02%	0.91%	1.14%	1.47%
Average	1.21%	2.24%	1.40%	2.06%	1.73%

Peak Daily Demand as a Percentage of Treatment Capacity

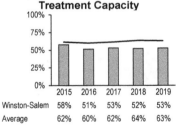

	2015	2016	2017	2018	2019
Winston-Salem	58%	51%	53%	52%	53%
Average	62%	60%	62%	64%	63%

Breaks and Leaks per Mile of Main Line Pipe

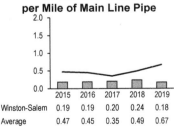

	2015	2016	2017	2018	2019
Winston-Salem	0.19	0.19	0.20	0.24	0.18
Average	0.47	0.45	0.35	0.49	0.67

Customer Complaints about Water Quality per 1,000 Meters

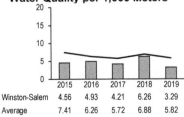

	2015	2016	2017	2018	2019
Winston-Salem	4.56	4.93	4.21	6.26	3.29
Average	7.41	6.26	5.72	6.88	5.82

Performance and Cost Data

WASTEWATER SERVICES

PERFORMANCE MEASURES FOR WASTEWATER SERVICES

SERVICE DEFINITION

Wastewater Services includes the collection, treatment, wastewater discharge, solids disposal, and billing related to sewer services. This service area includes the collection system after leaving the customer's outlet, lift stations, pretreatment, and treatment plants. Activities and costs include the operation, maintenance, and installation of infrastructure. Also included are costs and activities associated with billing and collection for sewer services and administrative activities, such as planning, engineering, and testing. This includes wastewater treated for reuse at the plant site and for other purposes. Excluded are potable water systems and stormwater systems.

NOTES ON PERFORMANCE MEASURES

1. Volume of Sewage per Account

This workload measure captures the amount of wastewater generated and received at the treatment plant relative to the number of customers.

2. Miles of Sewer Main Line Pipe per Square Mile of Service Area

The amount of sewer main line pipe per square mile shows the density of the pipe infrastructure to be maintained relative to the geographic size of the area served.

3. Number of Lift Stations per Thousand Accounts

This workload measure provides some idea of the amount of reliance on pumping in a system to supplement gravity-fed delivery. Lift stations also generate additional maintenance workload.

4. Cost per Thousand Gallons of Collected and Treated Wastewater

This efficiency measure shows total system costs relative to the volume of wastewater reaching treatment plants. Some wastewater does not make it to treatment plants.

5. Wastewater Volume in Millions of Gallons per FTE

This efficiency measure captures the number of workers the system is using relative to the volume of wastewater treated.

6. Customer Accounts per FTE

The number of customer accounts relative to the number of workers is another efficiency measure showing how many customers are being served per worker.

7. Percentage of Bills Collected

Collection of wastewater bills sent to customers is necessary to ensure revenues for system operation. Bills not collected reflect potential lost revenue to the system, but some loss is unavoidable.

8. Average Daily Treatment as a Percent of Permitted Capacity

A wastewater system needs sufficient capacity to meet not only average demands, but also peak demands. This measure looks at average daily demand relative to the wastewater system treatment capacity in a day. Some excess capacity is needed to allow for daily service variations and also to plan for future expansion needs.

9. Percent of Existing Main Line Pipe Rehabilitated or Replaced

As the wastewater systems age, pipe needs to be replaced to ensure that service will not be interrupted. This effectiveness measure captures the amount of current stock being replaced or rehabilitated during a given year.

10. Overflows Per 100 Miles of Main Line Pipe

Sanitary system overflows may be due to blockages or breaks in pipe. Keeping these breaks to a low level is an important measure of the effectiveness of preventive maintenance and system upkeep. Overflows, if large enough, may also represent a public health concern.

11. Sewer Backups per 100 Miles of Main Line Pipe

Backups in sewer pipes are another measure of potential maintenance concerns and potential public health concerns. Backups may also be a sign of insufficient maintenance.

12. Billed Sewer Effluents as a Percent of Treated Effluent

The volume of wastewater that is billed for relative to the volume received at the treatment plant is an effectiveness measure that points to potential losses in the collection system. Some loss is inevitable in sewer systems, and not all drinking water billed for is used in such a way that it should make it back to the wastewater treatment plant. But comparisons may reveal excessive infiltration or leakage.

Wastewater Services

Summary of Key Dimensions of Service

City or Town	Estimated Residential Population in Service Area	Service Area (in Square Miles)	Operating Treatment Plants	Average Daily Flow of Wastewater at Plants (in MGD)	Total Treatment Capacity for Wastewater (in MGD)	Miles of Gravity and Forced Main Lines	Number of Wastewater Accounts	Sewer System FTE Positions
Apex	58,726	24.0	1 + 1 jointly operated with Cary	3.9	9.7	296.5	19,723	25.0
Charlotte	1,093,901	546.0	7	91.0	123.2	4,393.0	264,978	516.0
Concord	92,567	105.7	0	NA	NA	586.2	37,043	33.0
Goldsboro	34,234	25.0	1	11.5	14.2	243.0	12,456	30.0
Greensboro	294,722	148.0	1	37.3	56.0	1,506.9	102,854	165.0
Hickory	37,478	65.0	3	6.4	16.5	541.2	15,924	44.0
Mooresville	41,000	44.0	1	4.9	7.5	325.0	15,207	37.0
Raleigh	582,098	299.0	3	51.8	80.2	2,511.0	185,672	348.0
Wilson	54,400	41.0	1	10.0	14.0	367.0	20,641	65.0
Winston-Salem	297,137	196.0	2	37.7	51.0	1,761.0	101,325	175.2

NOTES
MGD stands for millions of gallons per day.

EXPLANATORY FACTORS
These are factors that the project found affected wastewater services performance and cost in one or more of the municipalities:

Topography
Size of service area
Population density
Age of infrastructure
Growth of population and businesses

Explanatory Information

Service Level and Delivery

Wastewater services for the Town of Apex are managed by the Water Reclamation and Wastewater Collections Division under the Department of Water Resources. The system covers the area within the municipal limits.

Apex has one treatment plant, which uses bar screens, grit removal, biological nutrient removal (BNR), oxidation ditches, secondary clarifiers, sand filters, ultraviolet disinfection, aerobic sludge digestion, and rotary drum sludge dewatering as part of its treatment process. The Apex wastewater system has nutrient limits in place that restrict what can be discharged from the plant to protect water quality. Apex uses land application for biosolids resulting from treatment and also dries some biosolids as fertilizer pellets. Apex also pays for one-third of the operation of a separate treatment plant, which is jointly owned with the Town of Cary.

The town's system had no regulatory violations for the treatment portion of the system and three violations connected to the collection system during the fiscal year.

Conditions Affecting Service, Performance, and Costs

The costs of wastewater or sewer services as captured here do not include debt service but do capture depreciation of capital.

Municipal Profile

Estimated Service Population	58,726
Service Land Area (Square Miles)	24.0
Persons per Square Mile	2,447
Topography	Flat; gently rolling
Climate	Temperate; little ice and snow
Median Household Income	$84,000
U.S. Census 2016	

Service Profile

Total FTE Staff Positions	25.0
Treatment Plant	8.0
Line Crews	13.0
Billing/Collection	2.0
Other	2.0
Number of Treatment Plants	2
Total Treatment Capacity	9.7 MGD
Average Daily Flow	3.9 MGD
River Basin into Which System Discharges	Neuse
Miles of Gravity Main Line Pipe	258
Miles of Forced Main Line Pipe	39
Average Age of Main Line Pipe	15 years
Blocks in Sewer Mains	30
Number of System Breaks	24
Sanitary System Overflows	3
Number of Customer Accounts	19,723
Total Revenues Collected	$16,791,493

Full Cost Profile

Cost Breakdown by Percentage

Personal Services	16.1%
Operating Costs	44.6%
Capital Costs	39.2%
TOTAL	100.0%

Cost Breakdown in Dollars

Personal Services	$1,570,741
Operating Costs	$4,348,615
Capital Costs	$3,824,383
TOTAL	$9,743,739

Apex

Wastewater Services

Resource Measures

Wastewater Services Cost per Capita

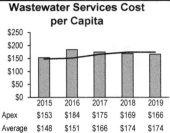

	2015	2016	2017	2018	2019
Apex	$153	$184	$175	$169	$166
Average	$148	$151	$166	$174	$174

Wastewater Services FTEs per 10,000 Population

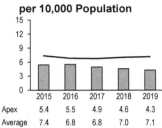

	2015	2016	2017	2018	2019
Apex	5.4	5.5	4.9	4.6	4.3
Average	7.4	6.8	6.8	7.0	7.1

Wastewater Services Cost per Customer Account

	2015	2016	2017	2018	2019
Apex	$479	$554	$527	$499	$494
Average	$421	$445	$494	$499	$492

Workload Measures

Thousands of Gallons of Wastewater per Account

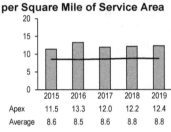

	2015	2016	2017	2018	2019
Apex	67.6	68.6	63.6	67.2	72.5
Average	116.4	121.0	135.0	124.8	146.8

Miles of Sewer Main Line Pipe per Square Mile of Service Area

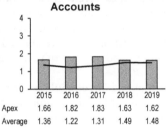

	2015	2016	2017	2018	2019
Apex	11.5	13.3	12.0	12.2	12.4
Average	8.6	8.5	8.6	8.8	8.8

Number of Lift Stations per 1,000 Accounts

	2015	2016	2017	2018	2019
Apex	1.66	1.82	1.83	1.63	1.62
Average	1.36	1.22	1.31	1.49	1.48

Efficiency Measures

Total Cost per 1,000 Gallons of Treated Wastewater

	2015	2016	2017	2018	2019
Apex	$7.09	$8.07	$8.29	$7.43	$6.81
Average	$3.94	$3.96	$4.07	$4.34	$3.83

Million Gallons of Wastewater per Wastewater Services FTE

	2015	2016	2017	2018	2019
Apex	39.9	41.5	42.6	49.6	57.2
Average	57.9	62.7	69.2	63.9	76.0

Customer Accounts per Wastewater Services FTE

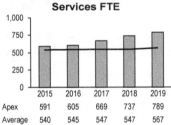

	2015	2016	2017	2018	2019
Apex	591	605	669	737	789
Average	540	545	547	547	567

Effectiveness Measures

Percentage of Wastewater Bills Not Collected

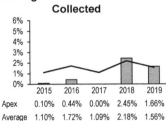

	2015	2016	2017	2018	2019
Apex	0.10%	0.44%	0.00%	2.45%	1.66%
Average	1.10%	1.72%	1.09%	2.18%	1.56%

Average Daily Treatment as a Percentage of Capacity

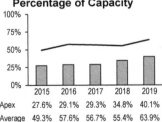

	2015	2016	2017	2018	2019
Apex	27.6%	29.1%	29.3%	34.8%	40.1%
Average	49.3%	57.6%	56.7%	55.4%	63.9%

Percent of Main Line Rehabbed or Replaced

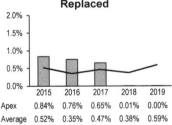

	2015	2016	2017	2018	2019
Apex	0.84%	0.76%	0.65%	0.01%	0.00%
Average	0.52%	0.35%	0.47%	0.38%	0.59%

Overflows per 100 Miles of Main Line Pipe

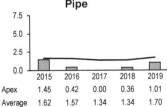

	2015	2016	2017	2018	2019
Apex	1.45	0.42	0.00	0.36	1.01
Average	1.62	1.57	1.34	1.34	1.70

Backups per 100 Miles of Main Line Pipe

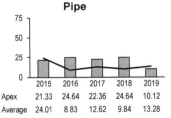

	2015	2016	2017	2018	2019
Apex	21.33	24.64	22.36	24.64	10.12
Average	24.01	8.83	12.62	9.84	13.28

Billed Wastewater as a Percent of Treated Effluent

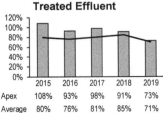

	2015	2016	2017	2018	2019
Apex	108%	93%	98%	91%	73%
Average	80%	76%	81%	85%	71%

Charlotte

Wastewater Services

Fiscal Year 2018–19

Explanatory Information

Service Level and Delivery

Wastewater collection and treatment are handled by Charlotte Water (CLTWater). This is a combined water and sewer utility for Mecklenburg County and the City of Charlotte. The department is run as an official City of Charlotte department. The service area corresponds roughly to the boundaries of Mecklenburg County.

There are seven wastewater treatment plants owned and operated by Charlotte Water. Each of CLTWater's treatment plants applies primary, secondary, and advanced treatment to the waste stream. The system does have regulatory limits in place on nutrient loads, which can be discharged in order to protect water quality. In addition to the treatment of wastewater, the system handles biosolids, most of which are applied to land (unless non-conforming) and then taken to the landfill.

The system had three regulatory violations connected to treatment issues and one regulatory violation connected to the collection portion of the system during the year.

Conditions Affecting Service, Performance, and Costs

Charlotte did not participate in the Benchmarking Project during FY 2014–15. No data are available for that year.

The costs of wastewater or sewer services as captured here do not include debt service but do capture depreciation of capital.

Municipal Profile

Estimated Service Population	1,093,901
Service Land Area (Square Miles)	546
Persons per Square Mile	2,003
Topography	Flat; gently rolling
Climate	Temperate; little ice and snow
Median Household Income	$46,975
U.S. Census 2016	

Service Profile

Total FTE Staff Positions	516.0
Treatment Plant	145.0
Line Crews	179.0
Billing/Collection	12.0
Other	180.0
Number of Treatment Plants	7
Total Treatment Capacity	123.2 MGD
Average Daily Flow	91.0 MGD
River Basin into Which System Discharges	Catawba and Yadkin
Miles of Gravity Main Line Pipe	4,258
Miles of Forced Main Line Pipe	135
Average Age of Main Line Pipe	33 years
Blocks in Sewer Mains	101
Number of System Breaks	102
Sanitary System Overflows	162
Number of Customer Accounts	264,978
Total Revenues Collected	$249,292,533

Full Cost Profile

Cost Breakdown by Percentage

Personal Services	22.1%
Operating Costs	33.7%
Capital Costs	44.2%
TOTAL	100.0%

Cost Breakdown in Dollars

Personal Services	$33,092,873
Operating Costs	$50,441,631
Capital Costs	$66,141,380
TOTAL	$149,675,884

Charlotte

Wastewater Services

Resource Measures

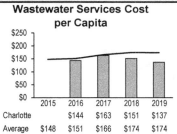

Wastewater Services Cost per Capita

	2015	2016	2017	2018	2019
Charlotte		$144	$163	$151	$137
Average	$148	$151	$166	$174	$174

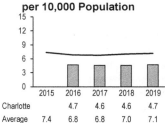

Wastewater Services FTEs per 10,000 Population

	2015	2016	2017	2018	2019
Charlotte		4.7	4.6	4.6	4.7
Average	7.4	6.8	6.8	7.0	7.1

Wastewater Services Cost per Customer Account

	2015	2016	2017	2018	2019
Charlotte		$544	$630	$624	$565
Average	$421	$445	$494	$499	$492

Workload Measures

Thousands of Gallons of Wastewater per Account

	2015	2016	2017	2018	2019
Charlotte		126.6	117.5	114.9	131.6
Average	116.4	121.0	135.0	124.8	146.8

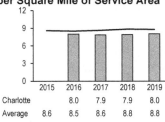

Miles of Sewer Main Line Pipe per Square Mile of Service Area

	2015	2016	2017	2018	2019
Charlotte		8.0	7.9	7.9	8.0
Average	8.6	8.5	8.6	8.8	8.8

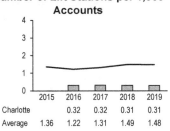

Number of Lift Stations per 1,000 Accounts

	2015	2016	2017	2018	2019
Charlotte		0.32	0.32	0.31	0.31
Average	1.36	1.22	1.31	1.49	1.48

Efficiency Measures

Total Cost per 1,000 Gallons of Treated Wastewater

	2015	2016	2017	2018	2019
Charlotte		$4.30	$5.36	$5.43	$4.29
Average	$3.94	$3.96	$4.07	$4.34	$3.83

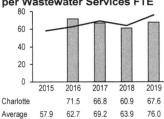

Million Gallons of Wastewater per Wastewater Services FTE

	2015	2016	2017	2018	2019
Charlotte		71.5	66.8	60.9	67.6
Average	57.9	62.7	69.2	63.9	76.0

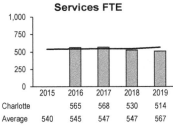

Customer Accounts per Wastewater Services FTE

	2015	2016	2017	2018	2019
Charlotte		565	568	530	514
Average	540	545	547	547	567

Effectiveness Measures

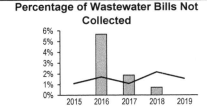

Percentage of Wastewater Bills Not Collected

	2015	2016	2017	2018	2019
Charlotte		5.67%	1.88%	0.72%	
Average	1.10%	1.72%	1.09%	2.18%	1.56%

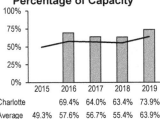

Average Daily Treatment as a Percentage of Capacity

	2015	2016	2017	2018	2019
Charlotte		69.4%	64.0%	63.4%	73.9%
Average	49.3%	57.6%	56.7%	55.4%	63.9%

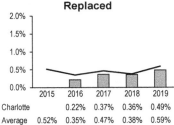

Percent of Main Line Rehabbed or Replaced

	2015	2016	2017	2018	2019
Charlotte		0.22%	0.37%	0.36%	0.49%
Average	0.52%	0.35%	0.47%	0.38%	0.59%

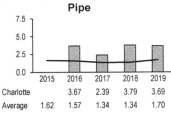

Overflows per 100 Miles of Main Line Pipe

	2015	2016	2017	2018	2019
Charlotte		3.67	2.39	3.79	3.69
Average	1.62	1.57	1.34	1.34	1.70

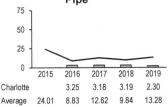

Backups per 100 Miles of Main Line Pipe

	2015	2016	2017	2018	2019
Charlotte		3.25	3.18	3.19	2.30
Average	24.01	8.83	12.62	9.84	13.28

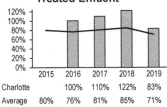

Billed Wastewater as a Percent of Treated Effluent

	2015	2016	2017	2018	2019
Charlotte		100%	110%	122%	83%
Average	80%	76%	81%	85%	71%

Explanatory Information

Service Level and Delivery

The City of Concord has a wastewater department that focuses on the inspection, maintenance, and repair of the wastewater collection system. Concord does not have its own treatment plant, making it unique among the benchmarking partner cities. Instead, treatment is handled by the Water and Sewer Authority of Cabarrus County, a regional system. All treatment and disposal of wastewater and biosolids are handled by the regional authority using two treatment plants.

The Concord wastewater collection system had three violations on the collection portion of the system involving sanitary system overflows.

Conditions Affecting Service, Performance, and Costs

The costs of wastewater or sewer services as captured here do not include debt service but do capture depreciation of capital.

Municipal Profile	
Estimated Service Population	92,567
Service Land Area (Square Miles)	105.7
Persons per Square Mile	876
Topography	Flat; gently rolling
Climate	Temperate; little ice and snow
Median Household Income	$50,863
U.S. Census 2016	

Service Profile	
Total FTE Staff Positions	33.0
Treatment Plant	NA
Line Crews	27.0
Billing/Collection	0.0
Other	6.0
Number of Treatment Plants	0
Total Treatment Capacity	NA
Average Daily Flow	NA
River Basin into Which System Discharges	Yadkin and Pee-Dee
Miles of Gravity Main Line Pipe	574
Miles of Forced Main Line Pipe	13
Average Age of Main Line Pipe	40 years
Blocks in Sewer Mains	3
Number of System Breaks	0
Sanitary System Overflows	3
Number of Customer Accounts	37,043
Total Revenues Collected	$17,684,744

Full Cost Profile	
Cost Breakdown by Percentage	
Personal Services	17.3%
Operating Costs	60.4%
Capital Costs	22.3%
TOTAL	100.0%
Cost Breakdown in Dollars	
Personal Services	$2,695,581
Operating Costs	$9,398,169
Capital Costs	$3,461,397
TOTAL	$15,555,147

Key: Concord ▪ Benchmarking Average — Fiscal Years 2015 through 2019

Resource Measures

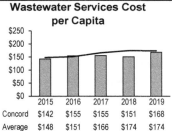

Wastewater Services Cost per Capita

	2015	2016	2017	2018	2019
Concord	$142	$155	$155	$151	$168
Average	$148	$151	$166	$174	$174

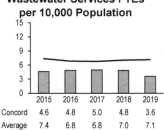

Wastewater Services FTEs per 10,000 Population

	2015	2016	2017	2018	2019
Concord	4.6	4.8	5.0	4.8	3.6
Average	7.4	6.8	6.8	7.0	7.1

Wastewater Services Cost per Customer Account

	2015	2016	2017	2018	2019
Concord	$375	$398	$395	$381	$420
Average	$421	$445	$494	$499	$492

Workload Measures

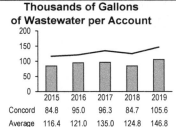

Thousands of Gallons of Wastewater per Account

	2015	2016	2017	2018	2019
Concord	84.8	95.0	96.3	84.7	105.6
Average	116.4	121.0	135.0	124.8	146.8

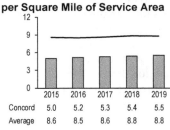

Miles of Sewer Main Line Pipe per Square Mile of Service Area

	2015	2016	2017	2018	2019
Concord	5.0	5.2	5.3	5.4	5.5
Average	8.6	8.5	8.6	8.8	8.8

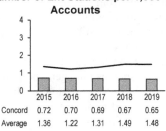

Number of Lift Stations per 1,000 Accounts

	2015	2016	2017	2018	2019
Concord	0.72	0.70	0.69	0.67	0.65
Average	1.36	1.22	1.31	1.49	1.48

Efficiency Measures

Total Cost per 1,000 Gallons of Treated Wastewater

	2015	2016	2017	2018	2019
Concord	$4.43	$4.19	$4.10	$4.50	$3.98
Average	$3.94	$3.96	$4.07	$4.34	$3.83

Million Gallons of Wastewater per Wastewater Services FTE

	2015	2016	2017	2018	2019
Concord	69.6	76.2	76.4	69.3	118.6
Average	57.9	62.7	69.2	63.9	76.0

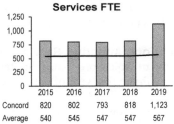

Customer Accounts per Wastewater Services FTE

	2015	2016	2017	2018	2019
Concord	820	802	793	818	1,123
Average	540	545	547	547	567

Effectiveness Measures

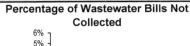
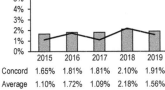

Percentage of Wastewater Bills Not Collected

	2015	2016	2017	2018	2019
Concord	1.65%	1.81%	1.81%	2.10%	1.91%
Average	1.10%	1.72%	1.09%	2.18%	1.56%

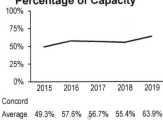

Average Daily Treatment as a Percentage of Capacity

	2015	2016	2017	2018	2019
Concord					
Average	49.3%	57.6%	56.7%	55.4%	63.9%

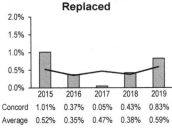

Percent of Main Line Rehabbed or Replaced

	2015	2016	2017	2018	2019
Concord	1.01%	0.37%	0.05%	0.43%	0.83%
Average	0.52%	0.35%	0.47%	0.38%	0.59%

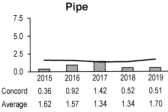

Overflows per 100 Miles of Main Line Pipe

	2015	2016	2017	2018	2019
Concord	0.36	0.92	1.42	0.52	0.51
Average	1.62	1.57	1.34	1.34	1.70

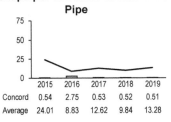

Backups per 100 Miles of Main Line Pipe

	2015	2016	2017	2018	2019
Concord	0.54	2.75	0.53	0.52	0.51
Average	24.01	8.83	12.62	9.84	13.28

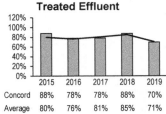

Billed Wastewater as a Percent of Treated Effluent

	2015	2016	2017	2018	2019
Concord	88%	78%	78%	88%	70%
Average	80%	76%	81%	85%	71%

Goldsboro

Wastewater Services

Fiscal Year 2018–19

Explanatory Information

Service Level and Delivery

Wastewater treatment in Goldsboro is a joint responsibility between the Public Works and Public Utilities Departments. The Public Works Director oversees both departments. The Public Works Department is responsible for the collection and distribution system lines. The Public Utilities Department is responsible for the operation of the water treatment plant, the water reclamation facility, and pump stations.

The sewer system covers the city of Goldsboro and receives wastewater from neighboring systems in Wayne County. Wastewater treatment is done by one plant with a total treatment capacity of 14.2 million gallons per day. The plant uses advanced biological processes to remove pollutants from the water. Besides removing oxygen consuming wastes, the facility is able to remove nutrients such as nitrogen and phosphorus to very low levels. The system has nutrient regulatory limits in place that restrict what can be discharged in order to protect water quality. All biosolids produced by the Goldsboro treatment plant are dewatered and then composted.

During the fiscal year, the system had two regulatory violations with the treatment portion of the system and no violations for the collection portion of the system.

Conditions Affecting Service, Performance, and Costs

The city of Goldsboro joined the Benchmarking Project in July 2017, with the first year of data showing for FY 2016–17.

The costs of wastewater or sewer services as captured here do not include debt service but do capture depreciation of capital.

Hurricane Matthew in October 2016 put stress on the wastewater system in Goldsboro due to the extensive flooding.

Goldsboro has improved its tracking system for a number of data items, which reflects greater accuracy in the most recent year.

Municipal Profile

Estimated Service Population	34,234
Service Land Area (Square Miles)	25
Persons per Square Mile	1,369
Topography	Flat; gently rolling
Climate	Temperate; little ice and snow
Median Household Income	$32,148
U.S. Census 2016	

Service Profile

Total FTE Staff Positions	30.0
Treatment Plant	10.0
Line Crews	5.0
Billing/Collection	6.0
Other	9.0
Number of Treatment Plants	1
Total Treatment Capacity	14.2 MGD
Average Daily Flow	11.5 MGD
River Basin into Which System Discharges	Neuse
Miles of Gravity Main Line Pipe	227
Miles of Forced Main Line Pipe	16
Average Age of Main Line Pipe	60 years
Blocks in Sewer Mains	8
Number of System Breaks	28
Sanitary System Overflows	4
Number of Customer Accounts	12,456
Total Revenues Collected	$7,385,664

Full Cost Profile

Cost Breakdown by Percentage

Personal Services	17.4%
Operating Costs	74.4%
Capital Costs	8.1%
TOTAL	100.0%

Cost Breakdown in Dollars

Personal Services	$1,224,903
Operating Costs	$5,237,044
Capital Costs	$573,187
TOTAL	$7,035,134

Goldsboro

Wastewater Services

Resource Measures

Wastewater Services Cost per Capita

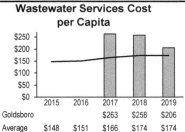

	2015	2016	2017	2018	2019
Goldsboro			$263	$258	$206
Average	$148	$151	$166	$174	$174

Wastewater Services FTEs per 10,000 Population

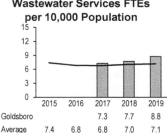

	2015	2016	2017	2018	2019
Goldsboro			7.3	7.7	8.8
Average	7.4	6.8	6.8	7.0	7.1

Wastewater Services Cost per Customer Account

	2015	2016	2017	2018	2019
Goldsboro			$810	$746	$565
Average	$421	$445	$494	$499	$492

Workload Measures

Thousands of Gallons of Wastewater per Account

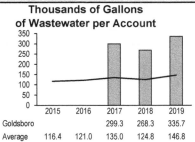

	2015	2016	2017	2018	2019
Goldsboro			299.3	268.3	335.7
Average	116.4	121.0	135.0	124.8	146.8

Miles of Sewer Main Line Pipe per Square Mile of Service Area

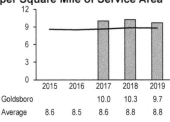

	2015	2016	2017	2018	2019
Goldsboro			10.0	10.3	9.7
Average	8.6	8.5	8.6	8.8	8.8

Number of Lift Stations per 1,000 Accounts

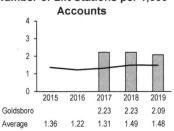

	2015	2016	2017	2018	2019
Goldsboro			2.23	2.23	2.09
Average	1.36	1.22	1.31	1.49	1.48

Efficiency Measures

Total Cost per 1,000 Gallons of Treated Wastewater

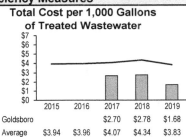

	2015	2016	2017	2018	2019
Goldsboro			$2.70	$2.78	$1.68
Average	$3.94	$3.96	$4.07	$4.34	$3.83

Million Gallons of Wastewater per Wastewater Services FTE

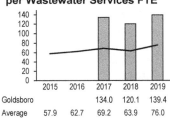

	2015	2016	2017	2018	2019
Goldsboro			134.0	120.1	139.4
Average	57.9	62.7	69.2	63.9	76.0

Customer Accounts per Wastewater Services FTE

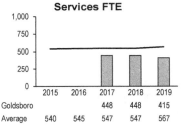

	2015	2016	2017	2018	2019
Goldsboro			448	448	415
Average	540	545	547	547	567

Effectiveness Measures

Percentage of Wastewater Bills Not Collected

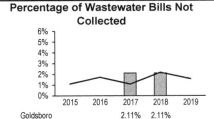

	2015	2016	2017	2018	2019
Goldsboro			2.11%	2.11%	
Average	1.10%	1.72%	1.09%	2.18%	1.56%

Average Daily Treatment as a Percentage of Capacity

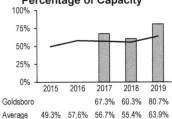

	2015	2016	2017	2018	2019
Goldsboro			67.3%	60.3%	80.7%
Average	49.3%	57.6%	56.7%	55.4%	63.9%

Percent of Main Line Rehabbed or Replaced

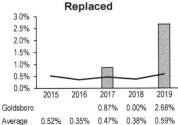

	2015	2016	2017	2018	2019
Goldsboro			0.87%	0.00%	2.68%
Average	0.52%	0.35%	0.47%	0.38%	0.59%

Overflows per 100 Miles of Main Line Pipe

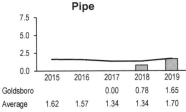

	2015	2016	2017	2018	2019
Goldsboro			0.00	0.78	1.65
Average	1.62	1.57	1.34	1.34	1.70

Backups per 100 Miles of Main Line Pipe

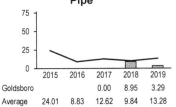

	2015	2016	2017	2018	2019
Goldsboro			0.00	8.95	3.29
Average	24.01	8.83	12.62	9.84	13.28

Billed Wastewater as a Percent of Treated Effluent

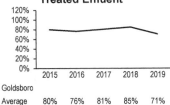

	2015	2016	2017	2018	2019
Goldsboro					
Average	80%	76%	81%	85%	71%

Fiscal Year 2018–19

Explanatory Information

Service Level and Delivery

Wastewater treatment in Greensboro is handled by the Water Reclamation Division. This is part of the Water Resources Department, which also includes stormwater and drinking water services. The director of water resources reports to the city manager. Services are provided to most of the City of Greensboro and to some addresses outside city limits within Guilford County.

Wastewater treatment in Greensboro is now handled by one treatment plant. In October 2017 one plant was decommissioned, with the effective capacity transferred to the remaining plant through a large construction upgrade. This plant uses advanced tertiary treatment. The system has nutrient regulatory limits in place that restrict what can be discharged in order to protect water quality. All biosolids produced by the Greensboro treatment plant are incinerated.

During the fiscal year, the system had twelve regulatory violations connected to the treatment portion of the system. Thirty-two violations connected to the collection portion of the system for sanitary system overflows were also experienced.

Conditions Affecting Service, Performance, and Costs

The costs of wastewater or sewer services as captured here do not include debt service but do capture depreciation of capital.

During FY 2015–16 a conversion to a new database used for tracking operations was undertaken. Some data were not available. The performance measure "backups per 100 miles of main line pipe" could not be calculated.

The full implementation of a new asset management system designed for utilities took place in FY 2016–17. Work orders are now assigned and tracked by more specific types of duties, which resulted in an increase in certain metrics over prior years.

Municipal Profile	
Estimated Service Population	294,722
Service Land Area (Square Miles)	148
Persons per Square Mile	1,991
Topography	Flat; gently rolling
Climate	Temperate; little ice and snow
Median Household Income	$40,760
U.S. Census 2016	

Service Profile	
Total FTE Staff Positions	165.0
Treatment Plant	52.0
Line Crews	87.0
Billing/Collection	7.5
Other	18.5
Number of Treatment Plants	1
Total Treatment Capacity	56.0 MGD
Average Daily Flow	37.3 MGD
River Basin into Which System Discharges	Cape Fear
Miles of Gravity Main Line Pipe	1,437
Miles of Forced Main Line Pipe	70
Average Age of Main Line Pipe	39 years
Blocks in Sewer Mains	37
Number of System Breaks	61
Sanitary System Overflows	11
Number of Customer Accounts	102,854
Total Revenues Collected	$62,660,247

Full Cost Profile	
Cost Breakdown by Percentage	
Personal Services	19.3%
Operating Costs	53.7%
Capital Costs	27.0%
TOTAL	100.0%
Cost Breakdown in Dollars	
Personal Services	$7,834,123
Operating Costs	$21,786,440
Capital Costs	$10,973,608
TOTAL	$40,594,171

Greensboro

Wastewater Services

Resource Measures

Wastewater Services Cost per Capita

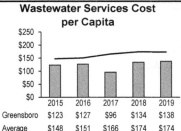

	2015	2016	2017	2018	2019
Greensboro	$123	$127	$96	$134	$138
Average	$148	$151	$166	$174	$174

Wastewater Services FTEs per 10,000 Population

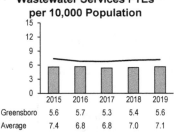

	2015	2016	2017	2018	2019
Greensboro	5.6	5.7	5.3	5.4	5.6
Average	7.4	6.8	6.8	7.0	7.1

Wastewater Services Cost per Customer Account

	2015	2016	2017	2018	2019
Greensboro	$343	$353	$268	$375	$395
Average	$421	$445	$494	$499	$492

Workload Measures

Thousands of Gallons of Wastewater per Account

	2015	2016	2017	2018	2019
Greensboro	118.2	124.9	119.3	112.2	134.3
Average	116.4	121.0	135.0	124.8	146.8

Miles of Sewer Main Line Pipe per Square Mile of Service Area

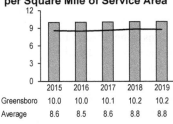

	2015	2016	2017	2018	2019
Greensboro	10.0	10.0	10.1	10.2	10.2
Average	8.6	8.5	8.6	8.8	8.8

Number of Lift Stations per 1,000 Accounts

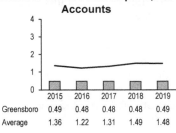

	2015	2016	2017	2018	2019
Greensboro	0.49	0.48	0.48	0.48	0.49
Average	1.36	1.22	1.31	1.49	1.48

Efficiency Measures

Total Cost per 1,000 Gallons of Treated Wastewater

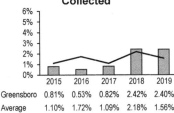

	2015	2016	2017	2018	2019
Greensboro	$2.90	$2.82	$2.25	$3.34	$2.94
Average	$3.94	$3.96	$4.07	$4.34	$3.83

Million Gallons of Wastewater per Wastewater Services FTE

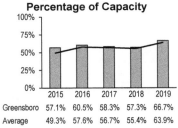

	2015	2016	2017	2018	2019
Greensboro	76.0	79.4	79.6	73.8	83.7
Average	57.9	62.7	69.2	63.9	76.0

Customer Accounts per Wastewater Services FTE

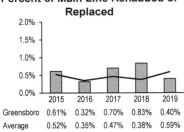

	2015	2016	2017	2018	2019
Greensboro	643	636	668	658	623
Average	540	545	547	547	567

Effectiveness Measures

Percentage of Wastewater Bills Not Collected

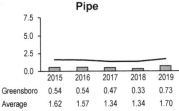

	2015	2016	2017	2018	2019
Greensboro	0.81%	0.53%	0.82%	2.42%	2.40%
Average	1.10%	1.72%	1.09%	2.18%	1.56%

Average Daily Treatment as a Percentage of Capacity

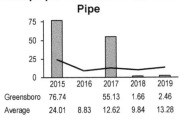

	2015	2016	2017	2018	2019
Greensboro	57.1%	60.5%	58.3%	57.3%	66.7%
Average	49.3%	57.6%	56.7%	55.4%	63.9%

Percent of Main Line Rehabbed or Replaced

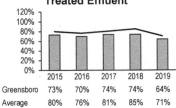

	2015	2016	2017	2018	2019
Greensboro	0.61%	0.32%	0.70%	0.83%	0.40%
Average	0.52%	0.35%	0.47%	0.38%	0.59%

Overflows per 100 Miles of Main Line Pipe

	2015	2016	2017	2018	2019
Greensboro	0.54	0.54	0.47	0.33	0.73
Average	1.62	1.57	1.34	1.34	1.70

Backups per 100 Miles of Main Line Pipe

	2015	2016	2017	2018	2019
Greensboro	76.74		55.13	1.66	2.46
Average	24.01	8.83	12.62	9.84	13.28

Billed Wastewater as a Percent of Treated Effluent

	2015	2016	2017	2018	2019
Greensboro	73%	70%	74%	74%	64%
Average	80%	76%	81%	85%	71%

Fiscal Year 2018–19

Explanatory Information

Service Level and Delivery

Wastewater is handled by the City of Hickory's Collection Division, which is part of Public Utilities under the Public Services Department. The service area covers the City of Hickory and several adjoining areas in Catawba County.

The system relies on three treatment plants to handle wastewater. One plant uses activated-sludge biological nutrient removal (BNR), the second uses oxidation-ditch-activated-sludge BNR, and the third uses conventional activated sludge. The entire system does not have nutrient limits in place at this time. Biosolids generated are handled as Class A compost.

The system in Hickory had two regulatory violations connected to the treatment portion of the system and seven violations connected to the collection portion of the system during the fiscal year.

Conditions Affecting Service, Performance, and Costs

The costs of wastewater or sewer services as captured here do not include debt service but do capture depreciation of capital.

Municipal Profile

Estimated Service Population	37,478
Service Land Area (Square Miles)	65.0
Persons per Square Mile	577
Topography	Gently rolling
Climate	Temperate; some ice and snow
Median Household Income	$35,353
U.S. Census 2016	

Service Profile

Total FTE Staff Positions	44.0
Treatment Plant	29.0
Line Crews	10.0
Billing/Collection	2.5
Other	2.5
Number of Treatment Plants	3
Total Treatment Capacity	16.9 MGD
Average Daily Flow	6.4 MGD
River Basin into Which System Discharges	Catawba
Miles of Gravity Main Line Pipe	498
Miles of Forced Main Line Pipe	43
Average Age of Main Line Pipe	47 years
Blocks in Sewer Mains	55
Number of System Breaks	6
Sanitary System Overflows	7
Number of Customer Accounts	15,924
Total Revenues Collected	$11,061,179

Full Cost Profile

Cost Breakdown by Percentage

Personal Services	38.6%
Operating Costs	43.7%
Capital Costs	17.6%
TOTAL	100.0%

Cost Breakdown in Dollars

Personal Services	$2,824,800
Operating Costs	$3,197,373
Capital Costs	$1,290,020
TOTAL	$7,312,193

Key: Hickory   Benchmarking Average —   Fiscal Years 2015 through 2019

Resource Measures

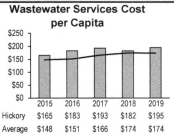

Wastewater Services Cost per Capita

	2015	2016	2017	2018	2019
Hickory	$165	$183	$193	$182	$195
Average	$148	$151	$166	$174	$174

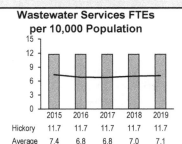

Wastewater Services FTEs per 10,000 Population

	2015	2016	2017	2018	2019
Hickory	11.7	11.7	11.7	11.7	11.7
Average	7.4	6.8	6.8	7.0	7.1

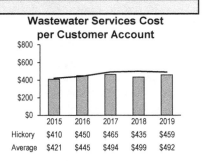

Wastewater Services Cost per Customer Account

	2015	2016	2017	2018	2019
Hickory	$410	$450	$465	$435	$459
Average	$421	$445	$494	$499	$492

Workload Measures

Thousands of Gallons of Wastewater per Account

	2015	2016	2017	2018	2019
Hickory	134.7	147.3	131.0	138.7	156.6
Average	116.4	121.0	135.0	124.8	146.8

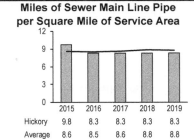

Miles of Sewer Main Line Pipe per Square Mile of Service Area

	2015	2016	2017	2018	2019
Hickory	9.8	8.3	8.3	8.3	8.3
Average	8.6	8.5	8.6	8.8	8.8

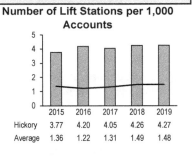

Number of Lift Stations per 1,000 Accounts

	2015	2016	2017	2018	2019
Hickory	3.77	4.20	4.05	4.26	4.27
Average	1.36	1.22	1.31	1.49	1.48

Efficiency Measures

Total Cost per 1,000 Gallons of Treated Wastewater

	2015	2016	2017	2018	2019
Hickory	$3.04	$3.05	$3.55	$3.13	$2.93
Average	$3.94	$3.96	$4.07	$4.34	$3.83

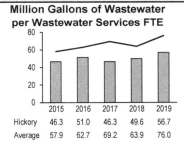

Million Gallons of Wastewater per Wastewater Services FTE

	2015	2016	2017	2018	2019
Hickory	46.3	51.0	46.3	49.6	56.7
Average	57.9	62.7	69.2	63.9	76.0

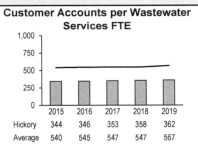

Customer Accounts per Wastewater Services FTE

	2015	2016	2017	2018	2019
Hickory	344	346	353	358	362
Average	540	545	547	547	567

Effectiveness Measures

Percentage of Wastewater Bills Not Collected

	2015	2016	2017	2018	2019
Hickory	2.47%	1.86%	2.24%	3.81%	2.25%
Average	1.10%	1.72%	1.09%	2.18%	1.56%

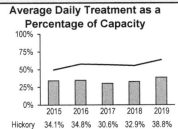

Average Daily Treatment as a Percentage of Capacity

	2015	2016	2017	2018	2019
Hickory	34.1%	34.8%	30.6%	32.9%	38.8%
Average	49.3%	57.6%	56.7%	55.4%	63.9%

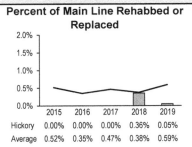

Percent of Main Line Rehabbed or Replaced

	2015	2016	2017	2018	2019
Hickory	0.00%	0.00%	0.00%	0.36%	0.05%
Average	0.52%	0.35%	0.47%	0.38%	0.59%

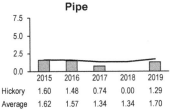

Overflows per 100 Miles of Main Line Pipe

	2015	2016	2017	2018	2019
Hickory	1.60	1.48	0.74	0.00	1.29
Average	1.62	1.57	1.34	1.34	1.70

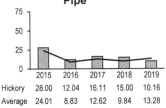

Backups per 100 Miles of Main Line Pipe

	2015	2016	2017	2018	2019
Hickory	28.00	12.04	16.11	15.00	10.16
Average	24.01	8.83	12.62	9.84	13.28

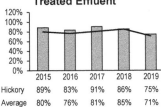

Billed Wastewater as a Percent of Treated Effluent

	2015	2016	2017	2018	2019
Hickory	89%	83%	91%	86%	75%
Average	80%	76%	81%	85%	71%

Mooresville
Wastewater Services

Fiscal Year 2018–19

Explanatory Information

Service Level and Delivery
The Town of Mooresville provides water service and wastewater services through the Public Services Department as an enterprise fund. Only the data for the wastewater services portion of the system are reported here. The system covers 44 square miles and serves approximately 41,000 people.

Wastewater is treated at one plant. The plant uses an extended aeration biological treatment with ultraviolet disinfection. The system does not currently have nutrient regulatory limits. Biosolids produced as a result of treatment are handled with a belt press and low temperature dryer. Class A solids are distributed to local farms, while Class B solids are transported to the landfill.

The system had no regulatory violations during the fiscal year for issues related to treatment and one violation connected to collections related to sanitary system overflows.

Conditions Affecting Service, Performance, and Costs
Mooresville joined the Benchmarking project in July 2018, with the first year of data showing for FY 2017–18.

The costs of wastewater or sewer services as captured here do not include debt service but do capture depreciation of capital.

Municipal Profile

Estimated Service Population	41,000
Service Land Area (Square Miles)	44.0
Persons per Square Mile	932
Topography	Flat; gently rolling
Climate	Temperate; little ice and snow
Median Household Income	$67,213
U.S. Census 2016	

Service Profile

Total FTE Staff Positions	37.0
Treatment Plant	19.5
Line Crews	15.0
Billing/Collection	2.5
Other	0.0
Number of Treatment Plants	1
Total Treatment Capacity	7.5 MGD
Average Daily Flow	4.9 MGD
River Basin into Which System Discharges	Yadkin Pee-Dee
Miles of Gravity Main Line Pipe	275
Miles of Forced Main Line Pipe	50
Average Age of Main Line Pipe	22 years
Blocks in Sewer Mains	19
Number of System Breaks	8
Sanitary System Overflows	6
Number of Customer Accounts	15,207
Total Revenues Collected	$15,148,131

Full Cost Profile
Cost Breakdown by Percentage

Personal Services	25.5%
Operating Costs	52.0%
Capital Costs	22.5%
TOTAL	100.0%

Cost Breakdown in Dollars

Personal Services	$2,594,949
Operating Costs	$5,280,591
Capital Costs	$2,286,155
TOTAL	$10,161,695

Mooresville

Wastewater Services

Resource Measures

Wastewater Services Cost per Capita

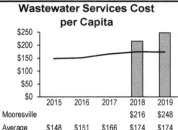

	2015	2016	2017	2018	2019
Mooresville				$216	$248
Average	$148	$151	$166	$174	$174

Wastewater Services FTEs per 10,000 Population

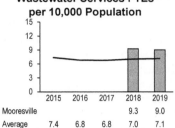

	2015	2016	2017	2018	2019
Mooresville				9.3	9.0
Average	7.4	6.8	6.8	7.0	7.1

Wastewater Services Cost per Customer Account

	2015	2016	2017	2018	2019
Mooresville				$586	$668
Average	$421	$445	$494	$499	$492

Workload Measures

Thousands of Gallons of Wastewater per Account

	2015	2016	2017	2018	2019
Mooresville				106.4	112.1
Average	116.4	121.0	135.0	124.8	146.8

Miles of Sewer Main Line Pipe per Square Mile of Service Area

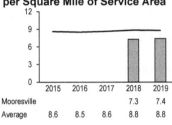

	2015	2016	2017	2018	2019
Mooresville				7.3	7.4
Average	8.6	8.5	8.6	8.8	8.8

Number of Lift Stations per 1,000 Accounts

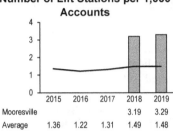

	2015	2016	2017	2018	2019
Mooresville				3.19	3.29
Average	1.36	1.22	1.31	1.49	1.48

Efficiency Measures

Total Cost per 1,000 Gallons of Treated Wastewater

	2015	2016	2017	2018	2019
Mooresville				$5.51	$5.96
Average	$3.94	$3.96	$4.07	$4.34	$3.83

Million Gallons of Wastewater per Wastewater Services FTE

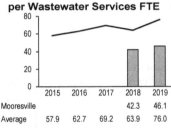

	2015	2016	2017	2018	2019
Mooresville				42.3	46.1
Average	57.9	62.7	69.2	63.9	76.0

Customer Accounts per Wastewater Services FTE

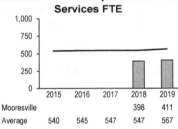

	2015	2016	2017	2018	2019
Mooresville				398	411
Average	540	545	547	547	567

Effectiveness Measures

Percentage of Wastewater Bills Not Collected

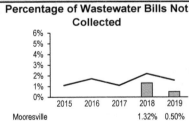

	2015	2016	2017	2018	2019
Mooresville				1.32%	0.50%
Average	1.10%	1.72%	1.09%	2.18%	1.56%

Average Daily Treatment as a Percentage of Capacity

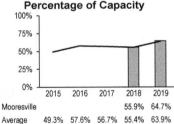

	2015	2016	2017	2018	2019
Mooresville				55.9%	64.7%
Average	49.3%	57.6%	56.7%	55.4%	63.9%

Percent of Main Line Rehabbed or Replaced

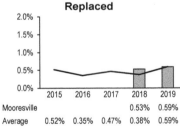

	2015	2016	2017	2018	2019
Mooresville				0.53%	0.59%
Average	0.52%	0.35%	0.47%	0.38%	0.59%

Overflows per 100 Miles of Main Line Pipe

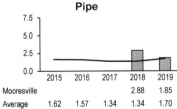

	2015	2016	2017	2018	2019
Mooresville				2.88	1.85
Average	1.62	1.57	1.34	1.34	1.70

Backups per 100 Miles of Main Line Pipe

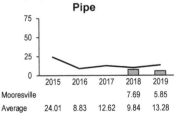

	2015	2016	2017	2018	2019
Mooresville				7.69	5.85
Average	24.01	8.83	12.62	9.84	13.28

Billed Wastewater as a Percent of Treated Effluent

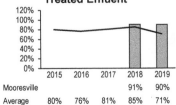

	2015	2016	2017	2018	2019
Mooresville				91%	90%
Average	80%	76%	81%	85%	71%

Explanatory Information

Service Level and Delivery

Public Utilities is a department within the City of Raleigh. It is a combined enterprise system that provides drinking water and sewage treatment services to the City of Raleigh and six merger towns: Garner, Rolesville, Knightdale, Wake Forest, Wendell, and Zebulon. The City of Raleigh also provides wastewater treatment for the Towns of Middlesex and Clayton. As of FY 2019, approximately 580,000 people live in the contractual service area of 299 square miles.

Wastewater is treated at three plants. The total combined treatment capacity at the three plants is 80.2 million gallons per day. The plants use primary treatment, a nutrient removal process for secondary treatment, and tertiary treatment along with biosolids treatment and land application. A portion of the treated effluent is distributed as reclaimed water. The system had no wastewater treatment violations.

Conditions Affecting Service, Performance, and Costs

Raleigh rejoined the Benchmarking Project in July 2016, with the first year of data showing for FY 2015–16.

The Utility has a full-functioning farm with a dedicated Land Management program consisting of 15 FTEs. The farm uses a portion of the biosolids produced at the plant as fertilizer to grow soybeans, corn, and hay.

The costs of wastewater or sewer services as captured here do not include debt service but do capture depreciation of capital.

Municipal Profile

Estimated Service Population	582,098
Service Land Area (Square Miles)	299.0
Persons per Square Mile	1,947
Topography	Flat; gently rolling
Climate	Temperate; little ice and snow
Median Household Income	$46,612
U.S. Census 2016	

Service Profile

Total FTE Staff Positions	353.5
Treatment Plant	140.0
Line Crews	34.0
Billing/Collection	132.0
Other	47.5
Number of Treatment Plants	3
Total Treatment Capacity	80.2 MGD
Average Daily Flow	51.8 MGD
River Basin into Which System Discharges	Neuse
Miles of Gravity Main Line Pipe	2,380
Miles of Forced Main Line Pipe	131
Average Age of Main Line Pipe	33 years
Blocks in Sewer Mains	NA
Number of System Breaks	198
Sanitary System Overflows	32
Number of Customer Accounts	185,672
Total Revenues Collected	$139,695,876

Full Cost Profile

Cost Breakdown by Percentage

Personal Services	37.2%
Operating Costs	43.2%
Capital Costs	19.6%
TOTAL	100.0%

Cost Breakdown in Dollars

Personal Services	$24,884,551
Operating Costs	$28,889,280
Capital Costs	$13,143,676
TOTAL	$66,917,507

Raleigh

Wastewater Services

Resource Measures

Wastewater Services Cost per Capita

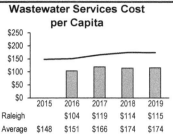

	2015	2016	2017	2018	2019
Raleigh		$104	$119	$114	$115
Average	$148	$151	$166	$174	$174

Wastewater Services FTEs per 10,000 Population

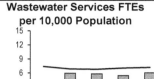
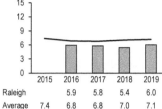

	2015	2016	2017	2018	2019
Raleigh		5.9	5.8	5.4	6.0
Average	7.4	6.8	6.8	7.0	7.1

Wastewater Services Cost per Customer Account

	2015	2016	2017	2018	2019
Raleigh		$337	$391	$353	$360
Average	$421	$445	$494	$499	$492

Workload Measures

Thousands of Gallons of Wastewater per Account

	2015	2016	2017	2018	2019
Raleigh		107.9	107.3	93.2	103.4
Average	116.4	121.0	135.0	124.8	146.8

Miles of Sewer Main Line Pipe per Square Mile of Service Area

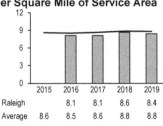

	2015	2016	2017	2018	2019
Raleigh		8.1	8.1	8.6	8.4
Average	8.6	8.5	8.6	8.8	8.8

Number of Lift Stations per 1,000 Accounts

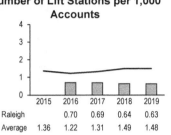

	2015	2016	2017	2018	2019
Raleigh		0.70	0.69	0.64	0.63
Average	1.36	1.22	1.31	1.49	1.48

Efficiency Measures

Total Cost per 1,000 Gallons of Treated Wastewater

	2015	2016	2017	2018	2019
Raleigh		$3.12	$3.65	$3.78	$3.49
Average	$3.94	$3.96	$4.07	$4.34	$3.83

Million Gallons of Wastewater per Wastewater Services FTE

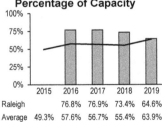

	2015	2016	2017	2018	2019
Raleigh		56.2	56.4	56.0	55.2
Average	57.9	62.7	69.2	63.9	76.0

Customer Accounts per Wastewater Services FTE

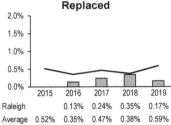

	2015	2016	2017	2018	2019
Raleigh		520	526	601	534
Average	540	545	547	547	567

Effectiveness Measures

Percentage of Wastewater Bills Not Collected

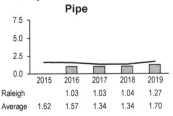

	2015	2016	2017	2018	2019
Raleigh			-0.98%	5.00%	
Average	1.10%	1.72%	1.09%	2.18%	1.56%

Average Daily Treatment as a Percentage of Capacity

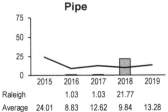

	2015	2016	2017	2018	2019
Raleigh		76.8%	76.9%	73.4%	64.6%
Average	49.3%	57.6%	56.7%	55.4%	63.9%

Percent of Main Line Rehabbed or Replaced

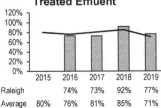

	2015	2016	2017	2018	2019
Raleigh		0.13%	0.24%	0.35%	0.17%
Average	0.52%	0.35%	0.47%	0.38%	0.59%

Overflows per 100 Miles of Main Line Pipe

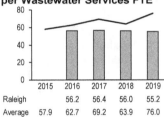

	2015	2016	2017	2018	2019
Raleigh		1.03	1.03	1.04	1.27
Average	1.62	1.57	1.34	1.34	1.70

Backups per 100 Miles of Main Line Pipe

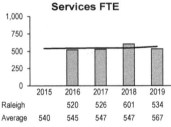

	2015	2016	2017	2018	2019
Raleigh		1.03	1.03	21.77	
Average	24.01	8.83	12.62	9.84	13.28

Billed Wastewater as a Percent of Treated Effluent

	2015	2016	2017	2018	2019
Raleigh		74%	73%	92%	77%
Average	80%	76%	81%	85%	71%

Wilson

Wastewater Services

Fiscal Year 2018–19

Explanatory Information

Service Level and Delivery

Wastewater in Wilson is handled by the Water Reclamation and Wastewater Collection Division, which is part of Water Resources in the Public Services Department. Billing for large customers is handled by Water Resources, but residential customer billing is handled by the Customer Services Division in the Finance Department. The system covers the City of Wilson and several small adjoining areas outside the city in Wilson County.

Wastewater treatment is handled by one plant. The treatment plant uses advanced five-stage biological nutrient removal with deep-bed filters with methanol and biological and chemical phosphorous reduction. The system had very stringent nutrient limits in place to protect water quality in the Neuse River basin. The system produced Class A and B biosolids, with most of this solid waste being composted. A small portion is applied on city land or other permitted farmland.

The system had no reported regulatory violations for either the treatment or collection portion of the system during the fiscal year.

Conditions Affecting Service, Performance, and Costs

The costs of wastewater or sewer services as captured here do not include debt service but do capture depreciation of capital.

Large capital improvements are being made to the Buckhorn Lake Dam and Wastewater Projects, which have been required to meet advanced nutrient removal standards.

Municipal Profile

Estimated Service Population	54,400
Service Land Area (Square Miles)	41
Persons per Square Mile	1,327
Topography	Flat
Climate	Temperate; little ice and snow
Median Household Income	$35,409
U.S. Census 2016	

Service Profile

Total FTE Staff Positions	65.0
Treatment Plant	31.0
Line Crews	28.0
Billing/Collection	3.0
Other	3.0
Number of Treatment Plants	1
Total Treatment Capacity	14.0 MGD
Average Daily Flow	10.0 MGD
River Basin into Which System Discharges	Neuse
Miles of Gravity Main Line Pipe	355
Miles of Forced Main Line Pipe	12
Average Age of Main Line Pipe	45 years
Blocks in Sewer Mains	285
Number of System Breaks	4
Sanitary System Overflows	4
Number of Customer Accounts	20,641
Total Revenues Collected	$14,302,000

Full Cost Profile

Cost Breakdown by Percentage

Personal Services	34.5%
Operating Costs	40.7%
Capital Costs	24.8%
TOTAL	100.0%

Cost Breakdown in Dollars

Personal Services	$4,422,355
Operating Costs	$5,226,747
Capital Costs	$3,180,234
TOTAL	$12,829,336

Wilson

Wastewater Services

Resource Measures

Wastewater Services Cost per Capita

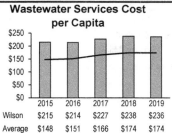

	2015	2016	2017	2018	2019
Wilson	$215	$214	$227	$238	$236
Average	$148	$151	$166	$174	$174

Wastewater Services FTEs per 10,000 Population

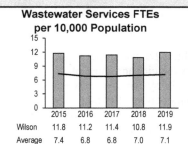

	2015	2016	2017	2018	2019
Wilson	11.8	11.2	11.4	10.8	11.9
Average	7.4	6.8	6.8	7.0	7.1

Wastewater Services Cost per Customer Account

	2015	2016	2017	2018	2019
Wilson	$584	$577	$596	$620	$622
Average	$421	$445	$494	$499	$492

Workload Measures

Thousands of Gallons of Wastewater per Account

	2015	2016	2017	2018	2019
Wilson	182.4	173.7	161.2	148.6	180.6
Average	116.4	121.0	135.0	124.8	146.8

Miles of Sewer Main Line Pipe per Square Mile of Service Area

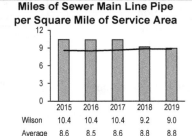

	2015	2016	2017	2018	2019
Wilson	10.4	10.4	10.4	9.2	9.0
Average	8.6	8.5	8.6	8.8	8.8

Number of Lift Stations per 1,000 Accounts

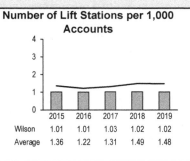

	2015	2016	2017	2018	2019
Wilson	1.01	1.01	1.03	1.02	1.02
Average	1.36	1.22	1.31	1.49	1.48

Efficiency Measures

Total Cost per 1,000 Gallons of Treated Wastewater

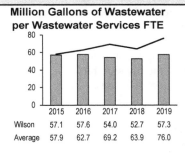

	2015	2016	2017	2018	2019
Wilson	$3.20	$3.32	$3.70	$4.17	$3.44
Average	$3.94	$3.96	$4.07	$4.34	$3.83

Million Gallons of Wastewater per Wastewater Services FTE

	2015	2016	2017	2018	2019
Wilson	57.1	57.6	54.0	52.7	57.3
Average	57.9	62.7	69.2	63.9	76.0

Customer Accounts per Wastewater Services FTE

	2015	2016	2017	2018	2019
Wilson	313	331	335	355	318
Average	540	545	547	547	567

Effectiveness Measures

Percentage of Wastewater Bills Not Collected

	2015	2016	2017	2018	2019
Wilson	0.70%	0.78%	1.41%	0.85%	0.95%
Average	1.10%	1.72%	1.09%	2.18%	1.56%

Average Daily Treatment as a Percentage of Capacity

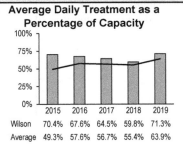

	2015	2016	2017	2018	2019
Wilson	70.4%	67.6%	64.5%	59.8%	71.3%
Average	49.3%	57.6%	56.7%	55.4%	63.9%

Percent of Main Line Rehabbed or Replaced

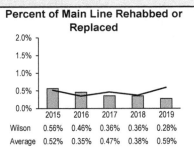

	2015	2016	2017	2018	2019
Wilson	0.56%	0.46%	0.36%	0.36%	0.28%
Average	0.52%	0.35%	0.47%	0.38%	0.59%

Overflows per 100 Miles of Main Line Pipe

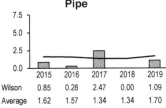

	2015	2016	2017	2018	2019
Wilson	0.85	0.28	2.47	0.00	1.09
Average	1.62	1.57	1.34	1.34	1.70

Backups per 100 Miles of Main Line Pipe

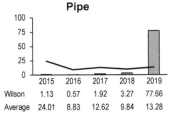

	2015	2016	2017	2018	2019
Wilson	1.13	0.57	1.92	3.27	77.66
Average	24.01	8.83	12.62	9.84	13.28

Billed Wastewater as a Percent of Treated Effluent

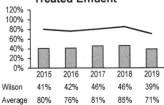

	2015	2016	2017	2018	2019
Wilson	41%	42%	46%	46%	39%
Average	80%	76%	81%	85%	71%

Explanatory Information

Service Level and Delivery

The Winston-Salem and Forsyth County Utilities Division operates a combined water and sewer system that covers the city and most of the remaining population of Forsyth County. The system also serves several adjoining areas in Davie and Davidson counties. Beyond water and wastewater, the Utilities Division also handles solid waste disposal. Operations are divided among several divisions by function.

The system has two separate treatment plants. The plants use conventional activated sludge with anaerobic digestion for treatment. The system currently does not have regulatory nutrient limits in place. Biosolids produced are disposed after first using thermal drying with subsequent reuse as a soil amendment.

During the fiscal year, the system had two regulatory violations connected to the treatment portion of the system and sixty-nine reported violations for the collection portion of the system connected to sanitary system overflows.

Conditions Affecting Service, Performance, and Costs

The costs of wastewater or sewer services as captured here do not include debt service but do capture depreciation of capital.

The city has used improvements in its GIS mapping systems and incident records to change the process by which the division ranks and proactively cleans pipes. This process is expected to lower the number of breaks and overflows.

Winston-Salem made improvements in their calculation of population served and area covered to improve the accuracy of their data. This had the effect of decreasing the reported population and size of the area served from earlier years. The changes seen in FY 2017–2018 are due to this improved estimation and not a change in services.

Municipal Profile

Estimated Service Population	297,137
Service Land Area (Square Miles)	196
Persons per Square Mile	1,516
Topography	Gently rolling
Climate	Temperate; some ice and snow
Median Household Income	$40,584
U.S. Census 2016	

Service Profile

Total FTE Staff Positions	175.2
Treatment Plant	83.0
Line Crews	65.0
Billing/Collection	8.2
Other	19.0
Number of Treatment Plants	2
Total Treatment Capacity	51.0 MGD
Average Daily Flow	37.7 MGD
River Basin into Which System Discharges	Yadkin
Miles of Gravity Main Line Pipe	1,725
Miles of Forced Main Line Pipe	36
Average Age of Main Line Pipe	50 years
Blocks in Sewer Mains	126
Number of System Breaks	82
Sanitary System Overflows	69
Number of Customer Accounts	101,325
Total Revenues Collected	$59,055,438

Full Cost Profile

Cost Breakdown by Percentage

Personal Services	26.1%
Operating Costs	35.4%
Capital Costs	38.5%
TOTAL	100.0%

Cost Breakdown in Dollars

Personal Services	$9,959,368
Operating Costs	$13,545,982
Capital Costs	$14,706,974
TOTAL	$38,212,324

Winston-Salem

Wastewater Services

Resource Measures

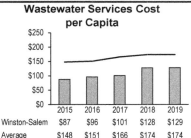

Wastewater Services Cost per Capita

	2015	2016	2017	2018	2019
Winston-Salem	$87	$96	$101	$128	$129
Average	$148	$151	$166	$174	$174

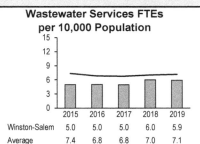

Wastewater Services FTEs per 10,000 Population

	2015	2016	2017	2018	2019
Winston-Salem	5.0	5.0	5.0	6.0	5.9
Average	7.4	6.8	6.8	7.0	7.1

Wastewater Services Cost per Customer Account

	2015	2016	2017	2018	2019
Winston-Salem	$333	$346	$362	$376	$377
Average	$421	$445	$494	$499	$492

Workload Measures

Thousands of Gallons of Wastewater per Account

	2015	2016	2017	2018	2019
Winston-Salem	110.8	124.0	119.1	114.0	135.8
Average	116.4	121.0	135.0	124.8	146.8

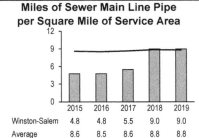

Miles of Sewer Main Line Pipe per Square Mile of Service Area

	2015	2016	2017	2018	2019
Winston-Salem	4.8	4.8	5.5	9.0	9.0
Average	8.6	8.5	8.6	8.8	8.8

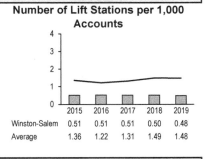

Number of Lift Stations per 1,000 Accounts

	2015	2016	2017	2018	2019
Winston-Salem	0.51	0.51	0.51	0.50	0.48
Average	1.36	1.22	1.31	1.49	1.48

Efficiency Measures

Total Cost per 1,000 Gallons of Treated Wastewater

	2015	2016	2017	2018	2019
Winston-Salem	$3.00	$2.79	$3.04	$3.30	$2.78
Average	$3.94	$3.96	$4.07	$4.34	$3.83

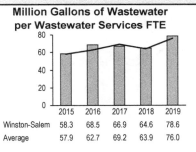

Million Gallons of Wastewater per Wastewater Services FTE

	2015	2016	2017	2018	2019
Winston-Salem	58.3	68.5	66.9	64.6	78.6
Average	57.9	62.7	69.2	63.9	76.0

Customer Accounts per Wastewater Services FTE

	2015	2016	2017	2018	2019
Winston-Salem	526	553	562	567	578
Average	540	545	547	547	567

Effectiveness Measures

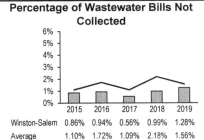

Percentage of Wastewater Bills Not Collected

	2015	2016	2017	2018	2019
Winston-Salem	0.86%	0.94%	0.56%	0.99%	1.28%
Average	1.10%	1.72%	1.09%	2.18%	1.56%

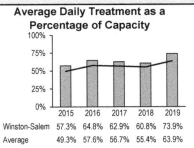

Average Daily Treatment as a Percentage of Capacity

	2015	2016	2017	2018	2019
Winston-Salem	57.3%	64.8%	62.9%	60.8%	73.9%
Average	49.3%	57.6%	56.7%	55.4%	63.9%

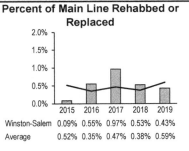

Percent of Main Line Rehabbed or Replaced

	2015	2016	2017	2018	2019
Winston-Salem	0.09%	0.55%	0.97%	0.53%	0.43%
Average	0.52%	0.35%	0.47%	0.38%	0.59%

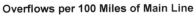

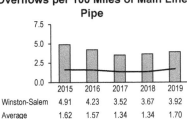

Overflows per 100 Miles of Main Line Pipe

	2015	2016	2017	2018	2019
Winston-Salem	4.91	4.23	3.52	3.67	3.92
Average	1.62	1.57	1.34	1.34	1.70

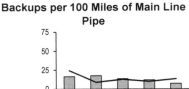

Backups per 100 Miles of Main Line Pipe

	2015	2016	2017	2018	2019
Winston-Salem	16.34	17.54	13.34	11.75	7.16
Average	24.01	8.83	12.62	9.84	13.28

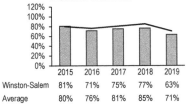

Billed Wastewater as a Percent of Treated Effluent

	2015	2016	2017	2018	2019
Winston-Salem	81%	71%	75%	77%	63%
Average	80%	76%	81%	85%	71%

Performance and Cost Data

CORE PARKS AND RECREATION

PERFORMANCE MEASURES FOR CORE PARKS AND RECREATION SERVICES

SERVICE DEFINITION

Parks and Recreation includes both passive and active recreation opportunities maintained and operated by a local government. For the purposes of this benchmarking effort, this includes core operational functions, such as parks, multipurpose recreation facilities, athletic facilities, greenways, and trails. This also includes programs and events.

However, Parks and Recreation departments frequently may include a variety of other activities and facilities. To support reasonable comparisons, this service benchmarking excludes these secondary recreational activities, including performance venues, museums, historic sites, golf courses, marinas/boat ramps, and professional stadiums. Also excluded are other non-recreational activities sometimes performed by parks and recreation departments, such as care of cemeteries; maintenance of rights-of-way along city streets; maintenance of facilities owned by a municipality but not parks-related; and maintenance of city lots. The dollars and people associated with these secondary and non-park activities are excluded.

Parks and Recreation does offer an important difference from many of the other services provided by local governments. Much of the objective of this service area is to provide facilities for use by citizens. Use of many of these facilities is not easily tracked. Many of the measures shown for this service area are accordingly measures of facility availability rather than the traditional workload type of measures seen in other service areas.

NOTES ON PERFORMANCE MEASURES

1. Land Acres of All Municipal Parks per 10,000 Population
This resource measure captures the amount of park land that is available relative to the population in the communities.

2. Recreation Centers per 10,000 Population
Recreation centers provide space for a variety of indoor recreational activities. This measure shows the number of centers relative to the population.

3. Swimming Pools per 10,000 Population
Indoor and outdoor pools are a desirable recreational facility. This resource measure captures the number of pools relative to the population.

4. Athletic Fields per 10,000 Population
Outdoor athletic fields are used for organized and informal recreation. This measure counts the number of formal athletic fields, including rectangular fields such as those for football and soccer, diamond fields as for baseball, and nondesignated fields that can be used for multiple activities. The count includes both natural grass and artificial-surface fields, where available.

5. Playgrounds per 10,000 Population

Formal playgrounds include a variety of fixed equipment, such as swings, jungle gyms, slides, and other apparatus. This measure captures these playgrounds relative to the population.

6. Miles of Trails per 10,000 Population

Outdoor trails of all types represent an important type of active recreation. This measure captures the total miles of trails in a community relative to the population. The miles total includes paved and unpaved trails and covers various types of trail, such as those for walking, bike riding, and equestrian riding.

7. Total Core Parks and Recreation Costs

This efficiency measure represents the level of spending relative to the park acreage in a community. Although funds may be spent on facilities and activities, this measure provides some comparison of the intensity of spending.

8. Acres of Park Maintained per Maintenance Full-Time Equivalent (FTE)

This efficiency measure compares the amount of acres in the park system relative to the number of FTEs used by a jurisdiction to provide maintenance.

9. Volunteer Hours in FTEs as a Percent of Paid Staff FTEs

Volunteers represent an important resource to help support Parks and Recreation activities. This efficiency measure compares the estimated amount of volunteer labor relative to the paid staff in order to provide a measure of the benefit these volunteers bring to a community.

10. Revenue Gained as a Percent of Total Core Parks and Recreation Costs

Parks and Recreation is a service that is primarily supported by general funding from a local government budget. But gaining additional revenues in the form of user fees, grants, donations, and sponsorships helps to leverage spending and provide services. This effectiveness measure shows how much revenue has been raised from these other sources relative to the total costs reported.

11. Acts of Vandalism per 10,000 Population

Vandalism damages parks and recreation facilities, making them unavailable or less useful to citizens. This effectiveness measure compares the number of acts of vandalism relative to the population to indicate the extent of this problem.

Core Parks and Recreation

Summary of Key Dimensions of Service

City or Town	Municipal Population as of July 2018	Core Parks and Recreation FTEs	Number of Parks	Park Land Acreage	Number of Recreation and Senior Centers	Number of Playgrounds	Number of Athletic Fields	Miles of Trails
Apex	52,909	41.5	13	618.3	1	12	27	20.8
Asheville	93,621	127.0	47	869.0	13	24	27	5.7
Chapel Hill	63,178	77.5	31	1,114.0	2	11	16	15.5
Concord	92,568	33.5	9	226.0	4	13	23	12.2
Goldsboro	33,636	40.5	14	233.0	3	11	23	5.5
Greensboro	292,306	173.3	425	9,155.3	12	105	75	95.8
Greenville	89,790	71.3	27	1,468.6	8	18	24	9.0
Hickory	40,932	50.0	26	558.0	8	40	25	16.1
Mooresville	41,255	78.4	24	370.0	4	13	28	10.9
Raleigh	464,453	765.3	175	6,127.0	41	96	100	134.0
Wilson	49,054	52.0	28	400.0	4	26	26	7.5
Winston-Salem	243,447	219.9	82	3,894.8	17	46	97	23.3

EXPLANATORY FACTORS

These are some factors that the project found affected core parks and recreation services performance and cost in one or more of the municipalities:

Youth Population
Total Acreage
Miles of Trails
Number of Facilities

Explanatory Information

Service Level and Delivery

The Town of Apex provides recreation services through the separate Parks, Recreation, and Cultural Resources Department. The city has priority use agreements with the Wake County School System in exchange for maintenance of areas used by the town.

The town has thirteen separate parks and sites. These parks cover 618 land acres; most of this area is currently developed. The city has nearly twenty-one miles of trails.

In addition to the core parks and recreational facilities, Apex has a performing arts center. The operation of this other facility is not included in the Core Parks and Recreation comparisons reported here. This facility is not included here in dollars or staff as part of core parks and recreation facilities and activities.

Conditions Affecting Service, Performance, and Costs

Municipal Profile	
Population (OSBM 2018)	52,909
Land Area (Square Miles)	21.55
Persons per Square Mile	2,455
Topography	Flat; gently rolling
Climate	Temperate; little ice and snow

Service Profile	
Parks and Recreation Staff	
Administrative Position FTEs	5.0
Maintenance Staff FTEs	25.5
Program and Facility FTEs	11.0
Other Staff FTEs	0.0
TOTAL	41.5
Number of Parks and Sites	13
Total Land Acreage in Parks	618.3
Miles of Trails in Parks	20.8
Recreational Facilities	
Indoor and Outdoor Pools	0
Recreation Centers	1
Outdoor Basketball Courts	15
Outdoor Tennis Courts	15
Playgrounds	12
Diamond Fields	13
Rectangular Fields	12
Other Athletic Fields	2
Picnic Shelters	11
Parks and Recreation Revenues	
User Fees	$1,089,168
Grants	$1,138,350
Sponsorships	$0
Donations	$0

Full Cost Profile	
Cost Breakdown by Percentage	
Personal Services	46.7%
Operating Costs	43.8%
Capital Costs	9.5%
TOTAL	100.0%
Cost Breakdown in Dollars	
Personal Services	$2,332,747
Operating Costs	$2,187,146
Capital Costs	$472,720
TOTAL	$4,992,613

Resource Measures

Core Parks and Recreation Services per Capita

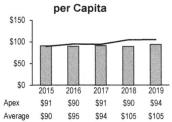

	2015	2016	2017	2018	2019
Apex	$91	$90	$91	$90	$94
Average	$90	$95	$94	$105	$105

Core Parks and Recreation Staff per 10,000 Population

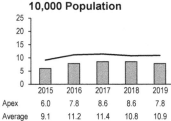

	2015	2016	2017	2018	2019
Apex	6.0	7.8	8.6	8.6	7.8
Average	9.1	11.2	11.4	10.8	10.9

Facilities Measures

Land Acres of Parks per 10,000 Population

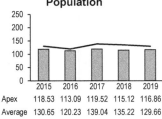

	2015	2016	2017	2018	2019
Apex	118.53	113.09	119.52	115.12	116.86
Average	130.65	120.23	139.04	135.22	129.66

Recreation Centers per 10,000 Population

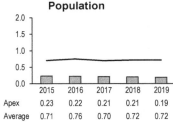

	2015	2016	2017	2018	2019
Apex	0.23	0.22	0.21	0.21	0.19
Average	0.71	0.76	0.70	0.72	0.72

Swimming Pools per 10,000 Population

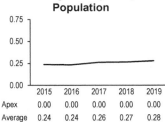

	2015	2016	2017	2018	2019
Apex	0.00	0.00	0.00	0.00	0.00
Average	0.24	0.24	0.26	0.27	0.28

Athletic Fields per 10,000 Population

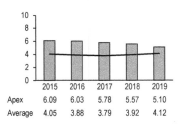

	2015	2016	2017	2018	2019
Apex	6.09	6.03	5.78	5.57	5.10
Average	4.05	3.88	3.79	3.92	4.12

Playgrounds per 10,000 Population

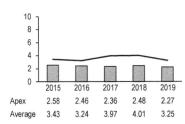

	2015	2016	2017	2018	2019
Apex	2.58	2.46	2.36	2.48	2.27
Average	3.43	3.24	3.97	4.01	3.25

Miles of Land Trails per 10,000 Population

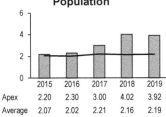

	2015	2016	2017	2018	2019
Apex	2.20	2.30	3.00	4.02	3.92
Average	2.07	2.02	2.21	2.16	2.19

Efficiency Measures

Total Core Parks and Recreation Costs per Acre

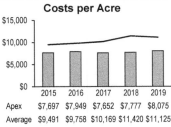

	2015	2016	2017	2018	2019
Apex	$7,697	$7,949	$7,652	$7,777	$8,075
Average	$9,491	$9,758	$10,169	$11,420	$11,125

Acres of Park Maintained per Maintenance FTE

	2015	2016	2017	2018	2019
Apex	31.6	31.6	26.8	27.5	24.2
Average	46.0	37.7	45.5	41.8	38.3

Volunteer Hours in FTEs as a Percent of Paid Staff FTEs

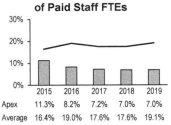

	2015	2016	2017	2018	2019
Apex	11.3%	8.2%	7.2%	7.0%	7.0%
Average	16.4%	19.0%	17.6%	17.6%	19.1%

Effectiveness Measures

Revenue Gained as a Percent of Total Core Costs

	2015	2016	2017	2018	2019
Apex	23.2%	22.7%	22.9%	26.3%	44.6%
Average	13.2%	13.6%	14.1%	15.1%	15.3%

Acts of Vandalism at Parks Facilities per 10,000 Population

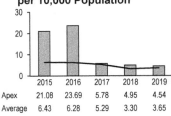

	2015	2016	2017	2018	2019
Apex	21.08	23.69	5.78	4.95	4.54
Average	6.43	6.28	5.29	3.30	3.65

Fiscal Year 2018–19

Explanatory Information

Service Level and Delivery

The City of Asheville provides recreation services through the separate Parks and Recreation Department. The city has formal agreements and partnerships with athletic associations, non-profits, universities, individuals, and for-profit organizations for the provision of recreational services.

The city has forty-seven separate parks and sites. These parks cover 869 land acres; about three-fourths of them are currently developed. The city has nearly six miles of trails.

In addition to the core parks and recreational facilities, Asheville has two large outdoor performance event sites and runs an eighteen-hole municipal golf course. The operation of these other facilities is not included in the Core Parks and Recreation comparisons reported here. These facilities are not included here in dollars or staff as part of core parks and recreation facilities and activities.

Conditions Affecting Service, Performance, and Costs

Municipal Profile

Population (OSBM 2018)	93,621
Land Area (Square Miles)	45.53
Persons per Square Mile	2,056
Topography	Hilly, mountains
Climate	Moderate; ice and snow

Service Profile

Parks and Recreation Staff	
Administrative Position FTEs	15.0
Maintenance Staff FTEs	41.0
Program and Facility FTEs	71.0
Other Staff FTEs	0.0
TOTAL	127.0
Number of Parks and Sites	47
Total Land Acreage in Parks	869.0
Miles of Trails in Parks	5.7
Recreational Facilities	
Indoor and Outdoor Pools	3
Recreation Centers	13
Outdoor Basketball Courts	15
Outdoor Tennis Courts	26
Playgrounds	24
Diamond Fields	19
Rectangular Fields	5
Other Athletic Fields	3
Picnic Shelters	11
Parks and Recreation Revenues	
User Fees	$636,441
Grants	$18,089
Sponsorships	$4,610
Donations	$10,913

Full Cost Profile

Cost Breakdown by Percentage	
Personal Services	52.1%
Operating Costs	35.9%
Capital Costs	12.0%
TOTAL	100.0%
Cost Breakdown in Dollars	
Personal Services	$6,389,933
Operating Costs	$4,405,555
Capital Costs	$1,473,283
TOTAL	$12,268,771

Key: Asheville ▨   Benchmarking Average —   Fiscal Years 2015 through 2019

Resource Measures

Core Parks and Recreation Services per Capita

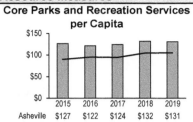

	2015	2016	2017	2018	2019
Asheville	$127	$122	$124	$132	$131
Average	$90	$95	$94	$105	$105

Core Parks and Recreation Staff per 10,000 Population

	2015	2016	2017	2018	2019
Asheville	10.5	14.6	14.4	10.2	13.6
Average	9.1	11.2	11.4	10.8	10.9

Facilities Measures

Land Acres of Parks per 10,000 Population

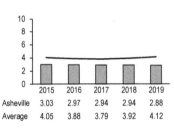

	2015	2016	2017	2018	2019
Asheville	97.36	95.58	94.52	94.54	92.82
Average	130.65	120.23	139.04	135.22	129.66

Recreation Centers per 10,000 Population

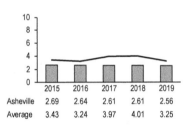

	2015	2016	2017	2018	2019
Asheville	1.23	1.21	1.20	1.20	1.17
Average	0.71	0.76	0.70	0.72	0.72

Swimming Pools per 10,000 Population

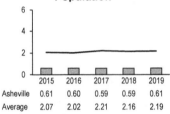

	2015	2016	2017	2018	2019
Asheville	0.34	0.33	0.33	0.33	0.32
Average	0.24	0.24	0.26	0.27	0.28

Athletic Fields per 10,000 Population

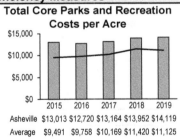

	2015	2016	2017	2018	2019
Asheville	3.03	2.97	2.94	2.94	2.88
Average	4.05	3.88	3.79	3.92	4.12

Playgrounds per 10,000 Population

	2015	2016	2017	2018	2019
Asheville	2.69	2.64	2.61	2.61	2.56
Average	3.43	3.24	3.97	4.01	3.25

Miles of Land Trails per 10,000 Population

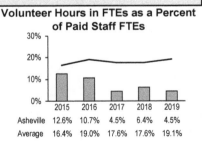

	2015	2016	2017	2018	2019
Asheville	0.61	0.60	0.59	0.59	0.61
Average	2.07	2.02	2.21	2.16	2.19

Efficiency Measures

Total Core Parks and Recreation Costs per Acre

	2015	2016	2017	2018	2019
Asheville	$13,013	$12,720	$13,164	$13,952	$14,119
Average	$9,491	$9,758	$10,169	$11,420	$11,125

Acres of Park Maintained per Maintenance FTE

	2015	2016	2017	2018	2019
Asheville	28.7	21.5	21.5	27.6	21.2
Average	46.0	37.7	45.5	41.8	38.3

Volunteer Hours in FTEs as a Percent of Paid Staff FTEs

	2015	2016	2017	2018	2019
Asheville	12.6%	10.7%	4.5%	6.4%	4.5%
Average	16.4%	19.0%	17.6%	17.6%	19.1%

Effectiveness Measures

Revenue Gained as a Percent of Total Core Costs

	2015	2016	2017	2018	2019
Asheville	11.7%	14.6%	18.4%	16.2%	5.5%
Average	13.2%	13.6%	14.1%	15.1%	15.3%

Acts of Vandalism at Parks Facilities per 10,000 Population

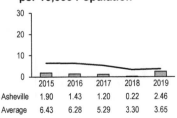

	2015	2016	2017	2018	2019
Asheville	1.90	1.43	1.20	0.22	2.46
Average	6.43	6.28	5.29	3.30	3.65

Fiscal Year 2018–19

Service Level and Delivery

The Town of Chapel Hill provides recreation services through the separate Parks and Recreation Department. The town has agreements with Orange County for use of the senior center and county resident participation in other programs. The town also has agreements with the Town of Carrboro, the Street Scene Teen Center, Holmes Childcare Center, and Chapel Hill-Carrboro City Schools.

The town has thirty-one separate parks and sites. These parks cover 1,114 land acres, much of which is currently undeveloped. The town has about sixteen miles of trails.

Conditions Affecting Service, Performance, and Costs

The Town of Chapel Hill began participation in the benchmarking project in July 2015, with FY 2014–15 being the first reporting year.

Municipal Profile

Population (OSBM 2018)	63,178
Land Area (Square Miles)	21.27
Persons per Square Mile	2,971
Topography	Flat; gently rolling
Climate	Temperate; little ice and snow

Service Profile

Parks and Recreation Staff

Administrative Position FTEs	7.0
Maintenance Staff FTEs	15.5
Program and Facility FTEs	55.0
Other Staff FTEs	0.0
TOTAL	77.5

Number of Parks and Sites	31
Total Land Acreage in Parks	1,114.0
Miles of Trails in Parks	15.5

Recreational Facilities

Indoor and Outdoor Pools	3
Recreation Centers	2
Outdoor Basketball Courts	7
Outdoor Tennis Courts	18
Playgrounds	11
Diamond Fields	7
Rectangular Fields	9
Other Athletic Fields	0
Picnic Shelters	8

Parks and Recreation Revenues

User Fees	$1,356,670
Grants	$0
Sponsorships	$82,630
Donations	$300

Full Cost Profile

Cost Breakdown by Percentage

Personal Services	47.3%
Operating Costs	41.7%
Capital Costs	10.9%
TOTAL	100.0%

Cost Breakdown in Dollars

Personal Services	$3,536,175
Operating Costs	$3,117,073
Capital Costs	$817,443
TOTAL	$7,470,691

Chapel Hill

Core Parks and Recreation

Key: Chapel Hill ▦ Benchmarking Average — Fiscal Years 2015 through 2019

Resource Measures

Core Parks and Recreation Services per Capita

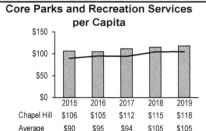

	2015	2016	2017	2018	2019
Chapel Hill	$106	$105	$112	$115	$118
Average	$90	$95	$94	$105	$105

Core Parks and Recreation Staff per 10,000 Population

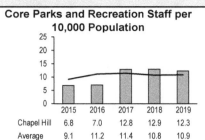

	2015	2016	2017	2018	2019
Chapel Hill	6.8	7.0	12.8	12.9	12.3
Average	9.1	11.2	11.4	10.8	10.9

Facilities Measures

Land Acres of Parks per 10,000 Population

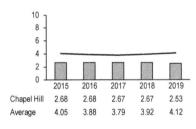

	2015	2016	2017	2018	2019
Chapel Hill	180.73	181.53	186.13	185.97	176.33
Average	130.65	120.23	139.04	135.22	129.66

Recreation Centers per 10,000 Population

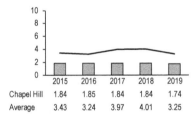

	2015	2016	2017	2018	2019
Chapel Hill	0.33	0.34	0.33	0.33	0.32
Average	0.71	0.76	0.70	0.72	0.72

Swimming Pools per 10,000 Population

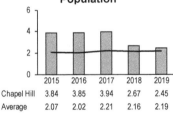

	2015	2016	2017	2018	2019
Chapel Hill	0.50	0.50	0.50	0.50	0.47
Average	0.24	0.24	0.26	0.27	0.28

Athletic Fields per 10,000 Population

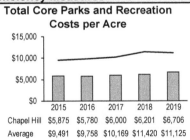

	2015	2016	2017	2018	2019
Chapel Hill	2.68	2.68	2.67	2.67	2.53
Average	4.05	3.88	3.79	3.92	4.12

Playgrounds per 10,000 Population

	2015	2016	2017	2018	2019
Chapel Hill	1.84	1.85	1.84	1.84	1.74
Average	3.43	3.24	3.97	4.01	3.25

Miles of Land Trails per 10,000 Population

	2015	2016	2017	2018	2019
Chapel Hill	3.84	3.85	3.94	2.67	2.45
Average	2.07	2.02	2.21	2.16	2.19

Efficiency Measures

Total Core Parks and Recreation Costs per Acre

	2015	2016	2017	2018	2019
Chapel Hill	$5,875	$5,780	$6,000	$6,201	$6,706
Average	$9,491	$9,758	$10,169	$11,420	$11,125

Acres of Park Maintained per Maintenance FTE

	2015	2016	2017	2018	2019
Chapel Hill	80.0	80.1	82.5	71.9	71.9
Average	46.0	37.7	45.5	41.8	38.3

Volunteer Hours in FTEs as a Percent of Paid Staff FTEs

	2015	2016	2017	2018	2019
Chapel Hill	29.8%	32.8%	17.4%	13.2%	10.8%
Average	16.4%	19.0%	17.6%	17.6%	19.1%

Effectiveness Measures

Revenue Gained as a Percent of Total Core Costs

	2015	2016	2017	2018	2019
Chapel Hill	22.8%	19.1%	17.3%	20.8%	19.3%
Average	13.2%	13.6%	14.1%	15.1%	15.3%

Acts of Vandalism at Parks Facilities per 10,000 Population

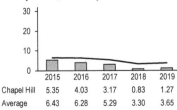

	2015	2016	2017	2018	2019
Chapel Hill	5.35	4.03	3.17	0.83	1.27
Average	6.43	6.28	5.29	3.30	3.65

Concord

Fiscal Year 2018–19

Explanatory Information

Service Level and Delivery
The City of Concord provides recreation services through the separate Parks and Recreation Department. The city provides an array of facilities and activities for recreation.

The city has nine separate parks and sites. These parks cover 226 land acres. The city has over twelve miles of recreational trails, most of them paved.

In addition to the core parks and recreational facilities, Concord has one large outdoor performance event site and one boat ramp. The operation of these other facilities is not included in the Core Parks and Recreation comparisons reported here. These facilities are not included here in dollars or staff as part of core parks and recreation facilities and activities.

Conditions Affecting Service, Performance, and Costs

Municipal Profile

Population (OSBM 2018)	92,568
Land Area (Square Miles)	62.80
Persons per Square Mile	1,474
Topography	Flat; gently rolling
Climate	Temperate; little ice and snow

Service Profile

Parks and Recreation Staff

Administrative Position FTEs	6.0
Maintenance Staff FTEs	0.0
Program and Facility FTEs	25.5
Other Staff FTEs	2.0
TOTAL	33.5
Number of Parks and Sites	9
Total Land Acreage in Parks	226.0
Miles of Trails in Parks	12.2

Recreational Facilities

Indoor and Outdoor Pools	1
Recreation Centers	4
Outdoor Basketball Courts	5
Outdoor Tennis Courts	14
Playgrounds	13
Diamond Fields	13
Rectangular Fields	7
Other Athletic Fields	3
Picnic Shelters	14

Parks and Recreation Revenues

User Fees	$354,240
Grants	$470,000
Sponsorships	$9,350
Donations	$0

Full Cost Profile

Cost Breakdown by Percentage

Personal Services	29.5%
Operating Costs	64.0%
Capital Costs	6.4%
TOTAL	100.0%

Cost Breakdown in Dollars

Personal Services	$1,754,514
Operating Costs	$3,807,410
Capital Costs	$382,643
TOTAL	$5,944,567

Concord

Core Parks and Recreation

Key: Concord ▦   Benchmarking Average —   Fiscal Years 2015 through 2019

Resource Measures

Core Parks and Recreation Services per Capita

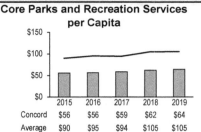

	2015	2016	2017	2018	2019
Concord	$56	$56	$59	$62	$64
Average	$90	$95	$94	$105	$105

Core Parks and Recreation Staff per 10,000 Population

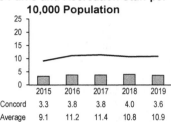

	2015	2016	2017	2018	2019
Concord	3.3	3.8	3.8	4.0	3.6
Average	9.1	11.2	11.4	10.8	10.9

Facilities Measures

Land Acres of Parks per 10,000 Population

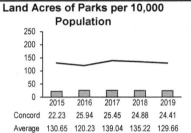

	2015	2016	2017	2018	2019
Concord	22.23	25.94	25.45	24.88	24.41
Average	130.65	120.23	139.04	135.22	129.66

Recreation Centers per 10,000 Population

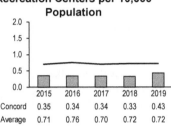

	2015	2016	2017	2018	2019
Concord	0.35	0.34	0.34	0.33	0.43
Average	0.71	0.76	0.70	0.72	0.72

Swimming Pools per 10,000 Population

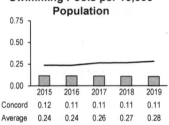

	2015	2016	2017	2018	2019
Concord	0.12	0.11	0.11	0.11	0.11
Average	0.24	0.24	0.26	0.27	0.28

Athletic Fields per 10,000 Population

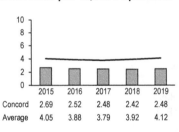

	2015	2016	2017	2018	2019
Concord	2.69	2.52	2.48	2.42	2.48
Average	4.05	3.88	3.79	3.92	4.12

Playgrounds per 10,000 Population

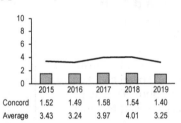

	2015	2016	2017	2018	2019
Concord	1.52	1.49	1.58	1.54	1.40
Average	3.43	3.24	3.97	4.01	3.25

Miles of Land Trails per 10,000 Population

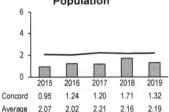

	2015	2016	2017	2018	2019
Concord	0.95	1.24	1.20	1.71	1.32
Average	2.07	2.02	2.21	2.16	2.19

Efficiency Measures

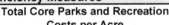

Total Core Parks and Recreation Costs per Acre

	2015	2016	2017	2018	2019
Concord	$24,980	$21,782	$23,056	$24,913	$26,303
Average	$9,491	$9,758	$10,169	$11,420	$11,125

Acres of Park Maintained per Maintenance FTE

	2015	2016	2017	2018	2019
Concord					
Average	46.0	37.7	45.5	41.8	38.3

Volunteer Hours in FTEs as a Percent of Paid Staff FTEs

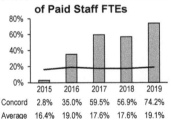

	2015	2016	2017	2018	2019
Concord	2.8%	35.0%	59.5%	56.9%	74.2%
Average	16.4%	19.0%	17.6%	17.6%	19.1%

Effectiveness Measures

Revenue Gained as a Percent of Total Core Costs

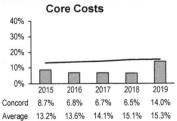

	2015	2016	2017	2018	2019
Concord	8.7%	6.8%	6.7%	6.5%	14.0%
Average	13.2%	13.6%	14.1%	15.1%	15.3%

Acts of Vandalism at Parks Facilities per 10,000 Population

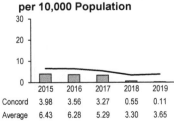

	2015	2016	2017	2018	2019
Concord	3.98	3.56	3.27	0.55	0.11
Average	6.43	6.28	5.29	3.30	3.65

Fiscal Year 2018–19

Explanatory Information

Service Level and Delivery

The City of Goldsboro provides recreation services through the separate Parks and Recreation Department. The department aims to serve the community through programs in youth athletics, adult athletics, seniors, and special populations both adult and youth. The city has a cooperative agreement with the public school system. The city has also formalized an agreement with the U.S. Air Force Base Seymour Johnson for the use of certain base facilities. County residents from outside the city are also users of the Goldsboro city system facilities and programmed activities.

The city has fourteen separate parks covering 233 acres. There are about six miles of trails, two outdoor pools, greenways, and a number of school indoor and outdoor facilities.

In addition to the core parks and recreational facilities, Goldsboro has a historic property and a farmers' market. The city also runs a municipal golf course. The operation of this course is not included here in dollars or staff as part of core parks and recreation facilities and activities.

Conditions Affecting Service, Performance, and Costs

The city of Goldsboro joined the Benchmarking Project in July 2017, with the first year of data showing for FY 2016–17.

There are no extra fees charged for non-resident users of Goldsboro's facilities. The department has teamed up with the Travel and Tourism Department to bring sports tournaments to Goldsboro. This helps expose more people to the city's offering of services and facilities.

Municipal Profile

Population (OSBM 2018)	33,636
Land Area (Square Miles)	29.41
Persons per Square Mile	1,144
Topography	Flat
Climate	Temperate; little ice and snow

Service Profile

Parks and Recreation Staff	
Administrative Position FTEs	5.0
Maintenance Staff FTEs	21.3
Program and Facility FTEs	14.3
Other Staff FTEs	0.0
TOTAL	40.5

Number of Parks and Sites	14
Total Land Acreage in Parks	233.0
Miles of Trails in Parks	5.5

Recreational Facilities	
Indoor and Outdoor Pools	2
Recreation Centers	3
Outdoor Basketball Courts	11
Outdoor Tennis Courts	18
Playgrounds	11
Diamond Fields	4
Rectangular Fields	13
Other Athletic Fields	6
Picnic Shelters	14

Parks and Recreation Revenues	
User Fees	$167,569
Grants	$2,743
Sponsorships	$37,684
Donations	$0

Full Cost Profile

Cost Breakdown by Percentage	
Personal Services	66.8%
Operating Costs	27.3%
Capital Costs	5.9%
TOTAL	100.0%

Cost Breakdown in Dollars	
Personal Services	$2,398,517
Operating Costs	$981,056
Capital Costs	$213,369
TOTAL	$3,592,942

Goldsboro

Core Parks and Recreation

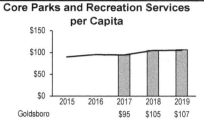

Key: Goldsboro   Benchmarking Average —   Fiscal Years 2015 through 2019

Resource Measures

Core Parks and Recreation Services per Capita

	2015	2016	2017	2018	2019
Goldsboro			$95	$105	$107
Average	$90	$95	$94	$105	$105

Core Parks and Recreation Staff per 10,000 Population

	2015	2016	2017	2018	2019
Goldsboro			13.3	16.1	12.0
Average	9.1	11.2	11.4	10.8	10.9

Facilities Measures

Land Acres of Parks per 10,000 Population

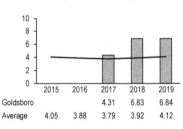

	2015	2016	2017	2018	2019
Goldsboro			48.51	50.47	69.27
Average	130.65	120.23	139.04	135.22	129.66

Recreation Centers per 10,000 Population

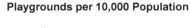
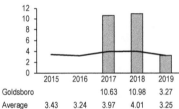

	2015	2016	2017	2018	2019
Goldsboro			0.57	0.59	0.59
Average	0.71	0.76	0.70	0.72	0.72

Swimming Pools per 10,000 Population

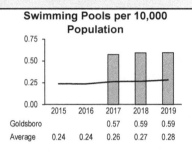
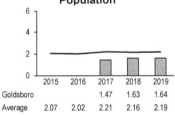

	2015	2016	2017	2018	2019
Goldsboro			0.57	0.59	0.59
Average	0.24	0.24	0.26	0.27	0.28

Athletic Fields per 10,000 Population

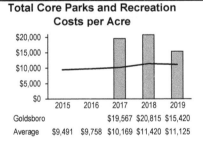

	2015	2016	2017	2018	2019
Goldsboro			4.31	6.83	6.84
Average	4.05	3.88	3.79	3.92	4.12

Playgrounds per 10,000 Population

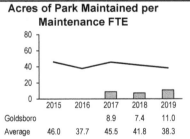

	2015	2016	2017	2018	2019
Goldsboro			10.63	10.98	3.27
Average	3.43	3.24	3.97	4.01	3.25

Miles of Land Trails per 10,000 Population

	2015	2016	2017	2018	2019
Goldsboro			1.47	1.63	1.64
Average	2.07	2.02	2.21	2.16	2.19

Efficiency Measures

Total Core Parks and Recreation Costs per Acre

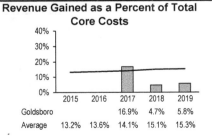

	2015	2016	2017	2018	2019
Goldsboro			$19,567	$20,815	$15,420
Average	$9,491	$9,758	$10,169	$11,420	$11,125

Acres of Park Maintained per Maintenance FTE

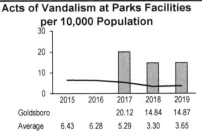

	2015	2016	2017	2018	2019
Goldsboro			8.9	7.4	11.0
Average	46.0	37.7	45.5	41.8	38.3

Volunteer Hours in FTEs as a Percent of Paid Staff FTEs

	2015	2016	2017	2018	2019
Goldsboro			0.5%	0.4%	1.2%
Average	16.4%	19.0%	17.6%	17.6%	19.1%

Effectiveness Measures

Revenue Gained as a Percent of Total Core Costs

	2015	2016	2017	2018	2019
Goldsboro			16.9%	4.7%	5.8%
Average	13.2%	13.6%	14.1%	15.1%	15.3%

Acts of Vandalism at Parks Facilities per 10,000 Population

	2015	2016	2017	2018	2019
Goldsboro			20.12	14.84	14.87
Average	6.43	6.28	5.29	3.30	3.65

Greensboro

Core Parks and Recreation

Fiscal Year 2018–19

Explanatory Information

Service Level and Delivery

The City of Greensboro provides recreation services through the separate Parks and Recreation Department. The city has several cooperative agreements with the local schools and some non-profits for the provision of services or use of facilities. The city provides a full array of recreational facilities and activities.

The city has 425 separate parks and sites. These parks cover 9,155 land acres; most of them are developed and include dedicated drainageway and open spaces. In addition, the city has a number of acres in water space as part of the parks system. The city has 98 miles of trails.

In addition to the core parks and recreational facilities, Greensboro has a large outdoor performance event site, a historic property, a famers' market, a boat ramp and marina, and operates two municipal golf courses, four municipal cemetaries, and four botanical gardens. The operation of these other facilities is not included in the Core Parks and Recreation comparisons reported here. These facilities are not included here in dollars or staff as part of core parks and recreation facilities and activities.

Conditions Affecting Service, Performance, and Costs

Greensboro did not report data for Core Parks and Recreation services for FY 2015–16.

Greensboro has been updating its lists of properties, including a number of drainage way and open space properties that were dedicated to the city but never accepted. These parcels have been added to the inventory of parks, which has increased the number of parks reported.

Municipal Profile

Population (OSBM 2018)	292,306
Land Area (Square Miles)	128.77
Persons per Square Mile	2,270
Topography	Flat
Climate	Temperate; little ice and snow

Service Profile

Parks and Recreation Staff

Administrative Position FTEs	19.5
Maintenance Staff FTEs	90.5
Program and Facility FTEs	63.3
Other Staff FTEs	0.0
TOTAL	173.3

Number of Parks and Sites	425
Total Land Acreage in Parks	9,155.3
Miles of Trails in Parks	98.0

Recreational Facilities

Indoor and Outdoor Pools	5
Recreation Centers	12
Outdoor Basketball Courts	46
Outdoor Tennis Courts	75
Playgrounds	105
Diamond Fields	39
Rectangular Fields	36
Other Athletic Fields	0
Picnic Shelters	39

Parks and Recreation Revenues

User Fees	$1,648,811
Grants	$53,193
Sponsorships	$14,400
Donations	$92,365

Full Cost Profile

Cost Breakdown by Percentage

Personal Services	60.3%
Operating Costs	39.7%
Capital Costs	0.0%
TOTAL	100.0%

Cost Breakdown in Dollars

Personal Services	$10,983,889
Operating Costs	$7,240,694
Capital Costs	$0
TOTAL	$18,224,583

Greensboro

Core Parks and Recreation

Resource Measures

Core Parks and Recreation Services per Capita

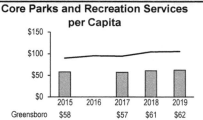

	2015	2016	2017	2018	2019
Greensboro	$58		$57	$61	$62
Average	$90	$95	$94	$105	$105

Core Parks and Recreation Staff per 10,000 Population

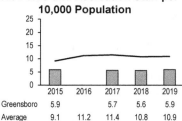

	2015	2016	2017	2018	2019
Greensboro	5.9		5.7	5.6	5.9
Average	9.1	11.2	11.4	10.8	10.9

Facilities Measures

Land Acres of Parks per 10,000 Population

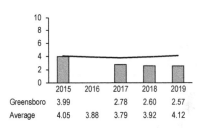

	2015	2016	2017	2018	2019
Greensboro	227.21		383.59	387.24	313.21
Average	130.65	120.23	139.04	135.22	129.66

Recreation Centers per 10,000 Population

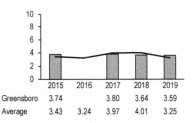

	2015	2016	2017	2018	2019
Greensboro	0.39		0.39	0.38	0.38
Average	0.71	0.76	0.70	0.72	0.72

Swimming Pools per 10,000 Population

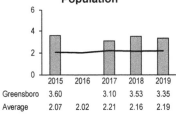

	2015	2016	2017	2018	2019
Greensboro	0.21		0.18	0.17	0.17
Average	0.24	0.24	0.26	0.27	0.28

Athletic Fields per 10,000 Population

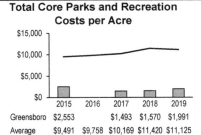

	2015	2016	2017	2018	2019
Greensboro	3.99		2.78	2.60	2.57
Average	4.05	3.88	3.79	3.92	4.12

Playgrounds per 10,000 Population

	2015	2016	2017	2018	2019
Greensboro	3.74		3.80	3.64	3.59
Average	3.43	3.24	3.97	4.01	3.25

Miles of Land Trails per 10,000 Population

	2015	2016	2017	2018	2019
Greensboro	3.60		3.10	3.53	3.35
Average	2.07	2.02	2.21	2.16	2.19

Efficiency Measures

Total Core Parks and Recreation Costs per Acre

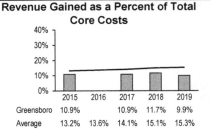

	2015	2016	2017	2018	2019
Greensboro	$2,553		$1,493	$1,570	$1,991
Average	$9,491	$9,758	$10,169	$11,420	$11,125

Acres of Park Maintained per Maintenance FTE

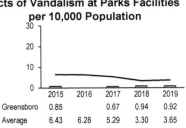

	2015	2016	2017	2018	2019
Greensboro	80.3		138.9	142.2	101.1
Average	46.0	37.7	45.5	41.8	38.3

Volunteer Hours in FTEs as a Percent of Paid Staff FTEs

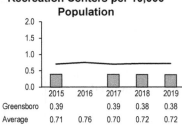

	2015	2016	2017	2018	2019
Greensboro	15.2%		16.3%	13.1%	8.2%
Average	16.4%	19.0%	17.6%	17.6%	19.1%

Effectiveness Measures

Revenue Gained as a Percent of Total Core Costs

	2015	2016	2017	2018	2019
Greensboro	10.9%		10.9%	11.7%	9.9%
Average	13.2%	13.6%	14.1%	15.1%	15.3%

Acts of Vandalism at Parks Facilities per 10,000 Population

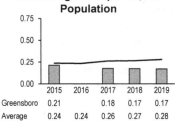

	2015	2016	2017	2018	2019
Greensboro	0.85		0.67	0.94	0.92
Average	6.43	6.28	5.29	3.30	3.65

Fiscal Year 2018–19

Service Level and Delivery

The City of Greenville provides recreation services through the separate Recreation and Parks Department. The city has a number of ad hoc or handshake agreements with other organizations but is moving to more formal agreements. Partner groups include Pitt County, local sports organizations, and concert entertainment groups.

The city has twenty-seven separate parks and sites. These parks cover 1,469 acres; about two-thirds of them are developed. The city has nine miles of trails.

In addition to the core parks and recreational facilities, Greenville has a large outdoor performance event site, a historic property, a boat ramp, a museum, and an eighteen-hole golf course. The operation of these other facilities is not included in the Core Parks and Recreation comparisons reported here. These facilities are not included here in dollars or staff as part of core parks and recreation facilities and activities.

Conditions Affecting Service, Performance, and Costs

Municipal Profile

Population (OSBM 2018)	89,790
Land Area (Square Miles)	35.58
Persons per Square Mile	2,523
Topography	Flat
Climate	Temperate; little ice and snow

Service Profile

Parks and Recreation Staff	
Administrative Position FTEs	8.0
Maintenance Staff FTEs	35.3
Program and Facility FTEs	25.0
Other Staff FTEs	3.0
TOTAL	71.3

Number of Parks and Sites	27
Total Land Acreage in Parks	1,468.6
Miles of Trails in Parks	9.0

Recreational Facilities	
Indoor and Outdoor Pools	2
Recreation Centers	8
Outdoor Basketball Courts	1
Outdoor Tennis Courts	20
Playgrounds	18
Diamond Fields	16
Rectangular Fields	5
Other Athletic Fields	3
Picnic Shelters	24

Parks and Recreation Revenues	
User Fees	$1,250,000
Grants	$0
Sponsorships	$0
Donations	$0

Full Cost Profile

Cost Breakdown by Percentage	
Personal Services	56.9%
Operating Costs	36.1%
Capital Costs	7.0%
TOTAL	100.0%

Cost Breakdown in Dollars	
Personal Services	$4,901,400
Operating Costs	$3,109,637
Capital Costs	$599,475
TOTAL	$8,610,512

Key: Greenville ▓   Benchmarking Average —   Fiscal Years 2015 through 2019

Resource Measures

Core Parks and Recreation Services per Capita

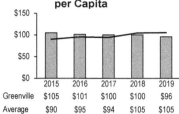

	2015	2016	2017	2018	2019
Greenville	$105	$101	$100	$100	$96
Average	$90	$95	$94	$105	$105

Core Parks and Recreation Staff per 10,000 Population

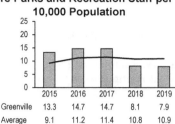

	2015	2016	2017	2018	2019
Greenville	13.3	14.7	14.7	8.1	7.9
Average	9.1	11.2	11.4	10.8	10.9

Facilities Measures

Land Acres of Parks per 10,000 Population

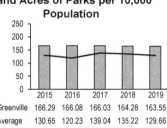

	2015	2016	2017	2018	2019
Greenville	166.29	166.08	166.03	164.28	163.55
Average	130.65	120.23	139.04	135.22	129.66

Recreation Centers per 10,000 Population

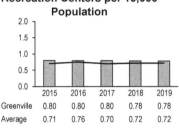

	2015	2016	2017	2018	2019
Greenville	0.80	0.80	0.80	0.78	0.78
Average	0.71	0.76	0.70	0.72	0.72

Swimming Pools per 10,000 Population

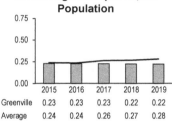

	2015	2016	2017	2018	2019
Greenville	0.23	0.23	0.23	0.22	0.22
Average	0.24	0.24	0.26	0.27	0.28

Athletic Fields per 10,000 Population

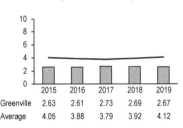

	2015	2016	2017	2018	2019
Greenville	2.63	2.61	2.73	2.69	2.67
Average	4.05	3.88	3.79	3.92	4.12

Playgrounds per 10,000 Population

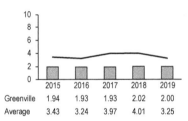

	2015	2016	2017	2018	2019
Greenville	1.94	1.93	1.93	2.02	2.00
Average	3.43	3.24	3.97	4.01	3.25

Miles of Land Trails per 10,000 Population

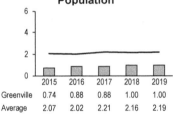

	2015	2016	2017	2018	2019
Greenville	0.74	0.88	0.88	1.00	1.00
Average	2.07	2.02	2.21	2.16	2.19

Efficiency Measures

Total Core Parks and Recreation Costs per Acre

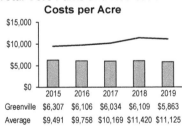

	2015	2016	2017	2018	2019
Greenville	$6,307	$6,106	$6,034	$6,109	$5,863
Average	$9,491	$9,758	$10,169	$11,420	$11,125

Acres of Park Maintained per Maintenance FTE

	2015	2016	2017	2018	2019
Greenville	51.5	38.2	38.2	41.6	41.7
Average	46.0	37.7	45.5	41.8	38.3

Volunteer Hours in FTEs as a Percent of Paid Staff FTEs

	2015	2016	2017	2018	2019
Greenville	9.9%	9.5%	17.9%	33.6%	34.2%
Average	16.4%	19.0%	17.6%	17.6%	19.1%

Effectiveness Measures

Revenue Gained as a Percent of Total Core Costs

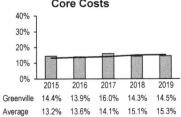

	2015	2016	2017	2018	2019
Greenville	14.4%	13.9%	16.0%	14.3%	14.5%
Average	13.2%	13.6%	14.1%	15.1%	15.3%

Acts of Vandalism at Parks Facilities per 10,000 Population

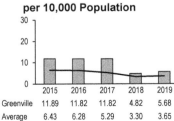

	2015	2016	2017	2018	2019
Greenville	11.89	11.82	11.82	4.82	5.68
Average	6.43	6.28	5.29	3.30	3.65

Fiscal Year 2018–19

Explanatory Information

Service Level and Delivery

The City of Hickory Parks and Recreation Department is a separate department under the city organization. The city has partnerships with other organizations to provide recreational services, including a priority-use agreement with local schools for use of facilities over other non-school users and a priority-use agreement with Catawba Valley Youth Soccer for use of city soccer fields.

The city has twenty-six separate parks and sites. This includes 558 acres of park acreage, mostly developed. The city has sixteen miles of trails.

In addition to the core parks and recreational facilities, Hickory has one historic property, one professional sports facility, one boat ramp, one museum, two community gardens, and a tower ropes course. The operation of these other facilities is not included in the Core Parks and Recreation comparisons reported here. These facilities are not included here in dollars or staff as part of core parks and recreation facilities and activities.

Conditions Affecting Service, Performance, and Costs

Municipal Profile

Population (OSBM 2018)	40,932
Land Area (Square Miles)	29.92
Persons per Square Mile	1,368
Topography	Gently rolling
Climate	Temperate; some ice and snow

Service Profile

Parks and Recreation Staff

Administrative Position FTEs	3.0
Maintenance Staff FTEs	26.5
Program and Facility FTEs	20.5
Other Staff FTEs	0.0
TOTAL	50.0

Number of Parks and Sites	26
Total Land Acreage in Parks	558.0
Miles of Trails in Parks	16.1

Recreational Facilities

Indoor and Outdoor Pools	0
Recreation Centers	8
Outdoor Basketball Courts	17
Outdoor Tennis Courts	16
Playgrounds	40
Diamond Fields	13
Rectangular Fields	12
Other Athletic Fields	0
Picnic Shelters	13

Parks and Recreation Revenues

User Fees	$205,199
Grants	$0
Sponsorships	$30,915
Donations	$51,500

Full Cost Profile

Cost Breakdown by Percentage

Personal Services	40.4%
Operating Costs	42.2%
Capital Costs	17.4%
TOTAL	100.0%

Cost Breakdown in Dollars

Personal Services	$2,185,353
Operating Costs	$2,279,159
Capital Costs	$939,400
TOTAL	$5,403,912

Hickory

Core Parks and Recreation

Key: Hickory ▨   Benchmarking Average —   Fiscal Years 2015 through 2019

Resource Measures

Core Parks and Recreation Services per Capita

	2015	2016	2017	2018	2019
Hickory	$113	$115	$117	$125	$132
Average	$90	$95	$94	$105	$105

Core Parks and Recreation Staff per 10,000 Population

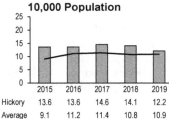

	2015	2016	2017	2018	2019
Hickory	13.6	13.6	14.6	14.1	12.2
Average	9.1	11.2	11.4	10.8	10.9

Facilities Measures

Land Acres of Parks per 10,000 Population

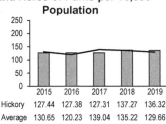

	2015	2016	2017	2018	2019
Hickory	127.44	127.38	127.31	137.27	136.32
Average	130.65	120.23	139.04	135.22	129.66

Recreation Centers per 10,000 Population

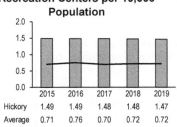

	2015	2016	2017	2018	2019
Hickory	1.49	1.49	1.48	1.48	1.47
Average	0.71	0.76	0.70	0.72	0.72

Swimming Pools per 10,000 Population

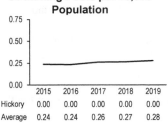

	2015	2016	2017	2018	2019
Hickory	0.00	0.00	0.00	0.00	0.00
Average	0.24	0.24	0.26	0.27	0.28

Athletic Fields per 10,000 Population

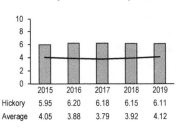

	2015	2016	2017	2018	2019
Hickory	5.95	6.20	6.18	6.15	6.11
Average	4.05	3.88	3.79	3.92	4.12

Playgrounds per 10,000 Population

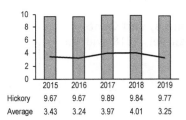

	2015	2016	2017	2018	2019
Hickory	9.67	9.67	9.89	9.84	9.77
Average	3.43	3.24	3.97	4.01	3.25

Miles of Land Trails per 10,000 Population

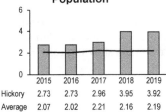

	2015	2016	2017	2018	2019
Hickory	2.73	2.73	2.96	3.95	3.92
Average	2.07	2.02	2.21	2.16	2.19

Efficiency Measures

Total Core Parks and Recreation Costs per Acre

	2015	2016	2017	2018	2019
Hickory	$8,875	$9,020	$9,184	$9,119	$9,684
Average	$9,491	$9,758	$10,169	$11,420	$11,125

Acres of Park Maintained per Maintenance FTE

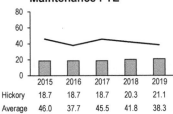

	2015	2016	2017	2018	2019
Hickory	18.7	18.7	18.7	20.3	21.1
Average	46.0	37.7	45.5	41.8	38.3

Volunteer Hours in FTEs as a Percent of Paid Staff FTEs

	2015	2016	2017	2018	2019
Hickory	50.1%	48.3%	47.7%	48.6%	60.4%
Average	16.4%	19.0%	17.6%	17.6%	19.1%

Effectiveness Measures

Revenue Gained as a Percent of Total Core Costs

	2015	2016	2017	2018	2019
Hickory	5.3%	6.2%	7.8%	6.4%	5.3%
Average	13.2%	13.6%	14.1%	15.1%	15.3%

Acts of Vandalism at Parks Facilities per 10,000 Population

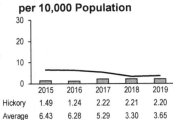

	2015	2016	2017	2018	2019
Hickory	1.49	1.24	2.22	2.21	2.20
Average	6.43	6.28	5.29	3.30	3.65

Mooresville

Core Parks and Recreation

Fiscal Year 2018–19

Explanatory Information

Service Level and Delivery

The Town of Mooresville provides parks and recreation services through a separate department. The department has five divisions: administration, parks services, recreation, athletics, and golf. The department also handles cemeteries. Neither the cemetery work or the golf course are included here in order to follow the benchmarking service definition.

The town has several formal cooperative agreements for providing services, including the Showcase Baseball Academy, the Mooresville Graded School District, Iredell-Statesville Schools, and the Convention and Visitors Bureau.

Mooresville has twenty-four separate parks and sites covering 370 land acres, most of which is developed. The town has eleven miles of trails in the parks.

In addition to traditional recreational facilities, Mooresville has a golf course, a farmer's market, a historic property and museum. A large outdoor performance event site is being designed and will bid out in the future. These facilities are not included here in dollars or staff as part of core parks and recreation facilities and activities.

Conditions Affecting Service, Performance, and Costs

Mooresville joined the Benchmarking project in July 2018, with the first year of data showing for FY 2017–18.

Municipal Profile

Population (OSBM 2018)	41,255
Land Area (Square Miles)	22.75
Persons per Square Mile	1,813
Topography	Flat; gently rolling
Climate	Temperate; little ice and snow

Service Profile

Parks and Recreation Staff

Administrative Position FTEs	4.0
Maintenance Staff FTEs	18.0
Program and Facility FTEs	52.0
Other Staff FTEs	4.4
TOTAL	78.4

Number of Parks and Sites	24
Total Land Acreage in Parks	370.0
Miles of Trails in Parks	10.9

Recreational Facilities

Indoor and Outdoor Pools	2
Recreation Centers	4
Outdoor Basketball Courts	7
Outdoor Tennis Courts	18
Playgrounds	13
Diamond Fields	17
Rectangular Fields	11
Other Athletic Fields	0
Picnic Shelters	22

Parks and Recreation Revenues

User Fees	$1,844,560
Grants	$10,000
Sponsorships	$20,000
Donations	$2,250

Full Cost Profile

Cost Breakdown by Percentage

Personal Services	34.8%
Operating Costs	51.7%
Capital Costs	13.4%
TOTAL	100.0%

Cost Breakdown in Dollars

Personal Services	$2,435,668
Operating Costs	$3,620,124
Capital Costs	$940,655
TOTAL	$6,996,447

Mooresville

Core Parks and Recreation

Key: Mooresville   Benchmarking Average —   Fiscal Years 2015 through 2019

Resource Measures

Core Parks and Recreation Services per Capita

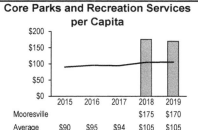

	2015	2016	2017	2018	2019
Mooresville				$175	$170
Average	$90	$95	$94	$105	$105

Core Parks and Recreation Staff per 10,000 Population

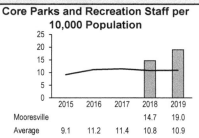

	2015	2016	2017	2018	2019
Mooresville				14.7	19.0
Average	9.1	11.2	11.4	10.8	10.9

Facilities Measures

Land Acres of Parks per 10,000 Population

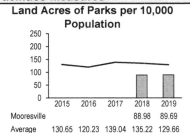

	2015	2016	2017	2018	2019
Mooresville				88.98	89.69
Average	130.65	120.23	139.04	135.22	129.66

Recreation Centers per 10,000 Population

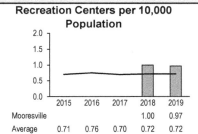

	2015	2016	2017	2018	2019
Mooresville				1.00	0.97
Average	0.71	0.76	0.70	0.72	0.72

Swimming Pools per 10,000 Population

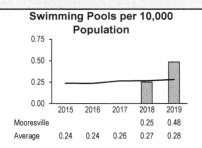

	2015	2016	2017	2018	2019
Mooresville				0.25	0.48
Average	0.24	0.24	0.26	0.27	0.28

Athletic Fields per 10,000 Population

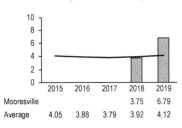

	2015	2016	2017	2018	2019
Mooresville				3.75	6.79
Average	4.05	3.88	3.79	3.92	4.12

Playgrounds per 10,000 Population

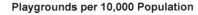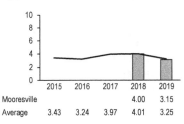

	2015	2016	2017	2018	2019
Mooresville				4.00	3.15
Average	3.43	3.24	3.97	4.01	3.25

Miles of Land Trails per 10,000 Population

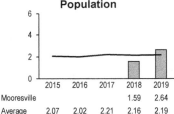

	2015	2016	2017	2018	2019
Mooresville				1.59	2.64
Average	2.07	2.02	2.21	2.16	2.19

Efficiency Measures

Total Core Parks and Recreation Costs per Acre

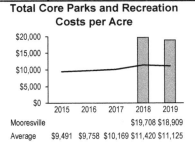

	2015	2016	2017	2018	2019
Mooresville				$19,708	$18,909
Average	$9,491	$9,758	$10,169	$11,420	$11,125

Acres of Park Maintained per Maintenance FTE

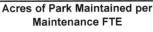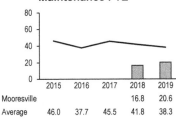

	2015	2016	2017	2018	2019
Mooresville				16.8	20.6
Average	46.0	37.7	45.5	41.8	38.3

Volunteer Hours in FTEs as a Percent of Paid Staff FTEs

	2015	2016	2017	2018	2019
Mooresville				7.9%	6.1%
Average	16.4%	19.0%	17.6%	17.6%	19.1%

Effectiveness Measures

Revenue Gained as a Percent of Total Core Costs

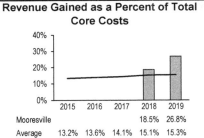

	2015	2016	2017	2018	2019
Mooresville				18.5%	26.8%
Average	13.2%	13.6%	14.1%	15.1%	15.3%

Acts of Vandalism at Parks Facilities per 10,000 Population

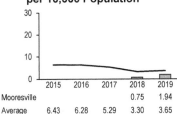

	2015	2016	2017	2018	2019
Mooresville				0.75	1.94
Average	6.43	6.28	5.29	3.30	3.65

Explanatory Information

Service Level and Delivery
The City of Raleigh Parks, Recreation, and Cultural Resources Department is a stand-alone unit within the city. The department is comprised of five divisions: Business Process Management, Park Development and Communications, Parks, Recreation, and Resources.

The department has a public/private partnership with the Dix Park Conservancy to provide funding for master planning and programming at Dorothea Dix Park. The city also has joint-use agreements and memorandums of understanding with other entities, including Wake County, the Wake County Public School System, NC State University, and local non-profit organizations.

Raleigh has a full array of recreational facilities available. The department plays a leading role in determining the quality of life and character of the Capital City. With over 6,000 acres of parkland, 134 miles of greenway trails, and over 1.3 million square feet of facilities, the department provides a wide range of creative programming opportunities that promote the social, cultural, mental, and physical well-being of citizens. The city's vision for its parks, recreation, and cultural resources system is "bringing people to parks and parks to people."

In addition to traditional recreational facilities, Raleigh has a large outdoor performance event site, historic properties, a performing arts center, boats ramps, and city museums. These facilities are not included here in dollars or staff as part of core parks and recreation facilities and activities.

Conditions Affecting Service, Performance, and Costs
Raleigh rejoined the Benchmarking Project in July 2016, with the first year of data showing for FY 2015–16.

Municipal Profile

Population (OSBM 2018)	464,453
Land Area (Square Miles)	145.65
Persons per Square Mile	3,189
Topography	Flat; gently rolling
Climate	Temperate; little ice and snow

Service Profile

Parks and Recreation Staff

Administrative Position FTEs	17.6
Maintenance Staff FTEs	174.6
Program and Facility FTEs	541.1
Other Staff FTEs	32.0
TOTAL	765.3

Number of Parks and Sites	175
Total Land Acreage in Parks	6,127.0
Miles of Trails in Parks	134.0

Recreational Facilities

Indoor and Outdoor Pools	8
Recreation Centers	41
Outdoor Basketball Courts	54
Outdoor Tennis Courts	112
Playgrounds	96
Diamond Fields	59
Rectangular Fields	0
Other Athletic Fields	41
Picnic Shelters	88

Parks and Recreation Revenues

User Fees	$10,032,633
Grants	$250,350
Sponsorships	$0
Donations	$940,544

Full Cost Profile

Cost Breakdown by Percentage

Personal Services	60.2%
Operating Costs	34.9%
Capital Costs	4.9%
TOTAL	100.0%

Cost Breakdown in Dollars

Personal Services	$33,659,679
Operating Costs	$19,542,839
Capital Costs	$2,743,637
TOTAL	$55,946,155

Core Parks and Recreation

Key: Raleigh ▨   Benchmarking Average —   Fiscal Years 2015 through 2019

Resource Measures

Core Parks and Recreation Services per Capita

	2015	2016	2017	2018	2019
Raleigh		$113	$121	$119	$120
Average	$90	$95	$94	$105	$105

Core Parks and Recreation Staff per 10,000 Population

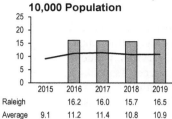

	2015	2016	2017	2018	2019
Raleigh		16.2	16.0	15.7	16.5
Average	9.1	11.2	11.4	10.8	10.9

Facilities Measures

Land Acres of Parks per 10,000 Population

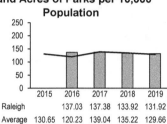

	2015	2016	2017	2018	2019
Raleigh		137.03	137.38	133.92	131.92
Average	130.65	120.23	139.04	135.22	129.66

Recreation Centers per 10,000 Population

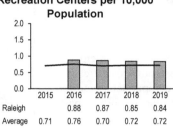

	2015	2016	2017	2018	2019
Raleigh		0.88	0.87	0.85	0.84
Average	0.71	0.76	0.70	0.72	0.72

Swimming Pools per 10,000 Population

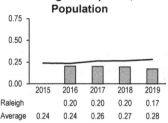

	2015	2016	2017	2018	2019
Raleigh		0.20	0.20	0.20	0.17
Average	0.24	0.24	0.26	0.27	0.28

Athletic Fields per 10,000 Population

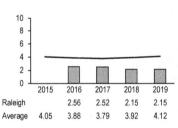

	2015	2016	2017	2018	2019
Raleigh		2.56	2.52	2.15	2.15
Average	4.05	3.88	3.79	3.92	4.12

Playgrounds per 10,000 Population

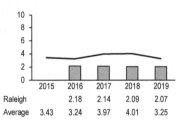

	2015	2016	2017	2018	2019
Raleigh		2.18	2.14	2.09	2.07
Average	3.43	3.24	3.97	4.01	3.25

Miles of Land Trails per 10,000 Population

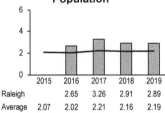

	2015	2016	2017	2018	2019
Raleigh		2.65	3.26	2.91	2.89
Average	2.07	2.02	2.21	2.16	2.19

Efficiency Measures

Total Core Parks and Recreation Costs per Acre

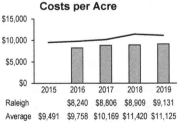

	2015	2016	2017	2018	2019
Raleigh		$8,240	$8,806	$8,909	$9,131
Average	$9,491	$9,758	$10,169	$11,420	$11,125

Acres of Park Maintained per Maintenance FTE

	2015	2016	2017	2018	2019
Raleigh		31.8	35.7	31.3	35.1
Average	46.0	37.7	45.5	41.8	38.3

Volunteer Hours in FTEs as a Percent of Paid Staff FTEs

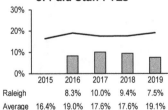

	2015	2016	2017	2018	2019
Raleigh		8.3%	10.0%	9.4%	7.5%
Average	16.4%	19.0%	17.6%	17.6%	19.1%

Effectiveness Measures

Revenue Gained as a Percent of Total Core Costs

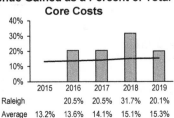

	2015	2016	2017	2018	2019
Raleigh		20.5%	20.5%	31.7%	20.1%
Average	13.2%	13.6%	14.1%	15.1%	15.3%

Acts of Vandalism at Parks Facilities per 10,000 Population

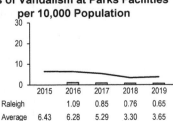

	2015	2016	2017	2018	2019
Raleigh		1.09	0.85	0.76	0.65
Average	6.43	6.28	5.29	3.30	3.65

Fiscal Year 2018–19

Explanatory Information

Service Level and Delivery

The City of Wilson Parks and Recreation Department is a separate department under the city organization. The city has partnerships with other organizations to provide recreational services, including the Wilson County Schools, the Wilson Youth Soccer Association, Wilson City Little League, Special Olympics, Youth Soccer Association, the Senior Games of North Carolina, and the Wilson Arts Council.

The city has twenty-eight separate parks and sites. This includes 400 acres, most currently undeveloped. The city has seven and half miles of trails.

In addition to the core parks and recreational facilities, Wilson has three boat ramps and one museum. The city also runs a municipal eighteen-hole golf course. The operation of these other facilities is not included in the Core Parks and Recreation comparisons reported here. These facilities are not included here in dollars or staff as part of core parks and recreation facilities and activities.

Conditions Affecting Service, Performance, and Costs

Municipal Profile

Population (OSBM 2018)	49,054
Land Area (Square Miles)	30.97
Persons per Square Mile	1,584
Topography	Flat
Climate	Temperate; little ice and snow

Service Profile

Parks and Recreation Staff	
Administrative Position FTEs	4.0
Maintenance Staff FTEs	16.0
Program and Facility FTEs	28.0
Other Staff FTEs	4.0
TOTAL	52.0

Number of Parks and Sites	28
Total Land Acreage in Parks	400.0
Miles of Trails in Parks	7.5

Recreational Facilities	
Indoor and Outdoor Pools	2
Recreation Centers	4
Outdoor Basketball Courts	7
Outdoor Tennis Courts	16
Playgrounds	26
Diamond Fields	11
Rectangular Fields	14
Other Athletic Fields	1
Picnic Shelters	19

Parks and Recreation Revenues	
User Fees	$525,000
Grants	$0
Sponsorships	$61,000
Donations	$0

Full Cost Profile

Cost Breakdown by Percentage	
Personal Services	57.3%
Operating Costs	34.3%
Capital Costs	8.4%
TOTAL	100.0%

Cost Breakdown in Dollars	
Personal Services	$3,174,632
Operating Costs	$1,901,492
Capital Costs	$464,716
TOTAL	$5,540,840

Key: Wilson ▨   Benchmarking Average —   Fiscal Years 2015 through 2019

Resource Measures

Core Parks and Recreation Services per Capita

	2015	2016	2017	2018	2019
Wilson	$106	$106	$112	$119	$113
Average	$90	$95	$94	$105	$105

Core Parks and Recreation Staff per 10,000 Population

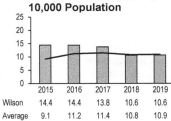

	2015	2016	2017	2018	2019
Wilson	14.4	14.4	13.8	10.6	10.6
Average	9.1	11.2	11.4	10.8	10.9

Facilities Measures

Land Acres of Parks per 10,000 Population

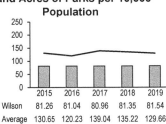

	2015	2016	2017	2018	2019
Wilson	81.26	81.04	80.96	81.35	81.54
Average	130.65	120.23	139.04	135.22	129.66

Recreation Centers per 10,000 Population

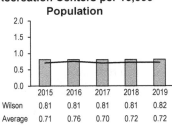

	2015	2016	2017	2018	2019
Wilson	0.81	0.81	0.81	0.81	0.82
Average	0.71	0.76	0.70	0.72	0.72

Swimming Pools per 10,000 Population

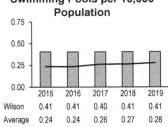

	2015	2016	2017	2018	2019
Wilson	0.41	0.41	0.40	0.41	0.41
Average	0.24	0.24	0.26	0.27	0.28

Athletic Fields per 10,000 Population

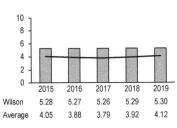

	2015	2016	2017	2018	2019
Wilson	5.28	5.27	5.26	5.29	5.30
Average	4.05	3.88	3.79	3.92	4.12

Playgrounds per 10,000 Population

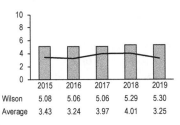

	2015	2016	2017	2018	2019
Wilson	5.08	5.06	5.06	5.29	5.30
Average	3.43	3.24	3.97	4.01	3.25

Miles of Land Trails per 10,000 Population

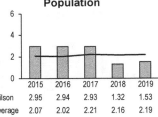

	2015	2016	2017	2018	2019
Wilson	2.95	2.94	2.93	1.32	1.53
Average	2.07	2.02	2.21	2.16	2.19

Efficiency Measures

Total Core Parks and Recreation Costs per Acre

	2015	2016	2017	2018	2019
Wilson	$13,062	$13,079	$13,802	$14,616	$13,852
Average	$9,491	$9,758	$10,169	$11,420	$11,125

Acres of Park Maintained per Maintenance FTE

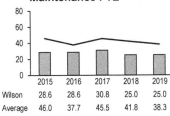

	2015	2016	2017	2018	2019
Wilson	28.6	28.6	30.8	25.0	25.0
Average	46.0	37.7	45.5	41.8	38.3

Volunteer Hours in FTEs as a Percent of Paid Staff FTEs

	2015	2016	2017	2018	2019
Wilson	8.1%	8.3%	8.6%	12.0%	12.9%
Average	16.4%	19.0%	17.6%	17.6%	19.1%

Effectiveness Measures

Revenue Gained as a Percent of Total Core Costs

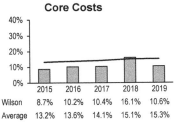

	2015	2016	2017	2018	2019
Wilson	8.7%	10.2%	10.4%	16.1%	10.6%
Average	13.2%	13.6%	14.1%	15.1%	15.3%

Acts of Vandalism at Parks Facilities per 10,000 Population

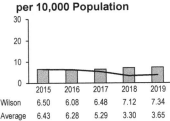

	2015	2016	2017	2018	2019
Wilson	6.50	6.08	6.48	7.12	7.34
Average	6.43	6.28	5.29	3.30	3.65

Winston-Salem

Core Parks and Recreation

Fiscal Year 2018–19

Explanatory Information

Service Level and Delivery

The City of Winston-Salem Recreation and Parks Department is a separate department under the city organization. The department is overseen by the advisory Parks and Recreation Commission, which has eleven members appointed by the mayor and approved by the city council. The city has formal cooperative arrangements with Forsyth County and various public-private partnerships with other organizations to provide recreational services.

The city has eighty-two separate parks and sites. This includes 3,895 acres of parkland, most of which is developed. The city has twenty-three miles of trails, about two-thirds of which are paved.

In addition to the core parks and recreational facilities, Winston-Salem has two large outdoor performance event sites, a historic property, one boat ramp, and one museum. The city also runs two municipal eighteen-hole golf courses. The operation of these other facilities is not included in the Core Parks and Recreation comparisons reported here. These facilities are not included here in dollars or staff as part of core parks and recreation facilities and activities.

Conditions Affecting Service, Performance, and Costs

Many Forsyth County residents make use of the city's parks and recreational facilities. Most of the city's facilities were built in the 1960s to 1980s and are aging. Several support services are in other departments to improve efficiency and reduce costs, including property maintenance and vegetation management.

Municipal Profile

Population (OSBM 2018)	243,447
Land Area (Square Miles)	132.55
Persons per Square Mile	1,837
Topography	Gently rolling
Climate	Temperate; some ice and snow

Service Profile

Parks and Recreation Staff

Administrative Position FTEs	24.3
Maintenance Staff FTEs	79.5
Program and Facility FTEs	114.1
Other Staff FTEs	2.0
TOTAL	219.9

Number of Parks and Sites	82
Total Land Acreage in Parks	3,894.8
Miles of Trails in Parks	23.3

Recreational Facilities

Indoor and Outdoor Pools	10
Recreation Centers	17
Outdoor Basketball Courts	23
Outdoor Tennis Courts	107
Playgrounds	46
Diamond Fields	47
Rectangular Fields	50
Other Athletic Fields	0
Picnic Shelters	51

Parks and Recreation Revenues

User Fees	$857,475
Grants	$638
Sponsorships	$11,300
Donations	$98,210

Full Cost Profile

Cost Breakdown by Percentage

Personal Services	53.4%
Operating Costs	34.5%
Capital Costs	12.1%
TOTAL	100.0%

Cost Breakdown in Dollars

Personal Services	$7,162,057
Operating Costs	$4,626,534
Capital Costs	$1,624,143
TOTAL	$13,412,734

Winston-Salem

Core Parks and Recreation

Key: Winston-Salem ▪ Benchmarking Average — Fiscal Years 2015 through 2019

Resource Measures

Core Parks and Recreation Services per Capita

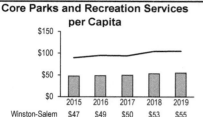

	2015	2016	2017	2018	2019
Winston-Salem	$47	$49	$50	$53	$55
Average	$90	$95	$94	$105	$105

Core Parks and Recreation Staff per 10,000 Population

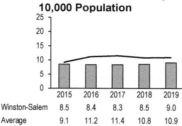

	2015	2016	2017	2018	2019
Winston-Salem	8.5	8.4	8.3	8.5	9.0
Average	9.1	11.2	11.4	10.8	10.9

Facilities Measures

Land Acres of Parks per 10,000 Population

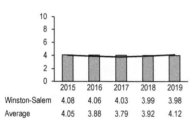

	2015	2016	2017	2018	2019
Winston-Salem	154.81	154.37	160.10	158.66	159.99
Average	130.65	120.23	139.04	135.22	129.66

Recreation Centers per 10,000 Population

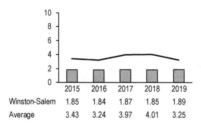

	2015	2016	2017	2018	2019
Winston-Salem	0.71	0.71	0.71	0.70	0.70
Average	0.71	0.76	0.70	0.72	0.72

Swimming Pools per 10,000 Population

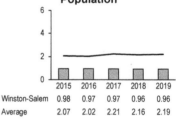

	2015	2016	2017	2018	2019
Winston-Salem	0.34	0.33	0.37	0.41	0.41
Average	0.24	0.24	0.26	0.27	0.28

Athletic Fields per 10,000 Population

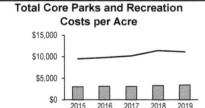

	2015	2016	2017	2018	2019
Winston-Salem	4.08	4.06	4.03	3.99	3.98
Average	4.05	3.88	3.79	3.92	4.12

Playgrounds per 10,000 Population

	2015	2016	2017	2018	2019
Winston-Salem	1.85	1.84	1.87	1.85	1.89
Average	3.43	3.24	3.97	4.01	3.25

Miles of Land Trails per 10,000 Population

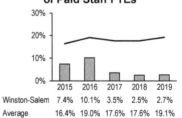

	2015	2016	2017	2018	2019
Winston-Salem	0.98	0.97	0.97	0.96	0.96
Average	2.07	2.02	2.21	2.16	2.19

Efficiency Measures

Total Core Parks and Recreation Costs per Acre

	2015	2016	2017	2018	2019
Winston-Salem	$3,060	$3,147	$3,104	$3,344	$3,444
Average	$9,491	$9,758	$10,169	$11,420	$11,125

Acres of Park Maintained per Maintenance FTE

	2015	2016	2017	2018	2019
Winston-Salem	48.9	51.2	52.9	48.3	49.0
Average	46.0	37.7	45.5	41.8	38.3

Volunteer Hours in FTEs as a Percent of Paid Staff FTEs

	2015	2016	2017	2018	2019
Winston-Salem	7.4%	10.1%	3.5%	2.5%	2.7%
Average	16.4%	19.0%	17.6%	17.6%	19.1%

Effectiveness Measures

Revenue Gained as a Percent of Total Core Costs

	2015	2016	2017	2018	2019
Winston-Salem	12.9%	8.4%	7.5%	7.8%	7.2%
Average	13.2%	13.6%	14.1%	15.1%	15.3%

Acts of Vandalism at Parks Facilities per 10,000 Population

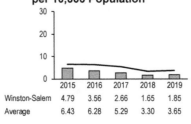

	2015	2016	2017	2018	2019
Winston-Salem	4.79	3.56	2.66	1.65	1.85
Average	6.43	6.28	5.29	3.30	3.65

CPSIA information can be obtained
at www.ICGtesting.com
Printed in the USA
LVHW060436081020
668216LV00011B/112

9 781642 380071